PERSPECTIVES IN RESOURCE MANAGEMENT IN DEVELOPING COUNTRIES

VOLUME 4

Land Appraisal and Development

Details of the Series

Perspectives in Resource Management in Developing Countries

1. Resource Management : Theory and Techniques
2. Population, Resources and Development
3. Ecological Degradation of Land
4. Land Appraisal and Development
5. Soil Deterioration and Conservation
6. Water Supply and Quality
7. Water Utilization and Management
8. Groundwater Assessment and Development
9. Bioresource Depletion and Conservation
10. Environmental Hazards
11. Scenic Resources and Tourism
12. Energy Resources and Environment
13. Degrading Atmospheric Resources
14. Integrated Watershed Development

About the Editor

B. Thakur is former Vice-Chancellor of L.N. Mithila University, Darbhanga and former Professor and Head of the Department of Geography, Delhi School of Economics, University of Delhi. He has more than four decades of teaching and research experience in resource management, natural hazards and urban development at the Universities of Ranchi, Patna, Waterloo, Akron, Delhi, North Dakota and Mithila. He was a Commonwealth Scholar at the University of Waterloo (Canada), Fulbright Visiting Professor at the University of Akron (USA) and Indo-Canadian Shastri fellow at York University (Canada). He has successfully supervised 21 Ph.D. and 35 M.Phil theses. Ten edited/ authored books and about 95 research papers in journals and as book chapters are to his credit. Professor Thakur has shouldered many responsibilities, such as Secretary General and President of National Association of Geographers, India (NAGI); Recorder and President of Earth System Sciences of Indian Science Congress Association; Editor and President of the Association for Geographical Studies (AGS), Delhi University; and Chairman of the Commission on Natural Hazards and Resource Management of NAGI.

Concept's International Series in Geography No. 5

PERSPECTIVES IN RESOURCE MANAGEMENT IN DEVELOPING COUNTRIES

VOLUME-4

Land Appraisal and Development

Edited by
BALESHWAR THAKUR
Former Professor and Head of the Department of Geography
Delhi School of Economics
Delhi University, Delhi

CONCEPT PUBLISHING COMPANY, NEW DELHI-110059

ISBN 13-978-81-8069-036-5 (Series) **ISBN 10-81-8069-036-9 (Series)**
ISBN 13-978-81-8069-619-0 (Vol. 4) **ISBN 10-81-8069-619-7 (Vol. 4)**

First Published 2009

Published and Printed by

Concept
Since 1974

Concept Publishing Company
Regd. Office:
A/15-16, Commercial Block, Mohan Garden
New Delhi-110059 (India)
Phones : 25351460, 25351794, *Fax* : 091-11-25357109
Email : publishing@conceptpub.com,
website: www.conceptpub.com

Editorial Office:
H-13, Bali Nagar, New Delhi-110 015, India.

Cataloging in Publication Data--*Courtesy:* D.K. Agencies (P) Ltd. <docinfo@dkagencies.com>

Perspectives in resource management in developing countries / edited by Baleshwar Thakur.
v. 4 ; cm. -- (Concept's international series in geography ; 5)
Contributed articles.
Includes bibliographical references and indexes.
Contents: v. 4. Land appraisal and development.
ISBN-13: 9788180690000 (set) ISBN-10: 8180690369 (set)
ISBN-13: 9788180696190 (v. 4) ISBN-10: 8180696197 (v. 4)

1. Natural resources--Developing countries--Management. 2. Sustainable development--Developing countries. 3. Natural resources--Developing countries--Management--Technological innovations. 4. Developing countries--Population--Economic aspects. 5. Developing countries--Population--Environmental aspects. I. Thakur, Baleshwar, 1943 II. Series: Concept's international series in geography ; 5.

DDC 333.7 22

Dedicated to
Chanda, my wife, who gave me help,
encouragement and inspiration

Preface

Thinking minds in the developing world today are deeply concerned at the massive quantitative expansion in the population size and the concomitant pressure on natural resources. This population pressure has often exceeded the carrying capacity of the land as traditionally used. It has resulted in loss of cultivated lands, disappearance of forests, soil erosion, energy crisis, ecological imbalances, pollution hazards, environmental harassment, regional water shortage and deterioration of water quality. Little wonder that we cannot maintain a growing population at a high standard of living without adequate natural resources. Thus, natural resource studies have become a subject of great importance in the perpetuation and enrichment of civilized human existence and, ultimately, even our biological survival.

The purpose of this multi-volume series is, therefore, to contribute to and provide scientific knowledge on natural resources in developing countries for their rational and sustainable development. It creates an understanding of the critical and decisive role that resource development and management play in today's society by an intelligent garnering of natural resources, restocking of forests and the achievement of a long-term rotational agro-forestry, arresting of soil erosion and depletion, prudent management of range and preservation of fish reserves and mammals.

Identifying current issues and responses of renewable and non-renewable resources, it suggests scientific techniques to permit greater flexibility and sophistication in the assessment of alternative management schemes, and demonstrates the role of new technological developments in their inventory and appraisal. Assessing the impact of natural hazards in resource management, it develops a scientific basis for integrated resource management and probes deeply into the questions of future resource supply as well as adequacy.

B. Thakur

Publisher's Note

Concept Publishing Company has successfully launched its multi-volume series entitled "Concept's International Series in Geography." Till date four multi-volume series have already been published and well received among the academic world. The details of the series are as follows:

1. Perspectives in Agricultural Geography, edited by *Dr. Noor Mohammad* (in 4 volumes).
2. Perspectives in Urban Geography, edited by *Dr. C.S. Yadav* (in 16 volumes).
3. Perspectives in Geomorphology, edited by *Dr. H.S. Sharma* (in 4 volumes).
4. New Dimensions in Agricultural Geography, edited by *Dr. Noor Mohammad* (in 8 volumes).

The present series was initiated about more than a decade ago. We have received in encouraging response from the scholars around the world. Although it took long time to see the light of the day, the problems in utilization and management of Natural Resources are still the same and a great concern for the sustainable development in the developing countries.

This series is planned in fourteen volumes. Each volume covers one particular natural resource, in detail.

Ashok K. Mittal
Publisher

Acknowledgements

More than a decade has elapsed since the multi-volume project was launched by the Concept Publishing Company. Many geographers and earth scientists have contributed advice, comments and ideas in the course of preparing this book. Particularly, I have greatly benefited from the interaction with Professor Bruce Mitchell, Professor R.P. Misra, Professor P. Dayal, Professor A.K. Dutt, Professor L.N. Ram, Professor V.K. Verma and Dr. K.V. Sundaram. I am grateful to all of them for their generosity of ideas and sacrifice of time. I owe many thanks to my colleagues particularly Mrs. Preeti Joshi, Dr. P.K. Parihar, Dr. Ramashray Prasad, Dr. Punyatoya Patra and Dr. Ritu Ahalawat who offered helpful comments in reviewing the articles. I would also like to acknowledge the encouragement and moral support. I received over the years from late Prof. C.P. Singh, Professor Noor Mohammad, Professor S.K. Aggarwal, Dr. Anu Kapur, Dr. R.B. Singh, Dr. R. Thakur, Dr. Phool Singh Bhusan and Dr. B.S. Dahiya.

Most importantly, the completion of this volume has been possible because of the tremendous support I received from the authors, particularly for their patience to cope with the delays on our part.

Some already published materials have also been reproduced, because these still have great relevance. I would like to offer my thanks to these authors and publishers who have allowed the use of copyright materials.

I express my deepest gratitude to Shri Ashok Kumar Mittal of Concept Publishing Company for his encouragement, support, suggestions and full dedication in creating a special working environment, who made possible the successful completion of this book. I appreciate Ashok's powerful cover and beautiful text design. The computer age made this endeavour more efficient and expedient. I am thankful to Shri Bachi Ram, Cartographer, for his cartographic assistance, Mrs. Neeru Sachdeva, Rajeev Ranjan Kr. Sinha, Punam Tripathi, Abhay Rajesh and Sarika Sharma for typing the manuscript.

I must thank my wonderful wife, Chanda, who gave me so much support, inspiration and practical help. I would specially like to thank my sons Dr. Sudhir Thakur and Rajiv Thakur, and daughter-in-laws Dr. Raj Rani and Madhuri, who took on onerous task of checking the completeness of the references for every chapter of the book.

Finally, I hope that the book will stimulate and generate a new thinking on natural resource management in general and developing countries in particular and would be popular among the students and teachers of natural resource management, administrators and policy makers.

B. Thakur

Contents

List of the Contributors

Abhimanyu Mahto, Head, Department of Geography, Marwari College. Ranchi (Bihar)-834001

Amal Kar, Principal Scientist and Head, Division of Natural Resources and Environment, Central Arid Zone Research Institute, Jodhpur-342003.

Anil Kumar, Univ. Deptt. of Geography, Bhagalpur University. Bhagalpur-812007.

Anthony K. Milne, Associate Professor, School of Geography, The University of New South Wales, P.O. Box 1, Kensington, NSW 2033, Australia.

Ashok K. Dutt, Professor Emeritus, Department of Geography and Planning, University of Akron, Akron, Ohio, 44325, U.S.A.

B. Thakur, Former Professor of Geography, Delhi School of Economics, Delhi University, Delhi-110007.

B.L. Sharma, Reader and Head, P.G. Department of Geography, Government College, Beawar (Rajasthan)-305901.

Bruce Koppel, Vice-President for Research and Education, East-West Centre, Institute for Economic Development and Policy 1777, East-West Road, Honolulu, Hawaii-96848 (USA).

Cleophas Lado, Dept. of Environment Science, University of Botswana, Private Bag 0022, Gaborone, Botswana.

D.J. Greenland, CAB International, Wallingford, Oxon, OX10 8DE, UK.

G. Venugopal, Chairman, Department of Geography, Ball State University, Muncie, IN, 47306, USA.

Hridai R. Yadav, Director, Rajiv Gandhi Institute of Wasteland and Rural Development, Palia, Gauriganj (Amethi), Sultanpur, U.P.

J.A. Bellamy, CSIRO, Division of Water and Land Resources, G.P.O. Box 1666, Canberra, Act 2601, Australia.

J.J. Basinksi, Assistant Chief, CSIRO, Division of Water and Land Resources, GPO Box 1666, Canberra, Act 2601, Australia.

J.R. Ive, Division of Wildlife and Ecology, CSIRO, P.O. Box 84, Lyneham, Act 2602, Australia, j.ive@cbr.dwe.csiro.au, ph.: 61 6 242 1703, fax: 61 6 241 3343.

J.R. McAlpIne, CSIRO, Division of Water and Land Resources, G.P.O. Box 1666, Canberra, Act 2601, Australia.

Jyotirmoy Mukhopadhyay, Jyotirmoy Mukhopadhyay, Senior Lecturer in Geography, Vidyasagar College, Kolkata, West Bengal.

K. Adinarayana Reddy, The author is currently working as a Research Officer in the Institute of Town Planners, G-A, Ring Road, Indraprasth Estate, New Delhi-110002, India.

Kevin M. Turcotte, Department of Geography, Ball State University, Muncie, IN, USA.

Mahamaya Chattopadhyay, Centre for Earth Science Studies, P.B. No. 7250, Akkulam, Trivandrum-695031.

Nageshwar Prasad, Professor. Post-Graduate Department of Geography, University of Burdwan, Burdwan-713104 (W.B.), India.

O.P. Thakur, Lecturer in Geography, Government Senior Secondary School, Kullu (H.P.)-175101.

P. Eaton, University Brunei Darussalam, Bandar Seri Begawan 3186, Negara Brunei Darussalam (Brunei).

P.B. Saxena, 16, Pragati Vihar, Saharshadhara Road, Dehradun-248001, U.P. (India).

Palak Bhardwaj, Research Scholar, P.G. Department of Geography, Govt. College, Beawar, 305901, Rajasthan.

Punyatoya Patra, Reader in Geography, Aditi Mahavidyalaya, Bawana, Delhi.

Qiming Zhou, Senior Lecturer, School of Geography, The University of New South Wales, P.O. Box 1, Kensington, NSW 2033, Australia.

R. Thakur, Reader in Geography, B.R. Ambedkar College, Main Wazirabad Road, Yamuna Vihar, Delhi-110094.

R. Nagaraja, National Remote Sensing Agency, Balanagar, Hyderabad-500037.

R.G. Gupta, Director (TYA), Delhi Development Authority, Vikas Sadan, I.N.A., New Delhi-110023.

S. Viswanatham, Regional Remote Sensing Service Centre, Jodhpur.

S.C. Kharakwal, Professor of Geography, B-70, Sector II, Defence Colony, Dehradun.

Srikumar Chattopadhyay, Centre for Earth Science Studies, P.B. No. 7250, Akkulam, Trivandrum-695031.

Sunando Bandyopadhyay, Department of Geography, Calcutta University, Kolkata-700019, W.B.

Surendra Singh, Central Arid Zone Research Institute, Jodhpur.

T.K. Ghosh, Regional Remote Sensing Service Centre, Jodhpur.

Introduction and Overview

B. THAKUR

Man rests on land for he is neither a fish nor a bird. Therefore, in a sense, land is his ultimate and most precious resource. It is perhaps regarded as a resource base rather than a resource itself (Mather, 1986). It is finite and fixed in place and most of the needs of humanity for food, clothing, shelter and energy come from the land (Davis, 1976, 11). Yet, the question of how best land can be developed remains obscure and problematic. Its appraisal and evaluation is essential for proper utilization which has been followed by a resurgence of interest by scientists and researchers during the 1970s through 1990s both in India and internationally.

Human Impact on the Land

It is a horrifying truth that the number of human beings and their domestic animals continue to multiply in underdeveloped countries. The swelling numbers of people have put increasing pressures on land resources and the environment. They had a greater impact on land through clearance and the land has become totally transformed. Much of the early clearance was for agriculture with pastures of clover and grasses for sheep and cattle. In recent years, the clearance of forests has been rapid and extensive as pressure on land has increased due to the ever increasing population competing for finite land resources. The pressure which the competition has engendered, coupled with unsuitable land use practices has led to degradation, erosion and eventually to complete destruction of the soil. The top soil has been lost because of over cultivation, improper irrigation, ploughed grassland and falling water tables. Even parts of the land most suited to crop production have been destroyed. Therefore, it is mostly agreed that vast areas of plants-based land resources have already been destroyed as a result of man's activities. In many developing countries, land well suited for food production is already in short supply. The quality of land has steadily deteriorated in many regions particularly as a consequence of soil erosion and salinity associated with agricultural activities. Also, the overuse of land has lowered the capacity of land to absorb moisture, and new technology and increased inputs have masked the effects of degradation which reduced the innate productivity of land in agricultural use (Chisholm and Dumsday, 1987, XVII). Further, the aesthetic appeal of the rural landscape has declined because of unsightly erosion and loss of trees and other native vegetation. There is a perception that land in its natural state is becoming increasingly scarce and socially vulnerable and more land should be set aside for national parks, recreation areas and flora and fauna reserves (Chisholm and Dumsday, 1987, XVII).

Taken together, the environment is being squeezed by the Third World's poor who destroy their resource base in order to stay alive. However, food production must meet the needs of the planet's billions of inhabitants, where demand for food and fuel has grown alarmingly. The need for food pushes agricultural use to the marginal lands and this has led to the expansion of cultivation and grazing into areas less suited to such uses and ecologically more fragile. As farming expands into fragile lands in order to feed growing populations, cultivation poses environmental risks leading to deforestation, soil erosion, soil infertility, loss of plants nutrients and organic matter and building up of salinity. Consequently, forest lands are being lost to agriculture; agricultural lands are being lost to urbanization and other uses. Simultaneously, there is increasing demand for more land to be allocated for wildlife, recreation, non-agricultural uses and maintenance of biodiversity.

In the face of these declining trends and expansion into fragile land, today, there has been enhanced environmental awareness for controlling land degradation as well as developing and managing land to increase agricultural production and to maintain harmony with nature. However, in many parts of the Orient, carefully terraced hillsides have maintained the productivity of valuable land resources even after thousands of years making agricultural landscapes in harmony with nature (de Souza and Stutz, 1994, 268). But, in general, in order to achieve environmentally sound, socially acceptable and economically feasible land use, the site-specific information of the land through systematic survey is basic to such achievement. Therefore, there is a need to set out ways of managing and developing land in the national interest taking into account its location, quality, purpose, its role as a basis for productive and sustainable agricultural production and in relation to changes in the technology of use. This can lead not only for its development but also to improvements in the productivity of land and their management. Land can be improved for a particular use by certain measures and it can also be improved by a certain kind of land use or at least sustained production can be assured (Chaturvedi, 1981, 61). If misuse and wastage of land has to be avoided, it should be used judiciously considering its capability and suitability for particular use (Chaturvedi, 1981, 61). Geographers have been active in land resource assessment and capability classification, with most of these efforts devoted to assessing the adequacy of agricultural land. A large number of geographers have developed analytical techniques to assess current and future land capabilities.

Land Evaluation

Land evaluation is the most important concept for developing and managing rural and urban land resources. According to Brinkman and Smyth (1973) land evaluation is the process of collating and interpreting basic inventories of soil, vegetation, climate and other aspects of land in order to identify and make a first comparison of promising land use alternatives in simple socio-economic terms. It means analysis, classification, quantification, assessment or appraisal of land resources which are made under whole range of existing physical and socio-economic conditions (De & Jana, 1997, 146). It is the process of estimating the potentiality of land for different kinds of use (De & Jana, 1997, 146). In fact, the basis of land evaluation method is nothing but a thorough assessment of land potentiality that promise to reveal much about the patterns, relations and processes underlying the rural land use. The most important challenge as well as problem in the evaluation of land is the improvement in the use of land. According to Young (1998, 40) the essence of land evaluation is to match kinds of land use with types of land. Thus, the focus of land evaluation is to identify the suitability of land for specified kinds of land use. Therefore, land evaluation is an essential tool for land use planning and knowledge about potentiality of land will help to take decision about crops to be grown and treatment to be made. Decisions about land use need to be made at national level, provincial, district level and the level of farm (FAO, 1976, 5). Whatever the land unit is selected for the purpose, each unit has a capability limit which can satisfy the human wants to a certain extent.

Appraisal of land resources is achieved by land capability assessment. Land classification is important and is of practical value in land development and land use planning. Capability and suitability are used interchangeably. However, there is subtle variation in how these terms have been adopted for the purpose of land evaluation classification. To be capable is to have the ability or strength to be qualified or fitted or to be susceptible and to be suitable is to be appropriate, fitting or becoming (Steiner, 1999, 364). In other words, capability is an inherent capacity of land to perform at a given level for a general land use, while suitability is a statement of adoptability of a given area for a specified land use type (Chaturvedi, 1981). It is essential to determine the optimum use of a particular piece of land, their problem and solution for a successful planning of land use. Land capability is determined by external land features, inherent soil characteristics and environmental factors. Since these conditions vary all over the world, a uniform method cannot be applied for land classification. Sharma (1981) has given a resume of land classification in some selected countries of the world and has also reviewed the inductive method of land classification. The fundamental purpose of land capability classification is to utilize the land resources according to their capabilities through rational planning (Mohammad, 1981, 9). The method of land capability classification is a systematic segregation of different kinds of land which are distinguished from one another by variation in the kind and degree of use imposed by soil characteristics, slope, climate, degree of erosion and other factors (Mohammad, 1981, 8-9). In other words, land capability classification is a grouping and grading of soil according to their potentialities and limitations, their capacity of producing agricultural crops and responsiveness to management practices (Mohammad, 1981, 8). However, capability cannot be measured either at macro or meso scales because detailed data are required. Therefore, unit of study is controversial. Various methods have been employed for rating the land into capability classes in different parts of the world.

Stamp (1942) stated that if land is to be used to be its optimal potential and every advantage taken of the concept of multiple use, a careful classification of land must be made. Stamp (1937) prepared a land classification suitable for a broad national policy of land resource conservation and land use planning of England, Wales and Scotland. He divided land into three major categories, that is, good (I), medium (II) and poor (III) quality land and ten subsequent types on the basis of site, elevation, slope, nature of relief, depth of soil, water conditions, texture etc. (De & Jana, 1997, 168-211). He plotted categories of land quality and land use on the Ordnance maps at 6 inches to the mile in three years (1930-32) with the help of some 22000 volunteers drawn from schools, colleges, universities and professional geographers (Martin and James, 1972, 224). Stamp (1948) distilled the country reports into *The Land of Britain: Its Use and Misuse*, a massive tome which was published in 1948. The book reflected of how the land was being used and progressively with how it should be used (Buchanan, 1968, 8). The maps and their documentary interpretation did help Britain in increasing its food production substantially (Shafi, 2006, 261). Stamp introduced the concept of Potential Production Unit (PPU) which examined the relationship of various types of land with reference to agricultural production. Potential Production Unit may be defined as the production from one hectare of average land whose management is in good hands and as the production can be increased through better technology, the word potential has been used (Shafi, 2006, 262). The second land use survey was inaugurated in 1960 under the direction of Alice Coleman. Data were again collected by field survey with schools playing an important role. From 1970 onwards, different methodologies emerged from those used by Stamp. It was not until the early 1980s that spatial and spectral resolutions of Landsat's Thematic Mapper provided an opportunity to map at a field-by-field scale (Fuller and Parsell, 1990, 1901-1917). Stamps remarkable achievement in coordinating the efforts of so many field workers and in assembling so much cartographic information into a unitary product is unlikely to be repeated (Fuller, Sheail and Barr, 1994, 181).

Land capability classification system has been alternatively defined by US Soil Service as a grouping of soil into special units, sub-classes and classes according to their potential uses (USDA, 1951; Klingebiel and Montgomery, 1961). This system evaluates land according to its limitations for its agricultural use like erosion of the land, location, slope, drainage, climate and soil characteristics. It classifies land into 8 classes: Class I is the least susceptible to erosion and Class VIII is the most susceptible. Class I lands are the most versatile. The limitations and needed conservation practices increase from Class I lands to Class VIII lands. Class I through IV are suitable for cultivation, whereas Classes V through VIII generally are not. Class I land is the most suitable for crop production, being flat, fertile and not vulnerable to erosion. Classes II and III may be used for growing crops but proper erosion control measures must be practiced. Class IV land is suitable only for limited cultivation. Classes V through VII are more suited for pasture, range, forest, wildlife or recreation. Class VIII land, being stony, infertile or very steep, is suitable only as wildlife habitat, wilderness or recreational areas. This classification scheme has been internationally accepted and is used in India, Malawi, Pakistan, Venezuela, South Africa and the Philippines. It is a mono-disciplinary soil science approach with emphasis on soil conservation and with consideration of climatic conditions, but without regard to economic and social aspects (Kappel, 1993, 56). However, the basic objective is to assess the degree of limitation to land use or potential imposed by land characteristics on the basis of properties (Kappel, 1993, 56).

Information Technology

Information technology provides the answer to the question of how the land of a particular location can be suitably used. It also captures the details of land for land resource planning by creating database. Since the early 1990s the information technology revolution assumes a paradigmatic shift in production processes and relations, the emergence of a new knowledge-based economy and a quantum leap into our information society. Information technology includes all forms of technology which is used to create, store and exchange information in its various forms (Vijayaditya, Shukla, Thakur and Malik, 2000). It is instrumental in capturing the details of land and helpful in assembling data required for land resource planning (Vijayaditya, Shukla, Thakur and Malik, 2000). GIS serves a number of applications from land inventory, land evaluation, land productivity assessment and land management and monitoring. Perhaps more significantly, GIS integrates databases, models for data analysis, decision support tools, computer hardware, software and human resources. Thus, GIS offers the ability and provides all the tools for digitizing the maps and presents the resultants maps. It is important to realize that GIS has the power to synthesize spatial information and better information leads to better decisions (Burrough, 1986; McRae and Burnham, 1981; Nagaraja and Gautam, 1996; Patra, 2004; Sharma, 1991 and Yadav, 1997).

Burrows (1986) book links GIS developments to the long history of land surveying and mapping in Europe and considers development of thematic mapping and quantitative spatial analysis as significant factors in evolution of GIS. GIS is defined as a class of mapping tools that made possible the integration of remote sensing, surveying and cartography. Emphasis is on characteristics, advantages and disadvantages of vector *versus* raster structures. Sources of possible error in GIS due to measurement and natural variation of the data and errors arising through processing are also discussed.

A practical use of GIS and remote sensing technology in a developing country has been documented by Zhou (1998) exposing the potential benefits of integration for regional development planning particularly in areas where the ecosystem is fragile, land productivity is relatively low and conflicts in land use have occurred.

Indigenous and Scientific Knowledge

The term indigenous knowledge has entered in land evaluation literature rapidly since nineties. It is also called as traditional ecological knowledge of indigenous people, peasant farmers and rural communities at large (Howitt, 2001, 35). Kuhn and Duerden (1996, 76) emphasize the increased integration of traditional ecological knowledge and western knowledge in formal resource management decision-making structures as an important element of the increased attention given to indigenous knowledge. Indigenous people are not literate, not healthy, not civilized and not us (Dodson, 1994). They are marginalized and excluded in the society. Thus, the focus to indigenous knowledge is long overdue. It represents a shift from the preoccupation with the centralized, technically oriented solutions of the past decades that failed to alter life prospects for a majority of peasants and small farmers in the world (Agarwal, 1995, 413-14). Indigenous knowledge is defined as a cumulative body of knowledge and beliefs transmitted from generation to generation about the relationships of living beings with one another and with their environment (Gadgil, Berkes and Folke, 1993, 151). Thus, indigenous people with a historical continuity of resource use practices often possess a broad knowledge base of the behaviour of complex ecological systems in their own localities (Gadgil, Berkes and Folke, 1993, 151).

While knowledge systems of traditional farmers must not be idealized, but they are widely respected and offer invaluable guidelines for development planners (Weinstock, 1984; Blaikie and Brookfield, 1987). Davidson (1976) derived a capability index based on the soils and slopes of 81 farms in north-eastern Scotland and compared results to farmers' opinion of their lands. It was observed that farmers on good land had conflicting opinions about its capability and farmers with poor land had an over-optimistic view of its capability.

Williams and Ortiz-Solorio (1981) showed that farmers in the valley of Mexico classify soil according to spatial variation in surface soil. They differ from scientists who perceive soil in three dimensions and emphasize presence or absence of diagnostic horizons. Sillitoe (1998) stated that scientific land and soil resource surveys have had only limited impacts locally on development and extension practice in the tropics. They are thought to have little relevance for subsistence farmers. Their failure to accommodate local social and cultural priorities is a factor. Soil scientists have, until recently, given little attention to other's understanding of soil or ethnopedology. The incorporation of the indigenous soil and land resource knowledge has recently been advocated to improve their relevance. But a common error is uncritically to impose a Western scientific model, which may distort understanding. The ill-informed, decontextualised knowledge that results may even promote negative interventions.

Kilic, Senal and Evrendilek (2003) have carried on use potential and suitability of 27 land mapping units of 4891 ha in Antakya for three different land use types: recreation-reforestation, residence and arable farming. For this purpose, soil and land data were used. The study showed that a total of 478 ha of land had the potential for residential use in the west and north of Antakya.

Through a case study, of a village of North-West Syria, an approach was adopted to integrate the knowledge of both farmers and land resource expert in order to promote adoption of new land use systems (Cools, De Paun and Deckers, 2003). This was done by comparing a farmer-led land suitability assessment with the results of an expert-led land suitability assessment so as to evaluate respective comparative advantages and complementarities. Some striking differences came out which were explained by participatory land evaluation.

Ryder (1994) stated that the survival of Dominican steepland farmers in the face of severe physical and economic constraints is proof of their ability to evaluate and till the land. The intimate empirical knowledge they have of their own land is a resource which should be used to verify results of land evaluation procedures. It is further stated that inhabitants of rural areas represent and invaluable but neglected source of information for scientists concerned with land evaluation in the Tropics.

Over the past 60 years, scholarly interest in land evaluation themes has increased dramatically, so much so that in 1976 the FAO (1976, 7) outlined six dimensions of the concept of land evaluation: (a) land suitability is evaluated for specific types of land use (land use may be defined either at a general level, such as, rainfed arable cropping or as a particular crop at a specified level of inputs, (b) evaluation includes a consideration of inputs and projected outputs (the level of material inputs is defined as are land improvements such as soil conservation or drainage and their overall impact is taken into account in predicting crop yields or outputs), (c) land evaluation requires specialists of different disciplines the land evaluation team must coordinate surveys and work in consultation with soil scientists, agroecologists, socio-economists and planners), (d) evaluation relates to the environmental and socio-economic conditions of the area (evaluations recommendations should relate to existing farming systems and to changes in land use which are technically feasible and socially politically acceptable), (e) suitability refers to use on a sustained basis (recommended land use must not cause soil erosion but must conserve the land for long-term production), and (f) evaluation involves comparison of more than one land use (improving the productivity of land use systems may involve introduction of new crops, changes in land management or other innovations in the existing farming system).

The Food and Agriculture Organisation (FAO) of the United Nations (1980) has suggested eight steps in the process of land evaluation: (1) defining objectives, (2) collecting the data, (3) identifying land uses, (4) identifying land units, (5) assessing suitability, (6) identifying environmental and socio-economic issues, (7) identifying the most suitable land use, and (8) planning land use.

Land Development

Land must be protected against degradation because there are considerable areas where land resources are insufficient to meet the food needs of the present and future populations. Land degradation has to be arrested and land must be restored to its original state or reclaimed to a new use after mining. Land development is an important element in land management as it includes change or transformation in the character of land to suit the needs of the society. Land development is the process for regaining land productivity which provides an efficient way of developing the available land resources and of improving the standard of living for the vast rural population. The main purpose of land development is to prepare the rudimentary land to a situation where land use types are matched with existing land quality. There is a growing realization of the overwhelming need for development of land but what kind of development is needed in a world where land degradation problem spills across political and administrative boundaries. Development potential is the process in which the regenerated land is maintained or developed in a sustainable manner in which the society gets maximum economic gain without affecting the quality of land (Patra, 2004, 177). What are the factors which affect the character of land development and what are the techniques which determine the development of land especially efficient, equitable and viable land development? Land development is concerned with reclamation of degraded lands, restoring damaged lands, restoration of mined land, wasteland development, and desertification control, remedial measures of water logging and salinity problem, rehabilitation of land, regeneration of different types of degraded lands, regeneration measures for gullied lands, rocky/ stony outcrops, sandy area and mining wasteland, and industrial wasteland. The problems of land development are aggravated by complex and inefficient and faulty land tenure systems. Therefore, the existing relationship between population and land has to be changed. Since the causes are tied to varied mixes of physical, social and economic conditions, the remedied must be diverse and tailored to the problems and needs of particular locales.

Wasteland Development

Singh (1978) studied the economics and geography of agricultural land reclamation in Koil tehsil of Aligarh district. *Jha* (1984) presented the effective utilization of different types of wasteland in the Birbhum district. The Academy of Sciences of ex-USSR (1958) has discussed the application of drainage and other scientific reclamation measures for the saline soils. *Sharma, Tripathi* and *Sharma* (1988) described various reclamation measures for usar land in the Sangrampur block of Sultanpur district. *Prasad* and *Yadav* (1969) have prepared a list of questions and answers for the alkali and saline soil reclamation and have also pointed out water quality, drainage measure, cultivation, sowing time, nutrient requirements, control of paste and diseases for reclamation. *Kumar* and *Pandey* (1989) determined the inherent characteristics of wasteland, causes and hazards for reclamation and controlling the destructive tendency operating over them. This work also provides necessary information required for conservation programme under which wasteland presently degraded by erosion can be improved. *Singh* (1962) presented the possibilities of reclamation of the cultivable wastelands which are being used as threshing grounds and sites for social and religious performance. *Yadav* and *Padmaja* (1985) attempted to reclaim usar land of Sultanpur district, revival and development by correlating various morphometric, climatic, hydrogenic, pedogenic factors and presented reclamation structures on the basis of quantifying values. *Yadav and Aggarwal* (1959) provided measures to reclaim saline and alkali soils along with assessment of their potential. *Shukla* (1988) studied the eroded lands of the Yamuna and Chambal rivers of Etawah district and provided empirical structure for ravine reclamation.

Sharma, Kumar and *Gough* (2000) determined the qualitative and quantitative success of rehabilitation plan used to revegetate limestone mine spoils in an area near Barna, North-west India. Rehabilitation success was achieved using a combination of rainwater harvesting techniques, soil amendment application approaches, plant establishment methods and the selection of appropriate germplasm materials (trees, shrubs and grasses). *Datta, deJong* and *Singh* (2000) stated that sustainability of irrigated agriculture is threatened by waterlogging, soil salinity and alkalinity. To reverse declining agricultural productivity, a combination of surface and sub-surface drainage, supplemented by improved irrigation management has been identified as the most appropriate strategy. The study analyses the cost of installing sub-surface drainage, the direct on-farm benefits of sub-surface drainage and the financial feasibility of the sub-surface drainage. *Kamel* and *Dapl* (2005) stated that Egypt has earmarked an ambitious desert land reclamation programme in order to increase total food production.

A very different approach that of eoho is taken by *MacLeod and Noble* (2001) to the directly related question, namely the rehabilitation of degraded semi-arid rangelands in Australia. They make the point that many landholders resist implementing remedial measures on the grounds that those measures are uneconomic to them. *Bradley* and *Grainger* (2004) stated while ecological resilience may explain why apparent symptoms of desertification are often temporary, soil resilience can prevent degradation resulting from over exploitation of land in response to drought and other constraints. *Arnolds* (2005) stated that organized soil conservation in Iceland began in 1907 as a response to reserve land degradation and desertification that was threatening the existence of several communities. Many of the threatening areas of accelerated soil erosion were fenced and seeded with sand stabilizers. They had a high success rate halting the advancement of sanddunes and other forms of highly accelerated erosion. During the last two decades there has been a gradual shift to more participating strategies, community involvement and ecosystem management for multiple benefits. These changes have greatly increased community involvement and stimulated conservation awareness and improved land use.

Patra (2006) has suggested some of the regeneration measures for land's potential development of Northern Highlands of Orissa like for degraded forest, forest blank, land with scrub, shifting cultivated land, gullied land, rocky/stony outcrop, sandy area, mining wasteland and industrial wasteland. She further states that village panchayat should be the sole authority to manage them with the help of local NGO, governmental organizations, corporate sector and village community by conducting meetings at regular intervals by keeping the accounts of land passbook and all economic issues.

Control of Desertification

Desertification is a pernicious problem that plagues millions of people in many parts of the world's arid, semi-arid and dry sub-humid areas. In recent decades, the international community has taken initiatives to address the problem and the efforts have accelerated since the adoption of the UN Convention to combat desertification in the mid-1990s. This paper by *Wang, Zheng* and *Yang* (2000) reviews the experience in the Asian region in implementing the conservation for combating desertification. *Jinfa* (1994) states that desertification has attracted much attention from the Central Government in China. About 10 per cent of the country's desertified land has been rehabilitated in the last few decades and the deterioration of another 12 per cent has been halted in North China. Scientific research has been greatly emphasized in China in this field, especially since the United Nations Conference on Desertification in 1977. Nationwide mapping and assessments of sandy desertification and water erosion have been carried out and field experimental stations for the study and control of sandy desertification have been established since UNCOD. National and regional maps of geomorphology, land resource and land use were completed in the 1980s to provide a basis for combating desertification and for rational land reclamation. China has achieved a number of remarkable successes in restoring degraded land during the last few decades. Sapotoer provides good example of combating the encroachment of shifting dunes in arid and semi-arid zones. Meanwhile, the introduction of improved land use patterns and agro-forestry rehabilitate degraded lands in the tropical and sub-tropical humid zones of South China has cut soil loss by 68 per cent in the Tangbeihe river basin of Xinguo Country, Jiangxi Province. Similarly, in the Jinhua-Quzhou basin, in the western part of Zhejiang Province, an experiment with eco-families and eco-villages has successfully demonstrated a better way of preventing the destruction of vegetation cover, restoring degraded lands, improving fuel, fodder and fertilizer supplies, increasing agricultural production and ultimately establishing a sound ecosystem. *Zhimin* and *Wenzhi* (2001) stated that due to over exploitation of land by the local people, desertification is a serious problem in central Tibet. Shifting sands have damaged farmlands and grasslands and have blocked traffic and buried water projects. They have suggested techniques for combating shifting sands including reformation of the agricultural structure, exploitation of new sources of energy and combination of mechanical and biotic measures. Desertification is estimated to affect about 25 per cent of the total land area of the world. Half of these desert regions are in developing countries. This phenomenon is one of the greatest preoccupations faced by mankind and should receive due attention from international organizations. The world's deserts are spreading and almost every continent is affected by desertification. What solutions can scientists offer? Developing arid lands in poor countries is a very complex and difficult process but it is not impossible. A number of conservation measures have been suggested by *Jodha* (—) in his paper on "Land-tenure problems and policies in the arid regions of Rajasthan". According to him, the measures such as sand-dune stabilization, shelter belt creation or the bunding work or the regeneration of rangelands through a variety of earthworks can be adopted effectively. Only on the basis of catchment rather than on the basis of individual farms or parts of the catchments.

Mining and Derelict Land

Mining is most destructive. In search for minerals the whole landform is destroyed. Land must be restored to its original state or reclaimed to a new use after mining. Mining is a total disturbance in which topography is radically changed. Its biological potential has to be restored, that is, restoring its original productivity of soil and vegetation replacement. It is estimated that about 184000 hectare has been abandoned in the Indian arid zone over the past 60 years following open-cast mining of limestone (Sharma, Kumar and Gough, 2000). The rehabilitation efforts of the mined land in arid regions have lagged behind those in more humid areas probably due to the harsh environmental conditions, lack of water for irrigation and lack of suitable technology. Successful mine-land rehabilitation can be evaluated using two main criteria: (1) stabilization of surface materials through appropriate landscape reconstruction, and (2) establishment of land development decisions involve substantial benefit and cost, many of which are yet to be assessed. As such, great care should be taken by a developer before he proceeds with an irreversible development decision. Since 1991, a collaborative research and development programme on biological reclamation of wasteland, land spoils and mining overburdens has been operating, aimed at breaking the dormancy of the rock surface and converting it into the production base for biomass generation through biological reclamation. *Basu* (—) is of the view that over 125 ha of such degraded areas have been reclaimed. In the industrialized countries, the land affected by mining represent an average of between 0.2 and 0.5 per cent of the total surface area of the country. The actions promoted for the restoration of damage lands are highly varied. In general, they start with the conservation of topsoil by means of sowing stabilizing plants, first herbaceous plants and then tree or bush seedlings.

Eweg, Lammeren, Deurloo and *Woldu* (1998) stated that the highlands of Ethopia suffer much from environmental degradation. The degradation was analyzed on sub-regional scale, using 25 × 25 metre grids. The USLE was employed to assess the potential and actual erosion risk. The research illustrates how a GIS can play an important role in supporting rehabilitation planning at both the farm and the sub-regional level.

Rhodes (2001) stated that the east coast were cleared for agriculture after the arrivals of European settlers in the 19th century. These slopes were subjected to severe erosion and loss of soil fertility, which ultimately threatened the regions economic well being. This article documents efforts to reverse the damage through tree planting.

Humphreys and *Groth* (2001) assessed the recovery of land which had been affected by extensive sheet erosion in a region south-west of Sydney, as a result of both grazing and cultivation for grain crops.

Improving both the efficiency and equity of the land development process has been identified by *Rojas* (1983). The author argues that the existing plantations—small holders structure is incapable of providing an efficient way of developing land resources and of improving the standard of living for the vast rural population. The long-term land development problems and issues in the Eastern Caribbean have been reviewed by *Rojas* and *Maganck* (1987) stating the overall scarcity of land resources creating conflicts among competing land uses and the fragility of the environment restricting land usage. The failure to resolve these conflicts in the past has led to the implantation of land distribution and land use structures that have deteriorated the quality of land resource base.

The twin problems of waterlogging and soil salinity are widespread in the irrigated lands of developing countries. In parts of India, especially in the states of Haryana and Punjab the sustainability of irrigated agriculture is being threatened by the emergence of waterlogging and salinity. About 35 per cent of the irrigated area is under canal command. It is in these areas especially that waterlogging and soil salinity occur. Main factors are the occurrence of large stretches of unlined canals and water courses, inadequacies in water distribution and, most importantly, the absence of an adequate surface drainage network. To reverse the declining trend in agricultural productivity in salt affected areas, a combination of surface and sub-surface drainage, supplemented by improved irrigation management has to be adopted.

Land Management

Land management implies strategies, control and direction to develop and conserve land resources so that agricultural production is enhanced in a region. It is a way to maximize lands potential benefits for use which should proceed in a systematic manner. The conservation and management of land resources help in the judicious planning of the use of land, identify the lands of special qualities for special purposes, plan to prevent irrational encroachment on good agricultural lands, suggest after careful survey a better use of village commons for pasture and social forestry and an overall development of the rural landscape and the preservation of the environment (Shafi, 1984). There are four major principles of land management: multi-functionality, sustainability, integration and subsidiarity (Kanda, 2000). The principle of multi-functionality indicates that land should be managed to deliver a wide range of benefits beyond food and fiber production. The fundamental principle is sustainability which means the use of land to meet changing human needs, while ensuring the long-term socio-economic and ecological functions of the land (Dumanski, Gameda and Pieri, 1998, 105). The principle of integration reflects that land management must be integrated with rural development. The last principle subsidiarity is a framework which reflects regional and local needs and aspirations.

It is important to mention five aspects of management so that land can be developed in the national interest taking into account its information, redistribution, land quality, land use and administration. Land information is prime requisite for making decisions related to land investment, development and management (Thakur, Khadanga, Venkatesh and Shukla, 2004). In order to achieve environmentally feasible land use, the site-specific information of the land through systematic survey is basic to such achievement. Land is precious resource and its information base must be continuously improved by updating land records and digitization of cadastral maps. Land records are of great importance to contemporary socio-economic imperatives and their revision and updating are necessitated for capturing the essentials of changes in social dynamics (Rai and Bhalla, 2000, 38; Saxena, 2005). Modernization of land records forms the base for all reform measures, therefore, regular updating of land records is essential. Land information system is a computerization process which assists in giving land particulars like ownership, revenue assessment and land classification (Rao and Shekhar, 2000, 35). LIS forms the micro-level land management tool while GIS is macro-level tool for decision-making. Both are computer-based solutions for addressing the requirements of land records management. Land management can be largely achieved on the basis of land ownership reform measures also. Access to land, improving tenancy, ceiling on land holdings, abolition of intermediaries and redistributing agricultural land in favour of less privileged classes are some of the steps towards the development and management of land resources. It is a move towards diminishing the existing land-man relations prevalent in rural society. However, it is quite amazing that despite the acute necessity to change the agrarian structure in many parts of the world, agrarian reforms have not been adequately executed. No less urgent and important is the requirement for better and more environmentally positive management of land quality for which a variety of indicators have been currently developed. Literature on land quality indicators is rapidly increasing (Dumanski, Gameda and Pieri, 1998). Land use is the sum total of all aspects discussed and emphasized above. It is an important index of the value attached by a society to natural resource management (Swaminathan, 2004, Foreword). Judicious and rational farming systems based on the principles of ecology, economics, gender and social equity and employment generation are the call of the day. Thus, integrated land use planning is widely reorganized as an important holistic approach to land resources development and management (Ravi Shankar, Raghavswamy and Gautam, 2003,1). It is concerned with finding out land fit for use, land with potential for use, land which appears useless, optimal and efficient utilization of land. Finally, management of land is controlled by government and administration with good policies. The Land Use and Conservation Board in the Department of Agriculture and Co-operation functions as the policy planning, coordinating and monitoring agency for scientific management of land resources. This agency has been assisted by the Indian Council of Agricultural Research (ICAR) and the National Bureau of Soil Survey and Land Use Planning (NBSS & LUP) in preparing detailed maps based on satellite imageries and GIS.

About the Volume

The twenty-eight chapters contained in the book range across the spectrum of land evaluation and land development policies with a focus on issues and management strategies. The purpose is to provide informative and interesting survey of many important areas from the developing countries. It is hoped that this book will inspire readers to become involved—individually and collectively—to work towards solutions to our pressing land development and management problems both in the rural and urban areas. The chapters follow a logical progression from basic principles of land evaluation through a survey of techniques to a discussion of what we can do to build and develop sustainable agriculture focusing on conserving degraded land and their reclamation. A central thesis of the book is that a better standard of living of the people of developing countries is possible if we are to preserve and conserve our valuable land resources by developing suitable techniques of land evaluation and their development. The land environment in which we live is a crucial part of the world.

Basinki has evaluated the land of a particular area in terms of its productivity, degradational hazard, and requirements for its management in generalized framework. He has suggested a number of land evaluation approaches including trial and error, land analogues and parametric and system analysis in a theoretical sense and discussed the requirements of relevant data, their analysis and giving different weights to various land classes.

Prasad and Mahto in their paper on Terrain Evaluation: Concept, Method and Application have provided the meaning of terrain and its evaluation and subsequently presented the terrain classification which is based on a number of properties like geology, surface elevation, surface forms, slope characteristics, plan profile, relative texture and conditions, nature of soil, vegetative cover, climatic variations and many other land characteristics. By giving the subjective considerations on the methodology of evaluation, the authors have presented a case study of Boreya village from fringe area of Ranchi city. Lastly, suggestions have been provided regarding terrain utilization in terms of developmental planning.

Sustainability of human life depends upon the produce of agriculture in terms of food supply and with the rise in population at a faster rate, the wide use of land is essential. Such land evaluation usually involves identifying either the most suitable location for a specified agricultural use or the most suitable use for a specified location. As sustained production should be the objective in both cases, there is a need to determine hazard potential as well as production potential. These contrasting, yet complementary, potential mimic in part diverse client responsibilities. Therefore, it is essential that a study's objectives influence the selection of the land evaluation approach as the relative emphasis that these potentials receive vary with the approach. Ive in his paper on Land Evaluation for Agriculture has dealt with the need of land evaluation and has demonstrated three essential ingredients of land evaluation. They are land use requirements, land unit characteristics and community requirements. The techniques available for matching land use requirements to land unit characteristics to meet community requirements are discussed including, including their relative strengths and weaknesses.

Yadav in his paper on Land Capability Classification: A Case Study of Sultanpur District has demonstrated that land capability is the best method to know the requirements of soil to produce the crop or to utilize it for agro-forestry, social forestry or any other purpose as per its suitability. The entire district is classed into four groups of land capability. The author is of the opinion that land capability study is a boon not only to the local level farmers but also to administrators, planners, scientists and researchers to develop their action plan. It also helps to regenerate the ecological imbalances and improves the socio-economic conditions of the deprived multitudes of the districts.

An inventory of wasteland has been made by Kumar in his paper on Wasteland Inventory: Step Towards Wasteland Development. This is a study on Karon anchal of Deoghar district of Jharkhand where wasteland has to be brought back under some use on the basis of their potential capability for development. He found that the use and conservation of wastelands are governed by relief, slope, erosion, stoniness, wetness, soil drainage, soil texture and soil depth and a composite index of all these factors determines the suitability of the wasteland unit.

Thakur and Saxena in their paper on the Higher Himalayan Beas Basin: An Analysis of Landform Systems, Soils and Land Use have analyzed the type and distribution of landform system to recognize the geomorphological regions and also to evaluate them in relation with the existing environmental residences of the Higher Himalayan Beas Basin. The study area has been categorized into three major geomorphological regions on the basis of relief, area-altitude relationship, dissection index, slope, drainage and geological structure, namely, (a) Dudhon-Dibika glacial tract, (b) Beas-Parvati Upper Kullu Thrust, and (c) Tirthan-Beas Lower Kullu Thrust Vale.

The landform system is found helpful in the evaluation of environmental resources by applying a new approach of Fractional Code Method (FCM). Based on this, a landuse pattern is identified to evaluate the suitability of land for different purposes.

Kharkwal has represented a study on the classification of terrain into morpho-cultural environmental units taking Khanda Basin on the lesser Garhwal Himalayas as an example. After analyzing the aggregate factors like physiography, hypsography, land use and other surface conditions, the basin has been classified into three morpho-cultural environmental zones, namely, (a) High mountain ranges, (b) Upper valley zones, and (c) Lower valley zones/combining landscape and parametric approaches. Their first level terrain systems have been recognized by relief factors. On the basis of orientations and aspects, eight second level terrain systems have been delineated. The third level terrain systems have been marked by parametric observations which are sixteen in number. Likewise, on the basis of morphometric and geomorphic characteristics, twenty-four fourth level terrain systems have been recognized. It is suggested that such hierarchy of units may be helpful in the planning of Himalayan basin for eco-development and watershed management.

The relationship of the catchment yield with terrain characteristics has been established by Chattopadhyay and Chattopadhyay. Analysis of monthly discharge data recorded in eight sub-catchments of the Kaberi river indicates that these sub-catchments can be distinctly grouped into three classes which is well manifested in their terrain characteristics also. Bivariate and multiple regression analysis bring out that the catchment area, area under hills and slope of the catchment yield.

Thakur and Patra assessed the biophysical characteristics of land affecting the land quality within the coastal ecosystem specially the Mahanadi Delta. The study area has been divided into a number of relatively homogenous land characteristic units with the mapping of their boundaries to provide necessary information of each type of units so that they can be evaluated for their quality. Based on the variables, landforms, soils and hydrology obtained from toposheets (1:50,000), the study area has been divided into a number of homogenous land characteristic units by using correlation technique and factor analysis. The study reveals that the Mahanadi Delta can be divided into eight land categories according to....The land characteristic features are not evenly distributed within the study area.

Land having high soil nutrients are found in three patches, extreme north, northern part, central part of delta. Land having medium and low nutrients are well distributed throughout the delta. But the land having low soil nutrients are found mainly towards the southern coast and south-western part of delta. Poor groundwater quality is found towards southern and north-eastern part of the delta. Waterlogged area is concentrated in the southern half of the delta. Infiltration rate of the soil is very high along the eastern central coast and low towards north-eastern part. Here, water quality is saline and alkaline. The land character of the north-eastern part of the delta is very interesting. Here, soil nutrient is very high, depth of groundwater is low and moisture content of the soil is high. Water quality is both saline and alkaline.

In order to test the relative performance of different digital remote sensing techniques *vis-à-vis* the conventional visual remote sensing in identification and mapping of the geomorphological features in the Indian desert, a study was undertaken by Kar, Ghosh, Singh and Viswanathan in the Pipar area of Jodhpur district, Rajasthan. Landsat TM and IRS LISS II images were used. It was concluded that the digitally edged enhanced FCCS often provide more terrain information than the standard FCC prints. Supervised classification and band rationing did not yield good results. However, supervised classification may be attempted in the terrain with distinctly separable special units. Principal Component Analysis provided many useful information, especially on lineaments. Proper interpretation of the colours in the FCCS of principal component analysis should be based on careful studies of the terrain features. The IRS satellite data products with resolution comparable to those in the landsat products, were found to yield equally useful information at a cheaper price than the products from landsat and other remote sensing satellites. For many simple applications the visual interpretation of the large-scale standard FCC prints with finer resolution are, however, easier and more cost-effective.

Mukhopadhyay in his article on Ecological and Economic Principles in Land Utilization: An Attempt Towards a Synthesis sets to resolve the apparent discord of the current economic principles with the ecological norms on the issue of utilization of land in general. The author is of the view that the general form of the present utilization of land on the earth is not wholly satisfactory as a number of problems stem from injudicious landuse in different places. The paper probes into the datum on which the traditional economic principles governing land utilization are based and it exposes the inadmissibility of some of the basic dicta of the economists from the perspective of ethics and psychology. It is found that the disagreement between the ecologic and economic principles has resulted from the development of the latter with a general disregard to the psychologic and ethical aspects of human beings. The discussion draws attention to the possibility of an alternative economic order that can reduce the ecologic-economic disagreement. The author pleads for the Gandhian economic model in this content.

The paper by Zhou and Milne on Computer-Assisted Land Resource Management Using Remote Sensing and GIS Technology has outlined a methodology to establish an integrated GIS for rangeland management on a regional scale. The emphasis has been on the techniques used for incorporating data sets derived from different sources into a well managed comprehensive geographical database. Focused on real-time or near real-time applications, the system is designed to use high frequency, low-cost remotely-sensed data such as NOAA imagery as the major source of real time information to be input to spatial models for natural resource management. Based on this regional image-based GIS, information useful for rangeland management can be provided to the land manager to assist decision-makers for the optimization of resource use.

Monitoring the land use change over the years, both positive and negative changes are essential for planning, management and environmental conservation. The paper by Nagaraja on Multidate Satellite Data for Land Use Change Analysis explains the utility of remotely sensed data for land use change analysis in the fast changing terrain of Chandragiri taluk of Chittoor district of Andhra Pradesh. Various land use and land cover categories are interpreted using 1973 and 1988 multi-spectral satellite data. The microwave data provides a new dimension for land use analysis due to its all-weather capability and its ability to discriminate the features based on indicators such as texture, surface roughness and corner effect, which are different from the optical data.

The major cause of malnutrition in the world today is poverty rather the inability to grow food. To relieve poverty, emphasis in agricultural research needs to be shifted to farming systems in environmentally disadvantaged areas, and to improvements in income generating activities. Greenland in his paper on Agricultural Research and Third World Poverty demonstrates the success achieved with intensification of rice-based rainfed farming systems as compared to the slow rate of adoption of improved fallow systems, where most research has been station-based. The results of on-farm research should be shared through networking, and supported by research conducted at institutions associated with the network, able to conduct such research.

Koppel in his paper on Sustainable Development, Poverty Alleviation and Limited Resource Farmers: Rethinking the Mission of Agricultural Support in Asia has outlined some of the challenges agricultural support systems face as they confront the problems of sustainable development and poverty alleviation. The paper briefly reviews some of the most important factors influencing the future of agriculture in Asia, examines the question of sustainability as a criterion for judging resource management, comments on the status of Asia's agricultural support systems and focuses on limited resource farmers, the group that may be most germane if agricultural research and extension are going to effectively increase their concern for both sustainable resource development and alleviation of rural poverty.

Prasad in his paper on Resource Potentials for Agricultural Development in Chotanagpur: Review and Reassessment reiterates that with adverse physioclimatic and socio-economic conditions, such as poor soil, undulating topography, water scarcity, poor infrastructural facilities, the Chotanagpur Plateau has been blessed with a number of resources which have potentialities for agricultural development. Because of higher topography the region is free from flood hazard. The low-lying lands and uplands within the plateaus are complementary to each other as the former gives good yield during excessive rain and the latter during drought condition. The rocks of most part of the plateaus are such that they retain rainwater during rainy season and oozes out slowly throughout the year, where it is exposed. The medium and minor irrigation projects have the potentialities for the development of agriculture. The pleasant climate allows people not to exhaust and facilitates hard labour. The demand on agricultural products has been increased with the development of mining, manufacturing and forest-based industries. All these have been discussed taking a number of case studies. Lastly, it has been concluded that on the basis of its resource structure, the plateau has an ample opportunity for agricultural development provided that the constraints are rightly assessed and developmental programmers are honestly implemented in appropriate time and in right direction.

The importance of rabi crops in the Middle Ganga Plain along with the changing patterns of vegetation in surrounding areas has been explained using AVHRR (NOAA) NDVI data by Venugopal, Dutt and Turcotte. AVHRR (NOAA) data is very useful for its high spatial and temporal resolution. The Normalised Different Vegetation Index (NDVI), a ratio of the near infrared of band 1 and visible of band 2 radiances, is very useful in conducting any study related to chlorophyll, because the ratioing of these two channels tends to be a better indicator of biomass rather than one band. In this study the Maximization methodology has been used as it reduces the lowering effects of NDVI values have been calculated for the study from May 1985 to April 1986. The result not only differentiates between the cropped area and the wooded mountainous area, but also recognizes that the rainy season in "all" cases may not be singlemost "green" (vegetative) period of the year. The months of October and February have also been other green periods due to improvement of irrigation and use of hybrid seeds over time.

In Rajasthan state the agricultural production has been increased in two ways: either by bringing the non-agricultural land under plough or by using all possible means of modern technologies. Sharma and Bhardwaj in their paper on Agricultural Land Development and Changes in Rajasthan demonstrated that in the long run, these led to overexploitation of soil to its maximum carrying capacity which consequently affected the soil condition adversely and generated the climatic environment like Rajasthan from 1950 to 1988-89. At the initial stage, the technical inputs and the mechanization of farming reflected the intensification of productivity. However, in the later period it has been interestingly observed that while the area under cereal crops has increased and crop land use intensified, even then the yield of most crops like maize, mustard, bajra, jowar etc. has decreased. The soil water regime has also been adversely affected.

Gupta has stated in his paper that urban land policy has become the most important instrument of planning, development construction, management and maintenance of urban spaces. The urban land policy has 8 important components: (1) Law of the land–modifications in various acts, (2) Planning and development of urban spaces, (3) Dispersal, (4) Control of land use, (5) Recapturing plus values of land, (6) Land management, (7) Maintenance of colonies, and (8) Conversion of lease-hold into free-hold. For a sound urban land policy, all these components should be studied and then decision taken.

Adinarayana Reddy in his paper on Urban Land Policies in India: Retrospect and Prospect has stated that because of unprecedented growth of urban population, the demand on urban land is increasing day by day. The main problem in India, is not shortage of urban land but its wasteful utilization. So the main aim of urban land planning is to ensure that land needed for urban development is supplied in need quantities, appropriate prices having regard to efficiency and equity in the allocation of resources. The paper attempts to review urban land policy which directly and indirectly controls and influences land development in India. The present land policy has several pitfalls regarding land use control and tax measurement. The land use controls are poor and inefficient without giving a single thought to the lower income group and previous laws. The main objective of the tax levies is generally to raise revenue rather than efficient use of land resources. Therefore, some direct and indirect measures should be taken to reform the policies. The direct measures include land readjustment and replotting, institutional rearrangement, alternative land tenure, etc. and indirect land measures include a well articulated property tax with regular and timely evaluation, imposing high tax rates on vacant lands, tightening up of the approval process to reduce un-social activities.

Land values in urban areas are dynamic because it is the result of many economic and social forces. However the nature and spatial distribution of land value is different in the cities in developed and developing countries. Comparing the land value surfaces of Akron (U.S.A.) and Madras (India), Dutt has emphasized that in the case of developed country cities the difference between the land values of the core of the CBD and the periphery is very marked compared to that of the developing countries. It is stated that because of multiple nuclei the cities in developed country possess significant peaks. On the contrary, in the central commercial areas of developing country cities the peak value denominates and the secondary peaks are universal. In other words, land value conforms to the traditional concept of distance decay with unicorn interruptions of local peaks.

The paper by Lado has demonstrated the main issues involving land tenure and ownership in the formulation of physical development plans for Eldoret, an emerging growth centre in western Kenya. Rapid urbanization in Eldoret has destabilized the balance between people, housing, employment, transport, electricity and water facilities. They are the results of colonial physical urban planning strategies. It is, therefore, suggested that Kenya has to develop its own indigenous philosophy for the acquisition of more land for urban infrastructure development. There is a need for a thorough and more comprehensive physical development planning strategies dependent on the local personnel and financial resources.

Bellamy and McAlpine in their paper on Estimating Food Production in Papua New Guinea have assessed the potential of the natural resources of Papua New Guinea for the development of food and cash crop production. It requires the assessment of natural resources and its functionality of population distribution and its functionality of population distribution and growth. The authors have dealt with four aspects of Papua New Guinea, namely: (a) Resource inventory, (b) Population and its distribution, (c) Different farming systems under operation, and (d) Crop eco-physiology. These groups are divided into a number of sub-groups. After studying these factors, a synthesis of information in done for the development of methodology of estimation. This gives scope for the assessment of crop productivity, land evaluation and food production and cash cropping as well as determination of critical areas in terms of intensification and degradation of land resource. In turn, a balanced estimation of food production potential can be achieved.

Yadav in his paper on Economics of Conserving Degraded Land for Agriculture has pointed out that agricultural land that is not treated properly gets degraded, input increases but output comes down. Land is limited resource and cannot be created or expanded. Thus, land which is degraded at one time can be reclaimed which can give very good return and in this context Yadav has taken up the study of the economics of conserving degraded land for agriculture with an example of Palia village, Gauriganj block of Sultanpur district. Land which is lying degraded for several years requires years to restore the soil fertility. In the beginning years of reclamation relatively the cost is higher but in later years the cost decreases and output increases. The reclamation cost also varies according to the suitability and capability of the land as well as the terrain of the area plus the extent to which the land is degraded. Reclamation can be taken as essential one in view of economic and environmental development by bringing additional degraded land under use.

Yadav in another paper on Strategies for Conserving Degraded Land observed that agricultural production through the application of science and technology has helped transforming Indian agriculture from subsistence type into commercial farming system. The research and development efforts, its impact is reflected in the achievement of the self-sufficiency in the food grain production whereby number of problems are faced as serious challenges due to increasing population, depleting land fertility, dryland etc. There is need to hold mission-oriented basic research particularly for wasteland which holds great potential for development focusing attention towards cropping system for irrigated and assured rainfall areas. For speedy diffusion of available innovations on wasteland well organized system to transfer of technology need to be developed. The use of appropriate channel in transmitting the information of wasteland technology is, therefore, of great importance.

Bandopadhyay in his paper on Reclamation of Sagar Island, West Bengal: Environmental Problems and Human Responses has stated that the reclamation of Sagar Island, an esturine island at the mouth of Hugli, West Bengal, was begun from 1811. This deprived the area of the natural process of delta building above the highest high tide and storm surge levels. After six cyclonic storms periodically devastated the island, a scheme of constructing storm refuges across the island, according to a specific site-plan, was undertaken in 1871. Currently, with population of 131,150 (1991 estimates), almost whole of the island is settled. Coastal erosion, salt water incursion, dune encroachment and sand blasting over agricultural areas are the major hazards it now faces. Coastal erosion is most severe in the eastern most section. The marginal earthen embankments of the island are inadequate for the sustained storm waves affecting the coast and show frequent breaches. Sand encroachment is mainly affecting the east central and eastern sections of the coastal zone. Afforestation programmes, in places have satisfactorily checked dune migration—even if temporarily. However, a sample opinion survey conducted in three sea-front villages of the island, shows some dissatisfaction about implementation management projects. Since a large outlay is inconceivable, hazard-prevention projects of the island should involve mobilization of the existing resources in a more rational framework.

P. Eaton in his paper on Wetland Management—Traditional Rights and Recreational Uses: The Tonda Wildlife Management Area of Papua New Guinea has stated that the relationship of land tenure to conservation has long been recognized as a significant one. It provides a motive for managing renewable resources and the means to do this by controlling access to these resources. There is a need to reinforce traditional rights and customary land tenure in order to conserve the wild life resources of a unique wetland area. This prevents overexploitation of resources whereby indigenous land owners may control the exploitation of their resources by outsiders. Further, the conservation policies will be more effective to protect and formalize these indigenous rights and customary practices. The case study for Papua New Guinea describes the efforts made towards conserving resources through customary tenure systems. These traditional conservation and tenure help to maintain a balance between rural societies and the natural resources that sustained them.

Thakur has investigated the genesis of the wasteland and their reclamation in the Damodar river basin. The study has revealed that ravine, gullied, derelict, waterlogged, degraded forest and weed-infected lands are responsible for making wastelands. Approximately, 50 per cent of Hazaribag, Bokaro and Giridih districts are under severe ravine erosion. Therefore, some major steps are required to be taken to reclaim these degrading lands. The Damodar Valley Corporation has made some strides in this direction like multipurpose dams on the Damodar river and its tributaries have been constructed to check the water seepage.

REFERENCE

Academy of the Science of U.S.S.R. (1958). "The application of drainage in the reclamation of the saline soils", *Translated from Russian*, Moscow.

Agrawal, A. (1995). "Dismantling the divide between indigenous and scientific knowledge", *Development and Change*, 26: 413-39.

Anderson, A.G. (ed.) (1980). *The Land Our Future: Essays on Land Use and Conservation*, Christchurch: New Zealand Geographical Society.

Arnolds, A. (2005). "Approaches to land care: A century of soil conservation in Iceland", *Land Degradation and Development*, 16(2): 113-25.

Bahren, T.S. (1981). "The utilization and management of land resources in Malaysia", *Geo Journal*, 5: 557-61.

Barrera-Bassols, N. and Zinck, A. (2003). "Land moves and land behaves: Indigenous discourse on sustainable land management in Pichataro, Patzcuaro Basin, Mexico", *Geografiska Annaler*, 85 A: 229-45.

Batabyal, A.A. (1998). "Land development and preservation over time and under uncertainty: A review and a research agenda", *Ecological Economics*, 25:233-38.

Bell-gam, W. (1988). *Land Reclamation and Environmental Management*, New Delhi: Sterling Publications Pvt. Ltd.

Biswas, A.K. (1993). "Land resources for sustainable agricultural development in Egypt", *Ambio*, 22(8): 556-60.

Blaikie, P. and Brookfield, H.C. (eds.) (1987). *Land Degradation and Society*; London: Methuen.

Bond, A.R. and Piepenburg, K. (1990). "Land reclamation after surface mining in the USSR: Economic, political, and legal issues", *Soviet Geography*, pp. 332-65.

Bosetti, V., Conrad, J.M. and Messinat, E. (2004). "The value of flexibility: preservation, remediation or development for. . .", *Environmental and Resource Economics*, 29(2): 219-29.

Bradley, D. and Grainger, A. (2004). "Social resilience as a controlling influence on desertification in Senegal", *Land Degradation and Development*, 15(5): 451-70.

Bradshaw, A.D. and Chadwick, M.J. (1980). *The Restoration of Land: The Ecology and Reclamation of Derilict and Degraded Land*, Oxford: Blackwell Scientific Publication.

Bradshaw, A.D. (1983). "The restoration of mined land", in A. Warren and F.B. Goldsmith (eds.) *Conservation in Perspective*, New York: John Wiley and Sons, pp. 177-79.

Bradshaw, A.D. (1984). "Ecological principles and land reclamation practice", *Landscape Planning*, 11: 35-48.

Brinkman, R. and Smyth, A.J. (eds) (1973). Land Evaluation for Rural Purposes, 17 International Institute for Land Reclamation and Improvement, Wageningen, The Netherlands.

Bridges, E.M. (1987). *Surveying Derelict Land*, Oxford: Clarendon Press.

Bryant, C.R. and Russwurm, L.H. (1982). *The City's Countryside: Land and Its Management in the Rural-Urban Fringe*, London: Longman.

Buchanan, R.O. (1968). "The man and his work", *Land Use and Resources: Studies in Applied Geography*; Institute of British Geographers, Special Publication No. 1: 3-11.

Buringh, P. (1986). "Land evaluation for agriculture in the tropics: A comparison of some new methods", in R. Lal, P.A. Sanchez and R.W. Cummings (eds.) *Land Clearing and Development in the Tropics*, Rotterdam: A.A. Balkema, pp. 29-36.

Burrough, P.A. (1986). *Principles of Geographical Information Systems for Land Resources Assessment*, Oxford: Clarendon Press.

Cha, Z., Lin, Z.M. and Luo, W. (2005). "Sustainable land management practices for rubber plantations in mountainous areas of Hainan", *Pedosphere*, 15(3): 404-08.

Chaturvedi, A. (1981). "The concept of land capability and suitability", in N. Mohammad (ed.) *Perspectives in Agricultural Geography, Vol. 3: Land Use and Planning*, New Delhi: Concept Publishing Company, 61-73.

Chiddick, D. and Millington, A. (eds.) (1984). *Land Management: New Directions*, Proceedings of the Land Management Research Conference held at Leicester Polytechnique, September 15-17, 1983, London: E & P.N. Spon.

Chishlom, A. and Dumsday, R. (eds.) (1987). *Land Degradation: Problems and Policies*, Cambridge: Cambridge University Press.

Choudhary, B. (1968). "Delimitation of land capability classes and its application in the land use planning of the Subarnrekha Basin", *Geographical Outlook*, 5: 95-102.

Choudhary, R.N.C. "Land classification on the basis of use capability: Arambagh Subdivision, Hooghly District, West Bengal", *Essays on Agricultural Geography*, Calcutta, 118-22.

Cools, N., De Pauwn, E. and Deckers, J. (2003). "Towards an integration of conventional land evaluation methods and farmers soil suitability assessment: case study in North-West Syria", *Agriculture, Ecosystems and Environment*, 95(1): 327-42.

Cornforth, I.S. (1999). "Selecting indicators for assessing sustainable land management", *Journal of Environment Management*, 56(3): 173-79.

Cullen, M. and Woolery, S. (eds.) (1985). *Second World Congress on Land Policy, 1983*, Boston: Oelgeschlager, Gunn and Hain Publishers.

Das, P.L. and Bhattacharya, R. (1978). "Criteria for land capability classification", *Geographical Review of India*, 40 (4): 340-44.

Das, P.L. and Bhattacharya, R. (1981). "Land capability classes *vis-à-vis* land use planning regions: A case study of Kaliaghai river basin", in N. Mohammad (ed.) *Perspectives in Agricultural Geography, Vol. 3: Land Use and Planning*, New Delhi: Concept Publishing Company, 61-73.

Datta, K.K., deJong, C. and Singh, O.P. (2000). "Reclaiming salt-affected land through drainage in Haryana, India: A financial analysis", *Agricultural Water Management*, 46: 55-71.

Datta, S.K. (1986). *Soil Conservation and Land Management*, Dehradun, International Book Distributors.

Davidson, D.A. (1976). "Terrain evaluation: Testing a technique in lower Deeside", *Scottish Geographical Magazine*, 92: 108-19.

Davidson, D.A. (1986). *Land Evaluation*, New York: Van Nostrand Reinhold.

Davis, K. (1976). *Land Use*, New York: Mc Graw Hill Inc.

Day, M.J. and Chenoweth, M.S. (2004). "The Karstland of Trinidad and Tobago, their land use and conservation", *Geographical Journal*, 170(3): 256-66.

DeSouza, A.R. and Stutz, F.P. (1994). *The World Economy: Resources, Location, Trade and Development*, 2nd Edition, New York: Macmillan College Publishing Company.

Dennington, V.A. and Chadwick, M.J. (1982). "Derilict and wasteland: Britain's neglected land resource", *Journal of Environmental Management*, 16: 229-39.

De, N.K. and Jana, N.C. (1997). *The Land: Multifaceted Appraisal and Management*, Kolkata: Sribhumi Publishing Company.

Diegnes, A.S. (1991). "The role of cultural diversity and communal participation in wetland management in Brazil", *Landscape and Urban Planning*, 20: 61-66.

Dodson, M. (1994). "The end of the beginning: Refinding aboriginality", *Australian Aboriginal Studies;* 1: 2-13.

Doubbday, G.P. (1974). "The reclamation of land after coal mining", *Outlook on Agriculture*, 8.

Dumanski, J., Gameda, S. and Pieri, C. (1998). *Indicators of Land Quality and Sustainable Land Management: An Annotated Bibliography*, Washington D.C: The World Bank.

Eaton, P. (1991). "Wetland management: Traditional rights and recreational uses: The Tonda Wildlife Management Area of Papua New Guinea", *Landscape and Urban Planning,* 20: 67-72.

Eden, M.J. (1978). "Ecology and land development: The case of the Amazonian rainforest", *Transactions of the Institute of British Geographers*, 3(4): 444-63.

Eden, M.J. (1990). *Ecology and Land Management in Amazonia*, London: Belhaven Press.

Eweg, H.H.A., Lammeren, R.V., Deurloo, H. and Woldu, Z. (1998). "Analyzing degradation and rehabilitation for sustainable land management in the highlands of Ethiopia", *Land Degradation and Development*, 9(6): 529-42.

FAO (1976). A Framework for Land Evaluation, Rome: *FAO Soils Bulletin 32*, pp.72

Fulier, R.M. and Parsell, R.J. (1990). "Classification of TM imagery in the study of land use in lowland Britain: Practical consideration for operational use", *International Journal of Remote Sensing*, 11: 1901-917.

Fuller, R.M., Sheail, J. and Barr, C.J. (1994). "The land of Britain, 1930-1990: A comparative study of field mapping and remote sensing techniques," *The Geographical Journal,* 16: 173-84.

Gadgil, M., Berkes, F. and Folke, C. (1993). "Indigenous knowledge for biodiversity conservation", *Ambio,* 22(2-3): 151-56.

Gerasimov, I.P. (1983). "Land resources of the world, their use and reserves, definition of land quality and agricultural potential by soil survey maps", *Geoforum*, 14: 427-39.

Ghosh, R. (2000). "Geological reconstruction of coal-mine disturbed lands in India's Jharia coalfield", in M.J. Haigh (ed.) (2000) *Reclaimed Land: Erosion Control, Soils and Ecology,* Rotterdam: A.A. Balkema, pp. 339-68.

Grainger, A. (1990). *The Threatening Desert: Controlling Desertification*, London: Earthscan.

Green, J.E. (1969). "The problem of reclamation of derelict land after coal strip mining in Appalachian", *The Southeastern Geographer*, 9: 36-47.

Greenland, D.J., Gregory, P.J. and Nye, P.H. (eds.) (1998). *Land Resources: On the Edge of the Malthusian Precipice?* New York: CAB International.

Gupta, R.K. (1981). "Ecological approach to land capability classification and regional planning", in N. Mohammad (ed.) *Perspectives in Agricultural Geography, Vol.3: Land Use and Planning*, New Delhi: Concept Publishing Company, 61-73.

Gupta, R.K. and Prajapati, M.C. (1983). "Reclamation and use of ravine lands", in Alam Singh (ed) *Desert Resources and Technology*, Jodhpur: Scientific Publishers, pp. 221-62.

Haans, J.C.F.M., Steur, G.G.L. and Heide, G. (eds.) (1984). *Progress in Land Evaluation,* Rotterdam: A.A. Balkema.

Haigh, M.J. (ed.) (2000). *Reclaimed Land: Erosion Control, Soils and Ecology,* Rotterdam: A.A. Balkema.

Haigh, M.J. (ed.) (2000). "The aims of land reclamation", in M.J. Haigh (2000) *Reclaimed Land: Erosion Control, Soils and Ecology,* Rotterdam: A.A. Balkema, pp. 1-20.

Harden, C. (1986). "Soil erosion and land capability evaluation in the upper Rio Pustaza Drainage, Eastern Ecuadorian Andes", *Mountain Research and Development*, 6 (11): 88-89.

Higgins, G.M. and Kassam, A.H. (1981). "Regional assessment of land potential", *Nature and Resources*, 17 (4).

Hoffman, D.W. (1976). "Soil capability analysis and land resource development in Canada", in G.R. McBoyle and E. Sommerville (eds.) *Canada's Natural Environment: Essays in Applied Geography*, Toronto: Methuen, pp. 140-67.

Howitt, R. (2001). *Rethinking Resource Management: Justice, Sustainability and Indigenous Peoples*; London: Routledge.

Humphreys, G.S. and Groth, B. (2001). "Land recovery following extensive sheet erosion at Menangle, New South Wales", in A.J. Conacher (ed.) *Land Degradation*, Boston: Kluwer, 255-74.

Hutchinson, C. (1985). "Remote sensing for arid zone development", in Y. Grandus (ed.) *Desert Development: Man and Technology in Sparse Lands,* Dordrecht: D. Reidel Publishing Company, pp. 201-17.

ICAR (1977). *Desertification and Its Control*, Indian Council of Agricultural Research, New Delhi.

Jeffery, R.C.V. and Chooye, P.M. (1991). "The peoples role in wetland management: The Zambian initiative", *Landscape and Urban Planning*. 20: 73-79.

Jha, B.N. (1965). "Land capability classification of the Kosi region". *Geographical Outlook*, 4: 75-80.

Jha, V.C. (1984). "Wasteland types and their effective utilisation in Birbhum district", *The Deccan Geographer*, 41: 231-42.

Jinfa, L. (1994). "China combats desertification", *Our Planet*, 6(5): 25-26.

Kanda, M. (2000). "Land resource management in India", www.pib.nic.in/feature/feyr2000/fsep2000/f120920001.html.

Kamel, S. and Dapl, C. (2005). "The economics of hybrid power systems for sustainably desert agriculture in Egypt", *Energy*, 30(8): 1271-81.

Kappel, M. (1993). "Methods of land evaluation and land use planning for rural areas: A review," *Transactions of the Institute of Indian Geographers*, 15(2): 53-69.

Kar, A. (1996). "Morphology and evolution of sand dunes in the Thar Desert as key to sand control measures", *Indian Journal of Geomorphology*, 1(2): 177-206.

Karmanov, I.I., Bulgakov, D.S., Karmanov, L.A. and Putilin, E.I. (2002).

"Modern aspects of the assessment of land quality and soil fertility", *European Soil Science*, 35(7): 754-60.

Kaul, R.N. (1996). "Sand dune stabilization in the Thar Desert of India: A synthesis", *Annals of Arid Zone*, 35(3): 225-40.

Kilic, S., Senal, S. and Evrendilek, F. (2003). "Evaluation of land use potential and suitability of ecosystems in Antakya for reforestation, recreation, arable farming and residence", *Turkish Journal of Agriculture and Forestry*, 27(1): 15-22.

Kirillova, T.B. and Ovchinnikova, V.H. (1975). "Predicting the reclamation of land after surface mining in the Central Chernozam Region", *Soviet Geography*, 16: 381389.

Kivell, P.T. (1987). "Derelict land in England: Policy responses to a continuing problem", *Regional Studies*, 21: 265-70.

Klingebiel, A.A. and Montgomery, P.H. (1961). *Land Capability Classification*, U.S. Department of Agriculture, Soil Conservation Service, Agriculture Handbook No. 210, Washington, D.C.

Kolarkar, A.S., Joshi, D.C. and Kar, A. (eds.) (1996). *Land Resources and Their Management for Sustainability in Arid Regions*, Jodhpur: Scientific Publishers, pp. 29-47.

Kuhn, R.G. and Duerden, F. (1996). "A review of traditional ecological knowledge: An interdisciplinary Canadian perspective", *Culture*, 16 (1): 71-84.

Kumar, A. and Pandey, R.N. (1989). *Wasteland Management in India*, New Delhi: Ashish Publishing Company.

Kumar, R. (1996). *Integrated Land Management: Scarcity to Surplus*, New Delhi: Society for Promotion of Wasteland Development.

Krishnamurti, Y.V.N and Adiga, S. (1999). "Remote Sensing and GIS for land use planning", in T. Haque (ed.) *Land Use Planning in India*, National Centre for Agricultural Economics and Policy Research, New Delhi, pp. 157-66.

Little, P.D., Horowitz, M.H. and Endre Nyerges, A. (eds.) (1987). *Lands at Risk in the Third World*, Boulder: Westview Press.

Mabbutt, J.A., Schneider, H.J. and Nava, R. (eds.) (1980). *Strategies for Improved Management of Latin American Drylands*, The United Nations University, Tokyo.

Mabbutt, J.A. (1980). *Research and Training for Management of Arid Lands*, The United Nations University, Tokyo.

Martin, G.J. and James, P.E. (1972). *All Possible Worlds: A History of Geographical Ideas*, New York: John Wiley and Sons.

Mather, A.S. (1986). *Land Use*, London: Longman.

MacLeod, N.D. and Noble, J.C. (2001). "Reconsidering the economic scope for rehabilitating degraded Australian semi-arid rangelands: Issues of control, process and integration", in A.J. Conacher (ed.) *Land Degradation*, Boston: Kluwer, 291-304.

McCormack, D.E. and Stocking, M.A. (1986). "Soil potential ratings: An alternative form of land evaluation", *Soil Survey and Land Evaluation,* 6: 37-41.

McGregor, D.F.M. and Thompson, D.A. (eds.) (1995). *Geomorphology and Land Management in a Changing Environment,* Chichester: Wiley and Sons.

McRae, S.G. and Burnham, C.P. (1981). *Land Evaluation*, Oxford: Clarendon Press.

Miles, C.W.N. (1976). "Land management and land use", in M.MacEwan (ed.) *Future Landscapes*, London: Chatto and Windus, pp. 74-85.

Ministry of Rural Development (2000). *Wasteland Atlas of India*, New Delhi.

Mohammad, N. (ed.) (1981). *Perspectives in Agricultural Geography*, Vol. 3: *Land Use and Planning*; Delhi: Concept Publishing Company.

Mohammad, N. (1998). "Management of common land resources in Uttar Pradesh: Some issues and problems", *National Geographical Journal of India*, 44: 49-54.

Nagaraja, R. and Gautam, N.C. (1996). "Role of remote sensing and GIS in wasteland management in India", in M.J. Eden and J.T. Pandey (eds.) *Land Degradation in Tropics: Environmental and the Policy Issues,* London: Pinter, pp. 144-54.

Nagaraja, R., Narayan, L.R.A. and Gautam, N.C. (1989). "Utility of landsat thematic mapper data for wasteland development", *National Geographical Journal of India*, 35: 38.

Nortcliff, S. (1982). "Developments in soil and land evaluation", *Progress in Physical Geography*, 6: 283-91.

Ochola, W.O. and Kerkides, P. (2004). "An integrated indicator-based spatial decision support system for land quality assessment in Kenya", *Computers and Electronics in Agriculture*, 45: 3-26.

Osemwata, O. (1989). "Ownership, control and management of land in Bendel State, Nigeria: The changing role of traditional rulers", *Land Use Policy*, pp. 75-83.

Pandel, G.S. and Thapa, G.B. (2004). "Impact of social, institutional and ecological factors on land management practices in mountain watersheds of Nepal", *Applied Geography*, 24: 35-55.

Parry, J.T. and Eden, M.J. (1996). *Land Degradation in the Tropics*, London: Printer.

Parviz Koohafkan, A. (2000). "Land resources potential and sustainable land management: An overview", in S.P. Gawande, *et al.* (eds.) *Advances in Land Resource Management for 21st Century*, New Delhi: Soil Conservation Society of India.

Patra, P. (2004). *Land Degradation, Regeneration and Development Potential in the Northern Highlands of Orissa,* Ph.D. Thesis, Department of Geography, Delhi University.

Pender, J. (2004). "Development pathways for hillsides and highlands: Some lessons from Central America and East Africa", *Food Policy,* 29(4): 339-67.

Prasad, R. and Yadav, J.S.P. (1969). *Alkali Soil Reclamation: Questions and Answers*, Karnal: Central Soil Research Institute.

Rhodes, D. (2001). "Rehabilitation of deforested steep slopes on the east coast of New Zealand North Island", *Una Sylva*, 52: 21-29.

Rai, K. and Bhalla, D.K. (2000). "Computerization of land records in India", *GIS Development*, 4 (4): 38-40.

Rao, T.R. and Shekhar P. R. (2000). "Land records computerization: Issues and Approaches", *GIS Development*, 4 (4): 35-37.

Ravi Shankar, G., Raghavswamy, V. and Gautam, N.C. (2004). "Land use management practices: Retrospect and prospect", in N.C. Gautam and V. Raghavswamy (eds.) *Land Use/Land Cover and Management Practices in India*, Hyderabad: B.S. Publication.

Rojas, E. and Meganck, R.A. (1987). "Land distribution and land development in the Eastern Caribbean", *Land Use Policy*, pp. 157-67.

Ryan, P.J. (1990). "Role of trees in controlling land degradation", in *Proceedings of the Land Degradation Conference,* Geographical Society of New South Wales, Sydney, pp. 47-57.

Ryder, R. (1994). "Land evaluation for steepland agriculture in the Dominican Republic", *The Geographical Journal*, 160(1): 74-86.

Saxena, N.C. (2005). "Updating land records: Is computerization sufficient", *Economic and Political Weekly*, January 22, 2005: 313-21.

Saleh, M.A.E. (1998). "Alternative land management approaches in the highlands of southwestern Saudi Arabia", *Environmental Conservation*, 25(4): 295-304.

Schaller, F.W. and Sutton, P. (eds.). *Reclamation of Drastically Disturbed Lands*, Madison: American Society for Agronomy.

Schnabel, S., Gonzalez, F., Murillo, M. and Moreno, V. (2001). "Different techniques of pasture improvement and soil erosion in a wooded rangeland in South-West Spain: Methodology and preliminary results", in. J. Conacher (ed.) *Land Degradation*, Boston: Kluwer, 239-54.

Schoenberger, P.J. and Wysocki, D.A. (2005). "Hydrology of soils and deep regolith: A nexus between soil geography, ecosystem and land management", *Geoderma*, 126: 117-28.

Schroeder, R.A. (1997). "Re-claiming land in the Gambia: Gendered property rights and environmental intervention", *Annals of the Association of American Geographers*, 87(3): 487-508.

Scott, G. and Pain, C.F. (1982). "Land potential", in B. Carrad, D.A.M. Lea and K.T. Talyaga (eds.) *Enga: Foundations for Development*, Armidale: University of New England, pp. 128-45.

Shafi, M. (1962). *Land Utilization in Eastern U.P.*, Aligarh: Aligarh University.

Shafi, M. (1968). "*Problems of wastelands in India*", *The Geographer*, 15: 1-15.

Shafi, M. (1984). "Geographer and the society with special reference to India", *Annals of the National Association of Geographers of India*, 5.

Shafi, M. (2006). *Agricultural Geography*; Delhi: Pearson Education.

Sharma, H.S. (1972). "Land capability classification of the lower Chambal Valley", *Symposium on Land Use in Developing Countries,* Calcutta.

Sharma, K.D., Kumar, S. and Gough, L.P. (2000). "Rehabilitation of lands mined for limestone in the Indian Desert", *Land Degradation and Development*, 11: 563-74.

Sharma, S.C. (1981). "The concept of land capability and suitability", in N. Mohammad (ed.) *Perspectives in Agricultural Geography, Vol. 3: Land Use and Planning*, New Delhi: Concept Publishing Company, 61-73.

Sharma, S.C., Tripathi, D.N. and Sharma, M.L. (1988). "Usarland reclamation measures in India with special reference to Sangrampur block, District Sultanpur, U.P.", in S.C.Sharma (ed.) *Utilization of Wasteland for Sustainable Development in India*, New Delhi: Concept Publishing Company, 285-302.

Sharma, V.K. and Shukla, P.N. (1988). "Yamuna and Chambal rivers eroded land and its reclamation in Etawah district, U.P.", in S.C. Sharma (ed.) *Utilization of Wasteland for Sustainable Development in India*; New Delhi: Concept Publishing Company, 359-68.

Sharma, V.K. (1991). *Remote Sensing for Land Resource Planning*, New Delhi: Concept Publishing Company.

Siderius, W. (ed.) (1986). *Land Evaluation for Land Use Planning and Conservation in Sloping Areas, Wageningen, The Netherlands:* International Institute for Land Reclamation and Improvement Publication No. 40.

Sillitoe, P. (1998). "Knowing the land: Soil and land resource evaluation and indigenous knowledge", *Soil Use and Management*, 14(4): 188-93.

Singh, A.L. (1978). *Economics and Geography of Agricultural Land Reclamation*; New Delhi: B.R. Publishing Corporation.

Singh, A.L. (ed.) (1997). *Land Resource Management: Felicitation* Volume in Honour of Prof. M. Shafi, New Delhi: B.R. Publishing Corporation.

Singh, B. (1962). "Distribution of culturable wasteland and possibilities of its reclamation in Chakia, Banaras", *National Geographical Journal of India*, 7: 59-72.

Singh, S. (1988). "Geomorphology and management of sand dunes in the Great Indian desert", in S. Singh and R.C. Tewari (eds.) *Geomorphology and Environment*, Allahabad: Geographical Society, Allahabad, pp. 616-29.

Singh, S. (1997). "Drifting sand hazard and its control in the Thar Desert", *Indian Journal of Geomorphology*, 2(1): 17-38.

Singh, S. and Das, D.C. (2000). "Land management and land use policy issues in India", in S.P. Gawande, *et al.* (eds.) *Advances in Land Resources Management for 21st century*, New Delhi: Soil Conservation Society of India, 94-108.

Singh, S. and Kar, A. (1995). *Desertification Control in the Arid Ecosystem of India for Sustainable Development*, Bikaner: Agro-Botanical Publishers.

Singh, S. and Shankarnarayan, K.A. (1986). "Dynamics, morphology and management of sand dunes in Great Indian Desert", in Alam Singh and M.L. Ohri (eds.) *Current Practices in Geotechnical Engineering*, Delhi: International Book Traders, pp. 23-47.

Singh, S. and Singh, R.P. (1995). "Wastelands and their rehabilitation in India", in R.P. Singh (ed.) *Sustainable Development of Dryland Agriculture in India*, Jodhpur: Scientific Publishers, pp. 473-96.

Sinha, P.P.K. (2000). *Land Reforms in India: An Unfinished Agenda*, New Delhi: Sage.

Smil, V. (1981). "Land use management in the People's Republic of China", *Environmental Management*, 5(4): 301-11.

Stamp, L.D. (1937). "Planning the land for the future", *Town and Country Planning*, 5: 118.

Stamp, L.D. (1942). "Principles of land utilization", *Agenda*; 1: 25-37.

Stamp, L.D. (1948). *The Land of Britain: Its Use and Misuse*, London: Longman Green and Company Ltd.

Steiner, F.W. (1999). "Land evaluation and suitability analysis", in D.E. Alexander and R.W. Fairbridge (eds.) *Encyclopedia of Environmental Science*, Kluwer Academic Publishing.

Stewart, G.A. (ed.) (1980). *Land Evaluation*, Melbourne: Macmillan.

Swaminathan, M.S. (2004). "Foreword", in N.C. Gautam and V. Raghavswamy (eds.) *Land Use/Land Cover and Management Practices in India*, Hyderabad: B.S. Publications.

Syres, J.K. and Rimmer, D.L. (eds.) (1994). *Soil Science and Sustainable Land Management in the Tropics*, Wallingford: Lab International.

Syres, J.K., Hamblen, A. and Pushparajoh, E. (1995). "Indicators and thresholds for the evaluation of sustainable land management", *Canadian Journal of Soil Science*, 75: 423-28.

Sys, C. (1980). "Land characteristics and qualities and method of rating them", in *FAO, Land Evaluation Guidelines for Rainfed Agriculture*, Rome: World Soil Resources Report, 5:23-49.

Thapa, G.B. and Pandel, G.S. (2000). "Evaluation of the livestock carrying capacity of land resources in the hills of Nepal based on total digestive nutrient analysis", *Agriculture, Ecosystem and Environment*, 78: 223-35.

Thakur, V., Khadanga, Venkatesh, D.S and Shukla, D.R. (2004). "Land management systems in India—Past, present and future". www.gisdevelopment.net/application/lis/overview/lisrp0004.htm

Tsoar, H. and Zohar, Y. (1985). "Desert sand dunes and its potential for modern agricultural development", in Y. Grandus (ed.) *Desert Development: Man and Technology in Sparse Lands*, Dordrecht: D. Reidel Publishing Company, pp. 184-200.

United States Department of agriculture (1951). *Soil Survey Manual*.

Velayutham, M. (2000). "Status of land resources in India", in S.P. Gawande, *et al.* (eds.) *Advances in Land Resources Management for 21st Century*, New Delhi: Soil Conservation Society of India, 67-83.

Vijayaditya, N., Shukla, D.R., Thakur, V. and Malik, L.N. (2000). "IT for land resources development and management", in S.P. Gawande, *et al.* (eds.) *Advances in Land Resources Management for 21st Century*, New Delhi: Soil Conservation Society of India, 63-66.

Volker, A. (1982). "Polders: An ancient approach to land reclamation", *Nature and Resources*, 18(4): 2-13.

Wang, S., Zheng, R. and Yang, Y. (2000). "Combating desertification: The Asian experience", *International Forestry Review*, 2: 112-17.

Werner, K. (1973). "Reclamation of land damaged by open-cast mining methods and results", *Biological Conservation*, 5: 277-80.

Whyte, R.O. (1976). *Land and Land Appraisal*, The Haque: Dr. W. Jank Publishers.

Winklerprins, A.M.G.A. (1999). "Local soil knowledge: A tool for sustainable land management", *Society and Natural Resources*, 12(2): 151-61.

Wong, M.H., Wong, J.W.C. and Baker, A.J.M. (1999). *Remediation and Management of Degraded Lands*, New York: Lewis Publishers.

Yadav, J.S.P. and Aggarwal, R.R. (1959). "Dynamics of soil changes in the reclamation of saline, alkali soils of the Indo-Gangetic alluvium", *Journal of Indian Society of Soil Sciences*, 7: 77-86.

Yadav, J.S.P. and Padmaja, S. (1985). "Reclamation of usar land in Sultanpur district: A case for rural development", *National Geographer*, 20: 45-53.

Yadav, R.S. (1997). *Remote Sensing in Land Evaluation*, Delhi: Rajesh Publications.

Young, A. (1973). "Rural land evaluation", in J.A. Dawson and J.C. Doornkamp (eds.) *Evaluating the Human Environment*, London: Edward Arnold, 5-33.

Young, A. and Goldsmith, P.F. (1977). "Soil survey and land evaluation in developing countries: A case study in Malawi", *Geographical Journal*, 153: 407-38.

Young, A. (1978). "Recent advances in the survey and evaluation of land resources", *Progress in Physical Geography*, 2: 462-79.

Young, A. (1998). *Land Resources: Now and for the Future*, Cambridge: Cambridge University Press.

Zhimin, L. and Wenzhi, Z. (2001). "Shifting sand control in Central Tibet", *Ambio*, 30(6): 376-80.

Zhou, Q. (1998). "Use of GIS technology for land resource inventories and modelling for sustainable regional development", *Ambio*, 27: 444-50.

Zonneveld, I.S. (1995) *Land Ecology: An Introduction to Lansdcape Ecology as a base for Land Evaluation, Land Management and Conservation*, Amsterdam: SPB Academic Publishing.

1

Land Evaluation: Some General Considerations

J.J. BASINSKI*

Introduction

The purpose of this paper is to consider some general features of land (or resource) evaluation including its aims, its place in environmental planning, the approaches and methods used and its data requirements. Land evaluation for agriculture, forestry and nature conservation — the three main forms of rural land use is discussed in more detail in the following section.

Land evaluation can be defined as assessment (based on local experience) or prediction (based on deduction from knowledge acquired elsewhere) of land quality for a specified use, in terns of its:

- *productivity;* e.g. yield or carrying capacity
- *degradation hazards*; e.g. erosion, salinization, pollution
- *management requirements*; inputs and techniques.

The object of land evaluation is to determine the physical, biological and ultimately economic and social consequences of the various land use options possible on different land parcels which make up a planning region (which may range from a single farm to the whole country). Thus, land evaluation is an essential middle phase in the land use or environmental planning process. It is preceded by a data acquisition phase concerned with the gathering of data concerning

* Reprinted with permission from Environmental Planning and Management eds. J.J. Basinski and K.D. Cocks, pp. 59-65, Commonwealth Science Council and the CSIRO Devision of Water and Land Resources, Canberra.

land characteristics and their effects on land use and *vice versa.* It provides the information necessary for the following phase concerned with choosing the most appropriate land use allocation pattern and management system. However, the importance of feedbacks in the planning process must be constantly stressed; planning goals, policies and scale determine the type of land evaluation, its criteria and land uses to be considered; these in turn determine what data should be sought through land surveys and other studies.

Approaches to Land Evaluation

There are several distinct approaches to land evaluation, which can be regarded as evolutionary states in the development of evaluation methodology, even though to some extent their development overlapped in time, and though they are not mutually exclusive (Nix, 1968; Angus *et al.,* 1974).

Trial-and-Error

This is the oldest approach to land evaluation and given time its end result is generally successful in evolving stable and viable land use systems. In fact, most of the well established land use patterns and practices existing today have been evolved largely or wholly through this approach. Its social costs are, however, considerable since each advance is usually achieved as a result of many failures. The strategy can be particularly dangerous when major changes in land use are tried over large areas, because it can lead to serious irreversible land degradation, such as erosion or salinization, well before these detrimental effects are recognized.

Trial-and-error is still the most widespread approach to land evaluation, with most farmers, foresters and other land users constantly engaging in experimentation. Unfortunately, apart from the major successes or failures, the results of these individual trials are seldom recorded so that experience gained is usually lost. Monitoring the effects of land use practices in selected areas and examination of these effects in relation to land characteristics would be of great help in future evaluation and planning of land use.

Land Analogues

Because of spatial variation in land characteristics (climate, topography, soils, vegetation) experience gained from land use trials is strictly applicable only on the site where the trial was carried out. To overcome this limitation many land evaluation methods are based on the concept of transfer by analogy, based on the assumption that all occurrences of a defined class of land ('land analogues') will perform similarly under the same or similar land use.

The success of the approach depends on valid identification of land analogues. In the past this was often based on the 'gestalt' concept which perceives land types as complex but recognizable entities and identifies them as such without separate consideration of individual land attributes. By now identification of land analogues is generally based on various land classification systems which take into account characteristics of individual land attributes. The usefulness of these systems depends on selection and weighting of appropriate classification criteria in relation to land use under consideration.

This is not always easy, since many important land characteristics (e.g. soil hydrologic properties) are difficult to observe, measure and map. They therefore have to be estimated on the basis of covariance with more easily observable attributes; the strength of covariance is sometimes open to doubt (Austin and Basinski,1978). Another problem in establishing land analogues arises from non-explicit methods of land classification, making them difficult to repeat in new areas.

Because the importance of individual land attributes varies for different land uses, a land evaluation based on analogues which are identified through general land classifications (which in turn result from multi-purpose surveys) is likely to be less accurate than one based on land classifications developed for specific uses. These may be based either on data provided by multi-purpose surveys or by special purpose surveys. Modern methods of computer storage of survey data offer new opportunities for special purpose classifications and hence improvement of transfer of information by analogy.

Parametric Approach

With this approach the effects of characteristics of each land attribute (parameter) on productivity or degradation hazards, or both, are evaluated separately and then combined according to some formula which can be naively simple or highly complicated. In contrast to the analogue approach based on discrete classes, the parametric approach aims to provide a continuous scale of assessment. It is, therefore, more strictly applicable to point locations (sites) than to land parcels, which are never entirely homogeneous.

Two kinds of parametric evaluation methods can be distinguished. One kind is based on the preconceived ideas of their authors and are derived from essentially qualitative observations and experience. These methods generally use arbitrary ratings of land attribute characteristics related to easily observable features. They also employ additive, multiplicative or more complex formulae representing their authors' ideas on the relative importance of different land attributes and the interactions between then. Results obtained by these methods are usually expressed in the form of relative indices or scores. Examples of these methods are numerous (McRae and Burnham, 1981). The Storie Index Rating (Storie 1933, 1944) is one of the best known systems of assessing land productivity, while the Universal Soil Loss Equation (USLE) (Peterson and Swan, 1979) provides a classic example of evaluating erosion hazards.

The second kind of parametric evaluation method is based on exploratory, quantitative analyses of the relationships between land characteristics and land performance. These analyses employ statistical correlation-regression techniques and their results are often expressed in terms of absolute, rather than relative, values.

In environments where a simple attribute has the dominating influence on land use, simple correlations can have very useful predictive value. Rainfall is one such attribute and has been widely used to predict crop yields (e.g. Fisher, 1924) and erosion hazards (Foster, 1977). Where more than one factor is important among various multivariate forms of statistical analysis can be used (e.g. Beier, 1973).

One of the major deficiencies of the correlation-regression analysis is that its results are generally location-specific and often cannot be validly extrapolated to other locations. They also represent a static approach to highly dynamic relationships.

System Analysis

This approach can be regarded as a logical development of parametric methods, made practical by modern electronic computing facilities. It differs from the parametric approach by recognizing the holistic, but generally extremely complex nature of relationship between land characteristics and land use. It also relies explicitly on the causal nature of these relationships.

In essence this approach involves resolution of complex systems into progressively simpler components and subsequent synthesis of these components into a conceptual representation (flow chart) and ultimately mathematical representation (model) of a real-life system.

The models can then be used, employing simulation techniques, to examine the likely outcomes of different land use allocations and different land management practices. A great advantage of this approach is that it makes it possible to integrate information about land and its use derived from various sources in a rigorous and explicit manner. This should not only improve the standard of land evaluation but also highlight major gaps in relevant knowledge.

Although in the past two decades system analysis and modelling have attracted many able research workers and vocal advocates, the practical impact on land evaluation has been limited. Few if any comprehensive operational models of land productivity and/or degradation exist today even though there are many partial models of separate components and processes; attempts to combine these tend to produce complicated and ill-balanced structures of limited operational use. The successful comprehensive models have been in general simple, combining a sound conceptual framework with concentration on a few key processes and the practical availability of input data.

The contribution of system analysis to land evaluation has been mainly in the field of yield responses to climatic variables. The use of soil variables has been less common, because of the lack of easily available soil data. Some attempts have also been made to model erosion and salinity hazards.

Data Requirements

Whatever the approach adopted, land evaluation requires two sets of data which provide information on:

- land attribute characteristics and their spatial and temporal distribution.
- functional relationships between these characteristics and land use consequences.

The first set of data is derived from land (or resource) surveys, which are mainly concerned with temporarily stable land attributes (such as topography, and soils), and from climatological and hydrological studies, concerned with attributes which vary with time. These data are usually collected at specific points. Their spatial interpolation and extrapolation is the main problem in converting them into information on land. Fortunately, various techniques of remote sensing and mathematical surface-fitting methods increasingly provide the means of overcoming this difficulty (Nix, 1983).

The second set of data, concerning functional relationship, comes from general experience, various monitoring records and from research which ranges from simple applied experiments to highly sophisticated fundamental studies. The inadequacy of these data, rather than data on land characteristics, is by now more serious in most countries as far as land evaluation is concerned.

It is most important that the two data sets should be properly balanced in terms of context, precision and accuracy. Unless an item in one data set is complemented by a corresponding item in the other, it is of little or no value. Unfortunately, this is often the case. Collection of balanced land and land use data could benefit greatly from international cooperation, and is a topic which warrants consideration.

REFERENCES

Angus, J.F., Basinski, J.J., and Nix, H.A. (1974). Weather analysis and its application to production strategy in areas of climatic instability. International Expert Consultation on the Use of Improved Technology for Food Production in Rainfed Areas of Tropical Asia.

Austin, M.P., and Basinski, J.J. (1978). "Bio-physical survey of techniques," In M.P. Austin, and K.D. Cocks (eds.) *Land Use on the South Coast of New South Wales*. CISRO.

Beier, W. (1973). "Crop-weather analysis model: review and model development," *J. Appl. Met.* 12, 937-47.

Fisher, R.A. (1924). "The influence of rainfall distribution on the yield of wheat at Rothamstead," *Phil. Trans. R. Soc. Ser. B.* 213, 89-142.

Foster, G.R. (ed) (1977). *Soil erosion: Prediction and Control*. Proc. National Conference on Soil Erosion. Soil Conservation Soc. Amer. Spec. Publ. 21. Ankeny, Iowa.

McRae, S.G., and Burnham, C.P. (1981). *Land Evaluation*. Clarendon Press; Oxford.

Nix, H.A. (1968). "The assessment of biological productivity," In G.A. Stewart (ed.) *Land Evaluation*. McMillan, Melbourne.

Peterson, A.E., and Swan, J.B. (eds.) (1979). *Universal Soil Loss Equation: Past, Present and Future*. Soil Sci. Soc. Amer. Madison, Wisconsin (USA).

Storie, R.E. (1960). Rating soils for agricultural forest and grazing use. In *Land Classification and Evaluation Section*, 4th Int. Cong. Soil Science. Amsterdam.

2

Terrain Evaluation
Concept, Method and Application

NAGESHWAR PRASAD and ABHIMANYU MAHTO

The term 'terrain' is defined as a tract or facet or a part of the landscape with more or less homogeneous or uniform properties of natural features (e.g., slope morphology, soil characteristics, drainage condition, vegetation cover, etc.) and configuration viewed with regard to its suitability for some specific purpose.

'Terrain evaluation, as a process, involves first *analysis*: the simplification of the complex phenomenon which is the natural geographic environment; secondly *classification*: the organization of data distinguishing one area from another and characterizing each; and thirdly *appraisal*: the manipulation, interpretation, and assessment of data for practical ends' (Mitchell, 1977: 5).

Terrains are evaluated for planning their better uses. 'Land planning is in essence the determination of the optimum use of every acre of land which must be elastic and can change from time-to-time adopt the changing conditions' (Stamp, 1950, 426). In the strict sense, to evaluate a terrain means to ascertain its extent or to express it in numerical form. Often, evaluation is taken to be synonymous with assessment which involves an estimation of value. So, the objective of terrain evaluation or assessment is to judge the value of an area for defined purpose.

Defining Terrain and Differentiating it from Other Seemingly Similar Terms

Terrain (alternatively spelt terrane) which has become popular with geographers very recently is a generic terms. It is a term of multiple connotation and varying use. The term is a derivation from *terrra,* a Latin word meaning thereby 'earth'. In its derivative adjective form the term *terrenus* (Latin) or *terrenum* (French) means 'earthen'or 'earthly'. Now the term 'terrain' or 'terrane' is frequently used in noun from. In the Oxford Dictionary this term means 'standing ground' or 'position'. It also means 'a tract of country considered with regard to its natural features, configuration, etc.' In Webster Comprehensive Dictionary (Encyclopaedic Edition), it means a place or plot of ground, a region or territory viewed with regard to its suitability for some particular purpose'. In Mill's Dictionary the term means 'a district or tract of land considered with reference to its fitness or use for a special purpose'. In geography, particularly in geomorphology, however, the term terrain or terrane is used to imply more or less all what are spelled out above. But this term has been long familiar in military use with the meaning that of 'battle ground, or a region suited for defence, fortifications, etc.' (W.C.D.). In geology, it was indicating a name for a connected series, group or system of rocks or formations or a stratigraphic subdivision. Sometimes, the term appears to have a wide connotation. It refers to 'any tract or region of the earth's surface, considered, as a purely physical feature, an ecologic environment, a geologic setting or as a site of some applied activity of man— an engineering location, an architectural setting or a landscape analysed in terms of military science' (Encyclopaedia of Geomorphology, Ed. Fairbridge). Both the military and geological usage has now become unusual, and at least in geography and geomorphology the term is never used in this specific sense. The term terrain, as the geographer uses it, appears to mean a tract or facet or 'a part of the landscape, usually with simple form, on a particular rock or superficial deposit, and with soil and water regime that are either uniform over the whole of the fact or if not, vary in a simple and consistent way' (Webster and Beckett, 1970: 54).

Terrain is thus a facet of land with more or less homogeneous or uniform properties, uniformity not only in relief, but also in slope morphology, soil characteristics, drainage condition, vegetation cover and other natural features. In one sense the term is used to denote a 'region' with uniform properties of natural features and configuration. Terrain is, therefore, 'the expression of the geological character, the soil and the surface geometry of the earth's crust' (Mitchell, 1977: 13) and 'terrain studies are natural studies usually with an emphasis on relief—soil, vegetation, and drainage' (Stamp, 1968: 451).

In the foregoing lines stress has been given on '*a facet with uniform properties of natural features, not one but many*' and '*specific or particular purpose*'. This stress differentiates the term terrain from many other seemingly similar terms, e.g., *topography, relief, landforms, land surface form* (Hammond, 1964), *physiography* and *physical environment, etc. Topography* means the general configuration of the land surface. This word is general and it does not indicate any surface with specific purpose. *Relief* is, too, exclusively geometric and does not comprehend earth materials or structure. 'The word *landform* itself is becoming very much debatable day by day in the present sphere of geographical knowledge' (Singh, 1974: 1). *Land surface form* has been coined to avoid genetic implication, but it does not include materials of the earth. '*Physiography* is an older term which includes not only surface form and geology but also climatology, meteorology and oceanography and indeed natural phenomena in general' (Mitchell, 1977: 4). *Physical environment* is too general to comprehend discussion with particular purpose '*Landscape* or *land* are perhaps the closest equivalents, but both are somewhat wider concepts than terrain and the former rather too strongly connotes the visual and artistic aspects' (Mitchell, 1977: 4). Thus, the term 'terrain' differs from all these seemingly similar words. Virtually, it conforms more to homogeneous inventory unit of potential land use assessment for specific or particular purpose.

Terrain Classification

Many parameters are measured in the classification of terrain (King, 1970; Van Lopik and Kolb, 1959; Speight, 1968; Ollier, 1978; Desai, 1968; Singh,1974; Mitchell, 1977; and Kumar, 1984). An objective method is based on measurements of a number of properties like geology, surface elevation, surface forms, slope, characteristics plain-profile, relative relief, dissection index, ruggedness index, drainage texture and conditions, nature of soil, vegetation cover, climatic variations and many other land resources. But there is no agreement which parameters are to be used or all parameters are to be given due consideration. It is natural because it is not logical to restrict certain parameters for all purposes in all regions on all scales. For example, climate may be an important property to be considered for macro-regions, but it has no significance in terrain-classification of a micro-level region, say, a village or a group of villages. Similarly, all those specialists who are concerned with raising economic plants and animals will consider mainly three properties of land apart from its location in terrain classification: soil condition's moisture regime and surface conditions including relief, gradient, permeability, topographic limitations and vegetal cover, etc. In case of civil engineering, on the other hand, considerations will be given to the 'suitability of ground for load bearing, which can be derived from the particle size distribution, impressibility and shear strength of the soil under different moisture conditions, and form its liability to erosion and flash flooding, which is a function of slope, permeability and surface roughness (Mitchell, 1977: 8). All these are to say that parametric approaches will be different for earth scientists, civil and military engineers, agriculturists of all types, foresters, hydrologists, urban, rural and recreational planners, meteorologists and archaeologists. Some of the properties for terrain-classification are, however, more or less common, because they are of concern to more than one type of use. Most users would agree over the importance of a central core of information about land, which would include such properties as slope, soil particle size distribution, and moisture regime, and each would require additional specific data of less general interest. Thus, such parameters are used for all purposes in all regions on all scales.

Apart from this objectivity, a certain amount of subjectivity is considered to be valid and necessary in selecting boundaries of terrain units.

Objectives of Terrain Evaluation

The evaluation of terrain varies according to the objectives of a study. Two terrain evaluation researchers, for example, commissioned to investigate a particular areas, say, one for agricultural planning and another for industrial or forestry or recreation or settlement sites etc., could disagree from the very beginning about the data which ought to be collected and factors which ought to be considered with due weightage. It also varies according to the scale of the survey, from area to area and from time to time. In general, in developed or developing areas the less valuable terrain is for agriculture, the more valuable it is for residential and recreational purposes. The requirements for these two types of terrain use are sufficiently similar to bring them into frequent competition. While agriculture tends to favour flat fertile areas of little aesthetic charm, recreational and residential development prefer the proximity of hilly or rocky or upland areas.

Thus, the main objective of terrain evaluation is to put the terrain to its appropriate use. For example, in an area which is primarily a rural centre engaged mainly in agricultural activities, an intensive and successful propaganda is being made for rationalizing agriculture. The terrains cannot be evaluated only for purposes other than agriculture. Cultivation is the main occupation of the people in such cases and a good portion of cultivated terrain is very much suitable for agricultural practices. So, this terrain use should remain unchanged otherwise the rural economy will decline. Only thing is that some improvements in management practices within the present agricultural use should be made possible. The evaluation of such terrains is required so that cost-benefit ratio is maintained and planning implementation becomes successful. Keeping this in mind, the terrain is evaluated first for agricultural uses, and, then, some measures are suggested for those terrains which are unsuitable or less suitable for agricultural uses.

Methods of Terrain Evaluation

The preceding discussion reveals that the methods of terrain evaluation will vary widely according to the objectives of study, type of data used, assumptions in the evaluation, the study area, intensity and scale of survey and type of suitability classification to be used. It is why there are numerous methods of terrain evaluation that have been developed to present terrain users with better comprehension and utilization of the terrain. The methods range from the adoption of one single indicator of terrain resources (e.g. soil) as diagnostic of its capacity or suitability for various uses to a combination of many terrain characteristics. Even for similar objectives, different countries have developed different methods and systems of terrain evaluation. It is quite natural because the range of possible uses of terrain and purposes of evaluation is so wide that no one method could take account all of them. Moreover, terrain evaluation is itself not an end, it is a means to an end.

Reference should be made to various methods of terrain evaluation, e.g., the American or the USDA (United States Department of Agriculture), Canadian, British, USSR, CSIRO (The Commonwealth Scientific and Industrial Research Organization in Austrialia), Oxford MEXE (Military Engineering Experimental Establishment), FAO (Food and Agriculture Organization), Framework for Land Evaluation, Parametric, Land System method and many others (Cooke and Doornkamp, 1978: 308-351; Davidson, 1980: 16-51; De, 1984, 3-8; Kumar, 1984: 30-37; Mitchell, 1977: 23-37; Oliver, 1978: 277-316; Osunade, 1979: 167-177). Quite clearly even a brief description of these methods is beyond the scope of this paper. The authors can, however, conclude that all the methods of terrain evaluation noted above are members of two groups, *landscape method* and *parametric method.* The *landscape method* describes a land unit as an area or group of areas throughout which a recurring pattern of topography, soils, and vegetation can be recognized. To a very large extent, this method is based on the interpretation of aerial photographs and areas with a recurring pattern of topography, soils and vegetation are mapped as individual land systems. The central concept is that in specific areas all the environmental characteristics will interrelate, resulting in distinctive patterns on aerial photographs. 'The approach is described as integrated because the method depends on identifying distinctive areas resultant upon the integration of environmental variables' (Davidson, 1980: 47). The *parametric method,* on the other hand, is defined as the classification and subdivisions of land on the basis of selected attribute values. This method is more precise than the landscape method, and being quantitative it allows numerical comparison and is suited to mechanical and computer data handling. Moreover, this method avoids subjective assessment while a certain amount of subjectivity is present in selecting boundaries of land systems. Therefore, the method currently in vogue is the *parametric.*

It is noted that both the methods have advantages and disadvantages. Landscape systems explain the fundamental causes of landscape differentiation; they assist reconnaissance; and they facilitate the appreciation of regions as a whole. But in this method, a certain amount of subjectivity is present. The parametric method, on the other hand, is more quantitative and less dependent upon subjective interpretations of landforms. But it is difficult to decide on the right parameters and the class limits to measure for any given land use.

'Despite the differences between them, however, the landscape and parametric methods should be thought of as ultimately complementary rather than conflicting. The relative advantage of each varies with circumstances' (Mitchell, 1977: 36). Each detailed study will require parametric approach and in every evaluation some amount of subjectivity will be present either in selection of variables or in ranking the attributes.

Application of Concept and Methods of Terrain Evaluation to Boreya

Study Area and its Potentialities

Boreya, a relatively large village (412.8 hectares/2586 persons in 1991) in Kanke block of Ranchi district in the State of Bihar, falls under the controlled area of Ranchi city which has facilitated the area with good linkages, bus stands, railway station, post offices, schools, technical institutions, colleges, universities, hospitals and many other urban amenities (Fig. 2.1). Boreya is itself facilitated with school, post and telegraph office, doctor's clinic, small hotel, bus stoppage, etc.

Boreya, though a very small unit of the Ranchi planation surface in the highlands of Chotanagpur presents a variety of topographic features consisting of residual hills, river valleys, terraced terrains and undulating surface of *dons* and *tanrs.* The variation in elevation (596 metres to 689.3 metres), land type (*tanr* III to *don* 1, Fig. 2.2), surface forms (Fig. 2.3, high hilly tracts and rugged terrain to undulating rolling and level lowlands) and slope (Fig. 2.4, below 1° to more than 20°) has greatly determined the drainage conditions and fertility, thickness and texture of soil. The streams and *nalas* (namely, Jumar, Potpoto, Dhora and Bargain) are ephemeral in nature and they are dry even in the rainy season during drought year. But the sand strata of the stream bed retains underground water, and this condition has been a good aspect for irrigation (Fig. 2.5, Mahto, 1985, 335). The soils range from sandy clay to sandy clay loam and clay (Fig. 2.6). These soils are, in general, poor in phosphates, nitrogen and humus, but comparatively rich in potash (Fig. 2.7). Boreya falls under sub-tropical humid climate. It has considerable areas under soils erosion (Fig. 2.8).

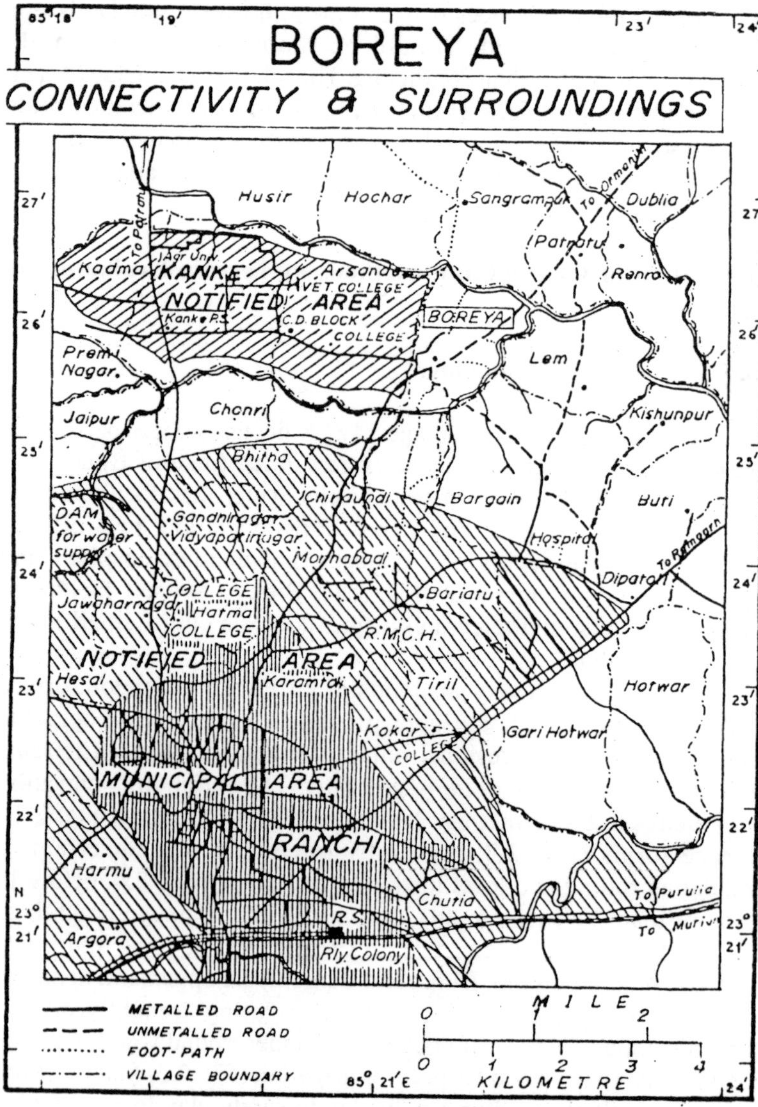

Fig. 2.1: Boreya: Connectivity and Surroundings

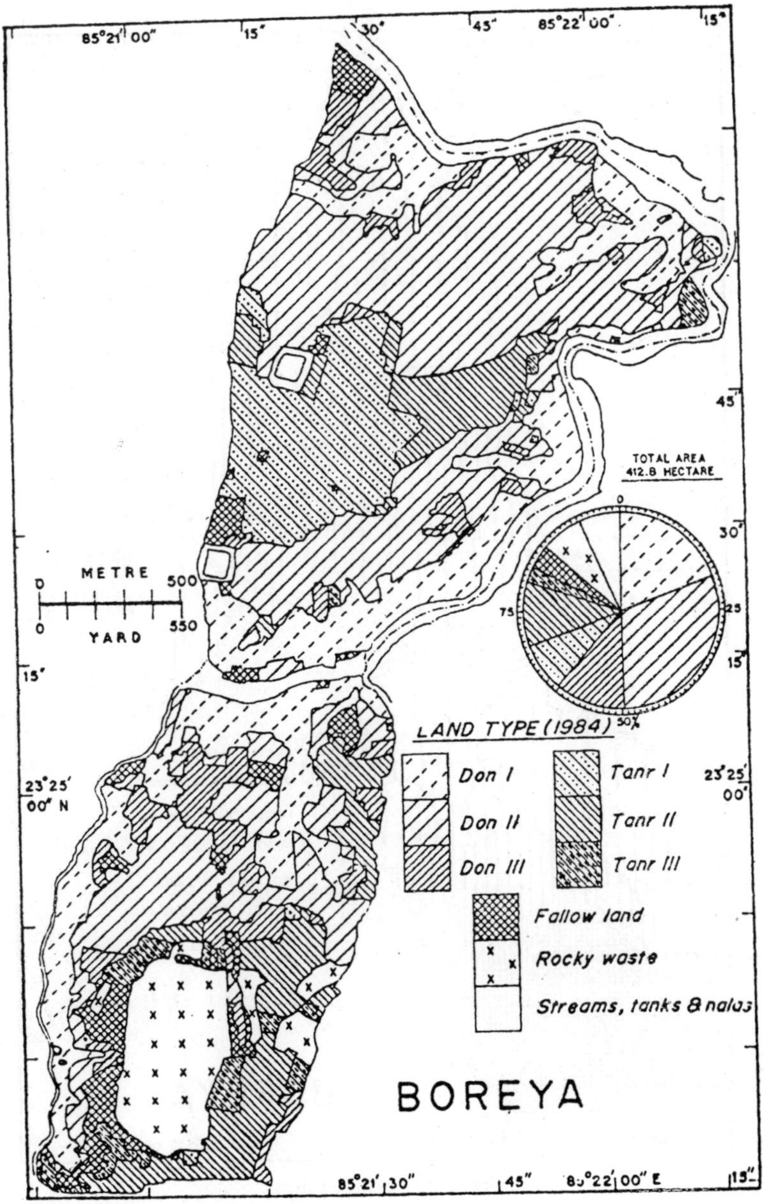

Fig. 2.2: Land Type

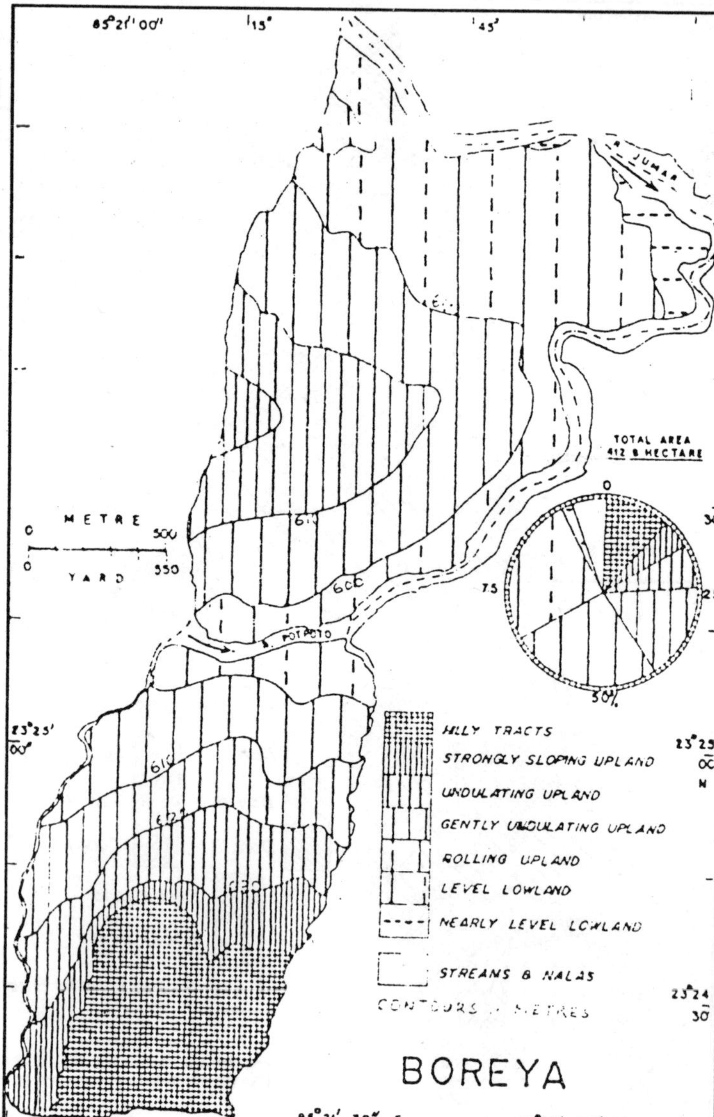

Fig. 2.3: Surface Forms

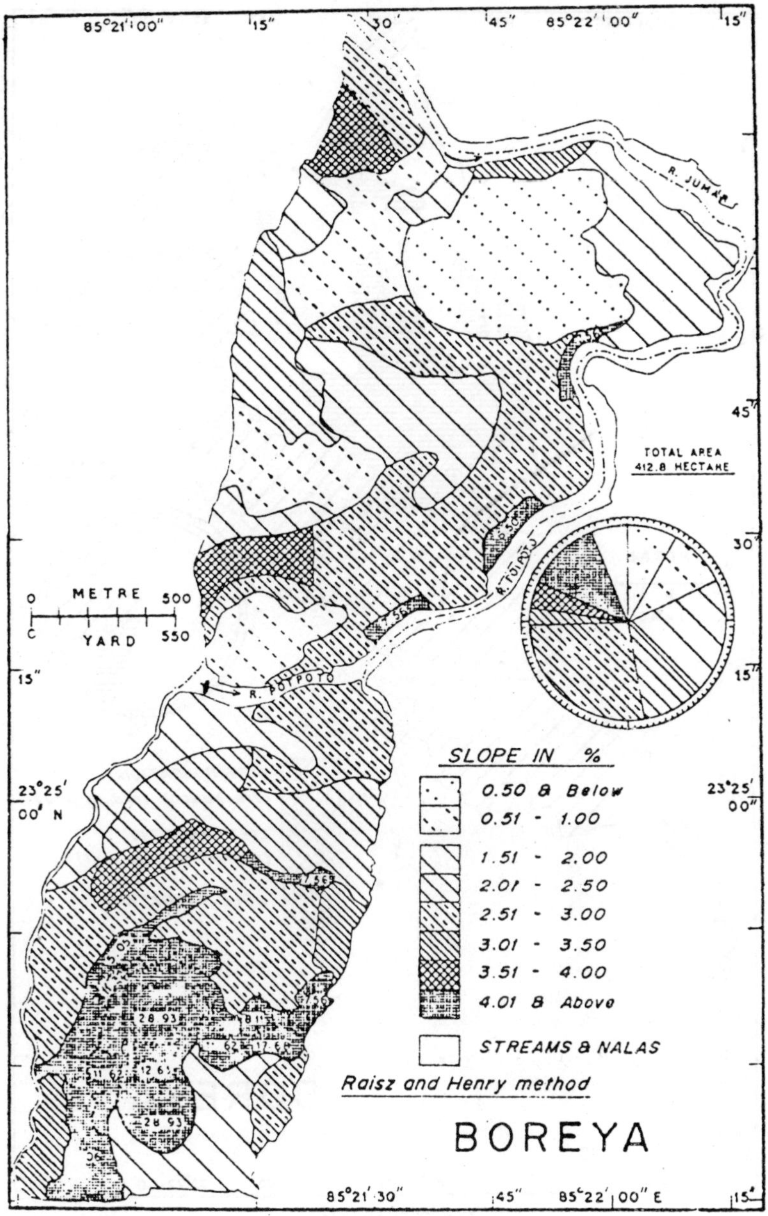

Fig. 2.4: Slope Categories

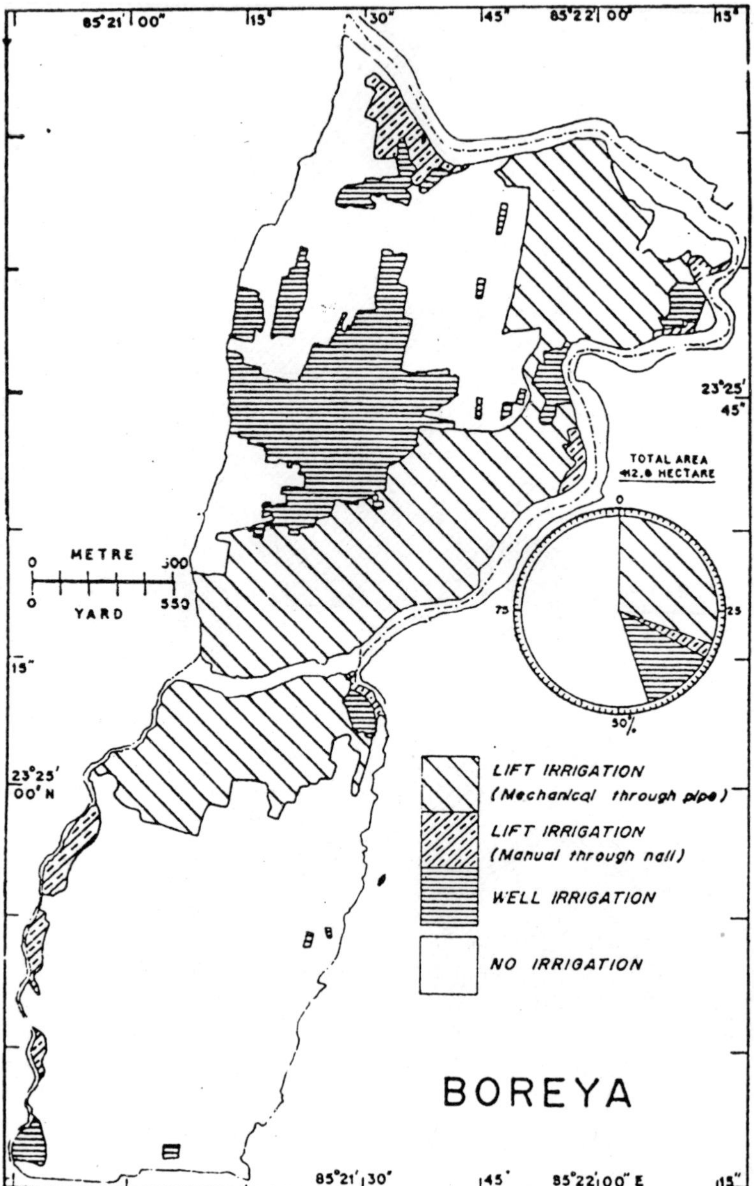

Fig. 2.5: Irrigation

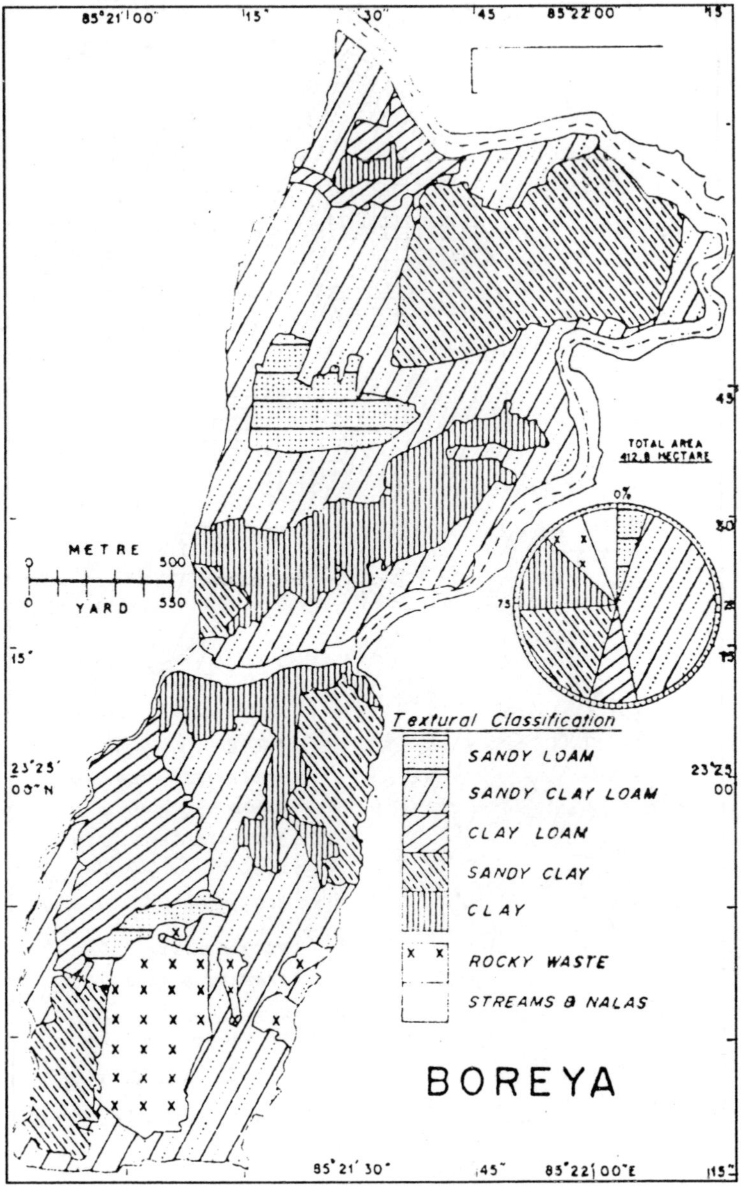

Fig. 2.6: Soil Type (Textural)

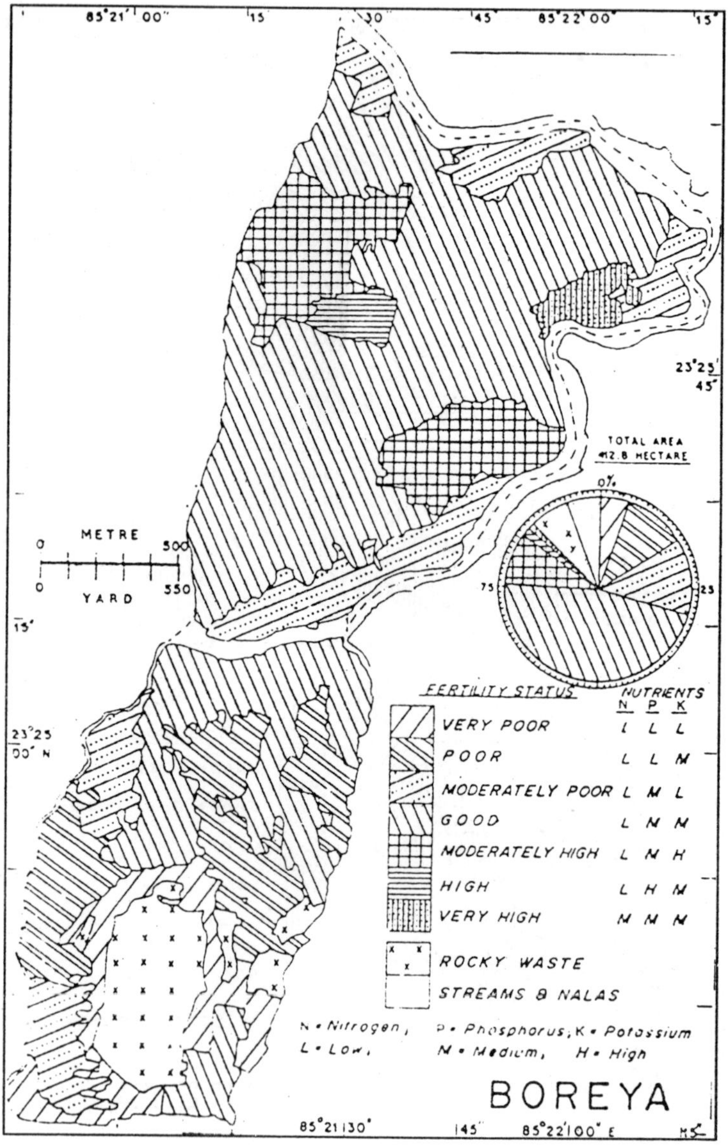

Fig. 2.7: Soil Fertility

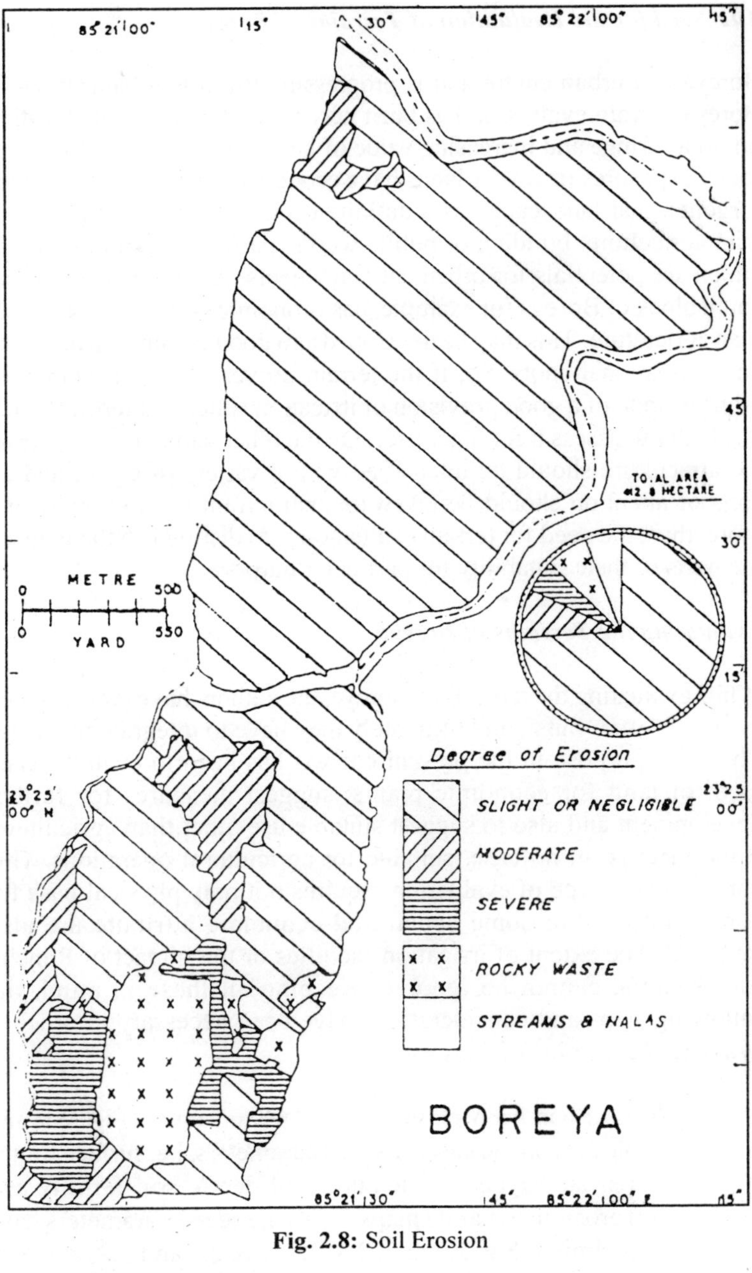

Fig. 2.8: Soil Erosion

The Need for the Evaluation of Terrains of Boreya

Boreya is a urban centre and is progressing towards urbanization. In Boreya, terrain evaluation has been necessitated owing to its location on urban fringe and increasing value of land. In such a situation, even rocky exposures or waster lands have economic value. It is sometimes forgotten that landscape has a definite economic value for use other than agriculture, building or public works, particularly in those areas which are potentials for urban encroachments. A good portion of the south block of Boreya for example, has economic values for uses other than agriculture. This may be developed as a good colony and aesthetic and recreational spots. So, if the terrain proves to be unsuitable for crops in spite of a good provision of irrigation water and fertilizer etc., it is better to assess it for other uses. On the other hand, the best terrain for agriculture should be intensified with a variety of crops, and all sorts of attention should be given to such terrain to grow more and more, thus, the need for terrain evaluation is to distinguish the units on the basis of their suitability for particular purpose.

Evaluating the Terrains of Boreya

While evaluating the terrains of Boreya, the authors have gone through many 'ifs' and 'buts', and ultimately they have to integrate the ideas. The main purpose in the present context has been to evaluate each facet of land for economic plants, suggest measures for further development and also to suggest suitable use other than agriculture, if the facet is, in no case, suitable for agricultural operations. This particularized type of evaluation requires not only physical base for consideration. but some social and economic attribute are also involved. The extent of irrigation facilities or the impact of Ranchi, for example, cannot be ignored. Keeping all these in mind, the following steps and considerations have been necessary in order to evaluate the terrains of Boreya:

(a) Boreya has been classified into terrain units (Fig. 2.9 and Table 2.1) on the basis of seven parameters, i.e. surface forms, slope, land type, soil texture, soil depth, soil fertility and soil erosion. Separate maps for all the seven parameters have been drawn (Fig. 2.2, 2.3, 2.4, 2.5, 2.6, 2.7 and 2.8) and they have been superimposed on a single map. Altogether 57 terrain units (Fig. 2.9) have been demarcated following the *Maull's girdle method.*

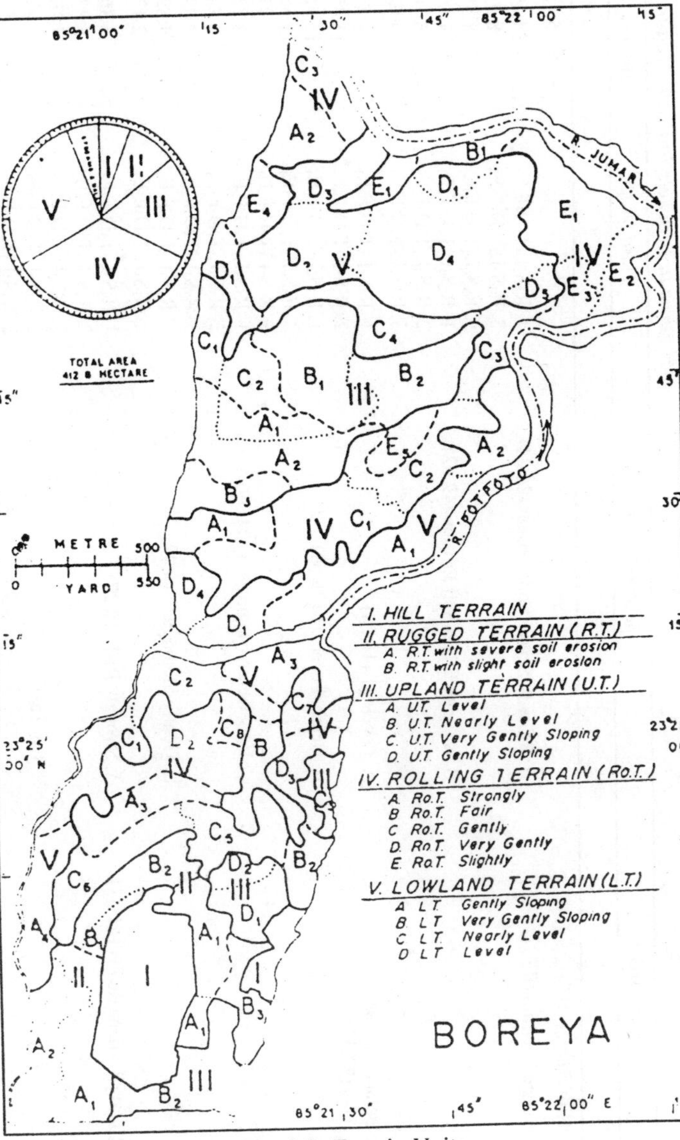

Fig. 2.9: Terrain Units

Table 2.1: Terrain Units

(Figures in Brackets Indicate Area in Hectares)

First Order	*Second Order*	*Third Order*	*Area in Hectares*
1	2	3	4
I. Hilly Terran (HT) (25.45)	–	–	25.45
II. Rugged Terrain (RT) (36.86)	A. RT with Severe Soil Erosion (24.24)	1. $R_1S_1L_2T_2D_1F_1E_3$	14.59
		2. $R_2S_3L_4T_4D_1F_3E_3$	8.07
		3. $R_1S_6L_2T_2D_1F_1E_3$	1.58
	B. RT with Slight Soil Erosion (12.62)	1. $R_2S_1L_2T_1D_2F_1E_1$	1.60
		2. $R_3S_1L_2T_1D_2F_1E_1$	6.10
		3. $R_1S_1L_2T_2D_2F_1E_1$	4.92
III. Upland Terrain (UT) (72.57)	A. Level UT (15.58)	1. $R_3S_7L_3T_1D_2F_6E_1$	4.13
		2. $R_3S_7L_3T_2D_2F_6E_1$	11.45
	B. Nearly Level UT (38.61)	1. $R_3S_6L_3T_3D_2F_6E_1$	13.15
		2. $R_3S_6L_2T_2D_2F_4E_1$	19.55
		3. $R_3S_6L_3T_2D_2F_4E_1$	5.91
	C. Very Gently sloping UT (11.39).	1. $R_3S_5L_2T_2D_2F_4E_1$	3.72
		2. $R_3S_5L_3T_1D_2F_4E_1$	4.84
		3. $R_3S_5L_2T_4D_2F_2E_1$	2.83
	D. Gently Sloping UT (6.99)	1. $R_2S_4L_2T_2D_2F_2E_1$	4.82
		2. $R_3S_4L_3T_2D_2F_2E_1$	2.17
IV. Rolling Terrian (RoT) (141.33)	A. Strongly RoT (18.27)	1. $R_4S_2L_4T_5D_3F_4E_1$	5.30
		2. $R_4S_2L_3T_2D_3F_4E_2$	5.87
		3. $R_3S_2L_4T_3D_2F_4E_1$	7.10
	B. Fair RoT (5.57)	1. $R_5S_3L_3T_2D_3F_3E_1$	2.43
		2. $R_3S_3L_4T_4D_2F_4E_1$	3.14
	C. Gently RoT (66.19)	1. $R_4S_4L_4T_5D_3F_4E_1$	16.23

(Contd.)

(*Contd.*)

1	2	3	4
		2. $R_4S_4L_4T_5D_3F_5E_1$	9.75
		3. $R_5S_4L_4T_2D_3F_5E_1$	9.11
		4. $R_4S_4L_4T_4D_3F_4E_1$	9.57
		5. $R_3S_4L_4T_2D_2F_2E_1$	7.08
		6. $R_3S_4L_4T_3D_2F_4E_1$	8.13
		7. $R_4S_4L_2T_4D_2F_4E_1$	4.09
		8. $R_4S_4L_4T_2D_2F_2E_2$	2.23
	D. Very Gently RoT (20.50)	1. $R_4S_5L_4T_2D_3F_5E_1$	4.57
		2. $R_4S_5L_4T_2D_2F_2E_2$	11.68
		3. $R_3S_5L_4T_4D_2F_2E_1$	4.25
	E. Low or Slightly RoT (30.80)	1. $R_5S_6L_4T_4D_3F_4E_1$	14.95
		2. $R_5S_6L_4T_4D_2F_3E_1$	5.00
		3. $R_5S_6L_4T_4D_3F_7E_1$	3.40
		4. $R_5S_6L_4T_2D_3F_5E_1$	4.41
		5. $R_5S_6L_4T_5D_3F_5E_1$	3.04
V. Lowland Terrain (LT) (112.31)	A. Gently Sloping LT (33.00)	1. $R_5S_4L_4T_2D_3F_3E_1$	12.32
		2. $R_5S_4L_4T_2D_3F_4E_1$	6.64
		3. $R_5S_4L_4T_5D_3F_4E_1$	7.24
		4. $R_3S_4L_4T_2D_2F_2E_2$	6.80
	B. Very Gently Sloping LT (5.87)	1. $R_4S_5L_4T_5D_3F_4E_1$	5.87
	C. Nearly Level LT (13.64)	1. $R_4S_6L_4T_3D_3F_3E_1$	6.35
		2. $R_4S_6L_4T_5D_3F_4E_1$	7.29
	D. Level LT (59.80)	1. $R_5S_7L_4T_2D_3F_3E_1$	7.99
		2. $R_5S_7L_4T_2D_3F_5E_1$	12.08
		3. $R_5S_7L_4T_2D_3F_4E_1$	5.60
		4. $R_5S_7L_4T_4D_3F_4E_1$	32.05
		5. $R_5S_7L_4T_4D_3F_5E_1$	2.08
Total Units 5	15	49	388.52

(b) To measure the terrain capability for agricultural purposes, all these parameters have been taken into consideration, because these are the permanent parameters. Besides, an important parameter has been added for this particular purpose, that is, extent of irrigation, because it plays an important role. It is an aid to terrain and it increases the productivity of land at least six-fold and generally a great deal more. Thus, for evaluation altogether 8 variables have been taken into consideration.

(c) Firstly, each variable has been awarded numerical scores to a maximum of 10, and this score 10 has been distributed proportionately among the components of each variable according to their quality (Table 2.2). For example, slope (S) scores a total of 10, and this has been distributed among components (S_1 to S_7) proportionately (S_1 = .36; S_2 = .71; S_3 = 1.07; S_4 = 1.43; S_5 = 1.79; S_6 = 2.14; S_7 = 2.50; Total = 10).

(d) All the 8 variables are not equally important for such evaluation of terrains. As stated earlier, irrigation is the most important factor which determines the capability of terrain for intensive and prosperous cultivation. It is one of the foremost factors that offsets the natural dominance on agriculture in Boreya to a great extent. The change in irrigation scenario 'has great impact on terrain characteristics' (Prasad and Mahto: 1987, 151). 'The terrains that were absolutely unsuitable for cultivation earlier have now come under good agricultural activities' (Prasad and Mahto, 1991: 110). It is, therefore, ranked first. In Chotanagpur where agriculture is grossly dependent upon natural concessions, slope is the single factor that broadly determines the extension as well as intensity of terrain use. Virtually, other variables like fertility, thickness and texture of soil, soil erosion, surface forms and land-type, all manifest aspects of slope. This is with this importance that slope is ranked second in importance among variables. Among soil characteristics, soil texture has been considered to be the most important, because its character can hardly be changed, while solid fertility can be increased by manuring and by other devices. The thickness of soil is important to a certain depth. Therefore, soil texture ranks third, and soil depth and fertility together rank fourth.

In case of agricultural planning soil erosion does matter, so it has been given due weightage by placing it in fifth in rank. Since slope has been given due weightage, surface forms and land-type have been placed together in sixth in rank.

Table 2.2: Ranking of Variable

Rank	*Variable*	*Weightage*
1.	Irrigation	6
2.	Slope	5
3.	Soil Texture	4
4.	Soil Depth and Soil Fertility	3
5.	Soil Erosion	2
6.	Surface forms and Land-type	1

With the above considerations, weightage has been given to each component of all the variables and the overall score index for each component has been obtained by multiplying the original score by weighted score (Table 2.3).

Table 2.3: Variables and Scores

Variable	*Symbol*	*Scores Assigned on the Basis of Quality*	*Weightage Assigned According to Rank*	*Total Scores Awarded*
(1)	(2)	(3)	(4)	(5)
A. Irrigation: Rank-First				
Area Irrigated below 25%	I_1	1	6	6
25-50%	I_2	2	6	12
51-75%	I_3	3	6	18
above 75%	I_4	4	6	24
Total		10		60
B. Slope: Rank-Second				
Strongly sloping	S_1	0.36	5	1.8
Rolling	S_2	0.71	5	3.6
Gently rolling	S_3	1.07	5	5.4
Gently sloping	S_4	1.43	5	7.1

(*Contd.*)

(Contd.)

(1)	(2)	(3)	(4)	(5)
Very gently sloping	S_5	1.79	5	8.9
Nearly level	S_6	2.14	5	10.7
Level	S_7	2.50	5	12.5
Total		10.00		50.0
C. Soil Texture: Rank-Third				
Sandy loam	T_1	0.7	4	2.7
Sandy clay loam	T_2	1.3	4	5.3
Clay loam	T_3	2.0	4	8.0
Sandy clay	T_4	2.7	4	10.7
Clay	T_5	3.3	4	13.3
Total		10		40.0
D. Soil Depth: Rank-Fourth				
Moderately deep	D_1	1.7	3	5
Deep	D_2	3.3	3	10
Very deep	D_3	5.0	3	15
Total		10.0		30
E. Soil Fertility: Rank-Fifth				
Very poor	F_1	0.36	3	1.1
Poor	F_2	0.71	3	2.1
Moderately poor	F_3	1.07	3	3.2
Good	F_4	1.43	3	4.3
Moderately high	F_5	1.79	3	5.4
High	F_6	2.14	3	6.4
Very high	F_7	2.50	3	7.5
Total		10.00		30.0
F. Soil Erosion: Rank-Fifth				
Slight or no erosion	E_1	5.0	2	10.0
Moderate	E_2	3.3	2	6.7
Severe	E_3	1.7	2	3.3
Total		10.0		20.0
G. Surface Forms: Rank-Sixth				
Hilly tracts	R_1	0.7	1	0.7
Rugged terrain	R_2	1.3	1	1.3
Upland	R_3	2.0	1	2.0
Rolling land	R_4	2.7	1	2.7
Lowland	R_5	3.3	1	3.3

(Contd.)

(Contd.)

(1)	(2)	(3)	(4)	(5)
H. Land Types: Rank-Sixth				
Rocky waste	L_1	1	1	1
Upland	L_2	2	1	2
Medium land	L_3	3	1	3
Lowland	L_4	4	1	4
Total		10		10

(e) Finally, the cumulative score for all the 55 terrain units have been obtained (e.g., for VA_1, $R_5S_4L_4T_2D_3F_3E_1\ I_4 = 3.3 + 7.1 + 4.0 + 5.3 + 15.0 + 3.2 + 10.0 + 24.0 = 71.9$). They were statistically grouped to find out terrain capability classes. For this purpose, the mean and standard deviation of the scores were calculated and the terrain units were put under various categories (Table 2.4, Fig. 2.10) to arrive at micro-regional variations.

Table 2.4: Terrain Evaluation

Tarrain Unit		*Scores x*	*Deviation from mean $\overline{x}$*	$(\overline{x}\ )^2$	*Terrain Units*		*Scores x*	*Deviation from Mean $\overline{x}$*	$(\overline{x}\ )^2$
II A	1a	19.2	–40.713	1657.548	IV C	5	40.5	–19.413	376.865
	1b	19.2	–40.713	1657.548		6	45.4	–14.513	210.627
	2	38.9	–21.013	441.546		7	64.8	4.887	23.883
	3	28.1	–31.813	1012.066		8	61.9	1.987	3.948
B	1	08.9	–31.013	961.806	D	1	57.3	–2.613	6.827
	2	29.6	–30.313	918.878		2	57.7	–2.213	4.897
	3	30.9	–29.013	841.754		3	53.7	–6.213	38.610
III A	1	70.6	10.687	114.212	E	1a	76.0	16.087	258.792
	2	65.4	5.487	30.107		1b	64.0	4.087	16.704
B	1	74.1	14.187	201.271		2	69.5	9.587	91.911
	2a	56.3	–3.613	13.054		3	85.2	25.287	639.432
	2b	50.3	–9.613	92.410		4	59.7	–0.213	0.045
	3	57.3	–2.613	6.828		5	85.7	25.787	664.969
C	1	59.2	–0.713	0.508	V A	1	71.9	11.987	143.688
	2	64.9	4.987	24.870		2	73.0	13.087	171.270
	3	45.7	–14.213	202.009		3	81.0	21.087	444.661
D	1	43.8	–16.113	259.629		4	49.2	–10.713	114.768
	2	39.5	–20.413	416.691	B	1	70.2	10.287	105.822
IV A	1	70.9	10.987	120.714	C	1	71.6	11.687	136.586
	2	46.6	–13.313	177.236		2	84.0	24.087	580.183
	3	47.9	–12.013	144.312	D	1a	77.3	17.387	302.308
B	1	57.2	–2.713	7.360		1b	65.3	5.387	29.020
	2	41.0	–18.913	357.701		2	61.3	1.587	2.518

(Contd.)

(Contd.)

Tarrain Unit		*Scores x*	*Deviation from –mean $\overline{x}$*	$(\overline{x})^2$	*Terrain Units*	*Scores x*	*Deviation from Mean $\overline{x}$*	$(\overline{x})^2$
C	1	80.4	20.487	419.707	3	81.1	21.187	448.889
	2	81.5	21.587	465.999	4a	71.8	11.887	141.301
	3a	73.0	13.087	171.269	4b	83.8	23.887	570.589
	3b	67.0	7.087	50.226	5	84.9	24.987	624.350
	4	59.8	–0.113	0.013				
Total		1447.2(a)		10767.272		1848.0(b)		6153.454

1147.2 + 1848.0 = 3295.2 Total units = 55

Mean = 3295.2 ÷ 55 = 59.913

$$\text{Standard Deviation} = \frac{\sqrt{(10767.272+6153.454)}}{55} = \sqrt{307.650}$$

$$=17.54$$

(f) No calculation was done for two terrain units of rocky exposures because agriculturally they are absolutely unsuitable.

(g) This method of terrain evaluation has proved to be very much appropriate because the authors could check the areas under various categories directly going to the field and it was found correct. It was possible because the area under study is small and there is an easy access to every terrain. Perhaps the most sensible approach to the problem is through the examination of personal preferences and prejudices. It is, however, a truism that perception of terrains varies within and between social and cultural groups and also varies with time.

Terrain Capability Classes

On the basis of detailed data contained in Table 2.4, a map (Fig. 2.10) of terrain capability classes has been prepared. A Terrain Value Profile has also been drawn which is based on measuring the percentage areas within a given region in each value category, and plotting the percentages as a frequency distribution (Fig. 2.11). Altogether 8 classes have been determined on the basis of 'mean ± S.D' principle of statistics. These classes are, thus, based on capability scores (Table 2.5)

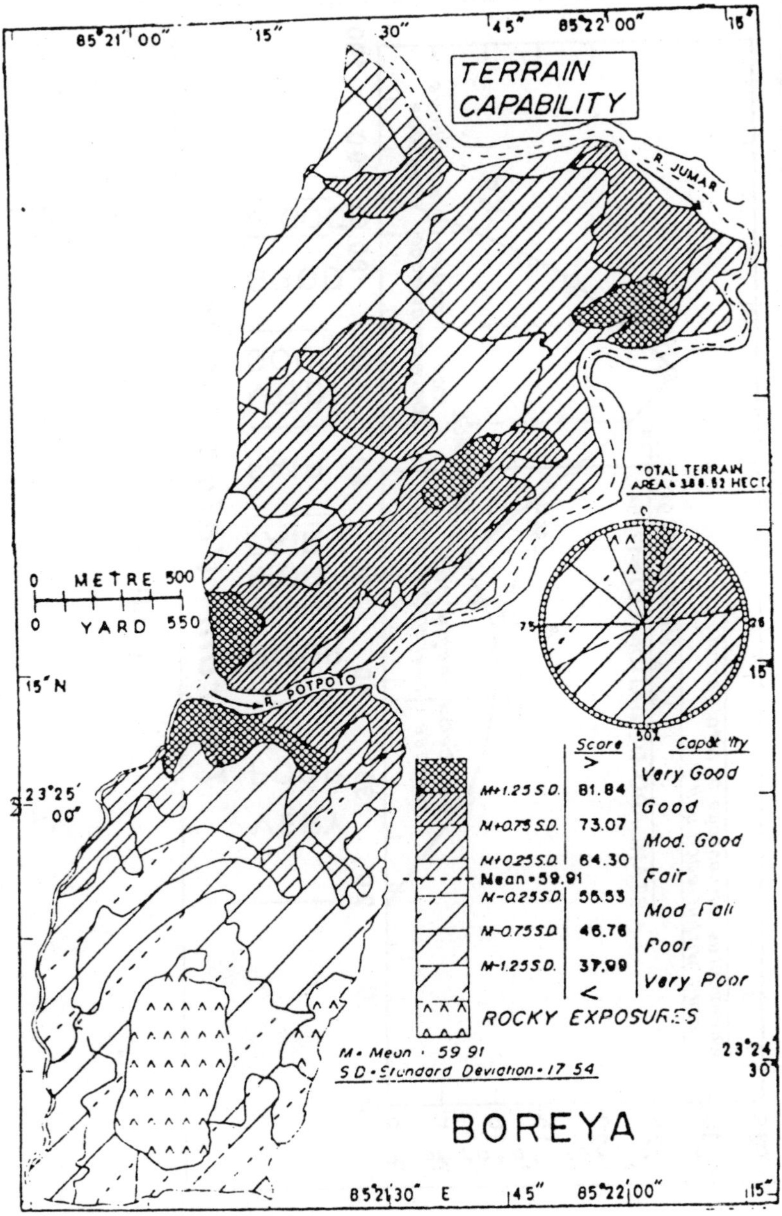

Fig. 2.10: Terrain Capability

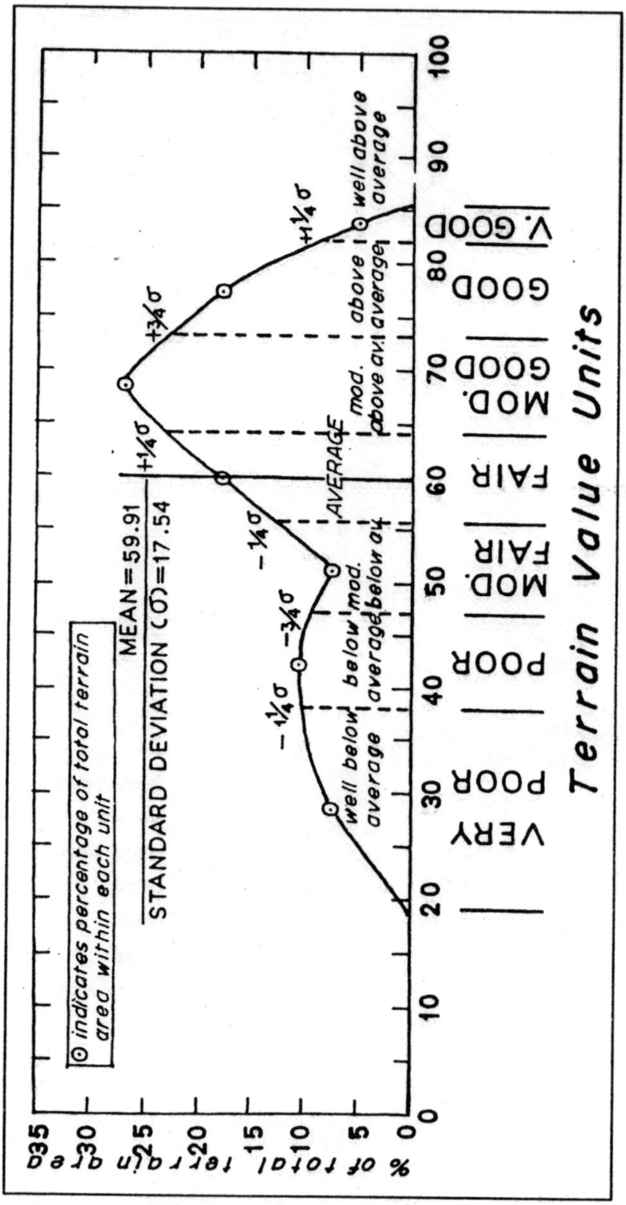

Fig. 2.11: Terrain Value Profile

Table 2.5: Terrain Capability Classes for Agriculture

Class	*Scores*	*Character*	*Area in Hectares*	*Percentage to the Total Terrain Area*	*Percentage to Individual Class of Block*	
					South	*North*
1.	Above 81.8	Very good terrain	19.81	5.10	57.0	43.0
2.	73.1–81.8	Good terrain	69.21	17.81	10.5	89.5
3.	64.3–73.0	Moderately good terrain	106.18	27.33	15.5	84.5
4.	55.5–64.2	Fair terrain	69.33	17.84	20.0	80.0
5.	46.8–55.4	Moderately fair terrain	27.84	7.17	100.0	00.0
6.	38.0–46.7	Poor terrain	42.11	0.84	86.0	14.0
7.	Below 38.0	Very poor terrain	28.59	7.36	100.0	00.0
8.	—	Rocky exposures	25.45	6.55	100.0	00.0
	Total		388.52	100.00	—	—

Very Good Terrain

This terrain is highly suitable for agriculture with very minor or no physical limitation to use. Surface is almost flat, soils are well drained, of moderate permeability, and are deep, medium textured, with good available of water capacity. This terrain includes mainly first class *don* and hundred per cent of the area is irrigated. Terrain units like IV E_3, IV E_5; V C_2, V D_4 and V D_5 (Table 2.1 and Fig. 2.9) are included in this class of terrain.

Table 2.5 reveals that this capability class occupies only 19.81 hectares of land (5.1%) out of which 57 per cent lies in the south block and 43 per cent in the north block. In the north this class is scattered in three patches while in the south it forms only one patch on the bank of the Potpoto. It is interesting to note that the north block though comparatively more developed has relatively less area under this class. It may be due to the fact that the terrains of the north block have been comparatively more exploited resulting in reduction of the terrain capability.

Good Terrain

This terrain is also very much suitable for agriculture, but it requires some moderate management practices like assured irrigation facilities, fertilizers and good ploughing, etc. Surface is undulating, soils are moderately well drained, moderately deep and medium textured. This terrain includes all types of *don, i.e.,* first, second and third class. But hundred per cent area is irrigated. The irrigation water has increased the capability of the terrain. III B_1; IV C_1, IV C_2, IV E_1 V A_3, V D_1 and V D_3 are included in this capability class.

Table 2.5 depicts that this capability class occupies 69.21 hectares (17.81%) of land, out of which only 10.5 per cent lies in the south block and 89.5 per cent in the north block. There are altogether five patches of this class, four of which lie in the north block (Fig. 2.10). It is noted that the upland terrain (III B_1) has come under this class owing to its assured irrigation facility and good soil condition because of nearness of the settlement-site.

This terrain, as a whole, can be used for more intensive cultivation.

Moderately Good Terrain

This terrain is also very much suitable for agriculture because it has minor physical limitations. In some cases the soil condition is moderate, in some irrigation is not available for 100 per cent areas. But the surface is almost flat and it includes mostly *dons*. This capability class requires some moderate management practices. The terrain units which have been included in this category are III A_1, III A_2, III C_2; IV A_1, IV C_3, IV C_7, IV E_2; V A_1, V A_2, V B_1, V C_1, and V D_4 (Fig. 2.9 and Table 2.1).

It is reveled by Table 2.5 that this capability class occupies the highest percentage (27.33) of land including 106.18 hectares of different terrain units. Like class 2 terrain, this terrain class is also dominated in the north block sharing 84.5 per cent of the total (Class 3). Out of 7 patches, five are distributed in the north. One interesting thing is that a single patch stretches for a long distance, firstly parallel to the Potpoto in the east and then it bulges in the north close to the Jumar (Fig. 2.10). It occupies almost half of this capability class.

Fair Terrain

This capability class of terrain is suitable for agriculture with slight obstacles such as rolling surface forms, moderately well drained soils, moderately slow or moderately rapid permeability or moderate depth of soil. This terrain has restricted choice of crops and demands careful management. At present, the units under this category are receiving irrigation water for 25 per cent to 75 per cent of their areas. If only this facility is provided, the terrain can be converted into a very good cultivated area. The terrain unit IV C_8 has such a facility where 100 per cent land is irrigated. III B_2, III B_3, III C_1; IV B_1, IV C_4, IV C_8, IV D_1, IV D_2, IV E_4; and V D_2 are the units which come under this terrain capability class (Fig. 2.9 and 2.10 Tables 2.1 and 2.4).

Table 2.5 and Fig. 2.10 reveal that this terrain class occupies the next highest percentage (17.84) including 69.33 hectares of about 10 terrain units. Like class 2 and 3, it is also dominated in the north block. Only three patches are there (Fig. 2.10) among which one is extending from mid-portion to the north-west and north in the north block. It alone occupies 49.51 hectares of land out of 69.33 hectares. In the south one patch can be observed near to the Potpoto. All these units have adequate qualities for the development of agriculture. It is under agricultural uses, but farm management can register an improvement with easy efforts.

Moderately Fair Terrain

This class of terrain is moderately suitable for agriculture with moderate obstacles such as upland and rolling surfaces, moderate depth of soil, moderate soil erosion and moderate texture of soil. No unit of this class is receiving irrigation water for more than 50 per cent of the area. Most of them receive limited irrigation water. Terrain units that come under this class are III B_2; IV A_3, IV D_3 and V A_4, all distributed in the south block of Boreya. This terrain requires very careful farm management. With the introduction of assured irrigation this can be developed as good agricultural land. Other devices like manuring, crop-rotation and contour-bunding, etc. are also essential.

This capability class occupies 27.84 hectares of land (7.17%) in three patches of the south block, one in the extreme south, another along the Dhora *nala* in the west and the third one in the mid-east (Fig. 2.10).

Poor Terrain

This class of terrain is marginally suitable for agriculture with severe obstacles, such as upland poor *tanrs,* rolling surfaces, sloping land, rapid drainage, shallow to moderate depth of soil, low to medium textured soil and moderate to severe soil erosion. Irrigation water is almost absent. It requires very careful management if planning for agriculture is made. The terrain units included in this class are III C_3, III D_1, III D_2; IV A_2, IV B_2, IV C_5 and IV C_6.

This terrain class occupies 42.11 hectares of land (10.84%) in altogether three patches — two large pactches in the south and one small (5.87 hectares) in the extreme north-west. This terrain is virtually girdling the rugged terrain of the south.

Very Poor Terrain

This terrain class is a rugged terrain girdling the hilly terrain of the south. It is with very severe limitations that made it generally unsuited to even moderate cultivation. Strongly sloping lands, severe soil erosion, shallow soil depth, rapid drainage and gullies are the severe obstacles which render it unsuitable for even moderate cultivation.

Rocky Exposures

This portion is virtually hilly terrain of Boreya which has rocky exposures. It has extremely severe limitations and, therefore, it cannot be rectified for cultivation. It is absolutely unsuitable for any amount of cultivation. That is why it has not been evaluated for agriculture, thus, it has no score.

Planning the Terrain Use

In the foregoing pages terrains of Boreya have been evaluated for agricultural uses. Quite obviously, zones have come out with their capability and suitability classes in terms of agricultural values. Since Boreya is a urban centre, its economy, though changing from subsistence to commercial, is still based on farming. The dominance of farming extends over most of the households of Boreya; so agriculture should be given priority, although the fringe farming and fringe farmers is Boreya differ from their more rural counterparts. The importance of agricultural value ought to be retained and the cultivated terrains that have high potentialities should not be transferred to non-agricultural purposes in any case. The first five classes (1 to 5) of terrains (Table 2.5 and Fig. 2.10) are suitable for agriculture in varying degree, and these have been facilitated with irrigation water provided by a number of schemes. These terrains are engaged in growing crops with a good diversity and intensity of cropping. Also the people of Boreya are more or less responding the development programmes initiated and implemented by government and private agencies. Therefore, the cultivated terrains of these five classes (moderately fair to very good terrains for agriculture) should be retained, with some exceptions, for agricultural uses, because agriculture is the backbone of the economy and it is providing and will provide a strong based for other economic and social developments (Fig. 2.12 and Table 2.6). An area of 221.78 hectares has, therefore, been demarcated for agriculture. Only thing is that agriculture requires improvements in management practices.

Table 2.6: Planned Terrain Use

Terrain Use	*Area in Hectares*	*% to Total Terrain Area*
Arable terrain	221.78	57.08
Pasture	37.76	9.72
Forestry and recreation	51.32	13.21
Settlements and arable terrain	59.03	15.19
Colony	18.63	4.80
Total	388.52	100.00

As regards other terrain classes (6 to 8), they can be put to non-agricultural purposes, e.g., forestry, recreation, settlement sites, etc. It should always be kept in mind that Boreya is a rurban centre, urban encroachment has already started, it is well linked with roads, its south block is contiguous to Morhabadi and a little away from Bariatu that are already urbanized and are parts of Ranchi city, and above all there has been daily intermingling of a large number of people of Boreya with Ranchi. Quite obviously, the planning of terrain use for non-agricultural purposes should be such that can keep pace with the urbanization and that can solve, if possible, some of the urban problems without any loss to the rurban environment.

Keeping all these in mind the following suggestions for planning the terrain use can be made:

Agriculture

The first five classes should be put to agricultural uses, because they have good potentials for such uses. Almost whole of the north block and one-third of the south block are included in such classes (Fig. 2.12).

The terrain use should be re-oriented with a flexible and dynamic plan aimed at providing maximum utility for every hectare of the cultivated terrain.

(a) At present all the portions of the existing and planned cultivated terrains are not getting facilities of irrigation water (Fig. 2.5). There are, however, a number of irrigation schemes working in Boreya, but they are not extending expected irrigation water to their command areas. Some portions of their command areas are still left unirrigated. These private and government agencies should assure the full and regular water supply to the fields.

(b) It has been observed that these life irrigation schemes with their intake wells on the bed of the rivers Potopoto and Jumar can provide irrigation facilities only to the lowland and rolling terrains. To ensure irrigation water on the upland terrains in both the north and south block high-diameter wells and big tanks should be constructed on the upper slopes, so that cultivated terrains on down-slope can be irrigated.

(c) Double and triple cropping areas are limited while terrains have potentials to grow more and more. These cultivated terrains should be brought under multiple cropping as well as diversification of crops.

(d) Since Boreya is a rurban centre and there is a high demand of such crops of daily uses, particularly vegetables a large acreage of cultivated terrain should be devoted to market-gardening. It will raise the economy of the people and, ultimately, it will lead towards prosperity in all spheres.

(e) The low yielding crops should be replaced by high yielding ones. Similarly, scientific crop rotation should be encouraged. The people of Boreya have adaptability to scientific programmes, so proper guidance by technical personnel will be beneficial for appropriate agricultural uses.

(f) The farmers should be given incentives to use chemical fertilizers and other modern devices to get the maximum return from the terrain.

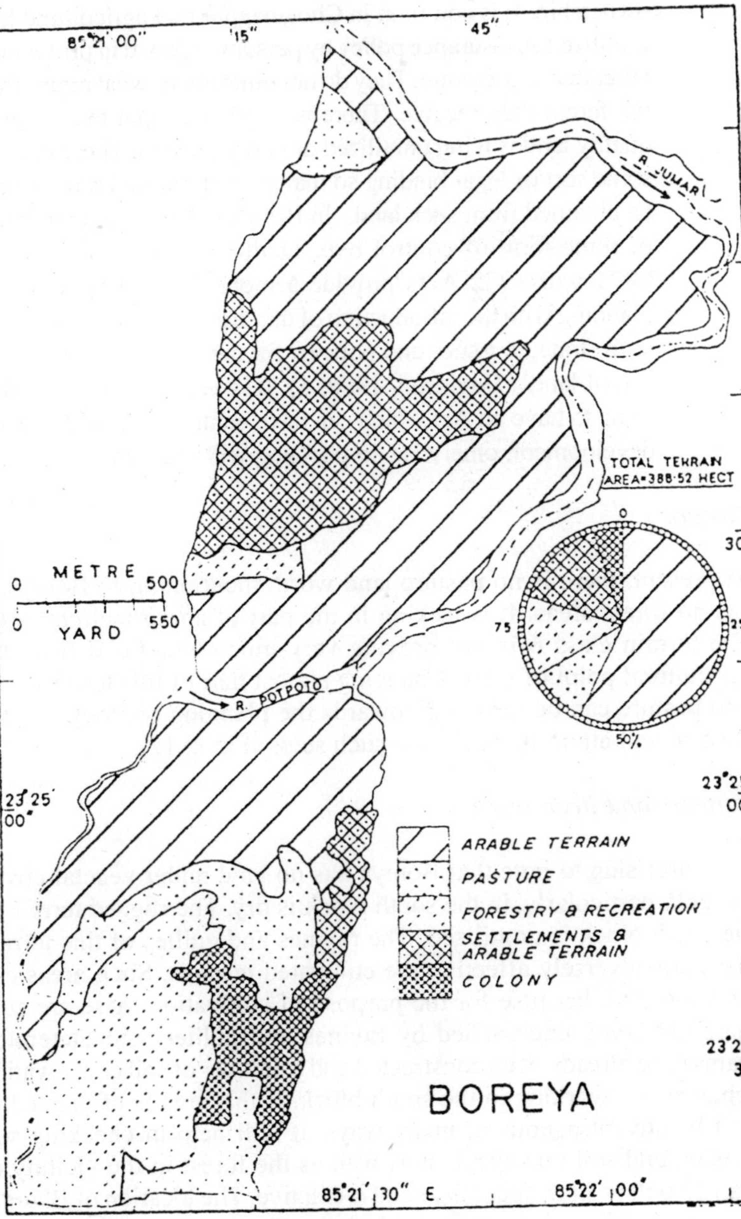

Fig. 2.12: Planned Terrain Use

(g) At last, but not of least importance, is the planning the land ownership. It is common in Chotanagpur that agricultural land is utilized as insurance policy by persons engaged in professions other than agriculture. They do not mind about what return from the farms they receive. There are instances that even a good quality land is lying unutilized or partly utilized. There must be some sort of legal binding so that at least minimum return can be obtained from such land. 'In Britain there is a long tradition of some form of control over landuse... . The more recent 1971 and 1972 Acts provide a more positive approach to planning with the introduction of the structure plans. These deal with strategic issues and policies for the development and the use of land' (Davidson, 1980: 5). It is very much essential in India to have an Act which can have control over land use and development, otherwise no planning will succeed.

Pasture

At present, there is no pasture land worth mentioning in Boreya. It has no forest areas. It is lacking in the part of an agricultural area. The terrain class 6 is not proving very much beneficial from the agricultural point of view. Changing almost half of this terrain class into pasture can be next step towards the planning of Boeya on the government authorites can take such steps (Fig. 2.12).

Forestry and Recreation

It is surprising to note that Boreya has no land under vegetal cover. Its look, particularly, in the south block is dry. The rugged terrain in the south block is unutilized. The ravines and gullies of this terrain class are adversely affecting the cultivated terrains. Such areas can be afforested, because for the purpose of cultivation these are sub-marginal being encroached by ravines and gullies. Silt Detention Dams have already been constructed and a number of soil conservation schemes are working in the south block. If this area is afforested, it will be advantsageous in many ways. It will help in checking soil erosion and soil management as well as the forest in the vicinity of Ranchi will be both decorative and recreative. The location of Bharam *Pahar* will be an extra aid to its beauty (Fig. 2.12).

Settlements and Industries

Portions of the terrain class 6, 7 and 8 can be developed for residential purposes, because they are otherwise less valuable and these terrain classes are laying contiguous to Ranchi. It is noted that C.C.L. (Central Coalfields Limited, Ranchi) has a plan to develop a colony for its employees over this terrain. It would be certainly a good use of this terrain. If it is not so, even then it is going to be developed as residential area in near future, because it is near to Ranchi and Morhabadi, and urban congestion of Ranchi has given here an attraction. It would be better if incentives are given to the people of Boreya to use such terrain for further settlement sites. It will save the land which is suitable for agricultural purposes. This terrain class can be utilized for industrial establishment, too, and it is not far from possibility because of Ranchi being an industrial complex.

REFERENCES

Cooke, R.U. and Doorkamp, J.C. (1978). *Geomorphology in Environmental Management*, Clarendon Press, Oxford.

Davison, D.A. (1980). *Soils and Landuse Planning*, Longman. London.

De, N.K. (1984). *Measuring Land Potentials in Developing Countries*, The University of Burdwan, Burdwan.

Desai, S.D. (1968). "Terrain Evaluation—Principles and Techniques." *The National Geographical Journal of India*. Vol. 14. pp. 258-64.

Fairbridge, R.W. (ed.) (1968). *Encyclopedia of Gemorphology*, Reinhold Book Corporation, Now York.

King, R.B. (1970). "A Parametric Approach to Land System Classification." *Geoderma* 4: 34-46.

Kumar, A. (1984). Terrain Evaluation and Wasteland Classification: A Paragmatic Approach *India Geographical Studies*, Bulletin No. 22. pp. 30-37.

Mahto, A. (1985). *Terrain Evaluation, Integrated Development and Change in Boreya*, Unpublished Ph.D. Thesis, Ranchi University.

Mitchell, C.W. (1977). *Terrain Evaluation: An Introductory Handbook to the History, Principles, and Methods of Practical Terrain Assessment*, Longman, London.

Ollier, C.D. (1978). "Terrain Classification: Methods, Applications and Principles," *Applied Geomorphology* (ed. by Johan R. Hails), Elsevier Scientific Pub. Co., Amsterdam.

Osunade, M.A.A. (1979). "Methodological Framework for Rural Land

Evaluation," *The National Geographical Journal of India,* Vol. 25, pp. 167-79.

Prasad, N. and Mahto, A. (1987). "Conservation and Utilization of Water Resources for Irrigation in India: An Assement," *Indian Journal of Landscape Systems and Ecological Studies,* Vol. 10.

Prasad, N. and Mahto, A. (1991). "Impact of Irrigation Development in a Hilly Area of Chotanagpur", *Indian Journal of Regional of Science,* Vol. 23.

Singh, R.L. (1974). 'Morphometric Analysis of Terrain', Bulletin No. 22, *National Geographical Society of India.* Varanasi, Presidential Address to Geology and Geography Section, 54th Indian Science Congress, Hyderabad, 1967.

Speight, J.G. (1968). "Parametric Description of Landform" in C.A. Stewart (Editor), *Land Evaluation,* Macmillan, Melbourne.

Stamp, L.D. (1950). *The Land of Britain: Its Use and Misuse*, London.

Stamp, L.D. (1968). *A Glossary of Geographical Terms,* Longman, London.

Van Lopik, J.R. and Koib, C.R. (1959). A Technique for Preparing Desert Terrain Analogues. *U.S. Army Corps. Eng. Waterw. Exp. Sta.,* Vicksburg, Miss., Tech. Res., 3-506.

W.C.D. (1982). *Webster Comprehensive Dictionary,* Encyclopaedic Edition. Vols. I and II, J.G. Ferguson Pub. Co., Chicago.

Webster, R. and Beckett, P.H.T. (1970). 'Terrain Classification and Evaluation Using Air Photographs: A Review of Recent Work at Oxford Photogrammetric," pp. 26, 51-75 (quoted in *Soils and Land Use Planning,* by Donald A. Davidson, 1980, Longman, p. 48).

3

Land Evaluation for Agriculture*

J.R. IVE

Land evaluation should be an inherent component of any attempt to ensure that our land resources are used in the best way possible. Agricultural land evaluation is no exception. As the world's population continues to increase and incomes rise so will the demand for land increase for both traditional and new land uses. Combined with a greater environmental awareness for sound land use decisions, the need for land evaluation studies will also increase.

Agricultural land evaluation can be seen as servicing two main tasks:

1. Identifying the most suitable location for a specified agricultural use (i.e. many locations — single use).
2. Identifying the most suitable agricultural use for a specified location (i.e. many uses — single location).

Obviously tasks involving a number of uses and a number of locations may also be considered, although strictly speaking such tasks involving a number of uses and a number of locations are more appropriate to the province of land use planning — particularly if the land uses being considered also include non-agricultural uses. In such situations land use planning will draw heavily upon the recommendations of land evaluation studies. In addition, agricultural land evaluation can also include studies which make management recommendations for a single use on one type of land.

---

* Reprinted with permission from Environmental Planning and Management eds. J.J. Basinski and K.D. Cocks, pp. 66-76, Commonwealth Science Council and the CSIRO Division of Water and Land Resources, Canberra.

Common to these tasks of agricultural land evaluation is the need for the land use recommendations from such studies to relate to sustained agricultural production, i.e. a choice is only made between agricultural land use alternatives which can be carried out indefinitely. A land use which can only be carried out for a few years may be the subject of a further land evaluation study specifically for defining management recommendations aimed at promoting sustained production. Alternatively, a non-sustainable land use may be excluded.

In addition, sustained agricultural production implies that land characteristics which indicate hazard potential or degradation risk (e.g. vulnerability to erosion or salinization) should be considered as well as those land characteristics which are indicative of agricultural production (output per hectare, dollar or man hour). This opportunity for consideration from two viewpoints is apparent in the development of several well known evaluation techniques which have been devised for agricultural purposes. Nevertheless, it is still possible to identify approaches which emphasize either the production potential (e.g. Ableiter and Barnes, 1960) or the hazard potential [e.g. USDA Land Capability Classification (Klingebiel and Montgomery, 1961)].

The relative attention paid to production potential *versus* hazard potential in an evaluation study should, however, depend mainly upon the requirements of the client commissioning the land evaluation study and not upon the approach selected. Commonly, the clients for agricultural land evaluation studies are government resource agencies who are responsible for ensuring that the utilization and development of the country's resources occur in a manner consistent with national policy. Such government resource agencies may, in turn, operate as managers or monitors of the land or alternatively they may provide a service to private land holders.

On the other hand, private land holders may instigate their own land evaluation studies. In contrast with government agencies who are concerned with agricultural land evaluation from the point of deciding upon infrastructure development, reconstruction assistance and long-term land preservation, private land holders are more likely to be concerned with location or selection of an agricultural enterprise, frequently with a shorter time horizon in mind than government resource agencies and possibly with greater emphasis on agricultural production rather than hazard potential or degradation risk.

The observation that private land holders are likely to have different reasons for undertaking a land evaluation study as well as having a different time horizon from that of government agricultural resource agencies raises another aspect of agricultural land evaluation, namely, that no technique can be expected to be universally applicable. Even to the extent that a number of techniques have an established record and are, therefore, considered standards [e.g. USDA Land Capability Classification Technique (Klingebiel and Montgomery, 1961)], no technique can be recommended universally for agricultural land evaluation. For example, in a comparative test of three techniques (Storie Index Rating, USDA Land Capability Classification, USDA Land Inventory and Monitoring System) for identifying prime agricultural land in North America where all techniques were originally developed, the techniques identified substantially different areas. The reasons for the inconsistency are traceable to differences in the three techniques (Reganold and Singer, 1979).

Because no approach can be considered universal it is necessary to clearly establish the aim of any particular agricultural land evaluation study prior to selecting an approach and then in turn, to select (and modify if necessary) a method which is appropriate to the approach selected for the study. For example, a number of aspects of the USDA Land Capability Classification have been the subject of modification during the course of its adoption (Table 3.1).

Table 3.1: Summary of the aspects of USDA Land Capability Classfication which have been the subject of modification

1. Number of Classes
2. Limiting Factors
3. Class sub-divisions other than on limitations
4. Quantifying the limiting factors
5. Rejection of assumptions.

Source. McRae and Burnham, pp. 74-133.

Because agricultural land evaluation is concerned with sustained utilization of the land resource direct approaches to land evaluation (e.g. agronomic trials over a few years) are of limited value apart from the role of supplementing indirect approaches (McRae and Burnham, 1981). Consequently, further review will be restricted to indirect approaches.

It is not intended to go into details of the range of approaches, methods or techniques (implied hierachy of increasing detail) available for agricultural land evaluation (see Davidson,1980; McRae and

Burnham, 1981 for such reviews), rather examples will be selected to illustrate some features of various approaches.

That aside, a broad outline of the FAO Framework (FAO, 1976) for land evaluation will be given, because, being a framework, it allows the individual user flexibility to tailor the Framework to the specific task at hand. In addition, as a relatively recent entrant into the field of agricultural land evaluation approaches it has been able to draw upon the experience gained from earlier approaches which have often been developed for narrower purposes.

The steps identified in the FAO Framework for land evaluation are:

- Initial consultations, concerned with identifying the objectives of the evaluation, and the data and assumptions on which it is to be based.
- Descriptions of the kinds of land use to be considered and the establishment of their land and social requirements.
- Description of land mapping units and derivation of land qualities.
- Comparison of land use requirements with types of land present.
- Economic and social analysis.
- Land suitability classification.
- Presentation of the recommendations of the evaluation study.

Although the Framework is presented in a linear or sequential manner, reconsideration of any or all of the preceding steps from any point within the Framework is accepted and encouraged. Consequently, it is possible to include relevant aspects or considerations (or conversely delete the irrelevant) which only become apparent during the course of the land evaluation study. Additionally, this feature can be used to advantage in providing an initial forum for attracting involvement by other parties in subsequent cycles of the framework.

The principles and procedure constituting the FAO Framework have been formulated with the intention of being usable anywhere in the world, and it is, therefore, as relevant for less developed countries as for developed countries. Likewise, it is intended to be implementable at any scale, from global assessments to detailed local studies for all rural land uses (but specifically excluding urban land uses) including forestry and conservation—land uses which will be the subject of the two subsequent papers. Such studies can be conducted by national or local government, by firms, farmers or individuals.

Experience to date indicates that there has been a marked upturn in the number of land evaluation studies undertaken and the use of their recommendations since the publication of the FAO Framework. However, a number of problems have been encountered, primarily when applied at the farm level. As a result, it has been suggested that for this situation there is a need for linking such a systematic approach of land evaluation with an appropriate farm decision-making model. At the same time, it has been suggested that evaluation for non-specific agricultural land uses is of comparatively little value (Davidson, 1982).

The FAO Framework aims to allocate a land use recommendation to each individual land mapping unit. The land mapping units are defined in accordance with the critical land variables for the land uses being considered in the study. The types of land uses considered for allocation are those judged relevant to the general physical, economic and social conditions prevailing in the area under study. Land uses can be defined at the major or general level (a qualitative or reconnaissance type of land evaluation). Alternatively, when defined at the more detailed level of the land utilization type it is possible to draft a set of technical recommendations appropriate to the area, in terms of produce, capital, labour requirements for example. The Framework also provides for multiple (i.e. more than one land use simultaneously on the same area) or compound land uses (i.e. more than one kind of use on the same area but not simultaneously).

As attention has been centred on the FAO Framework the following general discussion will use terminology consistent with that Framework, although other evaluation methods will be cited as examples.

The land evaluation recommendations can be broadly classed into one of two categories, namely (Hewitt and van Wambeke, 1982):

(a) proscription where the objective is to delineate areas where specified land uses are forbidden in the interests of good land use. For example, clearing of native forests on areas with steep slopes. The value of proscription is that, if properly used, it can reduce the time requirement of any subsequent planning study. However, prescriptive recommendations (which are usually incorporated into laws because they are easily implemented or monitored) are frequently criticized for being unduly negative.

(b) prescription is more positive in that it channels land use in the direction of the best land use. However, such directions usually take the form of recommendations lacking legal support and, therefore, a land user remains free to choose an alternative land use.

The selection between these alternative categories will depend upon the aims or objectives of the particular land evaluation study being considered.

Furthermore, there are two strategies one can take to scheduling a land evaluation study, namely:

1. Sequence or serial model where the land evaluation rating (and implied recommendations) is modified in a series of steps as one progresses from one level to another, i.e. soil, land and site.
2. Parallel model where the ratings are determined by simultaneously taking all factors into account with the resulting highest suitability being identified where the combined limitations are minimal. The FAO Framework is seen as being a parallel model.

The overall objective of any approach to land evaluation is to facilitate the development of land use recommendations which are made in a systematic, objective and reproducible manner. Such recommendations may be for diagnostic or predictive purposes. As already implied, a systematic approach to land evaluation requires three items of information:

1. biophysical and technological requirements of the agricultural land uses being considered.
2. biophysical characteristics of the land.
3. socio-economic factors relevant to the planning and management of the current and proposed agricultural land uses in the area under consideration. These include social and economic factors governing the supply of land available for a particular use and market demand for the production from that use.

These three items of input represent the three essential elements of land evaluation, namely, land uses, land and community requirements respectively (Hewitt and van Wambeke, 1982). Consequently, the task of agricultural land evaluation then becomes that of matching the requirements and characteristics in the light of the factors.

The matching of the land use requirements to the land unit characteristics for a single land use can be subdivided into a number of parts.

Firstly, the land use requirements must be defined so that the critical land variables can be specified. The FAO Framework regards critical variables as land qualities which usually are not simple land characteristics (e.g. if considering rice growing as a land use an impermeable subsoil would be a land use requirement and the corresponding critical land use variable may be low water infiltration rate) but rather derived from the land characteristics (e.g. hydraulic conductivity, pF curve etc. for the example cited).

The selection of critical land variables can be achieved by (Hewitt and van Wambeke, 1982):

1. Deductive selection, an approach by which critical land variables are selected by making inferences from the theory available on the subject. This approach is commonly applied as it makes maximum use of current knowledge and experience.
2. Inductive selection, on the other hand, involves selection of critical land variables by experimentation. Frequently, this approach is able to capitalize on the trial and error experience of existing and past users of the land. However, extreme care is needed when extrapolating beyond the area of the original observations.

Secondly, having established the critical land variables, it is then necessary to define levels of limitation severity. This is usually because production will decrease, the land will be degraded or costs will rise as the critical land variable becomes more limiting. This can be achieved by either (Hewitt and van Wambeke, 1982):

1. *Performance factor* — which relates decreased land use performance (e.g. in terms of yield) to increasing limitation severity, therefore, limitation severity levels can be used as performance predictors. Performance factor is of prime value for agricultural land evaluation.
2. *Cost factor* — relates increased costs to increasing limitation severity. Cost factor is usually expressed in money terms

and divided into the non-recurring and the recurring costs of overcoming the limitation.

In general, rating systems based on performance factor are more suited to land uses in which management inputs are minimal, whereas rating systems based on the cost factor are more suited to intensively managed land uses.

Thirdly, the critical land variables on each land unit have to be compared or matched with the requirements of a particular land use type. This step can be achieved by:

1. *Parametric methods* — critical land variables are assigned to parameters which express the variables as a percentage scale (0-100) or fraction (0-1). Each parameter represents a factor expressing limitation severity levels. Land qualities are then grouped into factors and the factors are combined to produce an overall rating [e.g. Storie Index (Storie, 1933)]. This method has the disadvantage of considering all qualities at one level of generalisation and consequently, the overall rating does not give any information on the nature of the limiting factors, and, as a result, the loss of qualitative information is large.
2. *Maximum limitation matching method* — highlights the critical land variables which require amelioration. Consequently, the approach serves as a management guide. As this approach is strongly prescriptive in approach it is criticized for not taking account of positive qualities that may be important if the limitations can be overcome.
3. Ranking of land units by subjective assessment, a method which enables an experienced evaluator to make full use of accumulated knowledge and allowance can be made for local conditions. However, such an approach lacks reproducibility and is vulnerable to challenge.

Multiple land use evaluation involves undertaking single land use evaluation for each alternative land use followed by the integration of all the single land use studies into one comprehensive set of recommendations. The decision between the candidate land uses is the role of land use planning, a topic of earlier consideration. In conclusion, three points should be seen as central to any agricultural land evaluation study:

1. The need to clarify the questions to be answered from the outset. The clarified questions will be determinants of the approach, methods and techniques selected for developing the answers.
2. The approach, methods and techniques chosen should allow recommendations to be made within the time frame proposed by the client.
3. Promotion and explanation of the recommendations by the evaluator is required to ensure that the recommendations are used to the fullest advantage.

REFERENCES

Ablelter, J.K., and Bownes, C.P. (1960). "Soil productivity ratings", In Land Classification and Evaluation Section of Transactions of the 4th International Congress of Soil Science, Amsterdam.

Davldson, D.A. (1982). "The assessment of land use capability", In 'LANDPLAN 1', Proc. 1st International Symposium on Soil, Geology and Landforms: Impact of Land Use Planning in Developing Countries, eds. P. Nutalaya *et al.* (Asian Institute of Technology: Bangkok).

FAO (1976). "A Framework for Land Evaluation," (FAO: Rome.) Gershmehl, P.J. (1980). Productivity ratings based on soil series: a methodological critique. *Professional Geographer*, 32, 158-63.

Gray, F., Nance, E.G., and Stiegler, J.M. (1979). Productivity of benchmark and key soils in Oklahoma. Agricultural Experiment Station, *Oklahoma State University Bulletin B-740.*

Hewitt, A.E., and Van Wambeke, A. (1982). Soil, land and site evaluation methods for land use planning. In 'LANDPLAN 1', Proc. 1st International Symposium on Soil, Geology and Landforms: Impact of Land Use Planning in Developing Countries, eds. P. Nutalaya *el al.* (Asian Institute of Technology: Bangkok).

Klingebiel, A.A., and Montgomery, P.H. (1961). Land capability classification. Soil Conservation Service, U.S. Department Agriculture Handbook No. 210.

McRae, S.G., and Burnham, C.P. (1981). *Land Evaluation*, Clarendon Press: Oxford.

Reganold, J.P., and Singer, M.J. (1979). "Defining prime farmland by three land classification systems", *Journal of Soil Water Conservation* 34, 172-76.

Storie, R.E. (1960). Rating soils for agricultural, forest and grazing use. In Land Classification and Evaluation Section of the 4th International Congress of Soil Science, Amsterdam.

4

Land Capability Classification
A Case Study of Sultanpur District

HRIDAI R. YADAV

Introduction

The alluvial deposits carried by the river system of Ganga, Gomti and their tributaries form the soils of the Sultanpur district. Horizon differentiation is not prominent. The textural variation is soil profile is apparent. The physiographic variations have contributed to the development of soils of various physical make up and chemical characteristics. Adjacent areas of Gomti river have predominantly coarse fragments soil, while farther from it have increasingly finer fragments. Coarse fragments variations are discernible in soils of different blocks of the Sultanpur district.

Soil survey organization of the Sharda Sahayak Command Area Development Authority carried out detailed soil survey in the Sultanpur district. The Department of Agriculture, Government of U.P. established important soil series and also land capability classification which is immensely valuable. The complete appraisal of soil productivity potentials and hazards and to devise management strategy for enhancing soil productivity, it was imperative to seek quantitative characterisation of physical and chemical properties of the soil. Therefore, a special survey was carried out by undertaking traverses through various sectors of the district. Major soil types and problem areas were identified based on the visual observations and preliminary examination of augured soil samples. Soil samples from different locations in each block were collected from 0-30 cm layer. These soil samples air-dried and ground to pass through 2 mm sieve,

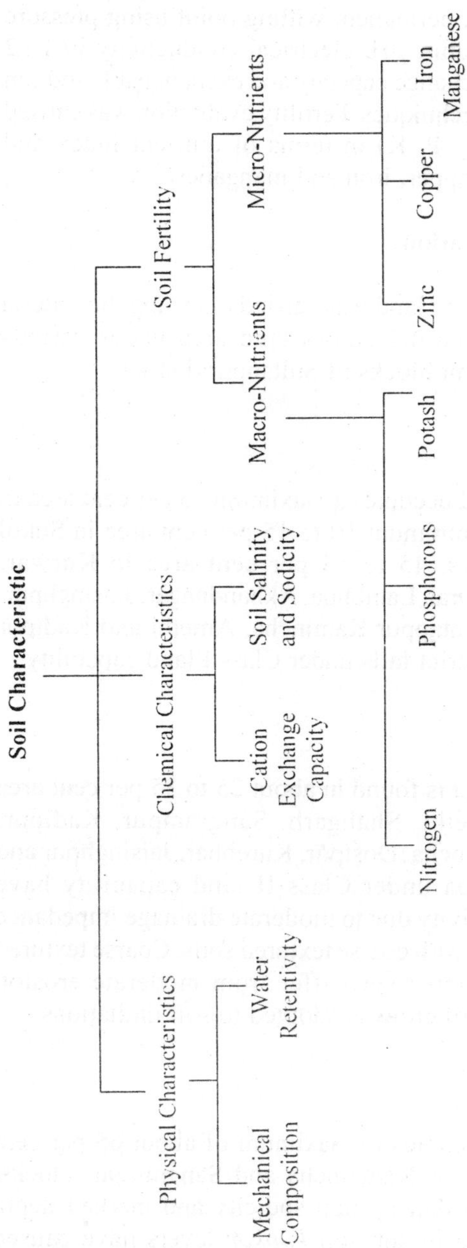
Soil Characteristic
Physical Characteristics
Chemical Characteristics
Soil Fertility
Mechanical Composition
Water Retentivity
Cation Exchange Capacity
Soil Salinity and Sodicity
Macro-Nutrients
Micro-Nutrients
Nitrogen
Phosphorous
Potash
Zinc
Copper
Iron
Manganese

were used for the determination of mechanical composition, water retentivity at field capacity, permanent willing point using pressure plate and membrane apparatus, *p*H, electrical conductivity in 1 : 2 soil-water extract, cation exchange capacity and exchangeable sodium percentage using standard techniques. Fertility evaluation was carried out for macro-nutrients (N, P, K) in terms of nutrient index and micronutrients, viz. zinc, copper, iron and manganese.

Land Capability Classification

Capability classification of the land was carried out using the criteria presented in Tables 4.1 and 4.2 shows land area under various capability classes in different blocks of Sultanpur district.

Class I

Land capability Class I land occupies a maximum 75 per cent area in the Jagdishpur block and minimum 10 to 15 per cent area in Sukul Bazar and Dostpur blocks. 45 to 53 per cent area in Kurwar, Musafirkhana, Jamon, Baldirai, Lambhua, Akhandnagar, Jaisinghpur, Kurebhar, Dhanpatganj, Pratappur Kamincha, Amethi and Kadipur blocks of the Sultanpur district falls under Class I land capability.

Class II

Class II land capability area is found in about 25 to 35 per cent area in Bhadar, Baldirai, Amethi, Shahgarh, Sangrampur, Kadipur, Lambhua, Pratppur, Kamaincha, Dostpur, Kurebhar, Jaisinghpur and Akhandnagra blocks. Area under Class II land capability have limitations to crop productivity due to moderate drainage impedance and soil sodicity. The areas with coarse textured soils. Coarse textured soil areas adjacent to Gomti river suffer from moderate erosion hazards where cultivation of crops is adopted to soil limitations.

Class III

Capacity Class III land occupies in maximum of about 65 per cent area in Gauriganj, Pratappur, Kamaincha and Sangrampur blocks. The marked drainage impedance, high sodicity and marked depth limitations to crop rooting in sub-soil *kankar* layers have caused limitations to crop productivity. Severe erosion and occasional inundation with flood water adjoining Gomti river are responsible for limitations in crop productivity.

Class IV

Class IV land capability occurs in a maximum of 18 per cent area in Sangrampur and about 5 to 10 per cent area in Musafirkhana, Sukul Bazar, Jomon, Bhetua and Gauriganj blocks. Crop productivity limitations in these areas arise from pronounced marshiness, very high sodicity and severe root zone restriction due to soil concretion, erosion hazard, soil wetness and root zone limitations.

Conclusion

Thus, the land capability classification is one of the best suited methods to know the requirement of the soil, to produce the crop or to utilize it for agro-forestry, social-forestry or any other purpose as per its suitability. The capability classification of the land of any area requires scientific, mechanized study of the soil at various levels but it is a fruitful exercise for the planners and the researchers alike. The land capability classification is also helpful in planning the wasteland development programmes for afforestation and agro-forestry purposes for its proper scientific planning for nursery raising, adoption of plantation schemes, soil and moisture conservation methods and other follow up and maintenance of the planted land to meet the increasing demand of the human and cattle population.

Land capability classification of the district was an asset to the Institute of Wastelands and Rural Development as well as to the District Administration of Sultanpur for developing micro-level action plan to develop the available wastelands for fuel wood, fodder, fibres, fruits, plantation programmes, fisheries programmes in the water locked areas and food grain production for better cropping pattern in the district. The land capability classification, irrigation, classification, fertility status of the soil was helpful in assessing the usarization process and its extent for future planning for required quantum of irrigation and fertilizers dozes to produce the better yield in the farmers yield. The farmers were suggested to utilize their land in a better cropping pattern system so that proper land productivity is obtained

Table 4.1: Criteria for Land Capability Classification

Characteristics	*Limitations*	*Land Capability Class*
Nearly level land with deep, well drained soils of satisfactory texture and structure: not affected by harmful factors like *kankar* granules, erosion, wetness and salinity/sodicity.	No productivity limitations; suitable for intensive cultivation of climatically adapted crops.	Class I No sub-class
Gently to moderately sloping land with deep soils of fairly satisfactory texture and structure; affected by moderate erosion, wetness and salinity/sodicity.	Productivity limitations due to moderate erosion, drainage impedance and wetness, droughtiness and salinity/sodictiy; cultivation of crops adapted to soil limitations.	Class II; sub-classes designated as erosion hazard IIe; soil wetness IIw and root zone limitation IIs.
Gently to strongly sloping land with moderately deep soils having very slowly permeable substratum; affected by marked erosion, wetness, presence of shallow water table and salinity/sodicity.	Productivity limitations due to severe erosion, marked drainage impedance and wetness, poor water holding capacity and high salinity/sodicity; cultivation with precautions against permanent land damage and careful selection of crops adapted to soil limitations.	Class III; sub-classes designated as erosion hazard IIIe; soil wetness IIIw and root zone limitations IIIs
Strongly sloping to steep land, deep to shallow sandy or concretionary soil with low moisture holding capacity; affected by severe erosion, pronounced marshiness/droughtiness and very high salinity/sodicity.	Productivity limitations due to very severe erosion, pronounced marshiness/droughtiness and very severe root zone limitations, occasional cultivation of crops in rotation with grasses.	Class IV; sub-classes designated as erosion hazard IVe; soil wetness IVw and root zone limitations IVs.

Source: Soil Survey Manual, All India Soil and Land Use Survey Organisation, I.A.R.I., New Delhi (1970).

Table 4.2: Area Under Various Land Capability Classes in Different Blocks of Sultanpur District (*in Hectares*)

Block	*Land Capability Class*										
	I	IIe	IIw	IIs	IIws	IIIe	IIIw	IIIs	IIIws	IVe	IVs
Musafirkhana	9109	4217	–	–	–	2698	–	–	–	–	840
Sukul Bazar	2005	–	–	12382	–	2884	–	–	–	–	1905
Jagdishpur	14955	–	1000	1993	–	997	–	990	–	–	–
Jamon	11047	6274	451	–	–	–	2513	1570	–	2161	–
Baldirai	10215	–	–	6810	–	–	3458	–	–	–	–
Amethi	6856	1530	–	2280	–	2270	–	2285	2285	–	–
Bhadar	5573	474	3981	318	789	–	–	2388	1592	–	–
Bhetua	4164	–	3665	–	–	796	–	7995	–	832	–
Gauriganj	5210	–	2084	–	–	–	–	6235	5295	–	–
Sangrampur	2260	2055	–	1568	–	1541	–	1000	–	1027	822
Shahgarh	4442	640	635	1524	2287	–	–	–	3176	–	–
Kadipur	10926	3924	5494	462	–	3524	523	1308	–	–	–
Lambhua	9066	1727	2159	4318	–	2190	–	2128	–	–	–
Pratappur	5460	1500	1367	1774	–	1638	1090	820	–	–	–
Kamaincha											
Dostpur	4024	1609	2682	5363	3218	1340	2145	3754	2682	–	–
Akhandanagar	11030	2200	1325	3197	2650	1325	2120	2650	–	–	–
Jaisinghpur	9914	3355	2854	905	–	964	2323	2223	–	–	–
Dhanpatganj	10552	4940	2245	1570	–	2444	–	900	–	–	–
Kurebhar	11602	3334	4440	1220	–	–	1610	–	–	–	–
Kurwar	9550	3255	2170	2605	–	1736	1085	1304	–	–	–
Dubepur	6717	1535	4606	2495	–	–	2687	1153	–	–	–
Bhadianya	7570	3154	1892	3575	–	1262	1682	1893	–	–	–

Source: Soil Survey Manual, All India Soil and Land Use Survey Organisation, I.A.R.I., New Delhi (1970).

from their respective land. Thus, the land capability classification is a boon not only to the local level farmers but also to administrators, planners, scientists and researchers to develop their action plan to meet the increasing demand of growing human and cattle population and to regenerate the ecological imbalances and improve the socio-economic conditions of the deprived and multitudes of the district.

5

Wasteland Inventory
Step Towards Wasteland Development

ANIL KUMAR

Introduction

The breaking of traditional social order of villages, perpetuating a sense of total indifference among the inhabitants who under old institution of village panchayats were collectively responsible for maintenance of common forest and grazing lands (Mukherjee, 1939), and because of the absence of a clear cut land policy administrative lapses have collectively introduced factors adversely affecting the efficiency of natural self-sustaining capability of land resources. Trying to use land for a purpose to which it was not adopted, and application of improper methods of resource utilization collectively resulted in marked deterioration of productive quality of land. The process of wasting of land is both natural and human-induced. It is difficult to separate them, but, it is the human interference with natural system which has in most of the places, gradually deteriorated the quality of land. These factors collectively or singularly are responsible for turning productive land into unproductive wastelands. Thus, conservation of land becomes an important issue in the present context of growing pressure of population on land resources for food, fuel, fodder and wood. Today, conservation means much more than prevention of exhaustion or depletion of soil. It means also that land should be put to the best use. The need of scientific method of enquiry becomes urgent to ensure optimum use of land. Hence, the correct assessment of each parcel of land and particularly of wastelands is essential both from the point of preventing the deterioration of its capability and for facilitating their economic use.

Wastelands merit our attention, both locally and regionally. Dealing with the problems related to the reclamation of the wasteland under productive unit of land resource is a matter of urgency and relevance to social policy (Georgii, 1973).

The term wasteland is not only confined to culturable and barren unculturable wastes but also includes within its broader term of definition all such land areas showing ailments of physical limitation rendering them useless or uneconomic to use to witch they are presently put to human exploitation of land resources by burning and cutting of vegetation, overgrazing of poor pasture, misuse and overuse of land without proper consideration of management, have subsequently exposed to leaching of soil nutrients and removal of humus rich top soil layer by erosion. Under such broad context many land areas officially included under forest, grazing land and other fallows will have to be declared wasteland. We can summarize wastelands as:

(i) areas losing its soil and fertility through pronounced erosion, wash and leaching,
(ii) land revealing such physical attributes which restrict or limit its use,

bad lands stony lands, base rocky surface, leached grounds with varying degree of restrictions.

Naturally lands previously under various uses before they lost their capability to sustain the needs of communities can be included under this category. Wastelands can be culturable or unculturable depending upon their physical attributes. It can be distributed in a region irrespective of terrain. Because most of waste lands still retains some inherent potentialities to support some specific use, they are considered potential as well as marginal lands which can be reclaimed to various uses on the basis of their limitation, and assessment of their capability under proper conservation and land management practices. It is obvious that the extent to which wastelands can be reclaimed under various land resources actually depends on relative behaviour of terrain, such as slope, soil, hydrology, erosion etc. Because of the wide differences in physical suitability for use, the inventory of wasteland is the first step towards their scientific reclamation and management.

Wasteland Inventory

Inventory of wasteland involves three sequential phases. The first phase is the assemblage of basic ground characteristics of wastelands. The inherent characteristics of each wasteland plots has to be identified with the help of field survey entries. The informations, thus, obtained can be used for formulating a general scheme of wasteland classification. The land inventory of wastelands has been carried out in Karon *anchal* of Deoghar district of Bihar. In making observation and measurements one is to be guided by the principles of genesis, by knowing relationship between physiography, soil and other features of terrain, and by the principles of land management. This is because these principles are helpful in making decisions about the significance of observed features. The descriptions are kept as objective as possible. Wasteland informations are collected following the criteria suggested in the soil survey manual. They are grouped three broad heads:

(a) *Geomorphic attributes*: Parent material, relief, slope, erosion, drainage.
(b) *Soil attributes*: Soil slope, texture, structure, depth, thickness of surface layer, stoniness, *p*H, permeability.
(c) *Vegetation attributes*: Surface condition, life form, size coverage, root penetration, land use.

Altogether 19 variables in the present study have been selected omitting other parameters after ascertaining quantitative influence and magnitude of influence. The land survey characteristics, thus, have provided sufficient information for classification of wasteland, limitations, and assessment of wasteland potential to support some specific landuse (Kumar, 1986, 1988, 1989).

The observed and measured values of the selected attributes of each wasteland plot in relation to their terrain site factors have been arranged in chart (sample of one page is included in Appendix I).

Classification of Wastelands

In the second phase of inventory, wastelands have been further compared and several plots with identical value have been further abstracted from the chart into one that is standard for the type. This scheme of grouping and classification of wasteland is based on number and type of most obvious terrain limitations (Kumar, 1984). The scheme is practical because this not only indicates physical limitations of wasteland plots, but, also provides information about potential hazards. This method is specially useful in selection of proper conservational measure and management practices while reclaiming wasteland plots for use.

Under this system, wastelands are first grouped into physiographic terrain classes such as hillslope, undulating upland and rolling upland terrains. These wasteland terrains are further subdivided into units and sub-units on the basis of limitations denoted by adding small roman letters as, r (relief), 1 (slope), e (erosion), s (stoniness), w (wetness) and d (depth of soil). These units of wastelands are again grouped according to potential of land containing similar limitations. They are designated capital roman letters like A (for limitations caused by sand and gravel in sub-soil), B (erosion hazards), C (problem of wetness due to poor soil drainage), E (problem of excessive gravel) and G (problem of root penetration due to shallow soil depth). Again by adding number variation of factors in a wasteland unit has been recognized. Wastelands are not only classified by this method but each sub-unit thus also explains the number of limitations and zonal variations of associated factors. They are sufficiently uniform in potential productivities and require similar conservational treatment.

In Table 5.1, wasteland plots of Karon *anchal* have been grouped into various wasteland units and sub-units according to progressively decreasing number of limitations within a terrain, and adjustments that are required before they can be reclaimed under proper management practices. It also sufficiently allows separate treatment of each plot.

Table 5.1 summarises that use and conservation of wastelands are influenced by the nature of relief, slope, soil, degree of erosion, wetness and stoniness of soil. One factor or several of them together has imposed limitations of land use. Presently, more than 20 per cent of the *anchal* area can be included under the category of wasteland.

Table 5.1: Wasteland classification in Karon *Anchal*

Wasteland Terrain Plot Unit/ No. Sub-Units.		*Wasteland Attributes (Limitation Factors)*							
		Relief	*Slope*	*Erosion*	*Types of Erosion*	*Stoniness*	*Soil Drainage*	*Soil Texture*	*Soil Depth*
(1)	(2)	(3)	(4)	(5)	(6)	(7)	(8)	(9)	(10)
Hill Slope Terrain Units									
1b-resd B_8	1	con	stro	mod	sheet	sev	sell	sandy loam	mod
Undulating Upland Terrain Unit									
2a(ii) Les–B3	9	nor	–	sev	gully/sheet	–	mod	loamy sand	mod
Les-B4	13, 45	–	–	–	–	mod	–	–	deep
Les-B6	30, 33	–	–	sev	–	–	–	–	shallow
Les-B7	20	nor	stro	mod	gully/sheet	mod	mod	loamy sand	mod
le-B15	12	–	–	sev	–	slight	well	–	deep
le-B16	44	–	–	–	gully	–	mod	–	–
le-B17	42	–	–	mod	sheet	–	–	–	mod
le-B18	22, 38, 44	–	–	sev	gully	–	–	–	deep
es-B19	25, 37	–	gent	–	–	mod	–	sandy loam	mod
es-B20	7, 8, 10, 18, 19, 23, 24, 43, 51	–	–	mod	gully/sheet	–	–	–	deep
es-B21	17, 21	–	mod	sev	–	–	well	loamy sand	mod
e-B22	4, 5, 6, 15, 27, 28, 29, 32, 34, 35, 36, 39, 46, 47, 48, 54	–	gent	mod	–	slight	mod	–	deep

(*Contd.*)

(*Contd.*)

(1)	(2)	(3)	(4)	(5)	(6)	(7)	(8)	(9)	(10)
rsw-cl	43, 50, 53	con	–	slight	sheet	mod	poor	sandy loam	mod
e-D2	14, 16, 41	nor	–	–	–	slight	well	loamy sand	–
lesd-F2	26	–	stro	mod	gully/sheet	mod	mod	–	–
e-F5	1, 2, 3, 32, 52	–	gent	sev	–	slight	well	sandy loam	–
s-F6	40	–	–	slight	–	sev	mod	–	–
Rolling Upland Terrain Unit									
2b-les-B2	28	–	strp	sev	–	mod	Well	–	deep
-les-B3	6, 20, 25	–	–	mod/sev	–	–	–	loamy sand	–
-les-B4	11, 22, 23	–	–	–	–	–	–	–	mod
esd-B5	2, 14, 19, 30, 38, 39, 40, 41, 44, 60, 61, 62	gent	mod	–	–	–	–	–	mod./ shallow
esd-B7	15	–	–	sev	sheet	mod	well	–	shallow
es-B14	1, 21, 24, 25, 43, 55, 65	–	–	mod	gully/sheet	mod	–	sandy loam	deep
Es-B17	4, 5, 20, 46, 47, 48, 51, 58, 59, 68	–	–	sev	–	–	mod	–	mod/deep
ed-B19	19, 31, 37, 38, 42, 53, 54, 66	nor	gent	mod	gully/sheet	slight	mod	sandy loam	mod/ shallow
e-B20	6, 7, 8, 9, 10, 12, 18, 26, 27	–	mod	sev	–	–	well	–	mod/ deep
e-B22	16, 17, 45, 50	–	gent	–	gully	–	–	loamy sand	mod
e-D2	29, 32, 34, 35, 36, 57	sub.nor	–	slight	Sheet	–	–	sandy loam	deep
s-D4	33, 56, 63	nor	–	–	sheet/gully	slight	mod	loamy sand	mod

Out of 5351 hectares of land, about 58 per cent (3078 hec.) is experiencing severe soil erosion. Intensity of erosion is slight in only 7 per cent (379 hec.) of wastelands.

The objective of classification is to determine the proper conservational method for treatment of land and management of wasteland for proper utilization based on land's potential capability. Inventory of wasteland provides base to organize various informations in determining the capability and suitability for specific uses.

The evaluation process has to clarify some pertinent questions such as whether particular land is suited for crop production? Can it be cultivated without causing soil erosion? Is it safe and pertinent to keep its use limited to grazing or production of fuelwood or timber? Each wasteland category has its peculiar problems and each one requires special approach to reclaim it. Before the reclamation, all land attributes have to be considered and their capability and suitability for optional land uses along with conservation and management aspect of land planning has to be determined. The first requisite to conservation of wasteland is to fit the use to the capability of land.

Capability Rating for Wastelands

The study of individual aspects of wastelands and considering several aspects of each unit simultaneously in land use plans are useful in wasteland development. A wasteland unit which may be deemed unsuitable for a particular land use based on one factor, such as slope may be suitable on the basis of another factor such as absence of stoniness. It may also be necessary to relate these factors to social and economic factors besides some basic pressing problem like soil erosion. This not only requires development of a method, which would provide the handling of a variety of data in a systematic manner with high degree of flexibility but also make possible to conservation element in development planning. It is a pre-established fact that the ecological system of the region has been tempered to a extent where degradation of various landuse initiated the encroachment of wastelands. So the basic aim of the study is oriented towards the problems of ecological imbalance and the extent to which ecological system can be re-established under a 'ecological planning method' (McHarg, 1969). Thus, the approach of the study is to emphasize the problems of wasteland development, through the assessment of the ability of wastelands to support development.

The first part of the study consisted of an inventory of terrain factors. This includes climate, geology, geomorphology, hydrology, soils and vegetation already discussed. Informations regarding these factors have been collected in some details from various maps, field investigations and records. It becomes necessary to combine various attributes at the third stage of inventory. To accomplish this value, each of the nineteen attributes is then encoded for each wasteland unit. This also involves selection of land use options for wasteland reclamation. The present study is restricted to determining the potential of wasteland, for forestry either as social forestry, afforestation, village woodland etc. or pastorage and for agricultural uses. Additional option is related to the conservation of soil in the preparation of a comprehensive plan. It has been then decided to select the land characteristics or environmental facts that would influence capability for the specific land use option. For the present evaluation the 19 wasteland terrain factors are selected. It is further decided that each factor or attribute would have no more than five sub-categories, and each has been given index number ranging from 1 to 5. The index numbers are for identification only, and the sub-classes of factors are arranged in a logical sequence, as from gentle to steep, slight to severe.

The second step is assigning capability values to each index number for each landuse option. The value of 1 indicates low capability and a rating of 5 indicates a high capability for the particular landuse option because of the importance of the given terrain factor capability values is defined as follows:

0. Not suitable	1. Very low	2. Low
3. Moderate	4. High	5. Very high

Under this scheme 0 capability value renders land useless for the particular landuse option. The total land capability value for that unit of land will be '0' regardless of how suitable the other attributes may be. For example, wasteland being considered for the pasture option will receive a capability rating of 0 for erosion if it is under severe erosion. Such land should not be reclaimed for pastorage, no matter how favourable the other terrain factors are. Similarly, a slope exceeding 50 per cent is not appropriate for either agriculture or pasture development. The capability value of 0 thus means that a wasteland unit with slope exceeding 50 per cent will not be allocated to any of these options regardless of the high capability rating of other factors. A slope of 0 to 5 per cent, in contrast, has very high capability for either agriculture of pastorage and is given a capability value of 5.

Some factors are more important to one type of landuse than others, that is why it is decided to assign a weight of 1 to 10 to each factor, while considering them for a single possible landuse. For each contemplated landuse a weighting or measure of relative importance has been assigned to each factor. The weighting is scaled form 1 to 10 as follows:

9-10	Very high importance
7-8	High importance
5-6	Moderate importance
3-4	Low importance
1-2	Very low importance

Suppose two wasteland terrain units are being assessed for agricultural use, the first with exceeding 50 per cent and the second with less than 3 per cent. The first cannot be cultivated normally, whereas a terrain with a slope up to 3 per cent can be cultivated easily and because slope is very important, a weight of 10 is assigned to it. When the individual capability rating is multiplied by the weighting value, a weighted capability value is obtained, which ranges from 0 to 40.

The land capability ratings for each wasteland terrain unit is obtained. When weighted capability values of all the factors for each landuse options are obtained, they are added together. The land capability rating for a particular landuse option is, then, transferred to the map and the values are, then, classified from high to no capability classes. The method is advantageous as a system for evaluating various characteristics in common terrain units. The resultant map of Karon *anchal*, thus, show the relative capability of each wasteland plot for three optional landuse, i.e. agriculture, pasture and forestry. (Figs. 5.1, 5.2, 5.3).

The wastelands of the *anchal* have been classified into five categories. Under the high capability rating wastelands have few restrictions and limitations. While low to very low capability rating means plots are more hazard prone and are better suited to forestry and controlled pastorage than any kind of farming. Table 5.2 reveals the comparative rating for three optional landuse in the Karon *anchal*.

Table 5.2 also reveals that a substantial hectare has no capability ratings under agriculture and pasture. Wasteland plots with this rating,

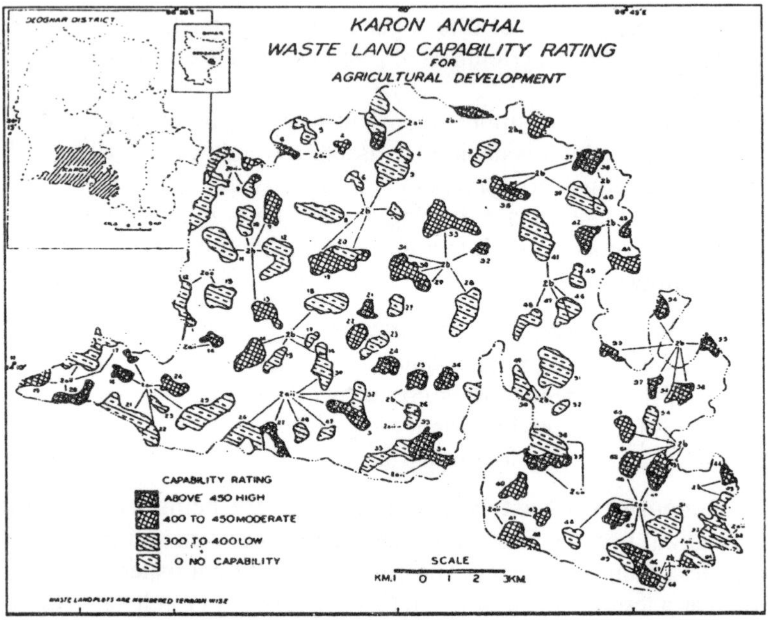

Fig. 5.1: Wasteland Capability Rating for Agricultural Development

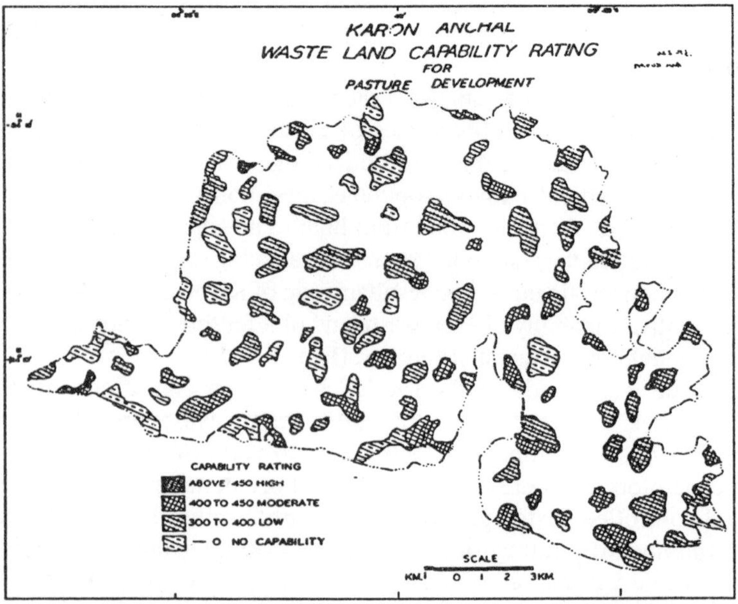

Fig. 5.2: Wasteland Capability Rating for Pasture Development

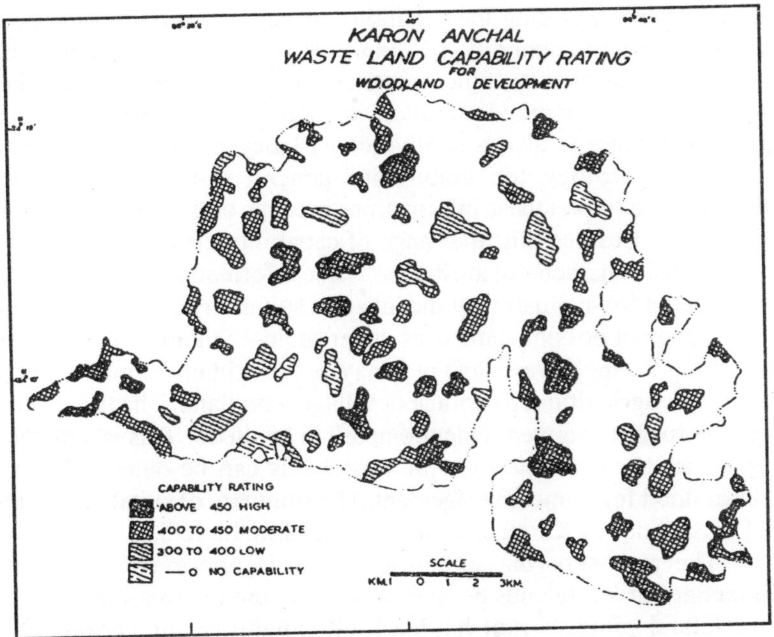

Fig. 5.3: Wasteland Capability Rating for Woodland Development

Table 5.2: Wasteland Capability Rating for Development: Karon *Anchal*

Capability Rating	*For Agriculture (hec.)*	*For Pasture (hec.)*	*For Forestry (hec.)*
High	1211.0	70.5	2281.5
Moderate	1018.5	995.5	1859.0
Low	105.0	2851.0	834.0
Very low	–	9.0	–
No capability	3016.5	1424.5	376.5

naturally, suffers from a number of limitations mainly erosion and stoniness which make reclamation under these specific land uses uneconomic and dangerous. But by simply protecting such wastelands from further interference from man and his animals a good green belt can be developed.

Wasteland Suitability for Development

The inventory of the various wastelands and tneir attributes provided informations regarding the capability of wasteland units and about factors like soil suitability, soil moisture, underground water level, soil erosion hazards etc. Since wasteland units differ from one another locally, there is marked variation in their inherent characteristics. However, there is also a relative consistency in the region due to climate, hydrology, topography and general soils. Thus, it is not difficult to interpret these informations in terms of the dominant factor or factors. Besides this, the range of capability classes also reflects the intrinsic character of attributes. These informations can be further considered for evaluation of the inherent suitability of wasteland unit for a range of possible land uses under socio-economic management planning. A single wasteland plot may be brought under management either for agriculture, pastorage or village woodland. The wastelands can be further grouped under compatible landuses. This is a method by which the characteristics of wastelands can be determined and understood for proper management. The summary of suitability rating of wastelands in Karon *anchal* is arranged in Table 5.3.

The map showing suitability rating is important in landuse planning for wastelands because it conveys the relative suitability of wasteland plots. A plot having high capability for various uses naturally has more favourable physical factors and only few restrictions. To develop such a plot will be both economic and wise. It will also provide wide range of choice to use it than a plot with low capability. Moreover, the present study is oriented to determine the ability of wastelands to support development and restoring their ecological balance. Map, thus tends to emphasize the suitability for development. During decision-making it is advantageous to have a clear understanding about the relative suitability of plots and what alternative best possible landuse can be safely supported by the land capability during planning because some specific optional use of land may seem more beneficial and economic. The map showing the inherent suitability of wastelands for a range of possible landuses can be superimposed on optional capability rating map to summarize the best possible use in relation to suitability for development. The summary of suitability map is given in Table 5.4.

In the present context, the suitability rating is aggregated from the weighted capability ratings for each wasteland plot. The method makes it clear that the capability factors related to optional land uses are very important in the determination of land suitability. The total scores for all the three optional landuses in the present case range

Table 5.3: Suitability Rating for Wastelands in Karon *Anchal*

Suitability Class	*Wasteland*	*Plots*	*Total Wasteland Area in Hec.*
High (rating more than 450)	Undulating Terrain (2aii)	4, 5, 14, 15, 16, 18, 20, 31, 32, 34, 36, 38, 39, 45, 46, 47, 48, 52, 53, 54.	747.5
	Rolling upland terrain (2b)	2, 4, 5, 12, 13, 18, 19, 21, 24, 25, 38, 46, 47, 48, 49, 50, 51, 52, 53, 55, 62, 63, 64, 65, 67, 68.	1234.0
Moderate (400-450)	Hill slope terrain (1b)	1	9.5
	Undulating terrain (2aii)	1, 2, 3, 6, 7, 8, 9, 11, 12, 13, 17, 19, 21, 22, 24, 29, 35, 40, 41, 42, 43, 44, 45, 50, 51	1012.5
	Rolling upland terrain (2b)	1, 6, 7, 9, 10, 11, 20, 22, 23, 26, 27, 28, 29, 32, 36, 37, 42, 43, 44, 45, 56, 57, 66	837.0
Low (300-400)	Undulating upland terrain (2aii)	10, 23, 25, 27, 28, 33, 37	383.0
	Rolling upland terrain (2b)	3, 8, 14, 17, 30, 31, 33, 34, 58, 59, 60, 61	551.0

Table 5.4: Suitability classes

Anchal	*Suitability Class (Showing Area in Hectares)*					
	Most	*2nd most*	*3rd most*	*4th most*	*5th most*	*Least*
Karon	652.0	2207.0	468.5	218.0	–	272.0

from more than 1350 to 750. These scores are divided into six groups and mapped separately for the *anchal* (Fig. 5.4).

Table 5.4 shows that upto 2nd most suitable category wastelands of the *anchal* are more economic to develop either for agriculture, pasture or woodlands. The cost of development will increase to lower

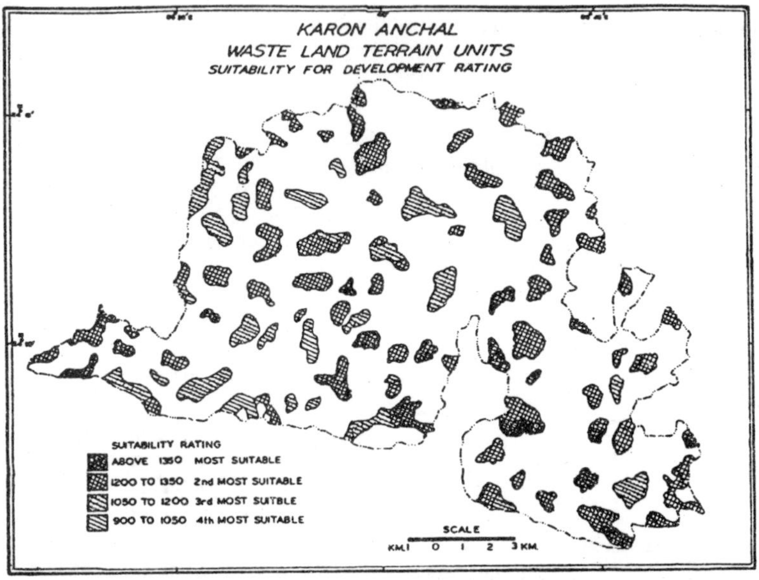

Fig. 5.4: Wasteland Terrain Units: Suitability for Development Rating

category besides the choice of use will become restricted. In 5th and the least suitability categories only those wastelands are included which have very low capability or have no capability, presentaly, as they are either rocky terrains or lands with several restrictions. It means that before wastelands are reclaimed for any use it is advisable to introduce appropriate conservation measure so that in long-term planning, these plots may improve their capability to support some sort of use.

The inventory of wasteland based on the recognition of physical limitation and their intensity is the prerequisite of wasteland reclamation for development. The inventory provides information to initiate measures to prevent further deterioration of land potentialities pertaining to their reclamation under some predicted possible optional use. The method can also be used at initial stage to determine the appropriate use of reclaimed plots for most suitable landuse based on the inherent capability determination.

REFERENCES

Georgii, Hnas W. (1973). "Global Ecological Effects," *Applied Science and Development*, pp. 136-43.

Kumar, A. (1984). "Terrain Evaluation and Wasteland Classification: A Pragmatic Approach," *Indian Geographical Studies, 22,* pp. 30-38.

—— (1986). "Application of Wasteland Terrain Evaluation in Integrated Rural Development," *Indian National Geographer,* I (1 & 2), pp. 16-36.

—— (1988) "Integrated Approach of Wasteland Capability Determination in Landuse Planning: A Case Study of the Deoghar District of Bihar," in P. Singh (ed.) *Problem of Wasteland and Forest Ecology of India.* Ashish Pub. House, New Delhi, pp. 89-114.

—— (1989) "*Wasteland Management in India,* Ashish Pub. House, New Delhi.

McHarg, T.L. (1969), *Design with Nature*, Natural History Press, New York.

Mukherjee, R. (1939), "Land Tenures and Legislation," Chapter II in *Economic Problems of Modern India,* Macmillan, London.

6

The Higher Himalayan Beas Basin

An Analysis of Landform Systems, Soils and Land use

O.P. THAKUR and P.B. SAXENA

The present study of the Higher Himalayan Beas Basin aims to analyse the type and distribution of landform systems (relief and slope) to recognize the geo-morphological regions of the basin and to evaluate them in relation with the existing environmental resources of the region. The pattern of a landform system signifies the type, mode and behaviour of land use pattern of a particular region. Thus, the study of landform system will be helpful in evaluating the environmental resources of the basin by applying a new approach of Fractional Code Method. The study further aims at diagnosing the nature and type of environmental resource depletion and to pinpoint the intensity and distribution of geo-catastrophic factors to treat them with ecological measures. This will also help to work out a trend of the suitability of landforms for varied rational uses of land in the context of the environmental development.

Geoidentity

The Higher Himalayan Beas Basin extends from 31° 27′ N Latitude to 76° 56′ E Longitude and from 32° 24′ N Latitude to 77° 53′ E Longitude (Fig. 6.1). Physiographically, the basin forms the central portion of the Western Himalaya (Himachal Himalaya). The Pir Panjal mountain range lies from north-west to south-east, dividing the watersheds of the Beas and Chandra rivers. The Greater Himalayan mountain range runs along the eastern margin and separates the catchments area of the Beas river form that of the Spiti and Sutlej rivers by the nature of its rugged terrain of snow, glaciers and voluminous streams and confined valleys.

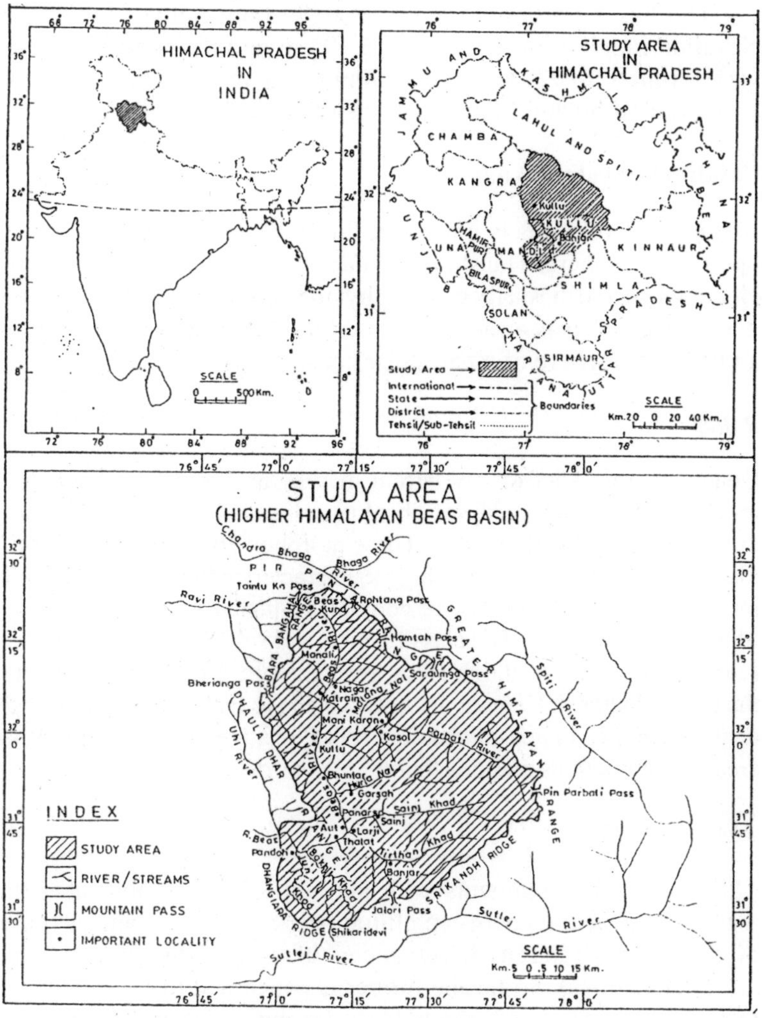

Fig. 6.1 Location Map

In the north-west, the basin is demarcated by the Bara Bangahal mountain range, the water divide between the rivers Beas and Ravi and the Dhalula Dhar range between the rivers Beas and Uhl. In the south-south-east Srikandh ridge (5,227 m.) and the Jalori pass (3,306 m.) in the southern tip and the Dhangiara Dhar (Shikari Devi 3,359 m.) in the south-wastern flank demarcate the boundary of the basin.

The basin encompasses an area of about 5,908 km^2 with an elevation ranging form 750 m to 6,395 m and the average gradient varies from 6° to 72° and more. Administratively, the basin occupies an area of Kullu and Mandi districts of Himachal Pradesh.

Landform System Analysis

A study of landforms is important for understanding their influence upon the biosphere. The study includes the characteristics of various elements of earth surface, i.e. physiographic, aspects, slope and drainage, which play an active role in soil genesis and land use forming a rational biosphere of a particular ecosystem.

Relief

Quantitatively, relief of any terrain may be analysed with the help of morphometry which analyses absolute relief and relative relief, slope drainage, and dissection index. These morphometric parameters help in diagnosing the terrain morphology to characterize the terrain into varied morpho-units which may also be correlated with the geological conditions of the concerned area. The classification and sub-classification of "Unit Landforms"[1] based on the above assessment form the bases to distinguish the terrain features. Keeping in view the above facts, the relief has been analysed in the context of absolute relief, relative relief, relief profiles, area height relations and dissection index as detailed below:

Absolute Relief

There are two components with the help of which absolute relief may be analysed: (i) between altitudinal zones discrepancies (based on contour map) and (ii) discrepancies of regional distribution (based on relief profiles). So far the former is concerned to the total height ranging from 750 m to 6,395 m in the basin encompassing an uneven distribution of latitudes, i.e. alluvial terraces, channel-bar and point-bar deposits river benches, interfluves, knick points, interlocking spurs, entrenched and ingrown meanders and glacial features at the higher elevation above 5,000 m.

After analyzing the morphogenesis of different relief features in relation to the altitude the Higher Himalayan Beas Basin has been divided into five relief regions (Fig. 6.2 and Table 6.1).

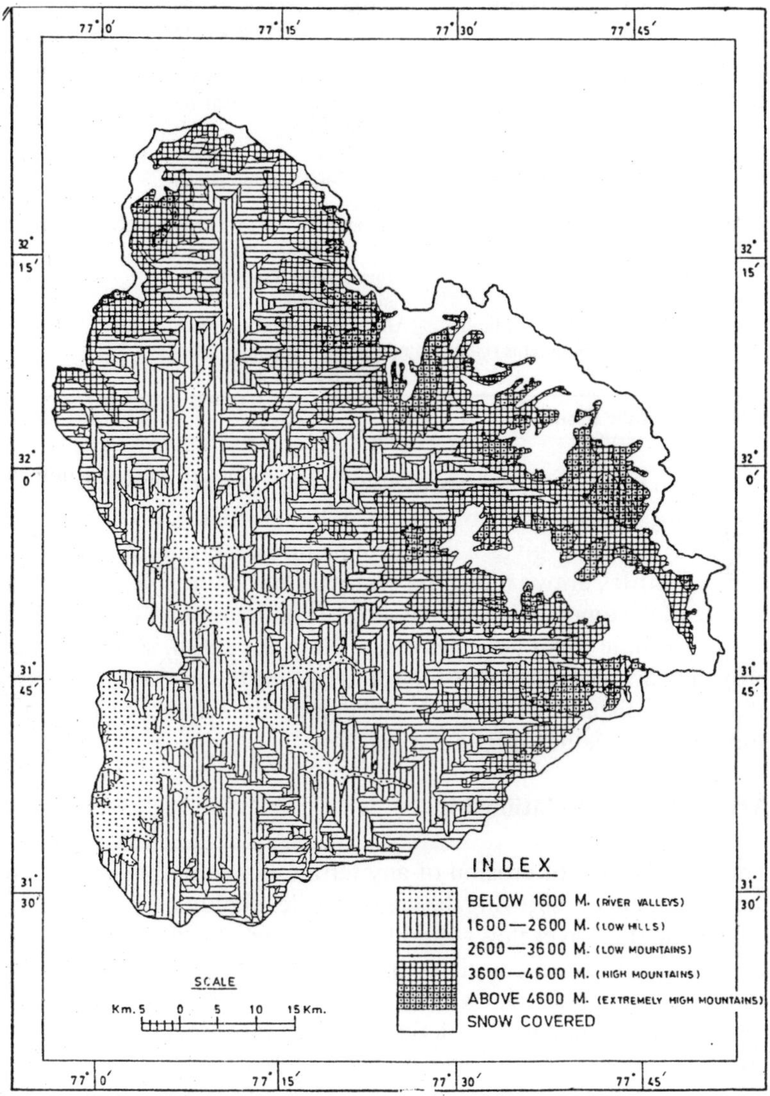

Fig. 6.2: Higher Himalayan Beas Basin: Relief Regions

Table 6.1: Relief Regions of the Basin

Altitude (in m)	*Types of Land-forms*	*Main Relief Features*	*Area in km^2*	*Area in %*
1. Below 1600	Low valleys (fluvial)	Alluvial deposits and terraces, channel and point bars, confluences and ingrown meanders	428.03	7.24
2. 1600-2600	Low hills (fluvial)	Confluences, river benches and interfluves	1386.43	23.47
3. 2600-3600	Low mountains (Glacio-fluvial)	Interfluves, low ridges, open gorges and knick points	1197.75	20.27
4. 3600-4600	High mountains (Glacio-fluvial)	Entrenched meanders, water divides, truncated cirques, spurs, knick points, hanging valleys, etc.	1194.75	19.46
5. Above 4600	Extremely high mountains (Glacial)	Aretes, horn peaks cirques, moraines, glacial lakes, hanging valleys, etc.	1746.53	29.56
Total area of the Basin			5908.49	100.00

It also becomes necessary to discuss the general nature of regional discrepancy with the help of different relief profiles. Since the contour map directly never gives a complete picture of terrain[2], the different terrain profiles drawn along the east-west direction gives a clear-cut picture of the topography and the surface configurations, the sharpness of the absolute relief becomes clear. Thus, the serial, superimposed, projected and composite profiles drawn along the east-west direction at an equal distance of the basin and depicts the sequence of summits and valleys together (Fig. 6.3 a and b).

Area-Altitude Relationship

The morphology of erosion of any terrain is mainly presented with the help of curves showing the area-altitude relations. Up to Dalashni village the Beas river flows into a broad U-shaped valley from 1-2 km. wide with unsorted classic sediments of all the grades. South of Dalashni, the river cuts a deep and narrow gorge at Aut-Pandoh section which indicates the action of the fluvial process. Dalashni of terminal moraine at and around Dalashni and the hanging valley of the Beas up to Dalashni suggests the glacial recession. In the Basin there are broad U-shaped valleys, in which some of the landforms

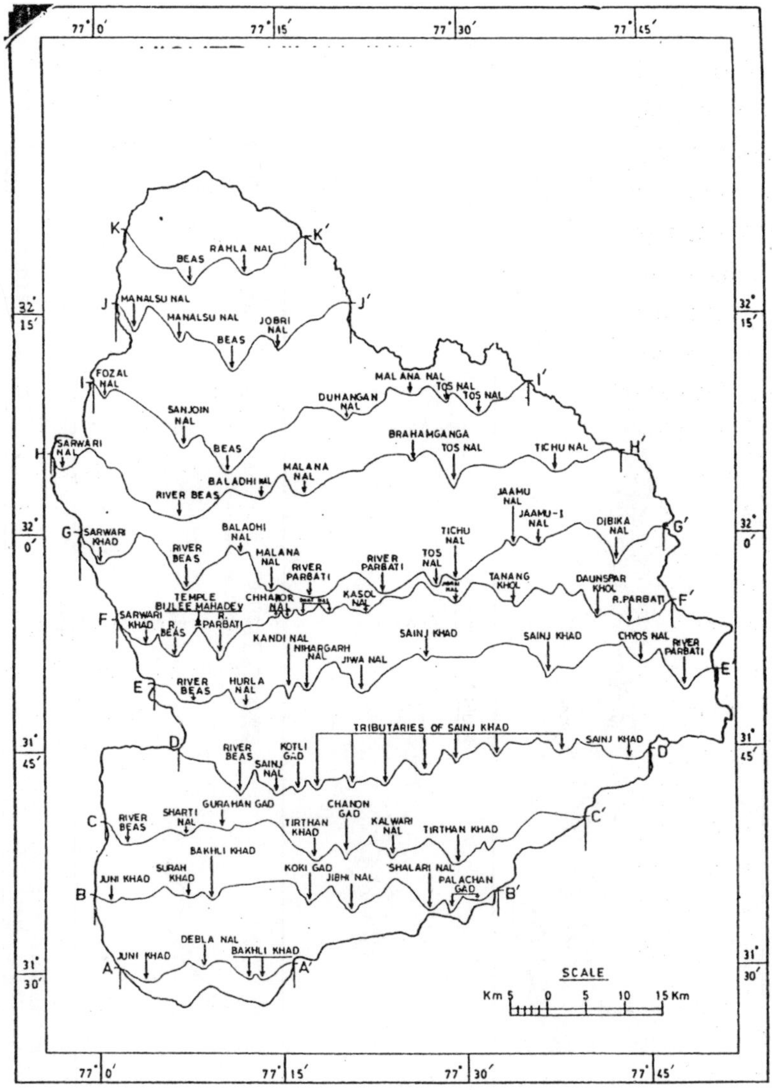

Fig. 6.3(a): Higher Himalayan Beas Basin: Distribution of Serial Profiles (Relief Profiles)

like coalescing piedmont forms, fan-cut terraces, interfluves and sand bars have been clearly observed. These later landforms are the outcomes of the fluvial processes.

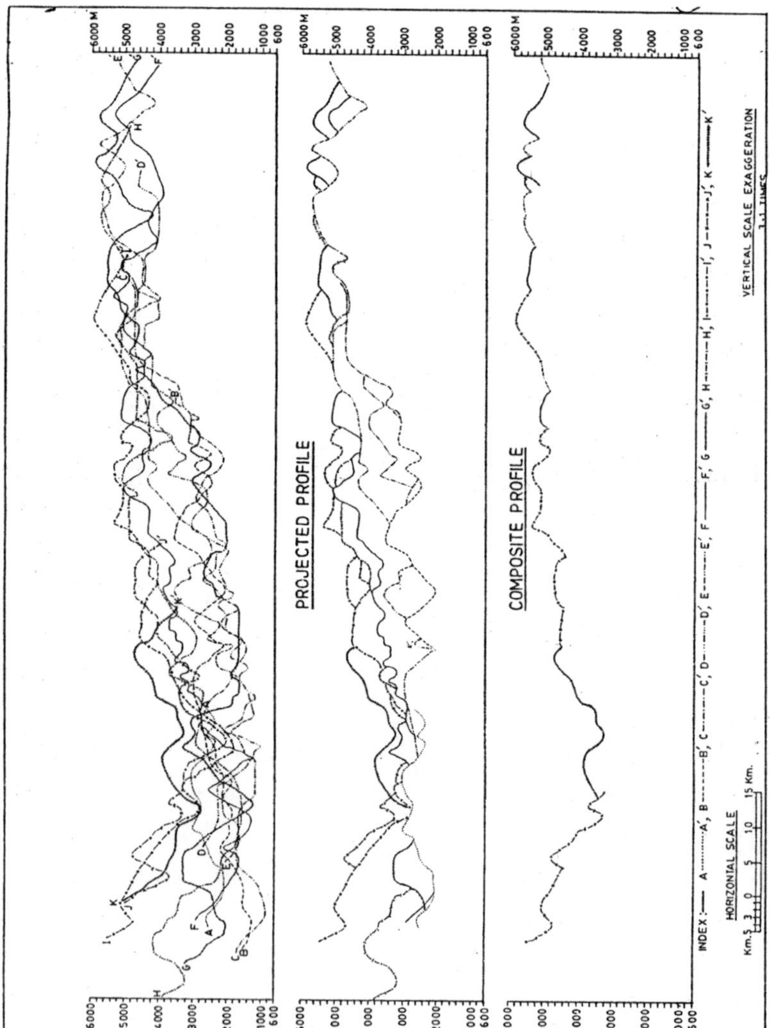

Fig. 6.3(b): Higher Himalayan Beas Basin Relief Profiles

Hypsometric Curve

Hypsometric curves may depict real geomorphic stage of river development. It has been used mainly as a measure to indicate the geomorphic stage because it expresses a percentage of landmass of the drainage basin or the proportion of the area at different elevations (laying below curve) yet to be removed by erosion. In the present study, percentage hypsometric curves have been drawn by involving two ratios, computed from map measurements (Table 6.2), i.e. relative height (*h/H*) on the ordinate where *h* is the height of the contour above the base and *H* is the total height of the basin and relative area (*a/A*) where *a* is the area enclosed between a given contour within the basin and *A* is the total area of the basin (Fig. 6.4).

Table 6.2: Area-Altitude Relationship

	Range of Altitude (in m.)	*%h/H*	*Area km²*	*Frequency %*
1.	Below 1200	16.67	155.65	2.63
2.	1200-1600	23.33	394.04	6.67
3.	1600-2000	30.00	575.08	9.73
4.	2000-2400	36.67	607.03	10.27
5.	2400-2800	43.33	707.38	11.97
6.	2800-3200	50.00	579.58	9.81
7.	3200-3600	56.67	478.00	8.09
8.	3600-4000	63.33	486.60	8.24
9.	4000-4400	70.00	560.74	9.49
10.	4400-4800	76.67	594.33	10.06
11.	4800-5200	83.33	529.61	8.96
12.	Above 5200	95.00	239.96	4.08
	Total area		5908.00	100.00

Table 6.2 reveals that the height group of 2,400 to 2,800 m encompasses the highest areal percentage, i.e. 11.97 per cent and the minimum area percentage, i.e. below the altitude of 1,200 m which recorded only 2.63 per cent area of the basin. The break in the slope of the curve is quite abrupt, i.e. about 45° between the height group of 2,800 to 3,200 m and above 4,800 m where the trend of the curve suddenly changes in an almost vertical slope (Fig. 6.4). On the whole, the hypsometric curve drawn for the basin reveals that the basin is passing through the early mature stage of the geomorphic development with the hypsometric integral of 51.21 per cent.

Altimetric Frequency Graph

The areal calculation of absolute height in each altitude range of 400 m per km^2 when plotted on graph and curve reveals the existence of erosion surfaces at different levels[3]. Both the altimetry frequency graph and the curve reveal two surfaces at 1,600 m and 5,200 m and above (Fig. 6.4). Its maximum proportion is constituted between 2,400 and 2,800 m altitude which occupies an area of 707.38 km^2, i.e. 11.97 per cent area of the basin. The minimum area between 3,200 and 3,600 m represents the erosional surfaces of the basin which covers an area of only 478 km^2, i.e. 8.09 per cent area of the basin. The abruptness of the curve below 1,600 m altitude reveals the effects of a severe erosion due to the excess of human interferences.

Relative Relief

Relative relief is one of the methods which may overcome the difficulty of presenting the three-dimensional relief characteristics with the help of two-dimensional maps. It visualizes the sharpness of relief which may not be expressed by profiles, altitudinal zones and area-height relation curves.

In the present study, the relative relief has been analysed by taking third order intra-basin as the smallest unit. The variation in elevations between the highest and the lowest points within the intra basins has been computed and found recorded that it ranges from 1,200 to 3,600 m which been grouped into seven categories.

Table 6.3 reveals that moderate relative relief encompasses in area of 844.02 km^2, i.e. 22.61 per cent area of the 36 intra-basins of the study region. Moderately high relative relief ranges from 2,100 m to 2,700 m covering 1,219.59 km^2, i.e. 32.67 per cent area of the 29 intra-basins. The area marked is actively affected by the Kullu thrust, over-grazing, deforestation, overlapping, etc. consequently, the area is experiencing maximum landslide occurrence and severe landform degradation. The high relative relief category varies from 2,700 m to 3,300 m and covers an area of 951.07 km^2, i.e.48 per cent area of the eight intra-basins. The very high relative relief shares only 718.04 km^2, i.e. 19.24 per cent area of the three intra-basins. The regions of this category

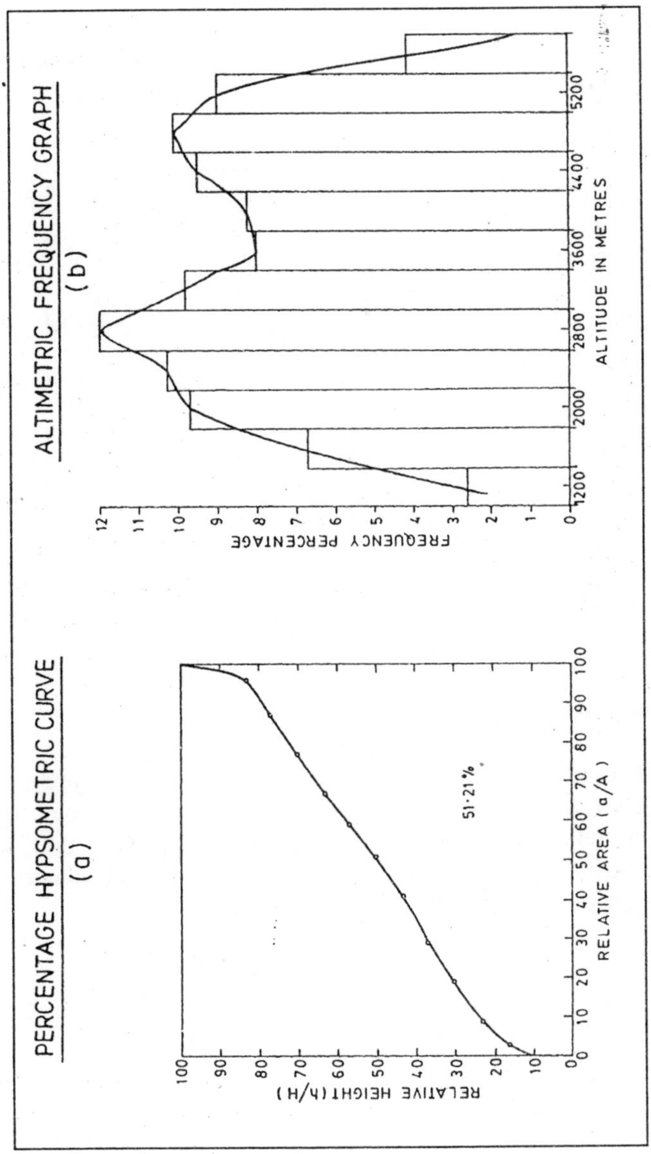

Fig 6.4: Higher Himalayan Beas Basin

are generally concentrated in the steep slope and high absolute areas which follows the general law that relative relief increases as the slope and absolute relief increases. In these areas with the help of heavy rains, steep slope and high absolute relief altogether increase the volume and velocity of water which consequently increase the intensity of erosion.

Table 6.3: Categorically Distribution of Relative Relief

Group (in m.)	*Area in km²*	*Area in %*	*Total Intra-Basins*	*Categories*
Below 2100	844.02	22.61	36	Moderate
2100-2700	1219.59	32.67	29	Moderately high
2700-3300	951.07	25.48	8	High
Above 3300	718.04	19.24	3	Very high
Total	3732.72	100.00	76	

The co-efficient of correlation between relative relief and absolute relief show the perfect correlation (+ 0.9068) when statistically correlated. The positive value of correlation reveals that the value of relative relief increases accordingly with the absolute relief. To know practically the relationship between the two variables, mentioned above, regression lines have also been drawn and found that there is a significant relationship between the variables (Fig. 6.5).

Dissection Index

Dissection index, the ratio of two variables of morphometry, i.e. relative relief and absolute relief within a definite area, has been analysed by taking third order intra-basin as the smallest unit. For the categorical distribution the range of values has been grouped into three categories (Table 6.4).

Table 6.4: Categorically Distribution of Dissection Index

Dissection Index Range	*Area in km²*	*Area in %*	*Total Intra-Basins*	*Categories*
Below 0.45	439.34	11.11	16	Low
0.45-0.65	1403.84	37.61	49	Moderate
Above 0.65	1889.54	50.62	11	High
Total	3732.72	100.00	76	

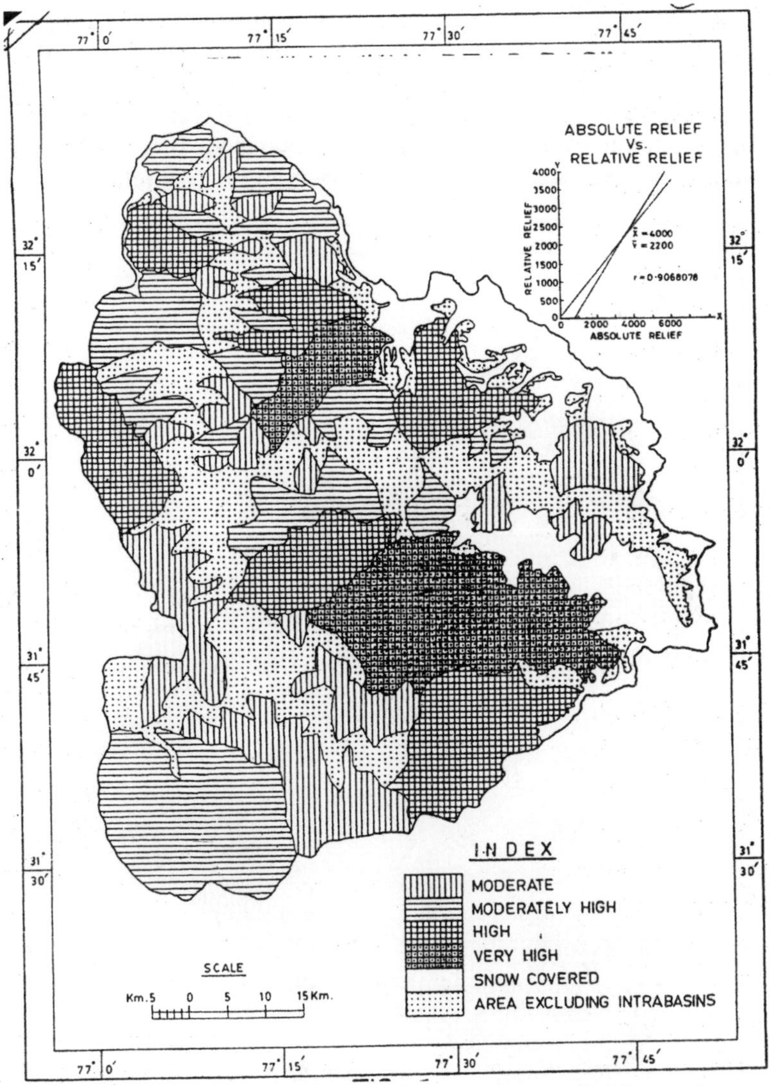

Fig. 6.5: Higher Himalayan Beas Basin: Relative Relief Categories

Table 6.4 reveals that the Low dissection index remains below 0.45 covering an area of 439.34 km^2, i.e. 11.77 Per cent of the 16 intra-basins of the study region. The moderate dissection index varies from 0.45 to 0.65 covering an area of 1403.84 km^2, i.e. 37.61 per cent of the 49 intra-basins. The high dissection index value varies from 0.65 to 0.73 and covers more than half of the area of the total intra-basins, i.e. 1,889.54 km^2 (50.62%) forming four major patches in the map (Fig. 6.6). The high dissection index enjoys high absolute relief, high to very high relative relief and steep to very steep gradient. This condition reveals that the high dissection index is not independent but highly associated with high to very high relative relief and high

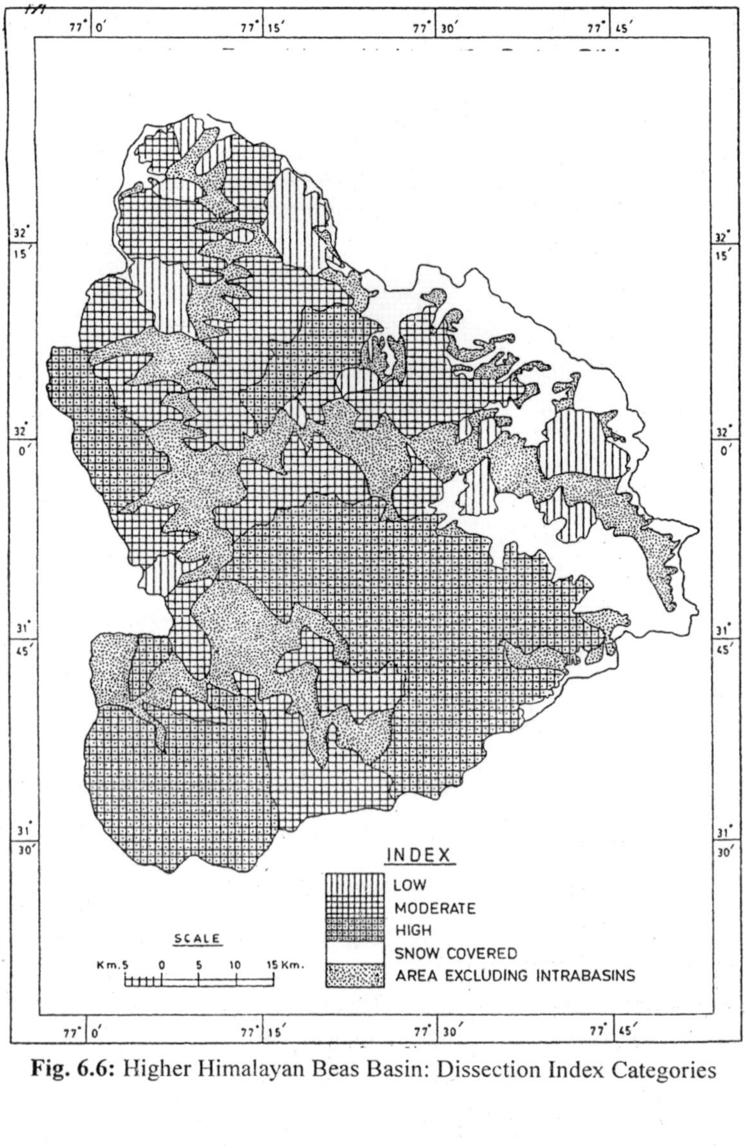

Fig. 6.6: Higher Himalayan Beas Basin: Dissection Index Categories

absolute relief. The said analysed results reveal the normal condition of the terrain. The increasing intensity of erosion, highly precipitous gradient and geological characteristics of the area affect the relative relief and are responsible for the high dissection index in the basin as a whole.

Slope

Slope is also an important aspect of landform study, which has been defined as an angular inclination of terrain between the hill-tops and valley bottoms, making with the horizontal datum. The area has been analysed by the Raisz and Henry method which reveals the slope ranging from 0° to more than 72°. It has been divided into the following categories (Fig. 6.7):

1. Gentle to moderate slope – Below 18°
2. Moderately steep slope – 18° - 54°
3. Steep slope – 54° - 72°
4. Very steep slope – 72° and above

In the area, it is marked the valley bottom area occurs under below 18° and generally the valley ranges from 6° to 36°. The higher degrees of slope are marked of more than 72° which is observed in higher water divides and where the terrain is incised deeply into sharp valleys which are generally rugged and steep ridges, overhanging bluffs and steep escarpments. The presence of gradient in broad patches in the higher elevations and higher gradient in narrow patches in the lower elevations is due to the uneven and immature topography of the region (a young phase of vertical upliftment).[4]

The slope conditions have their great influence on landuse pattern and human activities as they determine the nature and intensity of agricultural activities in a pronounced way. The area slope distribution table reveals the gradient-land use landform relationship in the basin (Table 6.5).

After completing the detailed study of relief, slope drainage, geological structure and morpho-units altogether with an intensive field study traverses, the Higher Himalayan Beas basin has been regionalized into three major geomorphological regions as follows:

1. Dundhon-Dibika Glacial Tract (Above 5,000 m).
2. Beas-Parbati Upper Kullu Thrust (Glacio-Fluvial uplands) (3,000-5000 m).

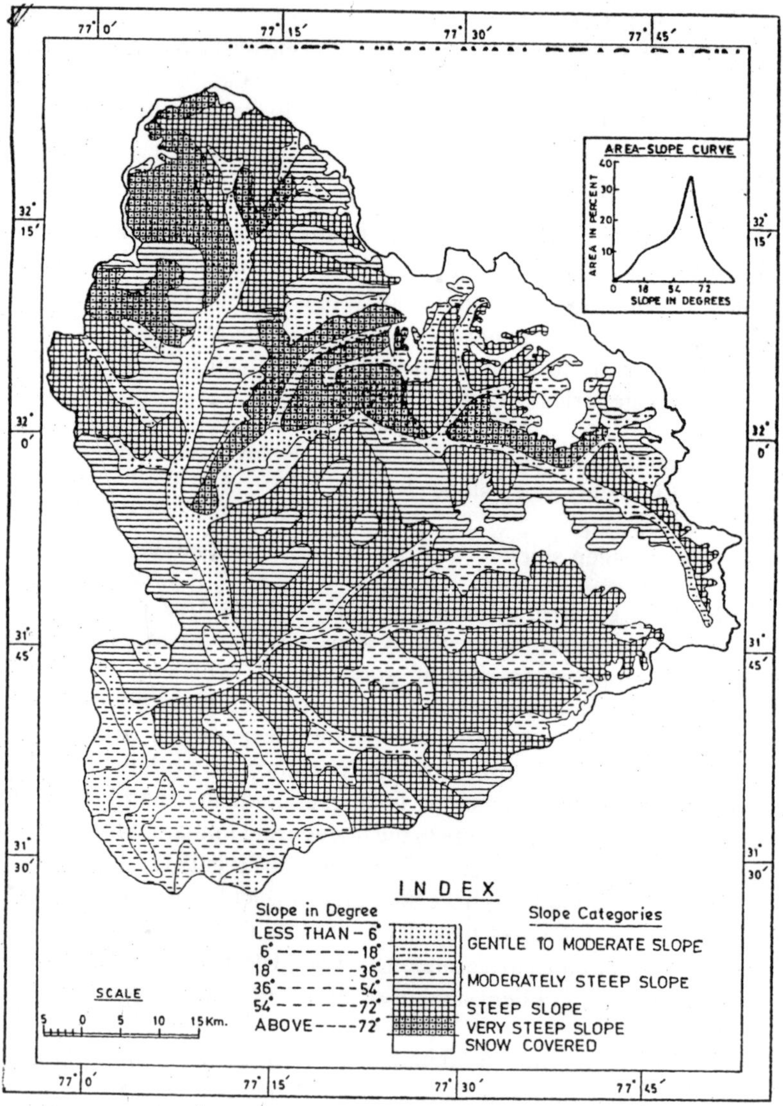

Fig. 6.7 : Higher Himalayan Beas Basin: Slope Structure

3. Tirthan-Beas Lower Kullu Thrust Vale (Below 3,000 m)
   3.1 Kullu Bowl
   3.2 Tirthan-Parbati Riverine Tract
   3.3 Bakhli-Juni Riverine Lowlands.

Table 6.5: Area Slope Distribution

Slope in Degrees	*Area in*		*Land use*	*Land Characteristics*	*Geo-catastrophic Processes*
	km²	*%*			
Below 18°	823.57	13.99	Human habitations, agricultural fields, orchards and scattered forest	Alluvial terraces, point bar and channel bar deposits, interfluves with recessional moraines, confluences, etc.	Landsliding, soil-creeping and mud-flowing.
18°-54°	1734.62	29.24	Human habitations, agricultural fields, orchards and forests	Terraces, interfluves, truncated spurs, low hills, etc.	Landsliding, soil-creeping, slumping, sludging and torrential run-off.
54°-72°	2027.39	34.27	Less human habitation, less agriculture and thick forest cover	Interlocking spurs, V-shaped valleys, water divides, high hills, etc.	Soil-creeping, landsliding, slumping, sledging and torrential run-off.
Above 72°	606.03	10.27	No habitation, least agriculture, thick forests and alpine pastures	Glacio-fluvial features like truncated cirque, sharp-edged ridges, water divides, groge and canyons, escarpment, etc.	Rock-shattering, slipping, falling, frost-shattering, etc.
	716.39	12.13	Snow-covered alpine pastures	Glacial features like horn peaks, aretes, cirque, etc.	Forst-shattering
	5908.00	100.00			

The first geomorphological region which ranges from 5,000 m to 6,395 m remains wholly covered with snow and glaciers and consists of about 716 km^2, i.e. 12.12 per cent area of the basin. The second region occupies about 31 per cent area of the basin which consists of mainly quartzite, gneisses, phyllite, schists, carbonaceous schists on which rectilinear, rectangular, triangular and irregular morphology of drainage intra-basin has been developed. The absolute relief varies from 3,000 to 5,000 m where the moderately steep to very steep slope has been marked. The third and most important geomorphological region varies from 750 to 3,000 m with the gradient ranging form 6° to 54°. Geologically, the region comprises intrusive granite, quartzite, green schists (meta basic rocks), slate phyllite, dolomite, limestone, etc.

From the detailed study, the Tirthan-Beas Lower Kullu Thrust vale geomorphic region has been sub-divided into three sub-regions, viz. Kullu Bowl which extends up to the locality of Palchan in the north and Panarsa in the south. It is about 1-2 km wide and about 60 km in length. The slope varies from gentle to moderately steep. The climatic conditions remaining the same, the time may come very soon when the Kullu Bowl may be called "Apple Bowl" of India. Physiographically, this sub-tract is very rigid and dissected where slope varies from 18° to 72°. Due to the neo-tectonic activities and presence of Kullu Thrust, the frequency of landslides has been recorded very high, i.e. 14 landslides per kilometre along the Aut-Pandoh section of the tract itself. The Bakhl-Juni Riverine Lowlands occupies the lowest part of the basin. Moderate to steep slope of the region varies from 18° to 72°. The Kullu Thrust is passing along the river Beas in the Aut-Pandoh section of the tract. Thus, the area is highly influenced by the geological structure of the region. Besides the geological disturbances, an excess of human interferences like deforestation, overlapping, overgrazing, unsystematic and over-quarrying of slates, unscientific blasting for road construction, etc., altogether stimulate the geo-catastrophic factors like landsliding, severe soil erosion and rock-sliding in the region. Consequently, these unwanted activities are responsible for the degradation of landforms and environmental conditions of the area.

Physico-Agro-Climatic Land Resource System

It is generally observed that the pattern of landform system signifies the type, mode and behaviour of the landuse pattern of that particular region. In order to evaluate the existing environmental resource system of the Higher Himalayan Beas basin, a physico-agro-climatic land resource survey has been carried out by applying a new approach of Fractional Code Method (Fig. 6.8). The factors taken into consideration are physiographic (relief, slope and aspect), agro-climatic conditions, soil fertility indexes and land use pattern of the basin. These factors have been codified in order to apply them in the fractional code method as noted below:

$$\text{FCM} = \frac{\text{Numerator}}{\text{Denominator}} = \frac{\text{Agro-climatic Condition} + \text{Soil Nutrients}}{\text{Altitude/Slope/Aspect/Land use}}$$

Numerator = Agro-climatic Conditions + Soil Nutrients

I. Agro-climatic Conditions

Code

Msh, where	M = Mid hills sh = Sub-humid
Htw, where	H = Higher hills tw = Temperate wet

II. Soil Nutrients

	Code Classification		
	Low-1	*Medium-2*	*High-3*
N = Organicarbon (%)	Below 0.5 (N_1)	0.5-1.00 (N_2)	Above 1.00 (N_3)
P = Phosphorus (kg. P_2O_5/hect.)	Below 20 (P_1)	20-50 (P_2)	Above 50 (P_3)
K = Potassium (kg. K_2O/hect.)	Below 125 (K_1)	125-300 (K_2)	Above 100 (K_3)

Classification according to the Agriculture Department:

Denominator

I. *Relief Regions/Altitude*

Code

1. Below 1,600 m (River Valleys)
2. 1,600-2,600 m (Low Hills)
3. 2,600-3,600 m (Low Mountains)
4. 3,600-4,600 m (High Mountains)
5. Above 4,600 m (Extremely High Mountains)

Fig. 6.8: Higher Himalayan Beas Basin : Physico-Agro-climatic Land Resource Evaluation (Fractional Code Method)

II. *Slope Categories*

Code

1. Gentle to Moderate Slope (Below 18°)
2. Moderate to Steep Slope (18° - 54°)

3. Steep Slope (54° - 72°)
4. Very Steep Slope (Above 72°)

III. *Aspect/Location*

Code

1. South-Western (Suitable for agriculture)
2. North-Eastern (Suitable for forest growth)

IV. *Land use Pattern*

Code

1. Agricultural Land
2. Forest Land
3. Alpine Pastures
4. Barren Land (unproductive)
5. Snow-covered (SN)

Thus, after analysing the physiographic characteristic (relief, slope and aspect), agro-climatic conditions, land use and chemical and mechanical properties of soil, nutrients from varied morpho-units of the basin have been depicted by digits in the map (Fig. 6.8). The analysis reveals that the Tirthan-Beas Lower Kullu Thrust Vale region of the basin is highly enriched with agricultural potentiality, where the valley terraces are represented by Msh, $\frac{Msh + N_2 + P_2 + K_3}{1111}$ which indicates that in mid-hills (Below 2000 metres) sub-humid region, the soil has medium organic carbon which ranges from 0.5 per cent to 1.00 per cent and phosphorus ranges from 20 to 50 kg. P_2O_5 per hectare and potassium ranges from 125 to 300 kg K_2O per hectare and *p*H value ranges from 5 to 7 in the basin. The latitude remains below 1,600 m and the slope varies form 6° to 18° under the south-western aspect which is occupied by human habitations, agricultural fields and fruit gardens. Similarly, the Beas-Parbati Upper Kullu Thrust glacio-fluvial uplands depicts the values of the code like $\frac{Htw + N_1 P_3 K_2}{4423}$ which indicates that in the High Hills temperate wet region, the soil has low organic carbon which remains below 0.5%, high phosphorus, i.e. above 50 kg. P_20_5 per hectare, and potassium is medium that ranges from 125 to 300 kg. K_2O per hectare in the basin.

The fractional codes as depicted in Fig. 6.8 reveals that the Tirthan-Beas Lower Kullu Thrust Vale is suitable for agricultural crops like rice and fruit gardening where physiographic, agro-climatic conditions and soil nutrients are well suited for the agricultural activities. The application of modern techniques in agricultural practices and irrigation facilities may increase the yield per hectare in the region. At the same time soil and landform conservation measures are required to be introduced to maintain the soil nutrients and also the scenic beauty of the region for the development of tourism.

NOTES

1. Leuder, D.R. (1959). *Aerial Photographic Interpretation.* McGraw Hill Book Co. Inc., London, p. 19.
2. Wooldridge, S.W. and Morgan, R.S. (1946). *The Physical Basis of Geography.* New Impression, London.
3. Baulig, H. (1939). Duex methods d' analyse Morphologique Appliques a' la hante Belgique Bull. Sec. Belge Etudes Geog. 9, pp. 165-84 in Durry, G.H. *Essay in Geomorphology* (ed.) Heinemann, London.
4. Sharma, V.P. (1977). Geology of Kullu Rampur Belt Himachal Pradesh. Memo, *Geol. Surv. Ind.* 106 (2) 235-407.

REFERENCES

Adrin Millias, Lacrais (1981), *Classification of Slope Movements.* Bull Liaison Lab. p. *et. al.* Special Vol. X. January, pp. 55-62.

Chopra, S. (1984), *Geomorphological Mapping of Part of Southern Fringe of Meghalaya.* Record, Geological Survey of India, 113, part IV, pp. 67-70.

Clark, I.J. (1966), Morphometry from Maps in H.G. Durry (ed.), *Essays in Geomorphology.* Heinemann, London. pp. 235-74.

Fort, M. (1978) Geomorphology of Ladakh, *Bull. Asso. Geogr.*, France, Paris 242, pp. 159-175.

Kumar, R. and Verma, Y.K. (1983), "Some Geomorphological Investigations Around Kud. Kashmir Himalaya," in *Geomorphology, Contributions to Indian Geography* (ed.) K.R. Dikshit. Heritage Publishers, New Delhi. pp. 72-84.

Marh, B.S. (1986), *Geomorphology of Ravi River,* Inter India Publications, New Delhi.

Mittal, R.S., Gohain, K. and Joshi, B.C. (1982), "A Geomorphic Analysis of a Part of the Ramganga Catchment Basin," in *Himalayan Landforms and Processes* (ed.) V.K. Verma and P.S. Saklani, pp. 1-28.

Raiz, E. and Henry, J. (1937), "An Average Slope Map of Southern New England," *Geographical Review* Vol. 27, pp. 467-72.

Saxena, P.B. (1987), *A Modern Approach in Geography for the Evaluation of Soils and Landforms Systems, Landuse Planning in Himalayan Eco-system of the Alkanada Basin (Garhwal Himalaya)*, pp. 1-108.

Sharma, H.S. (ed.) (1982), *Perspectives in Geomorphology*, Vol. IV, Concept Publishing Company, New Delhi.

Thornbury, W.D (1964), *Principles of Geomorphology*, John Wiley & Sons, New York.

Wadia, D.N. (1964), *Himalayan Geology*.

7

Classification of Terrain into Morpho-Cultural Environment Units

A Case Study of Himalayan Basin

S.C. KHARAKWAL

Any science starts with observation of the natural phenomena. In geography, map study seems to lead different investigators to different results. Moreover, terrain evaluation is still a subject composed of a number of concepts and techniques which have not attained the organic unity of a single academic discipline, and this can only be possible within the ambit of geography. Every fact of a landscape has a multitude of varied but intricately interrelated attributes which make them unique and complex to understand or simplify this complexity of terrain typology so that characteristics of different terrain facets can be identified, described and compared. The external land features, inherent rock and soil characteristics or surface materials, dominant land use and other environmental factors are the main attributes to be considered for the terrain classification in various orders. Thus the terrain evaluation, as a process, involves three successive stages—analysis, classification and appraisal. The typology of terrain units of various orders involves a set of activities, physical as well as cultural, leading to the morpho-cultural environmental units, which really present an overall picture of morphological and cultural environment and are very useful to understand the mountain ecology with an information store terrain.

The present area of study comprises a small basin, Khanda of the Alaknanda in the Lesser Garhwal Himalaya. Geographically, the Khanda basin lies between Latitude 30°7′ and 30°14′N and longitude 78°42′E and 78°52′E covering the total area of 104 km². With a maximum length of nearly 16 km, the width of the basin varies between 3 and 9 km. Nayagad, Nakotgad, Nandalgad, Garsarigad, Bichaligad and Kothargad are the main tributaries of the Khanda which give rise upto 6th order streams in the basin. The number of streams from the 1st to 6th order are 354, 81, 20, 6, 2 and 1 with the bifurcation ratio of 5.7, 3.0, 3.3 and 2.0 in respective orders.

The whole basin extends between the heights of 560 m and 2,100 m. Average slope of the basin varies between 10° and 35°. Nearly, 64 per cent area of the basin lies between the slope zone of 15-30°. About 87 per cent area has relative relief between 100-400 m, 100-200 m 21.2 per cent, 200-300 m 39.6 per cent and 300-400 m 26.2 per cent. Slates and unfossiliferous crystalline rocks are the main outcrops in the basin with orthoquartzites, grits, shales and silts at places.

Like other parts of the Lesser Himalays, major part of this basin is deforested. At places, the total forest area of this basin is only 29.4 km² which is nearly 28 per cent of the total geographical are a of the basin. Thus, the whole basin is badly denuded creating a severe problem of soil erosion and mass wasting. The area under vegetal cover at different altitudes is depicted in Table 7.1.

Table 7.1: Intensity of Vegetal Cover at Different Altitudes

Height (m)	*Forest Area (km²)*	*% to Total Forest Area*
Below 900	2.8	9.5
900-1200	3.8	12.9
1200-1800	17.5	59.6
Above 1800	5.3	18.0
Total	29.4	100.0

Patterns of Landuse

The whole basin has been divided into six height groups ranging from below 600 m to above 1800 m with an interval of 300 m. The area under different land use is given in Table 7.2.

Out of the total area of the basin, 28.13 per cent is covered by forests. Maximum forest coverage is found at altitudes of 1200-1800 m, 55.98 per cent area of the basin is covered by agricultural

Table 7.2: Magnitude of Land use According to Elevation

Height Group (m)	*Land use*					
	Forest Land		*Agricultural Land*		*Wasteland*	
	Area (km²)	*%*	*Area (km²)*	*%*	*Area (km²)*	*%*
Below 600	10.05	0.17	–	–	0.25	1.51
600-900	2.80	9.53	11.30	19.32	3.50	21.15
900-1200	3.80	12.92	22.80	38.97	7.50	45.32
1200-1500	7.50	25.51	17.53	29.97	2.25	13.59
1500-1800	10.00	34.01	6.50	11.11	2.80	16.92
Above 1800	5.25	17.86	0.37	0.63	0.25	1.51
Total	29.40	100.00	58.50	100.00	16.55	100.00

land, which is mostly confined under the height range of 900-1500 m. Only 15.84 per cent area of the basin is under wasteland, nearly 45.3 per cent of which lies under the height range of 900-1200 m, followed by 21.15 per cent in 600-900 m. It is also evident from the above analysis that with the increase in height, areal coverage of forests also increases; and, on the other hand, area under agriculture generally decreases. A number of physico-cultural factors are responsible for the distribution of wasteland in different elevations.

Intensity of various land use categories at different altitudes is obvious from the analysis in Table 7.3.

Table 7.3: Intensity of Land use at various Altitudes

Height Group (m)	*Land use (%)*		
	Forest Land	*Agricultural Land*	*Wasteland*
Below 600	16.7	–	83.3
600-900	16.9	64.3	20.8
900-1200	11.3	66.8	30.9
1200-1500	27.6	64.2	8.2
1500-1800	52.9	32.6	14.5
Above 1800	89.4	6.3	4.3

In addition to a number of physical factors, some cultural factors, viz. population pressure on forest and agricultural land, etc., have also been responsible for the magnitude and intensity of land use patterns in different elevations. The correlation values calculated for different variables are Elevation *versus* Forest Land—positive (+0.6760). Elevation *versus* Agricultural Land—Positive (+0.3760) and Elevation *versus* Wasteland—Negative (–0.3887).

After analyzing the general aggregate factors like physiography, hypsometry, land use and other surface conditions, the whole basin has been classified into morpho-cultural environmental units (MCEU). In the present study and analytical approach dividing the basin into a progressive segregation of groups to form a descending hierarchy is advocated. The aim of this approach is to include a number of variabilities in the terrain classification within the basin area. These variabilities are observed by the preliminary study of the lands at imageries of the area and also by the field reconnaissance. In the present method of terrain classification, two approaches—Land-scape and parametric—are combined together. The structure and morphology are mainly viewed in the landscape approach, while in the parameter approach numerical information of terrain, viz. height and magnitude of slope on various facets of landscape together with the nature of vegetal cover, etc., are considered. In this way, both the landscape and parametric approaches together can determine a real differentiation of an area into hierarchical structure of terrain types.

In the mountain terrain relief is the main factor influencing the physico-cultural environment of the place. Therefore, the "first level terrain systems" have been recognized by their relief factors. Thus, the whole basin is bisected into three such orders—High Mountain Ranges, Upper Valley Zones and Lower Valley Zones. In the mountain region, direction and aspect are also very influencing factors which bring many physiographic differentiations in various ways and thereby affect the physico-cultural environment of the terrain units. Keeping this in view, the "second level terrain systems" have been recognized which are eight in number. On the basis of parameteric observations, the "third level terrain systems" have been marked which in the present basin are 16 in number. Likewise, keeping in view the morphometric and geomorphic micro-details and their characteristics, the "fourth level terrain systems" have been recognized. The basin has 24 such systems or units. Such maps (Fig. 7.1) are the key maps presenting morphostructure, morphemetry and morphochronology of each form. The whole classification is detailed as below:

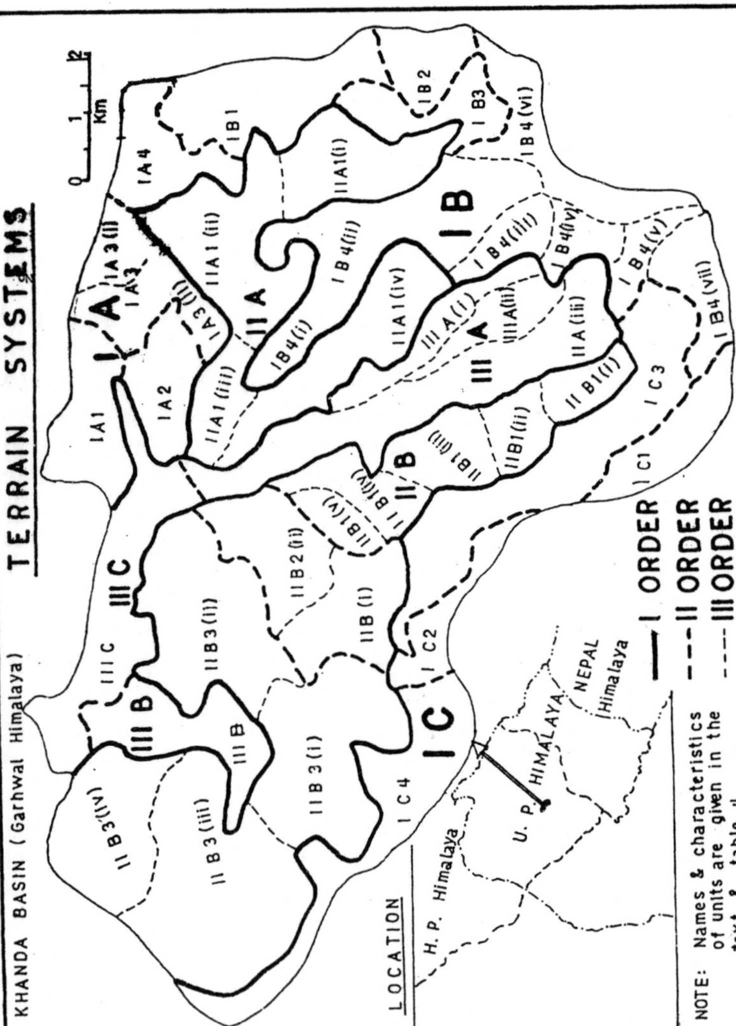

Fig. 7.1: Terrain Systems

Terrain Classification in the Khanda Basin (Systems and Sub-systems)

I. High Mountain Ranges
  (A) Northern Rages (Dharkot-Ghiri Range)
    1. Southern slope of Dharkot range
    2. Ridge top of Bachheli-Kathulsyun divide
    3. Sumari-Kulon spur
      (i) Sumari cirque
      (ii) Kulon spur
    4. Southern slope of Ghirikhal divide.
  (B) Eastern Ranges (Mehalchoridhar-Rajgarhdhar-Bubakhal Range)
    1. Mehalchoridhar
    2. Ulkagarhi hill top
    3. Western slope of Ulkagarhi
    4. Rama Ranadhar-Rajgarhdhar
      (i) Dhamkholi-Belgad spur
      (ii) Rajgarh dhar
      (iii) Ravines of Srikot gadhera
      (iv) Ravines of Bangwari gadhera
      (v) Bangwari spur
      (vi) Rama Ranadhar
      (vii) Bubakhal-Mandakhal ridge top
  (C) South-Western Ranges
    1. Nagdeve range
    2. Kandoliya-Kyunkaleshwar range
    3. Urban tract of Pauri town
    4. Ghurdauri-Chilangbita range

II. Upper Valley Zones
  (A) Valleys facing to west and north-west
    1. Nayalgad basin
      (i) Upper right hand gentle slope of Nayalgad
      (ii) Main Nayalgad valley
      (iii) Kathulsyun valley
      (iv) Gadsarigad valley
  (B) Valleys facing to north and north-east
    1. Higher valley slopes of the Nandalgad basin
      (i) Tholi-Chandola Rai tract

(ii) Chopra gadhera
(iii) Dhandri-Ryori tract
(iv) Masaun-Amkoti tract
(v) Barsiladhar spur

2. Kothargad basin
(i) Upper catchment
(ii) Lower catchment

3. Nakotgad basin
(i) Upper Baragad valley
(ii) Chardhar-Kesundra divide
(iii) Pisoli basin
(iv) Digoligad valley

III. Lower Valley Zones
(a) Main Valley Region of Nandalgad
(i) Jamnakhal-Pokhari spur
(ii) Dob-Srikot tract
(iii) Nandalgad main valley
(b) Nakotgad valley
(c) Main Khanda valley

Such maps are mere applied if the land use typology is also marked on each such terrain unit. Therefore, in the present study, the intensity of various land uses has also been calculated and depicted in the table, as is described in Table 7.4.

These terrain systems really present an overall picture of the morphological and cultural environmet and are very useful to understand the mountain ecosystems. These micro-facets of morpho-units are, therefore, more useful for an information store about the terrain. Such studies receive special attention in planning the Himalayan basins for eco-development or watershed management. It is to be noted here that these landscapes are not only of economic value for agriculture, engineering and other public works, but these have some aesthetic and recreational value which is now mere widely recogninsed. Therefore, planners in different disciplines would really be interested in such a store, which would abstract, sort and classify practically important data about terrain in such a way that it is rapidly and readily available.

Table 7.4: Terrain Systems and their Characteristics

Different Levels of Terrain Facet Units and Corresponding Codes	*Morphmetric Characteristics*				*Geomorphic and Other Surface Characteristics*	*Existing Landuse and Areal Coverage (% to Total)*			
	Relief Range (m)	*R.R. (m)*	*D.I.*	*Slope (O)*		*Agri.*	*Forest*	*Barron*	*Others*
(1)	(2)	(3)	(4)	(5)	(6)	(7)	(8)	(9)	(10)
I. High Mountain Ranges									
(A) North-eastern Ranges Codes: I A1	800-1080	280	0.26	30-40	Rocky exposures with flat saddle and very thin skeleton soils	8	12	70	10
A2	700-1109	409	0.37	35-40	Flat ridge with steep slope on all sides and skeletal soil cover	80	5	10	5
A3(i)	1060-1487	427	0.29	20-30	Old cirque with thick soil cover	50	–	40	10
(ii)	1000-1320	320	0.24	30-35	Regular slope with cliffs in higher parts	10	75	10	5
A4	1080-1400	320	0.23	45-50	Steep-sided valley slopes	70	5	25	–
(B) Eastern Ranges Codes: I B1	1200-1932	732	0.38	60-75	Steep to very steep wooded slopes	–	85	15	–
B2	1680-2088	408	0.20	60-75	Steep to very steep thickly wooded slope	–	100	–	–
B3	1360-1840	480	0.26	30-40	Irregular slopes, med. to steep slope on higher parts	60	7	30	3
B4(i)	740-940	200	0.21	20-30	Spurs with gentle-med. slopes	20	70	10	–

(Contd.)

(Contd.)

(1)	(2)	(3)	(4)	(5)	(6)	(7)	(8)	(9)	(10)
(ii)	800-1550	750	0.48	45-65	Steep to very steep thickly wooded slope with steep sided spurs	10	85	5	–
(iii)	1540-1850	310	0.17	70	Very steep sided gorge with ravine and gullies	–	60	40	–
(iv)	1400-1700	300	0.18	70	Region of steep ravines, spurs with rocky exposures	–	40	60	–
(v)	300-1740	340	0.20	60-70	Steep spurs with rocky exposures	–	60	40	–
(vi)	1650-2000	350	0.18	60-70	Elongated ridge top with a number of saddles and cols	–	90	7	3
(vii)	1400-1887	487	0.26	45-65	Elongated ridge with med-steep tops	–	90	7	3
(C) South-western Ranges Codes: I C1	1800-2143	343	0.16	50-60	Region of regular thickly wooded steep slope	–	85	13	2
C2	1800-2027	227	0.11	45-60	Thickly wooded ridge tops with steep slope	–	80	15	5
C3	1400-1800	400	0.22	25-35	Urban tract of Pauri town	5	–	20	75
C4	1100-1796	690	0.38	20-30	Med-steep sloping ridge tops	20	70	5	5
II. Upper Valley Zones									
(A) Valley facing to west and north-west									
Codes: II A1 (i)	1100-1580	480	0.30	20-25	Gentle to med. cultivated slopes with scarped cliffs at places	85	–	10	5

(Contd.)

(Contd.).

(1)	(2)	(3)	(4)	(5)	(6)	(7)	(8)	(9)	(10)
(ii)	800-1300	500	0.38	15-20	Open valley with gentle slope and densely settled and cultivated	80	3	7	10
(iii)	660-820	160	0.20	15-20	Fertile valley with open and wide agricultural terraces	80	–	20	–
(iv)	680-1580	900	0.57	20-30	Longitudinal range with a number of spurs	75	5	10	10
(B) Valleys facing to north and north-east									
Code: II B1(i)	1220-1440	220	0.15	10-20	Constantly sloppy terrain but densely cultivated	85	–	5	10
(ii)	1180-1440	260	0.18	15-20	Undulating slopes having concave and convex breaks of slope	85	–	10	5
(iii)	1080-1500	420	0.28	15-20	Gentley sloping open spurs and densely cultivated	90	–	5	5
(iv)	900-1380	480	0.35	20-25	Steep-sided valley walls	80	–	18	2
(v)	1160-1420	260	0.18	15-20	Elongated water divide	60	30	8	2
B2(i)	1080-1620	540	0.33	20-25	Mod. to steeply sloping open tract	70	15	5	10
(ii)	780-1200	420	0.35	30-40	Valley with very steep-sided walls	50	–	45	5
B3(i)	880-1520	640	0.42	35-45	Steep to very steep under valley slopes	55	15	20	10
(ii)	800-1370	570	0.42	20-30	Water divide with flat top	55	20	15	12
(iii)	900-1480	580	0.39	35-45	Steep terrain with regular slope	70	–	15	15

(Contd.)

(Contd.)

(1)	(2)	(3)	(4)	(5)	(6)	(7)	(8)	(9)	(10)
(iv)	700-1200	500	0.42	35-45	Steep-sided valley walls	75	3	10	12
III. Lower Valley Zones									
(A) Main valley region of Nandalgad									
Code: III A (i)	1300-1590	290	0.18	40-50	Longitudinal range with steep slope	20	50	30	–
(ii)	1060-1360	300	0.22	20-30	Zone of low-angled spurs	35	–	50	15
(iii)	760-1320	560	0.42	35-45	Main valley with river terraces	60	–	30	10
(B) Nakotgad valley Code: III B	700-1000	300	0.30	40-45	Eroded valley densely forested in its upper reaches	5	80	10	5
(C) Main Khanda valley Code: III C	560-1060	500	0.47	35-45	Deeply eroded valley with barren surface	5	10	85	–

8

Impact of Terrain Characteristics on Catchment Yield

A Case of Kabbini River Basin, Kerala

SRIKUMAR CHATTOPADHYAY and MAHAMAYA CHATTOPADHYAY

Sustainable development of land resources requires knowledge of hydrologic characteristics of an area and how these characteristics are related to various catchment parameters or terrain characteristics. Once relationship of catchment yield with terrain characteristics is established, the yield-modifying factors can be identified. This may, in turn, help proper management of catchments. This will ensure that, the yield pattern is not adversely affected due to human intervention.

Determinants of drainage discharge or yield can be categorized as atmospheric factors, catchments parameters and forest influences (Lee, 1980). Catchment parameters are the geofactors related to morphometry, morphology, lithology, pedology, etc., and forest influences refer to the land use/land cover.

Estimation of discharge on the basis of catchment characteristics has been widely attempted (Hedman and Osterkamp, 1982). Various models related to rainfall and run-off are used in hydrological studies. Rational method runoff curve number and Cook's method have been developed by using catchment characreristics (Schwale *et al.*, 1955). In fact, discharge of the ungauged streams are estimated on the basis of catchment parameters for various engineering works.

This paper intends to examine the relationship of various catchment parameters with drainage discharge.

The Study Area

The east-flowing Kabbini river basin, a sub-basin of the Cauvery system in the Wayanad plateau, has been selected for this study. Geologically, the area is characterized by the Pre-Cambrian formations of charnockites, gneisses and metamorphic rocks of the Surgur group. Western and south-western parts are charnockitic, while the major part of the basin is composed of gneisses. The Bavali fault running NW-SE is the most conspicuous structural feature in this area (Roy and Kumar, 1983). A number of lineaments traverse the area in different directions which are well pronounced in the layout of rivers and valleys. The three sets of prominent lineaments are WNW-ESE to NW-SE; NNW-SSE to NNE-SSW and NE-SW to ENE-WSW (Chattopadhyay and Chattopadhyay, 1989). Orientation of lineaments in these three directions might possibly correspond to the fractures developed along the strike and dip of the rock and the tensional fractures developed within the basement rocks (Fig. 8.1).

The river Kabbini and its tributary, Nulpuzha, possibly follow the direction of tensional fractures, i.e. NE-SW to ENE-WSW. The terrain is pronouncedly controlled by the lithology and structure.

A major part (85%) of this river basin is within the altitudinal range of 700 m to 900 m, although the highest point is above 2,000 m along the western drainage divide. On an average, this area receives around 3,500 m of rainfall, 75 per cent of which precipitates during south-west monsoon. Land use is dominated by plantations. The area is affected by widespread deforestation and land conversion. Broad valleys flanked by the steep slopes are notable features of this area.

Eight catchments, namely, Panamaram, Mananthody, Nulpuzha, Bavalipuzha, Kakavayal, Vazhavatta, Choorani and Manajat, which happen to be sub-catchments of the river Kabbani have been selected for this study.

Data Source

The catchment parameters have been worked out from the Survey of India toposheets of 1:50,000 scale in addition to the landsat images of 1:250,000 scale. Monthly discharge data for the period 1971-76 obtained from the Kerala State PWD have been used. Data for some recent years, although available, are not comparable. Attention has been paid to land use landcover data of the same period.

Fig 8.1 (a)

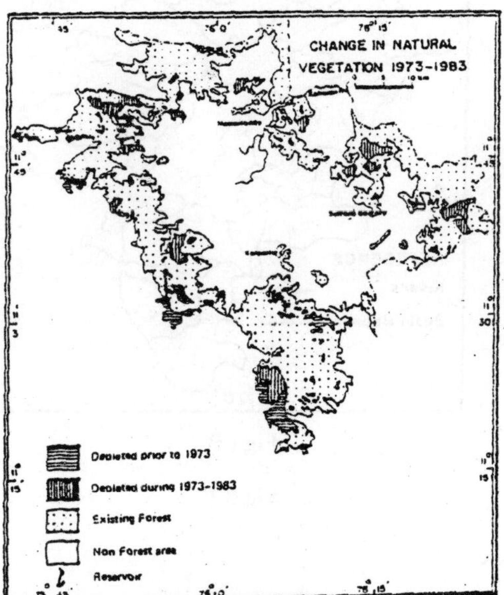

Fig 8.1 (b)

Fig (c)

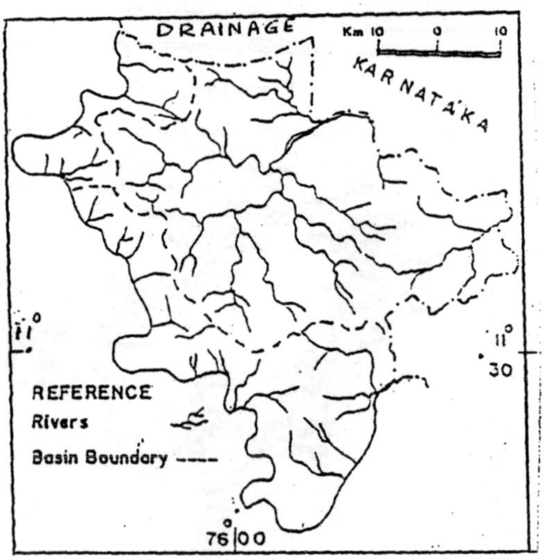

Fig (d)

Fig 8.1

Methodology

The monthly yield data as percentage to total average yield for each of the catchments have been worked out and plotted (Fig. 8.2).

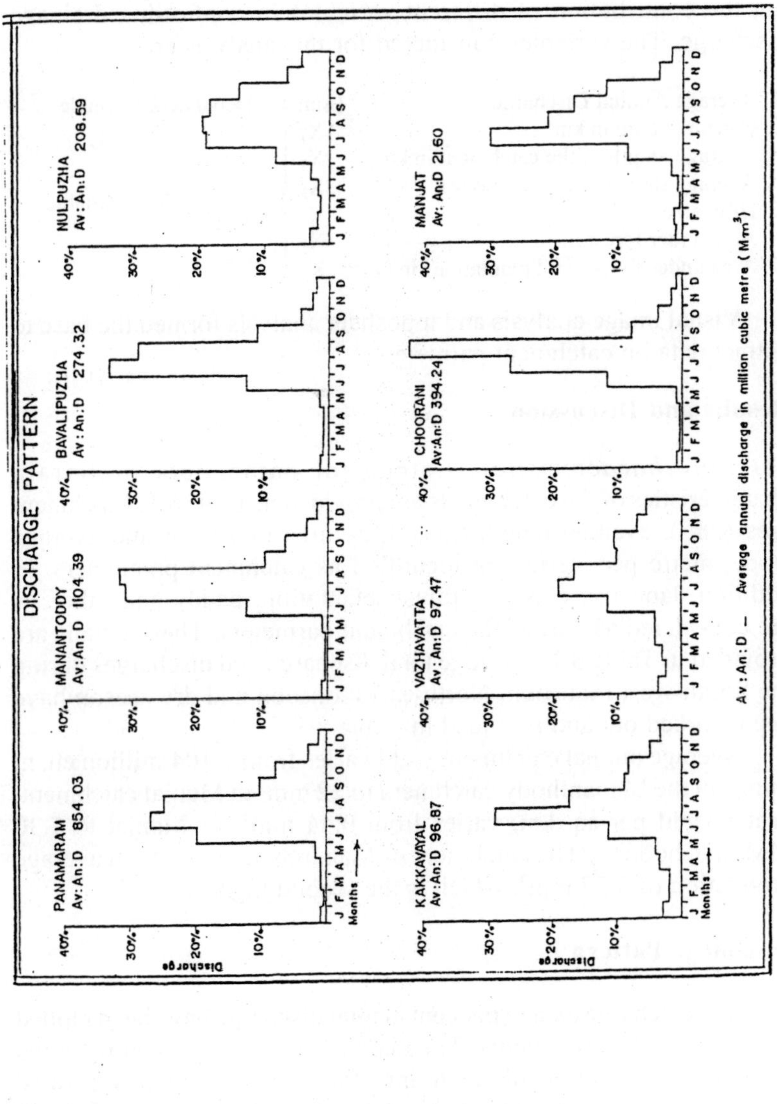

Fig. 8.2: Discharge Pattern

To understand discharge variabilities, bivariate regression analysis has been worked out by considering drainage discharge (D) and catchment area (A) in the first case and drainage discharge (D) and area under hills (HA) in the second case.

Multiple regression analysis has also been worked out to bring out the contribution of different variables in controlling drainage discharge. The variables considered for this analysis are:

1. Average Annual Discharge	(mm^3)	Dependent Variable
2. Catchment are in km^2	X_1	Independent Variables
3. Average length of the catchment in km	X_2	
4. Average slope (metre per metre)	X_3	
5. Hilly area in %	X_4	
6. Area under forest in %	X_5	
7. Area under forests and plantations in %	X_6	

Visual image analysis and toposheet analysis formed the base to extract data on catchment parmeters.

Results and Discussion

Terrain characteristics: Catchment parameters or terrain characteristics of the catchments are provided in Table 8.1. Catchment area (km^2), average length (km), hilly area (%) form and average slope, metre per metre, are identified as catchment parameters. In addition, land use classes—forest, plantation, paddy and others—are considered as part of the catchment parmeters. These details are provided in Table 8.1. Average total discharge and discharges during the South-west monsoon, North-east monsoon and dry season have been worked out and provided in Table 8.1.

Average annual catchment yield varies from 1,104 million cu. m (mm^3) in the Mananthody catchment to 22 mm^3 in Manjat catchment. Water yield per sq. km. varies from 0.44 mm^3 in Manjat to 7.30 MM^3 in Choorani. The catchment of Mananthody records an average production of 3.22 mm^3, which is the second highest.

Discharge Pattern

Monthly discharge data in per cent to total discharge have been plotted for all the eight catchments. The maximum yield has been recorded either in the month of July or August for all the catchments. Lowest yields have been marked for the drier months of February, March

Table 8.1: Terrain Characteristics of the Catchments

Sl. No.	*Name of the Catchment*	*Area (km^2)*	*Average Length (km)*	*Hilly Area (%)*	*Form $\frac{A}{L}$*	*Average Slope, metre per metre*	*Area (%)*				*Seasonal Discharge (in %)*		
							Forest	*Plantation*	*Paddy*	*Others*	*SW*	*NE*	*Dry*
1.	Panamaram	442	41	351	0.26	0.060	38	40	17	5	83	13	4
2.	Mananthody	342	30	25	0.38	0.044	50	14	14	22	85	12	3
3.	Nulpuzha	185	27	4	0.25	0.039	56	24	7	13	65	24	11
4.	Bavalipuzha	176	23	33	0.33	0.048	54	38	6	2	86	9	5
5.	Kakkavayal	68	20	1	0.17	0.027	–	67	25	8	67	17	16
6.	Vazhavatta	66	9	1	0.74	0.026	4	76	20	–	58	24	18
7.	Choorani	54	14	80	0.28	0.170	72	–	3	25	89	8	3
8.	Manjat	50	16	1	0.20	0.018	62	25	6	7	77	18	5

and April. Based on the monthly discharge pattern, the catchments can be classified into three categories.

The patterns shown by Nulpuzha and Choorani are the extremes and the other catchments are placed in between. The catchment of Vazhavatta record a pattern similar to that of Nulpuzha, although there is a big difference with respect to area and discharge. Considering the extreme cases of Nulpuzha and Choorani, it can be inferred that the catchment of Nulpuzha withholds considerable amount of rainwater and the river is perennial with a significant base flow. Choorani presents an opposite picture, where, very little amount of incoming precipitation is intercepted and rainfall directly contributes to discharge.

Discharge and Terrain Characteristics

Among the physical parameters related to catchment, area is the most significant in controlling the discharge variabilitites. After working out the correlation in exponential terms it has been observed that around 60 per cent variabilities of discharge can be explained by the catchment area alone.

The regression equation is

$$D = 0.886 \times A^{1.13} \qquad ...(1)$$

when D = Annual discharge

A = Area of the catchment

Correlation coefficient, $R = 0.78$

The positive and high correlations that exist substantiate the generally established relationship in the hydrological analysis.

The area-discharge graph (Fig. 8.3) indicates that six out of eight catchments show a normal trend. However, the high departure of Choorani and Manjat from the regression line need to be explained. Terrain characteristics of the catchments highlight that Choorani has a mountainous catchment with an average slope of more than 17 per cent. Also, it has bare rock exposures for a considerable area. This leads to generate tremendous overland flow, limiting infiltration potential. As a result, it records higher discharge compared to its area. Conversely, Manjat is completely flat with an average slope less than 2 per cent. Moreover, forests and plantations help interception of water in a flat area. Therefore, surface runoff is restricted and ground water recharge is high.

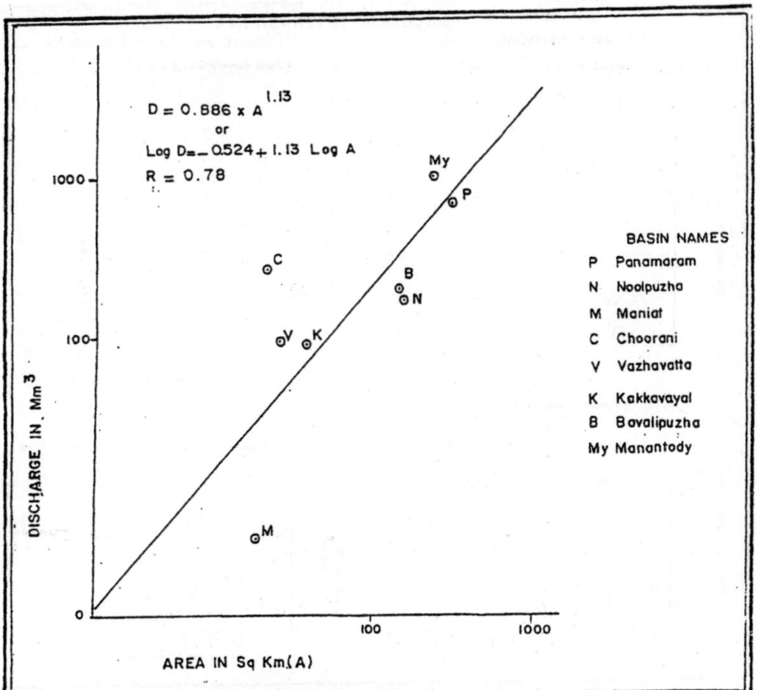

Fig. 8.3: Area—Discharge Graph

The next important parameter to influence discharge, particularly, in terms of seasonal variation is the area under hilly conditions in each catchment. In exponential terms, the regression equation in this case stands as

$$D = 89.13 \times H^{0.39} \quad ...(2)$$
$$R = 0.47$$

Where

D = Discharge
H = Area under hills in per cent
R = Correlation coefficient.

The scatter plot (Fig. 8.4) indicates that Mananthody and Panamaram show high positive departure and Manjat records high negative departure from the regression line.

As regards Choorani, the nearness to the regression line in this graph and the high departure in the earlier graph (Fig. 8.3) suggest that

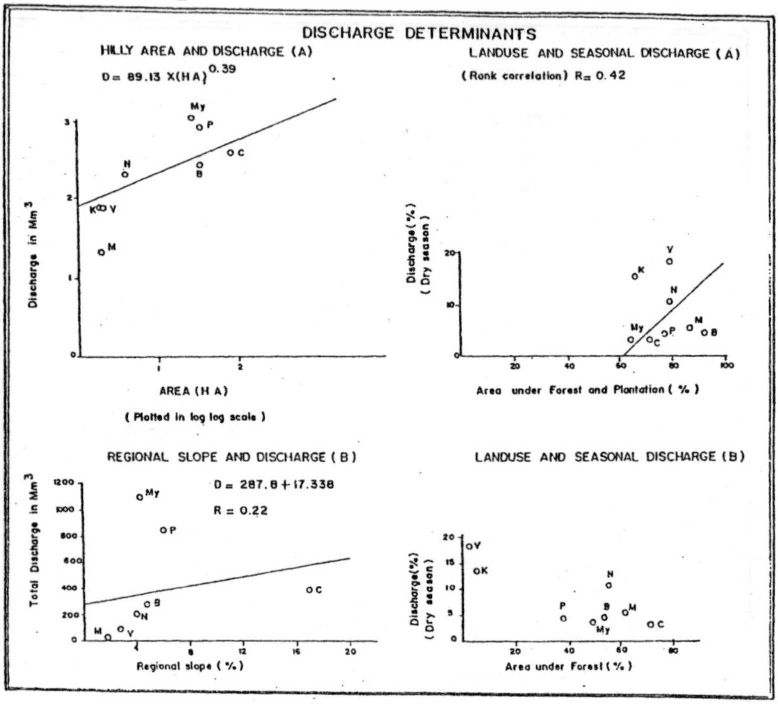

Fig. 8.4: Discharge Determinants

the discharge pattern of the Choorani catchment can be successfully explained by taking into account its hilly condition. It can be inferred from this, that, in the case of mountainous catchment, the discharge pattern or yield, primarily, depends upon steepness of the slope or hilly nature of the catchment as a whole.

The presence of hilly area does not much influence on the discharge of the bigger catchments like Manthody and Panamaram. The catchment area, average slope and length of the basin have a definite influence in these cases.

Slope is the other parameter that has been considered as important. The correlation coefficient is low—0.22—but important for a number of catchments as elucidated from the scatter plot (Fig. 8.4). In this case also, Manantoddy, Panamaram and Choorani record high departures from the regression line. The position of Manjat in the graph highlights that the slope is a very significant factor in this basin to generate discharge.

The foregoing discussion reminds that, the discharge pattern depends upon a number of terrain factors. It is difficult to explain the dispersions in bivariate terms as the catchment conditions are always subjected to local relief variabilities, which again influence discharge.

To understand the regulatory effect of land cover on the seasonality of discharge pattern, two scatter plots have been drawn by considering dry season discharge against (1) area completely under forests, and (2) area under forests and plantations.

There is no specific trend in the case of area under forests. However, taking into account the plantation area along with forests, the scatter plot shows some trend. Only rank correlation has been worked out and the coefficient stands at 0.42.

This apparently poor or non-correlation between land cover and discharge is attributable to the fact that catchments considered here are characterized by diversified terrain factors. The well-established plantations present a near-forest condition. Catchments of similar characteristics have to be selected for examining the influence of land cover over discharge in greater detail. It need to be mentioned here further that a number of streams in the Wayanad plateau are fed by seasonal and permanent springs, which do, substantially, modify the yield.

Multiple Regression Analysis

The multiple regression analysis brings out that around 74 per cent of the variabilities can be explained by considering the above listed variables. Regression co-efficients (B-value) of these variables and T-value are listed in Table 8.2.

Table 8.2: Regression co-efficients and T-value

Variable	*B-Value*	*T-Value*
Constant	–11.18	–.091
X_1	2.28	4.17
X_2	–0.74	–1.31
X_3	0.28	1.47
X_4	0.29	1.50
X_5	0.13	0.56
X_6	– 0.34	– 2.00

The discharge '*Y*' can be determined by the regression equation.

$$Y = -11.18 + 2.28\,X_1 -- 0.74X_2 + 0.28X_3 + 0.29X_4 - 0.34X_6 \quad ...(3)$$

The variable X_5 has been neglected due to very low B & T values. The significant aspect is that the length of the basin and area under plantations and forests are negative contributors to the discharge pattern. The travel time of water in an elongated basin is higher and, hence, there are strong possibilities of infiltration and percolation and also high evapotranspiration loss which naturally reduces discharge. Similarly, contribution of vegetation cover (forest and plantation) is negative as it enhances the infiltration capability by interrupting surface runoff and also contributes to higher evapotranspiration. Further, vegetation regulates the seasonality of discharge more than total discharge. It also smoothens peak flow.

Next to catchment area, the proportion of area under hilly conditions and slope are the other two variables that influence the drainage discharge pattern. Based on the equation 3 given above yields have been estimated for all the catchments (Table 8.3).

Table 8.3: Observed and Estimated Yields (MM^3) of the Catchments

Sl. No.	*Catchments*	*Observed Yield*	*Estimated Yield*	*Departure (%)*
1.	Panamaram	854	983	+15
2.	Mananthody	1104	732	–34
3.	Nulpuzha	209	365	+75
4.	Bavalipuzha	274	351	+28
5.	Kakkavayal	97	107	+10
6.	Vazhavatta	98	107	+10
7.	Choorani	394	100	–75
8.	Manjat	22	62	+182

The estimated yield is higher than the observed yield in all the catchments except Mananthody and Choorani. Choorani being a completely hilly catchment presents a different situation with a dominating overland flow. Although the hilly area within the Mananthody catchment is less (25%), the undulating condition enhances direct flow as is evident from the monthly discharge pattern.

What is evident from this analysis is that the catchment area plays a very significant role in determining the volume of discharge.

Conclusion

This study has indicated that catchment parameters, particularly catchment area and area under hills, are two important determining factors of catchment yield in this area. Land use records a smoothening effect on the hydrograph. As the externalities like contribution of springs on discharge could not be separated, the actual effect of the landuse/land cover as regulatory mechanism is not yet fully known.

Acknowledgements

Authors are grateful to the Director, Centre for Earth Science Studies, for providing facilities and permission to complete this work. Thanks are due to Sri Mohandas for drafting the maps and to Smt. Lails for the typographical work.

REFERENCES

Cattopadhyay, S. and Chattopadhyay, M. (1989). "Application of Remote Sensing in Terrain Analysis: A Case Study of the Waynad Plateau, Kerala, India", *Int. J. Remote Sensing*, 10(6): 1075-84.

Hedman, E.R. and Osterkamp, W.R., (1982). Stream Flow Characteristics Related to Channel Geometry of Streams in Western United States. *U.S. Geological Survey Water Supply Paper* 2193.

Lee, R. (1980), *Forest Hydrology,* Colombia University Press, New York.

Schwale, O.G., Firevert, R.K., Edminster, T.W. and Barnes, K.K. (1985), *Soil and Water Conservation Engineering,* John Wiley & Sons, New York.

Sinha Roy, S. and Ravindra Kumar, G.R., (1983). Geology of an Area in the Bavali Fault Zone of the Wayanad Schist Belt, North Kerala, Centre for Earth Science Studies, T.R. No. 25/1983.

9

Biophysical Characteristics of Land in the Mahanadi Delta

B. THAKUR and PUNYATOYA PATRA

NATURE OF PROBLEM

Along the eastern coastal tract of India, the Mahanadi delta is the most fertile land having a unique type of combined deltaic and coastal ecosystems. But, the land of this region is being observed to be degrading day by day due to the combined action of regular occurrence of flood, drainage congestion, saline water intrusion, waterlogging, over-irrigation, deforestation and faulty agricultural practices. During the rainy season most of the rivers exceed their normal channel capacity and attain the flood stage causing great havoc in this region. Despite all the efforts to reduce flood damage, the problem has continued to be serious and 40 per cent of this region is still prone to floods, drainage congestion and saline water inundation (Panda and Sinha, 1991). The western part is influenced by erosive action of recurrent floods and eastern part by salt water intrusion from the sea. The Water and Land Management Institute of Orissa (1988) reported that the production of paddy and jute has been decreasing since last one decade only due to salinization. The percentage of wasteland is increasing due to coastal sand encroachment and sand casting on the agricultural land during flood times. Deforestation has led to serious ecological imbalance in this region affecting soil erosion and water holding capacity. Therefore, the agricultural productivity in the delta region is comparatively low as compared to other deltas along the eastern coastal tract in the country. From the point of view of agriculture and land management problems, there is urgent need to better understand biophysical characteristics of land, i.e. alluvial feature, micro-erosional features and hydrological attributes within coastal ecosystem. Such a study may ultimate lead to detailed evaluation of land for their suitability and development for agriculture. For optimum production, it is necessary to examine the land characteristics which not only limits but also stands on the way of sustained development. The study of biophysical land characteristics is, therefore, essential especially in those areas where the forces of degradation are quite active.

Review of Literature

The number of geographers studying biophysical characteristics of land has increased substantially in the past three decades. An extensive literature has become visible and the presentation of papers at professional meetings has expanded notably. Geographer studies land in relation to human being, his past and present activities in so far as they exert a significant influence on the present and future uses of the land. A parcel of land may be suited to several uses at a given time. Its value does not depend on physical characteristics alone, but is greatly influenced by social requirements and economic considerations (Whyte, 1976, 2). Attention needs to be given to markets, population levels and growth rates, problems of land tenure, labour, transport of products and input etc. But, usually, the biophysical aspects of land area studied and mapped first to provide a geographical framework into which socio-economic dimensions area inserted later (FAO, 1990, 7). The establishment of a conceptual framework around which research can develop has been called for (Symons, 1978). Some land is better than other in the same use, and with the pressure of growing population in relation to a more or less fixed supply of land, it is important that variations of land quality should be studied and mapped. While topography, climate, soil and vegetation each has its own individual significance in the biological habitat or ecosystem, and therefore, in the development of agriculture, animal husbandry and forestry, it is the combined affect of all and the interactions between them which are important (Christian and Stewart, 1968, 233-80). Undoubtedly, soil plays an important role in evaluating the land for agricultural purpose. However, pragmatic land evaluation must take into account all land attributes—rock, relief, vegetation, water, animals and man—including the results of soil survey for land classification (Davidson, 1992). Rao and Vaidyanathan (1990) classified land of Krishna delta to their capability levels by giving due recognition to landform, soil and landuse pattern. Land suitability of the Madurai district has been evaluated based on physical aspects (Rao, 1985). Pant, Joshi and Jalal (1989) have classified the land of Kota Dun, Kumaon Himalaya into three capability classes on the basis of 8 variables, i.e. soil depth, soil texture, slope, erosion intensity, water holding capacity, sunlight condition, quantity of irrigation, accessibility and potential land use. While Singh (1989) classified the land of Manipur valley into three land capability classes on the basis of crop productivity; Singh and Ansari (1984) studied the fertility status of Aligarh soils on the basis of phosphorus, potash and nitrogen content and classified the lands of Aligarh district into four capability classes. Alam and Siddiqui (1984) have followed the same pattern. Yadav (1985) evaluated the distribution of *banjar* land at village level of the Sultanpur district in Uttar Pradesh, and Kumar and Pandey (1989) determined the capability of different types of wasteland of Deogarh district in Bihar. Nevertheless, much still needs to be done, and Agarwal *et al.* (1985) in their assessment of research on state of environment in India, called for more broad-based research on the wasteland of coastal tract.

Purpose of Study

The present study aims at the following: (1) to divide the study area into a number of relatively homogeneous land characteristic units with their boundaries mapped, and (2) to provide necessary information about each type of these units so that they can be evaluated for their quality. The paper is not meant to yield and understanding of the reasons or causes of land degradation, but it will help identify the regional pattern of its characteristics. As such, the paper makes no recommendation for an intervention to improve the land quality as this work requires going beyond the analysis of secondary data and finding out micro level evaluation at village level based on better estimates of land characteristics at sampled locations. However, the paper does provide some tentative evidence of characterisation of land quality.

Study Area

The Mahanadi delta is selected for study as it is a good representative of the Orissa coastal plain. There is no substantial work on biophysical characteristics of land of the Mahanadi delta. But, this region has been studied from many other geographical points of view. The regional geography of delta has been examined by Sinha (1995). Pattnayak, Tripathy, Sinha and Tripathy (1985) have described and analyzed urbanization patterns and urban systems in the deltaic area. Panda and Sinha (1988) have outlined different problematic areas of this region while studying flood hazards. Therefore, the proposed study would fill a gap in this field of research.

The Mahanadi Delta is the middle portion of the Orissa coastal plain and is triangular in shape. The apex is demarcated by Naraj Anicut where the main river Mahanadi enters the plain. The boundary is demarcated by Baragenguti-Brahmani-Pathsala Nai as the northeastern limit and Kuakhai Daya as the western boundary line. The region comes under the jurisdiction of three administrative subdivisions, viz., Kendrapara, Cuttack and Puri comprising 28 police stations. The geology of the delta is varied in lithology as well as age of rocks. The ancient crystalline rock—the Khondalites—occurs as isolated peaks within and at the reins of the delta. Next in age are the upper Gondwana sedimentary rocks found extensively in the delta head. Overlying the above, the deltaic sediments have been deposited throughout the Holocene period. They are further classified into older and younger alluviums. The highest lands are generally located along the river branches which dissect the delta, forming doabs. The doabs tend to slope down transversally from the river to the interior, and longitudinally from the delta apex to the coast. The flatness of the delta is disturbed by a number of micro topography, such as undulating hills, beach ridges, levees and patos' land. The Mahanadi river is divided into many distributaries forming doabs and a number of small islands. The density of drainage of this area is very high, i.e. about 0.61. Drainage is the major constraint to further agricultural development in the delta. About one-third of the area suffers from poor drainage. In fact, lack of adequate drainage is perhaps the most important constraint as it limits both yields and diversification of crops. A large length of unlined irrigation canals and distributaries allow greater seepage into underground strata and after become a direct source of waterlogging of low lying areas. The drains in the command area outfall into the area, Chilka lake or river. The outfall conditions in all the three cases vary widely and each has its own problem. Tidal fluctuations of the sea twice a day push sea water inland during high tides. During such period the drainage water does not get a chance to be discharged and piles up causing inundation of low lying areas. During the low tide period, the sea water which were pushed inland first gets drained out, then only drainage water has a chance to be drained out. The tidal level becomes higher during certain period of the month depending upon the phases of the moon. If the period coincides with the dual rainfall, the drainage congestion becomes more acute. The water level of Chilka lake remains at about 1.5 metres above mean sea level for most of the monsoon period. This creates drainage problem in southern portion and remains waterlogged for a longer period. Some of the drains outfall into rivers, where the water level often remains at higher level due to rainfall and controlled release from Hirakud dam. This also creates waterlogging for longer duration. The average annual rainfall is about 157 cm and during the rainy season the problems are aggravated. Most of the rivers attain flood stage and water gets diverted into the doabs through flood escapes. At the same time, the cyclonic storms also occur with fairly heavy rainfall. Thus, the efficiency of drainage outlets of these *doabs* is subjected to serious limitations, which, further accentuates the flood intensities. The damages brought by floods not only confine to the structural or erosional damage but also contamination of nearby land and waterbodies. The lowlands, swamps and marshes adjacent to the coast are filled up by tidal inundations and flooding of salt water which makes the valuable agricultural land unsuitable for cultivation. This also results the formation of saline soils and groundwater contamination. Saline inundation affects agriculture adversely to a great extent and prevents paddy cultivation and sometimes turns the soil permanently unfit for cultivation for decades to come till they are flushed out due to heavy flood or rainfall.

About ten per cent of the study area is lying barren because of unfavourable lithological conditions to support any human and plant life (Sinha and Chhotaraya, 1990). They consist of vast stretches of laterites in western margin, coastal sand in eastern side, wetlands in southern portion and hills of northwestern side which have been laid barren after deforestation. Due to deforestation, the sand dunes along the coast approach the fertile paddy fields during southwest monsoon when the wind velocity often exceeds 100 km per hour. Agriculture dominates economy of the delta and contributes 60 per cent of the domestic product. Net agricultural area is about 70 per cent of the total area. Paddy is the dominant crop.

Data Source and Methodology

For the purpose of this study, the delta is divided into 388 number of cells determined by latitude and longitude. Each cell represents $2.5' \times 2.5'$ grid with 20 km^2. Then, data on biophysical characteristics of land has been collected for each cell. The variables chosen are broadly grouped into: (a) Landform-relative relief, (b) Soils—laterite horizon; infiltration rate; nutrient content, such as phosphorous, potassium, calcium, magnesium; *p*H value; normal moisture content of the soil, (c) Hydrology—water quality determined by the total dissolved solids, alkalinity, chlorides, sodium content of water; groundwater depth; drainage density; and extent of waterlogging.

Data on water quality, such as total dissolved solids (TDS), chlorides, alkalinity, sodium; and average water depth were available from the Office of Chief Engineer, Department of Irrigation, Bhubaneswar. Data on soil nutrients, such as phosphorous, potassium, calcium, magnesium; *p*H value of soil; infiltration rate; and normal moisture content were obtained from Operation Research Group, Bhubaneswar. Drainage density and relative relief were calculated from the toposheets of the study area on the scale of 1: 50,000. The extents of waterlogging and laterite horizon were also calculated from the map 1:125,000 prepared by Orissa Remote Sensing Application Centre, Bhubaneswar.

On the basis of secondary data, the study area is divided into a number of homogeneous land characteristics units by using two statistical methods: Pearsonian product moment correlation coefficient and factor analysis. The former indicates the degree of linear association between two variables and is used to determine the basic structure of relations between the variables; the latter discovers the structure of a multivariate universe of data by revealing the clusters of closely related elements contained within the matrix of correlation co-efficient. The factor analysis with varimax rotation is employed to analyze the data matrix of 388 observation units to categorise the land. These analyses have been completed on computer by using SAS programme at Delhi University Computer Centre. Values for each selected variables were obtained for each of the cells and generalized choropleth maps were drawn.

Data Interpretation

The Pearson product moment correlation coefficient is calculated between each pair of the above mentioned sixteen variables to determine the basic structure of relations between them.

Table 9.1: Correlation Matrix (Land Variablses)

	V1	V2	V3	V4	V5	V6	V7	V8	V9	V10	V11	V12	V13	V14	V15	V16
V1									-0.11							
V2				-0.16	-0.15		0.12								-0.12	
V3																
V4					0.23						0.11		0.13		0.29	0.18
V5						0.4	0.39	-0.31			0.14		0.11	-0.13	-0.1	
V6							0.67	-0.21		0.11	0.14				-0.18	-0.16
V7								-0.13	-0.1		0.18				-0.15	
V8											-0.1				0.26	0.15
V9											-0.1	0.11			-0.54	
V10											0.24	0.3	0.37			
V11												0.14	0.31			
V12													0.14			
V13																
V14																
V15																0.33
V16																

Note: ± values are significant at 0.05. Probability level. Underlined figures are significant at .001 probability level.

V1= Relative relief
V2= Lateritic horizon
V3= Infiltration rate
V4= Phosphorous content of soil
V5= Potassium content of soil
V6= Calcium content of soil
V7= Magnesium content of soil
V8= *p*H value of soil
V9= Normal moisture content of soil
V10= Total dissolved solids of water
V11= Chloride content of water
V12= Alkaline content of water
V13= Sodium content of water
V14= Groundwater depth
V15= Drainage density
V16= Extent of waterlogging

Only the significant values at 0.05 probability level are shown in Table 9.1. Here the values are found to be low due to large number of observations, i.e. 388. The distribution of such significant values illustrates how much more diagnostic certain of the variables are than others within the total universe of data.

Total dissolved solids (TDS) of water are positively correlated with chloride, alkalinity and sodium content of water and potassium and calcium content of soil. The chloride content of water is positively related with TDS, chloride, sodium content of water, phosphorous, potassium, calcium, magnesium content of soil and negatively related with *p*H value of the soil and normal moisture content of soil. The sodium content of water is positively related with TDS, chloride, alkalinity content of water and phosphorous and potassium content of the soil. The average groundwater depth is negatively related with potassium content of the soil. Drainage density is positively related with extent of waterlogging, *p*H value of soil, phosphorous, calcium content of soil, and negatively related with lateritic horizon. *p*H value of the soil is positively related with drainage density, extent of waterlogging and negatively related with potassium, calcium, magnesium content of soil, and alkalinity content of water. Infiltration rate is not highly correlated with any other variable. At 0.07 probability level it is positively related with lateritic horizon and at 0.09 probability level it is negatively related with drainage density. Normal moisture content is negatively related with lateritic horizon, alkalinity of water, magnesium of soil and slope of the land. Lateritic horizon is positively related with magnesium content of soil and negatively related with drainage density, normal moisture content of soil, phosphorous and potassium content of soil. Phosphorous content of soil is positively related with potassium content of soil, drainage density, extent of waterlogging, alkalinity and sodium content of water and negatively related with lateritic horizon. Potassium content of soil is positively related with phosphorous, calcium, magnesium of soil and negatively related with average water depth, drainage density, *p*H value of soil and lateritic horizon. Calcium of soil is positively related with potassium, magnesium of soil, TDS, alkalinity of water and negatively related with drainage density, *p*H value of soil and extent of waterlogging. Magnesium content is positively related with potassium, calcium of soil, alkalinity of water, lateritic horizon and negatively related with drainage density, *p*H value, normal moisture content and extent of waterlogging. Slope is negatively related with normal moisture content. Extent of waterlogging is positively related with drainage density, *p*H value of soil, phosphorous of soil and negatively related with calcium and magnesium of soil.

The simple interpretation of correlation matrix gives the idea of relationship among the variables and their diagnostic importance. But it is not enough in delineating the areas of similar land type. Rough groupings can be done with the help of these variables, but it is a clumsy attempt to isolate the homogenous area. It is because of this complexity to handle such a large number of interrelated variables in the form of simple association that some form of multivariate technique is appropriate. The reason for the selection of factor analysis technique has already been discussed.

Dimensions of Land Differentiation

From the original data matrix of sixteen variables and 388 observations, 8 factors are extracted. These are orthogonal factors. All these factors explain 70 per cent of the total variance (Fig. 9.3). A detailed composition of these factors may be obtained from a close analysis of factor loadings. Factor loadings are presented in Table 9.2. The significant values have been underlined and considered for analysis. In this table factors are arranged according to the size of their exigent value for each factor. Factor loadings show the correlations of the variables with the factors and identify the land dimensions which are as follows.

Factor I: Soil Quality

This factor shows 16 per cent of the variance and explains soil quality, i.e. nutrient condition of soil. It is positively related with potassium (+.62), calcium (+.87), magnesium (+.87) of soil; and negatively related with *p*H value (-.19) of soil and extent of waterlogging (-.10). The low *p*H value of the soil has very less negative impact on this type of land category as the minimum *p*H value of the study area is 5.7 which is not very less from the ideal condition.

Factor II: Water Quality

This factor explains 12 per cent of the total variance and shows water quality. It is positively related with total dissolved solids (+.74), Chloride (+.70), alkalinity (+.21) and sodium (+.76) content of water and negatively related with average water depth (-.13). This table shows four variables having very high association with this factor.

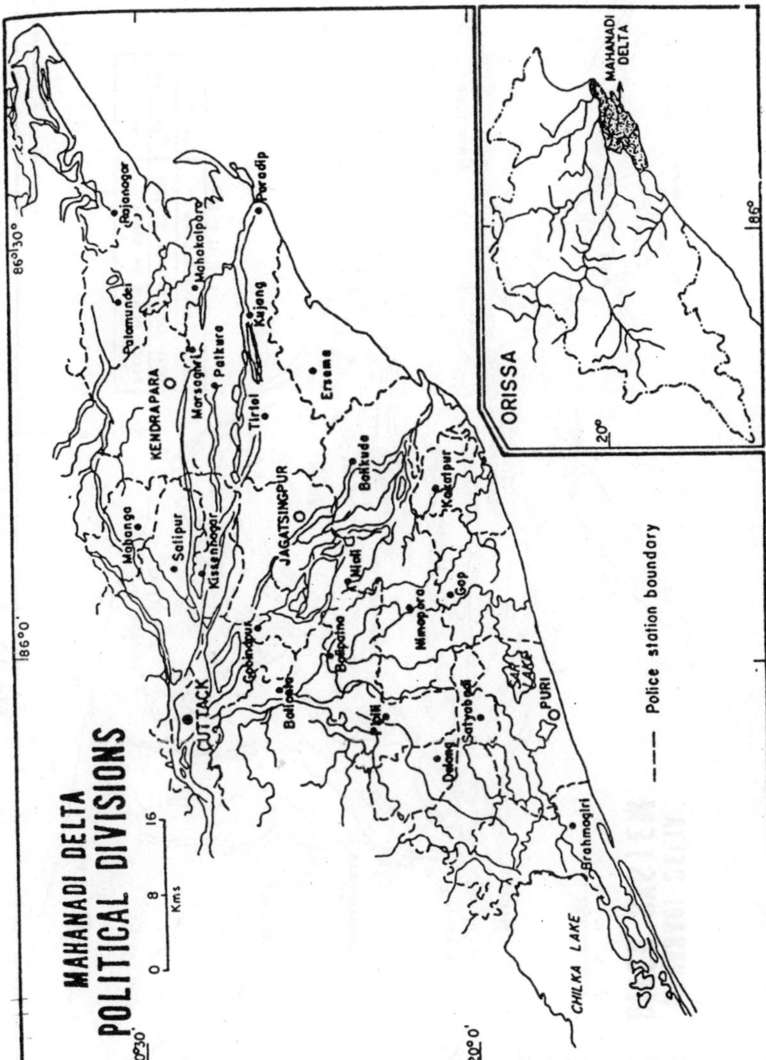

Fig. 9.1: Mahanadi Delta Political Divisions

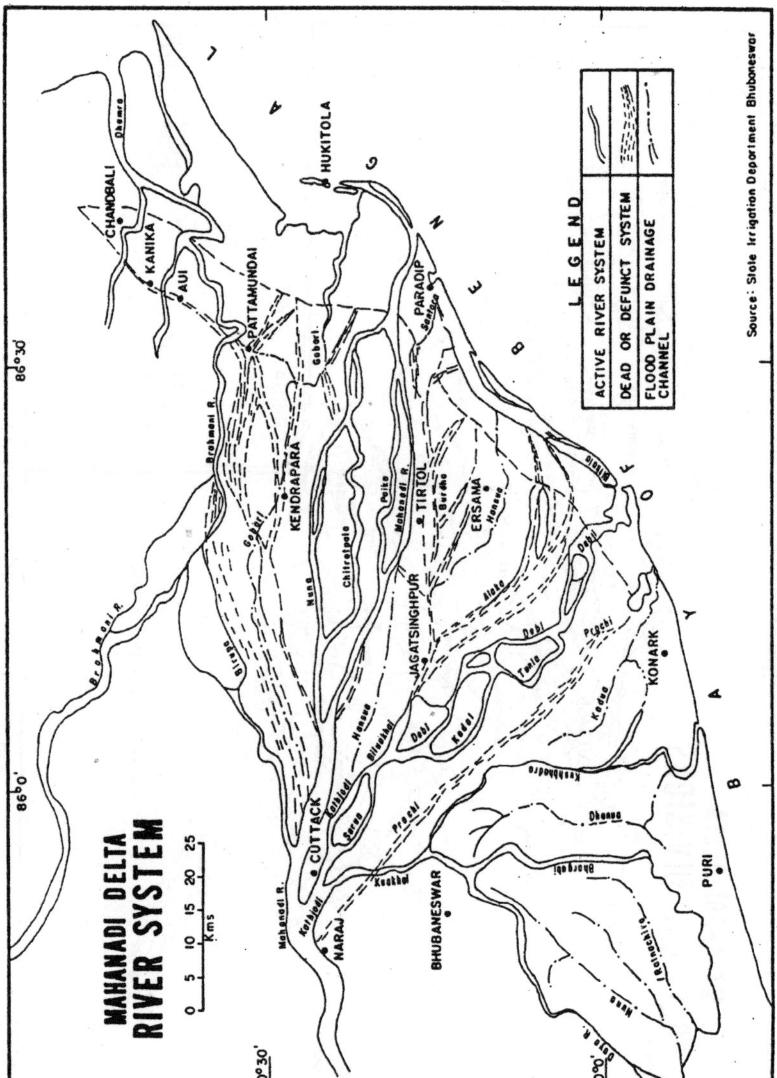

Fig. 9.2: Mahanadi Delta River System

Table 9.2: Factorial Structure of 16 Land Variables

Variables	*Factor Loading*							
	1	*2*	*3*	*4*	*5*	*6*	*7*	*8*
1. Relative relief slope	-0.030	-0.004	-0.006	-0.060	0.05	-0.050	0.95	0.010
2. Lateritic horizon	-0.009	0.030	-0.090	-0.850	0.00	-0.100	-0.06	0.050
3. Infiltration rate	0.003	-0.04	-0.10	-0.06	-0.02	-0.006	0.02	0.05
4. Soil phosphorus	0.03	0.03	0.59	0.22	-0.24	0.50	0.05	0.12
5. Soil potassium	0.62	0.04	0.01	0.14	-0.40	0.27	0.16	-0.01
6. Soil calcium	0.87	0.08	0.15	0.02	0.05	-0.04	0.01	0.02
7. Soil magnesium	0.87	0.04	-0.08	-0.15	0.05	0.09	-0.09	0.02
8. *p*H value of soil	-0.19	0.07	0.44	-0.08	0.50	-0.22	-0.19	0.23
9. Normal moisture content	-0.06	0.06	-0.08	0.86	0.005	-0.19	-0.13	-0.02
10. Total dissolved solids	0.06	0.73	-0.09	0.06	0.08	0.18	-0.03	-0.05
11. Chlorides	0.002	0.7	0.01	-0.04	-0.15	0.02	0.04	-0.09
12. Alkalinity	0.09	0.21	-0.12	-0.10	0.10	0.82	-0.07	-0.04
13. Sodium	0.07	0.76	0.07	0.06	-0.90	0.01	-0.02	0.10
14. Groundwater depth	0.05	-0.13	-0.08	0.05	0.08	0.12	0.12	0.07
15. Drainage density	-0.08	-0.07	0.79	0.06	0.12	0.03	0.06	-0.05
16. Extent of waterlogging	-0.10	0.06	0.68	-0.09	-0.10	-0.13	-0.05	-0.10

Factor III: Waterlogging Condition

This factor explains 9 per cent of the total variance and shows waterlogging conditions. It is positively related with drainage density (+.79), extent of waterlogging (+.68), phosphorous of soil (+.55), *p*H value of soil (+.44), and negatively related with alkalinity of water (-.12), infiltration rate (-.10) and calcium (-.15) content of soil. In the area where scores of this factor are high, content of phosphorous and *p*H value of soil are also high with drainage density and extent of waterlogging. So, if the excess water from this area can be drained out to other area, then, a number of crops can be grown in this region.

Factor IV: Soil Moisture Condition

This factor explains 8 per cent of the total variance and shows soil moisture condition. It is positively correlated with normal moisture content (+.86), phosphorous (+.22), potassium (+.14) content of soil and negatively related with alkaline content of water (-.15). The quality of land showing high scores of this factor is good as it is positively related with two main macro-nutrients and normal moisture content of soil, which are beneficial for crop production.

Factor V: Water Depth

This factor explains 7 per cent of the total variance which shows water depth. It is positively related with average water depth (+.80), *p*H value of soil (+.50), drainage density (+.12), alkalinity content of water (+.10); and negatively related with chloride of water (-.14), phosphorous of soil (.-.24) and extent of waterlogging (-.11). The land quality of the areas showing high scores of this factor is not so good. Here the water depth is high. The main soil nutrient, i.e. phosphorous content is very low. The soil is also little alkaline.

Factor VI: Alkaline Condition

This factor explains about 6 per cent of the total variance and shows alkaline condition. The factor is positively related with alkalinity (+.82), TDS content of water, (+.18), average water depth (+.12), phosphorous content of soil (+.50); and negatively related with *p*H value of soil (-.22), normal moisture content, (-.14) lateritic horizon

(-.10) and extent of waterlogging (-.13). The area showing high scores of this factor has poor land quality. The land is highly alkaline. Water is not abundantly available here. Even the normal moisture content of the soil is low. Only the soil nutrient. phosphorous is available here.

Factor VII: Relief

This factor explains about 6 per cent of the total variance. It is highly related with the slope (+.96) average water depth (+.12); and negatively related with *p*H value of soil (-.19) and normal moisture content (-.13).

Factor VIII: Dryness

It explains about 5 per cent of the total variance. It is positively related with infiltration rate (+.95), *p*H value (+.23) and phosphorous of soil (+.12) and negatively related with extent of waterlogging (-.11).

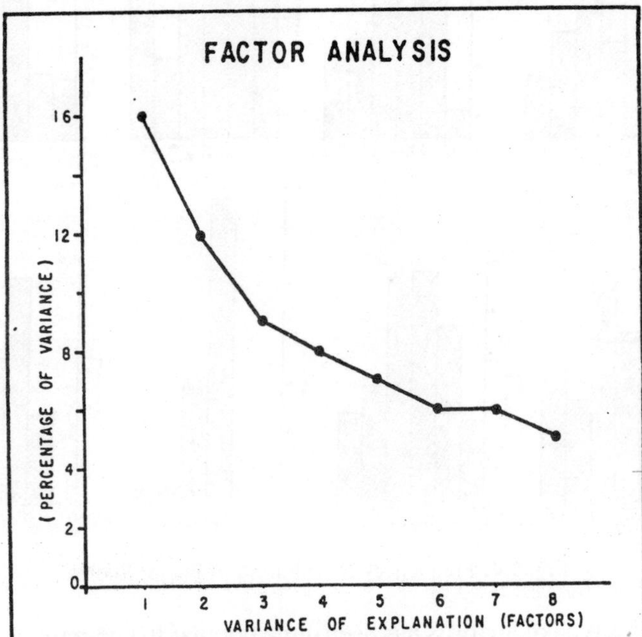

Fig. 9.3: Factor Analysis

Spatial Pattern of Factor Scores

Having identified the content of each of the eight principal factors, it is worth noting the principal features of factor scores on the maps. Factor score is the weight of factors on the units observed. It is the standardized measure of observed units. In case of the Mahanadi delta there are 388 observed units and 388 scores for each factor. The columns of the factor score matrix show the value for every areal unit on the factors that each column's value can be mapped to show the spatial pattern of the column factor.

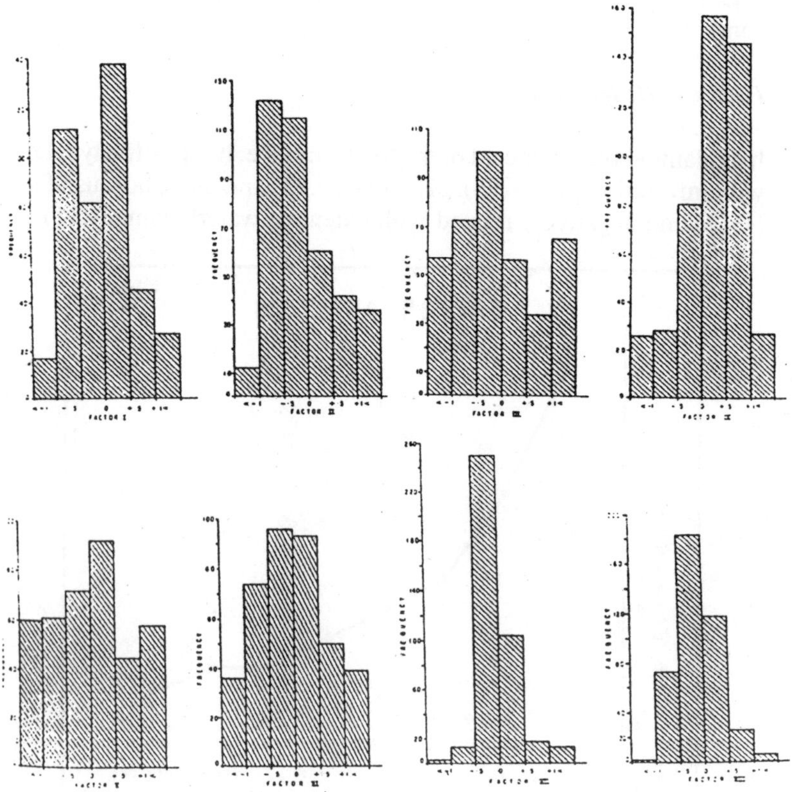

Fig. 9.4: Frequencey Distribution of Factor Scores

This type of analysis has been quite popular in geography. Figure 9.4 shows the frequency distribution and size of factor scores of each factor. The frequency distribution provides a guide to the selection of break points for the mapping of factor scores. The factor scores of all eight factors are divided into six class intervals ranging from high positive to high negative. The interpretation of each factor and their scores is provided in the following section.

Factor I Scores

Figure 9.5 shows the spatial distribution of factor I scores. Of the total area, 7.5 per cent of the land shows very high scores, i.e. more than 1, which is found mainly in Mahakalpara, Rajnagar, Ersama and Kendrapara police stations. The land having high scores, i.e. between .5 to 1.0 is found around the land with very high scores. This type of land covers 9.5 per cent of the total study area. The land with scores between 0 to +.5 is found mainly in Kendrapara, Salepur, and Gobindpur police stations and covers 22.7 per cent of the total area. The land with scores between -.5 to 0 is well distributed in the study area and covers 22.2 per cent of the total area. A large patch consisting of Satyabadi, Pipili and Brahmagiri police stations comes under this category. The land with low scores, i.e. -.5 to -1 is found mainly in Gop, Konark, Delang, Puri Sadar, Brahmagiri, Satyabadi, Balipatna, Gobindpur, Patkura police stations and covers 34.3 per cent of total land. The land with very low scores cover 3.8 per cent of the study area and are found in eleven number of cells. Lowest score of this factor which covers about 26 villages of Pipili police station. Of the total area, about 38.1 per cent of land has low soil nutrients (less than -0.5), 17 per cent of land has high soil nutrients (more than + 0.5) and remaining 44.9 per cent has medium soil nutrients. Land in Puri district does not have high soil nutrients.

Factor II Scores

Figure 9.6 shows the spatial distribution of factor II scores. Of the total area, 9.3 per cent of the land shows very high scores and is found mainly in almost all police stations of Puri district except Konark and Kakatpur and in some parts of Cuttak, Jagatsinghpur and Kendrapara districts. The land having high scores, i.e. between 0.5 to 1.0 is found very close to the land with very high scores. This category of land covers 10.8 per cent of the total study area. The land

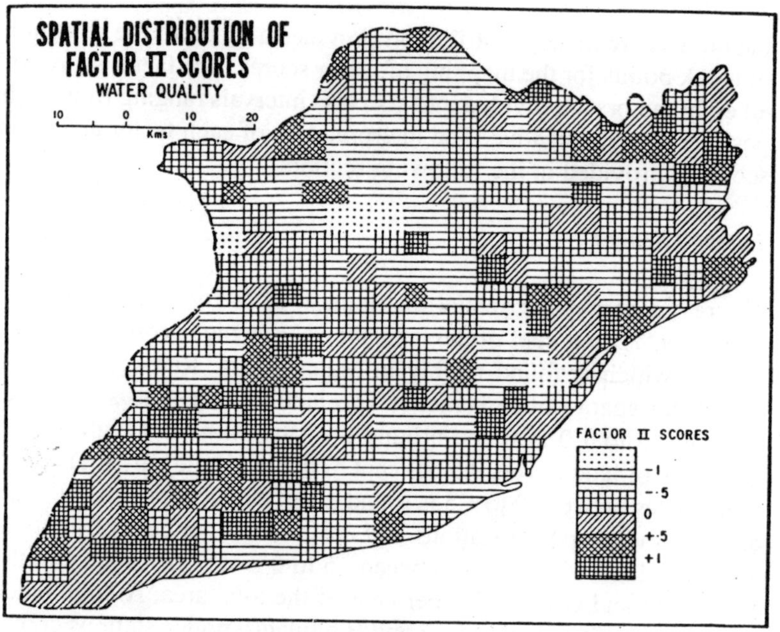

Fig. 9.5: Spatial Distribution of Factor

condition with scores between 0 to + 0.5 covers 15.7 per cent of the total area and is found mainly in Brahmagiri, Rajnagar, Pattamundai and Paradeep police stations. The land with scores between 0 to -0.5 is scattered throughout the delta and covers 29.6 per cent of the total area. The land with low scores, i.e. between -0.5 to -1.0 is found mainly in three patches. The first patch consists of parts of Salepur, Jagatsinghpur, Kishorenagar, Patkura, Tirtol, Mahanga, and Kendrapara police stations; and the second patch consists of Pattamundai, eastern part of Kendrapara and western part of Mahakalpara police stations. Some portions of Ersama and southeastern portion of Tirtol police station come under the third patch. All these land covers 31.5 per cent of the study area. The land with very low scores, i.e. less than -1.0 cover 3.1 per cent of the total area and is found in Kujang, Ersama and Jagatsinghpur police station. The highest score of this factor means the water quality of this area is the worst in the study area and covers 20 villages of Mahakalpara police station. Besides, very high score of this factor, which covers about 22 villages of Satyabadi police station.

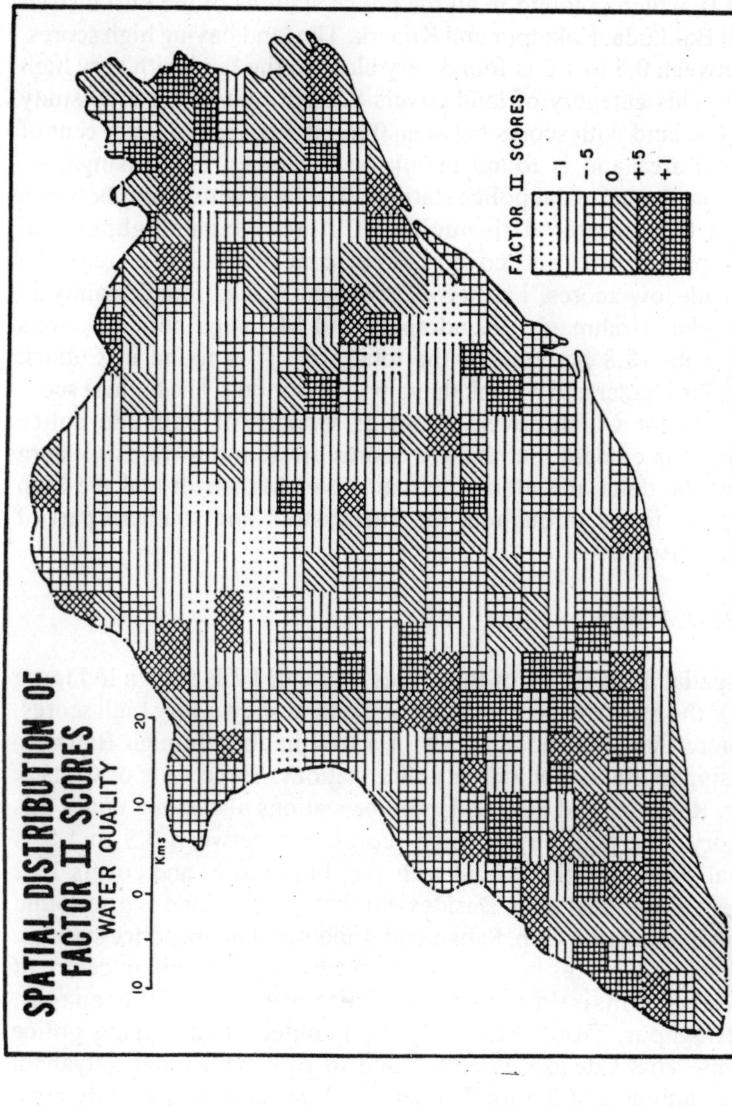

Fig. 9.6: Spatial Distribution of Factor II Scores

Factor III Scores

Figure 9.7 shows the spatial distribution of factor III scores. Of the total area, 17 per cent of the land shows very high scores, i.e. more than 1.0, which is found in all the police stations of the Puri district except Balikuda, Kakatpur and Konark. The land having high scores, i.e. between 0.5 to 1.0 is found very close to the land with very high scores. This category of land covers 8.8 per cent of the total study area. The land with scores between 0 to +0.5 covers 14.7 per cent of the total area and is found mainly in Brahmagiri, Jagatsinghpur, Balikuda, Pattamundai police stations. The land with scores between -0.5 to 0 is scattered throughout Cuttack, Jagatsinghpur and Kendrapara district and covers 26 per cent of the study area. The land with low scores, i.e. between -0.5 to -1.0 is found mainly in Puri Sadar, Brahmagiri, Kendrapara and Mahanga police stations and covers 18.8 per cent of the total area. It is found in Cuttack Sadar, Puri Sadar and Mahakalpara police stations. The highest score of this factor which covers about 25 villages of Balikudu police station. It is evident that the low scores are found towards western side of the delta and along the main river Mahanadi and the high scores are found throughout the Puri district and southern part of Cuttack district.

Factor IV Scores

The spatial distribution of the scores of factor IV is shown in Figure 9.8. Of the total area, 6.7 per cent of the land shows very high scores, i.e. more than 1.0 and is found in a row tracing through Balianta, Jagatsinghpur and Gobindpur police stations. Some parts of Cuttack Sadar, Rajnagar and Puri Sadar police stations also come under this category. The land having high scores, i.e. between 0.5 to 1.0 is normally found near the land with very high scores and covers 15.2 per cent of the total area. Besides, this category of land is also found in Nimapura, Pipili, Gop, Pattamundai and Kendrapara police stations. The land with scores between 0.0 to 0.5 is found mainly in centre of the delta consisting parts of Pattamundai, Kishorenagar, Jagatsinghpur, Tirtol, Mahakalpura, Paradeep and Kujang police stations. This category is also found in Brahmagiri and Satyabadi police stations and the total covers 43.3 per cent of the study area. The land with scores between 0 to -.5 covers 20.9 per cent of the

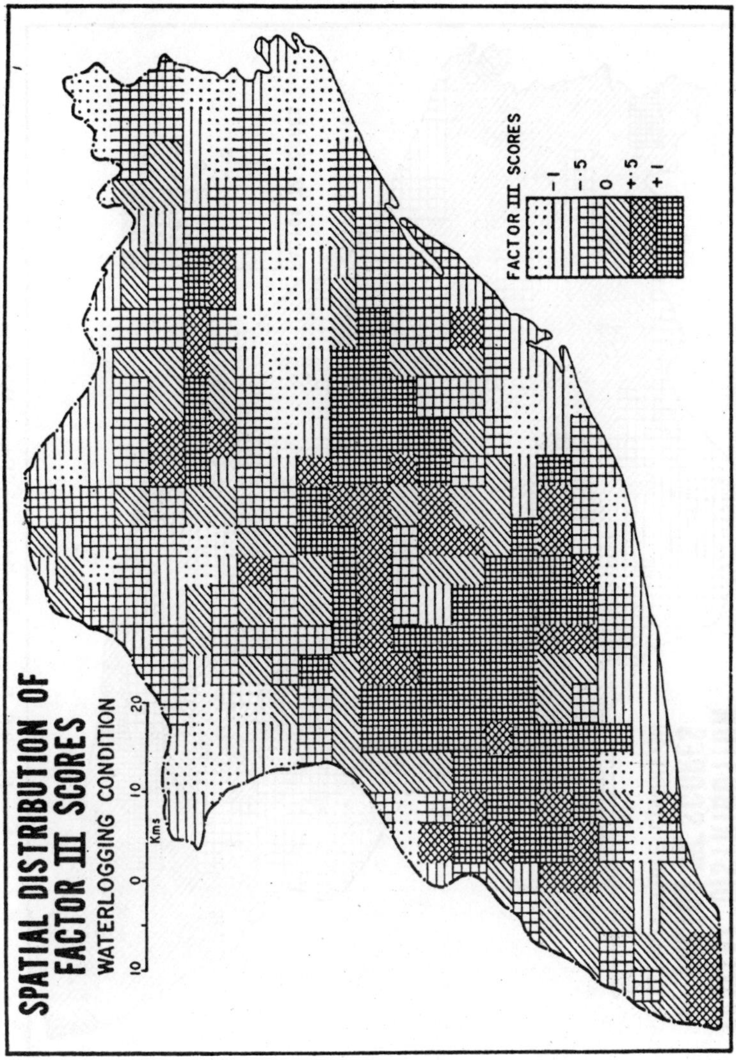

Fig. 9.7: Spatial Distribution of Factor III Scores

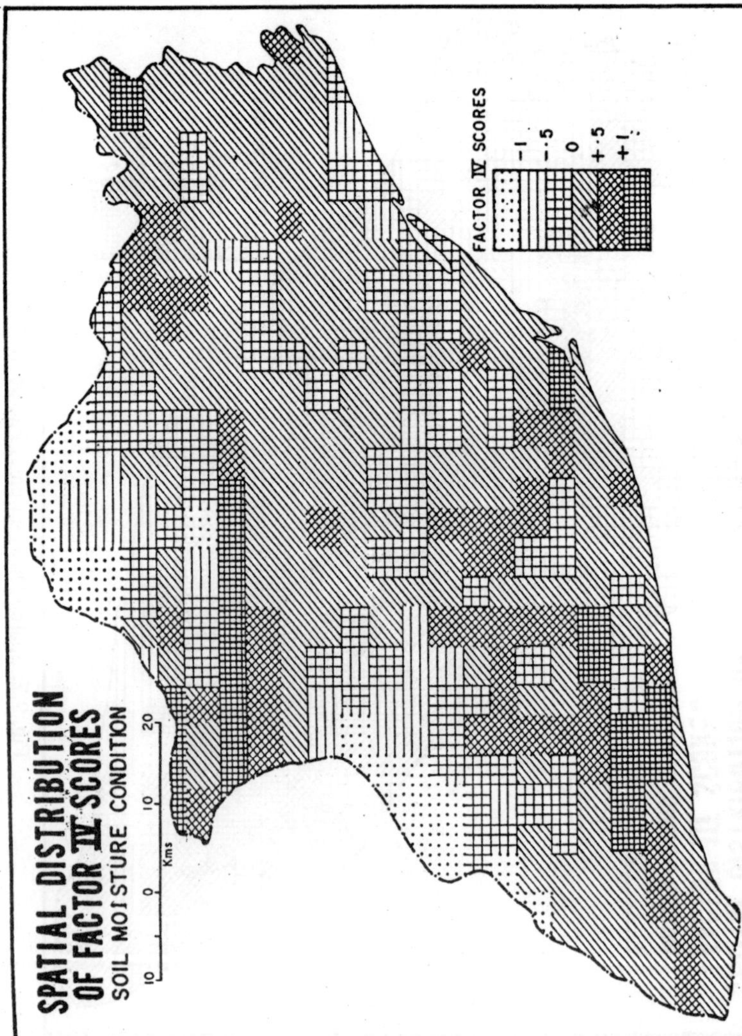

Fig. 9.8: Spatial Distribution of Factor IV Scores

total area and is mainly found near the periphery of the land with scores 0.0 to 0.5. The land with low scores, i.e. between -0.5 to -0.1 covers 7.2 per cent of the total area and is found mainly in three patches. The first patch consists of parts of Salepur and Kendrapara police stations; the second patch is found in Balianta and Balipatna police stations; and the third patch in Paradeep and Kujang police stations. The land with very low scores is found in two patches, i.e. in Mahanga, Kendrapara police stations and in Balianta, Pipili, Delang police stations and covers 6.7 per cent of the total area. The land with high moisture content is found mainly along the main river Mahanadi and northern side of Chilika Lake and along the muddy coast. The land with low moisture content is found mainly in the western and northern highlands and along some sandy coast.

Factor V Scores

The spatial distribution of factor V is illustrated in Fig. 9.9. Of the total area, 15.5 per cent of the land shows very high scores, i.e. more than 1.0, which is found mainly in two patches. The first patch consists of part of Kendrapara, Pattamundai and Mahanga police stations and the second patch is found in Nuagaon, Gobindpur and Nimapara police stations. The land having high scores, i.e. between 0.5 to 1.0 is found mainly nearly the and with very high scores. This type of land covers 15.7 per cent of the total study area. The land with scores between 0.0 to 0.5 is randomly distributed throughout the delta and covers 18.6 per cent of the total area. The land with scores between -0.5 to 0.0 is also found throughout the delta. One large patch of this category is found in the extreme southern portion of the delta. The land with low scores, i.e. between -0.5 to -1.0 covers 50.0 per cent of the total area and the land with very low scores, i.e. less than -1.0 covers 39 per cent of the total area. The latter is found mainly along the shores and southwestern part of the Puri district. The general trend is that the land with high water depth is found in north, northwestern and south central part of the delta and with low water depth is found along the coast. Besides these areas, the lands have medium water depth.

Factor VI Scores

The spatial distribution of factor VI scores is illustrated in Fig. 9.10. Of the total area, 9.3 per cent shows very high scores, i.e. more

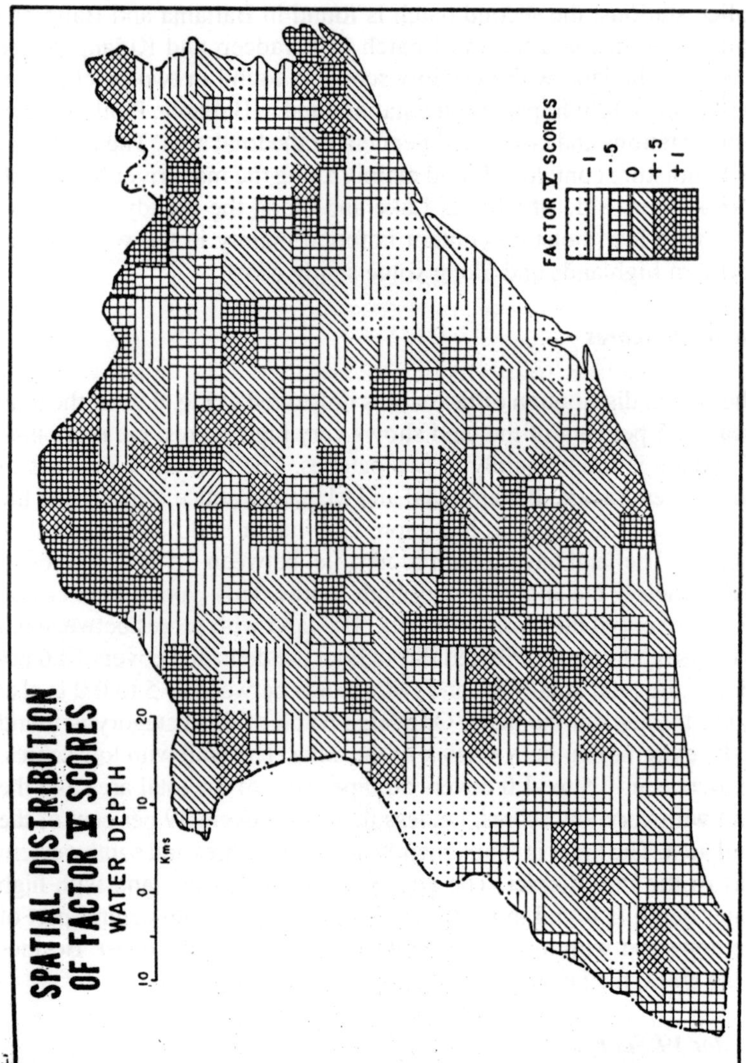

Fig. 9.9: Spatial Distribution of Factor V Scores

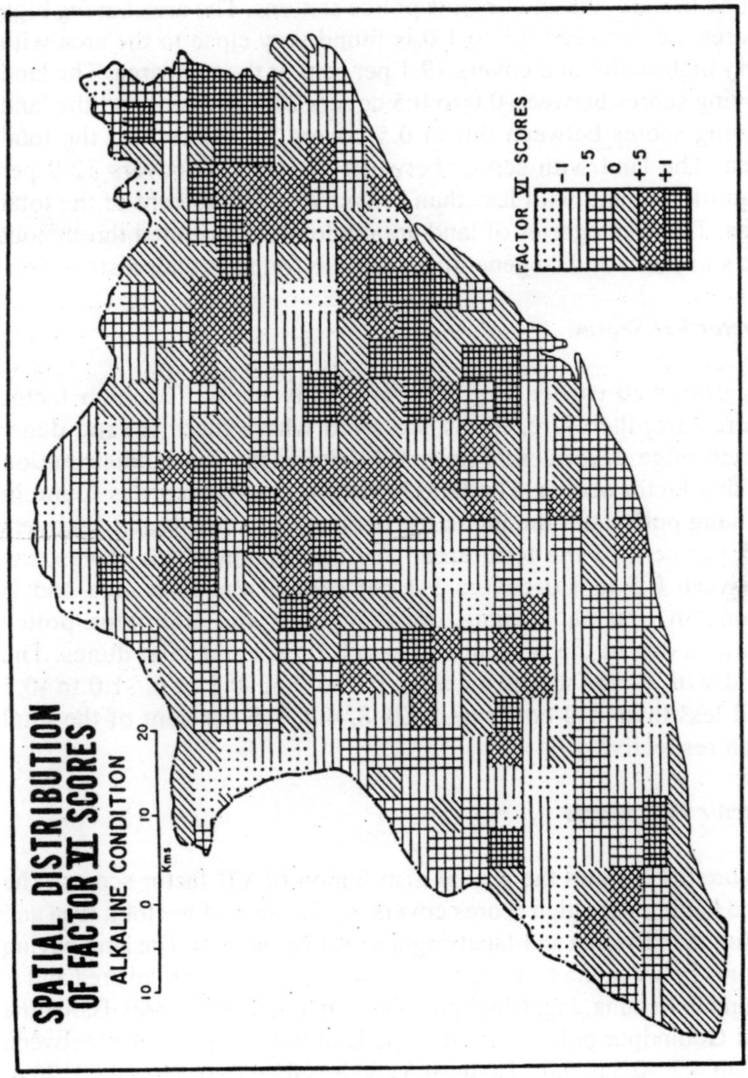

Fig. 9.10: Spatial Distribution of Factor VI Scores

than 1.0 and is found mainly in three patches. The first patch covers parts of Mahakalpara and the eastern side of Patkura police stations. The second patch is found in western side of Patkura police station, Kishorenagar and Jagatsinghpur police stations. The third patch is found in Balikuda and Ersama police stations. The area having high scores, i.e. between 0.5 to 1.0 is found very close to the area with very high scores and covers 19.1 per cent of the total area. The land having scores between 0.0 to 0.5 covers 24.7 per cent and the land having scores between 0.0 to 0.5 covers 24 per cent of the total area. The land with scores between -0.5 to -1.0 covers 12.9 per cent of land and with less than -1.0 covers 10 per cent of the total area. These categories of land are randomly distributed throughout the study area and no generalised trend is found in their distribution.

Factor VII Scores

As described earlier, the delta is mostly plain. The high factor scores are, therefore, found scattered where there is sand dune, beach ridge, levees etc. Figure 9.11 shows the spatial distribution of this factor scores. The land having very high score is found in Kujang police station due to the presence of sand dunes. It covers 0.5 per cent of the total area. The land having high scores, i.e. between 0.5 to 1.0 covers 3.3 per cent of the total area and is found in Ersama, Kujang, Jagatsinghpur and Balipatna police stations due to the presence of beach ridges and sand dunes. The land with factor scores between 0.0 to 0.5, -0.5 to 0, -1.0 to -0.5 and less than -1.0 cover 63.2, 26.8, 4.4, 1.8 per cent of the total area respectively.

Factor VIII Scores

Figure 9.12 shows the spatial distribution of VII factor scores. The land having very high scores covers 0.5 per cent of the total area and is found in Ersama and Jagatsinghpur police stations. The land having scores between 0.5 to 1.0 covers 13.6 per cent of the total area and is found in Ersama, Jagatsinghpur, Kendrapara, Pattamundai, Balipatna and Gobindpur police stations. The land with factor scores between 0.0 to 0.5, -0.5 to 0.0, -1.0 to -0.5 and less than -1.0 cover 47.3, 30.4, 6.7 and 1.5 per cent of the total area, respectively.

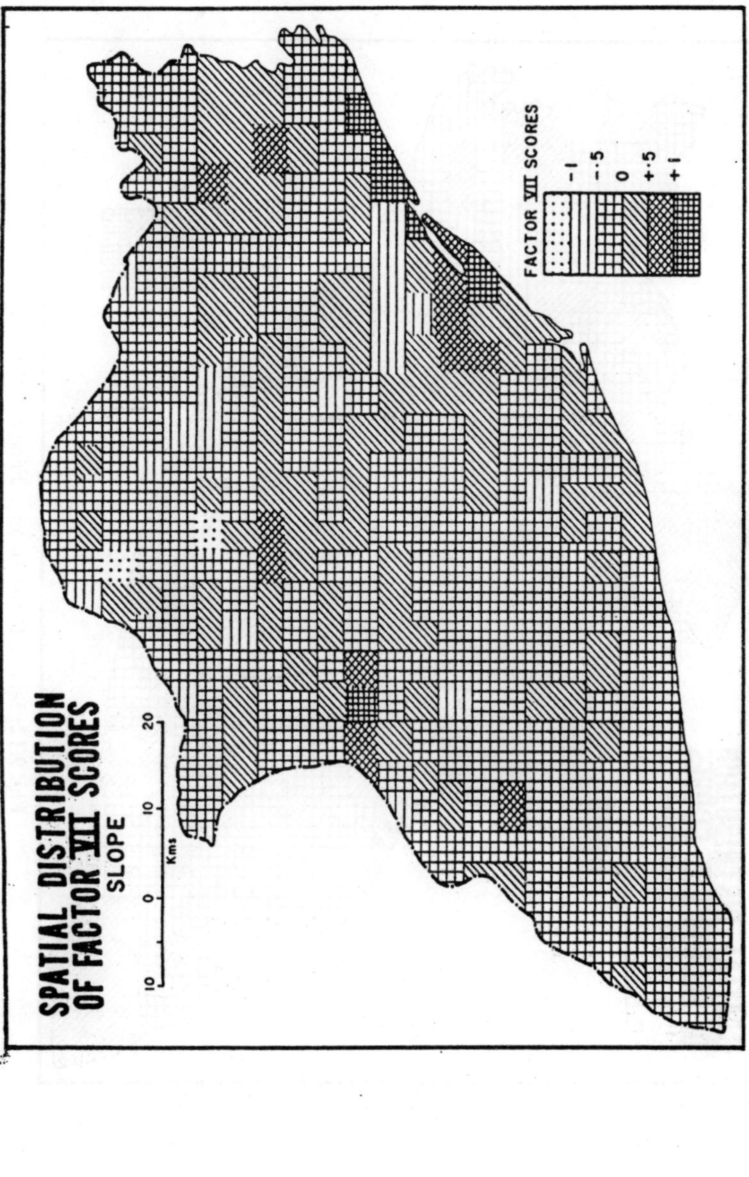

Fig. 9.11: Spatial Distribution of Factor VII Scores

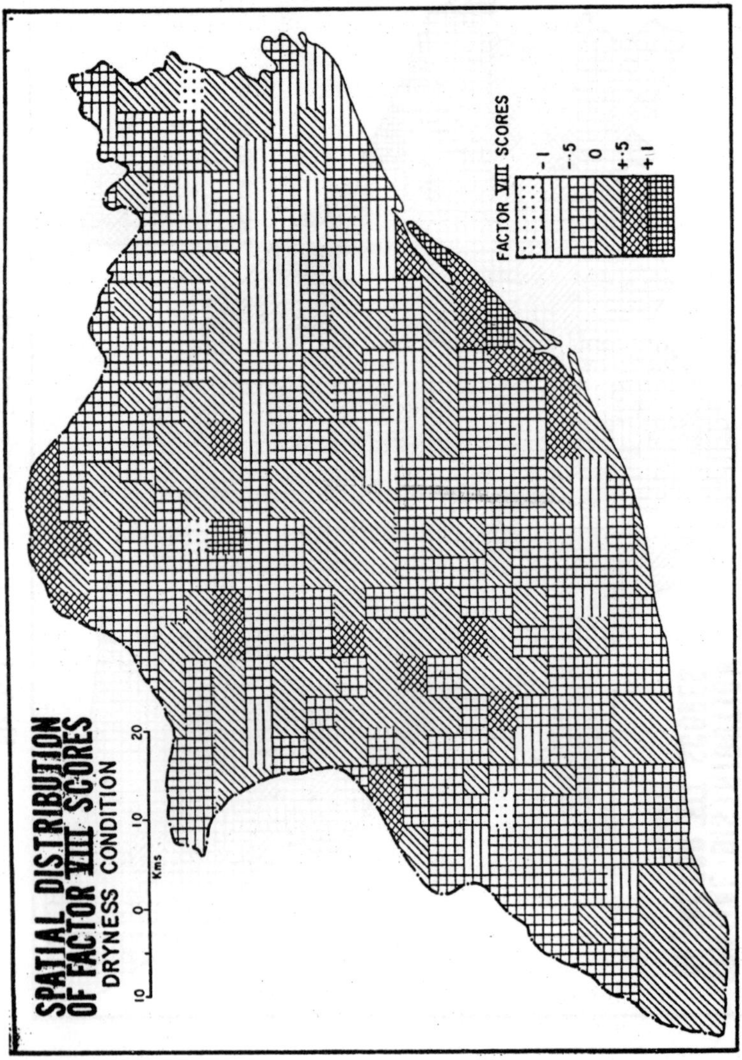

Fig. 9.12: Spatial Distribution of Factor VIII Scores

Land Characteristic Units

It is clear that the distribution maps of the eight factors reveal distinct areal patterns of each dimension. The final objective is to combine the evidence of first six factors to produce single composite framework of homogeneous land characteristics. The combination of first six factors has been selected because they together explain about 60 per cent of the total variance. In classifying the homogeneous area it has been kept in mind that there may be maximum homogeneity within group and maximum heterogeneity between different groups. There are some statistical techniques to delimit the homogeneous areas. Here the simple cross classification of the first four factor scores is attempted and very high scores of factor V and VI are taken into consideration to isolate the contiguous areal groupings. The selection of cutting points of factor scores is an important aspect in cross-classification. The cutting points should select meaningful divisions and a sufficient number of cutting points should be chosen to produce a reasonable number of divisions within each set of scores so that the number of homogeneous regions may be produced. Fig. 9.4 shows the frequency distribution of different size of factor scores. These maps have been considered in the selection of cutting points. The cutting points selected for factor I and II are as follows:

Factor I	*Factor II*
> 0.50	>0.50
0.00 to ±1.00	0.00 to ±1.00
<- 1.00	<-1.00

The cross-classification of factor I and II scores produces 9 types of combinations. These two factors account for nearly 28 per cent of the total variance in universe of the data. This cross-classification of the first two factors provides distinct break down of the delta into its component parts (Fig. 9.13). Nine breakdowns are:

1a Low score of factor I (defining soil nutrients) and factor II (defining quality of water)

1b Low score of factor I and medium score of factor II

1c Low score of factor I and high score of factor II

2a Medium score of factor I and low score of factor II

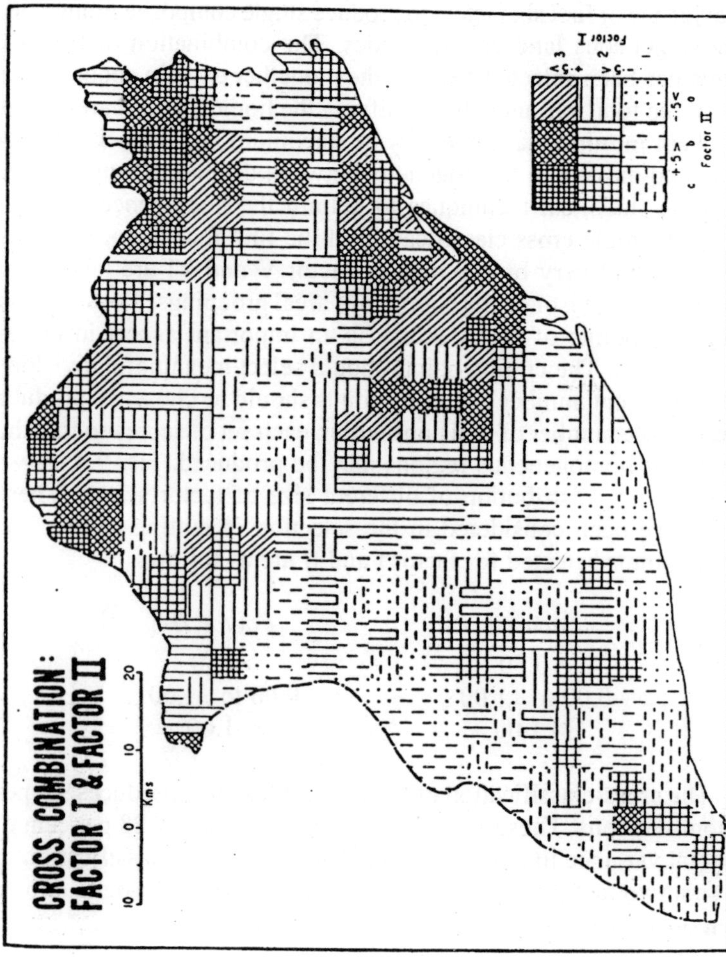

Fig. 9.13: Cross Combination: Factor I & Factor II

2b Medium score of factor I and medium score of factor II
2c Medium score of factor I and high score of factor II
3a High score of factor I and low score of factor II
3b High score of factor I and medium score of factor II
3c High score of factor I and high score of factor II.

In order to get some meaningful areal groups of 388 observed units, the above nine groups are reduced to five types. Two groups show little difference in their score values, therefore, they are combined to form one type. Thus, 3c and 3b are combined to form the land characteristic unit named as land having very high soil nutrients and poor quality of water (1) 3a and 2a are combined to form the land characteristic unit named as land having very high soil nutrients and very good quality of water, (2) 2c and lc are put together to form the land characteristic unit named as land having low soil nutrient and low water quality, (3) la and lb are combined together to form the land having low soil nutrient and good water quality (4). 2b is termed as land having medium soil nutrients and medium water quality (5).

On the basis of the cross-classification of these first two factors, the area is not divided into homogeneous land characteristic units, as they explain only 28 per cent of the total variance. To remove this problem, factor III and IV scores are also cross-classified like factor I and II (Fig. 9.14). Like the previous one, the cross-classification of factor III and IV provides nine breakdowns. These are:

la	Low score of factor III	(defining mainly drainage waterlogging conditions) and
	Low score of factor IV	(defining moisture condition of soil)
1b	Low score of factor III	and medium score of factor IV
1c	Low score of factor III	and high score of factor IV
2a	Medium score of factor III	and low score of factor IV
2b	Medium score of factor III	and medium score of factor IV
2c	Medium score of factor III	and high score of factor IV
3a	High score of factor III	and low score of factor IV
3b	High score of factor III	and medium score of factor IV
3c	High score of factor III	and high score of factor IV

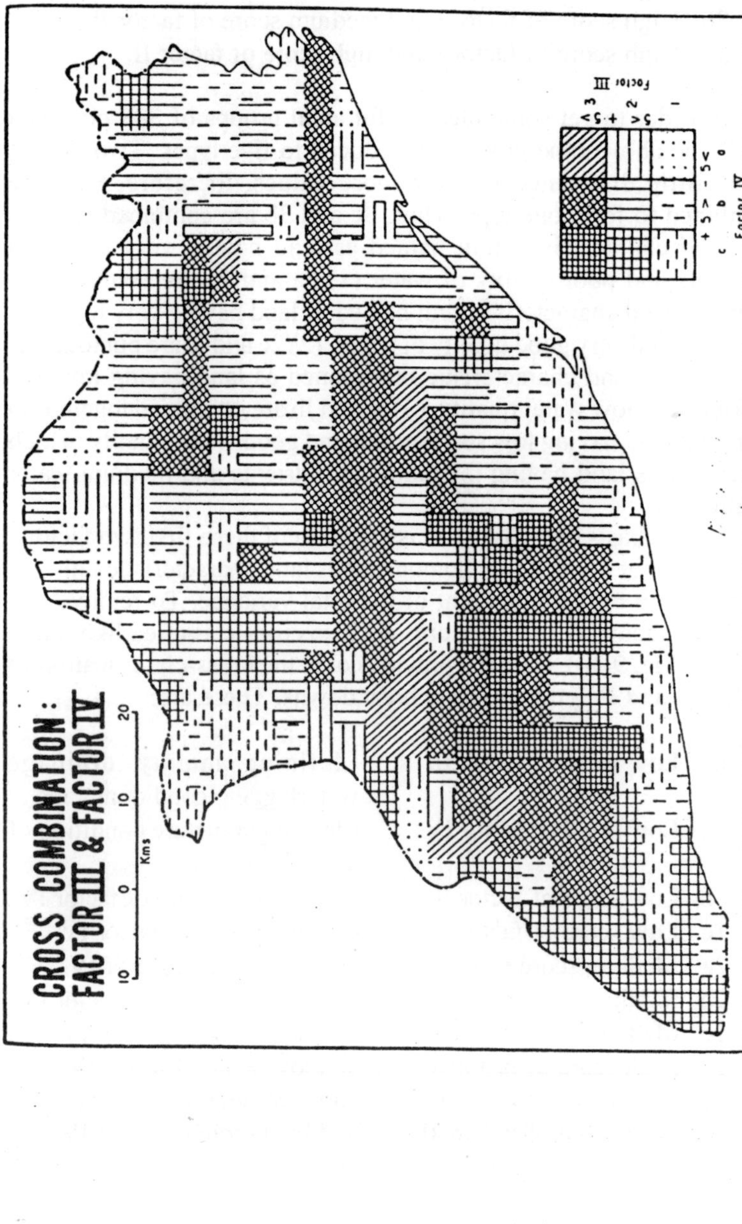

Fig. 9.14: Cross Combination: Factor III & Factor IV

Here, also 3b, 3c; lc, 2c; 3a, 2a; and la and lb are combined to form one type. The combination of 3b and 3c forms the land characteristic unit called as waterlogged area (1). But the combination of 3a and 2a does not form waterlogged area (2). In these land characteristic units, though the drainage density and extent of waterbodies are high, the soil moisture is low. When there is any seepage from drains or waterbodies and during flood time, the soil has the capacity to hold the water. The combination of lc and 2c forms the land having high moisture condition which is not waterlogged (3). The combination of la and lb forms the land having low moisture condition and no waterlogging condition (4). 2b is termed as the land having medium waterlogging problem and medium moisture (5).

In the final areal grouping of 388 units, the cross classification of factor I and II has been taken as base. Some changes, wherever required, are also incorporated considering the cross-classification of factor III and IV scores and very high score of factor V and VI. It is found that the waterlogged areas and areas having high moisture conditions are mainly found in the areas coming under 4th and 5th group of factor I and II cross-classification. In this case the latter characters of land lose their significance and are called as waterlogged or land having high soil moisture according to their dominance. The 5th group from factor I and II cross-classification and 3rd, 4th and 5th groups from factor III and IV cross-classification are deleted from the final land characteristic units as these characteristics of land are very common and dominated by other important characteristics. Besides very high scores of factor V showing land having very high water depth and very high scores of factor VI describing alkaline land are taken into account they dominate other characteristics. In the final areal grouping, personal field observation has also been taken into account. The final land characteristic units produced in this way are shown in Figure 9.15. The principal characteristics and quality of the various delineated areas are described in the following paragraphs.

Land with both Good Soil and Good Water Quality

This type of land covers about 33.5 per cent of the total area of the Mahanadi delta. It is found mostly in the northern part of the delta,

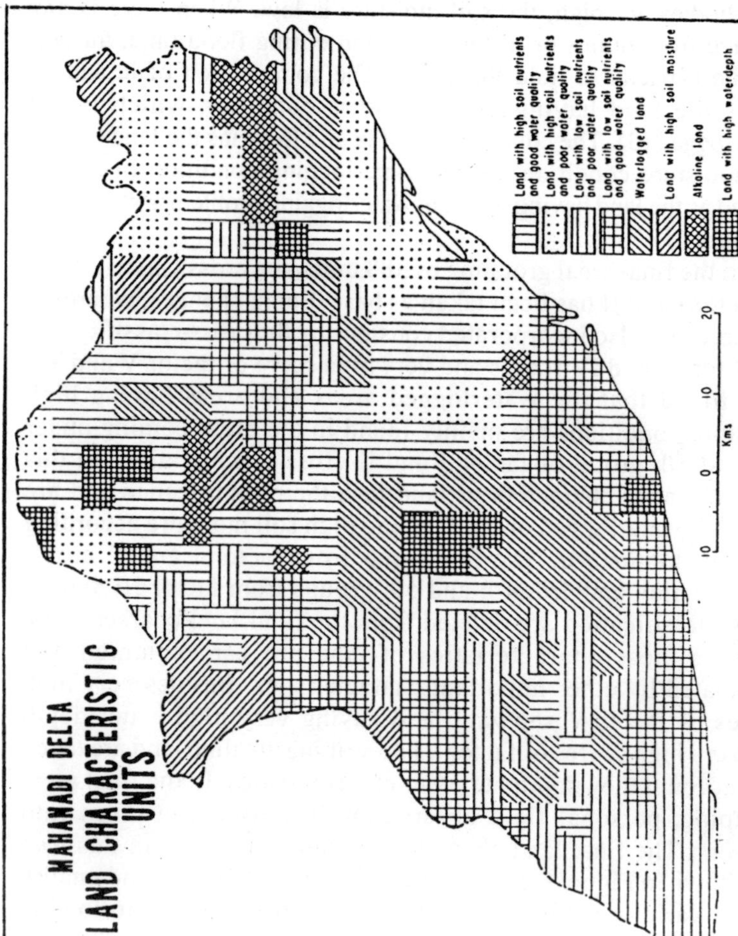

Fig. 9.15: Mahanadi Delta Land Characteristic Units

i.e. in Cuttack, Jagatsinghpur and Kendrapara districts. In Puri district, this type of land is very small. Large parts of the Kendrapara, Salepur, Jagatsinghpur and Tirtol police stations are covered under this land. This type of land shows very good quality of water as water contains low proportion of sodium chloride, total dissolved solids and fairly less proportion of alkaline content. The soil quality is also good in this region, i.e. potassium, calcium and magnesium percentage of the upper soil is high. But one important soil nutrient, i.e. phosphorous content of the soil is not high. The area coming under this type of land is not waterlogged, and the average water depth is little high. The latter does not have any negative impact as in extreme summer it does not go beyond 5 metre. Though in Puri district this type of land is less, but their quality is better than the same type of land of other districts of the study area due to its low water depth.

Land with Good Soil Quality and Poor Water Quality

This type of land covers 10.6 per cent of the total area of the study area and is found mainly in four patches. One large patch is found towards the northeastern part of the delta, i.e. in Mahakalpara and Rajnagar police station; the second patch is found along the coast of Ersama police station; the third patch in south of Tirtol and north of Balikuda police station; and the fourth at the northern extreme of the delta, i.e. in Mahanga and Kendrapara police station. This type of land shows very high quality of soil as the soil nutrients, i.e. potassium, magnesium and calcium contents are more than the 1st category of soil identified. But the water quality is poor. The total dissolved solid, sodium, chloride content of water is high. The 1st two patches of this are called Little Sunderban as mangrove forests and swamps are found here. The low water quality in this region is perhaps due to saline water intrusion during high tides. The drainage density is low in this area allowing sea waters easily to penetrate into the soil and contaminate groundwater. If the water quality is treated properly, this land may become the best of all in the Mahanadi delta which can give maximum production. Otherwise, if properly managed, a good mangrove ecosystem can be developed here which is the bare need during this time.

Land with both Low Soil and Low Water Quality

This type of land covers 14.5 per cent of the total area and is found mainly in low patches. The large patch is found towards southwestern part, i.e. north of lake Chilika. This covers most part of Delang and Satyabadi police station and some part of Pipili police station. Another patch is found in Kujang police station mainly in and around Paradip port. Besides, this type of land is also found haphazardly in Cuttak, Jagatsingpur and Kendrapara police stations. This category of land is the worst of all. However, it has been found that the larger proportion of this category is under forest or tree crops in comparison to other areas. But most part of this category is under cultivation, though the production is low. Here, the water quality is very bad, but the soil quality varies from medium to low. Some extent of this area is waterlogged and drainage density is moderately high. Therefore, this area is best for brackish water pisciculture. Besides, salinity resistant vegetation can be grown here to bring more area under forest, as the percentage of forest area is very low in the study area.

Land with Low Soil Quality and Good Water Quality

This type of land covers 15.0 per cent of the total area of the delta and is found in four patches. One patch is found along the southern coast, where the coastline is regular and covers coastal part of Puri Sadar, Gop and Kakatpur police stations; the second patch is found in doab II and doab IV; and the third and fourth patches are found in Balipatna and Pipili police stations, respectively. In this region the soil nutrients, such as potassium, calcium and magnesium are very low. But water quality is good though not very good. Sometimes, the question arises about the water quality of the first part, i.e. the land along southern coastline. It may be due to the combination of a number of factors like moderately high drainage density, moderately large area under waterbodies and regular coastline. In this region if the soil nutrients are applied properly the land can give good production.

Waterlogged Land

This type of land covers 13.7 per cent of the total area and is found mainly in the Puri district and southern part of Jagatsinghpur district. In this type of land, both the drainage density and extent of waterlogging is high. The soil moisture condition is also high. As the moisture condition is high, the soil has little capacity to hold the extra water. When there is seepage from drains, waterbodies and particularly during flood time, the extra water remains standing on the land. During rainy season the condition becomes very bad. In this region phosphorous content and *p*H value of soil are high. But due to waterlogging problem this land does not give high production during kharif season. If this type of land is properly cultivated during rabi season the production may rise to a considerable degree. People cultivate this land after March by irrigating from the drainage channels.

Land with High Soil Moisture

This type of land covers only 6.2 per cent of the total area of the delta and is found in four patches. The first patch covers almost all parts of Cuttack Sadar police station; the second in eastern part of Kissennagar and western part of Marsaghai police station; the third in Kendrapara police station; and the fourth in Balipatana police station. In this type of land, moisture condition is very high; but it is not waterlogged. The main soil nutrients, phosphorous and potassium content of soil are moderate here. Lateritic soil is totally absent and moisture content is so high that if monsoon fails, this type of land is less affected. Crops can be grown though the production becomes less.

Alkaline Land

This type of land covers 3.9 per cent of the total area and is found in northern part of Kujang, southern part of Mahakalpara police station, and in Kissennagar police station. The quality of this type of land is also bad. The alkalinity content of water is very high. The area is not waterlogged. The soil moisture is low and the soil quality is moderate. Only the phosphorous content of soil is high here. Overall, the water is unsuitable for drinking and irrigation purposes.

Land with High Water Depth

This category of land covers 2.6 per cent of the total area and is found in some parts of Mahanga, Salepur, Kendrapura Niali, Nimapara and Balipatna police stations. Here, the water depth is very high and the extent of waterlogging is low. But drainage density is farily high, phosphorous content of soil is low and the water is little alkaline.

Conclusions

Eight land dimensions have been identified in the Mahanadi delta on the basis of secondary data, using reliable statistical techniques. The eight dimensions identified by the factor scores reveal that they are not evenly distributed within the study area and there are spatial variations in their intensity. The factor score maps show that there are very little problems in some areas, and in other areas, a number of problems exist simultaneously. The delta has been divided into eight different land characteristic units on the basis of cross-classification of the important factors. The detail information about each type of these units has been provided for evaluation of their quality.

REFERENCES

Agarwal, A. (1982) *The State of India's Environment*, New Delhi: Centre for Science and Environment.

Agarwal, A. and Narain, S. (eds.) (1985) The State of India's Environment, 1984-85: *The Second Citizen Report*, New Delhi: Centre for Science and Environment.

Alam, S. and Siddiqui, M.F. (1984) "Fertility status of soils in different altitudinal zones of Garhwal Himalaya", *The Geographer*, 31 (l): 68 -76.

Christian, C.S. and Steward, G.A. (1968) *Proceedings of the Toulouse Conference*, UNESCO, Paris, 233-280.

Davidson, D.A. (1986) *Land Evaluation*, New York: Von Nostrand Reinhold.

Food and Agricultural Organisation of the United Nations (1990) *Land Evaluation for Development*.

Kumar, A. and Pandey, R.N. (1989) *Wasteland Management in India*, New Delhi: Ashish Publishing Company.

Panda, G.K. and Sinha, B.N. (1990) "Flood hazard of the coastal and deltaic environment of Orissa: A study of their nature and characteristics", in B.N. Sinha (ed.) *Ecosystem Degradation in India*, New Delhi: Ashish Publications House, 46-61.

Pant, B.R., Joshi R.C. and Jalal D.S. (1989) "Land capability classification model for Kota Dune, Kumaun Himalaya", in B.N. Mishra (ed.) *Land Utilization and Management in India*, Allahabad,: Chugh Publication, pp. 209-217.

Pattnayak, K.C., Tripathy, S.N., Sinha, B.N., and Tripathy, A. (1988) "Urban ecosystem planning in Cuttack-Bhubaneswar urban complex", in K.K. Dubey and A.K. Singh (eds) *Urban Environment in India: Problems and Prospects*, New Delhi: Inter-India Publications, pp. 375-385.

Rao, K.N. and Vaidyanadhan, R. (1990) "Landuse capability studies from aerial photo interpretation: A case study from Krishna delta," in B.N. Mishra (ed) *Land Utilization and Management in India*, Allahabad: Chugh Publications, pp. 1-19.

Rao, M.S. (1985) Land suitability of the Madurai district using remote sensing data, Tamil Nadu". *The Geographer*, 32(1): 81-92.

Singh, A.L. and Ansari, M.A. (1984) "Fertility status of Aligarh soils", *The Geographer,* 31(1): 32-42.

Singh, R.R. (1989) "Land capability classification in Manipur valley", *Geographical Review of India*, 47 (4): 59-66.

Sinha, A.K. and Chhotaraya, D.K. (1990) "An environmental appraisal of the Mahanadi delta in relation to geology and geomorphology", in B.N. Sinha (ed) *Ecosystem Degradation in India*, New Delhi: Ashish Publishing House, pp. 79-84.

Sinha, B.N. (1968) "Mahanadi delta", in R.L. Singh (ed.) *India: Regional Studies*, Calcutta: Indian National Committee for Geography.

Sinha, B.N. (1995) *Geography of Orissa*, New Delhi: National Book Trust.

Symons, L. (1978) Agricultural Geography, London: Bell and Hyman Ltd.

Water and Land Management Institute (1990) *Annual Report*, Pratap Nagar, Bhubaneswar.

Whyte, R.O. (1976) *Land and Land Appraisal*, The Hague: Dr. W. Jank B.V. Publishers, 233-280.

Yadav, H.R. (1985) *Genesis and Utilization of Wasteland: A Case Study of Sultanpur District*, New Delhi: Concept.

10

Comparative Study of Visual and Digital Remote-Sensing Techniques for Desert Landform Analysis Using Landsat and IRS Images

AMAL KAR, T.K. GHOSH, SURENDRA SINGH and S. VISWANATHAM

The utility of satellite data products in the field of land resources studies is now well recognized. In fact, since the launching of the first Earth Resources Technological Satellite (ERTS 1; renamed afterwards as Landsat 1) from the USA in 1972, satellite remote-sensing has gradually become a major source of information for studies in geomorphology, geology, soil survey, vegetation, water resources, land utilization and a host of other related fields. The vast improvement in the resolution of the images in recent years, judicious slicing of the electromagnetic spectrum, synoptic viewing of wider areas, case availability of the products, repetitive coverage of an area and case of mapping have all now made the satellite remote-sensing more indispensable, almost totally replacing the vertical aerial photographs, for resource identification and mapping. Data products of the Landsat Thematic Mapper (TM: 30 m resolution), Indian Remote Sensing Satellite IRS-1A (Liss I: 72.5 m; Liss II: 36.25 m) and the French SPOT (MLA: 20 m; PLA:10 m) satellite are now widely used by the researchers in India. Most studies are, however, being carried out through visual interpretation of the printed outputs, although several studies in this country and elsewhere have also indicated the vast potentiality of computer-aided (or digital) image-processing. The capability of the computer system to handle effectively a large amount of data within a short period of time and its ability to perform numerous analysis on the images within certain limits could hardly be achieved through visual interpretation of the printed output. On the other hand, the interpreter is the best judge on the accuracy of the units, whether drawn through machine processing or through visual interpretation. Through the use of his own intellect he can even produce better results from visual interpretation, without procession the image through computer. In the light of the above arguments the potential user becomes confused as to which technique is more useful and profitable for his purpose.

The present study was undertaken with a view to testing the relative performance of the different digital image-processing techniques *vis-à-vis* the conventional visual remote-sensing in identification and mapping of the geomorphological features of the Indian desert. Another objective of the study was to find out the application potentials of the IRS-1A images, as compared to the Landsat TM images, especially in the field of geomorphologic studies, both in respect of the visual interpretation and digital interpretation.

The methodologies were tested in the Kaparda-Tigra-Pipar-Tilwasni area in the south-eastern part of the Jodhpur district, covering 1,054 sq. km area. Many of the terrain features observed within the desert are represented here.

Methodology

The study was carried out in two stages. The initial study was carried out through visual interpretation of images followed by field survey. This was followed by digital image-processing. Hence, two different sets of methodology were adopted for the two stages.

(*a*) *Stage* I*: Visual Interpretation Techniques*

(i) Two 1:50,000 scale subscenes of the standard false colour composites (FCCs) of Landsat TM scene 148-042, dated January 9, 1986, were visually interpreted. The standard FCC is a combination of bands 2, 3 and 4. Single-band images were not tried, as earlier experiences indicated that standard FCCs provide much better information for landform mapping than the single-band images (bands 3 and 4).

(ii) The Survey of India topographical sheets of the area at 1:50,000 scale were also interpreted. Incidentally, these topographical sheets were prepared after interpretation of large scale aerial photographs and detailed field survey and, hence, have more than 99 per cent positional accuracy for the major features shown in the maps. The base map was, therefore, prepared from these topographical sheets.

(iii) The landforms were identified and marked on the FCC on the basis of their tone, texture and pattern, and the boundaries were transferred on to the base map.

(iv) A rapid field survey was carried out to confirm the boundaries of different units.

(v) Based on the above, the boundaries were readjusted and the final map was prepared.

Subsequently a similar exercise was carried out on the 1:250,000 scale FCC of the IRS-1A Liss-II B2 subscene of 32-49, dated December 8, 1988, to find out if the IRS products are comparable to the TM products.

(b) Stage II: Digital Image-Processing Techniques

(i) The computer compatible tapes (CCTs) of the Landsat TM scene 184-041, quadrant 1 (containing the area of interest) for April 18, 1987, were loaded in the VIPS 32 image-processing system that is configured around a VAX 11/780 host computer.

(ii) Since the generated images indicated a number of stripes the images were restored through *destripping*.

(iii) A raw FCC was generated from the combination of bands 2, 3, and 4.

(iv) Often the data from various wavelengths, registered in the multi-band images, convey almost the same information, as they fail to appear differently. To reduce such interband correlation in the multi-band data *principal component analysis* (PC) was launched through KLOEVE function that performs factor analysis. Band 1, 2 and 4 were used for the PC analysis. The resultant first new axis or component (PC 1) represented the maximum accounted variance (or information), while PC 2 and PC 3 represented gradually decreasing information.

(v) *Band ratioing* was carried out to reduce the inter-band correlation of information in two-band images. The ratio images were prepared by dividing the digital number (DN) in one band by the corresponding DN in the other and for each pixel. The function was especially launched to suppress the effects of vegetation and to enhance the terrain band palaceochannel features. The ratio outputs were obtained for bands 4/1, 5/1, 3/4 and (1-5)/(1+5).

(vi) A number of *filtering techniques* were also used to extract or enhance certain features in the images through pixel-by-pixel transformation of the image on the basis of the relationship of a pixel's grey level value with that in its neighbouring pixels, thereby removing the unwanted values from the data and highlighting some desired trends. Only spatial domain functions were used.

For *edge extraction* EXTCONT function was lauched with Kirsh operator "that provides maximum compass gradient magnitude about an image point, ignoring the central pixel" (RRSSC, 1988), and with Roberts operator that provides the DN to a pixel on the basis of total diagonal variation in the pixel values across it.

For *edge enhancement* of the features AMECONT function was tried through Roberts operator. The mixing factor was taken as 0.9.

All the functions were carried out on 3×3 pixel windows. TM bands 2, 3, 4 and 7 were used for the above purposes. In the first combination bands 2, 3 and 4 were used, wherein vegetation appears in red. In the second combination bands 3, 4 and 7 was used, wherein vegetation appears in green.

(vii) Apart from the above, attempts were made to classify the images on the basis of homogeneity of the spectral signature of pixels in different bands—a system known as multispectral classification. Although we had options for both the supervised and unsupervised classification schemes, *supervised classification* was chosen, wherein independent information on different terrain types, generated from the field-based knowledge and visual interpretation of FCCs, were used to define a number of training areas.

The maximum likelihood method was then used to perform the classification, especially through the stages of statistical analysis of the training areas, reliability test on those training areas and finally calculation of the probability of a pixel value occurring in different classes, followed by assigning of the most likely class to it. A pixel which hand a lower probability of belonging to all the classes defined through training areas was assigned to "reject class".

Subsequently, based on the experiences gained, some of the above techniques were tested on the Liss II B2 scene of 32-49, dated December 8, 1988.

The methods and general application potentials of the different digital image-processing techniques are described lucidly in Sabins (1978), Colwell (1983), Curan (1985), and RRSSC (1988).

Results

(*a*) *Stage I: Visual Interpretation of Landsat TM Data*

For the visual interpretation and mapping of the morphological features, criteria and characteristics, which could be tested in the digital processing stage also, were considered appropriate. Hence, the conventional system of classifying the older alluvial plain into depth classes was not attempted. Instead, a textuaral classification was carried out. Moreover, to accommodate the major mappable tonal variations in different units some less important sub-units had to be mapped (i.e. alluvial plain with granite outcrops). The following 11 landform units were identified and mapped, along with their sub-units (Fig. 10.1).

1. *Hills*: Isolated hills of granite and metamorphic formations occur near Rian, Rawaniyana, Soniya and Khejarala. 40 to 60 m high quartzite hills near Rian and Rawaniyana are elongated and narrow-crested. These appear as lighter streaks

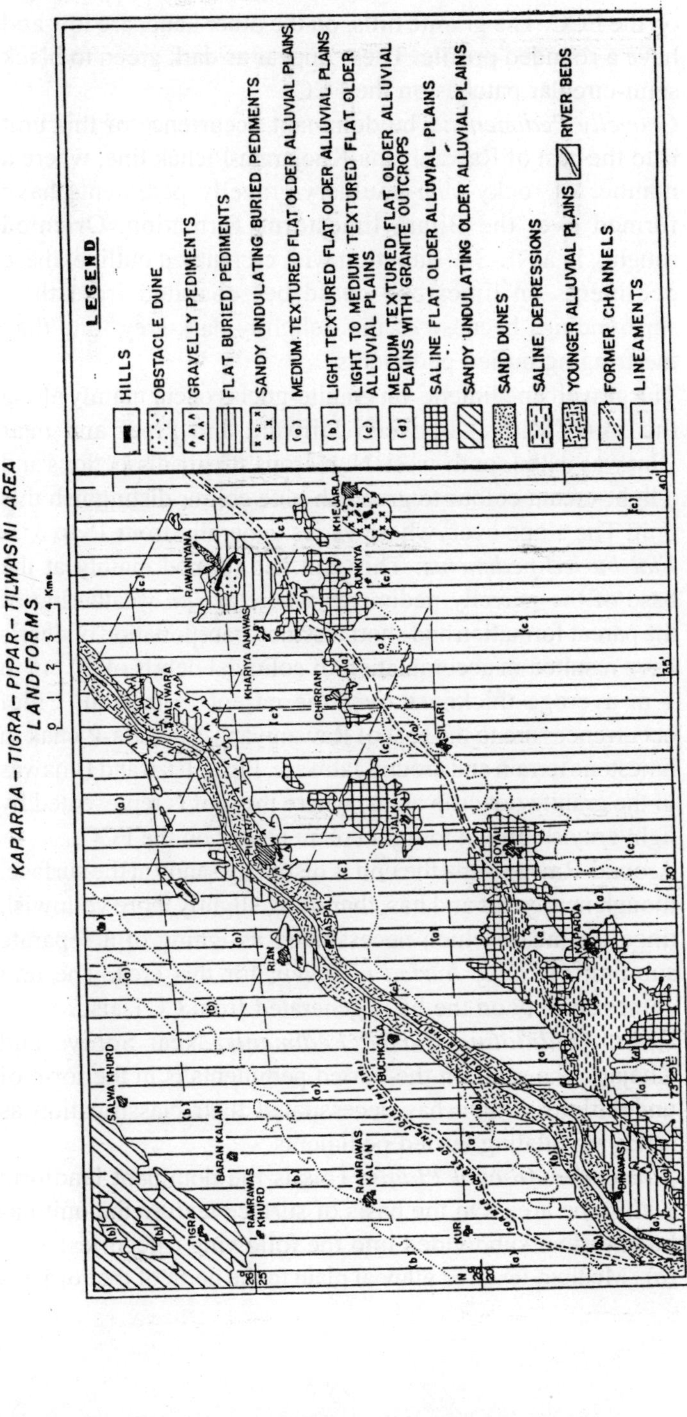

Fig. 10.1: Kaparda – Tigra – Pipar – Tilwasni Area

on the FCC. The granite hills, on the other hand, are low and have a rounded profile. These appear as dark green to black semi-circular patches on the FCC.

2. *Gravelly Pediments*: The dominant occurrence of this unit is to the east of Rawaniyana-Khejarala-Pichak line, where a number of rocky-*cum*-bouldery/gravelly pediments have formed over the Bilara limestorne formation. Oriented roughly in a NE-SW direction with crenulated outline, these pediments on limestone could be separated from their surroundings because of their slightly dark-grey tone than the fringing buried pediments.

   The gravelly pediments on granite-gneiss occur mainly along the Jojri (Mithri) between Jaliwara and Pipar and near Binawas in the south-west. Numerous stream dissections and a light-cream colour to greenish blue colour distinguish this unit. The slope everywhere varies generally from 1° to 3°.
3. *Flat buried pediments*: This unit has formed mainly at the base of the gravelly pediments where *in situ* weathering of the parent formation and short distance transportation of debris have resulted in accumulation of colluvial debris of 30 cm to 1 m average thickness over the parent formation. Chief occurrences are to the east of Rawaniyana-Khejarla-Pichak in limestone terrain and around Jaliwara, Pipar, Rian and Binawas in the granite out crop areas, where the unit is represented by light greyish brown to light cream colour on the FCC.

   Around Rawaniyana the unit is distinctly sandy at the surface, though nearly flat and has, therefore, slightly more yellowish tinge—a factor which necessitated assigning of a separate sub-unit of *sandy buried pediment* for this area. The unit comes sharply on the FCC generated from CCT also.
4. *Sandy Undulating Buried Pediments*: Near Soniya and Khejarla the sand on the buried pediments is in the form of undulations, which has necessitated their classification as sandy undulating buried pediments.
5. *Flat Older Alluvial Plains*: This is the dominant landform within the area. On the basis of surface texture the unit has been further subdivided into the following categories:

   (*a*) Medium-textured alluvial plain to the north of the Jojri and up to the limit of the light-textured alluvial plain further north and between the Jojri and the Kaparda Rann in the south,

(*b*) Light-textured alluvial plain, mainly in the north and north-west of the study area,

(*c*) Light-to-medium textured alluvial plain to the east and south of the Kaparda-Boyal-Anawas saline areas, and

(*d*) Medium-textured older alluvial plains with granite outcrops to the south-west of Kaparda.

While unit (a) is in dark brown to dark grey colour, unit (b) is in light yellowish brown colour, unit (c) has a mixture of both the colours and unit (d) has a dark bluish tinge over the brownish shed of unit (a).

6. *Saline Older Alluvial Plains*: In the central part of the study area the saline older alluvial plains occur as disjointed, roughly ENE-WSW oriented units between Khejarla and Binawas. The unit is easily marked from FCC because of its white to light brown colour with an occasional bluish tinge. The patterns created by these colours in the alluvial plains make the task of identification easier.

7. *Sandy Undulating Older Alluvial Plains*: This unit occurs to the north of Tigra-Salwa Khurd line and appears distinctly on the FCC with a light yellowish brown colour, superimposed by lighter yellow to white streaks of hummocks and dunes. The thickness of undulations and patterns created by the aeolian sand over the older alluvium are the main criteria for delineating its boundary.

8. *Sand Dunes*: A single dune of distinct longitudinal shape and height of 12 m occurs near Rawaniya. It could be identified properly on the TM FCC.

   The obstacle sand dunes occur at the foothills region of Rawaniyana and Soniya hills and are dissected. The unit could be sharply differentiated from the surrounding sandy terrain because of its tone and pattern.

9. *Saline Depressions*: The Kaparda Rann is the only major saline depression in the area. It has a milky-white tone, mixed with bluish tinge. Because of its white colour in the brownish-to-grey surroundings of the alluvial plain the unit's boundary is sharp and clear.

10. *River Beds*: The Luni and the Jojri (Mithri) are the only two major streams with a well-defined and mappable bed. The colour is white, but the pattern helps to avoid any possible misclassification with the saline depression of any other white areas.
11. *Younger Alluvial Plains*: This unit occurs along both the banks of the Luni and the Jojri as narrow strips and is widely cultivated. Wherever not presently under crops it appears on the FCC as light brown colour. In cropped areas it is in red colour. However, the unit is distinguishable from the surroundings because of its pattern.

Apart form the above, it was also possible to identify a few buried and abandoned stream courses. The most notable among these run through Khejarla and Anawas to the Kaparda Rann, while another major course was identified on the right bank side of the Jojri.

A number of lineament could also be marked across the area.

(b) Stage* II: *Digital Interpretation of Landsat TM Data

(i) The principal component analysis outputs were available in three planes of PC 1, 2 and PC 3, with gradually decreasing information content. Out of these, PC 2 was found very useful for lineament mapping. A number of E-W and N-S lineaments could be easily identified in the limestone terrain in the east and the sandy terrain elsewhere, some of them cutting across the present and former stream courses. The river Jojri appears to be structurally controlled at several places. At Pipar a number of lineaments cross each other. The FCC prepared from PC 1, 2 and 3 was, however, unintelligible. For example, the saline depressions, saline alluvial plains, rocky/gravelly pediments to the east of Pipar and the bed of the Luni appeared in dark green, perhaps because of higher reflectance. On the other hand, the course to the Jojri, parts of its younger alluvial plains and some of the medium-to-heavy textured older alluvial plains appeared in blue. The light-textured older alluvial plains appeared either in shades of yellow or in magenta. Many of the lineaments, however, appeared distinctly, as also the road network, including many village roads.

(ii) The ratio images did not yield satisfactory results, perhaps because of the month of imaging (April) when the land was dry and almost barren and reflectance from the sandy and rocky terrains was high in all bands.

(iii) Among the two filtering techniques the edge extraction method did not provide any desirable information for lineament mapping.

The edge enhancement techniques, however, proved to be very useful. The combination of bands 2, 3 and 4 provided sharp edges between the terrain types and most of the units could be easily separable visually from this output. The result was far better than the CCT-generated raw FCC and even slightly better, in some respects, than the FCC print that was available for visual interpretation. All the units identified through visual interpretation of FCC prints at 1:50,000 scale could be identified.

The combination of bands 3, 4 and 7 was, however, not so appealing, although the units were more or less distinct.

(iv) The supervised classification was launched on the standard FCC on bands 2, 3 and 4. After three attempts it was very much clear that a narrow range of spectral signature values over the scene, plus the occurrence of a dominantly limestone terrain in the east, were creating problems of accurate classification. Therefore, to counter the effects of mixing tones between the limestone and sandy terrains the image was split into two and classification was launched separately for the two areas. Finally, 10 major landform units were identified after amalgamation of some units (Table 10.1). For example, it was difficult to isolate the medium-textured alluvial plain from the light-to-medium textured alluvial plain. Similarly, the sandy undulating older alluvial plains could not be separated from the sandy flat or undulating buried pediments for similarity to tone. The hills and obstacle dunes had also to be merged together. The "reject class" was only 4.6 per cent.

Table 10.1: Landform Units Through Digital Image Processing (Supervised Classification)

	Units	*Pixels*	*Area* (*Sq.km*)	(*%*)
1.	Hills with obstacle dunes	25477	22.00	2.0
2.	Gravelly pediments			
	(i) On limestone	84491	76.00	7.3
	(ii) On granite-gneiss/metamorphics	17052	16.00	1.5
3.	Buried pediments	121189	110.00	10.4
4.	Flate older alluvial plains			
	(i) medium textured	361367	325.00	30.8
	(ii) light textured	254644	230.00	21.8
	(iii) with granite outcrops	2423	2.00	0.2
5.	Saline older alluvial plains	56490	51.00	4.9
6.	Sandy undulating older alluvial plains	66455	61.00	5.9
7.	Sand dunes	4289	5.00	0.5
8.	Saline depressions	37743	35.00	3.4
9.	Younger alluvial plains	44749	40.00	3.7
10.	River bed	34587	32.00	3.0
			1005.00	95.4
		Reject class	49.00*	4.6
		Total	1054.00	100.00

* Apart from true reject of 1.3 per cent the obstacle dune near Rawaniyana has been kept in the Reject Class.

Further processing and amalgamation of the units were carried over the output and a broad geomorphological-*cum*-geological map was obtained. A total of eight units could be mapped thus (Table 10.2) The former stream courses of the Jojri could be identified through the pattern created by association of colours. Some of the lineaments could also be identified due to a sharp break in tone.

However, there were some misclassifications.

(c) *Stage* III: *Comparison between IRS Liss II and Landsat TM Image Outputs*

The standard Liss II ECC print at 1:250,000 scale did not provide information comparable to that in TM FCC at 1:250,000 and 1:50,000 scales. This was, perhaps, because of the poor print quality and slightly poor resolution of Liss II images (36.25 m). Although most of the

Table 10.2: Broad Geomorphological-cum-Geological Classes through Digital Image Processing (Supervised Classification)

Unit	*Pixels*	*Area*	
		(Sq/km)	*(%)*
1. Limestone rocky/gravelly plains and ridges	84491	76.0	7.2
2. Granite-gneiss and metamorphic hills, plains and other outcrops	44952	40.0	3.8
3. Buried pediments	121189	110.0	10.4
4. Older alluvial plains	616011	555.0	52.6
5. Younger alluvial plains	44749	40.0	3.7
6. Sandy undulating plains and sand dunes	70744	66.0	6.4
7. Saline plains	94233	86.0	8.3
8. River beds	34587	32.0	3.0
		1005.0	95.4
	Reject class	49.0	4.6
	Total	1054.0	100.0

landform units could be identified, their boundaries were not clearly visible.

The principal component analysis highlighted the lineaments efficiently, both in the individual outputs of PC 1 and PC 2 and in the PC FCC (Fig. 10.2; *et al.*, 1989).

Band ratioing was not tried, nor was the edge extraction technique. The supervised classification was also not attempted, because of the misclassifications in the TM output.

On the other hand, the edge enhancement technique was tried, with a mixing factor of 0.9. The output revealed a sharp boundary between the units and thus helped in easy identification of unit boundaries (Fig. 10.3). All the units identified through visual interpretation of the TM FCC prints at 1:50,000 scale and the edge enhanced FCC output could be easily identified. The buried former channels could also be delineated from the output (Kar *et al.*, 1989).

Discussion

(a) Assessment of the Supervised Classification Outputs

The 10 major landform units appear to occur in their respective broad zones of occurrence. However, there are some distinct misclassifications in every unit due to similarity of signature in as different a unit as the

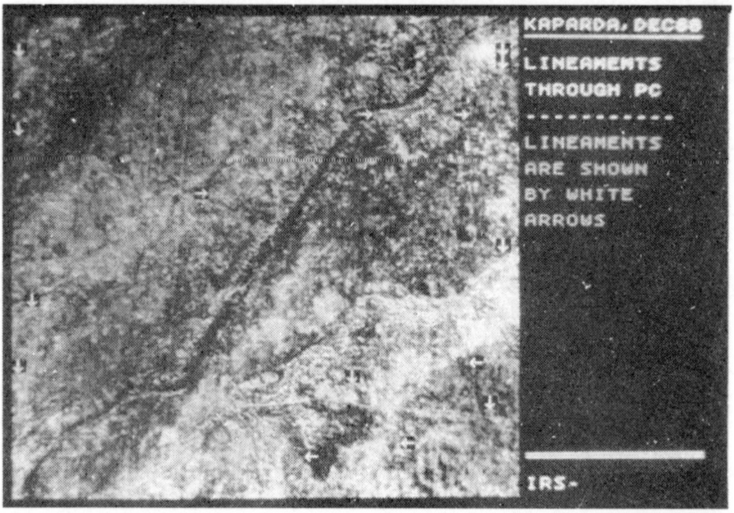

Fig. 10.2: Principal Component Analysis of Kaparda Area. Lineaments and Roads Get Highlighted. Original Output is in Colour, Generated from Liss II Scene of 8 December, 1988

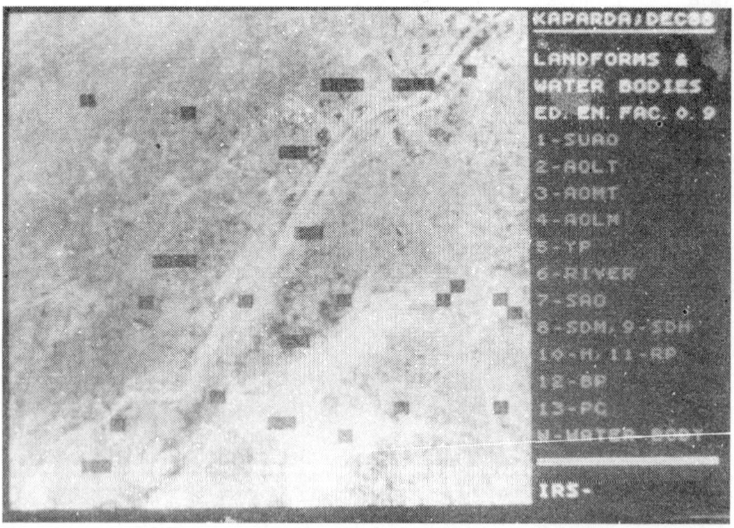

Fig. 10.3: Edge Enhanced FCC of Kaparda Area, with a Mixing Factor of 0.9. Unit Boundaries Get Sharpened. Original Output is in Colour, Generated from Liss II Scene of 8 December, 1988

limestone pediment and a sandy alluvial plain, or in the saline depression and a river bed. It is to be appreciated that the range of pixel values was very narrow and similar values occur in widely different units. Perhaps the data of a dry, cool season would have yielded better results. The other major factor of mixing was the occurrence of aeolian sand over almost all the units, so that the effects of it could hardly be erased from units where these are masking or affecting the major features. The following major misclassifications were noticed:

The colour of gravelly pediments on limestone-affected parts of the older alluvial plain to the east and south-east of Rawaniyana, especially between Mudaliya, Didiyaronki Dhani and Thilari Dhani. The pediment on granite-gneiss is partly affected by the colour of saline alluvial plain and saline depression, especially near Jaliwara. Parts of the older alluvial plain to the north of the Jojri are also affected by the colour of this pediment.

The buried pediments within the limestone terrain are affected along their fringes with gravelly pediments by the colour of light textured older alluvial plain. This is mainly because of the aeolian sand spread along the dissected slopes of gravelly pediments. However, the presence of the colour gives a misleading picture of the actual situation. In the south-west part of the buried pediment is affected by the colour of saline depression.

The amalgamated medium-textured and light-to-medium textured older alluvial plains have been recorded more correctly. To the north of Jojri the unit is affected by spotted distribution of the colour of light-textured alluvial plain, which is reasonably correct due to the nearness of the adjoining light-textured alluvial plain with much Aeolian sand.

The younger alluvial plains along the Luni and the Jojri are registered correctly, although the fringes of the saline depression and parts of medium-textured alluvial plains are also affected by its colour.

Apart from these drawbacks, representation of most other occurrences is fairly correct. As a first approximation it could be said that 70 to 80 per cent area is correctly classified and the rest is misclassified due to several constraints imposed by the spectral signatures, time of imaging, etc. Unfortunately, the 20-30 per cent misclassified areas could be very crucial. In a new area with only a little ground truth information one cannot be sure as to where those misclassified units should occur. This necessitates checking of the whole area through a conventional method. Further, the results did not improve upon the findings from the visual interpretation of TM FCC, even for a single category of landform, or for the paleo-channel.

(b) Assessment of the PC and the Edge-enhanced Outputs

As we had noted earlier, the PC outputs proved successful for lineament mapping, both from the TM and Liss-II scenes. Most of the lineaments are oriented N-S, NE-SW, E-W and NW-SE. Wherever these occur in association with favourable geomorphological features, there are possibilities of groundwater potentiality. For example, near Pipar city the crossing of a number of lineaments near the Jojri has great implications for groundwater. Similarly, one of the former courses of the Jojri on its right bank side has been cut through by an E-W lineament and, hence, many have some groundwater potentiality. The former buried channel that feeds the Kaparda saline depression has also been cut through by a major N-S lineament near Anawas, although the proximity of the saline alluvial plain and subsurface granite formation may lead to saline groundwater in the area.

Although the PC FCC failed to produce tangible units, density slicing may help in improving the situation. One of us (Amal Kar), while experimenting with soil brightness index mapping in another part of the sandy desert, fount that judicious density slicing of the processed output immensely improves the result.

The edge-enhanced FCCs through high-pass filtering were by far the best among the digitally processed images. However, these outputs are simply to improve the quality of the FCCs. Unlike in the supervised classification the interpreter, in this case, has to delineate himself the unit boundaries on the hard print of enhanced FCC. Nevertheless, the enhanced FCCs often provide better tonal differences than the standard raw FCCs available in the market. Moreover, depending upon the requirement, the interpreter can himself decide about the level of enhancement and act accordingly (Kar *et al*., 1989).

The units delineated from these outputs and from the standard FCC prints are also viable land resources units within the desert. Each of the units has its own potentials and limitations. Their correct mapping, therefore, provides the planners and decision-makers with a sound base for land resources planning.

Conclusions

The following broad conclusion are drawn from the above study.

(i) Outputs from the principal component analysis provide very useful information for lineament mapping. However, care should be taken during interpretation, because the edge gradients of many linear features like the road networks are sharpened in these outputs.

(ii) Edge-enhanced FCC often provides better information on the terrain conditions than the standard raw FCC print.

(iii) Further testing is necessary in different morpho-climatic situations within the desert to find out the potentiality of the supervised classification system. The test areas should not be large and should have distinctly separable spectral classes.

(iv) For most purposes, however, visual interpretation of large-scale FCCs with a finer resolution is easier and cost-effective. In this respect India's own IRS images, especially from the Liss-II sensor, have already been proven as a boon.

(v) The digitally enhanced IRS Liss-II images have also been found to be equally useful and more economical than the digital processing of Landsat images.

Acknowledgements

The authors would like to thank the Director and Head of the Resource Survey and Monitoring Division, CAZRI, and the Head, RRSSC, Jodhpur, for providing facilities to carry out the research.

REFERENCES

Colwell, R.N. (ed.) (1983). *Manual of Remote Sensing.* American Society of Photogrammetry, Virginia, USA; Vols. 1 and 2 (second edition).

Curan, P.J. (1985). *Principles of Remote Sensing.* Longman, London.

Kar, Amal, Singh, S., Ghosh, T.K., Vangani, N.S. and Dubey, J.C. (1989). Application Potentials of IRS-1A Data for Mapping Hydrogeomorphic Features in the Indian Desert. *Proc. Regional Workshop on Indian Remote Sensing Satellite Mission and its Application Potential.* CAZRI, Jodhpur; 54-58.

RRSSC (1988). *Lecture Notes on Digital Image Processing.* Regional Remote Sensing Service Centres (mimeo.).

Sabins, F.F. (1978). *Remote Sensing: Principles and Interpretation.* W.H. Freeman and Co., San Francisco.

11

Ecological and Economic Principles in Land Utilization

An Attempt Towards a Synthesis

JYOTIRMOY MUKHOPADHYAY

It is imperative to observe that 'ecology' and 'economics' have a common etymologic origin: the terms stem from the Greek 'oikos' that means house. The latter part of the term economics has its root in the Greek 'nemein' which stands for 'to manage'. In fact, the archaic meaning of 'economy' is the management of a household or family affairs with an implication as to the expenses. For 'ecology', on the other hand, the implication of a household was extended to denote environment—a concept too wide to make a facile comprehension—and the term entered into the store of English vocabulary from the German 'okologie' with a meaning of totality of interrelations between organisms and their habitat. It is unfortunate, however, that the use of these two terms has not only been different contextually, but also insidiously divergent, and it is now to be evidently admitted that they in their intent have eventually come in opposition to each other. The practical contraposition of these two concepts must have had their root in the fact that the makers of modern economics were prone to delineate their developing discipline by the postulate that human beings by their nature have material wants unlimited and all the activities that are centred around the unquenchable human thirst for goods and services are the constituents of the subject matter of economics. Economics, henceforth, has been regarded as a branch of social study that is directed to the description and analysis of production, distribution and consumption of commodities and services of pragmatic utility. It should be noted that economics, though a branch of social study of considerable importance, has paid surprisingly little attention to the development of human psychology, both individual and social, and to ethics in particular. It could well be an interesting exploration for psychologists, for historians and for human geographers besides the other social scientists to test the reality of the two different notions that the human beings are basically characterized by a mental trait that would make an 'economic man' as postulated in the dicta of the economists, or that, not material profit, but benefit and happiness, in the true sense of the term, is the ultimate goal of mankind in general. The notion of an 'economic man' actually reduces a human being into a mechanistic model—a person devoid of the essential moral and aesthetic elements that are to be expected in Homo-sapiens only and not in any other species of living creature of the world. It is a serious need for all of us, who are concerned with our individual and collective welfare, to reconsider that basic postulates of our academic thoughts and seek the principles that would not drag an academic discipline towards a specific direction in isolation, but would develop it with corrections by which it could be placed in harmony with others. At the turn of the 20th century A.D., one might well turn to the basic axioms with a frown to know whether it is true that the human beings are really ever so cursed to have their material wants quite unlimited or whether maximization of profit is an obvious human behaviour. The history of man has ample evidence to support the view that economic (here synonymous with material) prosperity paves the way for growth of a civilization, but as such it is means for something above it, and not itself an end. It could hardly be denied that the economic boon made the stage on which the Periclean Athens, the glorious Ancient India particularly under the Guptas, the Augustan Rome, the classical China under the Tang dynasty, the Elizabethan England, to name but a few, appeared, but these Golden Days of the human history had not just been periods of economic affluence like the periodic crests of a business cycle. In the contemporary world, economic development of a country does not necessarily mean its all-round development that can come into the sight by the attainment of a quality of life that is ever looked for.

The *raison d'être* of the present treatise lies in the question: whether the common economic principles for utilization of land resource could be in parity with that what aim at total development of a place for human habitation, i.e. with the directives of ecological norm? In other words, whether it can be possible to develop a logical and ethical frame that would put together the practically conflicting attitudes of the present-day economics and ecology in harmony? The need is serious, because at the terminal decade of the century of Technological Revolution, the human communities, even in the countries of the spectacular economic growth, find themselves at the threshold of a grave ecologic disaster. The peoples of the so-called Developing World have been continually planning for their desired techno-economic development only to experience eventually the disappointment as to their well-being and the quality of the environment. It is a fact that both the Developed and Developing Worlds are being afflicted by such present-day evils as air and water pollution, noise pollution, monstrous urban sprawl with amazingly high density of population, squatter settlements, traffic congestion, shortage of the necessary public facilities like school, college, public library and reading room, dispensary, hospital, park and playground, cinema and theatre, bank, market, post and telegraph office, and transport besides drinking water, electricity and above all, living space. Modern living means staying in an apartment in a high-rise concrete structure without the full-fledged family bonds that normally tie a person with others and thus make a cozy nest of society. Our history perhaps has never known such a cellular isolation of the human individuals until the howl of the Industrial Revolution that marks the emergence of our busy age. Since the high bang of that grandiose display of history, the water of our rivers are gradually becoming streams of increasing filth and dirt, the giant manufacturing agglomerates have been continually surpassing their previously set demarcations with alarmingly increasing congestion of population and traffic together with the sprawl of uninhabitable slums and squatter settlements, the forests with their wealth of magnificent wild life have fast disappearing and, above all, the incidence of mental sickness marital separation and divorce, suicide, juvenile crimes, cardiac troubles and carcinoma in most of the modern cities and metropolices have been quite significantly increasing much more than in the rural localities to foreshadow the dismal future of our once green planet.

What is the relation between the crises mentioned above with the principles of landuse on which we are to focus our present attention? One may naturally look for the relevance of these prefatory comments in a seemingly expectable unambiguous discussion about the principles of utilization of land resource from both economic and ecologic perspectives with a geographic datum. To highlight the rationale, it should be pointed out that landuse in its varying territorial-periodic, i.e. spatio-temporal aspects, can be regarded as the most sensitive variable that signifies the interaction between land and man, or the human response to the different physico-cultural milieux at any scale. The nature of landuse on any part of the earth could be viewed as the most open and definite testimony of the nature of human adjustment with the land with its varying properties, viz. locational (or positional), physical and cultural. An analysis of the nature of human response or adjustment on a land is diagnostic and prognostic as to the different aspects of both land and the human community that occupies it. A land is not just a piece of ground or a part of the terrestrial surface which is underlain by a certain type of rock and a certain characteristic flow of ground water, which has a typical surface run-off and surface morphology, a certain type of soil, natural vegetation and animals besides a typical general condition of its overlying troposphere, i.e. climate; in fact, the land has much more than all these physical elements which conventionally concern geographers; a land in any portion of the earth has an economic value, expressed in terms of money as its price which is very important when the question of its use or that need for the transfer of its ownership arises. As its surface form, it is to be noted, land value differs from place to place and from time to time and therefore, it is as much a geographic variable as climate, soil, natural vegetation, human society and human activities. A piece of land can be purchased, sold off and hired, and in the latter case, it returns a rent (that is considered as a factor price in economics) which is both a geographic and historical variable. Landuse should be viewed as a visible manifestation of the complicated and dynamic relations between the underlying terrain with its several attributes that are moulded or synthesized in a "complex" or physiotope (Neef, 1968), and the subtle, turbulent "soft" processes of human actions that are directed, on the background of their history, by different ideas, thoughts, pragmatic necessities, prejudices and obsessions which find their expression in the formulation of the principles. The human activities that occupy a land have their immediate social base and they are often guided by what might be called political motives. A analytical study of landuse, particularly from a comparative viewpoint, is expected to reveal all these facets in its correlated form and this role of landuse explains why its study has been traditionally regarded as of prime importance in the theory and practice of the classical geography.

The present discussion is a modest attempt to probe still deeper to explicate the role what landuse plays, or more correctly, could play in the territorial organization of society that concerns a geographer, and in such fields as geographic prognostication, human decisions in territorial and environmental context and above all, in the quality of human life, which connects the positivistic geography with ethics and psychology that have much to offer to the geographers. The central postulate of this essay is that the landuse of any part of the earth's surface reflects the human community what it truly is; in other words, a landuse is what a people want to make from a piece of land and basically, it is an outcome of human volition. In most of the previous researches landuse has been studied from the positivistic standpoint and the geographers did not burden themselves with the psychological and ethical questions. The present article steps out of the confine of the value-free geography and tries to enter to explore the realm of what may be called normative geography.

Background of Economic Principles of Landuse

It is a general postulate of the scientists of human culture that the history of human beings is evolutionary and progressive. A modern man believes that his ancestors were primitive people, for inferior to him, but slightly superior to the anthropoid apes. They might have had stronger physique, but obviously immature intelligence. Now-a-days, most of us unquestioningly accept the doctrine that the present-day state of mankind is the outcome of a continuous, unidirectional process of development of life-forms whose start is still wrapped up to us in mystery; that the modern man is the sign of the highest form that the Nature has so far created. If would be redundant to mention that the origin of this notion lies in the *Origin of Species* of Darwin in 1859 A.D., but it is important to point out that the influence of the theory of Darwin on the thoughts of our age is enormous. Though the biogeographic, palaeontogic, anatomic and embryologic evidence in favour of the Darwinian theory are spectacular, the Theory of Natural Selection is yet to have a sound, unquestionable cytologic and genetic base; it is yet to be proved and logically comprehended that all the primates stem from a common ancestor and Homo-sapiens have evolved according to the principle of random variation of the genetic cells of a particular species of anthropoid ape and by the process of Natural Selection. Homo-sapiens differ from all other creatures of the earth quite significantly in respect of their intelligence of what biologists speak about, and something more than that, which is called rationality. Man is defined as a rational animal, i.e. as a species that is characterized by two apparently contraposed components, viz. animality and rationality, the terms for proper comprehension outstrip the limit of our Natural Science. In fact, how the first man was born is still a conjecture among the scientists.

The purpose of this apparently digressive discussion is only to search the root of the economic motive of human beings. All the living creatures on the earth have to look, if not hunt, for food, most of them for shelter, and human beings amidst the all for their dress. Food, shelter and dress make the base of the life of a man; and, the demand for them makes what is called the fundamental economic motive; to get them human beings have to do some work that basically consists of assembling natural material resoùrces (land), labour, artifacts or equipments (capital) that are employed in acquiring the desired object, and à software structure as to the management that goes by the name organization. They look for the objects that are capable or seem to be capable of satisfying their want, i.e. the objects of utility, and by their works of many different kinds they try to increase the utility of the different objects they need. These works are generally called production. The aim of all these efforts is consumption, which does not very radically from that of the other species of animals.

What is supposed to differ for mankind from the behaviour of the other species is that the human demand seems to be virtually unending and extremely varied. It is not just confined to the want for food, shelter and dress for survival. Human beings do not want just to exist, but they desire to "live life". It is hard to explain the meaning of "living life" from the point of view of biology, though the prefix "bios" stands for the term life. Human life is not just a biologic existence, but truly more than it a mental one. Even the advanced primates, the most advanced of the mammals, cannot be said to possess mind in the proper sense of the term. Consciousness, behavioural response to various stimuli cannot be called mind. Mind is a distinct faculty, and Man, amongst all the living creatures, can have it in its nature form. The theory of Darwin is not adequate to explain the development of mind is Homo-sapiens.

Western psychology considers human mind to have three basic components, viz. feeling will and thought. Feeling is perceptual and it is dichotomous in the sense that it can be either pleasant (happy or attractive) or unpleasant (unhappy or repulsive). Man is always after pleasant sensations, be them visual, auditory, tectual, gustatory, or olfactory. This makes him selective in his will or wishes, or, from the practical point of view, in his wants. He wants the things that are capable of satisfying him and tries to avoid the things that make his feeling unpleasant. As to this selection, the human behaviour cannot be said to differ radically from that of the other animals. But he is distinguished by the third element of mind, i.e. thought. His feelings and wills can be value-free, as it is often the case, but his thoughts are intrinsically tied to another dichotomy that labels the worldly objects by the terms good or bad. A French proverb so says *Ce qui est bon est généralment cher; mais ce qui est cher n'est pas toujours bon.** The ethical trait at its variable extent of manifestation is characteristic of human beings.

The initial postulate of the economists that the human wants are unending and endlessly varied may now be judged from the viewpoint of human psychology. That because human beings have mind significantly developed as compared with the other species and the mind in general has a component which might be described as extra-ethical, i.e. a component which lies in the part of animality in mankind, the human beings are not satisfied just with the fulfilment of their basic needs, viz. food, shelter and dress. In fact, superfluity and extravagance are the characteristic traits of human beings as they do not want just to subsist like the other animals, but want to "live life". This is obviously a great development in comparison with the life of other living creatures. However, to interpret the phase "to live a life" is difficult, as the human beings themselves have different, often extremely varying, opinions on this question. Still, there can be, and in fact there is a consensus that all the human beings are basically motivated towards acquiring or attaining happiness. He demands many things, because he thinks that the goods and services he wants would meke him happy.

With a developing mind and a perpetual quest for happiness, men is exposed to the variegated world. For the majority of the people

---

* That which is good is generally dear; but that which is dear is not always good.

living on the earth, the initial necessity of food, shelter and dress has been met with the simple form of primary and secondary productive occupations. Yet, man is not generally satisfied when he is well fed, well clad, and quite securely sheltered from the external hazards. He wants more than what he at a moment gets, more and more. Not only that, he wants to reduce his labour in the production of goods and, therefore, he engages himself in search of machines that would work for him and thus make him free to enjoy the goods and services he desires with an increasing leisure time. Man's quest for leisure and recreation is a sign that he does not generally like to engage himself in work for all the time; his work is a means and not the end. He works not for the work's sake, but to fulfil his wants. How does it then differ basically from the animal behaviour—the pursuit for hunting? How does then the economists' postulate of the motive of profit maximization for an entrepreneur isolate the human beings from the trait of the other species?

Whether one does agree on this point or not, it can hardly be denied that the economic motives as postulated by such dicta as "unending and quenchless demand of human beings for commodities and services", "maximization of profit of the entrepreneur of a firm", "maximization of satisfaction for a consumer by bidding the highest price", have their root in some psychic elements of man, such as unjust, inordinate and unmitigated desire, unregulated acquisitiveness, illusive attitude about the real gain, unjudged egotism, a flair for material display, if not pomp and grandeur, jealousy and sometimes an obsession with money making. The material acquisitiveness of human beings comes form intense desire and avarice. One very significant feature of this kind of behaviour, i.e. the behaviour of an ideal "economic man" is his lack of proper consciousness and humane consideration about the other fellow beings, not only the human ones, but the others too, the "economic man" is perhaps deliberately thoughtless about the environment where he had his birth and physical growth and where he is now sustained. The economic system in which we are at present intricately woven regards the human beings as belonging to a number of classes, having special, rather imposed relations between themselves; here, a man exists as a producer and/or a consumer, as a labourer or an entrepreneur, as a creditor or debtor, or simply as a buyer or seller. This is a sort of relationship (which is sometimes claimed as the basic relationship among the human beings) where everybody is concerned just with him or herself and the wide, checkered surface of the earth—the geographers' arena—acts as a chessboard. It is no wonder why such a sophisticated mathematical development as the Game Theory has proved to be an effective model for the practicing economists of the present day.

Another division of mankind what the economic systems have inevitably led to is the partition of the people into two fuzzy sets, viz. poor and rich. It is one of the wonders that man with his spectacular achievements in the science and technology at the turn of the 20th century A.D., and with his long experience and knowledge helplessly, and often hopelessly finds the earth spectacularly scarred by poverty and its associates—famine, distress and inhuman living conditions. Millions of people in the Tropical world and a considerable number in the other parts of the world "live" below the indignitary datum, what has been called "the poverty line". In fact, the very existence and elevation of the poverty line is a mark of failure of the human beings to organize and sustain an agreeable and successful economic system, if not to acquire a true economic knowledge. Had the discipline of economics been aimed at to describing and interpreting the economic life and activities of the peoples of different lands and of different periods of time, it would have had to excavate the rugged surface of the theoretical models of economics to bring forward the rudimentary psychic elements implicit in human beings that motivate them to the activities to satisfy their wants. But for the human beings the importance of the question "What should they do?" is superseded by the interrogation, "What should they do?" Any branch of social studies is practically ineffectual, if it remains complacent within the bound of description and explanation, but it could become effective and successful if, by the knowledge gained on the positivistic ground, it goes ahead to get ideals, i.e. elevate itself to a normative level.

The argument in favour of the economic doctrines in vogue lies in the apparently realistic notion that the resources are scarce. In fact, modern economists define their discipline as a science that deals with the human activities in relation to the utilization of the scarce resources (Samuelson and Nordhaus, 1989). To judge the truth of this idea, one has to, once again, be out from the confine of the conventional economic dicta and step into the field of psychology and ethics. The obvious question is: how the Nature, so just as to the physical (i.e. extra-human) affairs, could be so unjust or unfair to a particular species of life? The subsequent interrogations are : whether the so-called scarcity of natural resources for the human beings is apparent, relative and subjective, or the sense of scarcity of resources is a perception or a mental image grounded on the characteristic of common human desire? Whether, if the scarcity be real, it is inherently natural or, to some extent, man-made? Is it not a fact that scarcity is a word for the poor and not actually for the affluent? Do the rich people really experience scarcity of material goods and services? If they do, then the term affluence would have no place in the real world.

So, it seems that the subject of economics needs some consideration as to its definition in the most comprehensive sense that would be compatible with the real-world situation. Aren't we in need of a science that would describe and interpret the affluence and poverty of human beings in different parts of the world and in different time? Here, clearly, the emphasis would be on the nature and level of consumption and not on the production of goods and services; the former is the end and the latter is the means. Why the discipline of economics should not be focused on the complexities of human consumption of commodities and services? Why should it not be aimed at formulating principles for material consumption which stands for satisfaction of wants of human beings? After all, the ultimate purpose of human mind is satisfaction and happiness.

To sum up, it may be stated that the economic principles are two-fold: positive and normative, i.e. they are as they are, and that could be as they should be. The positive principles are grounded, if not embedded, in the biologic motives that are centred around the animal-self of human beings. From it spring the urge to maximize profit (but not the benefit), and the instinctive inclination of material acquisition, "to earn more, spend more, and earn more" directive, and "to out-step other" behaviour of man. The normative principles are generated from a certain mental elevation wherefrom a man can look at the world as his true "oikos"—the home, and the fellow human beings not as competitors, but as co-workers or cooperators, not as customers or creditors, but as relations and friends in the spaceship floating through the boudless cosmos. The normative principles are indeed humane directives that crop out from ethics and aesthetics. Ecologic principles must necessarily have an ethical and aesthetic framework.

The Categories of Landuse : A Consideration

The first noteworthy classification of landuse was done by Sir Stamp in 1930-37. Sir Stamp's one of the most remarkable contributions to geography has been the mapping of the landuse of Great Britain at a scale 1 : 63,360, where he considered the following scheme of classification of landuse: (1) forest, (2) arable land, (3) meadow land and permanent grass, (4) health and moorland, (5) houses with gardens, orchards, nurseries, (6) land agriculturally unproductive, close buildings, pits, quarries, cemeteries and industries premises.

In fact, Sir Stamp's classification still stands as a classic in landuse study. All other subsequent classifications that are followed in different countries stem from it. In India, for example, the commonly held practices of landuse mapping is done under the following scheme: (1) forest, (2) land not available for cultivation and put to non-agricultural uses, (3) barren waste, (4) permanent pastures and grazing areas, (5) land under tree crops and grooves, (6) cultivable waste, (7) current fallow, (8) net sown area. The landuse maps of other countries show a little variation from the basic pattern of the above-described schemes.

What is actually the basic pattern or structure in the various schemes of classification of landuse data? Coleman (1969), the great worker in the study of landuse after Sir Stamp, has formulated a general model of landuse, where she considers the earth's land surface to have been covered by three dynamic, interacting sets as to landuse, which are: (1) wildscape, (2) farmscape, and (3) townscape. Wildscape is obviously the natural or primary form of the landscape, which has gradually and continually been replaced by farmscape, i.e. the landscape developed by the primary economic activities of man, chiefly by agriculture and animal hasbandry, which itself has been showing spectacular signs of recession by the growing townscapes around the unban nodes, where the secondary, tertiary and quaternary economic activities are conspicuously concentrated. All the three forms of landscape are not only different as regards their material content and features, but also they differ significantly as to the concentration or density of economic activities and output. Towns and cities are small in comparison with the farmlands and the latter are smaller than the vast natural forests, wild mountainous areas, tropical deserts, and polar areas or sub-polar tundras. Nevertheless, the towns and cities are the most effective centres of control of human activities and culture, and within themselves, they are so vatied and differentiated that the study of landuse is now being treated under two separate headings, viz. rural landuse and urban landuse. Study of urban landuse requires quite a different scheme of categorization of the land utilization data. However, we are yet to have a comprehensive, integrated and satisfactory taxonomy of landuse.

The relevance and importance of the categories or classes of landuse in a discussion of economic and ecologic principles that guide them could be appreciated on the background of the general model of Coleman. Whichever scheme of categorization of landuse a country follows, the categories of landuse must necessarily belong to any one of the three basic sets, i.e. wildscape, farmscape, or townscape. Wildscape is the testimony of the original ecology of human beings that was modified at the first stage by the technologic innovation of farming; it damaged the natural home of mankind and formed what may be called "the artificial ecology" of the first order; thereafter, the techno-economic changes led to the development of the nucleated form of human habitation based on manufacturing, trade and services, that trusted and distorted the green farmscapes giving rise to "the artificial ecology" of the second order with its increasing and unprecedented complexities as to human life. Man has moved far away from his natural home. We recall the saying of Winston Churchill:

"We shape our buildings and afterwards our buildings shape us."

The Economic Principles of Landuse : A Review

That the spatial variation of landuse is primarily due to economic factors could not escape the insight of Johann Heinrich von Thünen (1783-1850 A.D.) who has been noted as one of the early scholars to have formulated a convincing geographic explanation of landuse. According to von Thünen, profit is the most important factor that makes a producer choose a particular use of a piece of land. He has expressed profit by the formula: $P = V - (E + T)$, where P stands for profit, V for value of commodities sold, E for total expenses of production and T for cost of transportation of the commodities produced from the place of production of the market; with increasing distance from the market, T increasing resulting in the reduction of profit, and there is for each commodity, according to the theory of von Thünen, a specific distance from the market, where $P = O$, and beyond which P becomes negative. The specific distances of different commodities differentiate the areal cover of the commodities, in other words, differentiate land according to different characteristic uses. It is interesting to note that though von Thünen's theory was formulated to interpret the pattern of landuse in a model farmscape around an isolated town (the agricultural landscape near the city of Rostock in Mecklenburg, Germany, in the late 18th and early 19th centuries A.D.), it has been found to be explanatory to a considerable extent as to the variation of landuse of the agricultural tracts around the urban nodes today (Horvath, 1968), and its basic tenets prove to be an effective interpretative tool for the pattern of urban landuse in general. Landuse varies, because the units of land have different prices different places and a number of competitors or bidders for their occupation or ownership for a gainful purpose. A piece of land is put to a particular use as its occupier has been able to be a successful competitor, i.e. able to defeat others by paying the highest price for it. We, therefore, find the most accessible locales are occupied by offices and shops of the highest rank (the most profitable concerns) and the least accessible or physically difficult places are occupied by the poor or are simply left as wastes. Accessibility of a place is virtually not a separate factor because it reflects itself in the price of a land or its rental value. Land value has been considered as a basic differentiator of landuse (Alonso, 1964; Hurd, 1903; Ratcliff, 1949; Berry, 1959).

Mandal (1981), has listed a number of principles that guide variation of landuse. Most of the principles of the list are economic, though few of them have what may be called ecologic connotation. The principles as listed by Mandal (with their order in the list modified) are:

1. The principle of maximization of value returns for the user of land: it stems from the "desire to make use of most of the resources".
2. The equi-marginal principle : it implies "the division of fixed quantity of use among the number of different uses so that they apportion each use an amount sufficient for increment of a gain and every use might be put for maximum profit".
3. The principle of diminishing marginal rate of substitution : it implies that with the increase of production and consumption the increment of satisfaction diminishes; so, substitution of two uses of land are not necessarily quantitatively matched with each other.
4. The principle of diminishing marginal productivity: it states that with continuous increase of production of expansion, the increment of productivity gradually decreases; this is a

general law of economics.

5. The principle of specialization and comparative advantage: this is an economic principle that is directly controlled by geographic and environment variables.
6. The principle of first choice: it is related to the fifth one, but sometimes it reflects a social or political aspect.
7. The principle of alternative better use of land: this principle surely has an ecologic connotation.
8. The principle of increasing the efficiency and capability of land.
9. Fixation of cropping system around human habitation for least effort and less cost travel; this is undoubtedly an economic principle.
10. Optimization of the quality of landuse in relation to environment: this is both an economic and an ecologic principle, because it is directed to make the best possible utilization of land resource.
11. Conservation of land for future judicious use: this has also both economic and ecologic connotations.

In the discussion of the above-mentioned principles, the important question is: whether all the principles are congruous and compatible, with each other? If not, contradiction and confusion will arise before the planners and policy-makers. After all, landuse represents human decisions, either individual or corporate, taken in a territorial (environmental-spatial) context. The decisions are often dualistic in the sense that they are favourable to some, but injurious to others. A decision as to a particular use of a piece of land sometimes leads to raging conflict, strife and prolonged litigation.

The Ecological Directives for Landuse

Before launching on the discussion about the ecological principles of land utilization, a few naïve questions may be posed whose significance has some importance. The queries are:

1. Whether the current practice and the common pattern and development of landuse allover world are generally agreeable and satisfactory to us or not?
2. If the present pattern of landuse in most of the settled areas

of the earth be satisfactory, then how the growing menace of global pollution, excessively high density of population in certain places, slums and squatter settlements, civil disputes as to the encroachment and construction of undesirable buildings adjacent for?

3. If the common practice of landuse in most of the inhabited areas of the world be considered as for the most part unsuitable and disagreeable and be thought as a consequence of the characteristic practice of the present-day people engaged in the primary, secondary, tertiary and quaternary economic activities, then it is undoubtedly a serious and immediate exigency before us to take recourse to an alternative economic system that would result in an agreeable territorial disposition of landuse. But, the question: What is that alternative economic principle or system? Does it exist at all? If so, are all the people willing to shift from the pressing current practice to the relieving new one?

An ordinary man, who has never heard of the word "ecology" or "environment", intuitively knows that manufacturing plants, though a source of employment, are nevertheless a source of pollution of air and water and they disturb, if not disrupt, the natural habitat. The rural people in India who commute to the city for their work clearly confess that they live somewhat better in the villages or in the rurban settlements, but only for the sake of money they have to bear the noise and crowd of the giant cities. From the Calcutta downtown the commuters on every working-day evening simply walk for about 4 km to the station of the suburban railway as they cannot board the crowded buses and tram-cars that ply in numbers between the Central Business District and the suburban railway station. So, thousands of people who come from the rurban areas to the city find themselves misfit to the characteristic ecology of the bustling Calcutta; in fact, most of them walk the said distance both in their to and fro journey.

In comparison with a village, a town or a city is a large organizational unit and a metropolis is more so. The original ecological set-up is dissipated and is gradually being modified by the growing settlements and activities of the human community. The terminal threshold of the 20th century is in a serious demand of a science that could predict the critical stage or the probable limit up to which ecologic modification by human activities is permissible so far as the psychophysical well-being of man is concerned. The chief difference between the economic and ecologic postulates lies perhaps in the fact that the science of ecology, as our age-old proverb says, considers health as wealth, while in economics, money and objects of material utility make the storehouse of treasure. But the question is: what is of more utility to a person than his or her physical and mental well-being or health? If someone unfortunately loses health, then all other objects of utility, however valuable they might be, become simply useless. Human beings need to reconsider their thoughts and actions and fix up their goal in life. It is the human mind that decides, directs to act and imposes various changes; the entire cultural landscape may be interpreted as an outcome of the human decisions and imaginations, individual or collective, taken at different places, times and environments.

Therefore, it can hardly be denied that the economic motives or principles, as they are now-a-days or have been continuing to be for a long time, come in obvious contradiction to what the ecologists direct. This is so, because the first is pragmatic and the second is normative. But it is a serious question whether a normless pragmatism ever succeeds or results in a lasting benefit for the practitioners of the officious philosophy. The point is that the formulation of the principles, be them economic or ecologic, should of necessity admit that the world with its various phenomena is a platform of lessons that we are to learn, thereby rectify our pitfalls to make and re-make our notions about the principles of life that stem from an integrated and ordered entity.

The present article is directed to place the following assertions on the background of the discussion so far done:

1. Economic and ecologic principles should not be fundamentally different in their motivation, because the common goal of human life is the total well-being and welfare.
2. That the economic and ecologic principles practically contradict results from the fact that the practice of economics stem from the imperfect and impure principles, which should achieve inclusiveness and balance as to the objects it deals with.
3. The failure to materialize the first and the second proposition results in the imperfection, imbalance and undesirable incidence of landuse that are the source of many serious

troubles and hazards that mankind faces.

The prime ecologic directive is to save the Nature, that means to practice not that much a constructional engineering, but truly a conservational one. The philosophy is not to conquer the Nature by killing her, but to live together happily (Kristof, 1968). Homo-sapiens is not a species to be called "unnatural", as we are often used to think it so, but we are surely as natural, though different, as other species of life that thrive so luxuriantly on the surface of our planet. Therefore, our aim must not be to discolour the face of the earth by our unkind and unjust actions, because if the earth becomes grey, we cannot remain vivid. It is the verdant that vivifies.

Still the so much talked of ecologic directive is a far cry until a newer, alternative economic strategy is devised. The postulate is that we cannot go long by the path now we follow. The formulation of a principle is perhaps the most difficult adjudication that a man faces. The principles should not be partial, short-sighted and exclusive, because though human mind is used to perceive and conceive in a differentiated manner, the reality is, so far it has been comprehended, interlinked and all-inclusive. The dichotomy of economic and ecology principles is in fact a human distortion of the real-world image. Why should they at all be different? Why should not the principles conform to one another as they basically aim at a single destination—achievement of well-being, welfare and lasting happiness?

So the ecologic directive is sharpened to point out to find a new economic order—not one that aims at profit in a narrow sense, but one that aims to achieve maximum benefit and distribute it on the principles of humanity. Resource utilization is not hunting, nor is it an act of plundering or predation. The ecologic disaster that the mankind is now about to face is a predation pressure as the human beings have quite injudiciously utilized, if not preyed on, the earth's resources. The justification of this interpretation could be verified from the history of man.

Conclusion

The search for an alternative economic order is one of the most important issues before Man in the new millennium. Several experiments with different economic models have been done but none have been able either to wipe out the material distress and poverty of countless people or to keep our earth clean and safe. The economic principles would fail to achieve success, if they are kept confined within their traditional enclosure to ignore the other important aspects of Man. The economists should not expel the ethical questions from their study, as it is not logical to be unethical; the ethics constitutes the very essence of a human being. The alternative economics should also necessarily consider the psychologic aspect, because Man is effectively a mental entity; mind is the most superior to all the human organs. It would not be out of point to mention here that the Gandhian economics is a remarkable step towards the development of such an economic order. It does not ignore the ecologic directives. Much research, therefore, is urgently needed on the Gandhian economics, particularly as to its bearing on utilization of resources, employment and income, standard of living and quality of life, relation with the countries that follow different economies, and planning at local, regional and national levels. Models such as the Gandhian economics should not be dispelled outright with scorn or indifference, because we are yet to know and appreciate it fully and realize the economic and ecologic doctrines in harmony.

In India, the Panchayat (the local self-governing bodies) can formulate strategies that are to combine the economic and ecologic issues as to a collective need-oriented landuse planning. Of course, there must be a general conformity as to its design and legislative support as regards their implementation. Environmental laws should not overlook the economic problems, nor should the economic developmental plans ignore the environmental issues. A sound and comprehensive economic order, like the Gandhian economic model, is expected to satisfy most of the human needs, simply because the Gandhian doctrine is not only an economic or political theory, but also a philosophy.

REFERENCES

Alonso, W. (1964). Location and Landuse, Cambridge, Massachusetts. p. 16.

Berry, B.J.L. (1959). The spatial organization of business landuses, Chapter 3 in Garrison *et al.*, *Studies of Highway Development and Geographic Change,* p.62. Seattle, Washington.

Coleman, Alice (1969). A geographical model for landuse analysis, *Geography*, Vol. 54, No. 242, Part I, pp. 43-55.

Grotewold, Andreas (1959). Von Thünen in Retrospect, *Economic Geography,* pp. 346-355.

Horvath, R.J. (1968). Von Thünen's Isolated State and the Area around Addis Ababa, Ethiopia, Section: Economic Geography, *21st. Int. Geogrl. Cong.* New Delhi.

Hurd, R.M. (1924). *Principles of City Land Values,* New York.

Kristof, Ladis K.D. (1968). On the concept of conquest of Nature, Section-Historical and Political Geography, *21st. Int. Geogrl. Cong.,* New Delhi.

Mandal, R.B. (1982). *Land Utilization: Theory and Practice,* pp. 42-52, 111-14. Concept Publishing Company, New Delhi.

Neef, Ernst (1968). Der Physiotop als Zentralbegriff der Komlexen Physischen Geographie, Petermanns Geographische Mitteilungen (Gewidmet dem Internationalen Geographenkongress in New Delhi, 1968), 112. 1. Quartalsheft, Veb Hermann Haack, *Geographische-Kartographische Anstalt,* Gotha/Leipzig, pp. 15-23.

Ratcliff, R.V. (1949). *Urban Land Economics,* New York. p. 369.

Samuelson, Paul A., and Nordhaus, William D. (1989). *Economics,* McGraw-Hill Book Company (13th Edition).

Stamp, Sir L. Dudley (1950). *The Land of Britain, Its Use and Misuse.* Longmans Green, London (2nd Edition).

—— (1960) *Applied Geograph.* Penguin Books Ltd., Harmondsworth, Middlesex, England.

12

Computer-Assisted Land Resource Management Using Remote Sensing and GIS Technology

QIMING ZHOU and ANTHONY K. MILNE

Remote sensing technology is recognised to be an appropriate tool for rangeland management given that it can provide information on the state of land cover and biomass on a regular, continuous and near real-time basis (Pickup, *et al.*, 1993). However, to be meaningful for rangeland management, remotely-sensed data must be processed and interpreted in the context of geographical and historical information. It is now recognised that remotely-sensed data is of maximum value when it can be integrated into an efficient spatial data handling and processing system which has the potential to provide real-time management advice. Geographical information systems (GIS) offer a logical basis for such integration. It is widely accepted that geographical information systems, when incorporated with remotely-sensed data, offer farm managers a state-of-the-art tool for monitoring environmental conditions and allocating livestock in a spatially efficient manner under the prevailing rangeland conditions.

The aim of this study, therefore, is focused on establishing a regional geographical information system which, based on 1:250,000 map sheets, is capable of providing near real-time information for regional rangeland management. To achieve this objective, multitemporal remotely-sensed data derived from Landsat MSS and TM and NOAA-AVHRR have been integrated into a geographical data base together with information including weather records, land systems and cadastre. These data sets are then used in spatial models which describe relationships between range conditions and particular environmental parameters, such as weather, changes in soil moisture, vegetation phenology and land management activities such as grazing, cultivation and the clearing of natural areas. The goal of this system is to apply these spatial models to detect range conditions from real-time satellite and meteorological data. Based on this system, near real-time advice can be provided to the regional land manager to assist in decision-making for rangeland management, hazard control and environmental planning.

This chapter outlines the methodological framework of this project. It focuses on the techniques used for the design and construction of the integrated spatial data base which incorporates conventional geographical information and remotely-sensed data. The use of this integrated data base in spatial modelling for rangeland management is also discussed.

Study Area

The study area encompasses some 15,000 square kilometres in south-western New South Wales and corresponds with the area shown on the Pooncarie 1:250,000 Map Sheet (Fig. 12.1). Bounded by the Darling river to the west, the region is covered with aeolian sand deposits of Pleistocene age. These sand plains and dunefields form part of the eastern extension of the continental dunefields that have progressively migrated eastwards under the influence of a prevailing westerly wind system. The eastern margins of the sand plains abut against and overlie the riverine plains of the Murray basin of eastern Australia. Through the centre of the study region is a series of dry lakes which were once fed by a tributary stream of the Lachlan river. Six major lakes and numerous small depressions cover over 1,000 square kilometres and are linked by Willandra Billabong Creek. This system has been dry and inactive for at least the past 15,000 years.

The lake beds themselves are covered by chenopod shrublands of varying density. On the heavier clay soils *Atriplex vesicaria, Maireana pyramidata, M.appressa* and *M.aphylla* dominate with annuals, such as *Atriplex holocarpa, Atriplex lindleyi* and *Salsola kali* more widespread on the outer edges of the lakes.

Mallee woodlands occur on the sandplains and on much of the dunal ridge crests with the dominant species being *Eucalyptus dumosa*

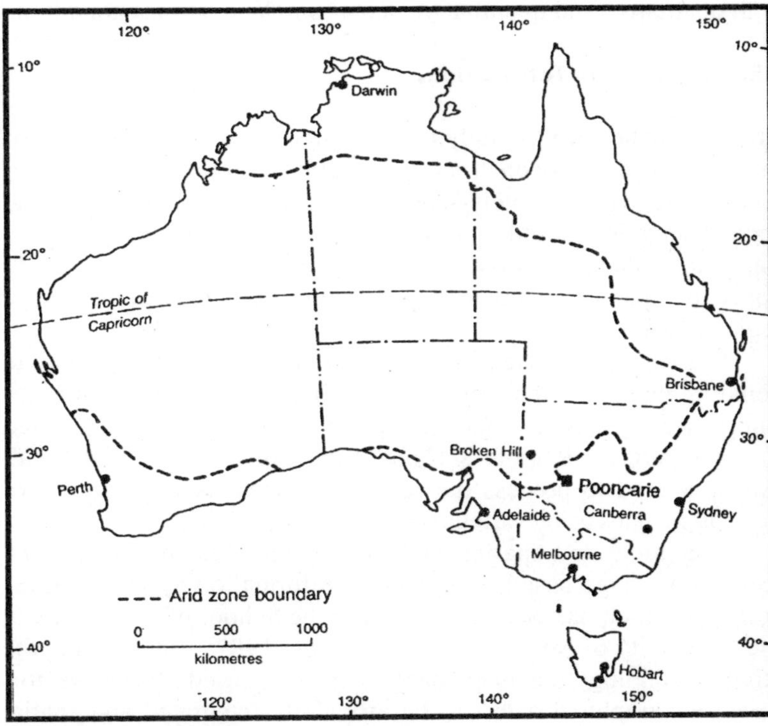

Fig. 12.1: Location Map of the Study Area

and *E.socialis. Triodia irritans* is the main understorey component. *Casuarina cristata* and *Hetrodendrum aleifolium* (Belah-Rosewood communities) occur mainly on the sandy red earths with an understorey dominated by saltbush. Dense stands of *Callitrus columellaris* are common throughout the Belah-Rosewood communities (O'Neill, 1986).

Climatically the region is semi-arid with a mean annual rainfall of approximately 250 mm spread evenly throughout the year. Records show, however, a high annual variability in rainfall with a high incidence of drought being experienced over the period of record (100 years for Mulurulu Station).

Sheep and cattle have been grazed in the region since the 1880s with current stocking rates ranging between 1 sheep to 4 hectares to 1 sheep to 11 hectares. Overgrazing, the clearing of selected areas for cultivation, fire and the invasion of woody shrubs on marginal land comprise the major threats to environmental conservation causing both qualitative and quantitative declines in land surface condition.

The Spatial Data Integration

The approaches of this study include three stages. The objective of the first stage is to construct an integrated spatial data base that incorporates both remotely-sensed and geo-based information. The second stage is focused on developing spatial models based on the integrated data base for rangeland management. The third stage is to apply the spatial models to near real-time land management on a regional scale.

The techniques used in this research include those in remote sensing image processing and applications of geographical information systems. A *Meridian* image processing system installed in the Centre for Remote Sensing at the University of New South Wales is used to process the remotely-sensed data and to derive vegetation maps using various types of auto-classification techniques.

The integrated spatial data base is handled by the *ReMAP* Relational Image-based Geographical Information System (RIGIS) software which has been developed in the School of Geography at the University of New South Wales (Zhou, 1987; 1989). Using the RIGIS technology, the image-based remotely-sensed data and vector-based geographical data can be efficiently integrated and spatial models can be developed based on these data sets using the geographical modelling operations supported by the ReMAP software.

Remotely-Sensed Data

Remotely-sensed information used in this study includes Landsat MSS and TM data and NOAA-AVHRR imagery. The geo-referencing of these data sets for selected dates or over certain periods of time provides an opportunity to examine the nature and extent of changes occurring in the surface conditions of the landscape within the constraints of both a spatial and a temporal framework.

The low resolution daily coverage obtainable from the NOAA-AVHRR sensors provides the potential at least to monitor conditions on a near day-to-day basis, but at a scale that may be insensitive to local variations in surface cover. Looking at regional changes across biomes, however, NOAA-AVHRR has proved to be a very effective means of identifying gross surface change. Given these characteristics NOAA-AVHRR will be used to flag changing landscape conditions and to locate target areas for more detailed analysis with Landsat MSS and TM data.

An equally valid approach to studying change within the area is to undertake detailed analysis of MSS and TM data in order to characterise the type of alterations occurring in the surface conditions and then seek to extrapolate these findings to a much larger region using NOAA data. Such an approach will be of necessity after the event, given the satellite return period and the time delay in acquiring data.

Both, however, depend on how well the geometric and radiometric properties of the two systems can be preserved and correlated to one another. Given the complexity and the need to minimise cumulative error in the data base, all remotely-sensed data have been subjected to an atmospheric correction procedure developed by Forster (1984). This procedure also takes into account the effects of sun angle differences and can be used to normalise multitemporal data sets.

The remote sensing imagery incorporated into the spatial data base includes annual Landsat MSS scenes for November 1984-1989; TM quarter-scenes centred around Lake Mungo for June 1989; October 1989 and February 1990; and NOAA-AVHRR data acquired weekly for the period October 1989 to March 1990. These images have been registered to the Australian Map Grid and resampled to pixel sizes of 25 metres, 50 metres and 1 kilometre for Landsat TM, MSS and NOAA-AVHRR, respectively. These data sets are then directly input to the ReMAP software system through the interface between the GIS and image processing system.

A suite of change detection procedures (Milne, 1988; Milne and O'Neill, 1990) including the use of albedo images are available to the authors which enable an objective assessment of surface reflectance conditions to be made in multitemporal comparisons. Ground data collection and sampling procedures designed for use with both Landsat and NOAA imagery (O'Neill, 1990; Williamson *et al.,* 1990) have been implemented in order to establish the relationship between the spectral record and ecological properties (samples taken in ground surveys) such as cover, biomass and the rate of grassland curing in rangeland environments.

Geo-based Data

Spatial data derived from traditional geographical sources in this study include land systems, geology, property and cadastre and ground sampling sites for vegetation cover and biomass measurement. These data sets provide ancillary information for remote sensing image processing and they also form the basis of land use and landscape related spatial models.

A land system is defined as "an area or group of areas throughout which there is a recurring pattern of topography, soils and vegetation" (Christian and Stewart, 1953). This information provides a comprehensive view of a particular land by integrating information, such as landform, soil and vegetation. For this study, the land system can provide basic information on soil and vegetation properties, hence, it can be incorporated into image processing to assist in the prediction of vegetation information from remotely-sensed data.

In a rangeland environment, land management activities are primarily related to land properties. Availability and use of land for grazing are also influenced by the spatial accessibility of man-made features on the landscape such as watering points, roads and residential sites. Therefore, knowledge about these features is essential for 'real world' land management.

The geo-based data sets integrated into the spatial data base include land systems and property boundaries from the 1:250,000 Pooncarie Land System Map; roads, watering points and residential sites from the 1:250,000 Pooncarie Topographic Map Sheet; geological information from the 1:100,000 Geology Map; and vegetation information such as communities and types from vegetation maps and samples around Lake Mungo area based on the research conducted by O'Neill (unpublished data). These geo-based data sets were initially digitised using a in-house digitising software and then edited and maintained using *ARC/INFO* vector-based GIS software package. As the ReMAP software package has efficient interfaces to the ARC/INFO software, the vector-based information can be shared by both systems and vector-to-raster conversion (or *vice versa)* is performed only when vector data need to be processed together with images in the spatial models.

Establishing the Integrated Data Base

Based on the remotely-sensed and geo-based data sets described above, the construction of the integrated data base has been conducted using the data base management capabilities of ReMAP. According to their spatial relationships, three primary data categories have been introduced into the comprehensive natural resource management data base. These are:

Tabular Information: This information presents general environmental characteristics for the region and normally does not exhibit great local variations within it. Although only few sample points exist within the study area, the time series related to each of these is relatively long. The information is derived from existing sources such as Bureau of Meteorology or from field investigations. These data sets are often presented as tables and can be directly input to the attribute data base managed by the *INFO* relational data base management system (RDBMS). Typically, this information is used for statistical analysis regardless of its spatial relationships. However, a spatial index can be established to link this information to spatial models which record the locations of these sample points (Fig. 12.2).

Cartographic Information: This type of information is available in the form of analogue maps which have been digitised and presented as vector digital files. The resulting vector spatial features were originally stored in the ARC data base and a vector-to-raster conversion performed to encode such features into ReMAP's spatial models. Since thematic maps often present information at nominal or ordinal levels of measurement, the vector-based information can be modelled as non-continuous surfaces in three-dimensional space. Attributes of these spatial features are often complex and include a number of data fields in each record. Such aspatial information is managed by INFO RDBMS as normal relational tables, regardless of whether a vector or raster structure might be employed by the corresponding spatial component (Fig. 12.3).

Image information: Remotely-sensed images are directly input into the spatial data base after geometric registration and resampling using the image processing system. Different from the cartographic information, which often has a simple spatial component but complex aspatial attributes, image information has a rather complicated spatial component but simple aspatial attributes. The only primary attribute for the raw image data is the digital number representing the ground spectral characteristic. However, after radiometric and atmospheric corrections, new attributes can be created for each digital number to present ground reflectance. With the new reflectance attribute, the

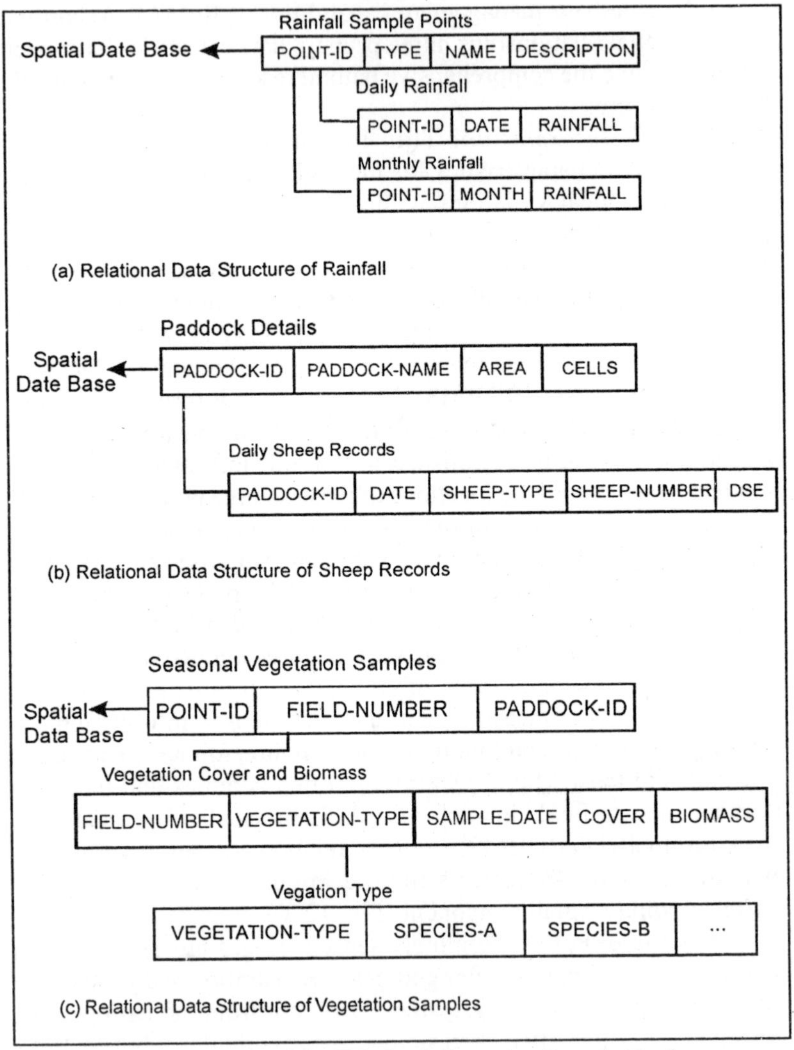

Fig. 12.2: Data Structure of the Tabular Information Encoded in the Geographical Data Base

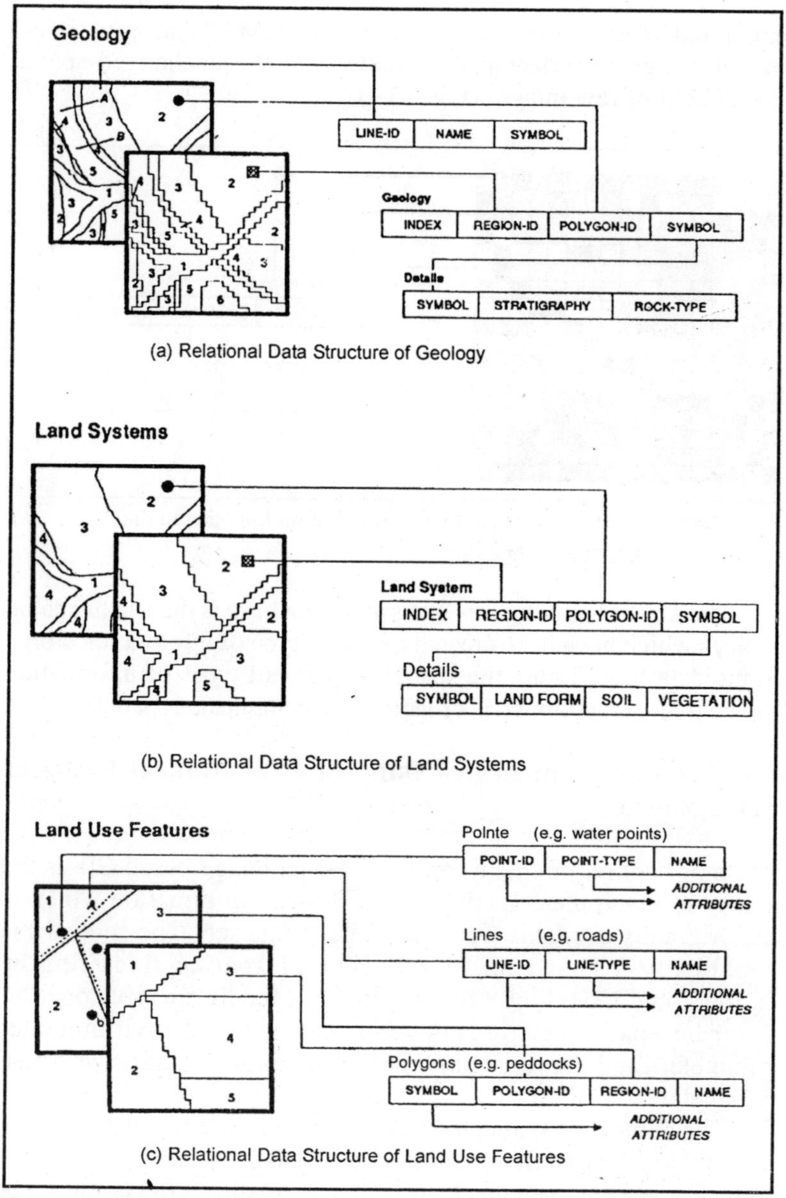

Fig. 12.3: Data Structures of the Cartographic Information Encoded in the Geographical Data Base

calibrated images can be retrieved from the ReMAP data base simply by selecting the reflectance attribute with the unchanged spatial component of raw images (Fig. 12.4).

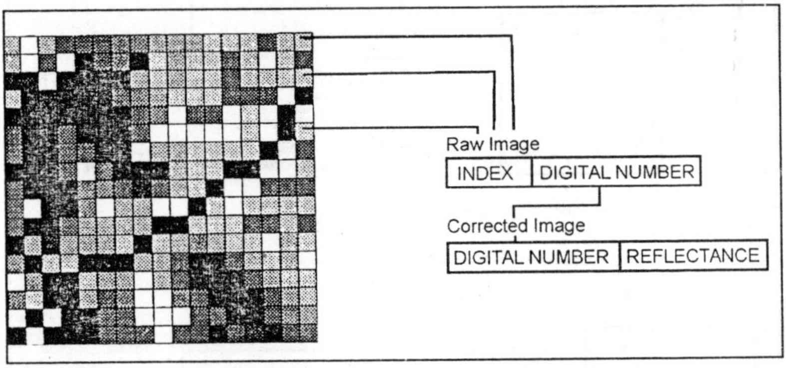

Fig. 12.4: Data Structure of the Image Information Encoded in the Geographical Data Base

The key to handling this integrated data base is the use of spatial indices which have been created for every type of information stored in the data base. Using the spatial indices, all types of information can be freely transformed in order to build complicated spatial models.

The Use of the Integrated Data Base for Natural Resource Management

An important requirement for this regional image-based GIS is the ability to manipulate spatial data to provide information which is not originally available from the primary data sets. The core of this capability is based on the concept of spatial modelling or cartographic modelling (Tomlin, 1983). Models are developed to describe spatial relationships between various environmental parameters and the results are recognised as a "synthesis" of these parameters.

The purpose of spatial models in this study is to translate spectral information derived from remotely-sensed data to a more meaningful form for land management; to estimate weather effects on range conditions associated with a variety of environmental parameters; and to model the relationships between demand and supply of rangeland resources.

The overall structure of the spatial models is outlined in Fig. 12.5. As shown in the figure, the input to the spatial models includes thematic information, such as land systems, geology, property boundaries, roads, residential sites and remotely-sensed data. Among these, the thematic information can be considered as "static" information which rarely changes in the time scales associated with rangeland management. Weather records and the information derived from remotely-sensed data can be considered as "dynamic" providing real-time data for change analysis. The purpose of the spatial models is to integrate the "static" (e.g. geology) and "dynamic" (e,g. vegetation cover derived from remote sensing) components in order to describe what is happening to land cover, how it has changed, how it is likely to change and what environmental and human factors are responsible for the change. Based on these descriptive models, near real-time information can be derived by updating the "dynamic" components of the input on a regular basis.

The output from these spatial models can, for example, provide land managers with information about vegetation status on a property basis. This information can be presented in both graphic or tabular form (Fig. 12.6) and a series of query processes can be developed to derive multitemporal information on natural vegetation resources. Using this information and land administrative records of the properties, thè balance between consumption and supply of vegetation resources can be quantified and land management practices initiated to optimise natural resource usage.

Concluding Remarks

This chapter has outlined a methodology to establish an integrated GIS for rangeland management on a regional scale. The emphasis has been on the techniques used for incorporating data sets derived from different sources into a well managed comprehensive geographical data base. Focused on real-time or near real-time applications, the system is designed to use high-frequency, low-cost remotely-sensed data such as NOAA imagery as the major source of real-time information to be input to spatial models for natural resource management.

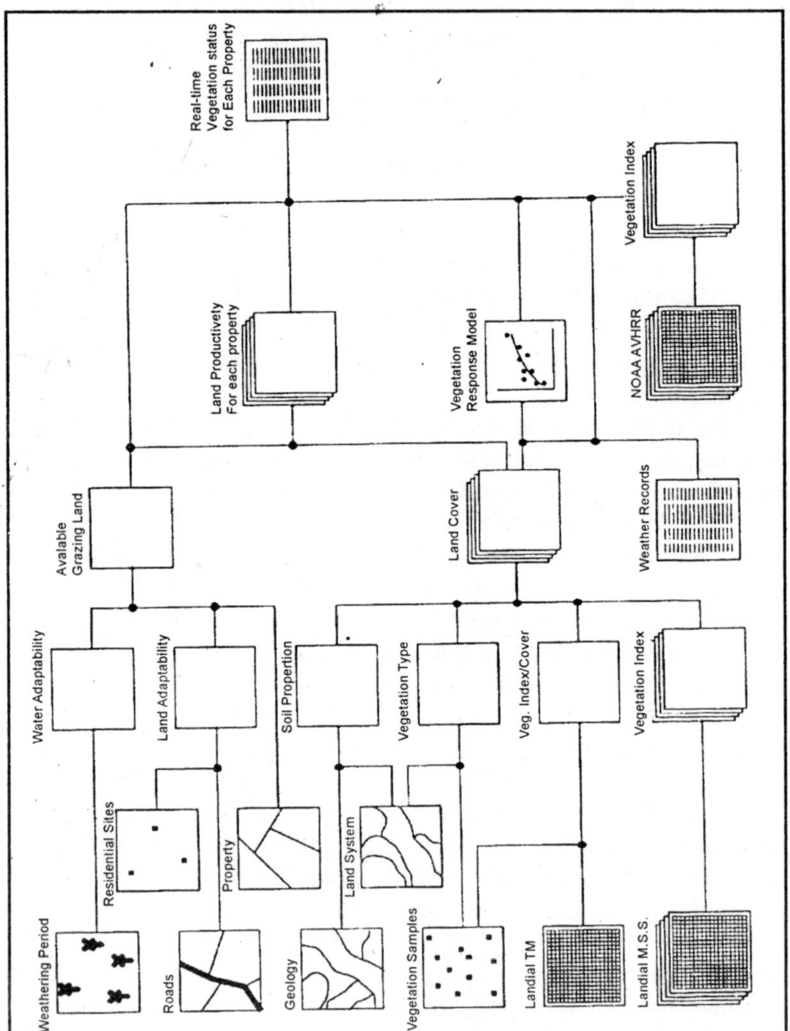

Fig. 12.5: The Structure of Spatial Models for Regional Rangeland Management

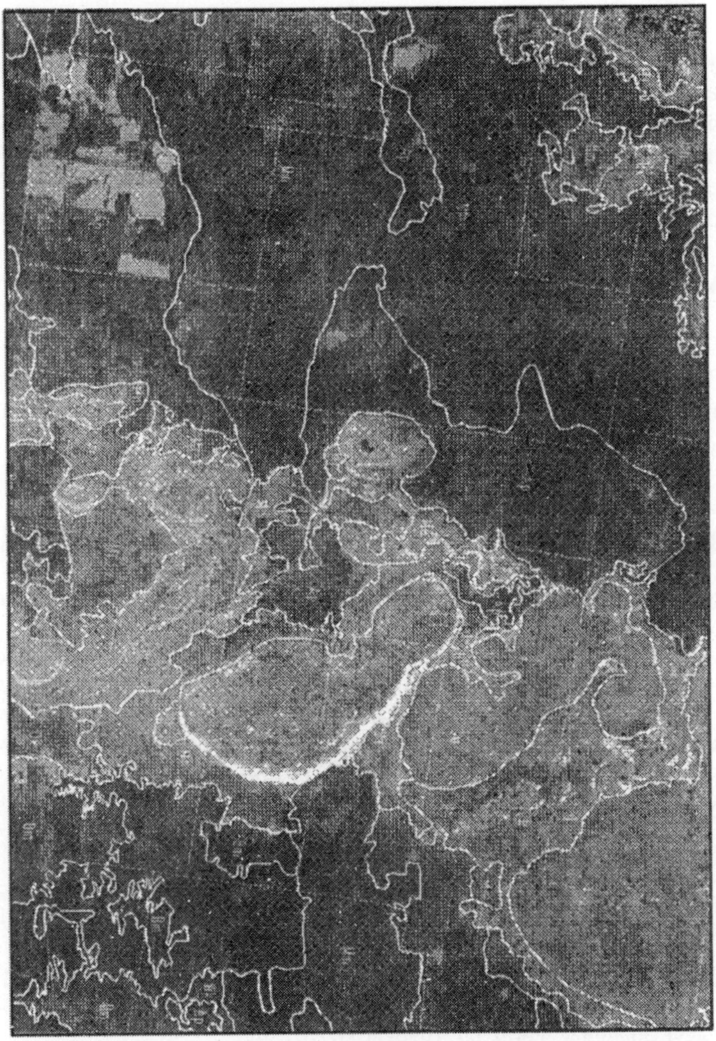

Fig. 12.6: An Example of the Graphic Output from the Integrated Geographical Data Base. The Background is Vegetation Index Derived from Landsat MSS Superimposed by the Vector Information Including Land System (Solid Lines) and Property Boundaries (Broken Lines). Based on this Integration, the Query Processes can be Developed to Summarise the Vegetation Status for Each Property (or Land System).

The final outcome of this image-based geographical information system is to be able to invert the spatial models developed so that range conditions can be predicted from real-time satellite and meteorological data. The real-time applications can also feedback to the system to improve the spatial models. Using this system, near real-time advice can be provided on a regional scale to the land manager and optimum use of the natural resources can be achieved.

Acknowledgements

The authors would like to thank Mr. John Owen of the School of Geography at the University of New South Wales for his assistance in digitising geographical data sets and producing cartographic output for this research.

REFERENCES

Christian, C.S. and Stewart, G.A. (1953). General Report on Survey of Katherine-Darwin Region, 1946, *CSIRO Australian Land Research Series,* No. 1.

Forster, B.C. (1984). "Derivation of Atmospheric Correction Procedures for Landsat MSS with Particular Reference to Urban Data," *International Journal of Remote Sensing,* Vol. 5(5): 799-817.

Milne, A.K. (1988). "Change Detection Using Landsat Imagery, in *Proceedings IGARSS'88 Symposium,* Edinburgh, pp. 541-44.

Milne, A.K. and O'Neill, A.L. (1990). "Mapping and Monitoring Land Cover in the Willandra Lakes World Heritage Region", *International Journal of Remote Sensing,* Vol. 11 (11): 2035-49.

O'Neill, A.L. (1986). *The Use of Landsat Dgital Data to Map Land Cover in the Willandra Lakes,* (Unpublished) M.Ap.Sc Thesis, University of New South Wales.

O'Neill, A.L. (1990). "Leaf Morphology and Sepectral Reflectance of Some Australian Plants", in *Proceedings of the 5th Australiasian Remote Sensing Conference,* Perth, pp. 1096-1103.

Pickup, G., Chewings, V.H. and Nelson, D.J. (1993). "Estimating Changes in Vegetation Cover Over Time in Arid Rangelands Using Landsat MSS Data", *Remote Sensing of Environment,* 43(3): 243-63.

Tomlin, C.D. (1983). *Digital Cartographic Modelling Techniques in Environmental Planning,* Doctoral Dissertation, Yale University.

Williamson, H.D., Milne, A.K. and Steer, J.L. (1990). "Using NOAA Data for Monitoring Pasture Biomass, Cover and Curing Rates", in *Proceedings of the 5th Australiasian Remote Sensing Conference,* Perth, pp. 228-34.

Zhou, Q. (1987). "Development of a Relational Image-Based Geographical Information System and its Application to Land Resource Studies using Landsat MSS imagery", *Proceedings of the 4th Australasian Remote Sensing Conference,* Adelaide, pp. 590-603.

Zhou, Q. (1989). "A Method for Integrating Remote Sensing and Geographical Information Systems", *Photogrammetric Engineering and Remote Sensing,* Vol. 55(5): 591-96.

13

Multidate Satellite Data for Landuse Change Analysis

R. NAGARAJA

Land is the most important natural endowment on which all the main activities are based. The interaction between man and land (soil), vegetation, water and other resources culminates in the development of landuse. A sequential development of landuse with time results in different land utilization patterns and trends.

Growing population and increased human activities are exerting pressure on limited land resources. This is evident from the decrease in the per capita available cultivable land from 0.48 hectare in 1951 to 0.26 in 1981 and most likely it may reach 0.15 hectare by 2001 A.D. The changing trends in the landuse pattern also indicate that by the turn of the century, the net sown area will increase from the present 143 million to 150 million hectares and at the same time; about 10 million hectares of productive arable land will be lost due to urban and industrial activity. Therefore, this unprecedented demand on land for agriculture, urban and industrial growth and mining besides for forests and pastures (apart from land degradation and erosion) calls for an optimum utilization of land. This requires timely and up-to-date information on the spatial distribution, location, extent, type and its pattern of change over a period of time for scientific landuse planning and management.

Ever since (1972) the remotely sensed data is available, the mapping of landuse/cover has gained importance. Prior to the launch of ERTS-1 in 1972 by the USA, the landuse details were collected by village officers and sample surveys, which lacked the spatial representation, reliability and, by the time the details were compiled and reached the planner, they became obsolete. But remotely sensed data due to its synoptic, unbiased and repetitive coverage provides reliable information on the spatial distribution of landuse. More so this is the only source for the inaccessible areas.

Present Scenario

Organization like the Central Arid Zone Research Institute (CAZRI), Jodhpur; National Remote Sensing Agency (NRSA), Hyderabad; Space Applications Centre (SAC), Ahemdabad; National Bureau of Soil Survey and Land Use Planning (NBSS & LUP), Nagpur; All India Soil and Land Use Survey, Delhi; and other State remote-sensing-centres have been engaged in landuse mapping using remotely sensed data in India. NRSA has carried out landuse surveys in parts of the country using MSS, TM, Pavan Tarra and recently SPOT and IRS data on different scales using digital and visual techniques. Wasteland mapping of the entire country on 1:1 M scale was completed using 1980-82 MSS False Colour Composites and estimated that they were about 53.3 million hectares (16%) of wastelands under eight different categories. As a sequel to this, at the behest of the National Waste land Development Board (NWDB), New Delhi, a detailed mapping of wastelands on 1:50,000 scale for 146 critically affected districts using Landsat Thematic Mapper (TM) data in Phases I and II, up to village level, have been completed and mapping of 84 districts using IRS-LISS-II data is under progress in Phase III. Presently, landuse/land cover mapping of all the States and Union Territories is being carried out on 1:250,000 scale for the Agro-climatic zone planning. IRS-LISS-I data for the seasons i.e. 1988 (Kharif) and 1989 (Rabi) has been used for mapping land use land cover details using hybrid techniques. As many as 274 districts are being mapped using visual interpretation techniques and 168 districts using digital analysis. The final map shows the spatial distribution of landuse details with special reference to the area under cultivation in Kharif and Rabi seasons and also area under double cropping.

Methodology

The methodology is essentially the visual interpretation of satellite data, i.e. Multi Spectral Scanner (MSS) data, of February 1973, and SPOT data of February 1988, for identifying and mapping different categories of landuse/land cover using standard visual image interpretation techniques which are based on tone, texture, shape, size, etc., in addition to the local knowledge. The preliminary interpreted details are ground-checked in order to verify the doubtful areas and, based on the ground verification, the landuse boundaries are finalized. Then, the landuse/land cover categories are transferred to the base map prepared from the typographical maps on 1:50,000 scale. Satellite data of Chandragiri taluk are shown in Fig. 13.1. The final landuse/land cover maps for the two periods are shown in Figs. 13.2 and 13.3.

Landuse/Land Cover Classification System

In the present study the landuse/land cover classification system is adopted based on the classification system developed by the National Remote Sensing Agency (1989). About 5 level I classes and 23 level II classes were identified and mapped using satellite data in the present study. Some of the level II classes could not be identified using MSS data due to its inherent limitation of low spatial resolution (80 m). The classification system followed is shown in Figs. 13.2 and 13.3 as Legend.

Spatial Distribution of Landuse/Land Cover in the Study Area

The spatial distribution of different landuses as on February 1988, was interpreted based on SPOT multispectral data and are shown in Fig. 13.3. The different landuse/land cover classes are briefly discussed in their dimension over space and time.

A. *Built-up Land*

It is defined as an area of human habitation development due to intensive non-agricultural use, where much of the land is covered by the infrastructures of residential, transportation, institutional, industrial, recreation and other utilities in association with water, drainage and vegetation punctuated by vacant lands. Tirupati, Renigunta, Chandragiri and Pakala are the major settlements identified and mapped in the study area. The built-up land in the study area covers about 3,388 hectare (2.40%).

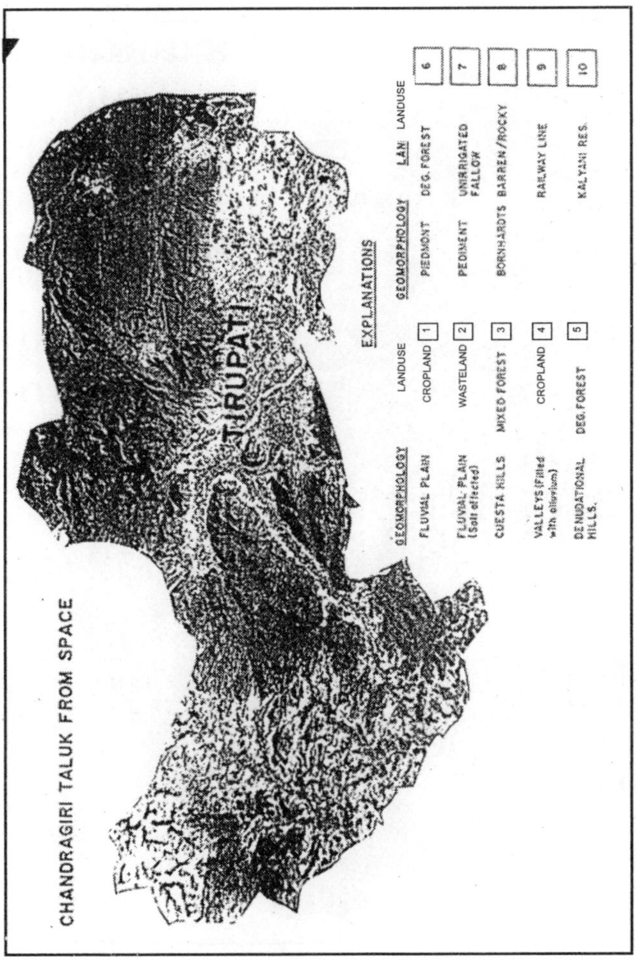

Fig. 13.1: Chandragiri Taluk from Space

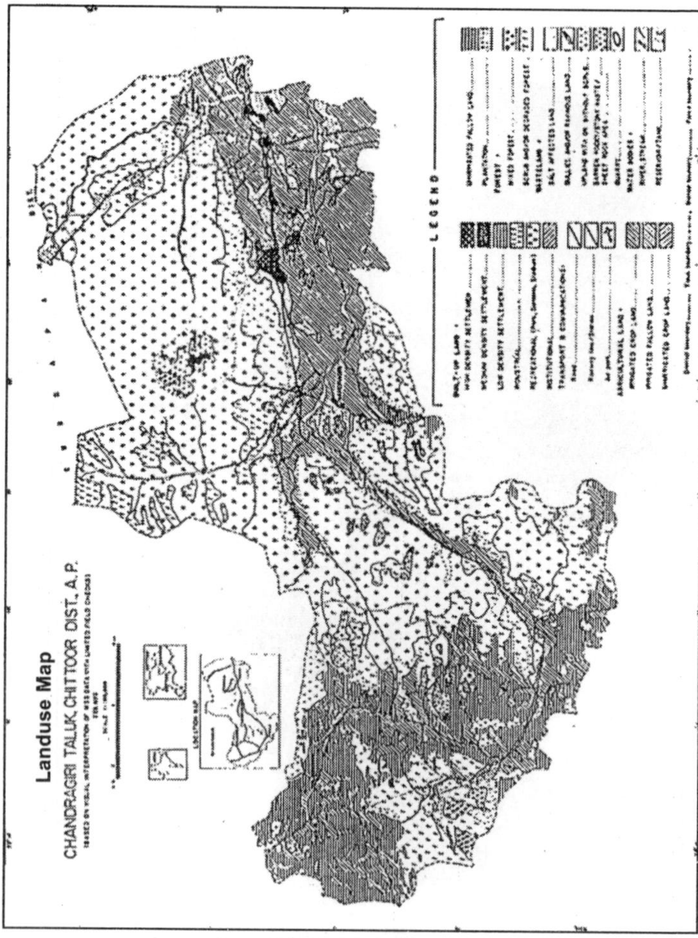

Fig. 13.2: Landuse Map: Chandragiri Taluk, Chittoor Dist., A.P. (Based on Visual Interpretation of MSS Data with Limited Field Checks)

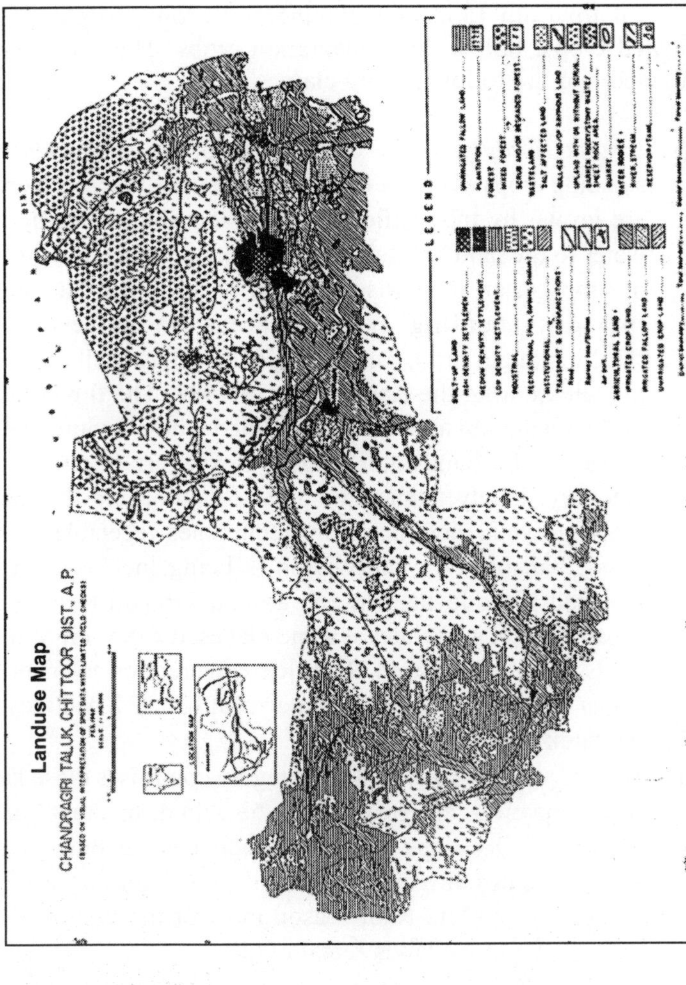

Fig. 13.3: Landuse Map: Chandragiri Taluk, Chittoor Dist., A.P. (Based on Visual Interpretation of MSS Data with Limited Field Checks)

B. ***Agricultural Land***

It is described as the land used for production of farm commodities, lands used for both food and commercial crops, irrigated and unirrigated crops, fallow land, plantation crops. This category is sub-divided into the following sub-classes.

(i) *Irrigated Cropland*: This category comprises those lands with standing crops as on the date of the imagery, where the crops are grown by the artificial distribution and application of water to the land to stimulate, or make possible, the growth of crops in an otherwise too arid or semi-arid climate. It includes standing cropped areas under reservoirs (Mallimadugu, etc.), tanks, dug wells, bore wells, etc., in the taluk during the Rabi season of 1988. The fluvial plain of Swarnamukhi and the valleys filled with alluvium, where surface and groundwater irrigation exist, are forms of this category. Paddy, sugarcane and groundnut are the major crops grown in these lands. In recent times vegetable, fodder grass, banana, etc., cultivation is being increased in the irrigated lands located in and around Tirupati to meet the urban demands. Of late, at some places, the top soil of these lands is being misused for brick construction to meet the urban demand. About 21.51 per cent (30,437 hectares) of the taluk falls in this category.

(ii) *Un-irrigated Cropland*: This category comprises those lands where the crops are grown with the help of natural climatic conditions. Dry crops, such as groundnut, jowar, other pulses, etc., are being cultivated in the study area. Since the imagery belongs to the late Rabi season most of the dry crops are harvested and the lands remain fallow.

(iii) *Irrigated Fallow Land*: These are those irrigated agricultural lands of cropped areas which are allowed to rest un-cropped for one or more seasons. This type of fallow land is mostly seen in and around Tirupathi and Regigunta urban settlements. It accounts for 1.40 per cent area (about 1,923 hectares) in the taluk. Sometimes the irrigated agricultural lands are kept uncultivated for a long time and are sold for urban construction activities to get much higher benefits.

(iv) *Un-irrigated Fallow Land*: These lands are those unirrigated agricultural lands which were lying uncropped at the time of imagery. About 14.69 per cent area (20,780 hectares) is covered by this category. At places these lands are being used for mango plantation which is the most suitable crop for these areas.

(v) *Plantation* : Lands being used for crops of longer duration for the purposes of large-scale production of cashcrops, mango, citrus and other forest plantations like eucalyptus, red sanders, etc., are included in this category. Since the aerial extent of most of these plantations is very limited, only large chunks of plantations are identified and categorized in this class and the small patches are generalized in the cropland. It accounts for only 0.4 per cent of the land (562 hectares) of the taluk. The young plantations which have been planted in recent times by the Forest Department in the notified forest land might have been mis-classified as degraded forest due to lack of sufficient canopy cover. However, wherever, correct ground data of such lands are collected they are classified under plantations.

C. *Forest Land*

About 67,878.54 hectares which account for 48 per cent of the total geographical area of the taluk are under the control of the Forest Department. The notified forest land has been classified under two sub-classes based on the density of forest canopy cover.

(i) *Mixed Forest* : Mixed forest lands are defined as those lands which are at least 20 per cent stocked by trees capable of producing timber or other wood products and which can exert influence on the micro-climate or water regime. It accounts for 13.91 per cent of the land (19,670 hectares) of the taluk. The forest mostly occurs on the slopes of quartzite (western) hills and the Mamandur valley consist of shales and phyllites. The occurrence and non-occurrence of forest depends upon rainfall, relief, location, biotic interference, etc. The hill slopes which receive more rainfall and less biolic interference are covered with mixed forest dominated by deciduous species. These forests contain red sanders (*Ptrerocarpus santalinus*), Yelama (*Anogeissis latifolia*), Yepi (*Hardwikia binata*), Karaka (*Terminalia chebula*), Billundu (*Chloroxylon swietenia*), Devadaru (*Erythroxylon monogynum*), Manga (*Rangia dumetorum*), Niruddi (*Dolichondron crispa*), Pedda bikki (*Gardenia latifolia*), Bikki (*Gardenia cummifora*), Thoda (*Ptersospermum subernifolium*) and Bamboosa species. The red sanders grown only in this region and nowhere else in India, and is mainly confined to the reserved forest of Chamala, Mamandur and Krishnapuram. This important species is being depleted in the region due to illicit and selective felling of this tree. Kesava Raju (1981) has indicated that the best quality red sanders grows in a tropical arid climate at an altitude ranging essentially from 400 to 700 m where very shallow to shallow brown coloured sandy loam of friable nature mixed with boulders covering Nagari quartzites or Pullampet shales of Caddapah upper group of Proterozoic age. Unless care is taken, there is every danger of this rare forest species getting completely extinct in the next few years. It is essential that the Forest Department take extensive plantation in the favourable areas.

(ii) *Scrub and/or Degrade Forest*: Lands as notified under the Forest Act and those lands with a vegetation cover less than 20 per cent of canopy cover are classified in this category. This is the major wetland category in the taluk covering 46,213 hectares (32.67%) of land. The degradation is associated partly with the precipitation-temperature regime and biotic interference. Most of the denudational hills of granitic gneiss and the western part of the quartzite hills form part of this category. The degradation is mostly occurring in the steep-slope areas (more than 15 degree slope) and are subjected to severe to very severe erosion. The uncontrolled grazing, illicit felling of trees for firewood and forest fire are some of the biotic factors which degrade the forest in the region.

D. *Wastelands*

Wasteland is defined as that land which is degraded and is presently lying unutilized due to different constraints. The lands are further sub-divided into the following sub-classes based on the type of constraint existing in that land:

(i) *Salt-affected Land*: The salt-affected land is generally characterized as the land that has adverse effects on the growth of most of the plants due to the action or presence of excess soluble or excess exchangeable sodium. Alkaline land has an exchangeable sodium percentage ES of about 15 which is generally considered as the limit between normal and alkali soils. The predominant salts are carbonate and bi-carbonate of sodium.

About 1.43 per cent area (2,024 hectares) of the taluk falls under this category. It is confined to Tirupati urban, Tirupati rural and Renigunta mandals in the taluk. These areas have brownish/whitish puff at surface and are easily identifiable on the satellite data. These lands are devoid of any vegetation and are subjected to severe erosion. At places, adjacent to the urban settlements, these lands are being used for construction of industries and other urban amenities.

(ii) *Gulled and/or Ravenous Land*: The gullies are formed as a result of localized surface run-off affecting the friable unconsolidated material and forms perceptible channels resulting in undulating terrain. The gullies are the first stage of excessive land dissection followed by their networking which leads to the development of ravenous land. In the study area only a small part of 145 hectares (0.10%) is classified under gullied/ravenous land. This erosion is noticed in Chandragiri and Tirupathi urban mandals along the Bhima and Kalyani rivers respectively in the piedmont plain.

(iii) *Upland with/without Scrub*: This is the second major wasteland category covering 12,890 hectares (9.11%) of the total geographical area in the taluk. The western mandals cover much more area under this category than the eastern. These lands have a very shallow to shallow reddish brown or greyish brown gritty soil cover with moderate slopes and are prone to sheet erosion. Sparse scrub and grass cover is common in these lands. These lands are being encroached upon for dry-crop cultivation wherever possible without proper land management.

(iv) *Barren Rocky/Stony Waste/Sheet Rock Area*: It is described as the rock exposures, often barren and devoid of soil cover and vegetation. It accounts for 2.41 per cent of the area (3,409 hectares) in the taluk. Most of the bornyards in the granite gneiss terrain are lying as barren peaks in the taluk.

(v) *Quarry*: The barren rocky areas which are located adjacent to the urban settlements and are easily approachable are being used for quarrying to meet the local (construction material) demands. Two major quarry places are identified and mapped in taluk—one near the Peruru village of Tirupati urban mandal and the other near the Ithepalli village of Chandragiri Mandal.

E. *Water Bodies*

This category includes all tanks/reservoir in the taluk which are covered with water.

Landuse/Land Cover Pattern of Change Between 1973 and 1988

The six mandals (earlier there were six taluks) comprising the taluk of Changragiri extended over 1,414.5 sq. km. (1,41,450 hectares). While there has been no change in the total geographical area in the taluk, the landuse pattern in the taluk has undergone significant changes in the last 15 years, i.e. from 1973 to 1988 (Figs. 13.2 and 13.3). Area under different categories and their percentage changes are shown in Table 13.1. The changes occurred in the taluk with respect to landuse/land cover during the above period are as follows:

(a) There is an increase in urban/built-up land from 1,371 to 3,388 hectares during the last 15 years. This increase in the urban/built-up land is mainly due to (a) increase in the population especially urban population from 1,09,366 to 1,75,624. The graph shows that there was very little increase in the urban population till 1951 and a steep increase from 1951 onwards (Fig. 13.4).

(b) Change in the Central place activity from piligrim to piligrim-cum-educational and then later to pilgrim-cum-education-cum-industrial. Since the presence of the famous piligrim town, Tirumala, the town central place activity was pilgrimage till the establishment of Sree Venkateswara University in the mid-1950s, since when the educational activity has also gained importance. From the mid-1970s the Tirupati urban complex has assumed importance in industrial development due to the creation of industrial estates. Tables 13.2 and 13.3 show the categorywise growth of industries during different periods in the taluk and reveals that industrial activities have been increasing from 1975 onwards.

(c) The area under agricultural land is more or less constant during the above period, i.e. 53,550 hectares (1973) and

Table 13.1: Area under Different Landuse and Land Cover Categories in Chandragiri taluk (1973-1978)

S. No.	Catagory	Feb. 1973*		Feb. 1988**		% change between 1973 & 1988
		Area in Hectares				
		Area	%	Area	%	
1.	Builtup land	1371	0.97	3388	2.40	+ 1.43
2.	Irrigated cropland	32520	22.29	30437	21.51	– 1.48
3.	Irrigated fallow	560	0.40	1923	1.40	+ 1.00
4.	Unirrigated fallow	20050	14.17	20780	14.69	+ 0.52
5.	Plantation	420	0.30	562	0.40	+ 0.10
6.	Mixed Forest	43259	30.58	19670	13.91	–16.67
7.	Scrub/degraded forests	24220	17.12	46213	32.67	+ 15.55
8.	Salt affected land	1552	1.07	2024	1.43	+ 0.36
9.	Gullied/Ravenous land	80	0.6	145	0.10	+ 0.04
10.	Uplands with of without scrub	15560	00.00	12890	9.11	– 1.89
11.	Barren rocky/stony/sheet rock area	1890	1.34	3409	2.41	+ 1.07
	Total	141450	100	141450	100	

Notes:

* Area estimated based on Landuse map prepared from satellite (MSS) data using Planimeter and Dot Grid method.

** Area estimated based on Landuse map prepared from satellite (SPOT) data using Planimeter and Dot Grid methods.

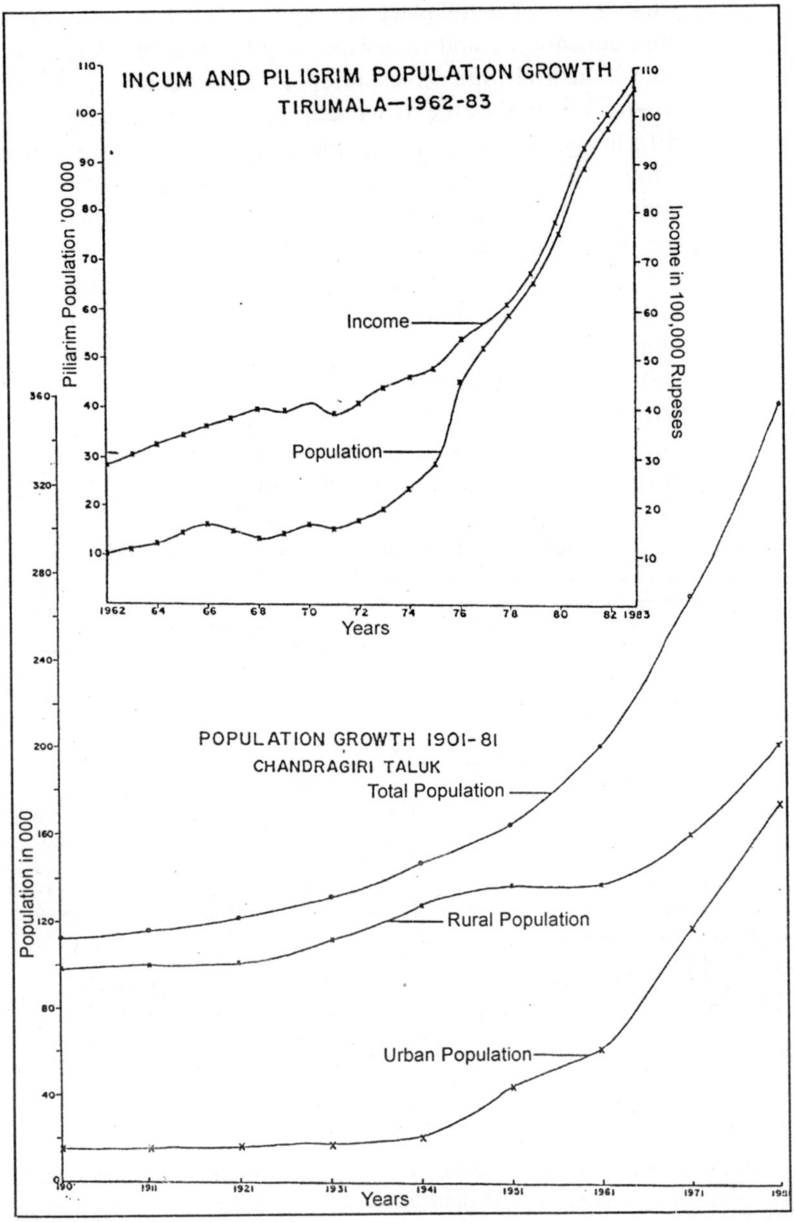

Fig. 13.4: Incum and Pilgrim Population Growth Tirumala—1962-83

53702 hectares (1988). However, there is a slight reduction in the irrigated crop land (about 1.48 %) maybe due to encroachment for urban activities in and around Tirupati, and also part of the irrigated lands have converted to saline/alkaline lands due to mismanagement. There was a slight increase in the irrigated fallow land (about 1%). The reason for this could be that some of the irrigated fallow land in and around Tirupati is kept vacant with the intention to sell it for urban activities for higher benefits. There is also a slight increase in the area under plantation crops due to increasing social forestry activity in the taluk.

Table 13.2: Growth of Large and Medium-scale Industries in Chandragiri Taluk

Sl. No.	*Period*	*No. of Units*	*No. of Workers*	*Captial Invesment (Rs. in lakhs)*	*Production (in lakh Tonnecs)*
1.	Before 1965	1 (1L)	500	60	55
2.	1965-70	4 (1L)	1020	234	215
3.	1970-75	3 (2L)	850	875	868
4.	1975-80	9 (2L)	1124	1036	1035
	Total	17 (6L+11M)	3494	2205	2173

Note : L—Large scale industries.
M—Medium scale industries.

Table 13.3: Growth of Small Scale Industries in Chandragiri Taluk

Sl. No.	*Period*	*No. of Units*	*No. of Workers*	*Captial Invesment (in Rs. lakhs)*	*Production Capacity (in lakh tonnes)*
1.	Before 1965	3	21	2.5	0.92
2.	1965-70	36	373	59.27	75.42
3.	1970-75	68	641	67.91	89.55
4.	1975-81	76	965	11.97	79.80
	Total	183	1600	249.08	246.20

(d) The taluk covers about 678.79 sq. km (48 %) under the notified forest area. The decrease in area under mixed forest from 30.58 per cent (1973) to 13.01 per cent (1988) of 23,589 hectares during the 15-year period was very significant and is attributed mainly to (i) large-scale felling of trees in the attributed forest land to meet the demands of firewood and building construction material of ever increasing population, (ii) illegal encroachment, (iii) forest fire, and (iv) overgrazing and other natural factors like recurring droughts in the region due to frequent failure of monsoons in the recent past. Correspondingly the area under scrub/degraded forest has been increased from 17.12 per cent (1973) to 32.67 per cent (1988). About 15.96 sq.km of the notified forest land (67,479 to 65,883) has become barren rocky area due to the erosion of top soil over steep slopes.

(e) The area under saline/alkaline area has been increased from 152 hectares (1973) to 2,024 hectares (1988) in the taluk. This increase could be due to mismanagement of land in the Swarnamukhi fluvial plain, lack of proper drainage, higher temperature, low rainfall, etc.

(f) The gullied and ravenous land in the taluk is mainly observed in the piedmont plain of the Tirupati hills and is developed due to the intensive erosion of the Kalyani and Bhima rivers. The loosely deposited sediments over the piedmont plain are eroded due to lack of vegetative cover. The area under this category has been increased from 80 hectares in 1973 to 145 hectares in 1988. Most of the area covering this unit is under the control of the Forest Department.

(g) The area under upland with or without scrub has decreased from 11 per cent (1973) to 9.11 per cent, i.e. 3,670 hectares in the taluk. The reason for this could be the marginal lands which are amenable to cultivation are brought under dry cultivation. Also part of these lands is converted into built-up area. This is found more in the western mandals than in the eastern mandals.

(h) There was an increase in the barren rocky/sheet rock/stony wasteland from 1.34 per cent (1973) to 2.41 per cent. The increase is mainly noticed in the notified forest land in the western mandals. Due to the removal of the vegetative cover

over the steep slopes, the top soil has been washed off by running water and the slopes are exposed as a barren rocky area. If the slopes are not covered with suitable vegetation, there is every possible danger that the slopes will become barren in years to come and cannot support any vegetation.

Conclusion

The study reveals that multidate remotely sensed data can provide information on landuse/land cover and its changes over a period of time. The high resolution data like SPOT will provide more details compared to low resolution data. Since the remotely sensed data is available in digital form, the computer analysis will provide more accurate and pixelwise information. The microwave data will provide as new dimension for landuse analysis due to its all-weather capability and its ability to discriminate the features based on indicators such as texture, surface roughness and corner effect, which are different from the optical data.

Acknowledgements

The author is grateful to Prof. K. Vitthal Reddy, Osmania University, for his guidance during the study. The author is also thankful to Prof. B.L. Deekshatulu, Director, NRSA, Dr. D.P. Rao, Group Head, Applications-1, and Dr. N.C. Gautam, Head, Landuse and Cartography Division, NRSA, for their valuable suggestions and permission to present this paper.

REFERENCES

Anderson, J.R., Hardy, E.E. and Reich, J.T. (1972). "Land Use Classification System for Use with Remote Sensing Data," *USGS Professional Paper 964*.

Census of India, (1981). *District Census Handbook*. Chittoor District. Pub. Census Operation, Hyderabad.

Director of Town Planning, (1974). "Draft Outline Development Plan for Tirupati", Unphblished Report, Director, Town Planning, Government of Andhra Pradesh, Hyderabad.

FAO, (1974). "Approaches to Land Classification," *Pub. Int. Inst. Aerial Sur. and Earth Sci.* (ITC), Enschede, The Netherlands.

Gautam, N.C. and Narayan, L.R.A. (1982). *Suggested Land Use/Land Cover Classification System for India Using Remote Sensing Techniques*, Mathura: Pink Pub. House.

Kesavaraju, K. (1981). "Geobotany and Bio-geochemistry of Red Sanders." (Unpublished Ph.D. Thesis, S.V. University, Tirupati).

Nagaraja, R. (1988). "Mapping and Monitoring of Forest Resources Using Multi-date Landsat Data: A Case Study of Andhra Pradesh," *Indian Geographical Journal*, Vol. 62 (1).

Vasudeva Reddy, P. (1984). "Land Use Analysis in Chandragiri Taluk, Chittoor District, Andhra Pradesh, India." (Unpublished Ph.D. thesis, S.V. University, Tirupati).

14

Agricultural Research and Third World Poverty*

D.J. GREENLAND

Poverty, rather than the inability to grow food, is the primary cause of hunger in the world today. There are some areas, particularly in Africa but also in other continents, where, from time to time, subsistence farmers have difficulty in producing sufficient food for themselves and their families, as recent climatic and political aberrations have shown. But the greatest number of malnourished people almost certainly exist amongst the landless labourers of Asia and the massive numbers of unemployed migrants who have moved into the shanty town areas of large cities in the Third World. These facts have important implications for the direction of agricultural research, particularly that which is conducted with the expressed purpose of helping developing countries solve their food problem. The objectives of higher yield and concentration on food crops rather than cash crops, or other income-generating activities, as has prevailed for the past three decades, may well be questioned.

Agricultural research which has helped to increase food crop production in subsidized agricultural systems in the developed world has tended to keep the price of food low. While helping urban populations, this has had a depressing effect on the incomes of unsubsidized Third (and First) World farmers and the rural workforce. The research which has raised the productivity of rice, wheat and other crops in developing countries has made food more cheaply available. This is to the advantage of the urban poor, but the depressed

* Reprinted with permission from *Developing World Agriculture*, Grosvenor Press International.

prices discourage some at least of the farming community, particularly those in disadvantaged areas where profit margins are least. It seems important, therefore, to address the question of where agricultural research should be directed if it is to be of greatest assistance to Third World countries and not to discourage their poorest communities.

Changes in Productivity and Poverty in the Third World

Over the past 25 years in the environmentally more favoured parts of Asia and Latin America, total production, production per hectare, and production per capita of food has increased. The primary source was the development of improved plant types of rice and wheat, which were able to utilize nutrients, particularly nitrogen, more efficiently. To realize the potential of these improved plant types, improved agronomic and other practices had to be introduced, particularly proper fertilizer application, pest control and land and water management.

Where conditions were suitable, and particularly where irrigation was available, all these elements were brought together and spectacular successes were achieved, leading to the use of the terms "Green Revolution", "miracle rice" and others. This helped to build the confidence of politicians and farmers, and those responsible for providing development aid, in agricultural research in Third World countries. It led among other things to the formation of the Consultative Group on International Agricultural Research (CGIAR) and the International Agricultural Research Centres (IARCs) supported by it.

Sometimes extravagant publicity also attracted the criticism of those who were concerned about the landless and others not benefiting from the changes. These included the farmers in the less advantaged regions. For example, improvements in rice yields have been much greater in the well irrigated areas of northern India than in the flood and drought-prone areas of eastern India and similar differences are found with irrigated and non-irrigated rice in the Philippines. Because total rice production has been much greater, prices have tended to fall in real terms. Where the higher production was sufficient to offset this fall in price, as well as the extra costs of production, the farmers benefited. But in the unfavoured areas, where little change in production occurred, the farmer was worse off unless governments took measures to support prices to farmers.

Several other adverse effects of the introduction of higher yielding food crop varieties, and the associated production techniques, have been described. Griffin[1], for instance, has drawn attention to the increasing impoverishment of the landless as modern crop production techniques have been introduced into Third World countries. This effect is nevertheless wholly or partially offset in some areas by the increased employment opportunities to which more intensive production methods give rise, and by the lower food prices[2] which benefit the landless labourers as well as the urban poor.

The problems of the disadvantaged rural communities have led many donor agencies and those concerned with international agricultural research to turn their attention from the problem of greater production where it is most easily obtained, to that of applying agricultural research to the relief of poverty.

Strategies for Disadvantaged Areas

Thus the Technical Advisory Committee (TAG) to the CGIAR in their Review of CGIAR Priorities and Future Strategies (1985) recommended increased attention should be given to the crops of disadvantaged areas—root crops and coarse grains—at the expense of rice and wheat, and greater attention to methods of improving production from poorer areas—lands where rainfall is erratic and irrigation not available and where soils are poor. The important and essential role which farming systems research has to play if changes are to occur in disadvantaged areas was only implicitly recognized in this review.

Although improved crop varieties and the elements of improved land management practices can be developed in station-based research, they can only be evaluated in the physical, social and economic environments in which they are to be used. In unfavoured areas, experience of the past two decades has shown that it is essential to link research station work with farming system studies conducted "on-farm" land involving the farmer if new technologies are to be developed which help the farmer. The great economic and social diversity, and of soil and other physical factors, that exists also requires special attention to be given to environmental characterization so that determination of the "extrapolation domain" becomes possible.

The importance of relating experiment station results to farmers' fields has long been recognized, although relatively few experiments on food crops were conducted on small farms in the tropics earlier than the "extension trials" with fertilizers in Ghana.[3] Such experiments with fertilizers were conducted on a much wider scale by FAO in its "Freedom from Hunger Campaign". While often successful as demonstrations, such trials did not take account of the wide range of circumstances which limit a farmer's options and determine his actions. The need to make a much more complete assessment of the factors controlling a farming system through more detailed on-farm assessments of the performance of crop varieties and changed management practices was recognised by Norman and by several other workers in the 1960s.[4]

Subsequently, the farming systems approach to agricultural research has crystallized as a methodology for evaluating, refining and extending improved production practices. Its importance in disadvantaged areas may be illustrated by considering specific examples—of the small rice farmer who does not have access to irrigation water, and the shifting cultivator in Africa.

The Iloilo Experience

The one resource common to almost all farmers in the tropics is a year-round temperature favourable to crop growth. If water is available throughout the year, several crops may be grown in succession. In some places, three and even four rice crops are produced in a year. But less than half of the rice farmers in Asia have the advantage of irrigation water. With rainfall concentrated in a single monsoon season, it has been difficult, without irrigation, to produce more than one rice crop per year. The introduction of a high-yielding, short-duration, pest-resistant variety, IR36, opened the door to a two-crop system for rainfed areas. Its testing and evaluation in farmers' fields showed that a double crop system was possible, but to be successful it had to be accompanied by a dry-seeding technique to ensure establishment of the first crop at the start of the rains, and to be used with a short "turnaround" time between crops. It was also necessary for the first crop to be processed quickly to release labour to establish the second crop.[5]

The appropriate technology, including design of small cheap threshers, was developed at the International Rice Research Institute (IRRI) in the Philippines, tested on rainfed farms at Iloilo, and rapidly adopted. The effect was not only greater income for the farmers, but more employment for labour and a boost to employment, not only because of the greater amount of labour required to handle the extra production but also because the small axial-flow threshers introduced to speed up the processing of the first crop were made by local manufacturers. The initial farming systems research project led to a larger, World Bank funded development project [Rainfed Agricultural Development (Iloilo) Project, RADIP], which has made a major change to prosperity in what had been a depressed area. At the start of the project, on-farm research was conducted on about 30 farms. This was accompanied by extension work in several nearby areas. Information exchange between the research project and the extension areas greatly accelerated the adoption of improved technology, and ensured involvement of a large group of farmers not only in evaluation, but in the research process. The second stage of the project, RADIP, involved more than 25,000 farmers.[6]

The methodology used at Iloilo has been described fully.[7] It is a cropping system, rather than a farming system, methodology. It has worked well in non-irrigated but otherwise relatively favourable lowland areas, where soils are rather easily cultivated and the onset of the wet season is reasonably certain. Attempts to extrapolate the success of the Iloilo project have shown how intensification of the cropping system is dependent on the characteristics of the physical environment—rainfall variability as well as seasonality, and soil and land types[5,6]—and have emphasized the importance of establishing the physical and social factors which determine the extrapolation domain.

The Iloilo experience was successful because the new technology was appropriate to the area, economically advantageous and received strong local support from all sections of the community. It has undoubtedly been advantageous to small farmers, and generated employment and so contributed to poverty relief amongst the landless. In general, cropping intensification is likely to operate in this way. It has been suggested that the new technology would have been successful without the study of the farming system—all that was necessary was good extension. This is unlikely. The "farming systems" group in fact fed back to the scientists developing the component technology essential information about its performance and the farmers' needs. The other advantage was that farmers were immediately exposed to and involved in the generation of the new technology. When it was successful they acted as extension agents, lauding its success to their colleagues, and so simplifying and catalysing the work of more formal extension.

The "Improved Fallow" Experience

The success of the Iloilo project may be contrasted with the slow rate of success in developing better farming systems for upland areas in Africa. One of the major impediments to agricultural development in Africa has been the failure to find a sustainable system for improved arable crop production in the humid and sub-humid tropical areas.

When population pressure is low and sufficient land is available for it to be left under natural vegetation for enough years to restore fertility after a short cultivation period, then shifting cultivation is an adequate system.[8] As population pressure intensifies, cropping periods are extended and the length of fallow shortened. Crop production declines rapidly and with it, income and food availability. As an alternative to shifting cultivation, planted fallows of trees, grasses and legumes to improve on the natural fallow have been studied for many years.[9] In spite of research station results to demonstrate their effectiveness, little farmer adoption has occurred.

Recently, much attention has been given to the use of *Leucaena leucocephala* in alley cropping or other systems.[10] A very similar system was in fact advocated much earlier and tried using alleys of *Acioa barteri.*[11] Leucaena (ipil-ipil, the "miracle tree") is valued for its leaves which can be used as animal feed, for its stems for firewood, for its nitrogen fixing ability and favourable effects on soil fertility, and for the fact that it makes an effective soil erosion barrier. The tree itself has, in fact, been widely adopted by farmers in Asia, primarily as a source of fodder. The regimentation of its use in "alley cropping" and the limitation of its use by cattle because of the trypanosomiasis problems are factors which have mitigated against its wider adoption. Farmers will undoubtedly modify alley cropping better to meet their needs as its advantages and limitations are understood by them, and on-farm research conducted with a farming systems perspective. The network recently developed by the International Institute of Tropical Agriculture (IITA) focused on alley farming should do much to accelerate its wider adaptation and adoption.

Several authors have stressed the importance of farmer involvement in the research process, particularly in the most disadvantaged areas where it is difficult to find successful innovations.[12] The farmer has found a way of surviving in these areas, and of organizing a social existence. New innovations have to fit not only the ecology in physical terms, but also the social and economic conditions in which the community lives. The failure to involve farmers in the design and evaluation of improved fallow systems in relation to their needs appears to have been a major limitation to their adoption. More than 50 years of failure in research on natural fallows might have been avoided if the research had been conducted concurrently on-farm, in a farming system context, as well as at research stations.

Sharing Farming Systems Research

From the two examples described above we can see the need for studies to be conducted with a farming systems perspective. Such studies involve many farms and farmers in a well characterised environment. It is also essential that the work be continued over a period of several years—at least five or six—and more if a cropping system involving woody fallows is to be studied. The work is, therefore, expensive, and normally requires an interdisciplinary team of scientists and field assistants to be assigned to the project for a lengthy period.[13]

For the results of such work to have a sufficiently broad impact to justify the cost it is important that the work not only has a wide extrapolation domain, but also is widely tested and adapted. Sharing of the work and results can be greatly facilitated through international networks.

There is now an increasing understanding of the way in which networks must operate to be successful on an international scale.[14] A prototype of such networks was the Asian Cropping Systems Network. Now, IITA, the International Livestock Centre for Africa (ILCA), the International Council for Research in Agroforestry (ICRAF) and the International Irrigation Management Institute (IIMI) all coordinate networks with the objective of sharing results on improved farming systems. A common feature of these networks is that national programme leaders are invited to meet once or twice a year to share results and discuss future actions. The networks are also normally associated with training programmes so that the field teams understand the methodology and objectives of the research programmes.

Participation in such networks is, of course, voluntary and requires a recognition by the national leaders of the advantages they derive. They will normally have to make a significant commitment of national funds to network activities, although coordination of the network may be funded internationally.[15]

One of the major successes of the farming systems approach is the identification of problems which require more detailed research. Different participants in a network often agree to take the lead in research on one of these topics, or an international centre may agree to do so, or the problem may be referred to a particular group of researchers, who have particular skills to apply to the problem.

A feature of the network model developed by the International Board for Soil Research and Management (IBSRAM) is the linkage between basic or strategic research and cells of the network. Support from basic research laboratories to assist in the solution of applied problems has been a feature of the work of the centres of the CGIAR system.

The coordination of international networks is expensive, and their effective management is not easy, but given funding and sensitive supervision, they offer an opportunity to tackle some of the more intractable problems of development in disadvantaged areas.

Increasing Income

Better management may enable production of food crops to be increased in disadvantaged areas. It will, however, be most unlikely to increase production to the levels obtained in more favoured areas. Frequently, it will do no more than help to maintain subsistence as population pressure grows. If an impact is to be made on income, it is usually necessary to find a subsidiary enterprise to food crop production. Such an enterprise has to be compatible with the farmer's circumstances. When he lives near subsistence, it has to be compatible with the farming system which produces the food on which he and his family survive.

Farmers, of course, are only too well aware of the need to have income generating enterprises. When an economic market for smallholder cash crops is established, they respond readily and rapidly—many examples with coconuts, cotton, coffee, cocoa, tobacco and other crops could be cited. Animal production as an adjunct to crop production is even more common and successful.

Outstanding rice farmers were invited to participate at IRRI's 25th Anniversary celebrations. They gave their insights on what makes an outstanding rice farmer—limited as they were to farms of less than 5 hectares.[16] Without exception they described subsidiary income generating enterprises maintained alongside rice farming.

The International Agricultural Research system has been slow to respond to the need to support income generating activities for small farmers. The 1985 TAC report to the CGIAR on priorities and future strategies suggested topics which might be considered in the future "assuming a gradual solution of the food issue". The topics involved:

(i) long-term issues regarding ecological management and conservation, and
(ii) energy concerns, but
(iii) "another area of concern for the long-term future will be improved technology for the world's important small-holder cash crops".

It recommended that priority be given to the inclusion of vegetables, coconuts and aqua-culture in the CGIAR system. Each of these are sources of income, and production of vegetables, coconut and fish is often conducted as a subsidiary enterprise to rice production. TAC also recommended that the CGIAR system should give high priority to livestock management systems for the grassland savannas and humid tropical forests.

The adoption of such income generating activities is, of course, dependent on compatibility with the farmer's system. He will only adopt new enterprises or changed techniques if they allow him to continue with methods for the production of his staple foodstuffs on which he knows he must rely. The farming systems approach is well suited to the study of integration of cash crops, animal production and fish ponds with an existing farming system.

Conclusion

Mellor[17] at the 1988 meeting of the CGIAR in Washington emphasised the continuing need for yield levels of the major staples to be raised, but also urged that the CGIAR should broaden its efforts "in the direction of labour-intensive agricultural commodities, such as horticulture, which are good for poverty alleviation, good for growth, and good for trade." There is now a structure in existence to serve the research needs to increase productivity of the major food crops, and given continued financial support it should meet those needs adequately. But too little has so far been done to help find ways by which the income of subsistence and near subsistence farmers may be enhanced.

Farming close to subsistence levels with traditional farming methods affords no opportunity for the land to support more people. For these areas improved varieties and methods of production of cereals, root crops, oil crops, animals and fish must be developed and evaluated under the farming conditions where they are to be used. Farming systems research methods are still evolving, but the essential components of "FSR" are now well understood.[18] On-farm research has to be associated with research station work, and one feeds the other with problems and potential solutions. The on-farm work, like networking, is relatively expensive, and it is desirable that the results and problems be shared as widely as possible, a process enhanced by networking.

The newer international centres, not yet part of the CGIAR, which have been established to foster a network approach to the problem of development in disadvantaged areas (ICRAF, IBSRAM, for instance) as well as the relevant activities at the existing CGIAR Centres, merit much stronger support in the immediate future, as an addition, not an alternative, to the current international research effort.

Acknowledgements

This article was first presented as the 1988 Blackman Memorial Lecture, Department of Plant Sciences, University of Oxford.

REFERENCES

1. Griffin K. (1974). *The Political Economy of Agrarian Change*. New York: Macmillan.
2. Scobie, G.M. and Posada, R. (1978). *Amer. J. Agric. Econ.* 60, 85.
   Lipton M. and Longhurst R. (1985). *CGIAR Study Paper No. 2*. Washington: The World Bank.
3. Nye P.H., Empire J. (1953). *Expt. Agric.* 21, 176.
4. Norman D.W. (1980). "Farming Systems Approach: Relevance to the small farmer". *MSU Rural Development Paper No. 5*: Michigan State University, East Lancing.

5. Morris, RA. (1984). A decade of on-farm research in lowland rice-based farming systems: some lessons, *Proceedings, Farming Systems Research Symposium,* Kansas State University.
   Price, E.C. (1982). *Cropping Systems Research in Asia,* pp. 709-20. Los Banos: International Rice Research Institute.
6. Rosario, E.L. (1985). *Agricultural Systems Research for Developing Countries* (ed. J. Remenyi) pp. 108-15, ACIAR Proceedings No. 11. Canberra: ACIAR.
7. Zanstra, H.G., Price, E.C. Litsinger, J.A. and Morris, R.A. (1981). *A Methodology for on-farm Cropping Systems Research.* Los Banos: International Rice Research Institute.
8. Nye, P.H. and Greenland, D.J. (1960). *The Soil under Shifting Cultivation,* Farnham Royal: CAB.
9. Nye, P.H.J. (1958). *West African Sci. Association,* 4, 31.
   Nye, P.H. and Stevens, D. (1962). *Agriculture and Land Use in Ghana* (ed. J.B. Wills) pp. 127-143. London: Oxford University Press.
10. Kang, B.T., Wilson, G.F. and Lawson, T.T., (1986). *Alley cropping, a stable alternative to shifting cultivation,* Ibadan: International Institute for Tropical Agriculture.
11. Charter, C.F. (1955). The mechanisation of peasant agriculture and the maintenance of soil fertility with bush fallows, *Proceedings CCTA Conference on the Mechanisation of Agriculture,* Entebbe, Uganda.
12. Chambers, R. and Ghildyal, B.P. (1984). "Agricultural Research for Resource-Poor Farmers: the Farmer-First-and-Last Model", *Agric. Admin.* 20, 1.
    Lightfoot, C., de Guia O and Ocado F. (1988). *Experimental Agric.* 24, 301.
13. Norman, D.W. and Collinson, M. (1985). *Agricultural Systems Research for Developing Countries* (ed. J. Remenyi). ACIAR. Proceeding No. 11. ACIAR, Canberra.
14. Plucknett, D.L. and Smith, N.J.H. (1984). *Science*, 225, 989.
    Greenland, D.J., Craswell, E.T. and Dagg, M. (1987). *Outlook on Agriculture,* 16, 41.
15. Webster, B., Valverde, C. and Fletcher, A. (1987). *The Impact of Research on National Agricultural Development,* The Hague: International Service for National Agricultural Research.
16. International Rice Research Institute (1986). *Insights of Outstanding Rice Farmers.* Los Banos: IRRI.
17. Mellor, J. (1988). Agriculture Development Opportunities for the 1990s—the Role of Research. Address at International Centres Week of the CGIAR, World Bank, Washington DC.
18. Merriil-Sands, D. and McAllister, J. (1988). "Strengthening the integration of on-farm client-oriented research and experiment station research in national agricultural research systems (NARS): Management Lessons from

nine country case studies", *OFCOR Comparative Paper No. 1*, pp. 66, The Hague: ISNAR.

19. Herdt, R.W. and Capule, C. (1983). *Adoption, spread and production impact of modern rice varieties in Asia.* Philippines, Los Banos: International Rice Research Institute.
20. Swaminathan, M.S. (1986). Building National and Global Nutrition Security Systems, pp. 417-49, in Swaminathan, M.S. and Sinha, S.K. (eds.), *Global Aspects of Food Production.* London: Tycooly Publishing.

15

Sustainable Development, Poverty Alleviation and Limited-Resource Farmers

Rethinking the Mission of Agricultural Support in Asia

BRUCE KOPPEL

Contemporary agricultural support systems in Asia's developing countries evolved principally to strengthen productivity growth for basic food and agricultural commodities. In the 1980s, these systems had increasingly to fulfil this mission while facing declining financial support and, in many instances, competition for technological advance from domestic and transnational proprietary agricultural research (Evenson and Pray, 1991). It is now apparent that agricultural support systems in Asia's developing countries face two additional challenges. These challenges do not simply impinge on the systems' capacities to address the productivity mission—they require in fact a redefinition of the support systems' mission. These two challenges are the issues of sustainable development and poverty alleviation. The issue of sustainable resource development has acquired wide recognition relatively recently, and has even become commonplace as an objective of national resource plans, but what it actually means for the mission and management of agricultural research and extension is less clear. The issue of poverty alleviation and the roles of the agricultural support system is not new, and indeed is the subject of an enormous literature, but it is still not clear that the full implications of this issue have been faced. What is clear is that together, both challenges may mandate a significant rethinking of what the mission of the agricultural support system is.

To speak of rethinking the mission of the agricultural support system is no small task nor is it a task that can usefully occur in a vacuum. Agricultural research and extension exist and have already played crucial roles in Asia's recent agricultural development. Any reassessments of the roles of agricultural research and extension should not do anything to weaken this system, but rather should emphasize directions in which the system can realistically and effectively move (cf. Echeverria, 1990). This paper is designed to contribute to this objective by indicating one way of determining what the challenges of sustainable development and poverty alleviation might mean for the mission of agricultural research and extension. To do this, the paper briefly reviews some of the most important factors influencing the future of agriculture in Asia, examines the question of sustainability as a criterion for judging resource management, and comments on the status of Asia's agricultural support systems. With these points as a background, the paper focuses on limited resource farmers, the group that may be most germane if agricultural research and extension are going to effectively increase their concern for both sustainable resource development and alleviation of rural poverty. Discussion focuses on a crucial distinction: between agricultural support fundamentally as a transfer process and agricultural support fundamentally as a transformational process.

Future of Agriculture

Since the early 1960s, overall production of major foodgrains in Asia has increased dramatically. For example, rice productivity increased from 1,500 kg per hectare in 1965 to over 2,500 in 1985 in South Asia and from close to 1,600 kg per hectare in 1965 to almost 3,000 in 1985 in South-east Asia. This growth is a result primarily of technological innovation represented by higher-yielding varieties and increased utilization of fertilizer, infrastructure improvement represented by significant investments in roads and irrigation and more intensive cultivation represented by double and triple cropping on newly irrigated fields and the opening of new agricultural areas.

At the same time, in parts of South and South-east Asia, per capita food production has grown only marginally and in some places, grain yields since the mid-1980s have shown evidence of levelling. This is a potentially troubling prospect given the complacency that appears to be setting in about agricultural development in Asia. A variety of factors, ranging from environmental degradation and urban expansion to economic mismanagement, civil disorder and political interference have been associated with declines in prime agricultural areas actually harvested with food crops. For example, food policy—the effort, in principle, to strike a balance between low consumer prices (consistent with reducing inflationary pressures on wages) and high producer prices (consistent with ensuring incentives for adequate domestic production and, possibly reducing incentives for rural-urban migration)—has had a mixed record and in many cases, may be suppressing both agricultural incomes and productivity without noticeably improving overall nutrition levels (Mann and Huddleston, 1986). Additional factors, including rural unemployment and population growth, have been associated with increases in marginal areas being utilized for food production. The combined result can be lower average productivity.

At least four additional reasons for existing or prospective problems in maintaining grain yields can be noted.

1. In some cases, drops (and rises) in agricultural production are statistical artifacts. For example, an extensive re-evaluation is currently underway in the Philippines where the National Census and Statistics Office is re-assessing a wide range of national statistics, including agricultural productivity estimates. Because these estimates were based on samples drawn from farmers participating in the Government's rice support programme, a programme that has experienced declining participation since the late 1970s, there are reasons to believe the Philippine production estimates may have been inflated. In many countries, statistical systems for estimating crop production have generally under-sampled more remote farmers. As the systems improve their coverage, reports of "declining" yield can be expected.
2. There is a growing problem pest resurgence. Extensive use of commercial pesticides by farmers who could afford them helped keep pest damage on rice and wheat down during the late 1970s and early 1980s. However, insect pests evolve

and adapt very quickly to environmental changes. There is evidence that the evolution of pests affecting Asia's major food crops is now outpacing the evolution of chemicals to control them. Pest problems are becoming more serious and there are no simple answers available in terms of "off-the-shelf" chemicals. Attention is turning to other strategies that might be more compatible with the realities of pest evolution and also more accessible by a wider range of farmers. But in the interim, vulnerability to serious pest problems is increasing.

3. There is a problem of irrigation deterioration. Investment in irrigation is one of the major chapters in the "Green Revolution" story for rice. In South Asia alone, projected need for new irrigation investment during the coming decade amounts to tens of billions of dollars. However, maintenance of existing irrigation facilities has proved less than satisfactory in many instances. Inadequate maintenance of irrigation facilities can seriously undermine productivity. For example, poor maintenance is frequently associated with poor drainage. Eventually, this leads to waterlogged soils. Improper canal maintenance can impede water flow, reducing the reliable irrigation service area. In the last few years, more attention has been given to irrigation management (including now the establishment of an International Irrigation Management Institute in Sri Lanka), but solving the problem will take considerable time and commitment. In the interim, productivity within many irrigation systems will continue to be less than what is possible and may even show signs of decline.
4. There is a transformation of rural labour markets in Asia which implies increasing levels of work and income diversification. In some cases, this process is a result of stagnant or declining agricultural productivity. Households are exporting labour (usually women and children) into other non-agricultural labour markets in an effort to maintain their welfare levels. Unfortunately, however, the withdrawal of labour from agriculture can lead to a downward spiral in productivity. In other cases, rural labour diversification is

> associated with rising agricultural labour productivity. In these circumstances, off-farm work becomes feasible as a welfare augmenting strategy. However, here too, if the withdrawal of labour and investment from agriculture is too aggressive, the viability of the household's agriculture base can be weakened. In both cases, labour diversification represents a significant challenge to an agricultural support strategy which assumes that all household members are full-time farmers.

Consequently, despite the successful agricultural production picture that can be seen in the aggregate for Asia, there are many warning signals to suggest that the foundation for maintaining this success is not impregnable. At the least, the aggregate picture masks considerable variability.

Challenge of Sustainable Development

There is considerable discussion these days of sustainable development. The amount of discussion could lead one to believe that there was consensus about what sustainable development was and that whatever it was, it was certainly a "good" thing to support. However, the consensus is largely accidental. At best, it represents endorsement. More commonly it represents acquiescence. For the most part, it does not represent commitment. The good news is that there is a broad idea about development strategy and objectives that people support. The bad news is that it is not clear what the idea is, what the implications of supporting this idea are for other ideas and their support, what sacrifices may be required if the idea is to be put into practice, and who will have to make these sacrifices.

As a result, agricultural support systems throughout developing Asia do not yet find themselves in a strong position to support purposeful action based on the idea of sustainable development. What exists is an accidental consensus, an indication of apparently growing coinciding global opinion. What does not yet exist, however, are sufficient indications of a shared and authentic commitment. These are required to yield an effective foundation for action. What is needed is an intentional consensus, one built up from an explicit and open dialogue, premised on a transparent exchange of information and ideas, consenting to multiculturalism, and accepting and supported by compatible social relations and political institutions.

Understanding the Problem: Accidental Consensus

What is sustainable development? At first glance, the answer seems to be simple: sustainable development is a rate and form of development that can be continued given specific natural and man-made assets. Factors which constrain continuance (e.g. absolute depletion of critical resources, high population growth relative to available resources, loss of access to critical resources, environmental degradation) have to be confronted. Better management of existing systems and alternative technologies and socio-economic arrangements are often advocated as solutions. That much appears obvious and is certainly worthwhile.

However, what happens if we ask: beyond notions of dependence and limits, what does sustainability actually mean? There are many answers. While many of the answers are offered with high degrees of self-assurance, on closer inspection many of the answers are inconsistent with each other. For example, neoclassical economic notions of sustainability focus on efficiency, market-determined growth in resources, and (predictable) equilibrium solutions to the allocation of resources. These notions are inconsistent at many points with sustainability as seen by ecology (Batie, 1991; Lele, 1991), where issues of instability, unpredictability, irreversibility, and the problems of absolute scarcity get strong emphasis. Yet, as acknowledged relationships between poverty and environmental degradation in the Third World and industrialization and environmental degradation in the First World suggest, the security of economic growth and the integrity of ecosystem development are strongly linked. But how?

The confusion about what sustainable development means is not limited to arguments about the relevance of disciplinary theories. Sustainable development is considered rightly to be a challenge for policy. As a policy problem, the sustainable development discussion is characterized by a split. Some see sustainable development as fundamentally a "technical" problem susceptible to technical solutions. Others see sustainable development as fundamentally a socio-political problem requiring socio-political solutions.

The language of this debate is often one that presents an ideology of neutrality on the one side and an ideology of imputed intent on the other (Koppel, 1987). This is important because it reveals that many of the arguments about sustainable development are not actually hypotheses about empirical issues, but rather demonstrations of ideological expectations. As a result, there are a few systematic empirical referents for sustainability. Indeed, and this may be surprising to some, we do not now have any agreed satisfactory ways of measuring sustainable development—in natural or managed biophysical systems (ADB, 1991; Carpenter, 1990).

That many governments now enunciate policies in terms of sustainable development does not differ with what has just been stated. The issue is how to assess both intentions and capabilities. There is a significant amount of new window-dressing in the development business, but we should not fool ourselves: the mannequins frequently are still the same and the clothes they wear are not necessarily new or different. For example, how many forest policies are now stated in the "new" idiom of sustainable development but rationalizing practices from the older idiom of open cutting and forced relocation of indigenous populations continue?

As a political and ethical problem, we have to recognize that the calls for attention to sustainable development are also (some would say primarily) calls for (re)distributions of the costs and benefits of development. These (re)distributions reflect both instrumental and expressive purposes. The question is whose values are being expressed and promoted, what is sustainable development an instrument for, and what power is being exercised over whom to achieve these values? When people demonstrate in Tokyo or New York to save the Brazilian rainforest, who are they really saving it for and who, in fact, are they saving it from? When sustainable development is translated as conservation, protection, and carefully regulated use of upland areas, for example, who actually benefits and who actually loses? We know that the answers depend significantly on who is exercising regulatory power and for what purposes and that these purposes are not necessarily derived from concerns about ecological sustainability (Contreras, 1991; Ferguson, 1990). Is it a scientific generalization or only a coincidence, for example, that sustainable development is more often a rationale for creating parks and preserves than it is for undertaking agrarian reform?

Finally, it is important to recognize the complex context in which the sustainable development issue rests. The sustainable development issue is in a cross-current of several quite different discourses. There is an international discourse, a local discourse and an interactive discourse. At the international level, the contours of many of the sustainable development discussions reproduce patterns identified by the North-South debates. Sustainable development is an agenda frequently advocated by affluent countries to developing countries. Developed industrial countries are telling countries in earlier stages of industrialization to reduce air pollution, protect forests, conserve energy, etc. At the local level, there is undeniably authentic local rural protest against resource destruction and resistance to attempts by urban middle classes to impose their own sustainable development agenda on rural peasant classes. An example is peasant resistance to logging in Thailand.

While these two discourses are well-established, a third discourse is emerging. It is about the interrelation of international action and local action. Peasant resistance may not be simply to other local parties, but may be directed at transnational actors. This is the case, for example, in the forest areas of Kalimantan and the tree plantations of Mindanao. The sustainable development discussion is part of and, in different ways, is representative of each of these three discourses.

Implications for Agricultural Support

It is argued that the key to sustainable development is the recognition of interdependence—temporally, spatially and functionally. We need to understand the linkages in development actions between the short-term and the long-term. This is where ideas about incrementalism, irreversibility and risk come into play. We need to recognize the linkages that development actions have across space and often the irrelevance of administrative and political boundaries as quarantines particularly for environmental problems. And we need to accept that development actions in one sector have consequences that are rarely restricted to that sector. We may have recently "discovered" energy-environment and poverty-environment linkages, but those linkages have a long history.

This multidimensional interdependence is not absolute nor uniform. Of particular interest is interdependence among three areas of concerns. The first two concerns are widely recognized: economic security (which can cover issues from growth to poverty amelioration) and environmental security (which can cover issues from conservation to exploitation). The third concern is democratic security (which can cover issues from accountability to participation).

The choice of democratic security as the third concern requires some additional explanation since it is especially important for understanding the implications of sustainable development for agricultural research and extension. Political security might have been chosen on the argument that the stability of political arrangements is a necessary correlate of (stable) sustainable development arrangements. This is agreed that there is an empirical association in many cases of stable political arrangements with economic and environmental security. However, that association should be viewed as a problem rather than as a desirable property. In a fundamental sense, sustainability is the continual making and remaking of a social contract. This is a contract about the nexus of risks and benefits from the intersections of the economy, the environment, and the polity. Both the contract and the processes of contracting define and reflect ideas about justice and equity in how those risks and benefits are allocated. It follows that what is crucial is not the stability of the State or the durability of any particular regime, but rather that the contract and the processes of contracting represent and are accountable to the broadest range of social interests. After all, sustainable development is not a technically determined or ideologically prescribed end state of relationships among economic, environmental and political security. Sustainable development refers to characteristics of processes for making choices about the interdependence of economic, environmental and political security—across different temporal, spatial and functional scales.

These processes are profoundly social and political. They are social because the issues of economic, environmental and political security are fundamentally issues about social relations, about how individuals and groups relate to each other through the sharing of risks and benefits from specific development paths. They are political because these are ultimately issues about the exercise, consequences and accountability of power. From this perspective, then, the issue of sustainable development is about the interdependence of economic security, environmental security and democratic security and the capability of societies to grasp and confront this interdependence. More than that, however, is the issue of how choices are identified and made when it may well be impossible to simultaneously maximize the properties and goals associated with each individual area of security (cf. Charoenwatana and Rambo, 1988).

Status of Agricultural Support Services

In the face of this variability, it is appropriate that attention is again turning to the roles of agricultural support services. The institutions comprising the support system have served as mechanisms for bringing goods and services both to and from rural areas in ways that have influenced the allocation of land, labour and capital within rural resource systems. The net effects of this system have been widely acclaimed as very positive (Evenson *et al.*, 1979; Pinstrup-Andersen, 1983; Ruttan, 1978).

However, we need to acknowledge that these same institutions also function as policy arenas that permit social, economic and political interests both within and outside the institutions operate to allocate scarce administrative resources (Burmeister, 1984; Chambers, 1983; Haas, 1979; Inayatullah, 1979; Koppel and Oasa, 1987; Korten and Alfonso, 1983; Lea and Chaudhri, 1983). As recognition of this point has expanded (de Janvry, 1985; Lipton, 1985), a sense of unease has grown that the institutions of the agricultural support system do not always permit market forces to operate and worse, that these institutions might be promoting interests that were inefficient. Today, this unease is expressed against a background of increased attention to policy reform, especially with regard to relationships between "government intervention" and market-determined price-formation processes. A fundamental generalization is repeatedly advocated in development policy discussions: economic development in rural areas is the outcome of policy reforms that reduce government intervention in rural commodity markets.

However, asked much less often is: what parts of government would this actually reference? What, for example, does the call for policy reform mean for the status of publicly-financed agricultural support services? Answers to these questions are not straightforward. After all, the state's relationships with rural society throughout Asia are multidimensional, employing policies, institutions and technologies as instruments. Rather than to criticize government role in agricultural development *per se,* it may be more worthwhile to first understand what the nature and impact of specific patterns of involvement are.

For example, while there are the equivalents of Ministries of Agriculture in every country, in almost all cases, governments' relationships with agriculture are only *partially* exercised by these Ministries. Moreover, the case can be made that the role of these Ministries in the overall food and agricultural policy formation and implementation picture is declining while the roles of other agencies, some only nominally connected to agriculture (such as Finance or Trade), are increasing. Strategies such as vertical integration and risk shifting through alliances between market power and State action have become important dimensions of change in the organization of rural commodity systems, as the Philippines under Marcos demonstrated. Control of virtually all major agriculture and food commodities— including coconut, sugar, rice, corn and wheat—were assumed by a variety of "Authorities" outside the normal agricultural support system.

The Philippine case is not unique. The acceleration of State intervention to control rural commodity systems, purportedly for purposes of stabilizing domestic prices and production in the face of volatile international markets appears to be a pervasive phenomenon throughout Asia from Japan to Burma (Canlas *et al.,* 1983; Clarete and Roumasset, 1983; Dell, 1983; De Leon, 1982; Harriss, 1984; Kruegger, 1974; Sathyamurthy, 1985). It is precisely against this background that what are now commonly called "parastatal" organizations have arisen. These are quasi-State corporations that have been delegated government powers to regulate, allocate and tax, but are not routinely accountable to "normal" government staffing, financial management and reporting conventions. Parastatals have acquired important roles as exclusive agents of the state for commodity trading in many countries of the region. These kinds of changes can have significant implications for the organization and performance of affected rural commodity markets and can be closely associated with the emergence (and State endorsement) of monopsony power in rural marketing systems. An often forgotten point is that what we usually think of as agricultural extension functions in this complex and frequently unfriendly environment.

Other developments are already present or on the horizon that can present additional problems for the support and mission of agricultural extension. For example, a technology transformation is in progress that is more far-reaching than the technological change that characterized the "Green Revolution". Science and technology are holding out the enticing prospect of substantially increased and less variable production, but in the framework of production systems that may be very different from those common today. Biotechnology already shows a significant potential not simply to modify (or in some cases enhance) existing technological bases of agricultural production, food processing and animal husbandry, but also to be very compatible with a restructuring of the economic, institutional and political foundations of Asia's agriculture (Brady, 1982; Buttel, 1983; Koppel, 1985; Randolph, 1984; Swaminathan, 1982).

For example, what will the hybridization of basic food crop seeds mean for Asia's small farmers, the vast majority of whom do not buy seeds? Will many farmers be motivated by expected economic benefits to buy seed or will income inequalities within agrarian Asia be exacerbated, with the better endowed farmers and millers capturing most of the benefits of technological developments such as hybridization? The broad changes associated with biotechnology have fundamental implications for the roles of public agricultural research and extension and for types and consequences of privatization that may occur in Asian agriculture. Who will be the agents and the benefactors of the more proprietary technology dissemination systems likely to be facilitated? What will the increasing privatization of germplasm-based research mean for the "publicly" supported agricultural support system? For international cooperation in technological improvements for Asia's agriculture? For the management of the specific natural systems where these germplasm materials currently exist in the wild?

Biotechnology is only one example of technology transformation. Other examples include the growing importance of processed foods in many Asian diets, the introduction of new preservation technologies that permit longer-term storage of perishable foods and the effects of transportation technologies on the marketing areas of various products. These are among the signs that post-production dimensions of Asia's food and agricultural systems are becoming more important. These are areas where extension has generally not been active. As the importance of these post-production dimensions increase, especially in terms of income and employment generation, will there be pressure on agricultural support services to extend assistance? Will competition for public financing of agricultural support services become more intense? Clearly these and other transitions have enormous implications for an agricultural development strategy that has strongly emphasized and encouraged public investment in agricultural support facilities.

Challenge of Limited-Resource Farmers

If Asia's agricultural support systems are going to make significant progress in addressing issues of sustainable development and poverty alleviation, it will most likely be through redefining their mission in relation to limited-resource farmers. These consist of those who have traditionally lacked access to agricultural support systems because of some limitation in their own resource endowment and because the support system is simply not available to them. They include, for example, approximately "one-half of Asia's rice farmers, who cultivate rain-fed upland and lowland rice, for which relatively little technological support is available. They also include farmers who cultivate irrigated lowland rice, which has received an intensive technological support, but who are too remote or poor to attract sustained attention from national agricultural support systems. Finally, these also include many farmers in the semi-arid tropics who have to depend on highly variable rainfall to grow their crops.

This will not be easy. A large portion of what has been learnt in the course of Asia's agricultural development experience during the last two decades has come from contact with a large group of farmers who are, relatively speaking, among the more well endowed, more accessible, more literate and more commercially oriented members of the agrarian community. By comparison, limited-resource farmers will expect their farming operations to directly support a broader range of household food and energy needs. They may not be incorporated into anything other than purely local commodity markets. They may be relatively less connected with the agricultural support systems that have driven much of Asia's agricultural development during the last two decades. They may be relatively more reliant on their own agricultural experience and orally transmitted cumulations of local agricultural knowledge than on research station science, formal extension and printed bulletins. They may live in communities with relatively less commercial and marketing infrastructure or government services, fewer opportunities for off-farm employment and possibly higher average incidence of unemployment, underemployment, episodic malnutrition and disease. They are unlikely to be anything other than marginal users of manufactured agricultural chemicals and what chemicals they do use are most likely to be fertilizers.

Limited-resource farmers are often referred to, in some short-handed way, as "traditional". But, in fact, what would this mean? Are the farmers traditional (in some cultural or psychological sense, for example) or are the technologies they use traditional (relative to some standards of "modernity", for example)? Does the term "traditional" convey the belief that such farmers are, in some fundamental way, different from other "non-traditional" farmers? If so, what is the basis of this fundamental difference? For example, are the differences based on the processes which yield decisions and behaviours about resource allocation and utilization or on the outcomes of these processes?

More generally, are the Green Revolution farmers and limited resource farmers simply two points on the same agricultural development curve, differing only in degree, or are they points on distinct agricultural development paths, differing in kind? Are the differences between these two types of farmers virtually inherent (and practically immutable) or predominantly acquired (and possibly transitory)? Do the differences reside in the structure of certain relationships, the operation of specific resource management processes, or in the fundamental roots and "rules" of resource allocation and utilization? These are difficult issues. If the differences are inherent, then the challenge represented by agricultural development may be quite substantial (Koppel, 1981). It means, for example, that much of what is known about one group would not necessarily apply to the other. If, on the other hand, the differences are acquired—for instance, as a consequence of significant spatial remoteness—then, in principle, it is only necessary to overcome or compensate for such an external "distortion" and more familiar strategies can proceed.

Inherent or transitory, it is necessary to understand why the differences occur and why they may be less tractable in some cases than others. One place to begin is by asking what is known about technology adoption and more specifically, what is known that might apply to limited resource farmers? Then we can ask what the answers to these questions mean for agricultural extension.

Technology Adoption Among Limited-Resource Farmers

Technology adoption among any kind of farmers can be reduced to some deceptively simple questions:

1. What is being adopted?
2. Who is doing the adopting?
3. Why is adoption occurring, and implicitly, why is adoption not occurring?
4. What happens after adoption has occurred?

It is important to emphasize that a good deal of what is known about how these questions can be answered for farmers in Asia has been learnt within the context of sponsored programmes of technology diffusion, usually among farmers who do not share most of the characteristics described earlier as being those of limited-resource farmers. This is not to suggest that such programmes have not reached limited-resource farmers. They have. However, there are some generalizations that need to be qualified or even reconsidered when limited-resource farmers are defined as a primary group of adopters.

1. *What is being adopted?*

Adoption research has worked best when this question could be answered unambiguously by identifying a specific material item (such as a seed or a cultivation instrument) that is either adopted or not adopted. In the last two decades what we have seen, however, is not the diffusion of specific material items alone, but rather an increase in deliberate efforts to encourage the adoption of packages of technologies, technology management practices and, in many instances, financial and marketing practices as well. The agricultural support systems may have been very clear about how all these different parts tied together so clear that they might have considered the packages to be really just one item for adoption. Certainly the descriptions of numerous "integrated" projects that were and are the vehicles for these efforts communicate the image of a merged package.

The lesson being learnt, however, is that the farmer's view of this package is not always the same as the support system's view. Some parts will appear attractive. Other parts will elicit less interest and enthusiasm. In fact, the farmer may not be seeing a package at all, but a collection of individual items. The reverse has also been true. A support system may believe it is recommending a specific, discrete item for the farmer's consideration. What the farmer may see, however, is not a discrete item but rather a solicitation to make commitments on time, land or labour that go beyond what the support system believes it is asking. The question that needs to be asked is: *Is enough understood about the limited-resource farmer and the limited-resource farm enterprise to know what it is that is actually being recommended?*

For example, consider botanical pest control strategy (Ahmed, 1984; Ketkar, 1976; Schmutterer, 1983). This is a strategy that employs plants with useful pest repellent properties, such as Neem (*Azadirachta indica*), that farmers could grow on their own fields to control pest problems. We recognize that evaluating this strategy may require rethinking some traditional research station criteria for assessing pest control performance. We also recognize, however, that we do not clearly understand what botanical pest control might mean to the farmer or what criteria the farmer might use to assess such a strategy. Is it a once-and-for-all practice? Is it a series of repeated or episodic practices? Do other aspects of farm management and household resource allocation have to be modified? If so, how much and in what ways? Can botanical pest control simply be compared to chemical pest control (the preference of the agricultural research system) or do the two strategies have other attributes that reduce their comparability? For instance, to what extent does a specific botanical pest control strategy have a role that exceeds the single function of pest management? What assumptions are made about resource requirements, management demands and the matching of costs and benefits? How do these assumptions compare to the way any specific botanical pest control strategy will relate to the land and labour management practices of limited-resource farmers? If we understand not simply what we expect botanical pest control to do (i.e. address pest management problems) but also what botanical pest control is within the context of the limited-resource farmer's relationship to specific parts of the natural environment, we may find ourselves with a better perspective on the question: what is the farmer being asked to adopt? For example, in parts of India and Pakistan, farmers have been using plant materials (especially Neem leaves) to protect grains in storage for generations (Ahmed and Koppel, 1987)—with virtually no encouragement from any agricultural extension system. We need to better understand the benefits (perceived and "real") of these practices as well as factors that help to explain why some farmers employ the practices and others do not.

2. *Who is doing the adopting*?

Many generalizations that can be drawn from the literature on technology adoption during Asia's Green Revolution assume that the adopter is a farmer, an individual, usually a male household head. If we saw the decision to adopt as a one-time decision, it was not unreasonable to focus on the individual we thought represented the farm enterprise and, in some visible way, could be identified with the decision.

Supporting this was a strong preference, if not an actual bias, in work by agricultural economists and extension agents to look for and find individual male household heads who were predefined both empirically (often through sampling frameworks which instructed them to contact male household heads) and theoretically (usually through theoretical frameworks that assumed the farm enterprise consisted of a single male manager who had family labour available for allocation). All this now seems to be changing.

One important example is the interest in considering farm households as collective decision-making entities (Fortmann, 1984; Roumasset, 1978; Smith and Gascon, 1980). Another example is interest in the role of indigenous farmer organizations in technology adoption and utilization. Certainly recognizing technology adoption as the outcome of a collective decision-making process is not novel. In fact, in some places, efforts to make the diffusion-adoption process an explicitly collective one were, and still are, visible in the context of sponsored technology-adoption programmes. In the 1970s, for example, local organization was certainly recognized by many national agricultural development programmes, but the local organizations recognized most often were the cooperatives organized by government, usually for purposes of improving the efficiency (that is, agent/client ratios and number of farmers contacted) of extension and credit services. Until relatively recently, the idea that effective collective decision-making influencing agricultural resource management might be operating outside of government-sponsored cooperative programmes was not widely shared.

Today, ideas in this area are changing, in part because even among the Green Revolution farmers, the performance record for sponsored cooperatives was perplexingly uneven (Castillo, 1983). Consequently, many practitioners now resist the temptation to state authoritatively "this mode of organization and decision-making always leads to this pattern of technology adoption, risk distribution and resource management while this other mode always leads to another pattern". Interest in indigenous farmer organizations, particularly in relation to irrigation and common property resource management, is increasing, but there is relatively little research to build on. Therefore, it is doubtful that agricultural support systems will be able to rely completely on lessons from their earlier experiences with more well-endowed agricultural communities to guide their work with limited resource farm communities. Instead, it is entirely possible that different starting points will be needed (Coward, Koppel and Siy, 1983).

More careful consideration also needs to be given to the distinction between technology adoption that follows from a single adoption decision or from a number of adoption decisions (Koppel, 1976, 1978). If the latter is the case, as it can be for any collection of tasks or technologies that have recurrent costs, it may be necessary to acknowledge the existence of different decision processes, different adoption curves, and even different decision-makers for various aspects of adoption commitments. In such circumstances many decisions are often decisions of degree—not simply "accept-reject"—that can be varied over time. If, indeed, a series of decisions are operating, what is the relationship between prior decisions and subsequent choices? How is this relationship organized socially? How is this relationship influenced by what is being adopted at any given point in time as well as who the effective decision-makers are at different points in time? An important point about adoption decisions follows: seen from the perspective of the technology generating and disseminating system, the process may be characterized as adoption. Seen from the perspective of the farmer, however, the process may be better characterized as *adaptation,* incorporating and modifying something into fuller compatibility with the farmer's specific situation (Rambo, Dixon and Wu, 1984; Ruddle, 1974).

In the context of a discussion about what is being adopted, it is quite natural also to be concerned with the corollary questions: from *whom* and from *where* is the technology *adopted?* Most discussions of agricultural development strategies associated with the successes of the 1970s can be located in reference to these corollary questions. However, if the discussion is about what technological strategy is being adapted, then attention shifts quite naturally to other corollary questions: by *whom* and to *what* is the technology being *adapted?*

3. *Why does adoption occur?*

Adoption research offers two broad types of evidence for answering this question: motivations and attributes. Research on individual motivations for adopting new technology has been extensive and has concentrated on answering two questions: Are farmers price (or benefit) responsive? Are farmers risk-averse? The research says repeatedly that farmers are price-responsive, which can be translated to mean that technologies which reduce marginal costs or increase average returns will be favourably viewed, *all other things being equal.* The research on risk offers the general insight that farmers, operating as they do in an aura of some uncertainty, determine and apply what amount to risk premiums when they evaluate new technologies.

Ecologists and anthropologists have also examined motivations for technological change among farmers and have pointed to some additional factors. Research on stability and uncertainty emphasizes that household subsistence and security are intimately tied to the agricultural enterprise. Consequently, farm households are visualized as trying to minimize episodes of variability (primarily in output) that can ultimately threaten the integrity of the family unit. Research on social, cultural and religious values that can influence perceptions about the generation and disposition of surpluses, the allocation of family labour, landuse intensity, financing production costs, etc., emphasizes that choice of agricultural technology is deeply embedded in a socio-cultural context.

Work on price responsiveness and risk aversion has tended to concentrate on the more surplus-oriented farmers. The "who" in this research has been predominantly the individual farm household head, although in recent years this kind of work has been extended to time and labour allocation within the farm household. Work on stability, uncertainty and values has tended to concentrate on the more subsistence-oriented farmers. The "who" in this case has tended to be the farm household (not necessarily defined in nuclear terms), with broader kinship relationships and village affiliations often considered as well.

Research on motivational aspects of technology adoption has been considerably better at explaining the adoption of specific technological artifacts (seeds, fertilizers, tractors) than it has at explaining the adaptation patterns for these artifacts or the adoption and adaptation of associated practices (for example, through patterns of complementary private investment in land infrastructure or reallocations of family, community and hired labour). For probably similar reasons, motivational research has not provided too many useful generalizations about the disadoption or abandonment of technology previously accepted. A special example is technology succession, the replacement of one technology by another. A well-known illustration is the rapid turnaround in seed variety choice demonstrated by large number of Asia's rice farmers, a turnaround that may say more about extension's effectiveness in getting seed materials to farmers than it does about farmers' reasons for replacing one variety with another. What are the dynamics of technology succession among limited resource farmers, especially among those farmers who are not currently well linked to the agricultural support system?

Motivational studies of adoption in the context of technological succession may need to be careful about assuming how an old technology and a new technology differ and why this difference would lead a farmer to replace one with the other. When is succession best understood as technologies *replacing* other technologies or as a cumulative and incremental process, occurring along a continuum of decisions, practices and investments. For example, much research labelled as agricultural mechanization actually focuses on the narrower issue of tractorization. However, among Asia's farmers, is mechanization most usefully seen as the adoption of a particular piece of equipment that is essentially discontinuous with prior tools, or as the cumulative enhancement of labour productivity by a progression of tools and skills? Most motivational research about technology adoption maintains a strong tendency to view adoption as a dichotomous (accept-reject) and one-time decision.

Adoption research implemented to focus on attributes rather than motivations can be seen, in part, as an attempt to ask: under what circumstances are generalizations about motivations likely to hold? This research asks: are attributes or characteristics of early adopters different in some systematic way from late adopters and from those who do not adopt? For example, if early adopters of new agricultural technologies are, as a group, more literate and educated than late adopters, then attention should be directed to understanding the relationships, in this case, between education, literacy and the adoption decision. Indeed, there is considerable research which correlates technology adoption with factors such as land size, land tenure, family size, land quality, market access, farm operator's age, average income, socio-economic status, level of living, etc. However, the research is more persuasive in providing descriptions of adoption than it is in accounting for delayed adoption, non-adoption, or disadoption. While the need to look beyond attributes of the individual to attributes of the individual's physical, social and economic environment has been recognized, the focus of that recognition has been understandably restricted. The question that has received most attention is: what are the relationships between characteristics and adoption behaviours of individuals and the levels of infrastructure (especially support services) which are available and to which they have access, etc.?

However, much work remains to be done if the question turns to relationships between individual characteristics, adoption behaviours, and attributes of the social organizational environment. For example, if higher literacy in an individual is associated with earlier adoption, what difference, if any, does it make if, in one case, a highly literate individual lives where the distribution of education is highly skewed to the low end or the high end? Income, land size, or land tenure can be substituted for education in the example. If adoption decisions are purely and entirely individual or household decisions, then the answer may be: "no difference". To the extent, however, that decisions are not that autonomous, then there may well be differences. In fact, research still only provides largely idiosyncratic examples of how and why social context, individual behaviour and technology adoption have configured in the ways they have.

Experience during the last few decades suggests that Asia's agricultural support systems know where technology adoption is more likely and rapid. This is knowledge accumulated through successful participation in the diffusion of Green Revolution technologies. However, most of this experience is based on technologies and associated development strategies that assumed essentially homogeneous end-users: specialized, relatively well-endowed and commercially oriented lowland irrigated wheat and rice farmers. Much less is understood about technology adoption by farmers who have not been the primary focus of agricultural development efforts in recent years. Moreover, and this is perhaps the most troubling, it is not certain what is generalizable from experience with the first group to efforts with the second. In the face of this, it follows that applied development efforts may need to rely less on generalized knowledge about technology adoption, opting instead to be more carefully informed by site-specific technology adoption research. This is, of course, part of what farming systems research appears to be about. It may also be the most promising course for any efforts that will focus on limited resource farmers.

4. *What happens after adoption has occurred?*

Adoption research traditionally has not concerned itself with this question, at least not as an empirical matter separate from attempts to explain why adoption occurs. An alternative view, however, has developed. Sometimes called "technology assessment", this view is that adoption research should not be restricted to the questions: Will it be adopted? Who will adopt it? When will they adopt it? Why will they adopt it? Two additional questions also need to be asked: How will the technology work? What happens if the technology is adopted? (Koppel, 1979)

The question of *how* a technology works encompasses the question of *whether* a technology works, but is also more than that. Awareness has broadened in the last decade that demonstrating the working of an agricultural technology in the carefully controlled environment of the experiment station really does not indicate whether the technology will work in other environments nor, what is even more important, what kinds of variability can be associated with the performance of the technology when it is inserted into different agro-ecological and farm management environments. As a result, on-farm research is becoming an accepted element of the agricultural research process. However, agricultural support systems are still attempting to understand how to make experimental sense out of the enormous variability in the off-station environment.

An example is the division of labour between on-farm and on-station research. For example, a review of existing research practices leads to the hypothesis that technologies or practices that are likely to be used in a relatively uniform way—which will be essentially independent of variabilities in other farm operations, and which will be applied under agro-ecological conditions similar to those on the research station—can be usefully assessed by basic testing on-station and verification on-farm. However, for technologies and practices that may not be applied with much uniformity, such as those which are specifically dependent on other farm operations, larger shares of the technology development and verification processes may need to occur on-farm.

The distinction that is really at issue is not where the research is physically taking place, but rather on what terms of reference, the research is being conducted and evaluated. Using experiment station methods on-farm really proves very little unless the methods used on-station are also close to farmer methods—for the farmers thought to be the end-users of the technology under development. As agricultural research moves towards greater immersion in on-farm research, it therefore needs to become more deliberate about what kinds of farms and farmers it chooses to work with. This is particularly important as agricultural research goes further than it has previously to develop technologies for specific types of farms and farmers, in some cases types with which it is not too familiar. The adoption issue surfaces before the technology research, when we ask: for what types of farms are we working?—not after the technology research, when we are implicitly in the position of asking: for what types of farms were we working?

Closely related is another question that, in one sense, is commonly asked and, in another sense, is very infrequently asked: *What if the technology is adopted?* This question is commonly asked through assumptions and expectations about benefits and costs that will accompany adoption. Increases in income, employment and output, or reductions in pests and weeds are already discussed. Other aspects of the question are not commonly considered. For example, environmental impacts of adopted technologies are often not given serious attention. This is partly a result of focusing on individual farmers and farm households as adopters and neglecting to aggregate and ask what the cumulative environmental impacts might be if concentrated adoption occurs in contiguous areas. It is also a result in some cases of inadequate knowledge about what kinds of environmental impacts may even be likely. In this context, it is possible to admit that predictive ecology is an infant science, but does it follow that longer-run environmental consequences should not be part of adoption research?

Sometimes the focus is more on who it is hoped will adopt the technologies than who actually might do the adopting. Identification of the latter group requires clarity about what kinds of resources (human, material, land, capital) will be required to make effective use of the technology; how the extension and diffusion systems are operating or are likely to operate in diffusing the technology and what all this may mean for: (1) which farmers will have early access; (2) which farmers will be most assured of getting supervision or assistance for early problems of acquiring and using the technology; and (3) how patterns of adoption by one group or type of farmers may influence the feasibility, rate, patterns and costs of adoption by other groups and types of farmers.

The question—what if the technology is adopted?—is really the question, what if the technology is *utilized?* The issue is not the accept-reject decision, but the graduated decisions involved in adapting the technology to the existing farming enterprise and resource endowment. It is important to improve not only how well the agricultural support system answers the utilization question for itself, but how well the agricultural support system understands how different types of farmers might answer that question. Such an effort might illuminate some benefits not considered; some possible consequences not anticipated. In either case, there are implications for technology development, verification and dissemination processes.

Attention to probable forms of utilization can also highlight another key issue: what kinds of variability are probable on the farm and what are the likely major consequences of this variability, in terms of the technology's performance and the farmer's welfare? For example, experience with chemical pest control shows that under certain circumstances, farmers may misuse this technology. They may mishandle or improperly mix chemical materials, application may be done incorrectly or at the wrong times, and so on. Such farmers have adopted chemical pest control technology, in the sense that they have acquired some of the material artifacts associated with the technology, but practice or utilization is not as hoped. In some cases, the result is uneconomic, a consequence the farmer may also see, resulting in substantial reduction or even termination of use, i.e. disadoption. In other cases, the result may have adverse health consequences, except that the farmer may not know this until it is too late.

Experiences like these illustrate the challenge of considering variability in utilization: What kinds of variability are probable? What are the probable causes of this variability? What are the likely consequences of the variability? In the illustration just discussed, we can hypothesize that sometimes there are basic incompatibilities between the support system's understandings and the farmers' understandings of plant-pest relationships and/or the roles of chemical pesticides to manage these relationships. In the same vein, what assumptions are now being made about the current utilization of botanical pest control strategies? For different kinds of farmers (and for different kinds of scientists), what will be "new" or "subtle" in the strategies extension may present that may be subject to variable interpretation or practice? Are there any forms of variability that should be worried about, such as variability leading to forms of environmental damage, or contaminated food, etc.? Are particular levels of utilization likely to influence and be influenced by variability in other parts of the farm enterprise, variability which may be an important part of the farmer's ongoing adaptation to changing environmental and ecological relationships, market conditions, labour opportunities, etc.?

Variability can be discussed in strictly biophysical terms—variability that is related to climate, soil properties, hydrological factors, etc. That kind of variability is routinely considered in the technology development process already. Another kind of variability, however, less routinely considered, comes from differences in farmer resource endowments and orientations. The very interest in limited-resource farmers, the desire to develop technologies that are, in the words of the former IRRI Director General, Dr. M.S. Swaminathan, "resource-neutral," *potentially* signals two important shifts that may be under way in understanding of variability being employed by agricultural support systems. One is a shift to consider a set of highly variable agro-ecological environments that were not formerly given sustained attention. The second is a shift to consider more deliberately the variabilities associated with farmer resource endowments. The latter shift, however subtle, represents a refocus from the farm as an essentially biophysical entity to a focus on the relationship between variabilities of the biophysicai entity and variabilities associated with the farm household—a social, cultural and economic entity.

Issues of utilization are strongly behavioural issues. They underlie the importance of understanding the farmer and the farm enterprise from the farmer's perspective. This doesn't mean that everything needs to be understood nor does it mean that component technological research has to be integrated for, and conducted on, a farm-by-farm basis. It does mean, however, that it is necessary to understand those relationships within the farmers' systems which most strongly influence how new technologies and practices will interact with the farm enterprise already in place.

Implications for Agricultural Research and Extension

Several strategies are available for translating the ideas and questions raised thus far into some operational procedures for learning about adoption, adaptation and utilization. However, such procedures cannot be considered independently of the institutional and programmatic context in which they will function. This means understanding how the research system, in particular, and the agricultural support system, more generally, visualize their relationships to farmers and what this visualization implies for the types of learning that are likely.

Fig. 15.1 offers a schema for visualizing the relationships between agricultural support systems and farmers and methodological strategies for learning about farmers. The figure asks two questions about assumptions:

(1) What is the agricultural support system's relationship to the linkage between what it does (its output) and the effects of what it does (i.e. adoption, adaptation and utilization by farmers). The question is not posed in administrative terms but rather in terms of the assumptions or "models" which guide what kinds of administrative relationships, communication flows and problem identification processes are probable. Two stylized possibilities are indicated. "Active" means the support system is involved interactively with farmers. "Passive" means that the support system's involvement is more unilateral. The fashionable phrases "bottom-up" and "top-down" are expressions of a similar distinction, but the hierarchical imagery of the phrases actually freezes us in the very way of thinking the phrases were presumably popularized to escape. "Active" and "Passive" can be hierarchical; they can also be collateral. The emphasis is on content, not necessarily position.

(2) The rows in Fig. 15.1 ask: what is the significance of farmers in the assumptions or "model" that the support system has of its relationship to farmers. Do farmers exist as a "Who," representing possibly complex and unique systems, that should be understood from within those systems? Or do farmers exist as a "What," known by the support system according to variables selected and defined by the support system itself? The stylized "methods" noted in the box are types of understanding which follow from the intersections of the two row and column questions. Essentially what Fig. 15.1 is attempting to convey is that the choice of method is a decision derived from the type of understanding of the adoption process a support system believes it needs.

ASSUMPTIONS	A Support System's Relationship to the Linkage Between What it Does and the Effects of What it Does is:	
	Active	**Passive**
THE FARMER	Adapts Utilizes Chooses Transforms	Adopts Accepts Follows
THE SUPPORT SYSTEM	Supports Learns	Sells Monitors Transfers
The Role of the Farmers in the Technology Generation and Diffusion Process is as a:		
WHO capable of defining own interests and needs	**Interactive-Based Understanding** Participation Experiential Systemic Analytic	METHODS
WHAT fits predefined category		**Indicator-Based Understanding** Confirmation Reconnaissance Systematic Hypothetical

Fig. 15.1: How to Support System Learns about Farmers

Basically, there are two kinds of choices:

Utilization: Where an agricultural support system is firmly oriented to utilization and adaptation objectives, it will be inclined to need an understanding of the farmer's context, provided in some sense, on the farmer's own terms of reference. This plus the tendency for utilization and adaptation objectives to establish requirements for recurrent support means that the support system will need to place itself in some *interactive* mode with the farmer. For example, the redefinitions of relationships between on-station research, agricultural extension and on-farm research that characterize the institutional innovations of farming systems research can be seen as illustrations of efforts to improve the form of communication between farmer and scientist.

Acceptance: If the support system's orientation is more towards acceptance objectives, then it will be inclined to need profiles of farmers and farms to facilitate monitoring and evaluation of acceptance rates, usually in terms of correlations with specific indicators of farmer characteristics. Many innovations and improvements in programme monitoring systems are illustrations of efforts to increase the availability and accuracy of such indicators for programme management purposes and are examples of this second choice.

If interactive research proceeds from the assumption that it is the difference in farming systems which mandates intensive understanding of specific systems, then indicator research proceeds from the assumption that it is common characteristics of farmers and farms which mandates extensive understanding of numerous systems. It is important to note that agro-ecological and socio-economic theory, in one form or another, is important for both types of research. For interactive research, theory is needed to provide some map for identifying a system and the key relationships in that system. For indicator research, theory is needed to identify variables and relationships and to attribute credibility to specific empirical indicators. Both approaches can fall victim to either of two fallacies: (1) they underemploy theory, become extremely empiricist, collect and possibly are overwhelmed by too much data, and avoid any clear conclusions or (2) theory's presence is so pronounced that data function more to illustrate theory than provide understanding about farmers.

Both types of research generate and support understanding about adoption, but they generate two different kinds of understanding. Interactive research does better at understanding what is happening and why in specific situations. It provides what can be called contextual knowledge. It is less useful for providing generalizations which can be applied to numerous other situations. This can be a problem for national agricultural support systems that are not characterized by capacities for regional variation in research trials and extension strategies or are otherwise accustomed to implementing standardized and uniform national recommendations. Indicator research does better at explaining what might happen in a large number of situations, what can be called generalizable knowledge, but it may be less adept at providing much insight about any specific situation. This can present a problem to more regionalized or decentralized national agricultural support systems, particularly if regional parts of the system are expected to develop adoption understanding that can directly support the formulation of national programmes as well as the development of their own more area-focussed programmes.

These two "types" of understanding, interactive-based and indicator-based, are not prescriptive or mutually exclusive, but rather are stylized characterizations of what is most likely. By inference, it is considered unlikely that a technology generation, verification and dissemination programme oriented heavily to acceptance rates would go to the trouble of interactive adoption research. Similarly, it is considered unlikely that a programme, heavily committed to technology utilization would be satisfied with indicator-based information about farmers. Most programmes, of course, will be somewhere in-between, varying with the stage the programmes are in, the possibilities represented by staffing and resource constraints, and the policy guidelines influencing the focus, level and pace of research. Each agricultural support system needs to ask where its programmes are and where they are heading in terms of the types of questions raised by Fig. 15.1.

Some Guidelines for a Minimum Beginning

Assuming that an agricultural support system knows where it is on Fig. 15.1 and that it is candid about what skills, resources and time may be available for any baseline research efforts related to technology adoption, adaptation and utilization by limited resource farmers, what can and should be done? It would be possible to identify a minimal and even common information base for a national programme, focused on limited-resource farmers. In fact, the focus should first and primarily be on the kinds of understanding needed. Consequently, it is essential that information-gathering methodologies should be seen as the means, not the ends. That is because what is needed most is not a minimum base of compatible information, but more fundamentally a minimum base of useful understanding. A baseline understanding needs to be developed of (1) who the limited-resource farmers are; (2) what characterizes their farming enterprises; (3) what their existing problems are; and (4) what strategies they currently choose to address these problems. In Appendix A, each of these categories of understanding are illustrated through a list of questions. The questions are not items for inclusion on a survey questionnaire, but rather examples of substantive areas of, understanding that would need to be developed.

Minimum baseline understanding can be obtained through several channels, depending on specific situations and orientations. Probably the most important methodological guideline that can be offered is this: the more contact there is between farmer, farm and scientist the better is the chance that the scientist will work from a vision of limited-resource farmers that leaps beyond stereotype and statistics. This contact can be obtained through participant observation, process documentation, rapid rural appraisal, group meetings in the field, or the like. In these cases, it is important to get away from the road, to talk to more than the male household head, to actually stand in farm fields, and to get beyond the obligatory ceremonial events that visits by research station scientists often generate. If surveys are to be conducted, they will be more useful when they are combined with some type of *prior.* experiential strategy that provides at least an overview of the field situation. Experiential information can guide the development of both the sampling frame and the actual survey instrument.

For efforts beyond the minimum understanding base, the issue is not the complexity of information but the communication patterns that will be established and used between farmer and scientist during the course of the technology generation, verification and dissemination process. This goes back to the discussion around Fig. 15.1 and the questions asked there: to what extent are agricultural support systems proposing to work *for* the limited resource farmer and to what extent are they proposing to work *with* the limited resource farmer?

This question has already led to a very substantial concern with farmer association's as an important component of contemporary agricultural extension strategies. However, here we believe it is important not to confuse means and ends. While interactive understanding can readily imply the utility of farmer organizations as the intermediary between individual farmers and the formal extension system, the presence of farmer associations does not necessarily endow extension arrangements with interactive attributes. We believe this point needs emphasis because it is unlikely that improvement of agricultural extension can be built on fads and fixes. What is needed instead are arrangements that are products of solid understanding of specific situations. For this reason, we want to briefly raise a few questions about the roles of rural organization in agricultural extension.

Roles of Rural Organization in Agricultural Extension

From the Philippines' *Zanjera* to Nepal's *Moeya* to Bali's *Subak,* indigenous irrigation associations, primary examples of locally organized resource management, are being "discovered" (Cernea, 1985; Coward, 1980; Dani and Campbell, 1986; Esman, 1982; Siy, 1982; Uphoff, 1982). This is the most recent phase of a tradition pioneered by the Comilla project (and innumerable others) advocating the role of farmer organizations as intermediate arrangements between individual farmers and the support system. At least two important issues have arisen during the course of this diverse experience. It is important to recognize and learn from these issues to ensure that innovations in agricultural extension are actually steps forward.

The first issue is the question: who governs (Bagadion and Korten, 1980; Illo and Chiong-Javier, 1983; Korten and Klauss, 1984)? This question becomes important to the extent that enhancing the roles of local organizations represents challenges to interests which pursue and maintain their own governance claims through manipulation of the policy management and institutional support system. The challenges do not always materialize. During the 1950s and 1960s, community development in South and parts of Southeast Asia "gave" rural communities a chance to provide certain amenities for themselves, but in most cases, there was no intent that rural communities (individually or as a group) were empowered to alter (favourably) any fundamental characteristics of their relationships with the State. Community organization strategies have attracted considerable new interest in recent years, but these strategies still appear to be unfolding within terms of reference that do not represent significant departures from basic relationships between the state and the rural periphery (Castillo, 1983; Goodell, 1983; Oommen, 1984). Illustrative are the moves towards decentralization in Bangladesh and Nepal promulgated at about the same time as decisions which strengthen the state's role in economic and political development and the co-evolution in Korea of a "New-Community" programme, with growing state participation in managing the economy.

This leads to a second issue, namely, what is the status of local organizational resources as rural resources? This issue is really the question: *what is governed?* "Old" rural organizational resources (such as the social organization of labour reciprocity, the household as a foundation of the division of labour, culturally or ethnically-based property management regimes) may be replaced by "new" ones (such as tenant or farm worker unions, local chapters of national political groupings, the privatization of natural resource management). Complex relationships between old and new organizational resources and other rural resources can result. What are the implications for the meanings of "local participation" and "local leadership?" What are the consequences for the viability of local governance strategies?

For example, considerable interest is being shown by rural development specialists in common property resource management systems. These are indigenous systems for managing and using natural resources involving the regulation of individual resource utilization patterns by collective norms and procedures. For instance, some communities in Nepal are reported to have established rules for cutting firewood and fodder and for harvesting fruits, timber and other products. These rules specify both individual and group rights to use the same piece of land. What is attractive about these systems is that they may represent indigenously organized (rather than externally imposed) cases of sustainable natural resource management.

However, recognizing that such systems exist has led to an idealization of the strategies, an idealization that might be very inappropriate. In many cases, common property resource management systems are being advocated as the "answer" to problems of maintaining sustainable productivity in degradable environments. However, social forestry and other common property resource management arrangements need to be assessed in the context of the types of demographic, social, economic and ecologic pressures operating in Asia's more "fragile" rural environments. Common property management cannot always be best understood primarily as a strategy for maintaining (or achieving) important stewardship relationships between Asian rural households and their natural environments. There will be times when common property resource management is better understood as a strategy to ration access to some natural resources, not necessarily in the interests of environmental welfare, but as a lactic for consolidating the state's role in more marginal areas. In the political economy of rural Asia, limiting access to selected natural resources can be a strategy for linking State power to the "rent-seeking" behaviour of rural (and often urban) elites. There are also reasons to suspect that the viability of common property management regimes will be quite sensitive to a variety of local factors such as population pressure, employment opportunities, and food security status (Blaikie, 1985; Khaleque, 1985; Putterman, 1985; Russell and Nicholson, 1981).

Consequently, whatever common property management and other "organizational fix" strategies for rural environmental management may be in theory, in practice they may be very different in food-deficit areas like Northeastern Thailand and Nepal's Terai or diversifying areas such as Northern Pakistan or Eastern Luzon in the Philippines. Because how these systems actually function is not well understood, there is reason to ask: what happens when such strategies are imported by the agricultural support system into existing customary land management systems? Where does "control" over natural resources effectively (if inadvertently) pass?

Conclusion

This paper has attempted to outline some of the challenges agricultural support systems face as they confront the problems of sustainable development and poverty alleviation. The paper argues that in practical terms the pressure to address these issues will come from the increasing contact support systems are having with limited-resource farmers. In that context, the challenges of sustainable development and poverty alleviation will take the form initially of understanding how limited resource farmers differ from the farmers better known by the agricultural support system.

In this process of reassessment that is already unfolding, an important distinction may emerge between the functions of the support system as fundamentally a *transfer* process and the functions of the support system as fundamentally a *transformational* process. For example, we often think of extension as the vehicle for transferring technology and knowledge from the agricultural research system to the farmers. Farming systems research has introduced new forms of complexity and interaction to the agricultural research system, but here too we are still frequently speaking of a (enhanced) technology transfer process.

However, the discussion of technology adoption among limited-resource farmers strongly suggests that many of the assumptions that permit a transfer emphasis to proceed may not be valid. The botanical pest control example suggests that we may be functioning in an area where continual learning and adaptation must be occurring—by both farmers and the support system. For example, extension as education has long been recognized, but the notion of continual learning as an element of this education has some interesting implications for how we might think about the central emphasis of agricultural extension.

Thinking about agricultural support not strictly as a transfer of knowledge and skills process but more broadly as a transformation of learning process (Hawkins, 1988) is a potentially important distinction for at least two reasons:

1. The distinction invites a more active emphasis on the learning that is actually occurring among farmers and support system personnel to complement a more traditional emphasis on the provision of inputs (technology and advice to farmers, funds and facilities to extension agents) that are assumed to support learning.
2. The distinction accommodates recognition that the learning associated with transitions in a farmer's commitment to productivity and an extension agent's commitment to more interactive-based understanding may not be strictly "vocational," but may also be a matter of orientation to new learning processes.

The paper has strongly suggested that much of what is known about technology adoption by farmers in Asia is not based on experience with limited-resource farmers. That may be a problem for developing both research hypotheses and practical expectations about technology adoption among limited-resource farmers. The word "may" is underlined, because we really don't know. Ultimately, what each agricultural support system must decide is: how well do the support systems now "know" limited-resource farmers? How well do the support systems *need* to know limited-resource farmers in order to properly evaluate the adoption, adaptation and utilization prospects of any agricultural development strategy? Once these questions have been answered, the systems can better determine how they need to be organized, managed, staffed and evaluated. In the course of this process, the support system is most likely as well to confront the challenges of sustainable development and poverty alleviation.

Appendix A

Guidelines for a Minimum Beginning

1. **Who are the limited-resource rice farmers?**
   - Where are the farmers who are not now part of the green-revolution complex?
   - How are these households distributed in terms of major agro-economic farm types?
   - What are the major demographic, economic and social characteristics of the households? What are the characteristics of household composition, organization and division of labour; of the levels, importance, variability and seasonality of off-farm and non-farm income sources and employment histories; of health, mortality and education; and of agricultural experience?
   - What are the households' food and energy consumption patterns, particularly intra-household food consumption levels? What are the variabilities in consumption? What are the effects of variabilities in food and energy consumption on health, savings and the maintenance of household integrity and welfare? How and from what sources are consumption demands supplied and what are the main variabilities in these supply systems? What, if anything, are households doing to smooth supply and consumption variabilities?
   - What are the characteristics of the communities where limited-resource farm households live, in terms of infrastructure and administrative services; ethnic, occupational and income diversity; demographic change (in particular, levels of in-migration, dependency ratios and household formation rates)?
2. **What are the characteristics of farm enterprises?**
   - What characterizes the household's security of access to land it cultivates? How was access acquired? How is access for children and heirs provided?

- What are the production levels, variabilities and disposition patterns for crops and animals raised?
- What is the current status of resource management practices including community, reciprocal, hired and family labour allocation, landuse patterns and intensity, and crop and variety choices? Have these practices changed in recent years? If so, how and why?
- What is the current status of environmental and ecological characteristics of lands utilized for agriculture? Are there problems? If so, what are the problems and what measures are being taken to manage and control the problems? Have the number, identity, or seriousness of problems changed in recent years? If so, how and why? If measures to manage and control environmental and ecological problems have changed in recent years, how and why?
- What are the characteristics of farm infrastructure such as equipment, tools, erosion control and water impoundment structures, and on-farm storage facilities?
- What characterizes patterns of accessibility to, and availability of, agricultural support services, such as markets; mills, storage and processing facilities; and input supplies, technical services and credit?
- What forms of local area coordination in resource management exist? How and when do these functions? What are their effects? How, when, to what degree and with what costs and benefits does any particular household participate in such arrangements?

3. **What are existing problems**
   - What is the frequency of problems in relation to important agricultural and family life-cycles? In relation to community resource management practices?
   - What are the locations of problems in relation to crop growth and utilization patterns, land management practices, soil and land forms, and proximity to houselots?
   - How can problems be characterized in terms of levels and variations?
   - What are the primary explanations for the levels, variabilities, frequency, duration and location of problems?
4. **What strategies are chosen to confront these problems?**
   - What are the major types of responses to problems, how do

these relate to resource management practices, and what, if any, extraordinary demands do any of these responses make on landuse, family or community labour, etc.?

— How are the types and levels of responses phased? When are responses initiated? What are the durations? How are responses related to other resource management functions?

— How were different resource management strategies learnt? From whom? When? Where? Are other practices known and not currently used? If so, why not? If other methods were previously used and discontinued, why?

REFERENCES

ADB (Asian Development Bank) (1991). *Economic Policies for Sustainable Development,* Manila: Asian Development Bank.

Ahmed, S. (1984). *Conference Report. Use of Indigenous Plant Materials for Pest Control.* Honolulu: East-West Center Resource Systems Institute.

Ahmed, S. and Bruce Koppel (1987). "Use of Neem and Other Botanical Materials for Pest Control by Farmers in India: Summary of Findings," in H. Schmutterer and K.R.S. Ascher, (eds.), *Natural Pesticides from the Neem Tree and Other Tropical Plants.* Eschborn, Germany: Deutsche Gesellschaft für Technische Zusammenarbeit), pp. 623-26.

Bagadion, Benjamin and Frances F. Korten (1980). "Developing Viable Irrigators Associations: Lessons from Small Scale Irrigation in the Philippines," *Agricultural Administration,* Vol. 7, pp. 273-87.

Batie, Sandra S. (1991). *Sustainable Development: Concepts and Strategies,* Paper presented to International Conference of Agricultural Economists, Tokyo, August 22-29.

Blaikie, Piers (1985). *The Political Economy of Soil Erosion in Developing Countries.* New York: Longman.

Brady, N.C. (1982). "Chemistry and World Food Supplies", *Science*, Vol. 218, November, 847-53.

Burmeister, Larry (1984). *State, Society and Agricultural Research Policy: The Case of South Korea,* Unpublished Doctoral Dissertation, Department of Rural Sociology, Cornell University.

Buttel, F. *et al.* (1983). *From Green Revolution to Biorevolution: Some Observations on the Changing Technological Bases of Economic Transformation in the Third World,* Bulletin Number 132, Ithaca, New York: Cornell University Department of Rural Sociology.

Canlas, Dante *et al.* (1984). *An Analysis of the Philippine Economic Crisis,* Quezon City: University of the Philippines School of Economics.

Carpenter, Richard (1990). "Biophysical Measurement of Sustainable Development," *The Environmental Professional,* Vol. 12, pp. 356-59.

Castillo, Gelia T. (1983). *How Participatory is Participatory Development? A Review of the Philippine Experience*, Manila: Philippine Institute for Development Studies.

Cernea, Michael (ed.) (1985). *Putting People First: Sociological Factors in Rural Development* London: Oxford University Press.

Chambers, Robert (1983). *Rural Development: Putting The Last First*, London: Longman.

Charoenwatana, Terd and A. Terry Rambo (eds.) (1988). *Sustainable Rural Development in Asia*, Khon Kaen, Thailand: Khon Kaen University.

Clarete, Ramon and James Roumasset, 1983, *An Analysis of the Economic Policies Affecting the Philippine Coconut Industry*, Manila: Philippine Institute for Development Studies.

Contreras, Antonio (1991). *Power and Discourse: From the World System to the Philippine Uplands,* Unpublished Ph.D. Dissertation, Department of Political Science, University of Hawaii.

Coward, E. Walter, Bruce Koppel, and Robert Siy, Jr. (1983). *A Conference Report: Organization as a Strategic Resource in Irrigation Development.* Honolulu: East-West Center Resource Systems Institute.

Coward, Jr., E. Walter, (ed.) (1980). *Irrigation and Agricultural Development in Asia: Perspectives from the Social Sciences*. Ithaca, New York: Cornell University Press.

Dani, Anis A. and J. Gabriel Campbell (1986). *Sustaining Upland Resources: People's Participation in Watershed Management,* ICIMOD Occasional Paper No. 3. Kathmandu, Nepal: International Centre for Integrated Mountain Development.

de Janvry, Alain (1985). *Technological Innovation in Agriculture: The Political Economy of its Rate and Bias.* Consultative Group on International Agricultural Research Study Paper Number 1, Washington, D.C.: The World Bank.

De Leon, Manual S.J. (1982). "Intersectoral Capital Flows and Price Intervention Policies in Philippine Agriculture", Doctoral Dissertation, University of the Philippines at Los Banos.

Dell, Sidney (1983). "Stabilization: The Political Economy of Overkill," in John Williamson, (ed.) *IMF Conditionality*, Washington, D.C.: Institute for International Economics, pp. 17-45.

Echeverria, Ruben G. (1990). *Methods for Diagnosing Research System Constraints and Assessing the Impact of Agricultural Research.* 2 Vol. The Hague: International Service for National Agricultural Research.

Esman, Milton J. (1982). *Local Organization and Rural Development. The State of the Art.* Ithaca, New York: Cornell University Center for International Studies.

Evenson, Robert E. and C. E. Pray, *et al.* (1991). *Research and Productivity in Asian Agriculture.* Ithaca: Cornell University Press.

Evenson, Robert E., *et al.* (1979). "Economic Benefits from Research: An Example from Agriculture," *Science,* Vol. 205, September 14, pp. 1101-07.

Ferguson, James (1990). *The Anti-Politics Machine: Development, Depoliticization and Bureaucratic Power in Lesotho*, Cambridge: Cambridge University Press.

Fortmann, Louise, 1984, "Economic Status and Women's Participation in Agriculture: A Botswana Case Study," *Rural Sociology* Vol. 49 (Fall), pp. 452-64.

Goodell, Grace (1983). "What Life After Land Reform?" *Policy Review,* Vol. 24, (Spring), pp. 121-48.

Haas, David (1979). *Interaction in the Thai Bureaucracy: Structure, Culture and Social Exchange*, Boulder, Colorado: Westview Press.

Harriss, Barbara (1984). *State and Market,* New Delhi: Concept Publishing Company, 1984.

Hawkins, John (1988). "The Transformation of Education for Rural Development in the People's Republic of China," *Comparative Education Review,* Vol. 31, pp. 266-81.

Illo, Jeanne Frances and Maria Elena Chiong-Javier (1983). *Organizing Farmers for Irrigation Management: The Buhi-Lalo Experience,* Naga City, Philippines: Ateneo de Naga Research and Service Center.

Inayatullah (1979). *Approaches to Rural Development: Some Asian Experiences.* Kuala Lumpur: Asian and Pacific Development Administration Centre.

Ketkar, C.M. (1976). *Utilization of Neem (Azadirachta Indica A. Juss) and its Bye-Products.* Pune, India: Directorate of Non-Edible Oils and Soap Industry, Khadi and Village Industries Commission.

Khaleque, Kibriaul (1985). *Insecurity of Land Tenure and Forest Management: A Case Study from Bangladesh.* Dhaka: University of Dhaka, Department of Sociology.

Koppel, B. (1976). "Sustaining the Green Revolution in the Philippines: How Many Diffusion Curves?" *Asian Survey,* Vol. 16 (April), pp. 355-64.

Koppel, B. (1978). "Private Investment in Agricultural Inputs and Sustaining the Green Revolution: Some Evidence from the Philippines," *Indian Journal of Agricultural Economics,* Vol. 23 (April-June), pp. 1-20.

Koppel, B. (1979). "The Changing Functions of Research Management," *Agricultural Administration,* Vol. 6 (April), pp. 123-39.

Koppel, B. (1981). "Food Policy Options for Secondary Regions: A Framework for Applied Research," *Food Policy,* Vol. 6 (February), pp. 33-46.

Koppel, B. (1985). "Themes on Genes: Comments on Biotechnology, Agricultural Research and Rural Sociology", *Rural Sociologist*, Vol. 5 (March): 79-88.

Koppel, Bruce and Edmund Oasa (1987). "Induced Innovation Theory and Asia's Green Revolution: A Case Study of an Ideology of Neutrality," *Development and Change,* Vol. 18 (January), pp. 29-67.

Korten, David C. and Felipe B. Alfonso (1983). *Bureaucracy and the Poor. Closing the Gap,* West Hartford, Connecticut: Kumarian Press.

Korten, David C. and Rudi Klauss (eds.), (1984). *People-Centered Development.* West Hartford, Connecticut: Kumarian Press.

Kruegger, Anne (1974). "The Political Economy of the Rent-Seeking Society," *The American Economic Review,* Vol. 64, pp. 291-303.

Lea, David A.M. and D.P. Chaudhri (1983). *Rural Development and the State: Contradictions and Dilemmas in Developing Countries.* New York: Methuen.

Lele, Sharachchandram M. (1991). "Sustainable Development: A Critical Review," *World Development* (June), Vol. 19, 6: pp. 607-21.

Lipton, Michael (1985). *Modern Varieties, International Agricultural Research and the Poor.* Consultative Group on International Agricultural Research Study Paper Number 2. Washington, D.C.: The World Bank.

Mann, Charles K. and Barbara Huddleston (ed.) (1986). *Food Policy. Frameworks for Analysis Action.* Bloomington: Indiana University Press.

Oommen, T.K. (1984). *Social Transformation in Rural India: Mobilization and State Intervention.* New Delhi: Vikas Publishing House.

Pinstrup-Andersen, Per (1982). *Agricultural Research and Technology in Economic Development.* New York: Longman House.

Putterman, Louis (1985). "Theoretical Considerations Regarding the Demise of Team Farming in China," (Typescript), Providence, Rhode Island: Brown University, Department of Economics.

Rambo, Terry A., John A. Dixon and Wu Tsechin (1984). *Ecosystem Models for Development,* Honolulu: East-West Center Environment and Policy Institute.

Randolph, Robert H. *et al.* (1984). *A Technology Assessment of Biological Nitrogen Fixation in U.S. Maize and Rice Production,* Honolulu: East-West Center Resource Systems Institute.

Roumasset, James A. (1978). *The New Institutional Economics and Agricultural Organization,* Honolulu: University of Hawaii, Department of Economics.

Ruddle, Kenneth (1974). *The Yukpa Cultivation System: A Study of Shifting Cultivation in Colômbia and Venezuela.* Berkeley: University of California Press.

Russell, Clifford S. and Norman K. Nicholson (1981). *Public Choice and Rural Development.* Washington, D.C.: Resources for the Future.

Ruttan, Vernon (1978). "The International Agricultural Research Institute as a Source of Agricultural Development," *Agricultural Administration,* Vol. 5 (November), pp. 293-308.

Sathyamurthy, T.V. (1985). *India Since Independence: Studies in the Development of the Power of the State,* Vol. 1, *Centre-State Relations: The Case of Kerala.* Delhi: Ajanta Publications.

Schmutterer, H. (ed.) (1983). *Proceedings. Second International Neem Conference,* Federal Republic of Germany: University of Giessen.

Siy, Jr., Robert Y. (1982). *Community Resource Management. Lessons from the Zanjera*. Quezon City, Philippines: University of the Philippines Press.

Smith, Joytee and Fe Gascon (1980). "The Effect of the New Rice Technology on Family Labour Utilization in Laguna." Paper presented to the Joint Workshop of the Agro-economic Survey and the International Rice Research Institute on Village Economy and Institutions. College, Laguna: IRRI.

Swaminathan, M.S. (1982). "Biotechnology Research and Third World Agriculture", *Science,* Vol. 218 (December): 967-72.

Uphoff, Norman T. (1982). *Rural Development and Local Organization in Asia*. Delhi: Macmillan.

Wade, Robert (1985). "Common Property Management in South Indian Villages," Paper prepared for Conference on "The Management of Common Property Resources in the Third World," Washington, D.C.: National Research Council.

16

Resource Potentials for Agricultural Development in Chhotanagpur
Review and Reassessment

NAGESHWAR PRASAD

It is a truism to say that the Chhotangapur region is handicapped by many physical, economic and socio-cultural aspects particularly in comparison to the adjoining areas of alluvial tracts of the middle and lower Ganga plains. If the region is adjudged with regard to agriculture, impediments appear to be more and more conspicuous because of the variety and differences of topographical features, gneissic-granite base, immature and less fertile soils, regular truncation and renovation of surface by erosion of in-process soils from upslope and deposition of poor soils over relatively good soils on the downslope, quick run-off rendering the streams ephemeral and underground water resources poor, inconsistency and irregularity of climatic features and many other socio-economic factors like poverty, illiteracy, backwardness, land-ownership, etc., which pose problems to the region in using good agricultural techniques, e.g. scientific rotation, use of improved seeds, fertilizers and modern implements and agricultural financing as well as organized marketing.

The present paper is not going to repeat the general statements of problems and measures which have become sometimes absolutely ideals, and only mental food and academic attainments are achieved. Born and brought up in this region the author is acquainted with the real problems and resource structure of the area. The region is not hopeless as many notions have been created by the people particularly coming from outside. The objective of this paper is, therefore, to offer clarifications of all these and correctly introduce the area to the planners, persons implementing the programmes and administrators involved in the development of this area.

Area of Chhotanagpur Considered for the Present Study

The term Chhotanagpur is variously used and hence opinion differ regarding its delimitation. Chhotanagpur is an administrative unit and refers, at present, to two Chhotanagpur Divisions—North and South of Bihar in India. It is also a geographical unit, a natural region which is the easternmost continuation of the Indian Peninsula lying to the south of the Middle Ganga plain. The regions implied by two terms, administrative and geographical, are coterminus for the most part but a good stretch is lying outside the administrative unit. Consequently, opinion differs on delimitation from physical geographers to cultural ones.

Dunn (1941: 11-12) and Singh (1969: 1) while studying geology and geomorphology respectively defined the Chhotanagpur plateau region as part of Bihar roughly bounded by the 500 ft. contour on the north, by the State of Orissa on the south, West Bengal on the east and Uttar Pradesh and Madhya Pradesh on the west. It is noted that Puralia district, now in West Bengal was part of Bihar, so it was included in the region. Later Ahmad (1965: 22) and Prasad (1973: 25-26) excluded the Purulia Upland from the Chhotanagpur Plateau, though it is physically very much associated with the plateau. Pandey (1970: 6) included only the present North and South Chhotanagpur Divisions.

Singh (1971: 37) in his most detailed book, *India : "A Regional Study,"* maintains the delimitation of the plateau as suggested by Dunn and R.P. Singh.

The Chhotanagpur Plateau, as a physical unit, undoubtedly sprawls extensively beyond the State boundary of Bihar towards Bengal, Orissa and Madhya Pradesh. But when the socio-economic and cultural aspects in relation to the physical data collection, compilation of information, etc. Physical boundary seldom coincides with administrative boundary. So, in such a study the administrative unit, at least at anchal level, is considered. Therefore, although the adjoining areas of Bengal, Orissa and Madhya Pradesh form part of the Chhotanagpur plateau on the rationale of physical geography, such areas cannot be included in the region of Chhotanagpur plateau for a comprehensive regional study. This is done, firstly, because of the difficulties in inter-State fieldwork, data collection and compilation of work. Secondly, it is a fact that outlying areas have been thoroughly integrated in altogether different cultural regions, administrative set-up, planning and projects. Moreover, the outlying areas like Purulia district and western portion of Malda, Burdwan and Birbhum districts in West Bengal are culturally different, particularly from the point of view of language, way of living, food habits, social consciousness, etc. Similar is the case with the outlying areas of Orissa and Madhya Pradesh.

Thus, the plateau of Chhotanagpur has a qualified definition and stands for those parts of the Chhotanagpur plateau which lie within the political boundaries of the State of Bihar. The political boundaries of the State have, therefore, been accepted as the limits of the plateau in the west, south and east. In the north, roughly 500 ft. contour makes the boundary with a compromise with the anchal boundaries (Prasad, 1973: 25-26).

Therefore the plateau of Chhotanagpur includes, at present, three full divisions and portion of two divisions (Table 16.1, Fig. 16.1), including 13 full districts, portions of 5 district and 223 anchals.

The region comprising an area of about 90,000 km^2, a little more than half of the State of Bihar and that of the whole of West Bengal, extends roughly from latitude 20°N to 25°20′N and from longitude 83°20′ E to 87°50′ E. It covers about 3 per cent of the total land surface of India.

The region is bounded by the South Middle Ganga plain or South Bihar plain on the north, the Lower Ganga plain and the Purulia-Bankura upland on the east, Orissa uplands on the south and Chhattisgarh Rimland and South Vindhyachal-Bundelkhand region on the west.

Resource Base

Physical Potentialities

The basement of Chhotanagpur is made of gneissic gneissic granite known as Bengal gneiss or Chhotanagpur gneiss. Sedimentary metamorphic, igneous intrusive and extrusive rocks are associated with this basement. A large part of such gneissic granite area is unsuitable for prosperous agriculture because of a thin veneer or no layer of soils.

Table 16.1: Delineation of Chhotanagpur*

Division	*Districts*	*Area (in km²)*	*Population (1981)*	*Anchals*
I. North Chhotanagpur		21053	6044782	All 52
	Dhanbad*	2996	2115010	All 10
	Giridih	6892	1731462	All 18
	Hazaribagh	11165	2198310	All 24
II. South Chhotanagpur		44331	7849759	All 100
	Gumla	9077	1017231	All 18
	Lohardaga	1491	229786	All 5
	Palamau*	12749	1917528	All 25
	Ranchi	7574	1823415	All 20
	Singhbhum*	13440	2861799	All 32
III. Santal Pargana's		13512	3717528	All 41
	Deoghar	2479	708828	All 14
	Dumka*	5518	1215542	All 7
	Godda	2110	713405	All 7
	Rajmahal	3405	1079753	All 13
IV. Bhagalpur (Part)		5389	1451072	Only 13
	Bhagalpur	2017	49584	Only 5 (Banka, Katoria, Chanan, Belhar, Bausi)
	Monghyr	3372	965268	Only 8 (Jamui, Lakshmipur, Jhajha, Chakai, Sono, Khaira, Sikandra, Halsi)
V. Magadh (Part)		5408	1740768	Only 17
	Aurangabad	1420	454984	Only 4 (Deo, Kutumba, Nabinagar, Madanpur)
	Gaya	2443	780551	Only a (Sherghati Amas, Imamganj, Dumaria, Garua, Fatehpur, Mohanpur and Barachatti.
	Nawada	1545	505233	Only 5 (Pakri Barawan, Kawakole, Gobindpur, Rajauli, Sirdala)
		89693	20813909	

* Recently Bokaro, Chatra and Garhwa have gained the status of new district truncating the portions of Dhanbad, Hazaribagh and Palamau respectively. Singhbhum has been divided into two districts—East Singhum and West Singhbhum. Palamau has now become a division comprising of two districts—Palamau and Garhwa. All the details are not available.

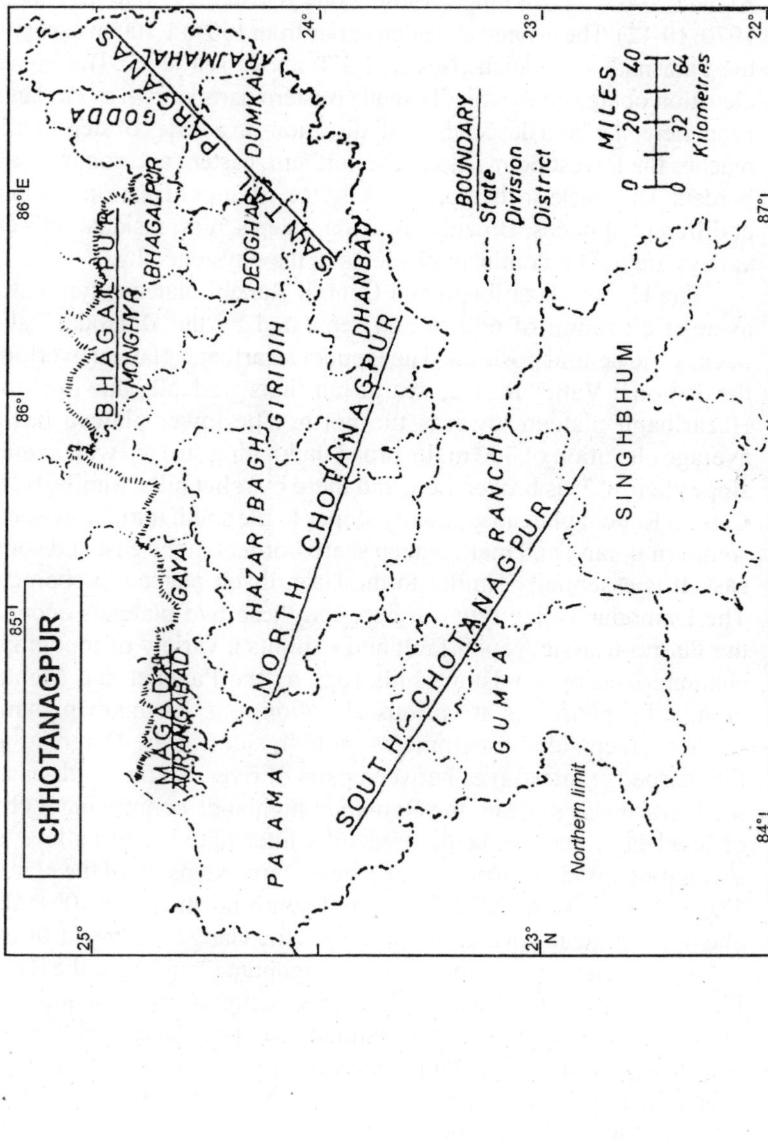

Fig. 16.1: Map of Chhotanagpur

Region of Great Physical Inequalities

The Chhotanagpur Plateau is a region of great physical inequalities and presents a rich panorama of topographic features (Dunn, 1941: 11-15; Ahmad, 1965: 22-26; Singh, 1969: 23-48; Prasad, 1973: 8-30; Pandey, 1970: 10-12). The general elevation varies from 150 to 1,100 m excepting the Parasnath hill which rises to 1,370 above sea level. The highest elevation obtains in the middle south-western parts known as *Pat* lands. From here, the land descends in all directions in a series of steps until it reaches the lowest points along the northern, eastern and south-eastern borders. The breaks in the slope mark the steep scarps of plateaus standing at different altitudes. Broadly speaking, steep scraps, residual hills and valleys are the predominant elements in the physiography.

The Upper Hazaribagh and Central Ranchi plateaus lying at an average elevation of 600 m and separated by the Damodar valley occupy the central position. The Upper Hazaribagh plateau overlooks the damodar Valley in steep scarps but sinks gradually into the lower Hazaribagh plateau towards the north. The lower plateau has an average elevation of 300 m. Its broad undulating surface with average slopes below 2° is broken here and there by relict hills. Similarly, the Central Ranchi plateau gradually slopes to the south into the dissected southern upland and makes steep scarp borders in the east and south-east. It is essentially similar to the Hazaribagh plateau in character. The Damodar valley lying in between these two plateaus occupies the Permo-triassic trough fault and exhibits a variety of topography characterized by sandstone hills such as the Panchet and Mahudi, undulating platforms at various elevation, e.g. Ramgarh planation surface, steep-sided escarpments on both sides of the Damodar and the scarpedge interfluves between pairs of river. To the north-east of the Hazaribagh plateau, the Rajmahal highlands comprising a chain of level lava plateau, sculptured hills interrupted with valleys and undulating divided surfaces mark the eastern extension of the plateau. The volcanic Rajmahal hills extend south-north rising 300-450 m above the plateau surface and overlook the Ganges in the north-east.

In the south-east corner lies the Singhbum plain below the Ranchi Plateau. It is studded with hills and is encircled by highlands. The granitic Chaibase plain, strewn with hills and boulders, and the mica-schist plains extending along the river Subarnarekha lie between the triangular mass of Dhanjori highlands in the south-east and the Dalma range in the north and north-west.

Such great differences in elevation and relief bring about strong contrasts in climate, natural vegetation, surface drainage, underground water and soil profiles, which, in turn, has a clear-cut impact on agriculture in terms of potential and development.

Limited Underground Water

On account of the relatively steep gradient and impervious nature of granite and gneiss, the underground water is limited over the larger areas of the Chhotanagpur plateau. The greater percentage of the regional precipitation flows down the steep slopes of the plateau in the form of surface runoff. Rainfall is distributed over four months of the year (mid-June to mid-October) while the remaining period is dry except for smaller cyclonic winter showers which are of uncertain character. Unlike the rivers of the adjoining plains, the Chhotanagpur streams are disconnected pools of stagnant water during the cold and hot seasons, but immediately after monsoonal showers in the hills they come down in sudden short-lived freshets. It is mainly due to their steep gradient that the torrents turn into senile, discordant and innocent looking streams after a few hours of the heavy downpours in the upper catchment area. Thus, both in terms of surface drainage and underground water in natural conditions the resource is poor especially when it is judged for agricultural operations and development.

Soil which is probably the fundamental aspect for agricultural prosperity of a region is related mainly to the parent rocks and drainage characteristics of Chhotanagpur. Chhotanagpur has the characteristic red soils of the gneiss and granite surface with four exceptions:

(a) The Damodar Valley where loose sandy soil has developed over the Gondwana sandstones.
(b) The high level laterite over the *Pats*.
(c) 'Regu' and lateritic soil over the volcanic lava-built surface of the Rajmahal highlands.
(d) The alluvium in the extreme north-east parts.

It is generally observed that the soils in Chhotanagpur are interfile and unsuitable for prosperous agriculture. It is true that the soils in comparison to the plains are of low fertility, but they are not absolutely useless. Actually fertility ranges from low to high and topography appears to have been the most potent factor in bringing about local variations. Besides, mineral composition matters much. Generally, low-lying areas, brooks or river valleys possess comparative fertile soil and there are agricultural activities in *dons* or lower valley areas. The introduction of irrigation facilities has made it more suitable and thereby agriculture of better economy.

Economic Potentialities

The Chhotanagpur Plateau is the richest mineral region in India. This is true not only of the monetary value of minerals produced but also of the remarkable diversity of the mineral which are available. The region accounts for 40 to 54 per cent of the mineral production of various minerals in India.

In certain minerals, it holds a key position. It produces nearly 100 per cent of India's copper and apatite, 95 per cent of kynite, more than 50 per cent of coal, mica, bauxite and china clay, and about 40 per cent of iron-ore. Chhotanagpur contains 80 per cent of India's known deposits of coal and nearly 100 per cent of coking coal. These minerals have developed a number of industries and to the development of the country these offer the greatest contribution.

Rich in Forest Resources

The region with more than one-third of its area under forest is richly endowed with forest resources. The forest products may be counted in hundreds and they are of economic and commercial significance in various ways. It is generally observed that forests repel or restrict population to their peripheries, but in this plateau the economy of the people is so inextricably bound up with forest that if the forest disappears the village disappears also, or in any case, the latter will find it most difficult to hold out. Thus, the forests have contributed to the economic prosperity of the people of the plateau. When minerals were not exploited and industries were non-existent, forest was the fountain-head of material property for the people of this region.

On the Industrial Map of the World

Chhotanagpur is considered to be one of the most highly industrialized tracts of India and finds a place in the industrial map of the world also. It offers very favourable opportunities for the growth of a variety of heavy and light, producer and consumer goods industries on large or small scale. A variety of forest and mineral-based raw materials are available in the region. The availability of good quality iron ore, coking coal and lime-stone provides an excellent advantage for the growth of the cycle of ferrous metal industries. Bauxite and copper ore, in association with the hydro-electricity of the Damodar Valley, provide a base for non-ferrous metal industries. Bamboo, *sabai* grass, timber, lac and other raw materials can feed paper, furniture and a host of other industries. Large-scale cement, chemical, glass, refracting industries may develop on the basis of limestone, quartz sand, coal and coke available in the region in abundance.

Inadequate Communication System

The communication system of the region includes railways, roads and airways. As the streams are characterized by gorges, faulted troughts and waterfalls, water communication is non-existence in Chhotanagpur. The existing lines of communication are of recent origin. Chhotanagpur ushered in the era of modern transport with the beginning of mineral exploitation and within half a century thousands of miles of metalled roads and a network of railways came into being. The density of roads and railways varies, however, widely in different parts of the plateau, and about 30 per cent of the total area of the region is still inaccessible by roads. All such inaccessible areas are more than five miles away from any category of roads. Similarly, about two-thirds of Chhotanagpur are yet to be effectively served by railways. It is on account of the physical obstacles, e.g. scarps, varying altitudes, fine texture of drainage, etc., that large sections have no rail communication and good roads.

All these enomic potentialities have a bearing on the prosperity and development of agriculture. The economic activities other than agriculture not only lessen the burden of population on agriculture, but they also enhance the status and purchasing power of the farmers and thereby boost the use of modern, appropriate and essential materials and techniques. The development of communication lines helps in marketing and movement of agricultural products rewarding the farmers with good returns.

Human Resource

Natural resources are defined by human perceptions and attitudes, wants, technological skills, legal, financial and institutional arrangements, as well as by political customs. What is a natural resource in one culture may be neutral stuff in another culture? The understanding of the people's relations with nature, their geographical behaviour as well as their feelings and ideas in regard to space and place is essential. With this view in mind the human resource of Chhotanagpur can be examined.

Table 16.2 reveals that in bout 90,000 km^2 of the total area of the Chhotanagpur Highlands, nearly 20.8 million people are residing with a density of 232 persons/km^2 as against 402 persons/km^2 in the State of Bihar and 221 persons/km^2 in India. This population shares 29.77 per cent of Bihar while it occupies 51.58 per cent of the total area of the State. The main working force is 31.11 per cent in comparison to 29.68 per cent of the State while it has 26.89 per cent literates in comparison to 26.20 per cent Bihar and 36.17 per cent of India. In both working force and literacy male population is dominating with shares of more than 75-80 per cent and 70-75 per cent respectively. It is, however, noted that North and South Chhotanagpur Divisions have a comparatively better percentage of literacy.

As regards percentage of the Scheduled Tribes (ST) and Scheduled Castes (SC) population a marked range can be observed (Table 16.2). In South Chhotanagpur Division the ST population is high with a percentage of about 43 followed by 37 in the Santal Parganas and 10 per cent in North Chhotanagpur Division. In Magadh Division the percentage is least, only 0.08 per cent. For the whole the State it is 8.31 per cent. The SC population, on the other hand, shares a high percentage in Magadh (32 %) followed by about 16 per cent in North Chhotanagpur and Bhagalpur Divisions and 9-10 per cent in South Chhotanagpur and the Santal Parganas in comparison to 14.51 per cent for the State. It is, however, important to note that more than 50 per cent and 45 per cent of the population is shared by ST and SC together in South Chhotanagpur and the Santal Parganas while in North Chhotanagpur they together share only about 26 per cent of the total population.

Some Notions about the Resources

Before we evaluate the resource of Chhotanagpur for agricultural prosperity and development, let us summarize some of the notions about the resource conceived particularly by persons living outside the region or social scientists not acquainted with the area fully or the planners making plans for the area sitting in their ivory towers.

Table 16.2: Human Resource in Chhotanagpur (1981)

Division	Area (in km²)	Population			Literates			Scheduled		Main Working Population		
		Total	Male	Female	Total	Male	Female	Tribes	Castes	Total	Male	Female
(1)	(2)	(3)	(4)	(5)	(6)	(7)	(8)	(9)	(10)	(11)	(12)	(13)
I. North Chhotanagpur	21053.0 (23.47)	6044782 (29.04)	3163561 (52.34)	2881221 (47.66)	1759077 (29.10)	1336006 (75.95)	423071 (24.05)	616247 (10.20)	971731 (16.08)	1701229 (28.14)	1505233 (88.48)	195996 (11.52)
II. South Chhotanagpur	44331.1 (49.42)	7849759 (37.72)	4017473 (51.18)	3832286 (48.82)	2307575 (29.40)	1636930 (70.94)	670645 (29.06)	3344968 (42.61)	773379 (9.85)	2551950 (32.51)	1992727 (78.09)	559223 (21.91)
III. Santal Parganas	13512.7 (15.07)	3717528 (17.86)	1899410 (51.09)	1818118 (48.91)	827400 (22.26)	636115 (76.88)	191285 (23.12)	1367868 (26.80)	311801 (8.39)	1227955 (33.03)	1008968 (82.17)	218987 (17.83)
IV. Magadh (Part)	5407.6 (6.03)	1740768 (8.03)	871063 (50.04)	869705 (49.96)	400485 (23.01)	306709 (76.58)	93776 (23.42)	1447 (0.08)	554850 (31.87)	537238 (30.87)	418002 (77.81)	119236 (22.19)
V. Bhagalpur (Part)	5388.9 (6.01)	1461072 (7.2)	745922 (51.05)	715150 (48.95)	302727 (20.72)	240734 (79.52)	61993 (20.48)	93915 (6.43)	229251 (15.69)	457203 (31.29)	374629 (91.94)	82574 (19.08)
	89693.3 (100)	20813909 (100)	10697429 (51.40)	10116480 (48.60)	5597264 (25.89)	4156494 (74.26)	1440770 (25.74)	5424445 (26.06)	2841012 (13.65)	6475575 (31.11)	5299659 (81.84)	1176016 (18.16)

Notes: (1) Figures in brackets show the percentage.
(2) In columns 4, 5, 6, 9, 10 and 11figures in brackets show the percentage to total population mentioned in column 3.
(3) In columns 7 and 8 figures show the percentage to total literates mentioned in column 6.
(4) In columns 12 and 13 figures show the percentage to total working population mentioned in column 11.
(5) Computation work has been done by the authors on the basis of data available from the primary Census Abstract, Part II B, Series-4 (Bihar), Census of India, 1981.

In Chhotanagpur, roads follow generally spurs, on either side of which are sloping lands with vegetation cover. Therefore, a person who is travelling through these roads for the first time forms the impression that the areas is full of forest, devoid of agricultural lands and there is no scope for agricultural operations and development on these sloping lands. He cannot view the *tanrs* and *dons* situated on the mid-slope and lowlying areas away from the forest as well as in the middle of the open vegetation cover. Many settlement sites are also out of sight giving the impression that the plateau area, in spite of being rich in natural scenery, is poor in land and human resources for agricultural development. This notion is wrong to a great extent and misleading too.

Incorrect Projection by Politicians

It is a general feeling that Chhotanagpur is full of tribal population or the tribes are dominating in number. The local politicians project this impression to make the term Chhotanagpur synonymous with the Jharkhand or Tribal Region with the intention that the demand for a separate Jharkhand state is justified. The shrewd politicians particularly from outside and sitting on the Opposition benches are nodding this notion to appease their voters, most of them knowing that it is a wrong projection and the movement would never succeed, if this wrong footing could be nodded all the time. The authors are not interested in the debate whether the movement of a separate State is justified or not, but it can be stated that the movement might succeed if there was no synonymity of the Jharkhand with the tribes. Table 16.2 and Appendix 1 reveal that excepting Gumla (73.55%), Lohardaga (58.67%) and Rajmahal (53.29%), none of the districts shares more that 50 per cent of the tribal population to the total population. The districts of Dhanbad, Hazaribagh, Giridih and Deoghar share not even more than 50 per cent. The purpose of revealing these facts in the present discussion is to show that the human resource for agricultural development should not be assessed on wrong projections.

Socially Advanced Communities

In Bihar four communities—Brahmans, Rajputs, Bhumihars and Kayasthas—are considered to be mentally alert and socially advanced.

They can carry out any work more efficiently and in an organized manner. Rest of the communities either belong to the backward classes or scheduled castes or scheduled tribes. In Chhotanagpur, the communities other than the four castes are dominating, the percentage of which in many pockets will be 100. "The tribal people are hardly sharp and quick in grasp" (Shafi, 1985: 2). The notion on this basis is that the region is undeveloped and backward agriculturally as well as in terms of other aspects owing to this dominance over population. It is also highlighted that the region will remain backward with this composition of population, and the only remedy to eradicate this constraint is to intrude the so-called forward castes into these backward communities. A considerable percentage of the people belonging to such forward communities also claim that they have played a significant role in the development of the region, whatever the degree of development. This is also a wrong notion to a great extent.

Programmes not Implemented Properly

It is stated that majority of the population particularly ST and SC are not responding to the development programmes meant for the area in regard to agricultural activities. But the fact is that the programmes are not implemented properly and honestly and because of the simplicity and peace-loving attitude of the people, they do not even know about the programme or if they do not struggle for the implementation. They do not struggle for the implementation. Their simplicity honesty and peace-loving attitude have been misinterpreted as their backwardness. Exploiting this, the implementing officials are very happy to get postings in this region, and they do not want to be transferred to places outside Chhotanagpur. Many of them have settled in this area.

It is considered that the resource pertaining to agricultural production is so poor that it cannot feed the people of Chhotanagpur. It is true in the present context, because a large number of persons have come to this area from almost every corner of the country with the development of mining and manufacturing industries. The resource is, nevertheless, insufficient to feed the old settlers.

Resource Appraisal

Hundred per cent correct estimation of available resources for agriculture in Chhotanagpur is difficult. Substantial differences may emerge depending upon analysts' interpretations of what constitutes a "resource" (Mitchell, 1989: 47). The present author will make an efforts to focus upon the inventory. A host of pertinent questions will be taken into consideration. What are the resources? How many of them are there? What is their condition? How available are they? What are the demands for them? How will changing prices, technologies and values effect future demands? How will different resource uses interact to influence future supplies? What opportunities exist to improve productivity? They will also try to determine whether existing agricultural activity represents the best of resources.

Agricultural Resource

Agricultural potentiality is a function of various factors including the physical, socio-economic and techno-organizational factors. Some of the aspects of resources for agricultural operations may differ from one region to another in their rank significance of importance, but there are resources which are common. The nature and extent of land; fertility, thickness and texture of soil; form and character of surface and underground drainage; Hydrographic characteristics of climate; potentialitis, facilities and extent of irrigation; extent of occupance, density and physico-mental status of the population; and social and economic institutions coupled with accessibility to markets, transport and communications, etc. are the common resources evaluated for the agricultural potentiality of a region.

Extent, Availability and Condition of Agricultural Resource in Chhotanagpur

In Chhotanagpur these resources are considered to be poor particularly when a comparative analysis is made with the adjoining Ganga plains of North Bihar and West Bengal.

It is true that cultivated lands in Chhotanagpur are not the blessed gift of nature like the alluvial tracts of the Ganga plains where man, at the initial stage of farming practices, threw the seeds and got the crops. Whatever patches of cultivated lands are observed in Chhotanagpur, they are owing to great human efforts made year after year right from terracing, embankments and levelling of lands along and across the river valleys, large and small alternating with spurs to patiently awaiting for rock-rotting for soil formation, regular sifting of boulders and stony materials for appropriate textural characteristics and applying crop rotation for the enrichment of soils with organic matter. Even for this human effort the area is limited. The scarps, rocky exposures, surfaces with a very thin veneer of soils, mountain slopes, areas with a dense vegetal cover are not to come under agricultural operations. It is why the net area sown in Chhotanagpur is only round 30 per cent of the total area as against more than 50 per cent of the whole of the State. The extent of land for agriculture as well as intensity and capability of agriculture is determined greatly by slope. "As the slope increases, the percentage of land under plough decreases" (Prasad, 1973: 58). As regard soils, natural and irrigation water, transport network and other components of agricultural development, the resource in Chhotanagpur is, no doubt, limited (see under Resource Base). But it is, at the same time, not disappointing.

It is noteworthy in this context that "the people of lowland Bihar have nominal marginal lands left for further operation of agricultural activities as they have utilized even the beds of runnels, channels and rivers at the cost of flood and devastation, but the highlands have few men and greater percentage of topographically usable land. They have even greater resources within the vaults of rough and rugged highlands. They await even further utilization (Singh and Kumar, 1970: 30).

Owing to topographic variation, Chhotanagpur is free from flood hazards. The region has an important character that is never experiences complete drought in respect of agriculture even in those areas where there is no provision of irrigation water as has been observed in the non-irrigated areas of the Ganga plains. It is because of the topographic variations. The low-lying cultivated lands, locally known as *dons*, get oozing water form the slope in the form of springs, may be miniature in form, throughout the year. The uplands, locally known as *tanrs*, on the other hand, are deprived of such natural endowments. Such conditions play a positive role in the agricultural production in an adverse situation. In case of excessive rain the uplands grow more than what in normal conditions while crops in the lowlands are subject to rotting. In the case of drought the lowlands grow more than in normal conditions while crops on the uplands yield a poor return. So, there is some sort of balance in the total quantity of production from *dons* and *tanrs* to a great extent. It should be noted, therefore, that when a family is partitioned among brothers and the landed property is fragmented, the arable lands are divided keeping this point in mind. No one prefers to take only *dons*, although the value of *dons* is much higher than that of *tanrs*. They prefer to share both types of arable lands, sometimes even sub-types like *don* I, II and III and *tanr* I, II and III.

Although the climate condition in Chhotanagpur has spatial variations due to plateau surfaces of different elevations ranging from below 150 to more than 1,100 m and seasonal variations owing to its monsoonal character, the climate is, in general, for most of the year, pleasant and energizing. It does not cause perspiration, exhaustiveness and weakness, so it facilitates hard labour in the agricultural fields.

In the Chhotanagpur plateau, the rain periodical, variable and irregular. It is also not uniform. Rivers, on account of steep gradient, drain off quickly. Contour irrigation and damming of small streams make up the vagaries of the monsoons.

The most useful and widely practised method of irrigation in the entire region consists of a succession of *bunds* or embankment thrown across the line of drainage, resulting in the formation of a chain of small reservoirs. In these reservoirs rain-water is accumulated. Irrigation is affected by cuts in the bunds which permit the stored water to flow down either through small artificial channels or through surface run-off. Sometimes, small embankments are constructed on higher slopes of hills or ridges to store water temporarily to irrigate the fields below by permitting the water to flow down or to percolate and keep the fields most (Prasad, 1973: 72).

For the better utilization of water resources in the Chhotanagpur plateau, a number of projects and schemes have been and are being planned and executed. These are of three kinds: major, medium and minor. Some of the major schemes are DVC, Vayurakshi project, Subarnarekha, North Koel and South Koel river schemes, Konar Irrigation project, etc.

Among the medium irrigation schemes, Kokro Irrigation Scheme (Ranchi), Khudia Weir Scheme (Dhanbad), Araj Irrigation Scheme (Palamau), Sona Weir Scheme (Singhbum), Bijay Weir Scheme (Singhbhum), Gumani Dam Scheme (Rajmahal), Ajoy Valley Project (Dumka), Souroo Dam Scheme (Singhbhum), Banki Right Irrigation (Palmau), Mohane Weir Scheme (Hazaribagh and Gaya) are important.

Besides these, numerous minor schemes are running from field to field, farm to farm and village to village in the form of small reservoirs across the stream, big tanks and high-diameter wells. Geological foundations in Chhotanagpur are unfavourable for sinking wells. Some of the areas are exceptions.

Most of the irrigation facilities available are used for the irrigation of paddy lands. In recent years irrigated areas under other crops particularly wheat and vegetables have increased and are increasing day by day.

It is expected that these schemes of irrigation will transform the agrarian economy of Chhotanagpur and hence all these should function to compose the irrigation environs within the campus of the Chhotanagpur plateau (Prasad and Mahto, 1991: 107-115).

The main working population (Table 16.2) in Chhotanagpur is more or less sufficient to carry on agricultural activities. It accounts for 31.11 per cent to the total population as against 29.68 per cent for the whole State of Bihar. This working force is maximum (33.03%) in Santal Parganas Division while North Chhotanagpur has 28.14 per cent. Chhotanagpur as a whole has no marked range of spatial variation of this resource, so agricultural activities with a similar intensity throughout the area can be viewed so far as human resource is concerned. The notion (see under Socially Advanced Communities) that the tribes, castes and backward communities are an inferior human resource is misleading. These people are in fact very hardy and energetic and they have in general faithfulness and sincerity to their work.

As regards social and economic institutions, Chhotanagpur has potentiality for agricultural development. The mining, manufacturing and forest-based industries have stimulated the growth of industrial and urban centres in almost all parts of the region developing therefor communications and transport systems, sometimes under compulsion and sometimes under development programmes. One cannot fail to notice that Chhotanagpur is in the grip of an industrial revolution and consequently rapid urbanization. Some of the districts like Hazaribagh, Dhanbad and Ranchi have registered 60 to 80 per cent urban growth rate during 1971-81. The whole of Dhanbad and parts of Hazaribagh, Giridih, Ranchi and Singhbhum districts are the areas of maximum concentration of towns. There are at present 5 Class I cities, 7 Class II, 14 Class III, 20 Class IV, 13 Class V and 5 Class VI towns in the region according to the 1981 Census (Tables 16.3 and 16.4) accounting for a total of 64 towns. These urban centres have great demand for agricultural products. The region is, however, lacking a developed network of communications and transport systems, organized marketing and other facilities provided for agricultural prosperity of a region.

Table 16.3: Class I Towns in Chhotanagpur (1981)

Urban Aggl./City (1 lakh +)	*Population (1981)*	*Growth Rate (71-81)*	*Rank in India*
1. Dhanbad	676736	+ 55.92	23
2. Jamshedpur	669934	+ 46.88	25
3. Ranchi	500593	+ 95.89	40
4. Bokaro Steel City	261240	+ 143.79	80
5. Bermo	101502	+ 46.42	207

Table 16.4: Towns in Chhotanagpur (Class I, II, III, IV, V and VI) (1981)

Class	*Town*	*Total population*
(1)	(2)	(3)
II. (50000-99999)	Patratu	99940
	Hazaribagh	80013
	Giridih	65446
	Ramgarh	65125
	Deoghar	58936
	Kumardhubi	54601
	Daltonganj	51944
III. (20000-49999)	Gumia	47731
	Chaibasa	45308
	Sahebganj	45109
	Jhumri Tilaiya	38703
	Dumka	31030
	Madhupur	29964
	Ghatsila	25152
	Lohardaga	23327
	Chatra	22761
	Gomoh	21951
	Garhwa	21515
	Itaki	20786
	Pakur	20004

(Contd.)

(*Contd.*)

(1)	(2)	(3)
IV. (10000-19999)	Khunti	18776
	Simdega	18440
	Chandrapura	14916
	Godda	14884
	Mihijam	14563
	Hussainabad	14447
	Noamundi	14363
	Jamtara	13888
	Bundu	13876
	Barki Saraiya	13772
	Maithon	13478
	Khelari	13267
	Gidi	12959
	Latehar	12523
	Rajmahal	12418
	Barughutu	12288
	Jadugora	11439
	Gua	10618
	Jhinpani	10472
	Gadhwa	10467
V. (5000-9999)	Basukinath	9359
	Muri	9318
	Bhojudih	9232
	Kiriburu	9034
	Nirsa	8868
	Chakulia	8711
	Seraikela	7865
	Panchet	7287
	Chandaur (Dhanbad)	6297
	Sini	5977
	Kharsawan	5756
	Malkera	5110
	Borio Bazar	5099
VI. (<5000)	Deorihalan	4755
	Meghhatuburu	3327
	Netarhat	2908
	Tenu	2441
	Chaitudih	2077

Demand, Changing Prices and Technology, Existing Landuse and Opportunities for Improvement

It is revealed that the growing population (see under Resource Base) and rapid industrialization and urbanization (see under Economic Potentialities and the foregoing Para) make a provision of great demands for agricultural products both for the people and raw materials for industries. The farmers of urban centres are getting high prices for their products from the urban population. This incentive has changed the technology, landuse pattern, system of farming and cropping pattern in such centres. This change has a conspicuous impact on the mobility and media exposure, settlement rationalization, educational development and normative patterns. From the study and observations of several rural and rurban centres of Chhotanagpur it can be concluded that, on the basis of its resource structure, Chhotanagpur has an ample opportunity for development of and improvement in agriculture provided that the constrains are rightly assessed and the development programmes honestly implemented at appropriate time and in the right direction. It is also noted that even rugged terrains can be used for improved agriculture with provisions of essential inputs. Boreya, a rurban centre of Ranchi city is one of the best examples, details of which are given for the validity of the present discussion.

Boreya : A Case Study

Space Relations of Boreya

The area in which the centre under study is situated is a relatively large village (412.8 hectares/2586 persons in 1984) in Kanke block of Ranchi district in Bihar extending from latitude 23° 24′ 16″ to 23° 26′ 30″ N and longitude 85° 20′ 44″ to 85° 22′ 17″E (Fig. 16.2).

Boreya falls under the controlled area of Ranchi city which has provided the area with good linkages, bus stands, railway station, post offices, schools, technical institutions, colleges, universities, hospitals and many other urban amenities (Fig. 16.2). Boreya itself is provided with facilitated like school, post and telegraph office, doctor's clinic, small hotel, bus stops, etc.

Physical Potentialities

Boreya, though a very small unit of the Ranchi planation surface in the highlands of Chhotanagpur presents a good panorama of topographic features consisting of residual hills, river valleys, terraced terrains and undulating surfaces of *dons* and *tanrs*. The variation in elevation (596 m to 689.3 m), land type (*tanr* III to *don* I), surface forms (high hilly tracts and rugged terrain to undulating rolling and level lowlands) and slope (below 1° to more than 20°) has greatly determined the drainage conditions and fertility, thickness and texture of soil. The streams and nalas which surround the study area on many sides are ephemeral, and they are dry even in the rainy season. But the sand strata of the stream bed retain underground water, and this condition has been a good aspect for irrigation. The soils range from sandy clay to sandy clay loam and clay. These soils are, in general, poor in phosphates, nitrogen and humus, but comparatively rich in potash.

Irrigation Facilities

Irrigation facilities have been an aid to the rugged and undulating terrains of Boreya because 45.11 per cent (186.20 hectares) of the total area of Boreya has irrigation facility which constitutes 57.44 per cent of the total cropped area (Fig. 16.2). Boreya has a variety of terrains with varied physical characteristics, and irrigation measures have become an aid to these terrains (Prasad and Mahto, 1987: 151). If irrigation schemes are implemented successfully and some other schemes come in advance to meet the failures of the former, only one-sixth of the land area in Boreya will be left as non-arable land. Rest of the terrains has agricultural potentialities and it is being improved with the urban impact.

Socio-cultural Potentialities

Even with regard to socio-cultural aspect, Boreya has been considered of poor potentialities because the Backward Communities, Scheduled Tribes and Scheduled Castes constitute the major portion of its population (91%). In the non-tribal group of population, the Scheduled Castes comprising the Ghasi, Kahar, Bhogata and Dhobi largely constitute the agricultural labour and domestic service classes. They

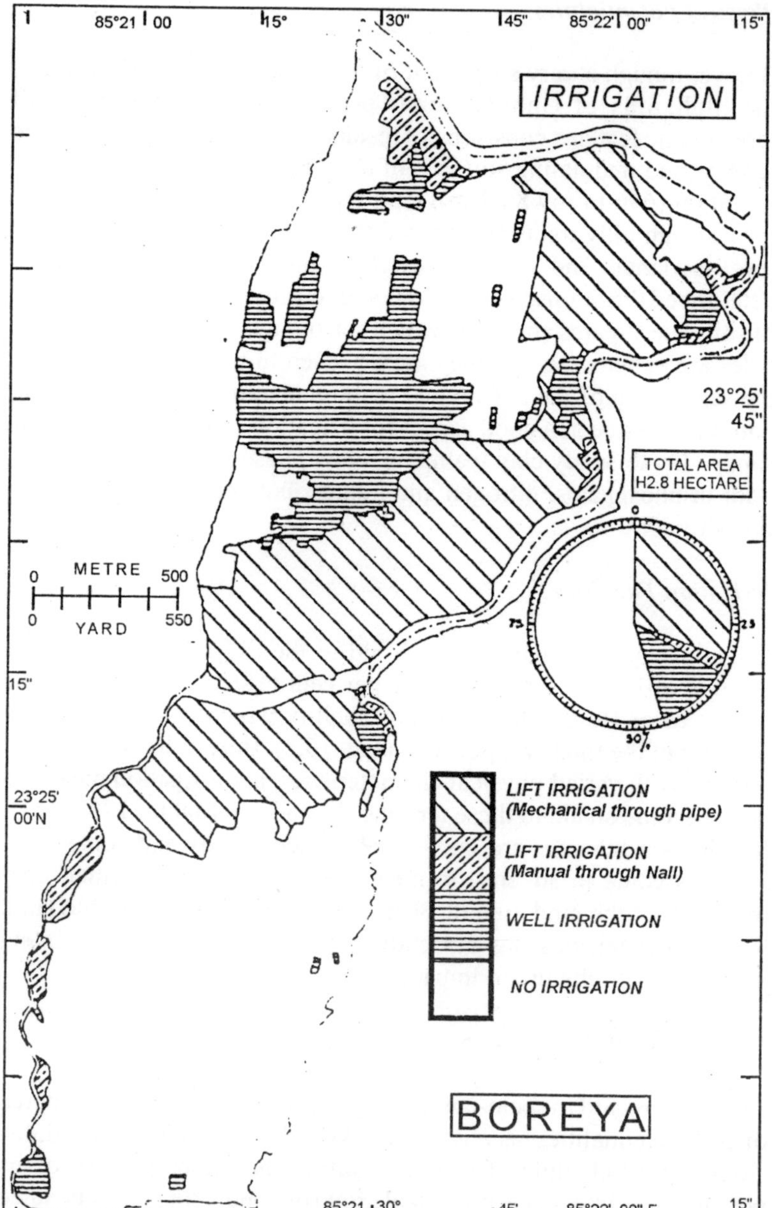

Fig. 16.2: Boreya: Irrigation

are generally landless people and represent the lowest level in the economic ranking of the social groups.

The Oraons and the Mundas, on the other hand, represent an entire economic scale ranging from landed aristocracy to landless labourer. The Backward community comprises eight castes. Kumhar, Lohar and Barber communities have no or insignificant landed property and they, too, like the Scheduled Castes represent the lowest level in the economic ranking of the social groups. Other castes, though trying their best to be on a par with the forward communities, are still treated as backward in the social, economic and political spheres. In Boreya about 38 per cent of the total population are literates.

Extent of Cultivation

At present the regularly cropped terrain covers 324.15 hectares and accounts for 84.14 per cent of the total terrain area and 78.52 per cent of the total study area. This extent of land under crops leaves a limited scope for further extension; thus the area is bound to adopt intensive type of farming by using improved seeds, chemical fertilizers, modern implements, and other agricultural devices. The present cropping pattern ranging from single-cropped area to triple-cropped area is an indication of this new trend. About 30 hectares and 94 hectares of land are under triple and double crops respectively. Thus there is a gradual shift of crops from subsistence to commercial (Mahto, 1985: 338).

The cultivated terrain, i.e. the regularly cropped terrain termed as net area sown is distributed over almost all the terrains except the hilly terrain. The rolling and lowland terrains offer a little land for uses other than agriculture. Most of the upland terrains are cultivated excepting those lands which are put to non-agricultural uses and other fallow lands. The rugged terrain permits no crops on a large portion of land. It is in the process of reclamation. This reveals the extent to which human responses have tamed and changed the local physical conditions owing to socio-economic developments and urbanization of the area.

An interesting feature of the cultivated terrain is its marked concentration and intensification in the north block where most of the terrain is under crop, and has a high and good diversification of crops. Some pockets of the cultivated terrain are so intensified that it can be compared with the alluvial terrain of the Gangetic Plain. In the highlands of Chhotanagpur where agriculture is "grossly dependent upon natural concessions" (Prasad, 1973: 57), such agricultural landscape is not very common. It does not mean that the terrains of Boreya are characterized always by high agricultural capability having good fertility, thickness and texture of soil, and other favourable components. It is virtually the growing consciousness and human responses to intensification and rationalization of the uses that have played and are playing some significant role in the changing and better agricultural scene of Boreya.

Some of the land is being reclaimed for cultivation. But it is not going to add a high percentage of land to the cultivated terrain. There is every possibility of urban encroachment, on the other hand, even upon the good cultivated terrain, which will reduce the acreage under cultivation. Therefore, the only way out to fulfil the demand for vegetables and other cash crops from Ranchi, and to make the balance between increasing value of land and production is to get the maximum return from the land by intensification of agriculture and scientific use of the terrain. Since the cultivated terrains are at present in a position to give returns to the people and the people are responsive to the natural endowments and development programmes, the cultivated terrain will show a rising trend in the graphs of production and crop diversification. The trend is already visible.

Cropping Pattern on the Cultivated Terrain

The present cropping pattern on the cultivated terrain of Boreya is an outcome of a long and constant process involving various natural, socio-economic and cultural factors. The prevalent use and pattern of cultivated terrain have been established through many successive trials and errors. The natural factors are not very much favourable, rather they have been made favourable for the cultivation of crops. If a single factor is to be enunciated responsible for the present cropping pattern in Boreya, it is the urban influence of Ranchi which has always compelled the farmers for more and more exploitation of terrain. On the other hand, a continuous growth of population, increase in per capita expenditure due to urbanization and limited opportunity of employment in the industrial sectors of Ranchi has led to concentration on cultivation and gardening. We have noted earlier that there is a very limited scope of further extension of cultivated terrain, and this is why intensity of farming has been a necessary alternative for livelihood of the people in Boreya. The present cropping pattern ranging from single-cropped area to triple-cropped area is an outcome of all these factors, and has emerged "as a means of self-preservation of societies that are hounded by their specific cultural norms" (Chakraborty, 1981: 139).

Table 16.5 and Fig. 16.3 depict the cropping pattern in Boreya. It is revealed that there is an ample scope for intensification of farming in Boreya; because out of 324.15 hectares of cropped area, only 30.32 hectares and 94.33 hectares of land are under triple and double crops respectively. The area under triple and double crops thus accounts for only 9.35 per cent and 29.1 per cent of the total cropped area. Therefore, the total or gross area sown which is the product of the addition of net area sown to the area sown more than once accounts for 479.12 hectares (199.50 hectares under single crop + 94.33 double × 2 + 30.32 triple × 3 = 479.12). It is 1.48 times the net sown area. There are some villages located in the industrial belt of the Damodar Valley Region where the gross area sown three to four times of the net area sown. All this is to say that intensification of farming has ample scope in Boreya, and the growing influence of urbanization on Boreya will result in more and more intensification of farming in the near future.

Table 16.5 : Cropping Pattern

Sl. No.	*Unit*	*Area*		*% to the Total Area*	*% to the Total Cropped Area*	*Gross Area Sown (in Hectares)*
		Acres	*Hectares*			
1.	Single-cropped area	492.99	199.50	48.33	61.55	199.50
2.	Double-cropped area	233.10	94.33	22.85	29.10	188.66
3.	Triple-cropped area	74.90	30.32	7.34	9.35	90.96
	Total cropped area	800.99	324.15	78.52	100.00	479.12
	Culturable waste	41.90	16.96	4.11		
	Current fallow	39.15	15.96	3.84		
	Rocky exposures	70.00	28.33	6.86		
	Streams, nalas and tanks	68.00	27.52	6.67		
	Grand Total	1020.04	412.80	100.00		

Note: The gross area sown (479.12 hectares) is about 1.48 times the net area sown (324.15 hectares).

Conclusion on the Discussion of Resource Appraisal

The previous discussion particularly on Boreya reveals that the resource potential of Chhotanagpur for agricultural activities is not so poor as though of by many evaluators. In the rugged and undulating terrains of Boreya agriculture is very much developed. Again, Boreya has dominance of ST, SC and Backward community population. But

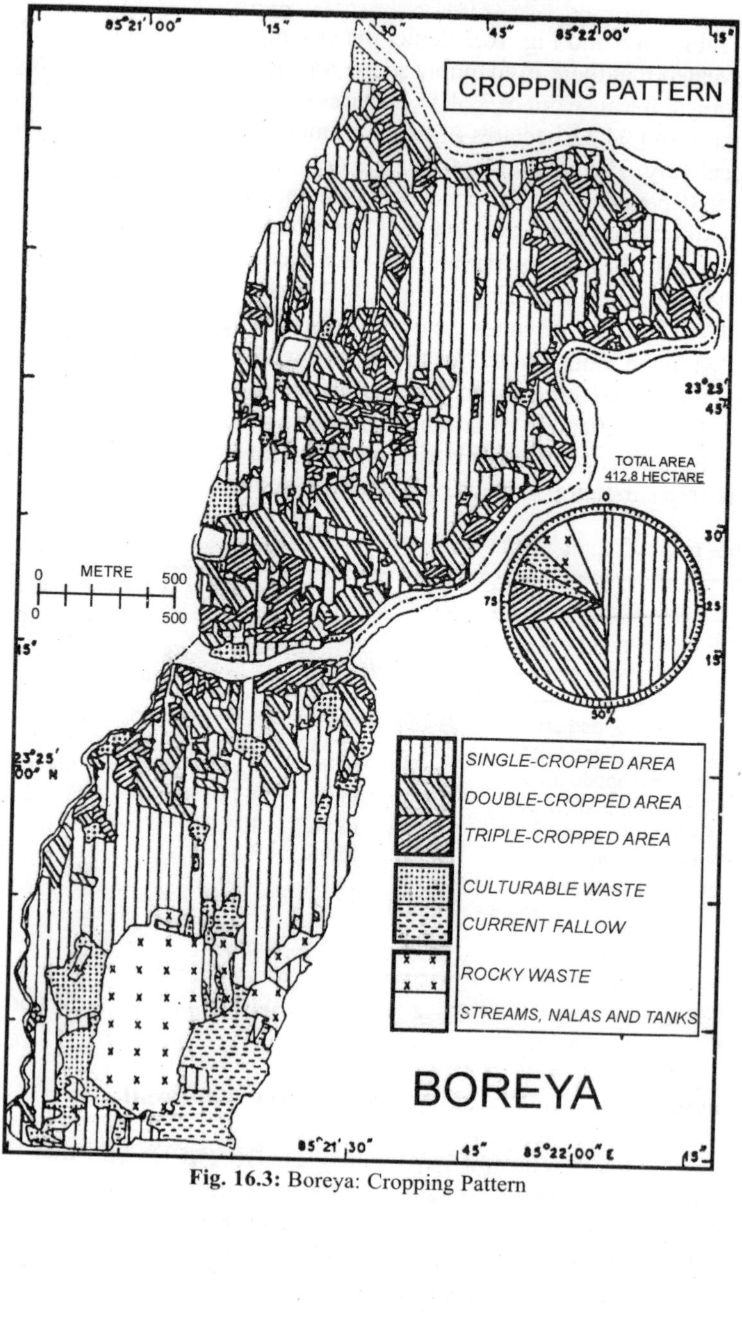

Fig. 16.3: Boreya: Cropping Pattern

it could not hinder the diversification and high intensity of the cropping pattern. There are, however, many areas in Chhotanagpur which are far better than Boreya in respect of physical potential, economic infrastructure and human resource. All these lead to conclude that if there is backwardness of agriculture in Chhotanagpur, it is not due to its resource structure but due to other constraints.

Problems and Constraints

In spite of having an adequate resource structure for agricultural operations. Chhotanagpur is a backward region with regard to this cultural landscape. All the districts are falling under medium, low and very low degrees of agricultural productivity (Prasad, 1984: 567-571). It is an undisputed fact that the region cannot complete with the adjoining plains in this regard even by the best efforts of the farmers and planners, but then the present state of development is disappointing. There are many problems and constraints which are emphasized in a general way, e.g. undulating and rugged surfaces, thin veneer of soils with low fertility, limited and seasonal water resource, inadequate irrigation facilities, unawareness of scientific rotation, uncommon use of improved seeds, chemical fertilizers and modern implements, undeveloped financing and organized marketing, fragmentation of holdings, dishonesty and carelessness in executing development programmes, lack of response from the farmers and so on. The author here is not going to discuss all these problems and constraints because it would just be a repetition of discussion made almost in every such study at many places. The author would like to concentrate upon some of the most pertinent constraints observed by him closely during the yesteryears.

Observation No. 1

The Konar Irrigation Project of Chhotanagpur envisages the construction of a main trunk canal and a number of distributaries to divert 49 cusecs of water from the Konar Reservoir to irrigate 0.63 lakh hectares of cultivated and culturable land of its command area (Latitude 23°49′50″ to 24°14′12″ N; Longitudes 85°41′43″ to 86°11′00″ E/0.975 lakh hectares) in the drought-prone districts of Hazaribagh and Giridih. The main trunk canal will be an open channel preceded by a tunnel to negotiate high ground therefor. The scheme is, of course, aiming at a success to be achieved as an endowment for the people of four anchals—Bishnugarh (Hazaribagh), Bagodar, Dumri and Nawadih (Giridih)—which have been neglected till now without the people of the area ever having an opportunity to feel that they have gained independence some forty three years ago (Prasad *et al.*, 1980). The people had great expectations when the Konar Dam was constructed in 1955 as a huge multipurpose reservoir at a cost of Rs. 4.48 crores but they became a dream gradually due to the negligence of the Government. They have, however, seen a new ray of hope for about 10 year when this scheme started working in the real sense. But the project, which was proposed to be completed phase-wise by 1984 at an estimate cost of Rs. 25.28 crores, is yet to be completed with an enhanced estimate of more than 100 crores.

The most vital point to which the author would like to draw attention and about which he has serious doubts is the capacity of the Konar reservoir, installed for this vast irrigation scheme. It is because of the incidence of soil erosion observed in the catchment of the reservoir. About 37 per cent of the total area is under soil erosion (Table 16.6).

Table 16.6: Statement of Erosion in the Konar Dam Catchment Based on Roy and Bhattacharya, 1967

Land Area (in hectares)	*Land (in hect.) Eroded, Eroding or Subject to Erosion*						
	Sheet Erosion			*Gully Erosion*			*Total Erosion*
	Farm Land	*Forest Land*	*Total*	*Outside Forest*	*Within Forest*	*Total*	
99152	17111	11320	28431	2187	5873	8060	36491
% over total land area	(17.2)	(11.4)	(28.6)	(2.2)	(5.9)	(8.1)	(36.7)

Murthy and Ayengar (1956) have estimated the life of the reservoirs of the Damodar Valley Project. They concluded that the total annual silt-deposit is 331, thousand cubic metres in the Konar reservoir while it has dead storage allocation of about 72,357 thousand cubic metres. So the life of the Konar reservoir is 219 years, i.e. 72537/331 = 219.

But personal observation reveals that the reservoir has been silting very fast and its life reducing gradually. The author has a doubt that its life will not exceed 100 or 125 years. Thirty-five years have already elapsed and the completion of the project is still expected. Thus, about one-third of the life of the reservoir will elapse by the time diversion of water into canals starts. Therefore, it is doubtful that the capacity of the reservoir will fulfil the demand for water. There is, thus, a threat to the irrigation potential due to the siltation in the reservoir. The author would, therefore, like to suggest that there is a necessity to arrest soil-erosion in the catchment area of the Konar reservoir to minimize the threat, because it is not economically feasible to remove the silt which is depositing in the reservoir. It may be possible to reduce its quantity by taking soil conservation measures in the catchment area. Afforestation along with other measures will not only save the land from disintegration and erosion, but add to the forest wealth also. The Damodar Valley Corporation is active in this respect but it should be intensified in view of such a vast irrigation scheme.

Secondly, to meet any unfavourable consequences, active thought may be given to some alternative arrangement. Another dam can be constructed at a suitable site which can be linked with the already constructed branch canals.

Observation No. 2

A dam of medium irrigation scheme had been constructed on the river Jamuna near Bishnugarh (24°02'N; 85°46'E) with a capacity of 3.91 million kilometres in the same year, in 1954-55. It has two canals to irrigate 1,458 hectares of land. But a situation has arisen now which poses a threat to the farmers year after year. The reservoir's irrigation potential has gone down to siltation when only 35 years have been elapsed. The public is put to so much inconvenience on account of inadequate water supply that they are led to believe that the reservoir might function only for another 10 years. So one will have to think twice before planning such a huge scheme of lakhs of rupees. It has also been observed that the canal water was not seriously used for agricultural purposes by the canal-side landowners till 1967. Even today, whatever amount of water is available from the canals is not used properly. Reasons? One of the most notable reason is that the most of the owners are businessmen, who do not care for a return from the land, they earn more in trade and commerce. They hold on the land for emergency reasons, for dowry or to unforeseen expenses like on accidents/diseases.

Observation No. 3

Harichak is a small urban centre, about four miles north of Giridih (24°12′N; 86°18′E), situated on the upland (*tanr*) but surrounded by terraced rice fields. The upland is rocky and has no potential for easy agricultural activities. Of many households, one family belongs to the farmer caste, *Koeri*. This family, by dint of hard work has dug a well cutting hard rocks and got the water for irrigation purposes. The vegetable farming in some limited fields is so rich that vendors from Giridh come to Harichak and purchase the fresh vegetables. Rest of the plots, even of better agricultural potentialities, are left uncultivated for most of the seasons of the year. Only paddy is grown. Reasons? The owners, excepting this family are interested more in business. They do not bother for a return from the land.

Observation No. 4

Barki Pona (Latitude 23°31′N: Longitude 85°28′E/area 623 acres) is a small village situated in the Damodar Valley region, 10 miles east of Ramgarh Cantt. in the district of Hazaribagh, Bihar. It has an area of 625 acres out of which 225 acres are bare rocky surfaces. Rest of the land, i.e. about 400 acres, are under intensive farming, some of the fields are quadruple cropped. It is interesting to note that some 800 wells, *katcha* and *pucca*, are there in 400 acres, about five wells in one acre on an average. Wells are the only source of irrigation and *latha-kundi* is dominating as the means of lifting water. There is no government or other development authority programme. But the agriculture is so prosperous that it is feeding many market centres like Ramgarh Cantt., Bhurkunda, Kuju, Bermo, Bokaro, Dhanbad, Jamshedpur, etc., with vegetables in all seasons. The main reason of this development is the habitation of more than 90 per cent farmer's caste, particularly *Koeris* living in this village who have love for land and who know to take the maximum return from land.

Observation No. 5

In the Ramgarh belt of the Damodar Valley in and around Barki Pona discussed in the preceding paras, there are unusual features of dug wells. Their diameter at the base is larger than that on the top. Again the cementing materials in between the layers of bricks are neither mud nor cement as is the usual case even in other parts of the same district. Only upper portions are plastered with cement. Logic? The farmers have valid logic in the context of local physico-economic conditions. The unusual greater diameter at the bottom facilitates the quick lifting of water from *latha-kundi* without getting obstructed against walls of the wells. The farmers have experience that if cement is put in between the layers of bricks, there will be no oozing of underground water to the well; and if mud is put, it will be washed into the well. It reveals that there is abundance of water oozing into the wells. Therefore, the gaps in between the bricks are filled in by granite chips or iron splinters of old pans of get the bricks and layers tightened maintaining the non-obstructed permeability.

Thus, there are many things to be observed which appear to be insignificant but they are associated with difficult problems and constraints for agricultural development. We have discussed only a few of them. Let us analyze our observations.

The five observations are virtually symbolic of many areas of Chhotanagpur. Sometimes planning for irrigation has been incomplete, sometimes unimplemented and in some cases irrational. On the other hand, users of water are sometimes unmindful and uninterested. Theoretically, irrigation should make double cropping possible, if not multiple cropping, but the bulk of the irrigated area in Chhotanagpur, still, constitutes to be single-cropped area. Indian farmers, by and large, lack the necessary knowledge to optimize irrigation use. The layman's concept of just flooding the crops with water at intervals has been found to be of not much benefit, rather, over-irrigation causes water-logging, salinity and alkalinity, and overall reduction in crop production. In many cases, multipurpose projects, major or medium, have been installed, but the proposals and targets have not been implemented properly in time and space. For example, the Konar Irrigation Project has been installed after 25 years of the construction of the Konar Dam. By the time the life of the reservoir has reduced and there is threat to the irrigation potential due to the siltation in the reservoir (Prasad, *et al.*, 1980). It has also been observed (Observation No. 2) that water is flowing in the canals and channels unutilized, because the land which is to be facilitated with irrigation water is owned by a person who is not at all interested in double or multiple cropping. For such persons culturable lands are just as secured wealth to be utilized in emergencies. These persons are earning enough either from business or service. On the other hand, Observations 3 and 4 reveal that farmers who love the land and for whom land is the only profession are getting maximum return even though no government planning has come to their aid. In such areas an additional provision of irrigation water would register much more development in agricultural operations. And this reflects the wrong land tenure system or ownership of land prevailing in the areas.

Observation No. 5 is indicative of the problems of being non-acquainted with the local circumstances. This unawareness sometimes leads to erratic programmes and planning. Can the well get water if the layers are cemented? Such mistakes are committed in many of the implemented programmes. This observation and the associated problem is just symbolic.

Remedial Measures

On the basis of the physical, economic and human resource potentialities available in Chhotanagpur (see under Resource Base) and their appraisal (see under Resource Appraisal) as well as on the basis of observations of selected areas (see under Boreya: A Case Study and Problems and Constraints) and experience of some notions (see under some notions about the Resources), the following measures may be suggested for the remedy of the problems and constraints and thereby for the development and prosperity of agriculture in Chhotanagpur:

1. Spatial allocations of resources and relationship between man and his environment on the complexity of regions should be understood. This requires interdisciplinary approaches particularly from geography, economics, law, public administration, business management and political science. Ideas from anthropology are very much required in this particular case of Chhotanagpur, because many traditions and customs are coming in the way. Perception and attitude studies to determine the adequacy of existing or proposed policies, plans and practices should be analysed.
2. There should be realization of the potential of land and labour by proper landuse planning, promoting agro-based rural industries, developing integrated farming systems and

strengthening socio-economic research to achieve optimum efficiency in the use of farm inputs.

3. Development of farm implements suited for small and resource-poor farmers to help them adopt modern technologies for crop, livestock, forestry and fish production should be given priority.
4. The detailed soil maps on 1:7920 (8 inches = 1 mile) of the whole of Chhotanagpur should be prepared to ensure the better landuse planning. The cadastral maps will be helpful because of their detailed plottings on 16″ = 1 mile scale.
5. The agro-climatic zones on micro-level should be demarcated and each zone studied in detail with regard to resource potential problems and requirements, social structure, attitude and perception of the people, etc. This will ensure non-failure of the programmes and planning. The Honours and Post-Graduate students particularly belonging to the disciplines of geography, economics, anthropolgy, botany, pedology, agriculture and management can carry this task as compulsory and major part of their syllabus under the guidance of qualified and interpreted teachers. An integrated cell can also be instituted for the purpose with sufficient grants from government agencies.
6. Irrigation is the most important factor which determines the capability of terrains for intensives and prosperous cultivation in Chhotanagpur. Water here is more valuable than land. Generally, productivity is increased at least six-fold when water is applied (Mukherjee and Prasad, 1985: 241). It is evident from the case study of Boreya that in spite of dominating rugged and undulating terrains, 79 per cent of the total area is under crops because of the remarkable development of irrigation in many respects, i.e. increase in the number of means and area under irrigation, improvement in the system and rationalization of irrigation water, etc. (Prasad and Mahto, 1987: 150). Near Bishnugarh also a vast stretch of drought-prone land in Urgi village, has been converted into an assured cultivated area only after the construction of a weir across the upper reach of the river Jamuna. Therefore, provision of irrigation water to every

field of Chhotanagpur will be a fruitful measure towards the agricultural development. But, at the same time, there must be an effective coordination and cooperation between the water management authorities, agricultural extension services and irrigators (Prasad and Mahto, 1987: 153). Gujarat has taken a lead where farmers' cooperatives receive water in bulk from the irrigation departments on a volumetric basis and then they do proper distribution of water amongst all the members of the society. The Kerala Government, too, has taken such a decision. This system in Chhotanagpur will be very beneficial and it is essential here too because of the limited water resources. As regard means, the major irrigation schemes can be avoided. The medium and minor schemes should be preferred. For small areas the Bandhara Irrigation System (Prasad and Jha, 1980-81: 81) will be found most useful. Under this system small weirs or Bandharas are constructed at a number of places across the river so that water spilling over from one Bandhara is checked by another downstream. From each Bandhara, canals are taken off to irrigate small areas and the water is controlled by a head regulator. It is advisable not to have a canal system of more than 8 m in length. The canal has its tail terminating in a low-lying area commanded by the Bandhara termed as *thal*. Once this type of system is introduced and developed the farmers themselves can maintain it.

7. Observation Nos. 2 and 3 reveal a vital constraint which, if not eradicated, is capable to nullify all the programmes and planning for agricultural development. The author has no reservation against any particular community and he also knows that it will require legal action and a sort of revolution; but for the development of the region and the State in particular and the country in general, measures must be taken so that agricultural land is owned only by those who have love for the land and who have the capacity to get the maximum return in terms of crops from the land. The principle of *one man, one profession* should be implemented and there may be a compulsion, too, that an averaged quantity

of production of three consecutive years is necessarily given otherwise the land will be seized and allotted to other interested persons.

8. The author has observed that there are persons of certain castes in Chhotanagpur who are rather more competent in farming. The Koeries are the most competent and they have expertise, something hereditary. Wherever they are engaged in farming, either Harichak or Barki Pona (see Observation Nos. 3 and 4) or other places, the agricultural prosperity is very much conspicuous. They have created a different scene in many villages of Chhotanagpur even by owning only some decimals of land. Such cultivated patches are like an oasis surrounded by uncultivated land particularly during the summer and pre-summer months.

The persons belonging to the Kurmi, Oraon and Munda are also basically farmers. It is not suggested and it is not possible, too, that all the cultivated lands should be transferred to these communities, but their expertise can be utilized and if necessary, they should be employed as supervisory staff to see that farming is practiced in a better and beneficial form.

Lastly, the author would like to confess that many areas are, still, left to be observed to identify the real problems and thereafter to think of appropriate measures. This paper is just a humble attempt to initiate some delegates with the expectation that other researchers will come forward to identify the basic constraints and suggest measures for the development of agriculture in Chhotanagpur.

Appendix 1

Human Resource in Chhotanagpur (1981)

Divisions/ Districts	Area (in km²)	Population			Literacy			Scheduled		Main Workers		
		Total	Male	Female	Total	Male	Female	Tribes	Castes	Total	Male	Female
(1)	(2)	(3)	(4)	(5)	(6)	(7)	(8)	(9)	(10)	(11)	(12)	(13)
I. *North-Chhotanagpur*	*21053.0*	*6044742*	*3163561*	*2881221*	*1759077*	*1336006*	*423071*	*616247*	*971731*	*1701229*	*1505233*	*195996*
1. Dhanbad	2996.0	2115010	1166126	948884	828264	608324	219940	192777 (9.09)	330767	595906	5482429	47477
2. Giridih	6892.0	1731462	876172	855290	414043	328410	85633	224678 (12.98)	225993	478199	417758	60441
3. Hazaribagh	11165.0	2198310	1121263	1077047	516770	399272	117498	198792 (9.04)	414971	627124	539046	88078
II. *South-Chhotanagpur*	*44331.1*	*7849759*	*4017473*	*3832286*	*2307575*	*1636930*	*670645*	*3344968*	*773379*	*2551950*	*1992727*	*559223*
4. Gumla	9077.1	1017231	503942	513289	265367	181986	83381	748181 (73.55)	51493	373112	272864	100248
5. Lohardaga	1490.9	229786	114254	115532	22495	14358	8137	134854 (58.67)	8280	17848	13486	4362
6. Palamau	12749.0	1917528	979955	937573	391388	305949	85439	351432 (18.33)	478225	620381	494529	125852
7. Ranchi	7574.1	1823415	942625	877790	638287	443050	195237	848997 (46.56)	98326	604276	475871	128405

(*Contd.*)

(Contd.)

(1)	(2)	(3)	(4)	(5)	(6)	(7)	(8)	(9)	(10)	(11)	(12)	(13)
8. Singhbhum	13440.0	2861799	1473697	1388102	990038	691587	298451	1261504 (44.29)	137055	936333	735977	200356
III. *Santal Parganas*	*13512.7*	*3717528*	*1899410*	*1818118*	*827400*	*636115*	*191285*	*1367868*	*311801*	*1227965*	*1008968*	*218987*
9. Deoghar	2478.6	708828	366811	342017	181913	142257	39656	108434 (15.30)	93210	205476	186914	18562
10. Dumka	5518.3	1215542	617645	597897	286707	222882	63825	574347 (47.25)	100255	424574	336636	87938
11. Godda	2110.4	713405	364522	348883	155554	122364	33190	209593 (29.38)	60036	229441	187730	41714
12. Rajmahal	3405.4	1079753	550432	529321	203226	148612	54614	475494 (53.29)	58300	368464	297688	70776
IV. *Magadh (Part)*	*5407.6*	*1740768*	*871063*	*869705*	*400485*	*306709*	*93776*	*1447*	*554850*	*537238*	*418002*	*119236*
13. Aurangabad	1420.2	454984	231139	223845	118473	90792	27681	56	120992	124476	105744	18728
14. Gaya	2442.8	780551	389829	390722	162411	123612	38799	417	304354	256300	191806	64494
15. Nawada	154406	505233	250095	255138	199601	92305	27296	974	129504	156466	120452	36014
V. *Bhagalpur*	*5388.9*	*1461072*	*745922*	*715150*	*302727*	*240734*	*61993*	*93915*	*229251*	*457203*	*374629*	*82574*
16. Bhagalpur	2017.3	495804	255303	240501	101592	79930	21662	49874	55710	156023	129691	26332
17. Munger	3371.6	965268	490619	474749	201135	160804	40331	44341	173541	301180	244938	56242

REFERENCES

Ahmad, E. (1965). *Bihar: A Physical, Economic and Regional Geography*, Ranchi University.

Chakraborty, S.C. (1981). "Crop-Combination, Regions of Eastern India", *Geo. Rev. of India*, Vol. 43, No. 2, pp. 138-54.

Dunn, J.A. (1941). The Economic Geology and Mineral Resources of Bihar Province, *Mem. of the G.S.I.* (Calcutta), Vol. 78, pp. 6-14.

Mahto, A. (1985). *Terrain Evaluation, Integrated Development and Change in Boreya*, Unpublished Ph.D. Thesis, Ranchi University.

Mitchell, B. (1989). *Geography and Resource Analysis*, Longman, London (Second Edition).

Mukherjee, P. and Prasad, N. (1985). "Irrigation in the Indian Context", *Modern Geographical Concepts* (ed. by N. Prasad, *et al.*), Prof. M.R. Chaudhuri Felicitation Volume, Burdwan.

Murthy, B.N. and Ayengar, N.S. (1956). Estimate of Life of Reservoirs included in the First Phase of Development of Damdar Valley Project." *Journal of Soil and Water Conservation in India*, Vol. 5, No.1.

Pandey, P. (1970). *Impact of Industrialisation on Urban Growth: A Case Study of Chotanagpur*, Central Book Depot, Allahbad.

Prasad, A. (1973). *Chhotanagpur: Geography of Rural Settlements*, Ranchi University, Ranchi.

Prasad, M. (1984). "Spatial Variations of Agricultural Productivity in Bihar", *Modern Geographical Trends* (Felicitation, Volume in Honour of Prof. Enayat Ahmad), Today and Tomorrow's Printers and Publishers, New Delhi.

Prasad. N. (1971). *Geography of Chhotanagpur (Bihar)* (A Survey of the Existing Literature), Department of Geography, Ranchi University, Ranchi.

Prasad, N., Gupta, S.N.P., and Sahu, S. (1979). "Geographological Assessment of the Konar Irrigation Project: A Study in Environmental Geomorphology", *Geographical Outlook*, Vol. XV.

Prasad N. and Jha, S. (1980). "Policy Formulation and Strategy for Landuse Planning in Ulatu: A Micro-Level Case Study". *Geographical Outlook*, Vol. XVI.

Prasad, N. and Mahto, A. (1987). "Conservation and Utilization of Water Resources for Irrigation in India: An Assessment", *Landscape Systems and Ecological Studies*, Vol. 10, No. 2.

Prasad, N. and Mahto, A. (1991). Impact of Irrigation Development in a Hilly Area of Chhotanagpur, *Indian Journal of Regional Science*, Vol. 23, No. 1.

Shafi, M. (1985). "Perspective on Agricultural Development in Tribal Areas with Special Reference to Chhotanagpur Plateau", Unpublished Paper Presented in Prof. E. Ahmad Felicitation Seminar at Ranchi on January 20, 1985.

Singh, R.L. (ed.), (1971). *India : A Regional Geography,* N.G.S.I., Varanasi.

Singh R.P. (1969). *Geomorphological Evolution of Chhotanagpur Highlands, India*, N.G.S.I., Varanasi.

Singh R.P. and Kumar, A. (1970). *Monograph of Bihar*, Bharati Bhawan, Patna.

Roy, D.K. and Bhattacharya, R.B. (1967). "Use of Air Photographs in Assessing Erosion in Upper Damodar Valley," *Journal of Soil and Water Conservation of India*, Vol. 5, Nos. 3 and 4.

17

Patterns of NOAA AVHRR NDVI Distribution in the Middle Ganges Plains and its Adjacent Areas and the Relationship with Rabi Crops

G. VENUGOPAL, ASHOK K. DUTT and
KEVIN M. TURCOTTE

Ever since the launch of Landsat 1, significant improvements have been made in increasing the spatial resolution of satellite sensors. Such improvements have led to a ground resolution of 20 metres in multispectral mode and 10 metres in panchromatic in the SPOT satellite system. These spatial resolutions are expected to increase in the future, thus, providing more information about very small areas on the surface of the earth. However, the temporal resolution of these land-resource monitoring satellites ranges from 16 to 22 days and are not as fine as the National Oceanic and Atmospheric Administration's (NOAA) satellites. Data captured by the Advanced Very High Resolution Radiometer (AVHRR) on board NOAA-6 through NOAA-11 with fine temporal resolution and coarse spatial resolution have been recognized as having good potential for regional and global-scale environmental monitoring. AVHRR provides multispectral data for the entire earth on a daily basis. These data have been used for many land resource applications (Gray and McCrary, 1981; Schneider *et al.* 1981; Townshend and Tucker, 1981). With the cooperation of Global Inventory Monitoring and Modelling Studies (GIMMS) several projects, such as desert locust monitoring, tropical deforestation, regional fire monitoring, continental land cover mapping, global vegetation phenology, global vegetation-CO_2 relationships and grassland monitoring were conducted using AVHRR data (Tucker *et al.*, 1984; 1985a, b, c; Malingreau *et al.*,

1985; Justice *et al.* 1985). Other studies of varying scales have also been conducted using such data for different parts have of the world (Tucker *et al.*, 1983; Narem *et al.*, 1986; Malingreau, 1986; Justice *et al.*, 1986; Hielkema *et al.*, 1986; Townshend *et al.*, 1987; Goward *et al.*, 1987; Turcotte *et al.*, 1988; Venugopal *et al.*, 1992; and more). The multitemporal nature of the data has helped researchers to address global and regional aspects of land remote sensing.

Nature of NOAA-AVHRR Data

NOAA-9 is a sun synchronized polar orbiting satellite system. It operates at an altitude or about 833 km which has an orbital period of about 102 minutes. The AVHRR on board this satellite system is capable of making two observations daily, one at 2.20 pm and the other at 2.20 am though subsequent crossings follow different orbital tracks. The time between the appearance of a similar node, the mean orbital period is 9.2 days. The configuration of the AVHRR sensor creates 1.1 km spatial resolution at nadir, a +56° scan. This translates to about 2,700 km swath width (kidwell, 1986). Analog data from the AVHRR sensors are digitized on board the satellite to a 10 bit precision ranging between 0 and 1023. The AVHRR aboard NOAA-9 has five spectral channels and the bandwidths are shown in Table 17.1.

Table 17.1: Spectral Bandwidths of NOAA-9 AVHRR Sensor

Channel	*Bandwidth (Micrometers)*	*Radiation Type*
1	0.58-0.63	reflective red
2	0.725-1.10	reflective IR
3	3.55-3.93	reflective and emitted IR
4	10.30-11.30	emitted IR
5	11.50-12.50	emitted IR

Though the sensor operates on five bands, the Normalized Difference Vegetation Index, (NDVI), a ratio of the near infrared (NIR band 1) and visible (VIS band 2), radiances (NIR–VIS) / (NIR + VIS) was used in this study. Channel 1, the reflective red, is sensitive to chlorophyll absorption of vegetation and, hence, negatively correlated with leaf biomass. Channel 2, the reflective infrared, is reflected due to leaf physiology and shows a positive correlation with biomass. Data from either of these channels could be directly used to study vegetation characteristics, but the ratioing of these two channels tends to be a better indicator of biomass rather than on band (Curran, 1980). This index is popular among many researchers because of its simplicity in calculation and high degree of standardization. Varying sun and sensor angles will have less effect on the ratio than on individual channels. Moreover, no assumptions are made on the numerical distribution of the data (Curran, 1980).

Normally NDVI values range from -0.5 for non-vegetated features to 0.60 for fully vegetated ones (NOAA,1986). It also provides a means of monitoring the density and vigour of green vegetation over growing areas of the earth (Kidwell, 1986). This ratio also yields a measure of photosynthetic capacity such that the higher the value of the ratio, the more photosynthetically active the cover type (Sellers, 1985. Clouds, water and snow have a higher reflectance in the red (visible part) and low in near-infrared portions of the spectrum. Ratioing will produce negative NDVI values for such surface features. Rock and bare soil will typically have similar values in both channels resulting in near zero NDVI values. However, green vegetation, due to absorption of red light for chlorophyll generation, produce low digital values while providing high values due to infrared reflectance. This will result the NDVI values to range from 0.1 to 0.6 for green vegetation. The higher values are associated with greater density and greenness of the plant canopy (NOAA, 1986).

Holben has stratified the NDVI response to a variety of land cover types, such as oceans, lakes, sandy deserts, grasslands, tropical rain forests, boreal forests and ice caps (Table 17.2).

Table 17.2 : Stratification of the NDVI response to broad scene components as measured from NOAA-7

Cover Type	*Planetary Albedo*		
	Channel 1	*Channel 2*	*NDVI*
Dense green leaf veg	0.050	0.150	0.500
Medium green leaf veg	0.080	0.110	0.140
Light green leaf veg	0.100	0.120	0.090
Bare soil	0.269	0.283	0.025
Clouds (opaque)	0.227	0.228	0.002
Snow and ice	0.275	0.342	– 0.046
Water	0.022	0.013	– 0.257

Source : Holben, 1986: 1419.

Several sampling procedures were performed by the National Environmental Satellite Data and Information Service (NESDIS) to the original 1.1 km Local Area Coverage (LAC) data to produce a 4.0 km Global Area Coverage (GAC) data. These GAC pixels are produced by averaging four out of five consecutive pixels every third scan line. The GAC data, thus, represent 4/15 sample of the high resolution LAC data set. Global data set used in this study was created from the GAC data with spatial resolution of 16 km. A complete description of NOAA AVHRR products is given by NOAA (1983) and Kidwell (1984).

Study Area and Objectives

The study area consists of the Middle Ganges plain and the adjacent areas north of it. It includes the northern parts of central Bihar, plains of eastern Uttar Pradesh and central parts of south-eastern Uttar Pradesh. In addition, the area also includes the southern fringes of the Himalayas. Thus, the area may be divided, from north to south, into three distinctive physical divisions. They are:

1. Himalayan fringe including parts of southern Nepal,
2. Middle Ganges plain, and
3. Northern fringes of Deccan Plateau (Fig. 17.1).

It is the Middle Ganges plain that covers about two-thirds of the area of study and the findings mainly relate to this part.

Using AVHRR NDVI data, this study aims to bring out the effects of the Rabi crop on the monthly NDVI values in the Middle Ganges plain of India (Fig. 17.2). The importance of Rabi crops grown during dry post-monsoon periods (January to April) is explained analyzing the monthly NDVI curves. Also explained are the green cover changes in some portions of the northern mountains and in the fringes of the Deccan plateau, south of the study area.

Methodology

Maximization Procedures

Maximization procedures have a tendency to reduce the lowering

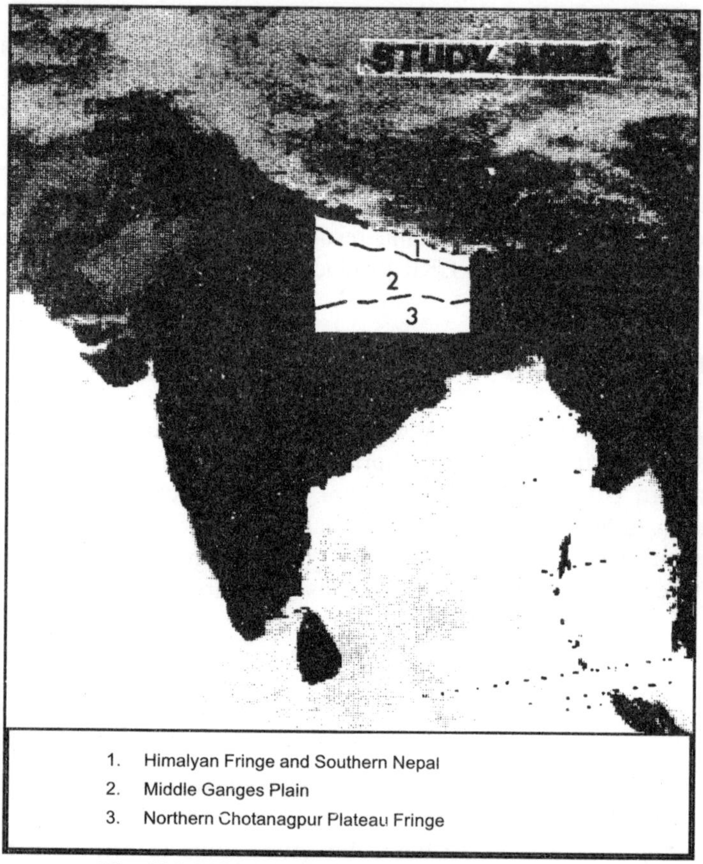

Fig. 17.1: NOAA AVHRR Imagery of the Study Area

effects of NDVI values resulting from cloud contamination, aerosol concentration and varying sun and illumination angles. Tucker *et al.* (1984) and Justice *et al.* (1985) reported that the AVHRR data are affected by cloudiness and atmospheric conditions. The presence of subpixel sized clouds, scattering by dust and aerosols and Rayleigh scattering tend to increase the values of channel 1 with reference to channel 2 thus reducing the NDVI values (NOAA, 1986). Holben and Fraser (1984) in their study found that data from extreme scan angles will result in low NDVI values. They also point out that the

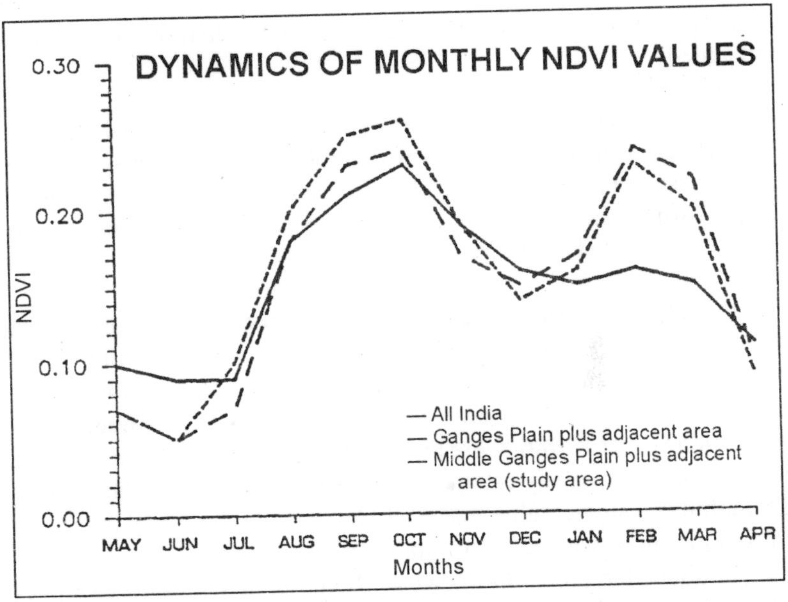

Fig. 17.2: Monthly Dynamics of NDVI Values for all India, all Ganges Plain and Middle Ganges Plain

processing done at the National Environment Satellite Data and Information Service (NESDIS) does not completely solve the problem of extreme scan angles. While discussing the maximization procedure NOAA pointed out :

> This eliminates clouds from the composite except for areas which were cloudy for all 7 days. Maximum value compositing greatly improves the product because atmospheric scan angle effects act to reduce the computed vegetation index. When several clear views of an area are obtained over the compositing period, NDVI values on days with haze, subpixel size clouds and high scan angle are eliminated (NOAA, 1984: 4).

Several researchers have applied this procedure to data sets of varying temporal lengths and spatial resolutions. Tucker *et al.* (1983) analyzed four months of Local Area Coverage (LAC) data and Malingreau (1986) examined three years of 15 km resolution data. Justice *et al.* in their study used a four week compositing interval selecting the highest NDVI values from individual weekly values and stated:

> At a regional scale the AVHRR enables monitoring of the seasonal dynamics of a wide range of vegetation types with respect to photosynthetic activity and provides a new means by which the distribution of major vegetation formations may be delineated and mapped (1986: 1471).

India being a monsoon country, and cloud cover being common, it becomes necessary to eliminate or to reduce possible cloud contamination. Hence, maximization procedure was performed on the four-week data. Fifty-two weekly AVHRR NDVI values, from May 1985 to April 1986, were processed so only the maximum of the four-weekly value was retained to represent one particular month. Though it is a single value that could have occurred at any one week of that month, it was taken to represent that month.

To understand the importance of Rabi crop in the Middle Ganges plain, the following steps were followed :

1. Monthly NDVI values were plotted for (a) entire India, (b) whole of the Ganges plain, and (c) the study area, the middle Ganges plain.
2. Monthly NDVI values were mapped for the Middle Ganges plain. For each month, one standard deviation around the mean was used as the class boundary to represent the average conditions as defined by NDVI. Classes above and below the monthly average represent luxuriant or poor vegetation conditions. Note that this does not necessarily refer to average crop conditions based on several years of data (that is, average yield). This procedure resulted in seven classes of varying NDVI intensity, thus representing the condition of vegetation for each month.
3. Monthly NDVI values were plotted to differentiate between the cropped area and wooded mountainous areas of the study area.
4. Distribution of monthly NDVI values using all-India mean and standard deviation was calculated to emphasize the importance of Rabi crop in the study area.

5. Monthly NDVI values were plotted on a graph showing the distinct variations in the three sub-regions of the study area (Fig. 17.3).

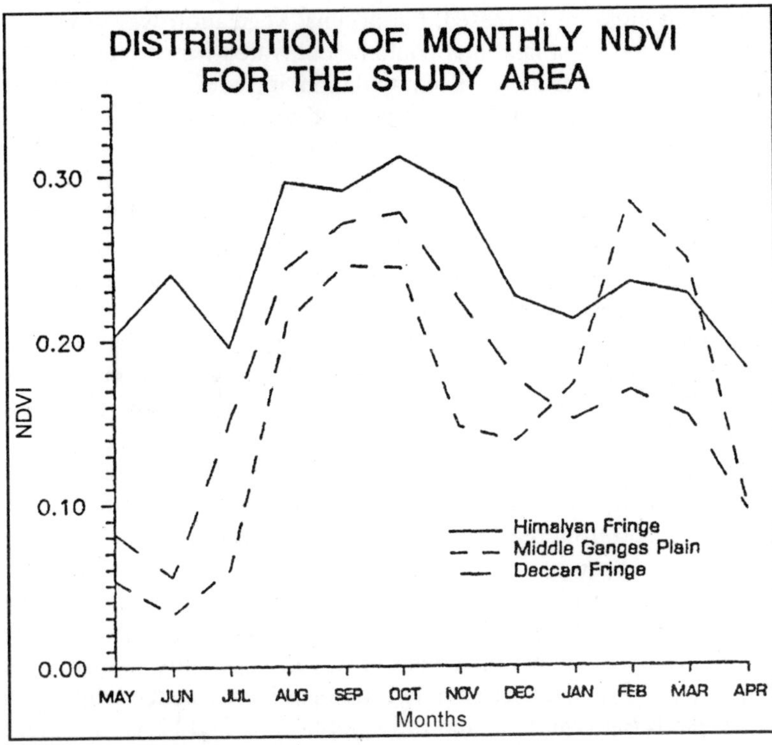

Fig. 17.3: Distribution of Monthly NDVI for the Study Area

Analysis

In analyzing the spatial distribution of NDVI, more attention is given to the Middle Ganges plain. The changing patterns of greenness (in NDVI values) in the mountainous areas and in the fringes of the Decan plateau are also explained. The Middle Ganges plain was originally covered by tropical monsoon vegetation. During the past 3000 years, the tropical monsoon forests and swampland grasses came under increased pressure of cultivation. When the Aryans moved eastward from their original habitat in the Punjab plains, systematical charring of the jungles took place in the Middle Ganges plain; entrance of Aryan civilization to a fully developed iron age greatly helped in clearing the forests. In Bihar, initially the Vedic Aryans settled in the higher parts of the plains forming two foremost domains: Vriggi with Vaishali (Janakpur earlier) as capital and Magadha with Rajgriha as capital. As population pressure increased, the original vegetation was gradually obliterated and most land that could be cultivated was brought under plough. With further increase in population, introduction of improved farming practices led to the cultivation of new crops, such as patato, corn, tomato and beans. Such high intensive use of land became more pronounced after the large-scale introduction of "Green Revolution". The Green Revolution was first introduced in Punjab in 1966 and in subsequent years other States followed. Green Revolution—the use of hybrid seeds, regulated irrigation or watering, timely application of fertilizers and pesticides—is a planned scientific agricultural technique. Failure to do a particular task at the right time could lead to lower yields. The Middle Ganges plain practised Green Revolution methods much after Punjab, Haryana and western Uttar Pradesh. There are also other reasons for such late implementation of Green Revolution in Middle Ganges plain. This region, primarily a rice-producing one, had to adopt this technique slowly because of the abundance of rain and periodic uncontrollable floods during the monsoon season. It was considered unproductive to use hybrid seeds of rice under such uncontrollable water conditions. It becomes a diseconomy because insecticides, pesticides and fertilizers are likely to be washed off during floods. Many other hybrid crops, however, especially wheat, were widely used here. Such usage of hybrid seeds increased the crop yields significantly between 1970 and 1984 (Tables 17.3 and 17.4). One piece of land is often used to produce two Rabi crops. The regulated use of water through irrigation, in this region, is possible only during the non-rainy seasons. Hence, the Kharif crops which are planted and nurtured during the rainy season (June-September) have not been able to make large-scale use of the total "Green Revolution" package. This is because the growing season is the monsoon season, with abundant and uncontrollable monsoon precipitation. On the other hand, the post-monsoonal Rabi crops (January-April) are highly suitable to be cultivated through the scientific Green Revolution methods. Ralatively low precipitation amounts and resulting application of irrigation water during the dry months provide optimum conditions for the best possible output from the hybrid seeds. Tables 17.3 and 17.4 show the cropped area, production and yield for a 15-year period. During this time, the production of Rabi crops, including wheat, in Uttar Pradesh and Bihar has more than doubled. During the same period Kharif crops have improved their production only slightly. In Bihar, during that 15 year period the yield of Rabi crops increased by 71 per cent while the Kharif crops showed an increase of only 28 per cent.

Table 17.3: Cereal (Foodgrain) and Wheat Production, Bihar—1970-1985

		1970-71	*1980-81*	*1984-85*
Cereal (Kharif)	A	6613.40	8730.80	6061.10
	P	5385.40	6626.50	6266.90
	Y	814.00	985.00	1031.00
(Rabi)	A	1650.00	1926.40	2063.50
	P	1509.00	2451.70	3225.40
	Y	914.00	1273.00	1563.00
Wheat (All Rabi)	A	1315.60	1754.80	1917.10
	P	1228.90	2305.70	3099.10
	Y	957.00	1314.00	1617.00

A : Area in thousand hectares.
P : Production in thousand tonnes.
Y : Yield per hectare.
Source : Area and Production of Principal Crops in India (1984-85). (New Delhi: Ministry of Agriculture, Government of India, 1986).

Table 17.4: Cereal (Foodgrain) and Wheat Production in Uttar Pradesh—1970-1985

		1970-71	*1980-81*	*1984-85*
Cereal (Kharif)	A	8562.10	8715.40	8774.50
	P	7295.50	8001.20	10830.00
	Y	856.00	918.00	1234.00
(Rabi)	A	7380.30	8894.30	9106.00
	P	9220.00	14420.60	16685.90
	Y	1249.00	1621.00	1832.00
Wheat (All Rabi)	A	5907.20	8118.90	8554.10
	P	7689.50	13385.00	15974.00
	Y	1302.00	1650.00	1867.00

A : Area in thousand hectares.
P : Production in thousand tonnes.
Y : Yield per hectare.
Source : Area and Production of Principal Crops in India (1984-85). (New Delhi: Ministry of Agriculture, Government of India, 1986).

In the Middle Ganges plain Rabi crops which are planted in January show a higher than average "green" content in terms of NDVI during February followed by March. In April, however, when heat and dryness intensify crops have matured and either are ready to be harvested or have already been harvested thus reducing the "green" content of the vegetation (so the NDVI). Furthermore, in the Middle Ganges plain, trees—mango for example—shed their leaves in January or February, while most of their new leaves and or blossoms start to appear at the same time. Therefore, in February and March, the young leaves and blossoms of varieties of trees tend to have a higher photosynthetic activity thus increasing the chlorophyll content. This condition is reflected as higher greenness (NDVI values) in the satellite images.

Comparing the monthly dynamics of NDVI of the study area with that of all India, it becomes clear that both Kharif and Rabi seasons are very significant in the study area. In general, on an all-India basis, Kharif crops have a greater importance. There is a primary peak of NDVI during September and October with a secondary peak during February and March. However, considering the Ganges plain plus the adjacent areas, the diagram (Fig. 17.2) shows two peak NDVI values of almost equal significance.

Analyzing the monthly distribution pattern of NDVI values (Figs. 17.4, 17.5, 17.6, 17.7, 17.8, and 17.9) it becomes clear that February and October are the most vegetated or "green" months. Small amounts of precipitation during these months provides the optimum conditions for crop growth. After the end of monsoon rains in October, the Kharif matures between November and December, leaving December to be relatively dry in the Middle Ganges plain. Similar dryness is exhibited after the maturation of Rabi crop during May and June. There are, however, two different orientations in the pattern of distribution of extreme dryness between December on the one hand and May/June on the other. In the former (Fig. 17.9), dryness broadens towards the east as the crops, in the east and in the Bengal plain, are sown early in the Kharif season. Therefore, there is a period in December when the land is left fallow. During May-June (Fig. 17.6), areas of extreme dryness broaden towards the west, a sign of high temperature and lack of precipitation there and as well as in the Upper Ganges plains and in the Rajasthan desert.

The misnomer that the rainy season is the single most green (vegetative) period is proven to be untrue for the Middle Ganges plain, because the distribution of NDVI values between July and September are not as pronounced as in February and March.

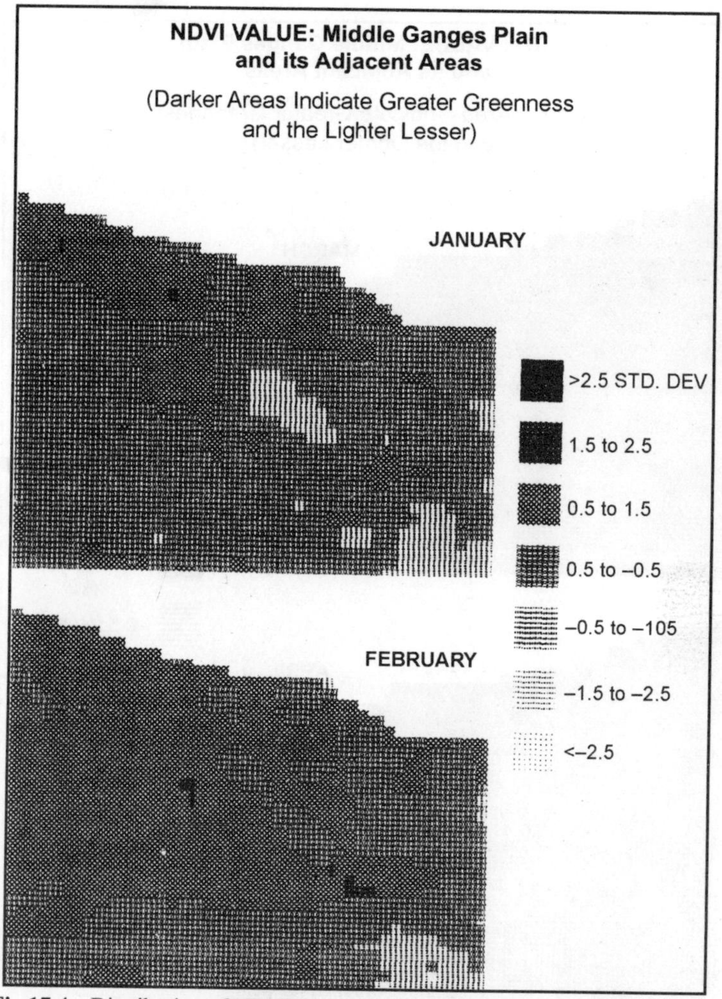

Fig.17.4: Distribution of NDVI for the study area, January-February, 1986. (NOAA data processed at the Laboratory for Information Processing and Mapping Sciences (LIPMaS), Ball State University, Muncie, IN.)

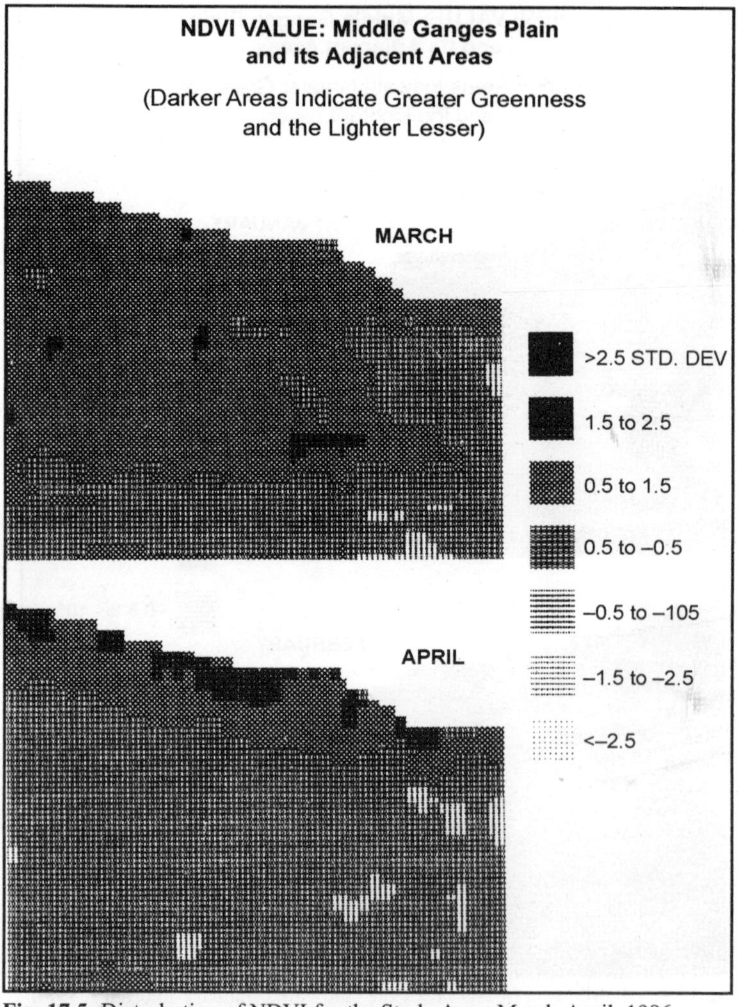

Fig. 17.5: Distrubution of NDVI for the Study Area, March-April, 1986. (NOAA data processed at LIPMaS.)

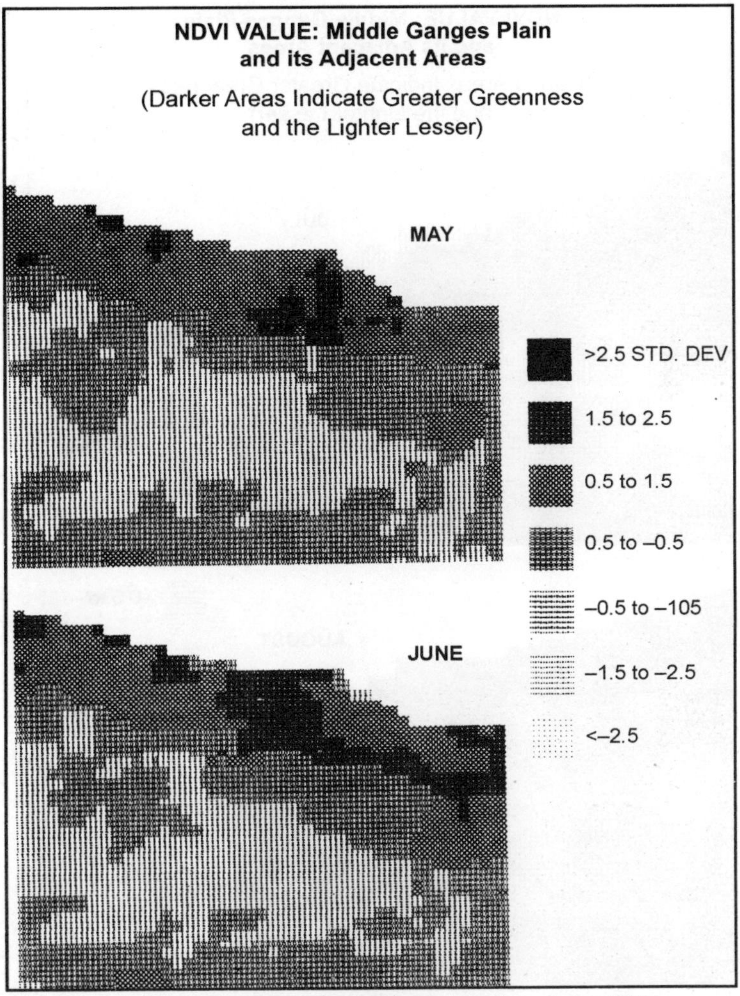

Fig. 17.6: Distrubution of NDVI for the Study Area, May-June, 1985. (NOAA data processed at LIPMaS.)

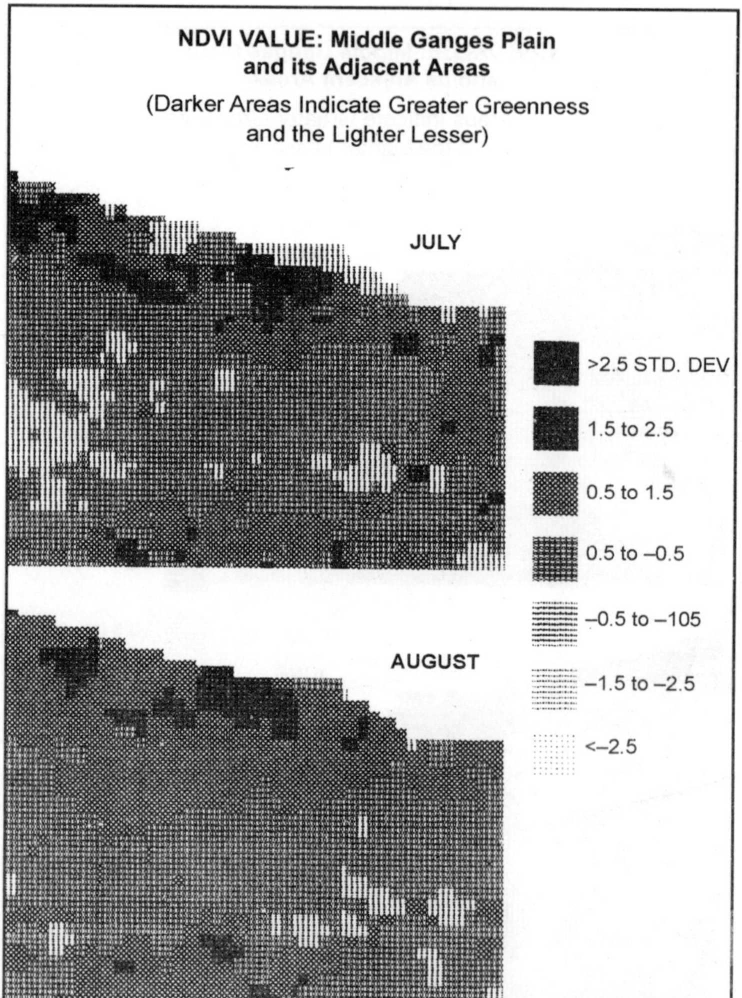

Fig. 17.7: Distrubution of NDVI for the Study Areas, July-August, 1985. (NOAA data processed at LIPMaS.)

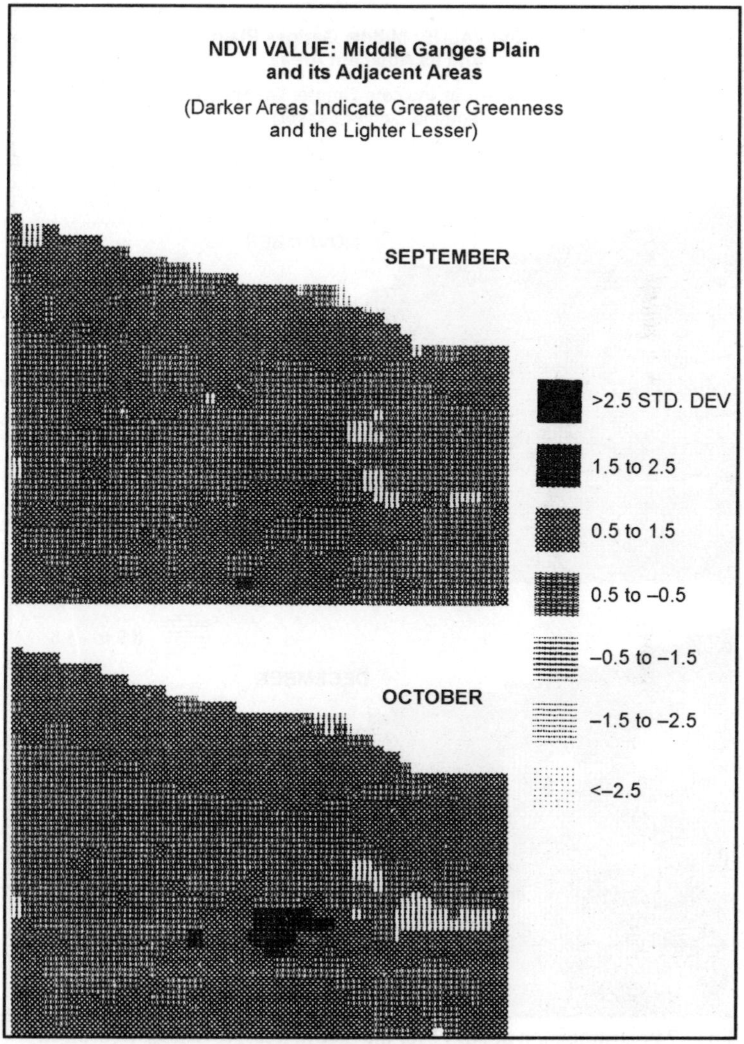

Fig. 17.8: Distrubution of NDVI for the Study Area, September-October, 1985. (NOAA data processed at LIPMaS.)

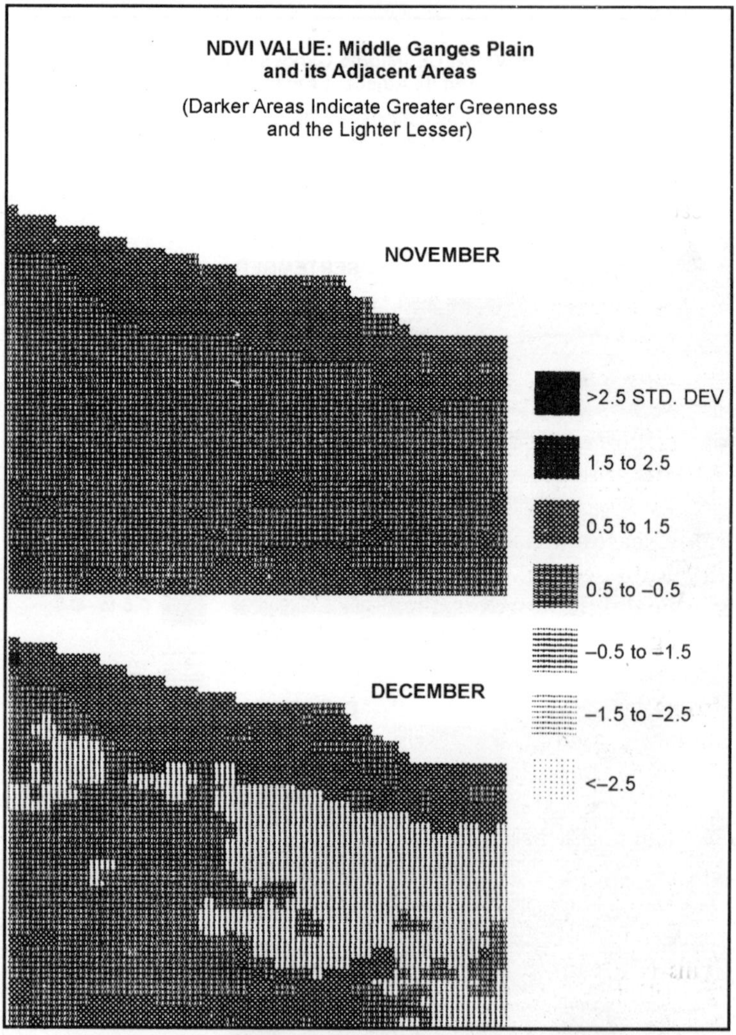

Fig. 17.9: Distrubution of NDVI for the Study Area, November-December, 1985. (NOAA data processed at LIPMaS.)

When the entire study area (Middle Ganges plain) is considered, a peaking of NDVI values is easily noticeable during September and October. During the rainy months the vegetation cover of northern mountain fringes increase the average monthly NDVI values of the study area. This is the result of the presence of forest cover in the mountains. Further, during the rainy months, July to September, the Middle Ganges plain is not only saturated by heavy rainfall (nearly 75% of the annual rainfalls during these months), but also flooded by the rivers. Wide areas are inundated creating several seasonal and permanent swamps. Thus, during the next July and August months of the rainy season, they prevent cultivation of crops as the fields are covered by water. Such swamps start to shrink from October. In the Middle Ganges plain this results in (a) less than optimum use of land for cultivation specially during July and August, and (b) cultivation of land where the water stagnates knee-deep. Some areas with small pinnacles of rice plant above the water do not show as "green" in the NOAA AVHRR images because water bodies tend to have low NDVI values. Thus, the study areas pronounced NDVI peak during the rainy season (Kharif season), though high, equals to that of the dry Rabi season. If we consider the middle Ganges plain as a physical unit, however, the NDVI values for the Rabi season will be higher than those of the Kharif season. The sowing of Kharif cropping is staggered for a longer period and such season varies from one part of the plain to the other. This is because of a longer moisture availability during this season compared to the Rabi cropping time. Hence, the growing season of Kharif lasts longest than that of Rabi.

There are certain similarities and dissimilarities between the fringes of the study areas, that is, the Himalayas and the Deccan plateau in the north and south respectively. Both these areas, being largely forested, show low NDVI values in February and March. This is because of the deciduous nature of vegetation found here. February-March is the season for these trees to shed their leaves. However, the Himalayan fringe in the north shows relatively higher greenness (NDVI) compared to the Deccan plateau because of the wet conditions there.

Conclusion

The study, using NOAA AVHRR NDVI values, records not only the natural phenomena of vegetation as it occurs year after year, but also brings out the importance of Rabi crops in the Middle Ganges plain. The study also recognizes that the rainy season in all cases may not be the single most "green" period of the year. Man-made changes in the form of extensive irrigation and use of hybrid seeds in a particular season may alter the traditional cropping pattern for good.

REFERENCES

Curran, P. (1980). "Multispectral Remote Sensing of Vegetation Amount", *Progress in Physical Geography* 4 : 315-41.

Goward, S.N., Tucker, C.J., and Dye, D.G. (1987). "Comparison of North and South American biomes from AVHRR observation,". *Geocarto International* 2 : 27-39.

Gray, T.I., and McCrary, D.G. (1981). "The Environmental Vegetative Index; The Tool Potentially Useful for Arid Land Management," *Proceedings of the Fifth Conference on Biometerology*, Anaheim, California.

Hielkema, J.U., Prince, S.D. and Astle, W.L. (1986). "Rainfall and vegetation monitoring in the savanna zone of the Democratic Republic of Sudan using the NOAA advanced very high resolution radiometer," *International Journal of Remote Sensing* 7 : 1499-1513.

Holben, B. and Fraser, R.S. (1984). "Red and near-infrared sensor response to off-nadir viewing." *International Journal of Remote Sensing*. 5 (1) : 145-160.

Holben, B.N. (1986). "Characteristics of maximum-value composite images from temporal AVHRR data", *International Journal of Remote Sensing*, 7 : 1417-34.

Justice, C.O., Holben, B.N. and Gwynne, M.D. (1986). "Monitoring East African vegetation using AVHRR data". *International Journal of Remote Sensing*. 7 : 1453-1474.

Justice, C.O., Townshend, J.R.G., Holben, B.N. and Tucker, C.J., (1985). "Analysis of the phenology of global vegetation using meteorological satellite data." *International Journal of Remote Sensing* 6: 1271-1318.

Kidwell, K.B., (1986), *NOAA Polar Orbiters User's Guide*. Washington, D.C. National Environmental Satellite, Data, and Infomation Service.

Malingreau, J. P., Stevens, G. and Fellows, C. (1985). "1982-83 forest fires of Kalimantan and North Borneo. Satellite observations for detecting and monitoring". *Ambio* 14.

Mallingreau, J.P. (1986). "Global vegetation dynamics : Satellite observations over Asia." *International Journal of Remote Sensing* 7 : 1121-46.

Nerem, R.S., Holz, R.K., Helfert, M.R. and Tapley, B.D. (1985) "Vegetation change detection from NOAA polar orbiting satellites," *Geojournal* 11 : 313-20.

NOAA, Satellite Data Service Division, (1986). *Global Vegetation Index User's Guide.* Washington, D.C. : National Environmental Satellite Data and Information Service.

Schnider, S.R., McGinnis, S.R., and Gatlin, J.A. (1981). Use of NOAA/AVHRR visible and infrared data for land remote sensing". *NOAA Technical Report,* NESS 84, USDC, Washington, D.C.

Sellers, P.J. (1985). "Canopy Reflectance, photosynthesis and transpiration". *International Journal of Remote Sensing.* 6 : 1335-1371.

Townshend, J.R. and Tucker, C.J. (1981). "Utility of AVHRR or NOAA 6 and 7 for vegetation mapping in *Matching Remote Sensing Technologies and their Applications Proceedings.* London : Remote Sensing Society.

Townshend, J.R.G., Justice, C.O., and Kalb, V. (1987). "Characterization and classification of South American land cover types using satellite data." *International Journal of Remote Sensing* 8 : 1189-1207.

Tucker, C.J. (1986). "Maximum normalized difference vegetation index images for sub-Saharan Africa for 1983-1985 ". *International Journal of Remote Sensing* 7 : 1383-84.

Tucker, C.J., Fung, I.Y., Keeling, C.D. and Gammon, R.H. (1985a). "The relationship of a global spectral vegetation index and atmosphere CO_2 concentrations", *Nature,* London.

Tucker, C.J., Holben, B.N. and Goff, T.E. (1984). "Intensive forest clearing in Rondonia, Brazil as detected by satellite remote sensing," *Remote Sensing of the Environment* 15 :

Tucker, C.J., Townshend, J.R.G. and Goff, T.E. (1985b). "African land cover classification using satellite data" *Science.* N.Y., 226.

Tucker, C.J., Vanpraet, C.L., Boerwinkle, E. and Easton, A. (1983). "Satellite remote sensing of total dry matter accumulation in the Senegalese Sahel", *Remote Sensing of the Environment* 13.

Tucker, C.J., Vanpraet, C.L., Sharman, M.J. and Van Ittersum, G. (1985c). "Satellite remote sensing of total herbaceous biomass production in the Senegalese Sahel : 1980-84", *Remote Sensing of the Environment* 17.

Turcotte, K.M., Kramber, W.J., Venugopal, G. and Lulla, K. (1988). "Analysis of regional-scale vegetation dynamics of mexico using stratified AVHRR NDVI data." *Technical Papers, 1989 ASPRS/ACSM Convention.* Baltimore, MD. 3. 246-57.

Venugopal, G. Dutt, A.K. and Turcotte, K.M., (1992). "The effects of Rabi crop and other vegetation cover on NOAA AVHRR NDVI in the Middle Ganges plains of India and adjacent regions in (ed.) R.P. Singh, *Environment Monitoring—Applications of Remote Sensing and GIS.* GeoCarto International. 121-33.

18

Agricultural Land Development and Changes in Rajasthan

B.L. SHARMA and PALAK BHARDWAJ

Agriculture is essentially a practice and a way of living of people in different environmental set-ups of the world. When we speak of environment that means the physical set-up of the land, climatic conditions and the soil texture invariably form the composite whole of the atmosphere in which different crops are cultivated. The human effort and the artificial aid of water (irrigation), fertilizers (NPK), methods and the systems of raising various crops are the other considerations of the eco-system in which we adopt agricultural practices.

A combination of natural and human effort makes agriculture a viable practice of cultivation of different crops in different parts of the world. The ingredients of differentiation in cropping patterns and systems all over the world are seen to have wide variations of natural resources as well as social systems.

Thus, a complex system of agriculture is the result of a complex network of an eco-system in an environmental set-up. There may be many more eco-systems in an environmental set-up of a region. Therefore, a regional perspective is enhanced for the better understanding of agricultural resource mobilization and preservation of eco-system in the traditional countries like India.

Resource Mobilization

The traditionality of farming was based on the environmental co-existence, where natural factors were least disturbed by man.

Whatsoever we cultivated the crops were grown according to the adaptability, not by man's initiation of efforts in order to grow and cultivate plants but it was entirely a natural process in which plants sustained their growth and development and yielded accordingly. But, later on, agricultural came under strenuous constraints of environmental change. The perceptibility of growth and development of techniques to raise productivity in the shortest possible time, i.e. reducing cropping season, using HYV seeds, fertilizers, etc. have undergone an ecological complexion of change in the agricultural scenario of the existing cropping pattern in particular and agriculture in general.

The story of growth and developments of Indian agriculture in terms of its environmental relationship is very much similar to that of other countries. A major change in this field has occurred after independence specially after Five Year Plans have been implemented. To divide Indian agriculture into phases is really a division of development of agriculture in to successive stages, which took place in the Five Year Plans one after another. Thus, the phases are nothing but a period of initiation of stages of agricultural development. In fact, India has withessed three such successive stages of its development under which Plan out lays were achieved . The following slogans were adopted in succession of plan period during the last 40 years.

(i) The extension of cultivated land (1950 to 1968),
(ii) To raise the productivity of land, and
(iii) Modernization of agriculture.

(i) First Phase : Extension of Cultivated Land (1950 to 1965)

The first phase of agricultural development was initiated soon after the independence of India, i.e. 1950, and lasted up to 1965, when the "Green Revolution begin." This period of about 15 years was taken as the starting point of rebuilding of agricultural infrastructure which had been totally ruined during the British rule in India.

The medieval period of European social system was imposed on the Indian agrarian society in which landlords, feudal organizations and jagirdar systems were well established. The land ownership, land tenurial system and size of land holdings were crudely organized which had divided the Indian society into big land holders as farmers on the one side and small land owners or without land as the peasant class, which constituted about 70 per cent of the total agrarian population, on the other.

Thus, the agricultural economy was totally at rampage and the rule of the land was the dominant factor in the society. Therefore, the first task of those with the responsibility of agricultural development was to reorganize the farming sector for which various Acts were passed and Ordinances issued by the Government from time-to-time. Just after independence and promulgation of the Constitution, land was redistributed by granting ownership and the tenurial system was relaxed. But, the problem listed with the size of holdings was a crucial one in the stubborn society like ours. The small size of the land holdings accounting for more than 70 per cent of the total operational holdings, were distributed unevenly not only in pieces but also in fragments. The social customs area also such that they land to further fragmentation of already small holdings till the land loses its existence.

Thus, overall changes in the process of reorganization of land reform took another 10 years. But in addition to this, by the 1960s, the Extension Programme was started under which more cultivated land was added to the existing one (Table 18.1). A case of this kind of extension of agricultural land may well be cited from the study conducted by Prof. Jasbir Singh (Fig. 18.1).

Changes in Landuse in Rajasthan

Table 18.1: Changes in Landuse in Agricultural Land During Four Decades in Rajasthan

('000 ha.)

Land Category	*1950-51*	*1960-61*	*1970-71*	*1980-81*	*1988-89*
NAS	9313 (27.2)	13112 (38.8)	15263 (44.6)	15268 (44.6)	11514 (47.0)
Fallow land	5815	5126 (15.2)	3646 (10.5)	4158 (12.1)	5140 (21.0)
Culturable Waste	–	6341	7926 (23.2)	6475 (18.7)	5985 (24.4)
Permanent Pasture and Grazing Land	–	1684	–	1834 (5.3)	1817 (7.4)
Total Agricultural Land % to Geographical Area	15138 (44.1)	26263 (76.1)	26835 (79.4)	27675 (82.1)	24456

Note : Figures in brackets are the percentage to the total land.

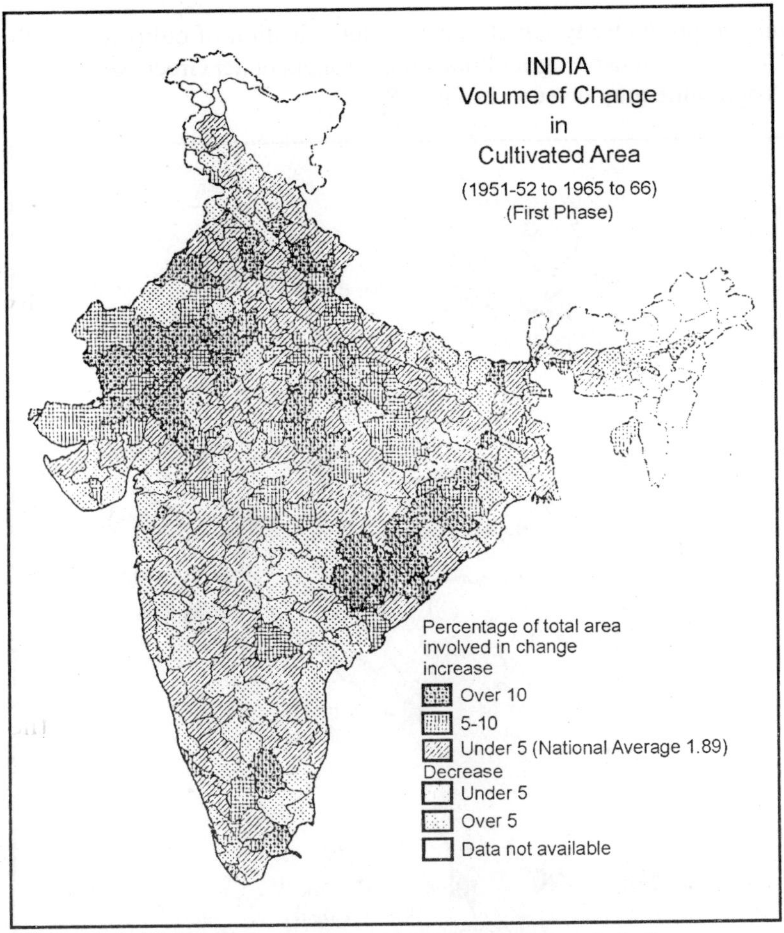

Fig. 18.1: Volume of Change in Cultivated Area in India.

(ii) Second Phase : To Raise Productivity and its Implications (Green Revolution 1968 to 1977)

By this time we had reached the second phase of development in which a drastic change was evident by 1968. This period is marked by the "Green Revolution" which not only ensured greater productivity of land but also brought self-sufficiency in the field of foodgrains. This could be achieved through raising productivity, efficiency and fertility of the soil. Thus, the slogan was provided for raising productivity which means intensification of cultivated land. (A case of intensive agricultural areas brought under Green Revolution Programme may be seen in Fig. 18.2).

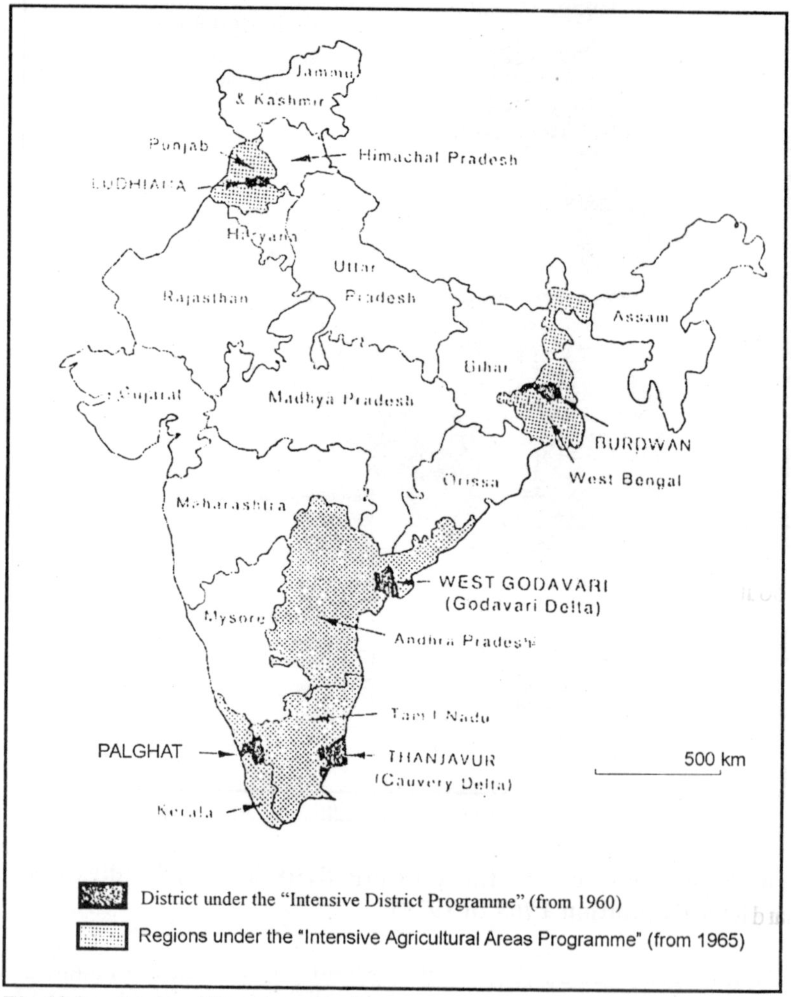

Fig.18.2 : Regional Development Programmes for the "Green Revolution" in India.
Source: Frankel, 1971, p. 2 modified.

To raise productivity it was necessary to provide adequate water to the crops and nutrients to the soil. Thus, a period of harnessing soil efficiency and fertility was marked with the advent of more use of fertilizers (NPK) and high-yielding seeds. This brought bumper production of foodgrains by 1977, and thus, self-sufficiency was achieved. But, the rising population trends were compelling the Indian agriculture to further increase foodgrain production which was not possible from the existing land conditions and prevailing social practices. Thus, a switchover to new techniques and methods of farming became inheritable by the 1980s.

The intensification and overexploitation of agricultural land during the three-phase programme was withnessed compelling land into declining productivity, diminishing returns and retarding of soil. To bring more land under cultivation was an extension programme of agricultural land, but to raise production from the existing cultivated land is to intensify land resources which means over-exploitation, in relation to efficiency and fertility of the soil, lending to conditions of exhaustion, land diminution and retardation. Best examples may be provided from the State of Rajasthan where radical changes have been recorded here.

If we look at the first and second-phase of programme, we may notice that land under cultivation increased from 27.2 per cent to 44.6 per cent of the total area. That means there was a sharp rise of about 17.4 per cent in the net area sown during the first phase—1950 to 1970. But it is interesting to note that there was no change in the N.A.S. during the second phase of 1970-1980, i.e. 44.6 and 44.6 respectively. This indicates that main emphasis was laid on the intensification of cultivated land for raising productivity. Because, this period marked an unprecedented rise in the foodgrain production under the Green Revolution (Table 18.2). In the Indian case the productivity is very well projected (Husain, 1979: 145).

The overall increase in the agricultural land was marked at 76.1 per cent to total land area in 1950 to 82 per cent in 1980. Here, the agricultural land includes net area sown, fallow land, and culturable waste, permanent pastures and miscellaneous land under trees, groves, etc.

The most fascinating features of this development marked in the State is the overall production trend during this period along with increase in the land area under cultivated crops like foodgrains, pulses and oilseeds. If we look at the various figures in Table 18.1, we find that there is not change in the land during 1971 to 1980 as discussed above, but production (Table 18.2) rose by 12 per cent over 1971. This was the trend in 1971 over the period of 1980, while area was not added to the existing land. Whereas area increased by 6 per cent and production by 11 per cent in 1971 over the period 1960-61. Thus there has been a sharp rise in production by 24 per cent over the 1960-61 period, i.e. 34 per cent to 58 per cent against the rise in area of about 6 per cent. There was no increase in area during 1970-1980, except a marginal one.

This leaves a clear impression of over intenfication of farming during the period of the second phase, i.e. 1970-80, and hence marked over-exploitation of the soil to its maximum carrying capacity. This is evident from indication available of soil exhaustion in different parts of the State. Declining soil fertility caused reduction in the yield which was reflected in the production.

During this period, i.e. by the 1980s, scientists and agronomists engaged in more researches to find out ways to control the increasing plant diseases and plant protection techniques. Because the application of heavy dozes of chemical fertilizers, and spray of pesticides caused heavy toxication and develop immunity in pests who sustain upon them. These areas developed into a large breading grounds later on.

First Phase Programme in Rajasthan

Pre-Green Revolution Period (1950-1965)

Table 18.2 : Production of Principal Commodities and Changes

(*in '000 tonnes*)

Principal Crops	*1950-51*	*1960-61*	*1970-71*	*1980-81*	*1988-89*
Cereals	3386 (84.2)	4550 (92.3)	4915 (75.0)	5348 (79.0)	4817 (80.7)
Pulses	498 (12.3)	1201 (24.4)	1102 (16.8)	150 (2.2)	63 (1.0)
Oilseeds	134 (3.3)	173 (3.5)	534 (8.1)	266 (3.9)	1089 (18.2)
Total	4018	4915	6551	6764	5969

Note : Figures in brackets are percentages to the total production.

The spectacular point of this phase was the use of modern techniques and machines through which intensification in farming was made possible. The widespread use of chemical fertilizers (NPK), without adequately educating the farmers in their use and in testing soil conditions, made the situation more complex in many ways. There was many glaring examples of retarding soils and soils reacting inversely on which no cultivation is possible till their appropriate treatment. Similarly, the intensification was brought by the wide-ranging use of the high-yielding variety (HYV) seeds, along with the mechanization of farming (Table 18.3) which brought changes in the soil atmosphere and generated conditions of infertility.

The impact and the rising trend in some of the facilities like fertilizers, mechanical power (tractor) and extension of irrigation projects can be seen in Table 18.3, which indicates their steady growth. These measures are beneficial but have also added more complexities to the farming system.

Second Phase Programme in Rajashan

Green Revolution Period (1965-1980)

Table 18.3 : Inputs in Agriculture

(*Area in '000 ha. fert. consumption in m.t.*)

Inputs	*1960-61*	*1965-66*	*1970-71*	*1975*	*1980-81*	*1988-89*
Fertilizers	N	868	46610		106623	
	P	300	22982		22982	
	K	–	5499		5499	
Mechanical (High power Tractor—Nos.)	–	42	106	240	370	54686
No. of Tractors per 1,000 ha. of cultivated areas	–	–	0.8	–	2.19	2.4
Irrigated Land	1823 (13.3)	1753 (13.8)	2173 (14.2)	2547 (16.9)	2895 (18.7)	3995 (30.0)

Note : Figures in brackets show the percentage to the total cultivated land.
Source : CMTE, Bombay, Vol. 2, pp. 7-12, 1982.

(iii) Third Phase : Modernization of Agriculture

We entered the third phase leaving behind the question of levels of agricultural development, passing through the first two phases. In the first-phase programme, we initiated effort to bring all the arable land under cultivation by mobilizing resources like the iron plough, tractor-driven machines, etc. Thus, hard soils could be broken enabling extension of agricultural land. But, the limit was reached with the availability of input resources like water (irrigation), fertilizers, seeds, etc.

The intensification of cultivated land was enhanced by raising productivity which was possible only after the use of HYV seeds, chemical fertilizers (NPK), irrigation facilities and new methods of farming practices. Thus, the resource mobilization was launched as the second phase of agricultural development. Because no further extension of cultivated land was possible and soil fertility limits were reached—the soil was exhausted.

Frequent cropping without fallow and rotation had gradually rendered the land infertile and hence retarded.

Having harnessed the available agricultured resources we launched a massive hunt for new resources to raise productivity, efficiency and fertility, during the third phase which was not possible only through the traditional methods and techniques of farming. So, we had to adopt some new measures for development. Thus, in the third phase of agricultural development which is purely a technical one, various measures were adopted, such as:

(i) Mechanical (technical use of machines),
(ii) Chemical (use of fertilizers and pesticides), and
(iii) Bio-cultural (hybridization of seeds, genetic-culture).

Introduction of technical inputs and mechanization of farming reflect the intensification of productivity not only at the State level but also at the country level. The rising production trend during the 1970s and even the 1980s was the direct result of the use of HYV seeds, fertilizers and irrigation. There was great increase in yield per hectare of foodgrains. The foodgrain production in 1988 was 138.4 million tonnes, while in 1990 it rose to 171 million tonnes well above the target of 150 million tonnes. Rajasthan contributed 6.7 per cent of the total production of the foodgrains. (A comparative statement of the yield and consumption of fertilizers can be seen in Tables 18.2 and 18.3.)

Cultural treatment is highly technical. It has been adopted only by those countries which have well equipped research laboratories and preservation facilities. In a biological treatment of plant genesis, desired plant species are developed and cared for in a certain set of conditions. Scientists have developed some varieties of rice which have low requirement of water, and of wheat which have a high tolerance capacity in the arid regions where water is saline.

Agricultural Potentiality

The variations in moisture during the cropping season profoundly influence the agricultural productivity. These variations are marked by high fluctuations from time to time. A peep into the agricultural drought conditions experienced in 1972 at Jaisalmer, Barmer, Jodhpur, and Bikaner districts of Western Rajasthan, with moderate conditions in Churu, Nagaur, Ajmer and Pali, is a case of moisture scarcity. Whereas, again in 1979, most of the western districts fell in the trap of a severe drought followed by in 1984-85 and 1986. The contrast between the regional patterns, i.e. eastern and wastern Rajasthan, indicates the impact of drought on the overall production and consequently the yield.

It is estimated during the year 1970 that the yield of millet was 4.7 q./ha. in western Rajasthan as compared to 5.2 q./ha. in the State. The decrease in the State's average rainfall was only 7 per cent during the year 1979, but the decrease in the pearl millet in the State was very high. If it is compared with the ones in the successive years of rainfall scarcity, in 1984, 1986 and 1987 in which the drop in the rainfall was recorded as 33 per cent, 37 per cent and 38 per cent respectively, the fall in production of Pearl Millet in the year 1987 was 73 per cent in western Rajasthan and 52 per cent in eastern Rajasthan. The decline in the yield was reported by 73 per cent and 77 per cent respectively. This trend indicates continuing declining trend even after 1979. The fall in production is attributed to two factors, viz.

(i) delay in sowing of the crops by nearly one month in the flood-affected districts of Jodhpur, Pali, Nagaur, Barmer and Jalore. There was a severe stress of water in the reproduction stage;

(ii) in the north-eastern districts of Churu, Jhunjhunu and Sikar the crop was affected by a severe water stress during its vegetative and reproductive stages. These conditions affect the growth and development of the plant in a particular period—during the growing stage.

Changes in Productivity

Changes in productivity due to late sowing or delay in cultivation due to failure of the monsoon or for other reasons is a case of change in the eco-system. Sharma (1987) has very characteristically described "the case of cotton harvesting in a late period and found an interesting development of micro-organism affecting the crop adversely. The incidence of heavy dodging of pesticides, oversupplying chemical fertilizers (NPK) and inadequate water, frequent ploughing without rotation are the factors that lead to change in productivity in a gradual process. Much more has been discussed about the environmental impact on crops due to changes in the harvesting period. The net result of these factors has been a major concern to all of us. It may be accepted that due to failure of monsoon, crops are adversely affected and there is a drop in production, or due to delay in harvesting, productivity is reduced to a considerable level. The untimely treatment of crops by fertilizers and pesticides, production drops much below the optimum level. But, a factor of change in the micro-organism, which causes change in the soil atmosphere, is rarely taken into consideration. It is forgotten that this factor alone is responsible for the change in the cropping pattern or reduction in the productivity level.

If this factor is applied and results are obtained from some of the key areas related to the crops grown in them the better realization may be known of some of the conditions responsible for the drop in the productivity level. For a better understanding may take the case of intensity of crop landuse in the 1971 and 1987-88 periods (Table 18.4).

If we look at the trends of crop land intensity in the various class categories of 1971 to 1988, we find an increasing trend in the medium to high and very high categories. In 1971, the number of district units found in the low category of intensity was 12 whereas in 1988 it dropped to 9 (Table 18.4), while in the high to very high classes the number increased in 1988 against the 1971 figures. It shows that more land was purt to crops in succession of years after as compared to 1971 (Fig. 18.3 and Fig. 18.4).

On the other hand, if we look at the yield trends during the successive years, i.e. 1981 to 1987 taking 1971 as the base year for various cereal crops, i.e. wheat, jowar, bajra, maize and mustard, the yield for these crops has dropped in some of the cases (Table 18.5).

It is quite interesting to note that while the area under cereal crops has been increased and crops landuse intensified, even then the yield has not improved to the expected levels. The yield of most of the crops under study with a few exceptions has increasingly dropped (Table 18.5). The yield of bajra has percentage-wise dropped from –57.6 in 1981 to –75.9 in 1988 over the 1977 period, maize has dropped from –29 to –69.3, and jowar from 30.5 to 54.6 per cent.

Table 18.4 : Intensity of Crop Landuse

S. No.	*District*	*Net Area sown*		*Total Cropped Area*		*Intensity %*	
		1971	1988	1971	1988	1971	1988
1.	Ajmer	397	330	458	372	115	112
2.	Alwar	500	419	698	538	140	128
3.	Banswara	206	207	255	287	123	138.6
4.	Barmer	1431	618	1436	632	100	102
5.	Bharatpur	535	371	675	457	126	123
6.	Bhilwara	318	296	413	395	130	133
7.	Bikaner	660	430	660	444	100	103
8.	Bundi	228	232	260	310	114	133.6
9.	Chittorgarh	347	349	449	488	129	139.8
10.	Churu	1234	964	1239	967	100	100.3
11.	Dholpur	–	136	–	169	–	126
12.	Dungarpur	124	91	167	116	134.6	127
13.	Ganganagar	1259	901	1353	1082	10.7	120
14.	Jaipur	813	676	949	855	11.7	126
15.	Jaisalmer	165	34	165	35	10	100
16.	Jalore	664	356	694	393	104.5	110
17.	Jhalawar	297	307	354	416	11.9	135.5
18.	Junjhunu	454	412	522	464	115	112.6
19.	Jodhpur	1202	649	1209	666	100.5	102.6
20.	Kota	586	581	681	741	107.6	127.5
21.	Nagaur	1228	994	1240	1024	100.9	103
22.	Pali	586	430	613	449	104.6	104
23.	Sawai Madhopur	501	476	589	571	117.5	120
24.	Sikar	550	440	589	501	107	113.8
25.	Sirohi	169	87	189	100	111.8	115
26.	Tonk	456	450	493	108	108	109.5
27.	Udaipur	353	275	475	340	134	123.6

Source : 1. Statistical Abstract of Rajasthan 1988, Districts of Rajasthan.
2. Agricultured Statistics and Plan Progress, 1971-73.

During this period, we find the use of fertilizers on an increasing scale. The State consumed about 460.8 mt. of nitrogen, 9403 mt. of phosphorus and 3135 mt. of potash in 1977 which rose to 106623 mt. of nitrogen, 22982 mt. of phosphorus and 5499 mt. of potash in 1981.

The use of high yielding variety (HYV) seeds during 1971-1988 in net area sown is another landmark in making agriculture a viable economy in the State (Table 18.2). The area under cereal crops of HYV seeds has been increased in almost all the districts with a high level of technological inputs of various kinds in order to achieve better results (Fig 18.5). But despite the fact that scientific agriculture is being done in most of the areas, the productive index available to this date indicates decreasing trends, reflecting our failure of achieving the targets (Table 18.6). This only reflects that the land has been exhausted so badly that it is no longer replenishable at places.

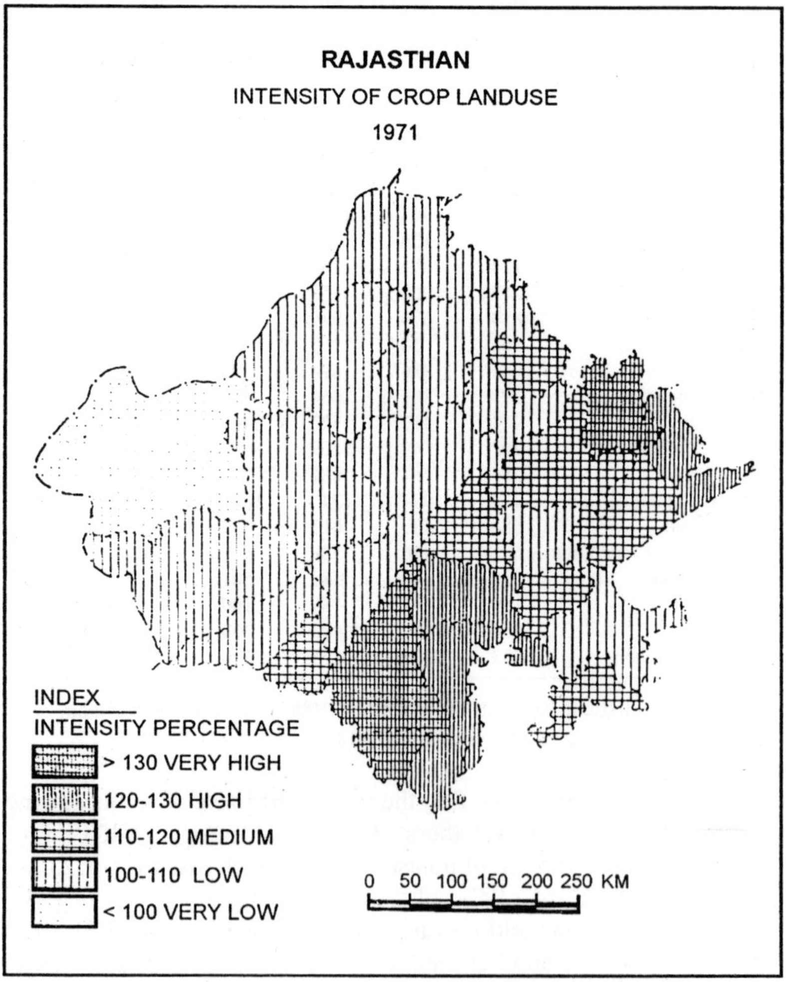

Fig. 18.3: Rajasthan: Intensity of Crop Landuse, 1971

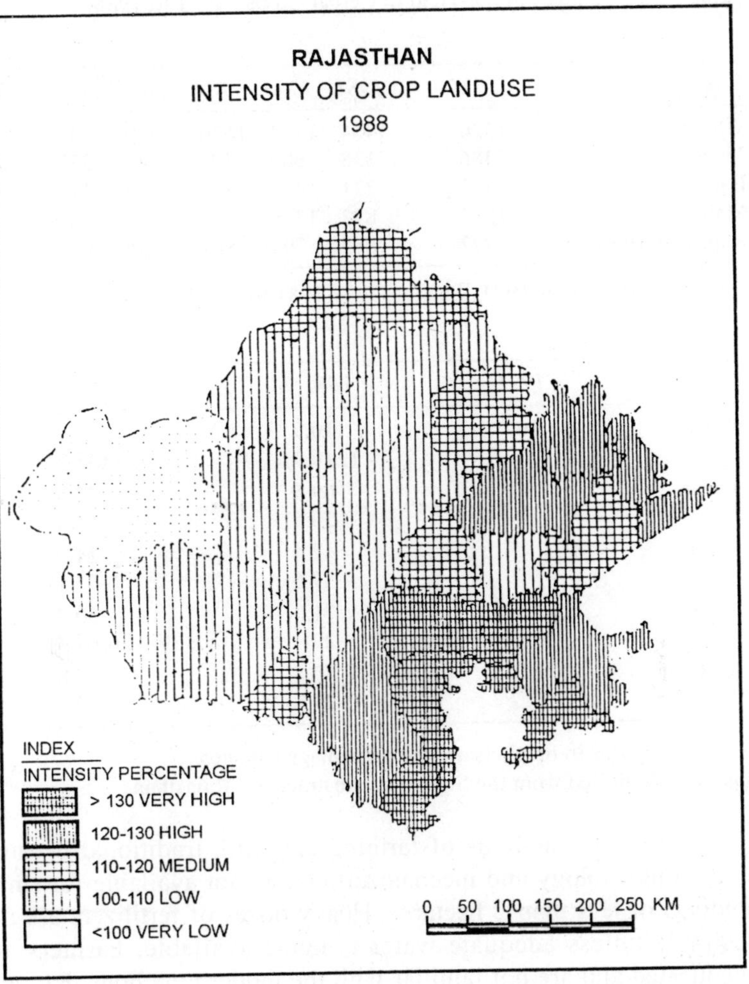

Fig. 18.4: Rajasthan: Intensity of Crop Landuse, 1988

Table 18.5 : Changes in the Yield of Cereal Crops : 1971 to 1988

(ha./kg.)

Crop	*1971*	*1981*	*1983*	*1984*	*1985*	*1986*	*1987*
Wheat	1320	1464	1594	1626	2209	1845	1897
Jowar	486	338	600	495	481	237	221
Bajra	521	221	491	364	153	192	130
Maize	1227	872	1376	1231	336	335	377
Rape and Mustard	972	685	791	801	736	859	854

Note: Yield Base Year 1971. Changes over 1981 to 1988 in % Agl.

(yield per ha./kg)

Crop	*1971*	*1981*	*1988*
Wheat	100	110.9 (+10.9)	143.7 (+43.7)
Jowar		69.5 (–30.5)	45.4 (–54.6)
Bajra		42.4 (–57.6)	24.9 (–75.1)
Maize		71.0 (–29)	30.7 (–69.3)
Mustard		70.4 (–29.6)	87.8 (–12.2)

Note : Figures in brackets are the percentage changes.
Source : Compiled from the Statistical Abstracts of Rajasthan.

In fact, our methods of farming are, still, traditional because modern technology and mechanization area not available for small holdings of less than 2 hectares. Heavy dozes of fertilizers are not desirable unless adequate water is made available. Farmers are uneducated and are not familiar with the modern methods. Farmers are changing cropping patterns according to their needs and desire for money.

All these factors, in the long run, are affecting our agricultural set up, leading to disturbed eco-system reflected in declining productivity. The realization of this fact has lately come. It is felt that the advantages of modern technology are no more helpful and useful in the traditional way of society like ours and thus raises the question of a sustainable agriculture for the future.

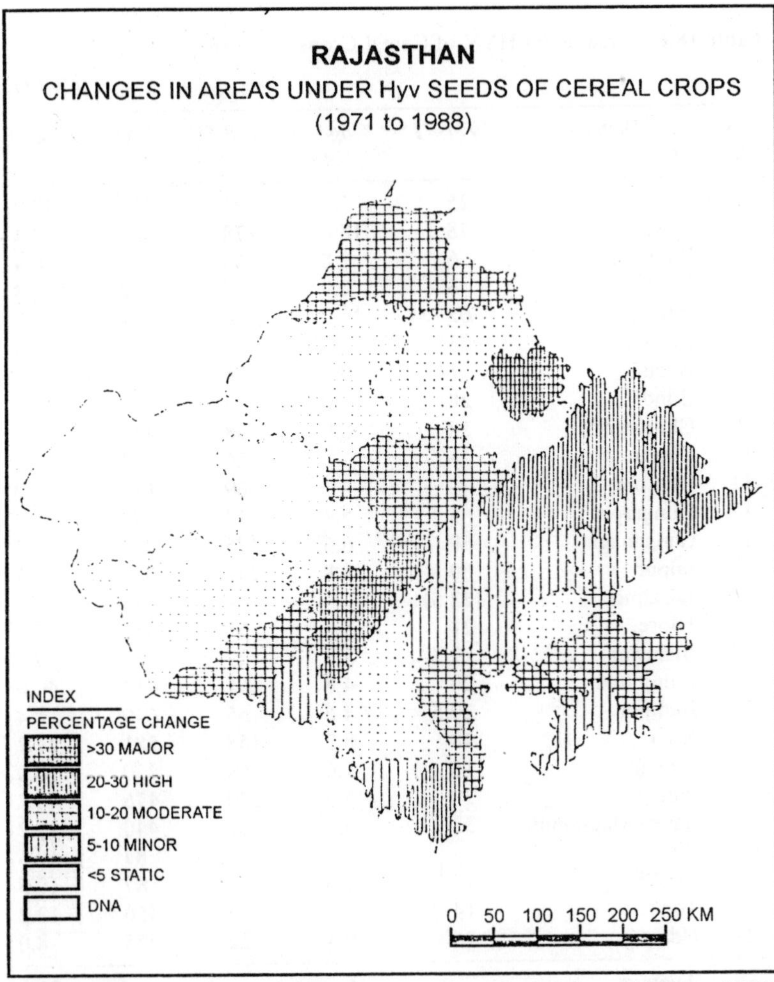

Fig. 18.5: Changes in areas under HYV seeds of Cereal Crops (1971 to 1998)

Conclusion

There is great stress and strain on agricultural land because of the rapid growth in the world population. It is estimated that by the year 2000 A.D. about four-fifths of the world's population of 6.1 billion will be living in the less developed region. This clearly reflects a great deal of pressure to find environmentally compatible means of not only maintaining but adding to the present agricultural production.

Table 18.6 : Area under HYV of Cereal Crops

('000 ha)

Sl. No.	District	1971-71*	%age to NAS	1988-89	NAS	%age
1.	Ajmer	25	7.5	57	330	17.2
2.	Alwar	78	18.6	178	419	42.4
3.	Banswara	6	2.8	63	207	30.4
4.	Barmer	6	0.9	15	618	2.4
5.	Bharatpur	62	16.7	138	371	37.2
6.	Bhilwara	23	7.7	40	296	13.8
7.	Bikaner	1	0.2	26	430	0.6
8.	Bundi	28	12.0	33	232	14.2
9.	Chittorgarh	28	8.0	68	349	19.4
10.	Churu	–	–	26	964	2.8
11.	Dholpur	–	–	69	136	50.7
12.	Dungarpur	5	5.4	12	91	13.1
13.	Ganganagar	60	6.6	175	901	19.4
14.	Jaipur	60	8.8	232	676	34.3
15.	Jaisalmer	(22.5)	–	–	34	–
16.	Jalore	21	5.8	61	356	17.1
17.	Jhalawar	12	3.9	27	307	9.1
18.	Jhunjhunu	20	4.8	165	412	40.0
19.	Jodhpur	29.5	4.6	55	649	8.4
20.	Kota	48	8.2	158	581	27.2
21.	Nagaur	16	1.6	69	430	16.0
22.	Pali	30	6.9	220	476	46.2
23.	Sawai Madhopur	32	6.7	67	440	15.2
24.	Sikar	–	–	17	87	19.5
25.	Sirohi	11	12.6	17	87	19.5
26.	Tonk	14	3.1	55	450	12.2
27.	Udaipur	26	9.4	22	275	8.0
	Average		6			21

*Agricultural Statistics and Plan Progress, 1971-72, p. 78 Rajasthan, Jaipur Statistical abstract 1988, Directorate of Economic Statistics, Jaipur.

There is sufficient evidence to mark the changes in agriculture as discussed in the light of the phased programme of developmental plans in the country and the State as well. The use of various kinds of aids, i.e. fertilizers, HYV seeds, new techniques, methods and machines, etc., brings into focus the increasing pressure to raise production, on the one hand and alarming population growth and demand for food, on the other. Thus, a balance between population growth and production has to be maintained through the compatible means, i.e. productivity, efficiency and fertility. The use of pesticides and new known methods and techniques of farming are the additional means to raise production. Chemical agents play an important role in creating advantageous developmental conditions of crops to protect them against diseases, pests and also against adverse abiotic environmental factors. However, when large amount of chemicals are used, in a broadest sense, there is a risk of upsetting the biologically stable balance resulting in unforeseeable consequences.

Thus, environmental compatibility is essentially a condition of harvesting plants in harsh environments, extreme temperatures, inadequate water, retarding soil, etc. In this context the moisture regime variation is an important controlling factor which directly affects productivity. If we look first to this factor in the State (Rajasthan) we find wide-ranging variations along with other climatic conditions controlling agricultural productivity.

REFERENCES

Buchel, K.H. (1984). "The Future of Chemistry," *Plant Research and Development,* Vol. 20, pp. 7-22.

Bugernrieder, A. (1982). *Plant Research and Development,* Vol. 16, p. 95.

Bohle, H.G. (1991). "Twenty Years of Green Revolution in India." *Applied Geography and Development*, Vol. 37, pp. 21-38.

Charmbers, R. (1986). "Beyond the GR...", *Applied Geography and Development,* Vol. 37, pp. 21-38.

Chetterji, P.C. & Sexena, S.K., (1987). "Canal Irrigation of Arid Zone in Rajasthan, and Its Ecological Implications," *Desert Ecology*, pp. 223-58.

Falkner, F.R. (1938). *"Die Trackon grenze deo Ragenfedbaus in Afrika* (The Desert Limit of Dry Farming in Africa)." *Pet. Geogr*. 84, pp. 201-14.

Hanagarth, W. (1989). "Ecology and risk spreading agriculture in the small holding...," *Plant Research and Development*, Vol. 30, pp. 76, 101.

Husain, M. (1979). *Agricultural Geography*. Inter-India Publication, New Delhi.

Kostrowicki, J. (1980). World Types of Agriculture, *IGU Commission's Report*. Warsaw, Poland.

Klingane, F. (1982). Do Developing Countries Require Chemical Plant Protections", *Plant Research and Development*, Vol. 16, p. 80.

Ramkrishna (1987). "Moisture Regime Variation and Agricultural Productivity in Rajasthan," *Desert Ecology*, pp. 37-64.

Roonwal, M.L. (1977). *Natural Resources of Rajasthan,* Vol. 2, pp. 616-71, Jodhpur.

Schrieiber, D. (1981). *Applied Geography & Development*, Vol. 17, pp. 29-43.

Schiedecken, W. (1981). *Applied Geography and Development*, Vol. 17, pp. 45-57.

Sharma, B.L. (1987). *Problem and Perspectives of Watering of Crops*, Concept Publishing Co., New Delhi.

Sharma, B.L. (1987). *Environmental Impact Assessment*, Landscape Ecology, pp. 5-13.

——, (1990). *Applied Agricultural Geography*, Rawat Publications, Jaipur.

——, (1991). *Dryland Farming*, Daya Publishers, New Delhi.

——, (1983). "A Typological Analysis of Agriculture in Rajasthan States," *Geographica-Polonica*, Vol. 46.

Shafi, M. (1991). *Agricultural Productivity and Regional Imbalances*. Concept Publishing Co., New Delhi.

Singh Jasbir (1974-75). *An Agricultural Atlas of India*. Kurukshetra.

Spitz, P. (1987). "The Green Revolution Re-examined in India," in B. Glasser (Hrsg), pp. 56-78. Berlin. *Applied Geography Development*, Vol. 37, p. 38.

Sachs, I. (1984). "The Food Energy Problems", in M. Levy and J. Robinson (Hrsg), Energy and Agriculture, Interaction Futures, Policy Implications of Global Models, *Applied Geography and Development*, Vol. 37, pp. 21-38. Germany.

19

Meaning, Scope and Statutes of Urban Land Development

R.G. GUPTA

There is no dearth of land. Taking an overall average density of 125 persons per hectare, the population of the entire world may easily be accommodated in a small area of the country like U.K. or West Germany. Out of an area of 3.28 sq.km of our country, hardly 5 percent is under settlements and the rest is under agriculture, forestry, mining, water courses, etc.

Land is a natural resource gifted by nature, as such it is to be shared by all living on its surface irrespective of caste, colour and creed. Hence, the Government is the only agency to ensure a balanced development and distribution of land amongst the people. The Government, therefore, must have a complete control over all the land available in a country. The land can thus easily be used for the social and economic welfare of the nation through socialization and rational distribution measures. This can be done only by the Government which should, therefore, exert control over planning, development, disposal, management and the pricing of land.

There is a big variation in the price of land. In Delhi, it is sold at different prices varying form Rs. 500 to Rs. 1700 per sqm. in the public sector to Rs. 3,000 to Rs. 8,000 per sq.m. in the private sector. To quote an example, developed land in the resettlement colonies in 1990, is allotted on a hire-purchase basis at the rate of Rs. 500 per sq.m. reserved rates for residential plots, EWS and LIG was Rs. 825 and 1,075 per sq.m.; for MIG Rs. 1,400 per sq.m. ; Self-Finance Scheme (SFS) Rs. 1,700 per sq.m.; for commercial plots in district centres Rs. 10,000 to 15,000 per sq.m. ; allotment of land for parks and playgrounds at the rate of Re. 1 per annum; for educational institutions average Rs. 500 per sq.m.

It is a fact that developed land at a cheaper and affordable rate is required for the extension and improvement of existing settlements, preservation and improvement of historical sites, monuments, and other areas of unique and aesthetic social and cultural values; protection and enhancement of environment along the river fronts, in pilgrimage centres and tourist centres.

In most of the town land should be developed at cheaper rates and should also be made available at the same rate to the society at large, for the benefit of the society and not for individual.

Development of Land

Development of land includes internal and peripheral development, viz. levelling, dressing, laying of internal and peripheral infrastructure, viz. water supply, sewerage, drainage, electricity, gas lines; construction of roads and service roads, bus stops, dustbins, milk booths, development of parks, playgrounds and open spaces, development of sites for various community facilities, laying of trunk infrastructure, viz. water lines, sewer lines, drains, electric lines, telephone lines, gas lines, construction of Master Plan roads, over-bridges, under-brides, flyovers; bus terminals, street furniture; sites for various community facilities of higher order, viz. colleges, general hospital, research institutions; sources of potable water by way of construction of treatment plants, systems of sewage disposal, generation of power, etc. Development of any land is a time-consuming process; the colonies whose development was started nearly eight to ten years back are not completely developed hitherto. So, it has become a continuous process. Development is always seen in terms of a long-term perspective.

In order to foster balanced development in a co-ordinated and integrated manner in any urban settlement, formulation of an appropriates Urban Land Development Policy is a must.

Urban Land Development Policy

The Urban Land Development Policy should have the following seven components:

1. Law of the land and modifications in various Acts;

2. Planning and development;
3. Dispersal;
4. Control of land-use;
5. Recapturing plus values of land;
6. Land management; and
7. Maintenance of land.

Law of the Land—Modifications in Various Acts

(*i*) *Proposed Modification in the Land Acquisition Act, 1894-1985*:

(a) Whenever there is a case of acquisition of land for trunk services/infrastructure, i.e. water supply, sewerage, drainage, power, telephone lines, major roads, rail lines, flyovers, road over and under bridges, water treatment plants, sewage disposal plant, etc. the following steps should be followed:

- Sections 4, 6 and 17 of the Land Acquisition Act should be applicable together the irrespective of whether the area is lying vacant, has built-up structures of fake religious buildings.
- In such cases, the entire process of survey, planning, Sections 4, 6 and 17 of the Land Acquisition Act, taking over possession of the land, alternative allotment of urban spaces and payment of compensation, etc., should not take more than six months.
- Once a plan of trunk infrastructure/important facilities is finalized and approved, these services should be demarcated on the site with stone pillars. Due publicity should be made with the help of location plans, announcements, public notices, radio and TV, so that the public is apprised of the situation and does not squat/encroach on the land earmarked for these facilities. It has been seen that many of the unauthorized colonies have come up in the green areas or in the pockets required for the trunk infrastructure due to non-availability of information to the public. It is suggested that there should be active public participation in the acquisition of land.

- Alternative allotments may be in terms of developed plots or built-up flats, should be made to the affected families whose lands are being acquired within a period of six months from the date of notification under Sections 4, 6 and 17 of the Land Acquisition Act.
- The amount of compensation to be paid to the party should be adjusted in the alternative allotment of plot/built-up tenements to be made.
- Alternative allotment should be made to the tenants also subject to other necessary terms and conditions.
- Cost of alternative allotment of developed plots or built-up flats should be charged to the project of laying trunk infrastructure.

(b) There should be a legal provision in the Act regarding allotment of alternative accommodation, may be in terms of developed plots or built-up flats or urban space in all the cases of land acquisition, so that people are not uprooted and harassed. These allotments would be subject to the condition that he/she or his/her dependents do not have any other property in the Union Territory of Delhi, and other administrative measures, terms and conditions.

(c) Stay orders should be granted only in genuine cases. It has been experienced that in the garb of stay orders people encroach on public lands.

(d) Preference should be given for alternative allotment to the affected parties in the construction of trunk infrastructure and Master Plan roads of 30m. and above R/W's.

(e) Planned development of Delhi should be well defined in terms of write-ups and maps.

(*ii*) *Proposed Modification in the Slum Clearance and Improvement Scheme*:

(a) A brief description of the Slum Areas Improvement and Clearance Act, 1956:

- Chapter I (Section 3) deals with the declaration of slum areas.

- Chapter III (Sections 4, 5, 6, 7 and 8) explains how a particular area can be improved and developed/re-developed.
- Chapter IV (Sections 9, 10, and 11) deals with the declaration of a slum area as clearance area, and then how to pass slum clearance orders in order to get the area cleared and then redeveloped.
- Chapter V (Sections 12 to 18) deals with the acquisition of land/property in slum areas, on the basis of five years' gross rent or three years' net rent of the property in question.

(b) Suggested modifications in the Scheme of Slum Clearance and Improvement:

- As per the 1981 census 3.2 lakh families were living in 2,170 hectares designated slum areas. So far in the last three decades, no substantial acquisition of land/property has been made. Only a few pockets have been declared as Clearance Ares and the DDA has not succeeded in getting them cleared. The idea of acquiring land under this Act is completely impractical and as such, should be modified.
- After studying the details of improvements made in the slum areas of Delhi by the authority during the last two decades. The following conclusions come to light. These conclusions should be considered at the time of modifying the Slum Areas Improvement and Clearance Act.
- Name of the Act should be changed to "Improvement and Development of Habitat in Sub-Standard Areas".
- The entire area of 2,170 hectares designated as Slum Area under the Clearance and Improvement Act, 1956, should be declared as development area of the Authority under Section 12(1) of the Delhi Development Act. Responsibility of planning, developing, re-developing, clearing and rebuilding the entire area of 2,170 hectare which is bounded by Boulevard Road, Roshanara Road, Road No. 40, metre-gauge line near Patel Nagar, Ranjit Nagar, Shadipur, Khanpur, Pusa Road, Punchkuin Marg, Railway Line from Tilak Bridge to Minto Bridge, Bahadurshah Zaffar Marg and Mahatma Gandhi Road should be with the Slum Department of the

Authority, irrespective of the nature of the area, landuse and type of project, whether remunerative or non-remunerative.

- All the roads acquired for slum schemes should be the property of the Slum Department. Expenditure and receipts should be debited/credited in the account of the scheme. There should be a clear cut policy that profits from the commercial projects would be used to subsidise projects for the Economically Weaker Sections of the people of the slum areas.
- It is also recommended that whenever any action in the slum areas is taken, it should be for the entire system, or sub-system. So far, more than 20,000 tenements under the slum scheme have been constructed without taking care of other components, i.e. for their place of work and enjoyment. The result is that all the quarters have not been occupied by the families who were living in the slum areas. This is mainly due to the reason that no comprehensive proposal at any stage for the entire system or sub-system has been worked out. People are generally reluctant to shift till their place of work and enjoyment is also made available at the new place. Now there is a strong feeling that shifting of people should be avoided to the extent possible.
- Allotment of built-up laws should be on the basis of hire-purchase system.
- Building bye-laws should be modified completely and then enforced strictly.
- Maintenance of services, viz. water supply, sewerage, drainage, sanitation, electricity, roads, service roads, parks and playgrounds should always remain with the local authorities, i.e. Municipal Corporation of Delhi. This is a very important function and should be given practical shape and taken care of in all the areas.
- All the capital works as listed below should be with a development authority like the Delhi Development Authority:
  - Construction of tenements for the rehabilitation of families to be shifted from the slum areas, if any.
  - Building of social infrastructure on Government properties/evacuee properties.

- Clearance of slum areas (if any) and then rebuilding of urban spaces.
- Improvements in slum areas in terms of physical and social infrastructure.
- Development/construction of remunerative projects in slum areas.

(*iii*) *Proposed Modifications in the Delhi Development Act, 1957*:

(a) Section 6 (Objects of the Authority) should be well defined, as under:

- Preparation, monitoring, review and implementation directly and indirectly of the Master Plan proposals concerning physical, social, economic infrastructure.
- Environment of landuse controls as envisaged in the Act.
- The acquisition and development of land for various activities of the planned development of Delhi.
- Making developed lands available to various agencies in the public, co-operative and private sectors for house-building activity.
- The promotion of a sufficiently dynamic housing programme.
- Development of residential, industrial, commercial and ancillary centres of work.
- In exercise of its role as custodian of the Master Plan, the DDA has to coordinate the activities of either specialized agencies, such as DESU, MCD, NDMC, CPWD, PWD, Delhi Administration, DTC, WS & SDU, DSIDC, DTDC, DLPPC, MTPR, etc., who are also concerned with the planned development of Delhi.
- Development of any other project necessary for the planned development of Delhi.
- DDA shall be responsible directly or indirectly for all the works concerned with the capital works of the city. In no case, she should enter the service functions of the local bodies.

(b) Section 8 (Preparation of Zonal Development Plan) should be modified as most of the zonal plans prepared in Delhi are incomplete, inaccurate and have taken more than 10 to 15 years. This section should be completely modified to the extent that a zonal plan should have (i) a proper base map, (ii) traffic and transportation plan, (iii) land ownership map, (iv) plan of physical infrastructure, (v) plan of social infrastructure, (vii) plan of economic infrastructure, and (vii) a financial plan.

(c) Section 24 (Budget of the Authority) should be revised completely and may be as follows:

- There should be a Perspective Plan of short and long-term projection of financial requirements based on physical targets, correlated with and acquisition, planning, development and construction of urban spaces including availability of building materials.
- A proper planning and programming of financial resources should be made every year before they are included in the budget.
- There should be a system of performance budget or annual plan with a close coordination between physical and financial achievement.

(d) Sections 37, 38 and 40 (Power of the Authority to levy betterment charges, assessment and collection). As per these sections, betterment charges can be collected after a work is done in any area. In Delhi, there are more than 1000 unauthorized and unauthorized-regularized colonies spread over an area of about 5,000 hectares with a population of about 1.5 million. It is not possible, first to develop these colonies and then to collect betterment or development charges. As such, there should be a modification in the Act that development charges can be collected simultaneously with the development works and if not paid, they can be taken as arrears of land revenue.

(IV) LAND ACQUISITION AND DEVELOPMENT SCHEME, 1959:

The Land Acquisition and Development Scheme is at the National Scheme Lines and is for the grant of loans to State Governments for bulk acquisition and development of land for house building and connected purposes. This came into enforcement on October 20, 1959, with the following features:

(a) Financial assistance under the scheme will be provided to the State Governments in the shape of loans with a rate of interest at 4 per cent per annum, to be repayable in 10 annual equated installments, with a moratorium period of five years.
(b) The loan would be used for acquisition and development of land for different purposes.
(c) While making allotment, preference would be given to those who are eligible for aid under the various housing and slum clearance schemes in over of priority noted below:

- Slum Clearance Scheme.
- Subsidized Industrial Housing Scheme.
- Low Income Group Housing Scheme.
- Middle Income Group Housing Scheme.
- Rental Housing Scheme for State Government Employees.

(d) Plots intended for commercial or commercial-*cum*-residential purposes shall be sold by public auction or open tender except for the above five categories. Other plots can be disposed of on the pattern as the State Government may consider appropriate.
(e) The State Government shall, however, ensure that there is no loss to the project and the entire profit gained by the sale of and for commercial purposes, and to persons in higher income groups, would be used for the purpose of reducing the price of land to be utilized for public housing for people falling in the group of LIG and below.
(f) Other conditions for allotment of land would be as under:

- Not more than one plot to an individual.
- The land would be given on lease-hold basis.
- Building should come up within a reasonable period of time.
- Avoid speculation in land.
- Prohibit misuse of land.

- Prevent transfer or resale of plot/house to persons not eligible for the benefits of the scheme.
- Discourage transfer or resale of plots/houses.

(v) *Control of Land Values in the Urban Areas of Delhi*:

(a) Private investment in housing should be facilitated.
(b) Setting up of colonies by private developers should be discouraged.
(c) No allotment should be made to any of the institutions till it serves the interest of Delhi.
(d) Developed land should be provided to various institutions.
(e) All the land acquired under the scheme will be nazul land and will vest in the President of India and will be given out in his name only on lease-hold basis to local bodies and private parties including cooperative house building societies, industrialists, individuals, institutions, etc.
(f) As a general policy, disposal of developed land should be made by public auction except in the following cases:

- Alternative allotment of land.
- Shifting of non-confirming industries.
- To low-income-group people.
- To cooperative house building societies.

(g) Ground rent should be charged at a nominal rate of Re. 1 per annum per plot for the first five years. Thereafter the annual ground rent shall be payable at 2½ per cent of the premium originally paid. The rate of ground rent will be subject to revision after every 30 years.
(h) The following conditions shall govern the allotment of land whether by auction or otherwise:

- One plot for one family in the entire Union Territory of Delhi, except in the case of persons living in a congested locality.
- The structure on the allotted land should be completed within two years.
- The plot cannot be transferred before 10 years from the date of allotment, that also after payment of 50 per cent of the unearned increase of the value of the plot.

- It was decided that the entire responsibility for the acquisition, development and disposal of land under the scheme should be that of the Chief Commissioner, Delhi (now Lt. Governor).

(*vi*) The Government of India modified the scheme of Large Scale Acquisition, Development and Disposal of Land on July 18, 1967. The scope, of the scheme was increased and the following activities were added:

(a) Flatted Factories.
(b) Single-storeyed sheds for group industries.
(c) Warehouses.
(d) Bus Terminals.
(e) Parking sites for idle trucks.
(f) Car parking.
(g) Development of district, community, local and convenient shopping centres.
(h) Construction of special markets, as cycle market, vegetable market, etc.
(i) Acquisition and development of land in Narela.

(*vii*) Scope of "Large Scale Acquisition, Development and Disposal of Land" further enhanced. The Government vide its order of December 18, 1969, further enhanced the scope of "Large Scale Acquisition, Development and Disposal of Land" to the extent that any other development project which the Lt. Governor, Delhi, considers essential for the implementation of the Master Plan of Delhi and the zonal plans, subject to the condition that such projects are self-financing, can be undertaken.

(*viii*) Scheme further modified and the then Ministry of Works and Housing (now Ministry of Urban Development) further modified the scheme vide its order of February 5, 1970, to the extent as given under:

(a) Allotment of residential plots to persons belonging to LIG and MIG with a decision on the size of plots, income category and reservation of plots for Members of Parliament, Councillors of Metropolitan Council/MCD, salaried classes, Schedule Castes/Tribes etc.

(b) Registration of new co-operative house building societies on group housing pattern.

(c) Allotment of land to owners and tenants of properties in areas which have been declared as clearance areas under the Slum Areas Improvement and Clearance Act.

- Allotment of plots to persons owning houses/plots in congested localities.
- Realization of premium/price of plots in instalments according to the stage of development.

(d) The scheme was further considered and modified *vide* an order of May 5, 1974. In this order, premium to be charged on a plot earmarked for college purposes in Dhaula Kuan was considered and it was decided that a rate of Re. 1 per sq.yd. may be charged irrespective of whether the plot forms a part of "General Development Scheme" or an individual case.

(e) Lastly, the Government vide its order dated April 29, 1976, decided to modify the scheme for the allotment of and for the construction of 8662 sheds by DSIDC.

(*ix*) Conversion of Leasehold into Free-hold (Notification in the *Hindustan Times* of 13.3.1991):

The Government has decided to establish two separate funds—the General Pool Residential Accommodation Fund and the Delhi Urban Development Fund—from the proceeds of the one-time conversion charge, including surcharge for conversion of lease-hold rights to free-hold rights for properties in Delhi.

The Government recently announced a modified version of the order sanctioning conversion of lease-hold rights to free-hold rights for properties in Delhi in case of residential leases of less than 500 sq.m.

The funds would be utilized for housing, including construction of general pool accommodation and also for the urban development of Delhi.

It has been decided that the benefit of the conversion would be allowed for residential leases in Delhi administered by a public agency in respect of properties up to a size of 500 sq.m. Janata, LIG, MIG and SFS flats, as well as those allotted by the Delhi Development

Authority as also flats/tenements of group housing societies on land leased by the Delhi Development Authority.

Plots up to 50 sq.m. and Janata flats of DDA would be allowed conversion free of charge.

In the present order, the rates specified have been formulated on an incremental basis from one slab to another on the lines of the Income Tax Formula. The incremental rates are higher for the higher area slabs.

The one-time conversion charge to be paid in lump sum shall be as follows:

For Plots (as also for Flats/Tenements of Group Hosing Societies on Lands Leased by DDA of Plinth Area Exceeding 125 sq.m.)

Plot Area in sq.m.	*Conversion Fee (in rupees) to be calculated on the following basis*
Upto 50	Nil
Above 50 & up to 150	7.5% of notified land rate per sq.m. for area above 50 sq.m.
Above 150 & up to 250	Conversion charge applicable for 150 sq.m. plus 10% of notified land rate per sq.m. for area above 150 sq.m.
Above 250 & up to 350	Conversion charge applicable for 250 sq.m. plus 15% of notified land rate per sq.m. for area above 250 sq.m.
Above 350 & up to 500	Conversion charge applicable for 350 sq.m. plus 20% of notified land rate per sq.m. for area above 350 sq.m.

For Flats/Tenements allotted by DDA and its Slum Wing on leasehold basis

Category of Flat/Tenement	*East Zone*	*North and West Zone*	*South Zone*
Janata	Nill	Nill	Nill
LIG	3000	9000	12000
MIG	4250	12750	17000
SFS(II)	6200	18750	25000
SFS(III)	7500	22500	30000

For Flats Constructed by Group Housing Societies on Land Leased by DDA

Plinth Area of Flat/Tenement	*East Zone*	*North and West Zone*	*South Zone*
Below 30 sq.m.	Nill	Nill	Nill
Above 30 & up to 50 sq.m.	3000	9,000	12000
Above 50 & up to 75 sq.m.	4000	12750	17000
Above 75 & up to 100 sq.m.	6250	18750	25000
Above 100 & up to 125 sq.m.	7500	22500	30000

As far as DDA flats and tenements are concerned the conversion rated are based on a zone-wise, category-wise basis of different types of flats.

For cases where there has been a transfer of property by the original lessee through power of attorney, there will be just a levying of a surcharge of $33\frac{1}{3}\%$ and above the normal conversion fee. This greatly simplifies the earlier order where a two-stage process was required for regularization.

However, no unearned increase will be recoverable. Whereas the earlier Government had laid down that the option for conversion would be available for a period of only six months, for exercising the option for conversion. However, for the period up to March 31, 1992, the land rates applicable for the purposes of calculating the conversion fee will be at the current notified land rates which have been effective from April 1, 1987. After March 31, 1992, conversion fee will be based on the land rates to become effective thereafter.

The option for conversion shall be applicable only in respect of properties where the land-use prescribed in the Master Plan Zonal Development Plan is residential.

For areas where rates have not been notified by the Ministry of Urban Development, the residential land rates notified by DDA for the area would be applicable.

In all cases of conversion, the conveyance deeds shall be registered on payment of stamp duty and registration charges and the consideration amount for this purpose shall be the amount of conversion charges, including the surcharge where applicable.

(*x*) *Jhuggi Jhompri Removal Scheme (Shanties Removal and Resettlement Scheme)*

The scheme was initiated long back in 1958 approved by the Union Cabinet on January 4, 1960, and modified by it on November 12, 1962. The Scheme has been modified from time-to-time depending upon the magnitude of the problem, size of the plot and demand of the time.

Following are the factors concerning the modifications and revisions in the scheme:

(a) Size of plot; initially about 5,000 plots each of 67 sq.m. and 45,000 of 21 sq.m. were developed in the 1960s. In the 1970s about 150,000 plots each of 21 sq.m. were planned and developed. In 1980s, the size of the plots was further reduced form 21 sq.m. to 18 sq.m. 15 sq.m. to 12.5 sq.m., and 10 sq.m. A study is required to determine the size of plot with relation to magnitude of the problem, number of squatters and their affordability.

(b) Up to the 1970s and early 1980s physical infrastructure has been provided on a community basis in terms of hand pumps, water taps, latrine blocks of suitable locations, street lights with no individual water, sewer and electric connections. In already developed resettlement colonies up to the 1980s the Municipal Corporation of Delhi is laying physical infrastructure on an individual basis, but the cost per plot of this system called "additional facilities" would be around Rs. 5,000 per plot.

Now there is a thinking to provide physical infrastructure on a Group basis, i.e. one W.C. for three families, one bathroom for six families, one water tap for six families, etc. This has been proposed and adopted in Delhi based on studies conducted in Maharashtra and Delhi.

(c) Ultimately, all these colonies have to be linked with piped water, sewerage through pipes, covered storm water drains and individual electric connections. A decision is required about the norms on which water supply per family should be provided. Standard of 50 gallons per day per capita in general colonies cannot be adopted here. So, if it is reduced to 20 gallons per day per capita for water and 16 gallons per day per capita for sewage would be adequate.

(d) In resettlement colonies up to the 1980s minimum width of road was 5 m and it is adequate. These roads were provided to give access to back-to-back plot of 3m × 7m size in rows. Now, there is a strong feeling not to provide any plots back-to-back in rows but on a Group basis by grouping 6, 7 and 8 plots around a common private courtyard 7 sq.m. that each to be used by all the families, meaning thereby, the system of provision of access roads to individual plots has been eliminated and the approach to individual units is through clustered common courtyards.

(e) The cost of development of the plot is increasing day by day. The cost of development per plot including the cost of land was Rs. 800 in the early 1960s when the scheme was initiated. It increased to Rs. 1,250 in 1972 and again increased at Rs. 1,860 as per the Government of India Order dated September 5, 1980.
The present cost of development of a plot of 18 sq.m. including the cost of land and without any subsidy in physical infrastructure at peripheral and internal level would be more than Rs. 25,000.

(f) Maintenance of services in these colonies has become a gigantic problem. Twelve lakh people, i.e. 13 per cent of Delhi's population, live in these colonies, without paying single penny as property tax. In addition a lot of public funds have to be spends to maintain services in these colonies.

(g) All the land acquired for the scheme used or to be used should be the property of the Department. Expenditures and receipts for the development and construction of urban spaces should be debited and credited in the account of the Scheme. There should be a clear-cut policy that profits from commercial development as part of the JJR Scheme would be credited to be account of the Scheme and surpluses would be used as subsidies for the system.

(h) A material bank for the supply of cheap and good building material should be created in all the major colonies for the benefits of the needy people.

(i) DDA should act as a co-ordinator to all the authorities who are reasonable for the maintenance of the services, plying of buses, supply of milk and other services like telephone booths, etc.

(xi) Conversion of Licence Fee System to Hire/Purchase System in Resettlement Colonies

Thinking has been going on since the 1980s and decisions have been taken by the Government of India *vide* their letter No. 14014/4(203)73/DD IIB-Vol.II dated September 4-5, 1980s and letter No. K/19011/2/78/DD IIB (Vol. II) dated December 18, 1982, but, so far, implementation has not been carried over. So far, more than

240,000 families are living in various resettlement colonies mostly in structures on 21 sq.m. plots and some on 67 sq.m. plots; 50-60 per cent are original allottees, 35 to 40 per cent unauthorized occupants and the balance tress-passers. Premium to be charged from these three categories should be different due to their status and method to take over plots from DDA or otherwise. Amounts to be charged from these three categories should be as under :

From the original allottees : As per the order of the Government of March 15, 1977, an amount of Rs. 1860 should have been charged. On this, an additional amount of Rs. 4470 is being spent for provision of additional facilities (individual water, sewer and power).

Like this, the total cost per plot is Rs. 1860 + Rs, 4,470 = Rs. 6,330. There is a decision to charge only two-thirds of this cost, i.e. Rs. 6,330 × 66.7% = Rs. 4,420 per plot.

The approved policy to charge interest at 5% per annum on Rs. 1,250 and ground rent at 2.5% on the premium Rs. 1,250 for 10 years. This works out to Rs. 940. In addition to this Rs. 300 per plot is deficiency charges.

The total amount comes to Rs. 4,220 + Rs. 940 + Rs. 300 = Rs. 5,460 or say Rs. 5,500.

It is stated that the licence fee paid up to March 15,1977, would be adjusted in the premium and to this extent rebate will be given. It is also proposed to give a further rebate of Rs. 500 per plot if lump sum payment is made.

In brief, the system of payment for the original allottee would be as under :

- If payment is made in lump sum, then Rs. 5,000 per plot (i.e. with a rebate of Rs. 500 per plot).
- Those who do not pay in lump sum may be given the option to pay in equated quarterly instalments with different rates of interest based on the period opted for payment as under :

Period of Instalment	*Rate of Interest*	*Mode of Payment*
0 - 5 Years	5%	Quarterly
6 - 10 Years	7%	"
11 - 15 Years	9%	"

Incentive for less interest has been allowed in accordance with the period of payment in order to boost the recovery within a short time.

For unauthorized occupants, the Government has decided to charge an amount of Rs. 9000 per plot from unauthorized occupants with a deficiency charge of Rs. 500 per plot. The revised amount for this category would be as under:

(a) If payment is made in lump sum then Rs. 8,500 per plot (i.e. with rebate of Rs. 500).
(b) If payment is made in 3 annual instalments then break-up of Rs. 10,000 would be Rs. 3,300 per annum for the first two instalments and Rs. 3,400 for the third instalment.
(c) If payment is made in 5 annual instalments then the payment would be made at the rate of Rs. 2,200 per year to make a total amount of Rs. 11,000.

After the decision regarding grant of lease-hold rights and its terms is announced, the beneficiaries should be allowed to apply for the same within a prescribed period. All such allottees and unauthorized occupants who do not apply for lease-hold rights in time shall be charged a licence fee of Rs. 150 per month and those who do not pay the prescribed instalments in time shall be charged interest for belated payment at the rate applicable in DDA.

(d) For tress-passers it is proposed to charge the market rate which varies form colony to colony.

Planning and Development

This is a large subject and has not been dealt with here. A few brief of paras are requested here.

Dispersal

A sound Urban Land Policy should have dispersal of land by the public authority to government departments, cooperatives and the private sector on some reasonable basis with rules and regulations. Land should be dispersed after its full development, and if not, then at least semi-developed land should be dispersed except in specific cases of bulk allotment to Government bodies like PWD, LIC, or State Housing Boards. Even in such cases, it should be ensured that development conforms to the prescribed norms, zoning regulations, standard and period.

Calculation of Actual Price

Calculation of the actual price of a developed land should be done after taking the following components into consideration:

(i) Cost of acquisition of land and cost of rehabilitation of affected parties and alternative allotment.
(ii) Cost of internal infrastructure.
(iii) Cost of internal roads.
(iv) Cost of development of parks, playgrounds and open spaces—sites for various public facilities at neighbourhood level ;
(v) 25 per cent of the cost of trunk infrastructure.
(vi) 25 per cent of the cost of major roads except National Highways, State Highways and district roads.
(vii) 20 per cent of the cost of public and semi-public buildings.
(viii) 20 per cent of the cost of beautification of the town.

Rational Distribution of Price

There should be a rational distribution of price of land for different uses.

An example has been quoted here. Assuming that the cost of land on the basis of the formula, X is the percentage of cost of land for different uses can be as under. But the value of X (developed land) would vary from location to location, depending upon the status of the town, etc.

— For EWS, 50 per cent of X;
— For LIG, 75 per cent of X;
— For MIG X;
— For HIG 2X;
— For district parks, playgrounds and open spaces, 5 per cent of X;
— Sites for educational and health facilities, 10 per cent of X;

— Sites for commercial use, 10X;
— For shifting of non-conforming industrial units, 76 per cent of X;
— For new industries 4X;
— For informal sector (commercial and industrial use) X.

A Case Study Work-out Economics of a Neighbourhood

To work out economics of a neighbourhood of 15,000 population different activities has been divided into following three heads:

(i) Activities concerning the subsidized sector.
(ii) Activities concerning the no-profit-no-loss sector.
(iii) Activities concerning the profitable sector.

The entire system has been worked out in such a way that the Government finances are not strained too much. A neighbourhood having 15,000 population with all the essential physical and social infrastructure, roads and buildings for community facilities and houses for different income groups would cost Rs. 2,982 million with a break-up of:

— Rs. 148.59 million in the subsidized sector.
— Rs. 63.3 million in the no-profit-no-loss sector.
— Rs. 78.26 million in the profitable sector.

The financial position would be as under :

	(In Rs. millions)
— Loss for subsidized sector	Rs. 28.2
— Profit from profitable sector	Rs. 22.5
— Income from ground rent per year	Rs. 1.5

Part of the loss can be covered by auctioning some of the residential plots for high-income group. This entire exercise has been given in *Planning and Development of Towns*—R.K. Gupta.

Control of Landuse

The control of landuse can be exercised through :

1. Enforcement of the Development Act.
2. Zoning regulation and landuse planning.
3. Direct intervention, i.e. by creating land banks, development of land, and its disposal/dispersal.
4. Legal controls, e.g. compulsory registration, changes in administrative boundaries, development and building permits.
5. Fiscal controls, e.g. property taxes, tax penalties, and tax incentives.

Recapturing Plus Values of Land

The unearned values, resulting from changes in the use of land, change in the ownership of land or change in the intensity must be subject to an appropriate recapture by public bodies. This can be done in the following ways:

1. Levy of appropriate taxes, e.g. capital gains, land taxes, betterment charges, development charges and particularly taxes on unused or underutilized land.
2. Periodic and frequent assessment of land values in and around cities and determination of the rise in such values after every; five years, and then to collect a part of this increased value as incremental land tax after every five years.
3. Instituting development fee, permit fee or building fee on all developments.
4. Leasing out the land in such a way that part of the future incremental value which is not due to the efforts of the users is kept by the community, e.g. public authority, at the time of transfer of land or change of use or change in intensity.

Land Management

The entire land should be disposed of only on lease-hold basis, except small holdings up to 30 sq.m.

The Government or the Development Authority should have the power to resume the land for the implementation of the Master Plan and also to receive part of the unearned income.

The land should be allotted on perpetual lease, but the term of lease should provide for revision of amount of ground rent at periodic intervals which should be long enough to enable the lessee to may proper use of the land so allotted. A period of 30 to 40 years is appropriate for this.

No sale or transfer of lease-hold right should be permissible during the first five years, so that land is not taken by those who do not require it for immediate use. After five years, sales and transfers may be permitted on the basis that a substantial part of the unearned income comes to the government or to the Development Authority, to further use it for the purpose of development or any similar activity.

Resumption of land should be provided in the case of misuse of land, or breach of any of the terms of lease conditions.

Calculation of ground rent in Delhi is on the basis of 2.5 per cent of the amount of premium but now it is being considered as excessive and unreasonable. It would be only reasonable to have an upper limit of the ground rent also, otherwise a plot of and of 200 sq.m. for residential use sold at a rate of Rs. 5,000 per sq.m. would carry a ground rent at the rate of Rs. 125 per sq.m. per annum, which seems to be rather on a much higher side. The upper limit can be 1 per cent of the actual price of land of that time when the plot was auctioned/disposed of.

Calculation of reserve price at the time of auction should be based on the following factors:

(i) Actual cost of the plot as defined in this chapter.
(ii) Prescribed use of the land.
(iii) FAR.
(iv) Relative importance of the locality/town or status of the area.
(v) Any special advantage, e.g. close to a landscape feature, water course, lake, etc.
(vi) Cost of management of disposal of the system.

Maintenance of Colonies

Problems of maintenance of land start with inhabit any of a colony and its development. The system of maintenance of a colony depends. On the municipality, its structure and resources available with it. Maintenance of a colony includes maintenance of parks, playgrounds, open spaces, scavenging of roads/service roads, drains, collection and disposal of garbage, to maintenance of continuous supply of water, power and disposal of sewage etc. To give an idea about the cost of maintenances, the DDA in 1985 was incurring an expenditure of Rs. 250 million per annum or Rs. 100 per plot per month for the maintenance of only resettlement colonies. Maintenance of a colony irrespective of land use, size, status should remain with the MCD.

To bear the cost of maintenance, municipalities are empowered to collect property tax, scavenging tax, fire tax and general taxes. Rates of taxes for different uses are different. Since small municipalities have meagre resources, they are not capable of spending money for the maintenance of different types of services under their jurisdiction. In such cases, the Government has to help financially.

20

Urban Land Policies in India
In Retrospect and Prospect

K. ADINARAYANA REDDY

Introduction

Owing to the rapid pace of urbanisation and industrialisation, towns and cities have been growing at a phenomenal rate, in a rather haphazard manner in recent decades. This unprecedented expansion of urban population is causing an exceptionally rapid increase in the demand for urban land. To worsen the situation, land values in our cities have sky rocketted to dizzy heights in recent times. Apart from a fairly long tradition of planned urban development and land-use controls a number of significant policy initiatives have been taken in this direction during the past three decades or so. Yet, the fact that accessibility of serviced land is getting more and more problematic for large proportion of urban population, particularly in larger cities, shows that, all is not well with our land policies and programmes. The purpose of this chapter is to review the policies and landuse control measures taken to deal with urban land problem and to set out the issues germane to more effective policy measures in this field.

Urbanisation—Its Impact on Urban Land

To the extent, process of urbanisation and the urban land market operations are interrelated. A reference to the trends and dynamics of urban growth is necessary to put the urban land issues in perspective.

In 1901, about 25.9 million persons (10% of total population) of the country lived in urban areas. Their number went up to 159.7

million (23.3% of total population) by 1981. This means during a period of eighty years as many as 133.8 million persons were added to the urban areas (i.e. 6.46% annual growth rate). According to an estimate by the Registrar General of India, urban population is likely to reach the figure of 230 millions (27.5%) by 1991 and 326 millions (33.1%) by 2001 A.D.

Given the unprecedented growth of urban population, it should not be difficult to estimate the extraordinary demands it generates for urban land in terms of infrastructure, shelter, and other facilities. However, in the absence of any systematic monitoring of the developments in this respect, except for certain impressionistic details, and some pragmentary data on landuse, very little is known, as to how these demands are being met. Practically all the cities are beset with inadequate supply of serviced land to a greater or lesser extent, speculative holding of urban land having further limited its supply. Given the existing structure of urban incomes and patterns of land ownership, the urban land market at best caters for the needs of upper and middle income groups. The low income urban majority is worst affected in the process; for not only their shelter needs, but their sources of livelihood also stand jeopardised for want of access and security of land tenure. Most of the cities still carry the colonial legacy of wasteful use of scarce land resources. In most of the cities land is misused, underused and carelessly used; large private gardens and clibs with extensive open grounds limit the amount of living space in favour of exclusive upper income landuses (Harris,1978).

According to a recent analysis of landuse and density patterns undertaken by TCPO in 95 cities in the population range of 1,00,000 and above, vacant land constituted 11-25 per cent of the developed area and that as much as 37-48 per cent of the total area was lying underdeveloped or used for agricultural purposes (TCPO, 1979). Besides, it seems relevant to mention that there are instances of large extent of valuable land under public ownership in various cities which if properly utilised would not only ease the land problem, but also bring in tax revenue, solely needed by the local bodies. Further, existence of high density slums and squatter settlements in the midst of substantial chunks of vacant land gives the impression that the real problem is not the shortage of land, but its efficient and equitable use. TCPO has also attempted to work out estimates for future land requirements, which have been put at 4.21 million and 5.67 million hectares in 1991 and 2001 respectively (TCPO, 1983). This broadly implies that about 1.27 million hectares of land would be additionally required for urban use during 1971-2001. How to augment the additional land resources and in what manner the land within the urban limits will be planned and developed will remain to be important task in land management.

Meaning of an Urban Land Policy

According to Bauer and Gergen (1968) the term 'policy' is used to describe "those parameter-shaping acts "and "strategic moves" that direct an organisation critical resources towards perceived opportunities in a changing environment. According to Lichfield (1978), it is part of development policy employed in the implementation of urban and regional plans which are directly related to the role of urban land. Therefore, an urban land policy is a set of parameter shaping measures designed to give direction, coherence and continuity regarding the role of land in the implementation of urban and regional development plans. In general, the objective of an urban land policy is to facilitate an equitable distribution of access to land and an efficient land utilisation, or as Lichfield puts it, "...to ensure that land needed for urban and regional development is supplied in need quantities, appropriate prices, having regard to efficiency and equity in the allocation of resources" (Lichfield, 1978).

In some countries, urban land policy is systematically formulated and documented by a specially created commission. But many developing countries, including India, urban land policies are mainly in the form of successive legislative enactments aimed at solving specific problems as they have arisen. As such, there is a possibility that new laws are passed without regard to past rules, and this may result in confusion and conflict in urban land policy.

A Review of Contemporary Urban Land Policy

Public authorities in India have for long, exercised powers to intervene in the urban land market for execution of public works. However, it was only in early sixties that some important initiatives were taken with respect to urban land problem. Two major developments merit attention in this context: (1) Initiation of a bold policy experiment in the form of scheme for large scale land acquisition, development and disposal in Delhi as a part of the first master plan for Delhi (1961-81), and (2) Appointment of a high level urban land policy committee by Government of India in 1963. The Committee in its report submitted in 1964 underlinded the need for a long-term land policy considered largescale land acquisition, development and disposal as one of its important prerequisites. The objectives laid down for the policy include :

1. Optimum social use of urban land,
2. Making land available in adequate quantity at the right time and for reasonable prices both to public agencies and individuals,
3. Encouraging cooperative community effort and bonafide individual builders, and
4. Preventing 'concentration' of land ownership in a few hands and safegaurding the interests of the poor sections of urban population.

The committee have also recommended, that the state governments should initiate action on implementation of different measures. Although there is no definite information to indicate as to what the various measures have been implemented and found useful in solving the problems of urban land in various states, the general impression is that, except in few situations like Delhi, the implementation of these measures do not appear to have made any significant impact on the problem. This is sufficiently evident from the conditions of living in most of the cities and towns. Much of the thinking at national level as embodied in the successive five year plans, is in the line with the recommendations of the aforesaid committee. The three dominant concerns of the plans in this regard have been, excessive increase in urban land prices, concectration of land ownership and use of land as a resource for urban development. The instrument of public acquisition of land has been one of the most important measures which is applied to solve many serious problems like speculation and unearned increments and indiscriminate conversion of agricultural land. The legal measure for effectuating acquisition procedure is provided in the Land Acquisition Act, 1894. This act provides for payment of compensation based on market value of land as on the date of preliminary notification plus a solatium of

15 per cent. But up to date the performance of different development authorities is unsatisfactory.

The actual experience of public land acquisition over the past several years reveals that the entire process of acquisition takes as much as 10-15 years resulting in freezing of land for long periods of time and excessive delay in execution of development projects (Ribeiro,1986). The basis of compensation as provided in the Act has been a subject of persistent debate in recent years and yet definite views seems to emerge. The recent amendment of the Act in 1984, has besides streamlining the acquisition procedure, raised the rate of solatium from 15 per cent to 30 per cent. The effects of these changes in the Act have yet to be assessed.

The most significant initiative for urban land reform came through the Central Urban Land (Ceiling & Regulation) Act, 1976, which sought to curb land speculation and bring equitable distribution of land in urban agglomerations. The main objectives of this Act are, "imposing a ceiling on vaccant urban land, acquiring land in excess of ceiling limit, regulating building on the land so as to prevent land speculation and profiteering and distributing land equally to serve the common good". To say the least, its implementation has, apart from other market distortions restricting the supply of land, been observed more in giving exemptions than in gaining surplus land above the prescribed ceiling limits in various categories of cities. According to a critic "It is unfortunate, but true that the Urban Land (Ceiling & Regulation) Act has not only been a failure in the sense that the objectives set by the policy makers, could have not been achieved but also (and worse) that the result has been just the opposite of what was envisaged. The Act was intended to curb speculation and price rise in land, both have touched new heights in the post Act era" (Wadhwa, 1983).

Land-use Controls

Land-use control is very much necessary for efficient urban land policy, but they are neither efficient nor equitable in their operation. A World Bank paper while criticising the land-use controls commented "In the developing countries, land-use regulation is almost complete failure as the policy is intended to implement a land-use plan to meet current needs for land for all income groups at a reasonable price, to permit orderly change and to increase property tax revenue. It fails because of poor and inefficient planning, and because regulations are made without regarding how the land is already being used" (Courtney, 1978). Indian planning laws are loosely based on the English planning legislation. The system is too rigid and cumbersome, lacks public understanding or support and the various bodies within the city are unable to coordinate their activities (McAuslan, 1985).

Zoning and sub-division regulations and building bye-laws are another type of negative controls. A systematic evaluation of the impact of zoning and sub-division regulations, which constitute the principal tool of implementing such plans, is yet to be made. They have the effect of harassing the squtterer and self-builder, of imposing unrealistic standards on such people and turning their efforts to house themselves into criminal activities. Such regulations are complex and full of technical terms. To get official approval to build or extend a house, one must fill in long and complicated forms, often in triplicate, and submit plans drawn to a particular scale. A recent report from the Planning Commission's Taskforce on "Housing and Urban Development" has been very critical of Indian Urban planning and land development policies damning them as "narrow, unrealistic, devoid of concern for the urban poor, misusing the coercive powers of the state for misguided development, concentrating of monopoly powers of development in a single public authority, lack of co-ordination in sectoral development, and devoid of people's participation at all stages of development process".(Dutta, 1983).

Land Taxation and Other Measures

The urban real property is subject to a wide range of central, state and local taxes. The underlying objective of the tax levies is generally to raise the revenue, rather than their use as a tool for efficient use of land resources.

Property tax is by far the most important tax imposition on the urban real estate property. More than 50 per cent of the revenue of local bodies in India are derived from property taxes. The vacant land is not taxed in most of the cities, except in few cases like Bangalore, Calcutta, Delhi, Bombay and Ahmedabad. However, even in such cases because of low rates and laxity in administering the tax, it has not proved effective in either inducing more efficient use of land or in checking land speculation.

Besides property tax, capital gains tax merits a mention because of its bearing on the crucial question of mopping up the unearned increase in land values. Under this tax, capital gains arising out of land held for less than three years is added to ordinary income and on land held for a longer period of the gain is taxed as ordinary income. Unrealised capital are not taxed due to the validation difficulties. However, the problem in administering capital gains tax on land values is the under reporting of sale transactions. The above rather rudimentary discussion of measures concerning urban land-use and development would be incomplete without a reference to the sites and services and slum improvement programmes undertaken in recent years to improve the accessibility of the poor to land and shelter and the readjustment schemes carried out in certain states. Site and service schemes are envisaged as a part of EWS housing and apart from the funds mobilised by HUDCO, allocations are made in the national plans.

The foregoing analysis, though sketchy in some respects, bring out that, the policy initiatives and measures taken so far with regard to urban land-use, generally represents a set of disjointed efforts without any concious efforts at their coordination, and that these lean heavily on direct public intervention in urban land markets and land-use controls and regulations. These measures have, by and large, failed to cope with increasing demand for serviced land at a price affordable by majority of urban poor. The growth of slums and squatter settlements and proliferation of unauthorised development in all major cities provide the most telling evidence of these. What strategy needs to be adopted to meet the existing deficiencies and prospective increase in urban land requirements. There is as such an imperative need to understand and analyse indepth the economic and spatial processes governing the growth of these and other towns undergoing rapid growth to formulate effective land policy measures.

While there can be hardly any disagreement about the objectives of urban land policy as set out earlier, no single policy instrument can meet the situation adequately. Adequate and timely supply of serviced land is key requirement both to check speculative increase in land prices and to improve its access to the poor. The experience of achieving this through large scale land acquisition, development and disposal as in Delhi, is far from satisfactory and raises serious doubts upon development authorities' capacity for planning, management and disposal of land (Huyek and Kaplan, 1973).

Urban Land Policy : Some New Directions

The following direct and indirect measures will form a framework for the future urban land policy. While the indirect measures are aim at curbing land speculation and increased supply of private develope land, the direct measures are to be concerned with making available increased volumes of developed land through the direct participation.

Indirect Measures

1. Reduction of the degree of uncertainity in the land market through increased planning information by the concerned public authority is the key to check land speculation.
2. Tightening up of the approval process for land development would also reduce uncertainty concerning the future.
3. A well articulated property tax, with regular and timely evaluation would also regulate the land market by bringing in surplus land in the market which it becomes uneconomic to hold it as an income yielding asset.
4. Imposing high tax rates on vacant lands will be a positive measure to control the speculation.
5. Installation of a proper land price information system in urban areas would help in two ways:
   (a) for paying compensation when land is acquired, and
   (b) for assessing various types of direct taxes.
6. Taxation of land profits often called as betterment levy charge should be effectively collected from the beneficiaries of the urban development projects.

Direct Measures

Land Readjustment and Replotting

An alternative to large scale acquisition, development and disposal of urban land through a public agency is land readjustment, involving pooling of land from various owners who receive back a portion of their land in serviced condition, with the balance used for access, community facilities and to be sold to recover the cost of land development. A varient of land readjustment called plot reconstitution has been used in Gujarat, Maharashtra and Tamil Nadu under town planning schemes.

Institutional Rearrangements

In the light of implementation problems of Delhi land policy (Jha, 1983), one could think of alternative institutional approaches such as:

— Separation of land planning and site plotting,
— Controlled privatisation in land development, and
— Exploiting public-private collaboration in land development.

Alternative Sources of Finance

It is possible to consider the alternative financing arrangements for urban land development through

— Land taxation,
— Plan finance, and
— Institutional finance,

such that the interests of the land owners are protected, the land needs of the urban poor are met and the urban land prices are kept in check.

Alternatives in Land Tenure

Assuming the need for public land development to meet the growing needs of urbanisation, one could think of alternatives to the existing lease hold plot allocations to the user with restrictive condition for tenure transfer. Three such alternatives could be considered even under a nominal lease hold system:

— permitting free transfer,
— granting user licence, and
— acquiring future development rights.

Directions of Policy Reform

Ideology of Policy

Although there is some degree of ideological consistency in urban land policy in India in terms of equity, the operational dimensions of such a policy has virtually negated its realisation, both under a public purpose urban land development strategy and through the implementation of the urban land ceiling legislation. In any workable system of urban land policy, it is important to consider all the three of its conceivable goals: (1) equity, (2) efficiency, and (3) revenue along with the degree of trade-off among these in terms of a broad social consensus. It is important to recognise the fact that the politico-economic environment of each country would determine the extent of tolerable tradeoff among competing policy goals.

Policy Design

A proper design of policy is made after considering alternative strategies to achieve the goals and objectives of the policy. In the case of Indian urban land policy it is clear that such an exercise was not done. The policy parameters were declared independently of the operational imperatives, resulting in non-realisation of, and conflicts in urban land policy goals and objectives. We have indicated a set of alternative strategies, so that under each of these options it is possible to estimate the social costs and benefits. It is only after a careful evaluation of such costs and benefits that an optional policy design must be indicated.

Policy Iteration

It is equally important to continually monitor the operation of an urban land policy and evaluate it at periodical intervals, so that the lessons learnt and difficulties encountered could be fed back into reformulation of its goals and objectives. It is only through such an iterative approach to policy making that an urban land policy could be realistic and capable of producing desired results.

Urban Land

A Political Problem

Inadequate and irrelevant laws reflect and legitimise an inadequate and irrelevant urban land policy. But, it by no means follows that relevant, carefully drafted laws will lead to relevant policies. The fact that the interests of powerful land owners and elites, well represented in the state and local bodies is also one of the factors responsible for this situation. The urban elites who drafts the laws, does not want to reduce his own privileges and increase the rights of the poor.

The ultimate question is how we can device an abuse free legal and administrative system to implement a basic human needs strategy in respect of urban land policy. Urban land policy is inevitably a matter of politics. Any alternatives in urban land policy are political and not merely technical, economic or judicial matter. While reports on urban land policies can be useful in drawing attention of policy makers to what is happening elsewhere and the possibilities for reform, nothing will happen without the political will to reform.

Concluding

This chapter attempts to give a review of the urban land policy and the land measures which directly and indirectly control and influence land development in India. At present there are enough control measures in the urban land development process. These are necessary to prevent haphazard land development especially in view of the possible widespread undesirable side-effects of large scale development. What is lacking is policy measures which can stimulate and provide incentives for the types of land development which are in line with government policy and at the same time discourage what is commonly termed "land refrigeration". In this respect Indian urban tax measurements can be substantially improved to play a more effective role. To sum up, the present urban land policy has several pitfalls. Therefore, serious thinking should be given to eliminate deficiencies and pitfalls, which have so far characterised the urban land policy. Based on the experiences so far, a new effective and efficient land policy has to be formulated so that it will have a better prospects for its smooth implementation and for the effectuation of declared objectives.

REFERENCES

Bouer, R.A. and K.J. Green (1968). *The study of policy formulation*. The Free Press. New York.

Courtney, J. (1978). "Urban land-use regulation" in H. Dunkerly and C.M. Whitehead (ed.) *Urban Land Policy : Issues and Opportunities*, World Bank Publication.

Dutta, A. (1983). "Planning of Urban Development : The Basic Policy Issues." *Nagarlok*, Vol.15, No. 4.

Harris, N. (1978). *Economic Development, Cities and Planning : The Case of Bombay*.

Huyek, V. and Kapian, M. (1973). *Guidelines for Establishing and Administering Land Development Agencies in Developing Countries*. USA.

Jha, G. (1983). "Land Nationalisation in Delhi: A Policy Analysis." *Nagarlok*, Vol.15, No. 2.

Lichfield, N. (1978). "What is Land Policy." Working Paper International Centre for Land Policy Studies, London.

McAuslan, P. (1985). *Urban land and shelter for the poor*.

Ribeiro, E.F.N. (1986). "Urban Land Policies and Land Use Control Measures in India: A review." Proc. of National symposium on *Urban Land Policy* held at New Delhi.

TCPO, New Delhi (1979). *Study of urban land-use and density patterns in India*.

TCPO, New Delhi (1983). *Urban land-use and density patterns in India*.

Wadhwa, K. (1983). "An Evaluation of the Urban Land Ceiling Legislation—A Case Study of Ahmedabad." *Nagarlok*, Vol. 15, No. 2.

21

Nature of Urban Land Values in Developed and Developing Countries

ASHOK K. DUTT and G. VENUGOPAL

Nature and Spatial Distribution of Land Value

Many studies of the distribution of land value indicate that the distribution is very uneven within an urban unit. If the distribution of land value is mapped as a three-dimensional statistical surface, one can notice many small points standing out prominently as peaks of high value, and many others as valleys of low value, the intermediate zone being a mixture of high and low values. Homer Hoyt (1960) provides a striking description of distribution of land value in Chicago. He by different maps, explained the presence of a peak value near the CBD and low values near the periphery. However, from many studies conducted in different parts of the world, particularly in the United States, three distinguishing features of distribution have been identified. They are:

1. A peak value area in the Central Business District, the value declining with increasing distance towards the periphery of the city.
2. Higher land value along major thoroughfares and declining away from them.
3. Local peaks of land value in the inter-sections of major traffic routes.[1]

Though these patterns are identified under Western conditions, the same patterns can be distinguishable in non-Western cities also.

However, there are some basic differences in land value gradient and location of land uses in the non-Western cities. A diagrammatic resentation of a land value profile for Madras, India, is provided in Fig. 21.1. In Madras, the land value gradient is more gentle than that of the Western cities. In all levels of land value gradient, in Madras and most other cities of India, a mixture of land use prevails. A study conducted by Pannel on Taiwan reveals similar situations (Pannel, 1973).

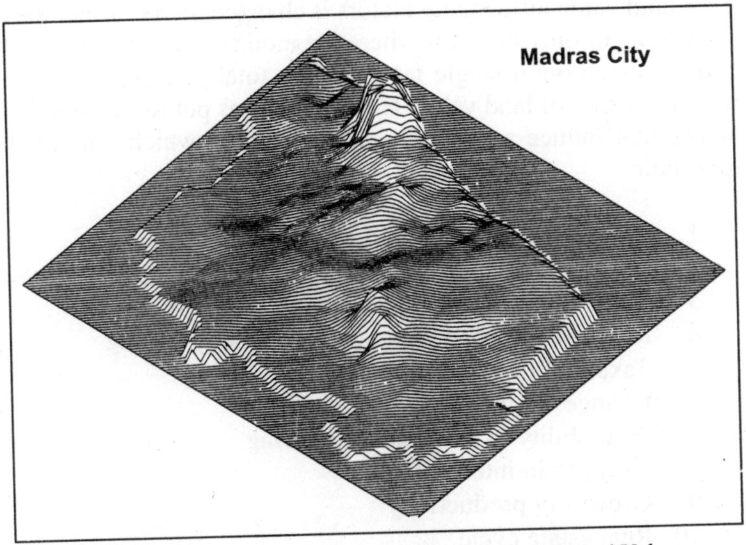

Fig. 21.1: Three Dimensional Statistical Surface of Land Value (A Southwest View)

Various urban geographers and land economists have commented that land value responds inversely to distance from the CBD and from the thoroughfare intersections. McKenzie (1933) has plotted the land value profiles from the central parts of Chicago, Cleveland, Detroit and New York and explained how rapidly land value drops from the high peak point at the commercial centre. Although land value responds inversely to distance, the variation per unit is not the same for all three major land use types, commercial, industrial and residential. Moreover, the change in value for a unit distance is not uniform in all directions. Usually, the direction of growth shows a lower inverse relation than others. The range of value, i.e., the difference between highest and lowest values, for any land use also varies. Normally the highest range occurs in areas devoted to commercial use, because of differential accessibility and locational factors. Land used for industrial and residential purposes can never reach the peak value attained by commercial use.

Urban land values are dynamic in nature. Since land value is the result of many economic and social forces operating in an urban area, it could be changed by modifying anyone of those forces. When one of the land value influencing factors is changed, it may affect the city as a whole, or only that part where the modification took place. It is hard to search out a single factor that is totally responsible for the dynamic nature of land value. Hoyt (1960) has put forth a number of factors that induce a change in land value of which ten are most important:

1. Population growth and distribution
2. Development in transportation and communication networks
3. Modification in transport technology
4. Methods of urban planning, particularly zoning
5. Taxation, its nature and rate
6. Changes in monetary policy
7. Availability of real estate financing
8. Changes in interest rates
9. Growth in productivity
10. Real estate cycle.

Maurice Preston (1963), discussing the factors affecting land value, puts forward a similar set of factors. He has also considered the change in human tastes and fashions that can affect land value. In the modern world, people select places to reside or to locate some commercial establishments, based on perception and image about a particular location. Perception, does to a certain extent, influence land value. These two sets of factors provided by Homer Hoyt and Maurice Preston, are the result of many studies in American cities, and need not have the same validity in cities of the developing countries. The factors that affect land value in such countries depend on the social and economic conditions of those societies. Abrams (1964) has put forth a set of factors that have validity in modifying land value in the developing countries:

1. Concentration of land ownership in the hands of a few.
2. Low tax rate for vacant land.
3. Land ownership—a traditional, prestigeous social status.
4. Lack of alternative investments.
5. Inflation in the economy.
6. The prospect of value appreciation due to State's development programmes.
7. The reluctance of State in compulsary purchase of land.

The concept of urban land value is a complicated one. Some principles that govern land value in the developed West, do apply to non-Western cities. Good examples are the relationship between land value and commercial use and location of lots. Under Indian circumstances, there are some other factors that influence land value, such as the proximity to the temple for the Hindus, nearness to public markets, bus terminals, railway stations and employment centres.

All lands have some monetary value; but some parts of the city command a higher price than others. Desirability, accessibility, and the degree of available amenities account for such differences in value. There is a strong association between land value and location. Location decides the land use; commercial activities need a favourable location for their survival. Ely and Moorehouse (1924) discussing the peculiarities of urban land points out that the first and foremost peculiarity of urban land is the overwhelming importance of location. A distance of one kilometre in agricultural land may not affect land value as adversely as in an urban area; a few hundred metres from the centre of the city produce great differences in value. A similar part is played by the location of the parcel; a corner lot fetches a higher value than one in the middle of the block or street. It has been estimated that in the main streets of Cleveland, a corner lot is worth 72 per cent more than an inside lot. This is true in the case of many Indian cities. A keen competition to occupy a corner lot results in an increase in land value.

Why are some grounds more valuable than others? As is the question, so the answer is also simple; it is desirability. Different economic activities have different requirements. Commerce requires a better location, transportation and accessibility. But residences require a quiet surrounding with better amenities. The differential desirability causes variations in land value.

The Central Business District is but one, albeit the largest, of a number of commercial areas in a city. If land values are higher towards the peak land value intersection (PLVI) of the CBD, they should also rise towards the other commercial areas. Berry (1963) illustrated this idea through the so-called "circus tent" diagram that depicts a major land value peak in the CBD and smaller peaks in outlying retail centers. Such a concept is quite applicable in the post-World War II U.S. cities, when they developed multiple neuclii. Empirical evidences given by Knos (1968) and Downing (1973) also support this contention. It follows that locations of smaller commercial and transportation centres would restructure land values in a city.

In the American urban scene, the automobile has brought about a revolution in the land uses: (a) declining rate of growth of retail business in the CBD; (b) increased concentration of office, management, and finance-related land uses in the CBD; greatly increased pace of suburbanization with high class residences moving outwards from the central parts of the city; and establishment of peripheral and suburban shopping complexes. The revolution has increased traffic congestion and parking problems in the CBD, while many suburban areas, became more accessible because of the newly constructed highways. As a consequence, it might be expected that the inverse relationship between land values and distance from the peak land value intersection (PLVI) would tend to weaken with the passage of time. Yeates (1965) examined this in the Chicago area at decennial intervals from 1910 to 1960. His study substantiated the hypothesis that land values decline with distance from the CBD for the whole city at each time period. His study also noted continuous decline in the strength of the association between the two variables. Further, it indicated that in Chicago there was an upward trend of land values at the periphery. This change of land value in one American city is perhaps not unique and, in the future the trend might become more pronounced. Although the existence of such a trend in American cities is indirectly supported by recent literature on suburbanization (Guest, 1975), no study of urban land values specifically designed to reinforce Yeates' (1965) findings are known to the authors. Similar trends have also been observed in other westernized countries, for example, South Africa (Boaden and Hart, 1975). Dutt and Khan paper (1982) presented 15 years after Yeates (1965) Chicago study, re-examined these relationships and found out the following based on a case study of a U.S. city, Akron, Ohio.

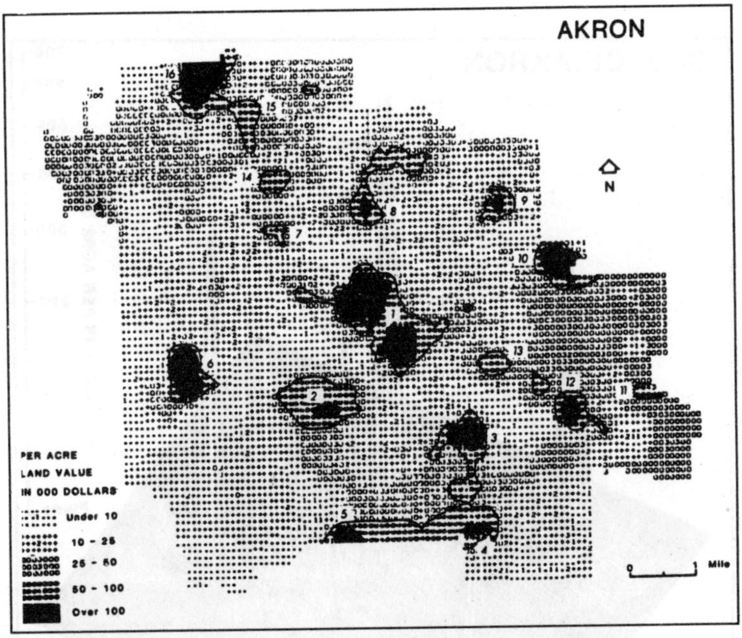

Fig. 21.2: Distribution of Land Value 1977

1. The spatial distribution of land values in Akron is quite irregular (Fig. 21.2). Although the maximum values are still located in the CBD, a number of other high value peaks occur in the city. These peaks correspond with the intersections of major business thoroughfares and the locations of large shopping centres (Fig. 21.3).
2. An inverse relationship was found between land value and distance from the PLVI in the CBD, but the strength of the relationship is statistically insignificant. Thus, a progressively declining and wakened relationship, found by Yeates in Chicago of 1960, seems to have matured in Akron by 1977 to a stage where statistical significance had disappeared. In the future, this relationship is expected to weaken even further.
3. The inverse relationship between distance and commercial land value is relatively stronger compared to other relationships, but the absence of a strong correlation reflects the influence of peripheral and suburban shopping complexes.

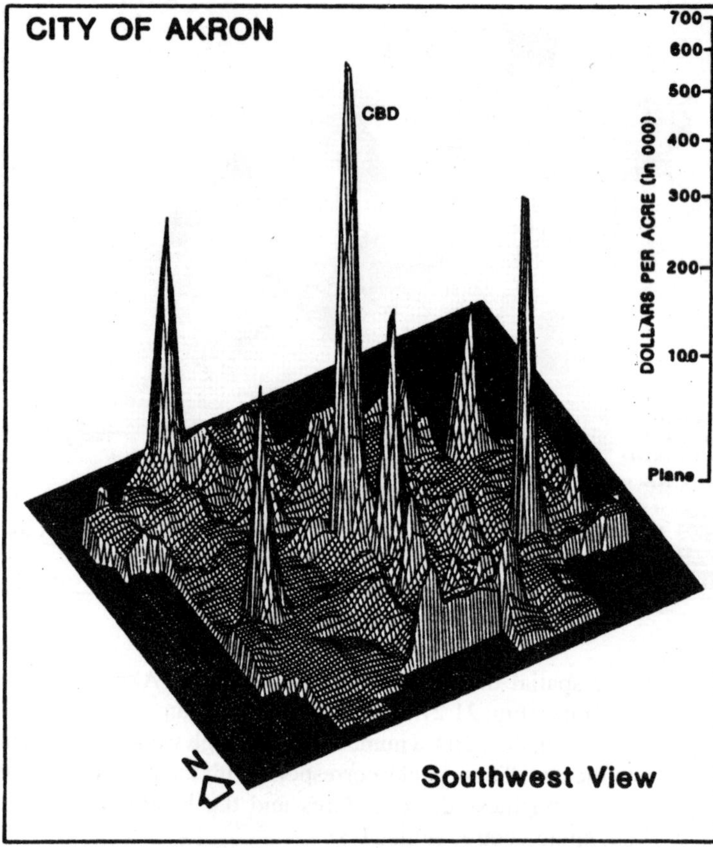

Fig. 21.3: Land Value Surface

4. Residential land values gradually increase away from the city centre. Higher residential land values near the periphery of Akron, an industrial city with a stagnant downtown are indicative of what has happened in many American cities. The effects of suburbanization and modern shopping complexes located in the outskirts of the city are reflected in the positive association between residential land value and distance from the CBD. Moreover, these two factors seem

to have contributed heavily to the development of a pronounced multi-peaked surface of land values in contemporary American cities.

5. Among the selected set of independent variables, value of buildings and improvements is the most important determinant of land value in Akron. Since this variable is an indicator of the intensity of land use, this finding is not surprising.
6. An expected inverse relationship between lot size and distance was discovered, but lot size itself was not an important determinant of land value in Akron.

Marked regional/sectoral differences in the pattern of land value were observed in Akron. This reflects the differential growth pattern of the city, and the regional/sectoral variations in land use characteristics.

Dutt and Khan study demonstrates a very weak inverse relationship between land value and distance from the PLVI in the CBD. The regression results also suggest that physical distance, even though a common surrogate for accessibility, is no longer a strong predictor of urban land value. The multiple regression model used in this study, however, did not prove satisfactory in eliciting the major determinants of land value in the city of Akron. Inclusion of more appropriate variables and the use of "dummy" and interaction variables in corjunction with the sectors or zones of the city would probably make the regression model more useful. Nonetheless, the statistical insignificance of the distance/land value relationship illustrates that the American city, as exemplified by Akron, may have entered a phase in history characterized by multiple peaks of land value and higher values for residential uses in the periphery.

Spatial Distribution of Land Value in Madras

The spatial distribution of land value in Madras can be understood with the help of a land value map and a three dimensional statistical surface provided in Figures 21.1 and 21.4. Land value is unevenly distributed in Madras city and conforms to the traditional concept of distance decay, with minor interruptions of local peaks in thoroughfare intersections.

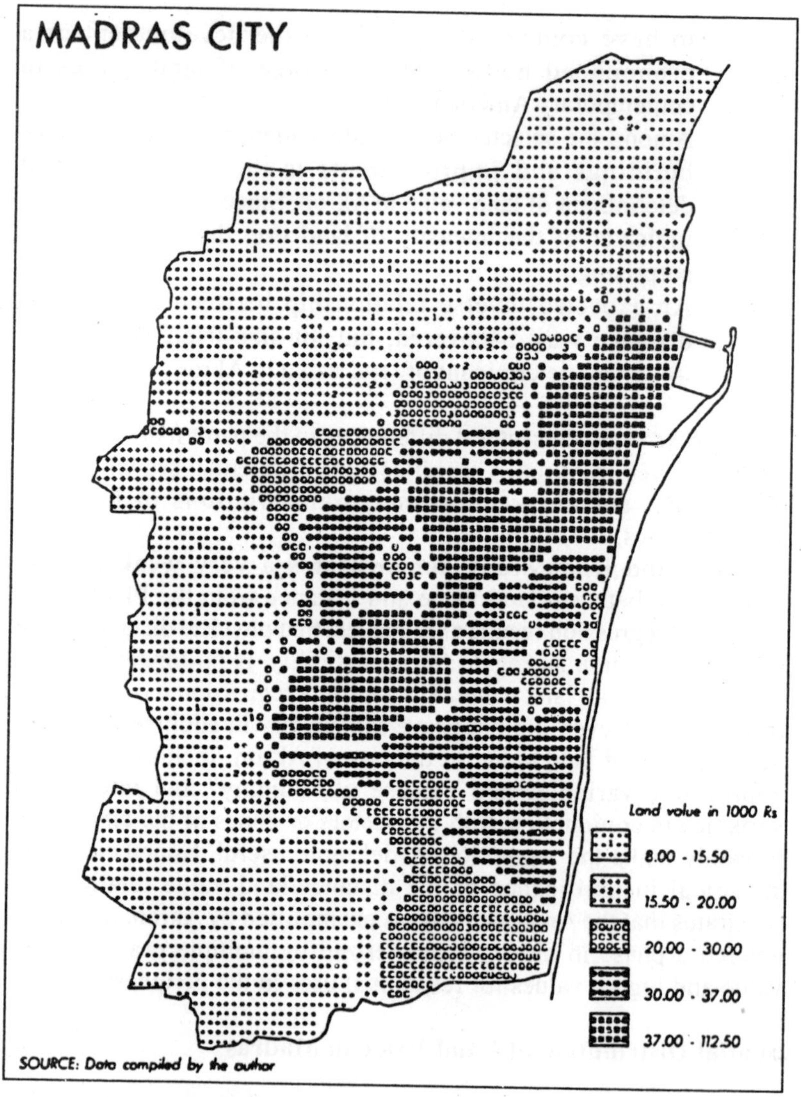

Fig 21.4: Distribution of Land Value, 1971

These figures (Figs. 21.1 and 21.4) show an area of high land value in the CBD and its vicinity, that extends as a ridge towards the southwest. This high land value ridge follows the commercial axis of Madras along Anna Salai. As in any other city, the high land value is due to the concentration of commercial activities, both in the CBD and along the major thoroughfares.

A general profile of land value at different distances from the PVI, shows the nature of declining values towards the periphery (Fig. 21.5). Assuming that the PVI of Madras has a 100 per cent value, within a distance of one kilometre, land value falls to 50 per cent and to 25 per cent in the next one kilometre. Many studies of land value indicate a direct relation between commercial land use and land value. When profiles of land value and commercial area are analyzed together (Fig. 21.5), this relationship is brought out clearly. Apart from the CBD, the neighbourhood business centres and regional business centres also show relatively high land values in Madras. There are two local peaks, one in the vicinity of the Anna Salai-Walajah Road intersection and the other in Thyagaraja Nagar.

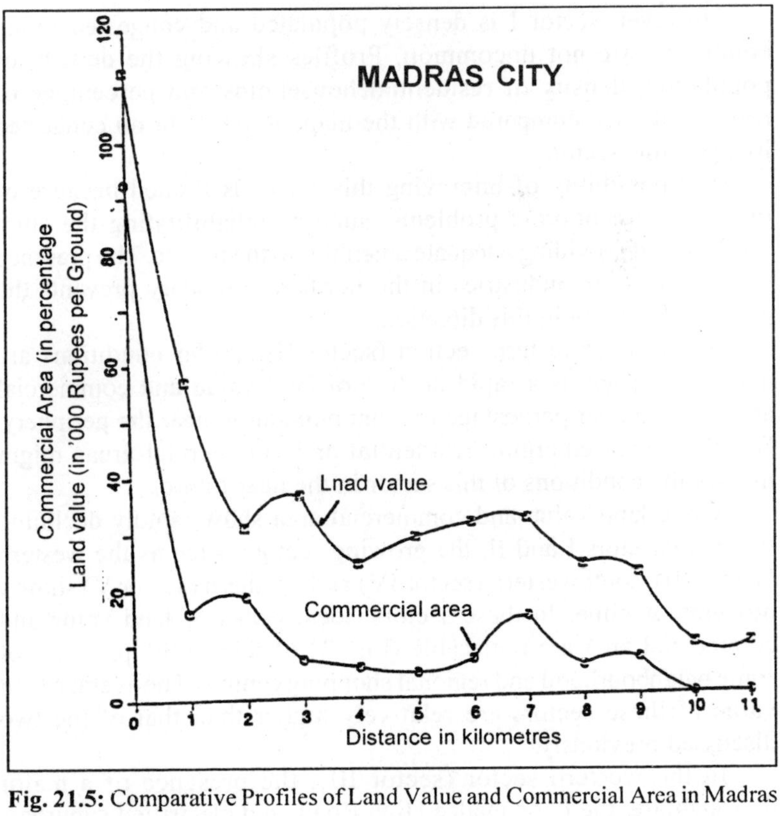

Fig. 21.5: Comparative Profiles of Land Value and Commercial Area in Madras

The land value declines unevenly from the PVI. Values fall sharply towards the north and northwestern sectors, and moderately in others. Such sectoral differences could be attributed to the differential growth of the city, the growing directions being the south and southwest. From the inception of the city, the northern section had been a residential area for low class and caste migrants. The majority of the people of this section (sector I) have been classified as slum dwellers; the area officially classified as slum is also high compared to the other sectors. The average income of these slum dwellers is not high, since a majority of them are not well qualified and are engaged in low paying jobs. No major commercial centres can thrive in such low purchasing power areas. Moreover, the presence of the CBD close by inhibited the development of large commercial establishments.

However, sector I is densely populated and congested living conditions are not uncommon. Profiles showing the density of population, density of residential households and percentage of residential area, compared with the maps throw light on congested living in this sector.

The possibility of improving this sector is limited because of many socio-economic problems, such as rehabilitating the slum dwellers and providing adequate amenities to the people. The presence of many noxious industries in the northern boundary prevents the growth of the city in this direction.

In the northwestern section (sector II) similar conditions are noticeable, such as a rapid decline of land value and commercial area and a higher percentage of slum population near the periphery. But the newly emerging residential and commercial areas might modify the conditions of this sector in the near future.

While land value and commercial area show rapidly declining trends in sectors I and II, the growing sectors, such as the western (sector III), southwestern (sector IV) and southern (sector V) show a moderate decline. In these sectors, local peaks of land value and commercial area are noticeable (Fig. 21.6) due to the presence of some neighbourhood and regional shopping centres. The average land value of these sectors are relatively higher than that of the two discussed previously.

In the western sector (sector III), the presence of a major thoroughfare, the Poonamalee High Road, and electrified suburban

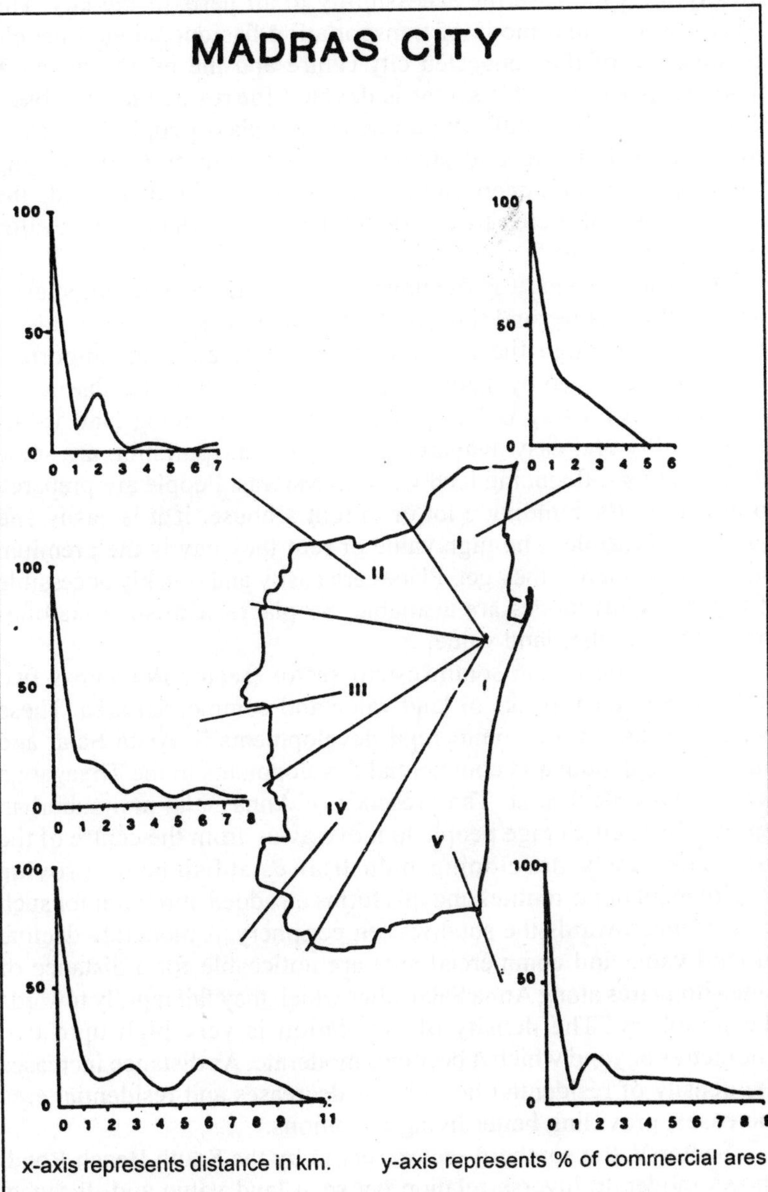

Fig. 21.6: Profiles of Commercial Area by Sectors

railway lines increase the accessibility to all parts of the city. The existence of a dual mode of transportation has encouraged people to move out of the congested city centre and the nearby areas. A major proportion of this sector is devoted for residential purposes, especially for the middle and upper middle class people. However, low income housing and slums are not uncommon. Increasing residential area and decreasing residential households towards the periphery provide better living conditions which influence land value to a certain extent.

The suburban railway running west to a distance of six kilometres turns south, and beyond this point only bus transport is available in this sector. Though the Poonamalee High Road is an important thoroughfare served by many major and minor roads, the absence of the suburban railway is felt in the form of a declining land value. Accessibility and easy availability of mass transportation are some of the factors influencing land value in Madras. People are prepared to pay more for building a lot or to rent a house, if it is easily and quickly accessible. The high value or rent they pay is the premium on the convenience they get. Places are easily and quickly accessible if two transport modes are available. So places with such facilities command a higher land value.

The profile of the southwestern sector (sector IV) shows two well marked local peaks of land value and commercial area. These peaks are due to the commercial developments in Anna Salai and planned residential and commercial developments in the Thyagaraja Nagar-Mambalam area. The presence of Anna Salai and suburban railway lines encourage people to move away from the centre of the city. The newly developing industrial establishments provide employment opportunities and this forms an added attraction for such movements towards the southwesten periphery. A moderate decline in land value and commercial area are noticeable for a distance of nine kilometres along Anna Salai, after which they fall rapidly towards the periphery. The density of population is very high upto two kilometres beyond which it becomes moderate. As distance increases the density of residential households decreases and residential area increases, providing better living conditions.

Sector V, the southern sector, served by the South Beach Road, shows moderate inverse relation between land value and distance. One of the oldest residential areas, Triplicane, with a famous Hindu Shrine, commands a high residential and commercial land value.

Wealthy Hindus prefer to live close to the temple, and this religious perception puts a premium on land for both residential and commercial purposes. Adjacent to Triplicane, along the coast, is an area of relatively low land value that is caused by the presence of many public and semi-public buildings. These areas were not subjected to sale for a long time and the assessors have only included the inflationary factor to the original value. This has caused a low land value region in the centre of a large tract of moderately high land values. Land values rise again towards the south due to residential and commercial need for land. Some better quality residential areas such as Mylapore, Luz and Raja Annamalipuram, along with commercial activities are located here. Moreover, Mylapore with another old temple adds to the attraction of these areas.

Throughout this sector commercial activities are well distributed, especially in the road intersections. Density of population and density of residential households are relatively high in the Triplicane-Chepauk area and moderate towards the periphery. The increasing residential area and decreasing households provide better living conditions. These factors increase land value even towards the periphery. While all other sectors record an average value of Rs. 8,000 to 21,000 per ground near the periphery, this sector records between Rs. 21,000 to 30,000 per ground. The increasing industrial developments in the south and excellent transport facilities have increased the demand for land, and hence, land value.

From the above discussion, the existence of an association between land value and land use, especially commercial, is brought out. The CBD has a higher proportion of land devoted for commercial purposes and so a high land value. Both commercial area and land value decline from the CBD towards the periphery of the city. However, the relationship between land value and land uses has to be statistically substantiated.

Conclusion

Land values evolve as cities grow. Some areas, particularly, those are associated with commercial land uses, attain higher values compared to others. In the case of developed country cities the difference between the land values of the core of the CBD and the periphery is very marked compared to that of the developing countries. Because of multiple nuclei the developed country cities have significant secondary peaks while in the central commercial areas of the developing country cities the peak value dominates and the secondary peaks are minimal.

NOTE

1. There are several studies done on the general behaviour of land values. Good examples are Warren R. Seyfried, "The Centrality of Urban Land Values." *Land Economics*. Vol. XXXIX, No. 3, August 1963, pp. 265-285; Duane S. Knos, "Distribution of Land Values in Topeka, Kansas," in B.J.L. Berry and D.F. Marble, (eds.), *Spatial Analysis: A Reader in Statistical Geography* (New Jersey: Prentice Hall, 1968), pp. 269-289; and Richard M. Hurd, *Principles of City Land Values* (New York: Real Estate Record Association, 1903).

REFERENCES

Abrams, Charles (1964). *Man's Struggle for the Shelter in an Urbanizing World* (Cambridge, Mass.: MIT Press), p. 56.

Berry, B.J.L. (1963) Commercial structure and commercial blight. *Dep. Geogr. Res.* Paper No. 85 University of Chicago, Chicago, IL.

Boaden, B.G. and T. Hart (1975) Spatial and temporal change in residential land values on the Witwatersrand. *South African Geogr. J.* 57:51-59.

Downing, P.B. (1973). Factors affecting commercial land values: An empirical study of Milwaukee, Wisconsin. *Land Econ.* 49:44-56.

Dutt, Ashok K. and Khan, Abdullah, A., "Multi-Peaked Urban Land Values: City of Akron Case," *Ohio Journal of Science.* Vol. 83, No. 3 (1980), pp. 114-119.

Ely, Richard T. and Edward W. Morehouse (1924). *Land Economics* (New York: Macmillan), p. 75.

Guest, A.M. (1975). Population suburbanization in American metropolitan areas, 1940-1970. *Geogr. Analysis* 7:267-83.

Hoyt, Homer (1939). *One Hundred Years of Land Values in Chicago.* (Chicago: University of Chicago Press).

Hoyt, Homer (1960). Dynamic Factors in Land Values (Washington. D.C.: Urban Land Institute, *Technical Bulletin No. 37*).

Knos, D.S. (1968). Distribution of land values in Topeka, Kansas. In: B.J.L. Berry and D.F. Marble (eds.), *Spatial Analysis: A Reader in Statistical Geography.* Prentice Hall, N.J. pp. 269-289.

McKenzie, Roderick D. (1933). *The Metropolitan Community* (New York: McGraw Hill).

Pannel, Clifton W. (1973). *Tai-Chung Tai-Wan: Structure* and *Function* (Chicago: The University of Chicago, Department of Geography, Research Paper No. 144).

Preston, Maurice (1963). "Capital Gains Taxation and the Value of the Land," Peter Hall ed., *Land Value* (London: Sweet and Maxwell).

Yeates, M.H. (1965). Some factors affecting the spatial distribution of Chicago land values. 1910-1960. *Econ. Geogr.* 41:57-70.

22

Some Aspects of Urban Land-Use and Development Planning Strategies in Eldoret, Kenya

CLEOPHAS LADO

Introduction

With urbanization taking place at high rates in developing countries, especially Africa, the question of supply of land for urban developers, and its subsequent development and management, has attracted the attention of policy-makers and scholars, usually in relation to housing, income distribution, planning and environmental issues.

The UN Committee on Housing, Building and Planning noted in the mid-1960s that one of the most important problems created by the process of rapid urban growth taking place in most countries of the world was frustration of the rational urban land use through land misuse and rampant speculation (UN, 1973). The UN Habitat Conference of 1976 pointed out that land was a scarce resource whose use and management should be subject to public surveillance (UN, 1976). Wilcox (1983) pointed out that among the more fundamental limitations on the ability of most cities in Asia to improve their existing urban land-use conditions include its rising costs, the difficulties of acquiring it for public and social objectives, the apparent lack of means to recover a significant portion of the increase in land value generated by the urbanization process, and the impediments to ordering land uses. Similar problems have been highlighted by Armstrong (1986, 1987) and World Bank experts in the late 1970s (Dunkerley, 1983).

The two and half decades of political independence in Kenya have injected little change, if any, in the philosophy, concepts, legislation, personnel and techniques by which the country's major urban centres have been planned (Banyikwa, 1990). Indeed, urban planning continues to be influenced by ideas and methodologies essentially derived from the country's colonial past thus giving rise to different urban land-use zones and patterns. While post-independence adjustments in spatial structures of Kenya's main urban centres may reflect changes in objective conditions and policies, they primarily symptomize a dependence on urban planning framework of the colonial administration as demonstrated by Eldoret, an emerging growth centre in western Kenya (see Fig. 22.1).

Generally, developing countries have experienced three great periods of urban growth, namely: pre-colonial, colonial and post-colonial (Ikhuoria, 1987); and each stage has given rise to a special type of urban land-use pattern.

Prior to the coming of Europeans to Kenya, there were no urban centres in the interior parts of the country. The only townships that existed were along the coastal strip founded on trading activities in the Indian Ocean (Soja, 1968). Except for the coastal region towns (e.g. Mombasa, Malindi, Kilifi), urban development including the growth of the capital city (Nairobi) was associated with the contraction of the Mombasa-Kisumu railway line between 1896 and 1901, and the subsequent occupation of the land by the Europeans.

One of the most notable environmental changes in Kenya has been the phenomenal growth of urban centres. In 1931, there were twenty-four urban centres, which increased to fifty-five in 1952. Over the same period, the proportion of Kenyans living in urban centres of over ten thousand people increased from 6.7 per cent to 10.5 per cent; and by 1963, the proportion had risen to 19.2 per cent (Soja, 1968). In addition to population growth, the other major dynamic component of rapid urban growth in Kenya is the spatial manifestation of intensive economic activities. Kenya's urban area represents a complex association of population concentration, housing/residential, communications and transport development, commercial, industrial and institutional land-use patterns.

This myopia has been acquired through a superficial interpretation of existing urban growth and land-use planning models including zonal, sectoral, multiple nuclei and additive which have provided the basic reference material for this endeavour. Discussions of the theoretical roots underlying the zonal and sectoral land-use models are usually concerned with an urban population differentiation process over space, and predicted particular patterns of residential districts (Banyikwa, 1989).

The spatial organization of Kenya during the colonial period closely followed the Mombasa-Kisumu railway network and its branches. The urban centres which developed away from the railway network were mainly associated with the maintenance of law and order, and these centres were carefully laid out with regard to the preservation of adequate land for Government use and providing for business, leisure and health.

The 1965-1970 Development Plan was the first Government policy document to stress the need for balanced development in Kenya (Kenya, 1965). This was to be achieved through sectoral development undertaken in the rural areas. The plan emphasized that the substantial spatial inequalities existing in terms of levels of incomes and so on should be relatively minimized. The issues facing planners in Kenya since then has been, that priority is given to the less-developed rural areas, including the policy that 'development money' should be invested where it yields the largest increase in net output. This clearly favours the development of areas with abundant natural resources, good arable land, transport and power facilities and where people are receptive to and active in the development process.

The first real statement of the Kenya's spatial policy was provided in the 1970-1974 Development Plan which focused on the decentralization of urban growth to other towns besides Nairobi and Mombasa. The urban centres designated were Kisumu, Kakamega, Eldoret, Nakuru, Thika, Nyeri and Embu. These centres were selected as, and perceived to be, key settlements by ethnic communities within the different regions.

In effect, the 1979-1983 and 1984-1988 Development Plans emphasized the role of urban centres in national development planning using the concept of 'rural-urban balance'. Indeed, rural areas were to be closely-knit to urban markets for supplies of farm inputs and consumer goods, and for outlets of farm produce in the hope they would become an integral part of the monetary economy. The Plans also stressed that a rapid rate of population growth was essential for the realization of the objective that urban centres should be widely dispersed yet closely-linked to the larger urban centres for access to the basic services they cannot supply for themselves.

The justification for the selection of Eldoret, Uasin Gishu District headquarters as a case study is mainly based on the following reasons: First, Eldoret's favourable location with respect to the markets in Western Kenya, Uganda and Sudan, its position as a railway nodal town, its rich and rapidly developing agricultural hinterland and the availability of vital infrastructural facilities, make it an ideal or excellent choice for export-oriented industries. This augurs well for its future socio-economic growth and development. Second, most of the major industrial complexes such as Raymond Woollen Mills, Ken-Knit and Rai Plywood have been established and are expanding their enterprises to meet the increasing demand for their manufactured products in the country. Third, the establishment of the Kerio Valley Development Authority (KVDA) headquarters makes Eldoret the critical integrated regional development and urban planning centre. Fourth, the establishment of new institutions of higher learning such as the Eldoret Polytechnic and the first generically-planned University (Moi University) in Kenya, has attracted more people to the urban centre as the core of innovative activities, pursuing relevance and excellence in the full range of physical and human environmental endeavours. Hence, the town will most likely witness demographic changes with an upsurge of incoming population requiring a relatively wide range of social and economic services, all of which must be planned in order to avoid inevitable problems created by the rapid and unplanned urban growth and development. Finally, Eldoret may be conceivably regarded as the new provincial headquarters of the largest Rift Valley Province in Kenya if it was to be divided into half. Thus, Eldoret has emerged as one of the largest and most important urban centres in Western Kenya and therefore, provides an empirical and mature case study by examining the land-use and urban planning strategies.

After setting this case study within a review of the relevant urban planning literature, the chapter intends to achieve the following objectives: First, a brief historical account on the urban development and land use is provided. Second, the nature and issues of land tenure and ownership and the extension of Eldoret municipal boundaries during the relatively short urban history are elucidated. Third, the land-use and physical development plans and strategies likely to be significant in the present and future establishment and maintenance of a satisfactory or sustainable urban environment in Eldoret are then examined. The chapter generally concludes that there is need for a serious re-examination of the land tenure system and the question of whether the Kenya Government should recapture the "unearned increments" of the benefits of urban growth. With respect to the latter question, land or property taxation is identified as fundamental. In view of an inadequate land use and appropriate physical development planning strategies for Eldoret, the chapter recommends an urgent broad-based, and overall urban growth and development strategy.

An Historical Urban Development in Eldoret

Eldoret is located in the Uasin Gishu District in the highlands west of the Rift Valley Province. These highlight rise sharply from the western edge of rift; and the level of the western highlands drops to an average of 2,200 m, between higher ground on each side. The land then falls gently westwards to the shores of Lake Victoria. Eldoret itself lies at an altitude of 2,084 m above mean sea-level, 48 km north of the Equator, close to the international trunk road linking Nairobi and Kampala (Uganda) and Juba (Sudan). The Uasin Gishu Plateau which rises in the east of Eldoret towards the Elgeyo-Marakwet Escarpment has extensive level or gently-sloping areas. The River Sosiani divides Eldoret into two parts, and flows westwards through the town to the Selby Falls (see Fig. 22.1).

Eldoret developed as a result of the activities of White South African settlers (Boers) who were encouraged through a newspaper advertisement to migrate and settle in Uasin Gishu District. This was done with the hope that the railway line which was by then under construction to Uganda would pay itself once the settlers started to transport their goods. Indeed, the settlement of the Boers in the district was part of the East African Protectorate authorities in encouraging immigration of the settlers/farmers into Kenya in 1909 (Mbwagwa, 1978). This is because the British settlers had surveyed most of the country and therefore, decided to maintain or keep the best farming areas of the 'White Highlands' for themselves and did not want the Boers' intrusion.

Those settlers who responded were on arrival in 1909, shown Uasin Gishu Plateau (referred to by the British as The 'Murram Pit', a marginal land unsuitable for farming) as the area for settlement. Thus, with relatively good and cool weather and constant reliable rainfall which the British did not anticipate or real Boers transformed the 'Marram Pit' into a relatively land.

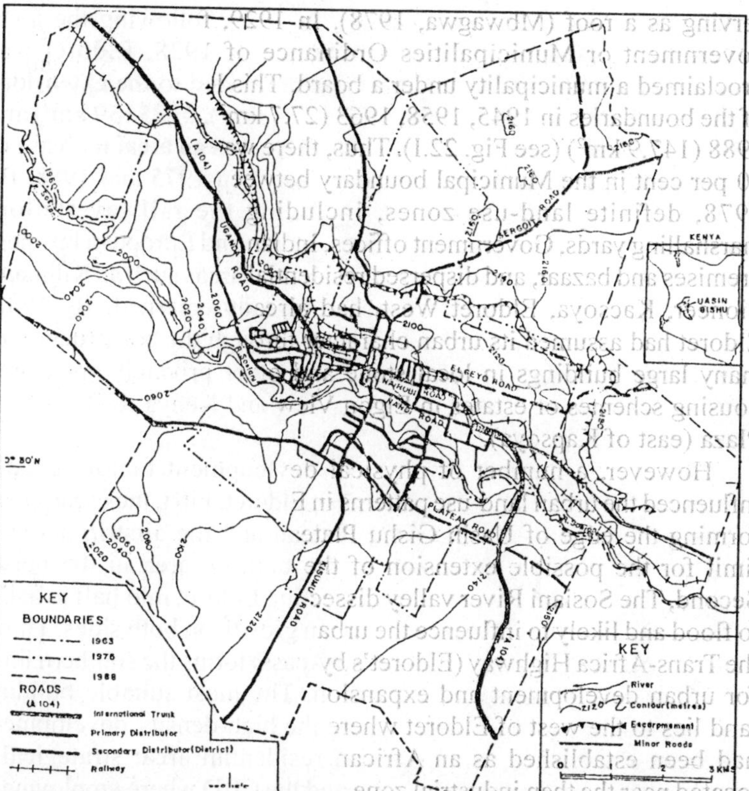

Fig 22.1: Eldoret Municipal Past and Present Boundaries and Road Net work.

Eldoret itself began in 1910 as an isolated post office, establsihed for the convenience of farmers and acted as a service and administrative centre. The original site for the post office was an unattractive stony piece of land known as 'Fram 64' which no farmer wanted. The apparently empty terrain in the area suggested lack of friction in its appropriation. The pre-urban nucleus, Eldoret was a name '*Eldore*' (meaning in Maasai, place of rock) became a railway encampment in 1924 when the first train arrived at after the Kenya-Uganda Railway was completed, thus leading to the emergence of a new era in urban development.

Eldoret was declared a township, with an area of 1,121 ha. in the Official Gazette on November 14, 1912, when it consisted of no more than a row of Government offices and shops, constructed of stone, mud-plastered walls and small pieces of timber fixed onto rafters serving as a roof (Mbwagwa, 1978). In 1929, following the local government or Municipalities Ordinance of 1928, Eldoret was proclaimed a municipality under a board. This led to the extensions of the boundaries in 1945, 1958, 1963 (27.7 km^2), 1975 (59 km^2) and 1988 (147.9 km^2) (see Fig. 22.I). Thus, there was an areal increase of 40 per cent in the Municipal boundary between 1975 and 1988. By 1978, definite land-use zones, including the railway station, marshalling yards, Government offices, Indian and European business premises and bazaar, and dispersed residential areas such as Kilimani, Pioneer, Kacsoya, Eldoret West, had already emerged. By 1988, Eldoret had assumed its urban character through the construction of many large buildings in local stone and other privately sponsored housing schemes or estates in Elgon View and Kenya Re-Insurance Plaza (east of Kapsoya).

However, a number of physical devleopment factors greatly influenced the urban land-use patterns in Eldoret. First, the escarpment forming the edge of Uasin Gishu Plateau and the airstrip act as a limit for the possible extension of the built-up area in the north. Second, The Sosiani River valley dissecting Eldoret into half is liable to flood and likely to influence the urban growth on both sides. Third, the Trans-Africa Highway (Eldoret's by-pass) forms the southern limit for urban development and expansion. The most suitable building land lies to the west of Eldoret where the high-density development had been established as an African residential area; strategically located near the then industrial zone and the CBD where employment opportunities were concentrated (see Figs. 22.2 and 22.3).

The CBD and settlements west of Eldoret were inhabited by the Asians, while the eastern part (where the terrains of land favoured high-cost/low-density housing development) was reserved for the Europeans. These settlements included Kapsoya, Elgon View and Ortillepville estates. Thus, the residential settlement structure of the town clearly reflected the aspirations of the colonial administration with a clear line of segregation, racial or ethnic. In effect, the current settlement pattern maintains the *status quo* of the past colonial urban policy, in that the eastern cart of Eldoret remains as a highcost housing estate where plots are relatively large exceeding 1/3 ha or more, and dominated by the high income-earning population. Medium-cost housing lies in the west. The CBD consists of residential housing units located behind or above shops, bars, hotels and restaurants and other commercial buildings especially along the Uganda, Moi, Oloo

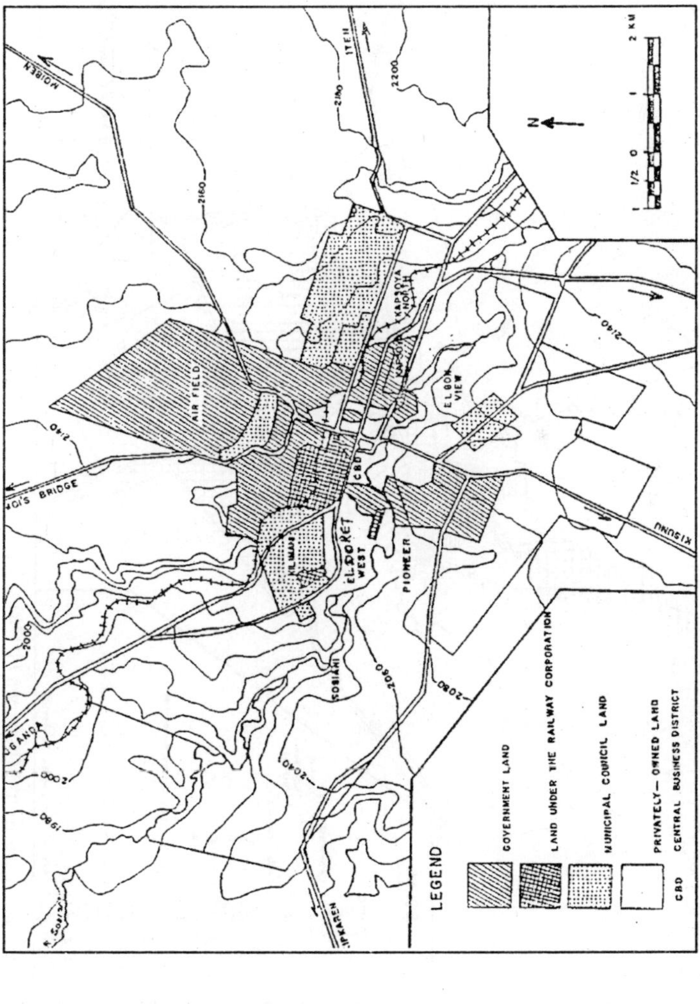

Source: Adopted from Mbwagwa (1978).

Fig. 22.2: The Pattern of Land Settlement in Eldoret

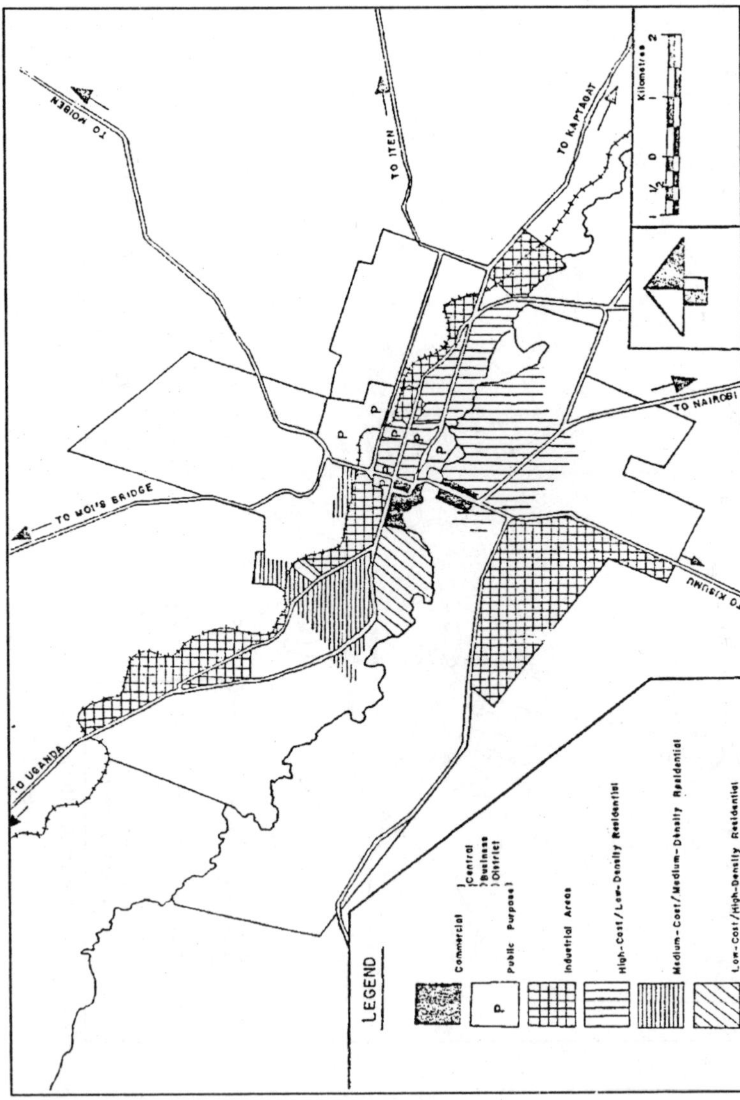

Source: Adopted from Mbwagwa (1978).

Fig. 22.3: Development of Land-use Pattern in Eldoret

and Oginga Odinga Streets and Kenyatta Avenue. These dwellings are generally overcrowded and dominated by medium and low-income people. Low-cost housing is still concentrated on the eastern part of Eldoret.

Planned residential densities for different social groups should, therefore, be understood in terms of colonial creation and perpetuation of class differences in Eldoret. The resulting physical design of residential neighbourhood units should also be seern as a spatial expression of class divisions in the urban economy and society. Indeed, the physical planning recommendations perpetuating social segregation in urban residential structure therefore managed to remain in vogue and escaped unquestioned. Yet in reality, to plan for anything but the most superficial changes in a capitalist society is to risk bankruptcy and to go out of business.

In this context, the people allocated the use of the low-density residential neighbourhoods have access to more spacious land than the rest of the urban-community. The low-density residential neighbourhoods such as Kapsoya, Ortillepville, Elgon View, and Pioneer boast the use of paved roads, lighting on all streets, water supply to each housing unit, electricity supply and linkage to the central sewerage system. The medium-density residential neighbourhoods such as Eldoret West and Upper Hill areas enjoy paved roads, lighting on collector roads, water and power supply to each housing unit and septic tanks.

The high-density residential neighourhoods covering Hururaa, Langas, Kamukunji, Bahati Yetu, Shauri Yako, Mwiyenderi enjoy lighting on collector roads and communal water stands and pit latrines. Beyond these planned residential neighbourhoods, exist bourgeoning squatter settlements both within and at the outskirts of the town, and these do not have any formal social services. Thus, in a country where the doctrine of egalitarianism has been advocated, the continued preservation and further development of neighbourhoods differentiated in terms of area and infrastructure demonstrates a gross departure from equality among citizens, and this is nothing short of urban apartheid (West, 1987).

It is worth noting that early settlers in Eldoret were guided by the 'no-man's land' notions to land acquisition, private rights in land ownership and land speculation (Hill, 1949). The combined effect of these led to large tracts of land being alienated as private property with little regard to future community needs of the budding urban settlement. Houses were occasionally erected on these lands and, as a result, dwellings were scattered over relatively large areas marking the areal extent of vested interests in land ownership. Consequently, land-use patterns developed not through organized physical planning but through chance and choice of the increasing population. In fact, population growth forms an important element of urbanization process in Eldoret. The urban population grew from 7,500 (1945) to 78,943 (1988) with an increase of 9.5 per cent (see Table 22.1). Thus through lack of land-use development control and vehement respect for private rights of land ownership, the morphology of Eldoret resembles wild-west appearance (Mbwagwa, 1978).

Table 22.1: Changes in Areal Extent and Population Growth in Eldoret. 1945-1988

Year	*Area (Km^2)*	*Population*
1945	—	7,500
1958	—	9,900
1963	27.7	14,890
1975	59.0	34,500
1978	65.9	56,443
1988	147.9	78,942

Source: Hallinian and Morgan (1967) and Kenya (1979).

Land Tenure and Ownership in Eldoret Municipality

Land tenure arrangements in Africa have generally deep roots in the traditions of the tribal societies, and have exerted the greatest influence on the economic organization and development of pastoralism and agriculture (Lado, 1989). In fact, the land tenure system embodies those legal and contractual or customary arrangements whereby the local people have access to the productive opportunities on the land (Dunkerley, 1983).

The land tenure system in the Rift Valley Province in general and Uasin Gishu District in particular was mainly based on the Maasai tribal or communal arrangements made during the second half of the 18th century. Indeed, during the pre-colonial era to about 1880, the Maasai land tenure was mainly based on nomadic pastoralism. This involved the priority of access of one clan or family to each part of the land or territory and preservation of some parts of the grazing area (*oloopili*) for use in certain seasons only, particularly in drought, or for use by certain classes of stock such as calves in the special (*oloopololi*) areas. Within such an arrangement, the Maasai pastoralists moved through the whole territory open to them depending upon the availability of grazing (pastures) and water. Such management systems can only support a low level of human and livestock population.

Lacking adequate knowledge on the ecological requirements of the 'traditional' Maasai pastoral system, the British colonial administration and white settlers did not consider their customs of livestock management and were incapable of determining the amount of land required for use of indigenous peoples. Though the so-called 'native land policy' aimed at providing sufficient land for the needs of the peoples, the interpretations of sufficiency were vague and inconsistent (Dilley, 1966) . The Europeans often did not take into consideration the land tenure system and the rationality of Maasai land-use.

Following a major review of the situation in the range areas in Kenya in 1960, the colonial authorities adopted the policy of land registration as part of the development programme for the 'Maasai pastoralists. The objective was to give the land itself a value which could be used as collateral for supporting the financing of development.

The initial land adjudications in Eldoret were made on an individual basis, which in some cases, took little account of the tribal structure, 'traditional' land-use practices or local allegiance of the individual, but rather more of the political or economic stature of the applicant. By 1964, it became very clear that the different patterns of land ownership as outlined below developed as a consequence of land speculation and accumulation, capital penetration into the rural areas, incomes inequality and the influx of immigrants into Eldoret. Thus, the concept of 'title deed' to land evolved and the wealthy people began to amass vast areas of land. Many of the local people whose ancestral lands were expropriated did not have legal claims toland, and hence population pressures in densely populated areas rendered some people landless.

Whereas the land within the 1963 boundary extension was Government land, the 1975 and 1988 boundary changes brought into the jurisdiction of the Municipality substantial private agricultural lands that were previously owned by the White Settlers. Large estates were thus bought by individuals or land purchase co-operatives, having enough capital, and subdivided among shareholders, who in turn erected rental units or turned them over squatter to housing. Indeed, land ownership within the current boundary extensions has been influenced by the Africanization of the former settlers' farms especially after the country's independence in 1963. Because of the rather acute housing shortage as a result of the increasing population in Eldoret, the previous farm areas such as Kemboi, Huruma, Langas, Mwiyenderi and Kamukunji (see Fig. 22.4) are now used almost exclusively for urban housing.

The land tenure in the medium-cost/medium-density housing in the Pioneer Estate is mainly freehold in which the owners have absolute rights, and this is the area that has been so difficult for the Municipal authorities to control because, unlike freehold title, there is no specification for the plot coverage and/or the number of dwelling units permissable per plot. Consequently, a number of terraced houses have been built with up to 75 per cent plot coverage (Mbwagwa, 1978). However, a large proportion of this area has been acquired and planned by the Municipality for medium and high density residential settlements.

The different types of land-ownership within the Municipality are depicted in Table 22.2 and Fig. 22.2. The most significant feature emerging from Table 22.2 is that 51.3 per cent of the total population of Eldoret was housed in privately-owned land. This resulted from the influx of the population into the town, and the situation has not been commensurate with the establishment of public housing particularly for the low-income group of people. In this context, it would, therefore be unreasonable for the Municipal authorities to demolish unplanned housing as this will aggravate the already critical housing shortage. Consideration should be given to the improvement and integration of the existing squatter settlements into the future urban land-use planning. Additionally, there is need to improve the infrastructural facilities in the unplanned housing estates, and to encourage the private and other major corporations to participate in the housing development for the low- and medium-income earners.

Table 22.2: Land Tenure and Ownership in Eldoret Municipality, 1978

Type of Ownership	*Area (in Ha.)*	*Total Population Accommodated*
Government/Municipal land	3,925	19,625
Kenya Railways Corporation land	1,570	7,850
Privately-owned land	5,793	28,968
TOTAL	11,288	56,443

Source: Mbwagwa, R.K. (1978).

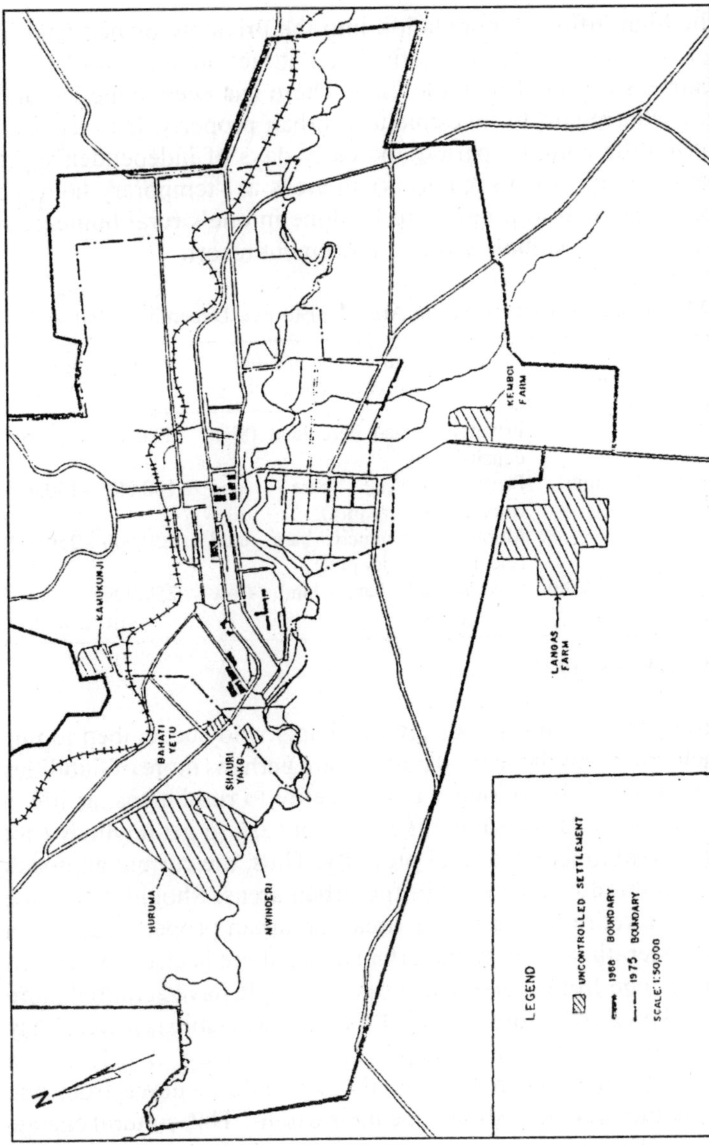

Source: Adopted and Modified from Woweru & Associates (1981).

Fig. 22.4: Uncontrolled Settlements after 1974 and 1988 Boundary Extensions

The high influx of population into the privately-owned land in Eldoret is a consequence of its financial attraction and affordability or cheapness depicted in Table 22.3. There has been some cultural changes with regard to investment in urban property. It is reported that during the colonial period and early days of independence the accepted outlook was to regard urban areas as "temporary homes", and for investment in property to be done in one's rural home, as a social and status symbol, and as a retirement resort.

Table 22.3: Prices of Plots in Select Areas in Eldoret, December, 1990

Area	*Land-Tenure/Type of Land Development*	*Price (Ksh)*
Huruma Langas	Privately-owned bare land (high density plot)	50,000 – 100,000
Kldoret West Huruma	Privately-owned bare land (medium density plot)	100,000 – 150,000
	Municipal Council bare land (medium diencity plot)	200,000 – 250,000
Ortillepville Elgon View	Government bare land (low density pest)	250,000+

Source: Fieldwork, 1990.

However, to many senior civil officials who succumbed to this approach, their grandiose rural edifices are perhaps more of liabilities than assets. For it is no longer easy to retire to rural areas, as life is hard there, while at the same time it is not easy to get anybody (not even relatives) to live in a rural property. Thus, the current approach is that one should first invest in the urban areas. Should it become necessary to retire to one's rural area, the urban property can be an income-generating asset. In the urban areas, there is also a perceived cultural change from shared premises, as people have acquired more wealth and preferred more privacy. Property ownership is increasingly seen as a social status symbol and stabilizing factor. A person in a rented or government property is always liable to move from one area to another as landlords change their whims. This cultural change is considered to have led most people to acquire urban property mainly in the privately-owned lands already with title deeds.

Lack of sources of capital is the most important factor which is considered to have motivated many people to seek land. Borrowing of money from the financial institutions such as banks is brought in crushing bureaucracy, and very difficult. Moreover, one of the most common conditions for a loan is possession of real property, complete with title deed. This certainly encourages some households to seek for land in privately-owned lands where title deeds exist, and no bureaucracy and easier to obtain. Besides, these lands are highly valuable and easier to convert to liquid money should financial conditions arise.

While it is not easy, now-a-days, to acquire Government or Municipal council land (a lot of lobbying, personal connexions and acquaintances, follow-ups, and sometimes outright cash is necessary) because of its financial constraint, it cannot easily be sold over its acquisition cost or value. The sale of Government bare land is illegal although it is secretly done. Sale of some development on land is allowed, but is subject to capital gains tax.

On the supply side, the bureaucracy to acquire, plan and survey Government/Municipal land is very long, and negotiations are usually very protracted. Declaration of an area as "a planning area" could easily be done by the urban authorities, but sanction must be obtained from various offices including the Ministries of Lands, Local Government, President's Office, Treasury and Kenya African National Union (KANU). Moreover, within the urban authority, co-ordination and co-operation between functional officers and councillors is always strained. Land layout schemes, valuation schedules and land surveying maps, must be approved and request forms signed by the departments of Lands, Planning and Surveying. Bureaucracy alone, even considering issues of resources, is a great constraint to the provision of Government planned land.

But an equally grave problem is lack of resources, particularly with regard to the question of compensation. Under the best circumstances, the Government has limited resources to pay compensation yet, people put up quite substantial investments on unplanned land. In this context, compensation is limited to the value of developments, excluding land calculated on a depreciated replacement cost basis to reflect, for example, the age and condition of the property. Thus, after valuation of property the affected household is normally assessed to get cash which cannot put it in equivalence, assessed from the acquired property's use value. Moreover, even after assessment, money is not readily available for payment which may take several months or years.

Once land is allocated, there is little follow-up by the Government authorities as to whether land is developed or not. As such, land suitable for re-allocation is unknown. Re-allocation of idle land would no doubt contribute to land available for development, but in Eldoret, re-allocation is rarely resorted to. The failure by the Government to devise a system of recovering the money sunk into planned land and to realize revenue from betterment noted above, implies that it has to rely on new funding every year. As most governments are resource-starved, only limited amounts can be annually mustered, meaning that the supply of land cannot be appreciably increased.

Considering some of the problems encountered in the acquisition of Government lands in Eldoret, it was informally reported that a privately-owned plot could be bought for more than Ksh. 150,000. Thus, Government owned land is indirectly related to the rapidly-escalating and quite unprecendented land values and prices for the types of land ownership in Eldoret. Indeed land is at a premium reflected in rising land values due to industrial, commercial and residential requirements.

Private land acquisition accompanied by speculation led to the accumulation of large tracts of land in the hope that once the town expanded, the value of holdings would increase. Until 1963, all the land around the Municipality was used for agricultural purposes and owned on family/group basis. Afterwards, family/group tenure was changed to individual freehold titles, thus signifying the official internalization of a new tenurial system, primarily private ownership of land in Eldoret.

Land owned by the Government is managed on its behalf by the Commissioner of Lands who therefore acquires it for use by the Municipal authorities. The Kenya Railways Corporation owns all the land along the railway line and served by railway siding. Land can only be acquired either through purchase or compulsory means. In the latter case, this can only be executed by the Commissioner of Lands who has all powers to acquire private farm lands for public development or re-development. The administrators sought to bring into the Municipality for development control purposes areas such as Kemboi, Kamukunji and Langas which are associated with high-density unplanned land-use patterns.

In fact, up to the 1975 boundary extension, there was no definite urbanization policy with regard to the provision of infrastructural and community-based facilities such as roads, schools, health and recreational centres. The implications for land delivery for industrial, residential, public and other community-oriented facilities are bound to confound the Municipality financial strategies for increasing public land bank in Eldoret.

As a result of the land tenure situation, Eldoret has a very little space for public facility development; and it is generally constrained in terms of centrifugal growth. Compulsory land acquisition for public facility is a very complex issue, and indeed it has also proved to be a protracted and politically difficult process delaying urban land-use planning and development programmes.

On the other hand, the Government seems to believe that compulsory land acquisition and allocation is an end in itself, since many times it allocates land (such as in Huruma and Langas) which is net ready for development and unserviced and does not attract development capital. Besides, the above land was allocated from incomplete or unapproved survey or town planning maps which cannot be used to issue certificates of title, a prerequisite to getting development capital. Moreover, all this land was allocated completely devoid of the usual infrastructure facilities. This is a recipe for land non-development, and many households easily point to this reason for doing nothing on their plots considering the current inflation rate in the construction and building industry; it is economical in terms of savings, to construct without waiting for services which may not be forthcoming for many years.

This suggests that non-developing households simply have no capital or do conduct a similar undertaking elsewhere. For the households with capital, it becomes uneconomical to invest in an unserviced slow-developing area, since with completed but isolated properties, such a neighbourhood cannot be let or occupied because it is unsafe, inaccessible and lacks supportive infrastructural facilities. These are some of the distribution consequences of land-use patterns in Eldoret. However, the constraints of land acquisition were later to be used as a basis for designing different land assembly mechanisms. The strategy adopted was based on servicing of privately-owned land by using a variety of modes of participation and partnerships in the physical development plans between the public and private sectors. For example, land held by land-buying companies (e.g. Kamukunji) was ripened for urban development in this strategy in Eldoret.

The Eldoret Physical Development Plans and Strategies

The colonial impact leading to shaping urban morphology in Kenya is channelled through the contribution of British planning consulting firms, as the instrument directly shaping the urban growth programmes and their spatial configuration. In this content, master plans mainly based on western urban development, are formulated in such a way that they achieve a minimum of their intended objectives because planners do not relate theory to practice. Rather than assist an urban authority solve the basic problems in the urban environment, planning consulting firms thus consider their role merely as carrying out projects as some popular trademarks—Project Planning Associates-shows. The implementability of the master plans' content and spatial efficiency to the users is none of their concern (Banyikwa, 1989). After all, a consultant cannot really be held responsible for constraints in master plan implementation, because nowhere in the contract is it made part of the deal.

In effect, for planning to achieve the intended objectives of an orderly, sustainable urban environment, implementation of the essential elements sensitive to the needs of the underprivileged population is vital. This would imply that the physical planners should first survey and map the actual intended landscape and identify the peoples priorities, problems and needs, and then draw their plans accordingly. Indeed master plans drawn in offices without correlation to its easy implementation and practicability become inappropriate or irrelevant. But the implementation of this may encounter far more difficulties than the preparation of the plan itself mainly due to its inappropriateness to the socio-economic urban environment. For example, urban development programmes may be constrained by lack of funds due to misappropriation, embezzlement and corruption, and structural adjustment programmes imposed by the World Bank and International Monetary Fund (IMF) conditionalities.

The first real statement of the Kenya Government's urban spatial policy was provided in the 1970-74 Development Plan focused on the decentralization of urban growth to other towns (e.g. Kisumu, Kakamega, Eldoret, Nakuru, Thika, Nyeri and Embu). These towns were selected as 'growth centres' and perceived to be key settlements by ethnic communities within the different regions. These centres were to be closely-knit to the major urban centres such as Nairobi and Mombasa for supplies of farm produce in the hope they would become an integral part of the monetary economy in Kenya.

Eldoret has had two main physical development plans specifically prepared to deal with the issues and problems that accrued from the

Municipal boundary extensions, which resulted into uncontrolled periheral settlements such as Huruma, Kemboi, Kamukunji and Langas Farms (see Fig. 22.4).

Urban growth in Eldoret is characterized by the approaches and methodology similar to those of the 1947 Colonial Capital Plan for Nairobi (Halliman and Morgan, 1967). In 1974 the Department of Physical Planning invited a British consulting firm, Sir Alexander Gibb and Partners Company to work and produce a master plan for Eldoret. Therefore, contracted to plan the growth of the town, this consulting company produced 'Eldoret Structure Plan' (ESP) (see Fig. 22.5) for the period 1975-80, which recommended that the town should take the needs of different residential and industrial areas into consideration. Indeed, the plan was based on a 'directional grid growth' concept where the major new direction of growth was northeastwards between the long-term alignment of the Trans-Africa Highway (i.e. A104 road) to Uganda. In effect, the potential of ESP for urban development can be argued to be a strategy which is a mixture of both 'a creative and linear growth,' entailing a substantial concentration of development in the periphery of the existing built-up area; and that additional growth would be located along a 'corridor' mainly along both sides of the Sosiani River (see Fig. 22.2).

The ESP accepted the structure and land values created by the wild-west approach and proposed that the town should develop naturally out the then existing land use. A separation of industrial zones from other uses such as roads, roundabouts, public open spaces, residential neighbourhoods and a spectacular civic centre was proposed as the ideal planning strategy. This land-zoning concept was derived from the 'garden-city' ideas typical of the British Urban Planning Tradition fo the 1930s (Armstrong, 1986). The architecture-planner's contribution to land-use change in Eldoret was cast in terms of layout and visual appearance, conformity with accepted residential land-use pattern, densities and development principles.

In general, the ESP is to define the role of Eldoret as a major urban centre in socio-economic development of the country, and to link that role with the physical planning of the Municipality, as well as provision of a comprehensive infrastructure and community facilities particularly to the new residential areas resulting from the boundary extensions. Consideration was also given to stimulate housing construction by the private sector, resolution of traffic congestion and parking along the Trans-Africa Highway especially

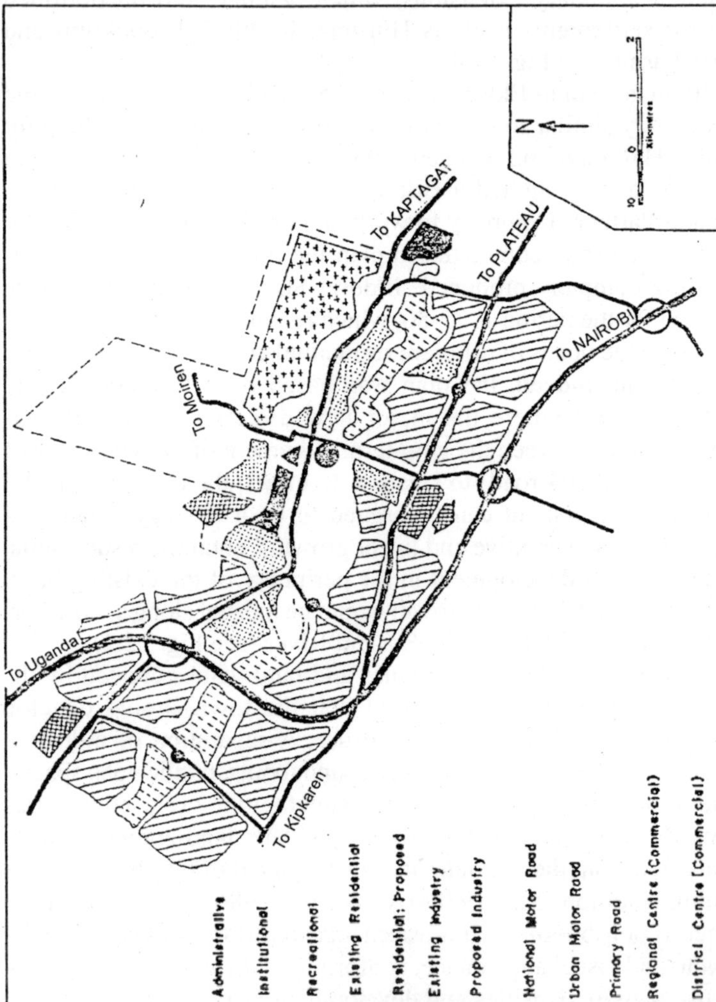

Source: Republic of Kenya (1973 and 1975).

Fig. 22.5: Eldoret Structure Development Plan

during the peak hours by restricting the on-street stoppages, and to provide alternative parking spaces (e.g. fringe ones). The ESP also aims at a consistent community education and mobilization programme for the urban population so as to attain an attitude and appreciation about the role of urban infrastructure for sustainable environment; and to set aside land for urban facility development when or wherever needed by the planning authorities.

The cost of implementing the ESP was estimated to be Ksh. 256 million (i.e. 8.5 million US$) to be met by the Government which consequently was able to release only half of the above amount in 1975. However, the Government was faced with some financial constraints such as the deteriorating terms of export trade, local currency devaluation, budget cuts on public spending imposed by the World Bank. There were also local problems associated with misappropriation and embezelment of funds and general corruption among the town planners.

In this context, the ESP could not achieve all its intended objectives due to the persistent problems of lack of infrastructural and community services such as health centres and schools especially in the high and medium residential areas; and the reluctance of private land owners to provide the land for the establishment of public infrastructural facilities; squatting in public open spaces due to the influx of people into the town, and the deteriorating condition of the Trans-Africa Highway characterized by many pot-holes and traffic congestion. The SSP is envisaged to be too costly as it requires a lot of funds and many specialists for its implementation. Thus, the issues of the direction of urban expansion, road network and street layout pattern, and distribution of different land-use zones or patterns are the major considerations of urban master planning other than the efficient functioning of the town.

In 1980 the Government formulated and adopted the Eldoret Physical Development Plan (EPDP) for the period 1980-85 which forms the basis of a detailed implementation schedule for the long-term planning as the second strategy. The broad objective of EPDP is to rationalize land-use development by implementing the strategy that provides the basic framework for the realization and promotion of the best possible land-use in the Municipality (Kenya, 1980). The provision of water reticulation, sewerage, road network, housing, education, health and electricity are the main facilities to be dealt with accordingly. The major effect of these measures is that

Government recognition has been given to the plot owners in the sprawling peripheral settlements, to the extent that they have more or less security in land tenureship and hence are encouraged to develop more decent low and medium-density housing with the basic infrastructural services.

The EPDP is basically a typical land-zoning technique which perhaps offers the physical planning authorities the most significant strategy for the achievement of rational land-use patterns and development efficiency in an urban environment. In its broadest sense, zoning not only demarcates and/or organizes an urban area into discrete land-use patterns but also controls the extent or intensity of development in each zone. Land zoning usually comprises two interrelated strategies-land-use and development-density delimitations which are the basic framework of EPDP. The former is mere comprehensive but the latter is quite limited in scope.

There are several interrelated potential benefits to be achieved from land-zoning system:

(a) It ensures that those land uses generating external economies of scale upon one another tend to locate in the same zone thus stimulating self-sustaining growth.

(b) It reduces the external costs or diseconomies created by one user on others by separating them. Thus, the value of a housing area can be maintained by separating them from an industrial land user with its consequential environmental and external health costs.

(c) It ensures that the available land is utilized economically to its maximum and best value, and that the development conforms to the acceptable standards of physical conditions.

(d) It ensures that health, safety and amenity elements of public interest are maintained, and that the public sector is also able to gain the economies of scale in the provision of infrastructural services.

The disbenefits of land-zoning system may accrue from its restriction of land-use in each zone to one or two particular types. Indeed, a person wishing to change the use of his plot or building must, according to the law, obtain permission from the local authority. In processing the applications for 'change of user,' the authority and other associated personnel may make conditions in accordance with the requirements of each area and the types of development activity.

The land-use delimitation under the EPDP involves the demarcation of the Municipality land into specific and exclusive areas including residential, industrial, recreational, educational, public purposes (e.g. church, community, social centres and clubs, post office, police stations, cemeteries); and public utility (e.g. sewerage, water reserviour and treatment works, commercial and transportation). In each category, the zoning further details sub-categories, for example, residential land can be sub-divided into high-density/low-income and low-density/high-income areas. Similarly, industrial land is further sub-divided as light and major areas.

Land-development-density zoning entails a limitation of the total amount of development or building allowable on available site or plot within a specific land-use area. In this context, the zoning specifies three main elements—permissible minimum plot size (PS) and maximum plot ratio (PR) (known as floor-space index or floor-area ratio) and maximum permissible plot coverage (PC). In some cases, there is also a specification as to the maximum number of dwellings per plot allowable especially for the residential land-use pattern.

Regarding the devleopment-density zoning, only residential land use is dealt with in the EPDP by using PS, PR, PC and a number of dwellings per plot to delimit the type and total development possible in each residential zone. The EPDP organizes the existing and proposed residential zones into categories depending on whether they are, in high-medium and low-density areas. The high-density residential zones are proposed to have a minimum plot size of either 0.03 or 0.04 of an hectare, a maximum permissible PR of 0.50 and PC of 0.50 of an hectare depending on the availability of main sewer. if there is no sewer connection, then the PR and PC are reduced to 0.25 ha. to allow the use of septic tank.

The medium-density residential zones comprise the following main categories:

(a) Where the minimum PS in either 0.099 or 0.1 of an hectare, the PR is 0.50 and PC is 0.33, and flats and maisonettes are permissible;
(b) Where PS is 0.4, PR is 1.25 and PC is 0.75 of an hectare, high rise flats are developable; and

(c) Where PS is 0.4, PR is 0.75 and PC is 0.35 of an hectare, flats and maisonettes are allowable. On the other hand, the low-density residential category was prepared to have a minimum PS of 0.2 an hectare, maximum PR or 0.5 and PC of 0.3 of an hectare, and flats or maisonettes are prohibited.

Although the EPDP discusses proposals for non-residential land-use, it does not specify its development-density zoning; and even when discussing the land-use delimitation, it is very general and quite tentative in nearly cases of non-residential land-use pattern. Two examples in regard to commercial and transportation land-use will suffice to illustrate this point. In order to reduce congestion of commercial activities within the CBD, the EPDP proposes that local centres be established in the residential areas such as Kapsoya, Ortillepville, Elgon View and Sosiani.

In effect, this may well be a relatively good strategy for dealing with the over concentration of Eldoret's CBD. But when it is done without due consideration of the existing and proposed nature of CBD's development and efficiency of land-use (which could well be catered by development densities proposed), it does not lend itself to a good appreciation of the strategy. Regarding transportation, although noting rightfully the need for a detailed transport study, EPDP proposes a considerable realignment of the main roads including Trans-Africa Highway.

It should be noted that urban development plans such as the ESP and EPDP have generally been implemented and financed by the Government or through borrowing from non-government institutions (e.g. World Bank) and only minimally through direct revenue, with the latter being mainly used for debt-servicing. Local authorities in the country generally face difficulties in generating sufficient revenues for the implementation of physical development plans including urban infrastructure projects. For example, over the last few years, the Local Government Loans Authority (LGLA) (the main channel for Government funding to local authorities) has experienced financial constraints, to the extent that it probably seems to have deviated from recycling funds among the local authorities to merely seeking project-specific funds from the Treasury for onward transmission to the local administration.

Against the financial background noted above, some of the urban infrastructure development projects contained in the EPDP for implementation received funds from various sources. As in the case of the ESP, the EPDP has some financial problems as outlined below.

Water supply and sewerage, for example, received a total of Ksh. 15.8 million. However, this has led to the existing sewerage treatment works at Kapsoya being overloaded thus leading to the pollution of Sosiani River especially during the dry season due to relatively low dilution by water. Road network development has received Ksh. 10.5 million from the World Bank, but this was not sufficient considering the rapid expansion of Eldoret. Thus, in Langas residential area a main arterial road and water main had been, provided, whereas the provision of electricity along the main road is half complete. In the Kamukunji residential area, main access road has been constructed and its sub-division plan is currently been processed.

The investment on housing totalling Ksh. 15.2 million as a bank loan has not achieved its full objective of house construction on site and service projects. Only a few estate houses have been constructed in Kapsoya and Elgon View residential areas. Thus, the increase in housing stock is minimal and acute housing shortage persists. The investment on education, health and social services totalling Ksh. 10.2 million (as loan from financial institutions and LGLA) has not been significant. In particular, there has been no substantial investment on recreational facilities except the town hall clubs established in Kapsoya and Eldoret West, and only one health centre has been built in Huruma over the period. In effect, the development control or land-use zoning requires elaborate and expensive 'policing' in the EPDP which requires the adoption of an appropriate planning system supported by the availability of local personnel and limited financial resources.

Conclusion

This chapter has demonstrated the main issues involving land tenure and ownership and the formulation of the physical development plans for Eldoret which are bound to be crucial in the creation and continuation of its sustainable urban environment. The issue of privately-owned land examined is very significant and hence is a clear message for policy-makers and physical urban planners. This phenomenon has been recognized especially in the urban centres of developing countries (Waweru and Associates *et al.*, 1981) as directly and positively related to the rapidly escalating, normally quite unprecedented high land values and prices for all land-use patterns. The existing pattern of land tenure and ownership is the consequence of land speculation and accumulation, increase of population growth and the penetration of capital into the Eldoret Municipality. Additionally, the colonial land-use policies and expropriation and adjudication played a greater role.

The implications for land delivery for industrial, residential (especially for the low-income population), and public and community-oriented facilities are bound to constrain the physical planning strategies for increasing the public 'land bank' in Eldoret. Thus, if land is not acquired from the private owners by the Government probably through Estates Development Fund (EDF) or LGLA at the current prices, it is likely to be very expensive considering the country's rapid population growth rate of 3.8 per cent per annum (Kenya, 1979).

The Government/Municipality considers its land acquisition programme to be a major mechanism in the drive to provide mere shelter and prevent the growth of unplanned land development without infrastructural services.

The Government would well be advised to go neighbourhood by neighbourhood, servicing, allocating and ensuring land development as it goes along. An administrative measure is the establishment of site offices or area development authorities whose duty would be to ensure the infrastructural development of their areas.

The Government surveying standards are too costly and hence require a revision downwards to ensure more surveyed land. Block survey followed by simple inter-block demarcation is considered quite sufficient. Use of aerial photography for (partly) settled up areas has been suggested as a cheaper and efficient alternative strategy (Mbwagwa, 1978). Bureaucracy in the land surveying, and its allocation and issuing of title deeds should also be minimized.

Where it is obvious that some households are unable to develop the allocated land, re-allocation should be swift by issuing short-term offers for land which could be converted into long-term as dedication to its development is confirmed. The bureaucracy to obtain money loan for land development should be minimized, and the insistence on a full title deed is unnecessary particularly if the idea of an area development authority is acceptable which can therefore vouch to the authenticity of the applicants for finance.

In regard to land tenure and other financial issues is the question of recapturing 'unearned increments' for public purposes and the benefits of urban growth. The most significant strategy in this connection is land or property taxation which should be seriously examined by the local authorities. It should be noted that it would incidentally be unimaginative to rely on a rating system even if a regular revaluation strategy could be pursued, hence alternative methods of collecting unearned increments should be considered possibly through additional rating.

In fact, is Eldoret Municipality not able now to handle the administration of property taxation as the most vital source of venture, rather than rely on the valuation section of the Department of Lands in Nairobi? Would such a move not only relieve the above department of large towns such as Eldoret in order to concentrate on the small local authorities and other land issues so as to facilitate more frequent valuations as righfully requested by the rating legislation, and hence broaden the scope of land-tax base and hence the revenue? Eldoret Municipality should, therefore, seriously address itself to these and other related questions to sustain financially its urban environment.

Rapid urbanization in Eldoret has continued to destabilize the balance between people, housing and employment. Attendant to this, have been inadequacies in transport, housing, electricity and water facilities. It is evident that the physical development plans adopted in Eldoret have raised expectations about the management strategies to control urban pressure, but they have achieved very little by way of creating a desirable urban structure. The practice of theory and strategy of land zoning both in terms of land-use delimitation and land development-density delimitation, has been quite limited in scope.

These physical planning strategies must therefore assume part of the responsibility for their ineffectiveness in creating a sustainable urban environment in Eldoret. Their ineffectiveness resulted from the colonial concepts, philosophies and themes of consulting firms and applying them in Eldoret, irrespective of differences in environmental conditions. What appears, quite clear is that there is need for a thorough and more comprehensive physical development planning strategies, which are less sophisticated and more appropriate and dependent on the available local personnel and financial resources. This would involve all aspects deemed likely to impinge on the future of the place such as economics of the town, environmental and physical issues, land, housing, industry people's priorities and problems and transport development. In short, more broadly-based and overall growth strategy appears to be more desirable. Consideration should be given to the improvement and integration of the existing squatter settlements into the future urban land-use planning and to encourage the private sector to participate in the housing development especially for the low-income population. The potential for future urban development and land-use strategy in Eldoret should be a mixture of both 'accretive and linear' growth. It would entail a substantial concentration of development in the periphery of the existing built-up area, and that additional growth would be located along a 'corridor' mainly along both sides of the Sosiani River.

The financial resources for Eldoret should be broadened and the Government financial institutions such as the LGLA also be set on a sound footing, to be able to mobilize, avails and manage these resources for sustainable urban environment and development programmes. Boundary extensions and adjustments need to be made after a detailed physical planning studies and land surveying, and these should also be linked with a comprehensive infrastructure development particularly for the newly-added areas into the Municipality.

The Government Estates Development Fund for the acquisition of more land for urban infrastructure development should be revived. Such acquired land should purely be used for public purposes, and people's education on land issues and their commitment to this understanding at various levels ought to be consistently clear. In general, Kenya has yet to develop its own indigenous philosophy and approach in order to transform the signatures left behind by the foreign and colonial physical urban planning strategies not only in Eldoret but also in other urban centres.

REFERENCES

Armstrong, A.M. (1986). 'Urban Planning in Developing Countries: An assessment of Master Plans for Dar es Salaam, Tanzania, *Singapore Journal of Tropical Geography*, Vol. 7, No. 1, pp. 25-40.

Armstrong, A.M. (1987). Urban Control Campaigns in the Third World: The Case of Tanzania, *Occasional Paper Series*, No. 19, Geography Department, University of Glasgow.

Banyikwa, W.F. (1989). 'Effects of Insensitivity in Planning Land for Urban Development in Tanzania: The Case of Dar es Dalaam', *Journal of Eastern African Research and Development,* Vol. 20, pp. 186-201.

Dilley, M.R. (1966). *British Policy in Kenya Colony*, Barnes and Noble, New York.

Dunkerley, H.B. (ed) (1983). *Urban Land Policy, Issues and Opportunities*, Oxford University Press, Washington D.C.

Halliman, D.M. and Morgan, W.T.W. (1967). 'The City of Nairobi', in Morgan, W.T.W., *Nairobi: City and Region*, Oxford University Press, London, pp. 61-71.

Hill, M.F. (1949). *Permanent Way: The Story of the Kenya and Uganda Permanent Way*, East African Railways and Harbours, Nairobi.

Ikhuoria, I.A. (1987). 'Urban Land-Use Patterns in a Traditional Nigerian City: A Case Study of Benin City', *Land Use Policy*, Vol. 4, No. 1, January, pp. 62-75.

Kenya, Republic of (1965). *African Socialism and its Application to Planning in Kenya*, Government Printer, Nairobi.

Kenya, Republic of (1973). *Rift Valley Province*, Regional Physical Planning Department, Nairobi.

Kenya, Republic of (1975). *Eldoret Structure Plan, 1975-1980*, Department of Physical Planning, Nairobi.

Kenya, Republic of (1979). *Population Census*, Central Bureau of Statistics, Nairobi.

Kenya, Republic of (1980). *Eldoret Physical Development Plan, 1980-1985*, Department of Physical Planning, Nairobi.

Lado, C. (1989). 'Traditional Agricultural Land Use and Some Changing Trends in Maridi District, Southern Sudan,' *Land Use Policy*, Vol. 4, No. 4, October, pp. 324-40.

Mbwagwa, R.K. (1978). *The Impact of Industrial Growth on Housing in Eldoret, Kenya*, Unpublished M.A. Thesis, University of Nairobi.

Soja, S.W. (1968). *Geography of Modernization of Kenya*, Syracuse University Press, Syracuse.

U.N. (1973). *Urban Land Policies and Land Use Control Measures*, Volume 1, UN Publications.

U.N. (1976). *Report on Habitat*, United Nations Conference on Human Settlements, Vancouver, 31st May-11th June.

Waweru and Associates, *et al.* (1981). *Third Urban Housing Project: Interim Report*, No. 2, Vol. Bl, Eldoret Project Report for the Republic of Kenya, Ministry of Urban Development and Housing, Nairobi.

West, M.E. (1987). *Apartheid in Southern African Towns, 1968-1985*, Institute of International Studies, University of California, Berkeley.

Wilcox, D.L. (1983). 'Urban Land Palicy Where The Population Bomb Has Already Exploded,' *Habitat International Journal*, Vol. 7, No. 5/6, pp. 36-46.

23

Estimating Food Production Potential in Papua New Guinea

J.A. BELLAMY and J.R. McALPINE

Introduction

This paper describes a project to assess the potential of the natural resources of Papua New Guinea (PNG) for the development of village-based food and cash crop production. The project is being carried out jointly by the PNG Department of Primary Industry and the CSIRO Division of Water and Land Resources. It involves the determination of both the current use and developmental potential of the natural resources of PNG for food and cash crop production, and their relation to population distribution and growth. The project will not produce either prescriptive or indicative environmental plans for agricultural production, this being solely the prerogative of the PNG Government. It aims, however, to produce information relevant to environmental planning and, equally as important, a system for effective use of that information.

The identification of the role of the use and management of natural resources in food production and cash cropping is being made in the context of a country in which: many areas are virtually unused, and those that are being used vary greatly in the population they support; the population is relatively small (3 million people) and has a growth rate of 2.5 per cent per annum; over 80 per cent of the population is reliant on traditional village-based subsistence production for food supplies; and villagers have considerable aspirations to gain income from cash cropping within the traditional village resource use framework.

Assessing resource potential in this situation requires investigations both of the nature of the resources themselves and of the farming systems applied to them.

Farming Systems

One of the main problems in attempting to make an assessment of the potential of the PNG natural environment for increased agricultural production is that three distinctly different economic sectors are involved. The three sectors are:

1. Traditional subsistence food production systems which take place within a village resource use framework. In this sector, environmental planning for agricultural production is based on detailed traditional knowledge of local resource productivity in respect of local traditional agricultural cropping systems. This body of knowledge is not codified in a form that makes it answerable to environmental planning and management, either at the level of Provincial or National Planning, or in terms of the techniques of 'Western' science. Consequently, the subsistence sector, while being the largest agricultural sector and the most extensive in terms of use of the PNG environment, operates largely outside any governmental planning framework. This does not mean that central and local government activity does not influence the subsistence sector. For instance, while the traditional village agricultural sector lies outside the field of direct governmental planning, carry-over from planning in other sectors may indirectly influence food production either in a beneficial or deleterious way. For example, government initiatives such as education and infrastructure development (e.g. roads) influence internal migration, which, in turn, may affect labour input and hence productivity of village-food systems.
2. Small holder cash cropping occurring within the same village resource use framework as that used for subsistence food production. In this sector cash cropping involves either tree cropping for export (e.g. coffee, cacao) or fresh vegetable production for urban markets. This cash crop sector is distinctive in that decisions concerning production are local

and subject to the same resource constraints as those applicable to traditional subsistence food production. Given that this sector relies on only small or modest capital investment, cash crops may be introduced into an environment that could be considerably less than optimal but still profitable. Although the degree of governmental planning activity is greater than for the subsistence sector, it is still largely indirect (for example, provision of marketing agencies, small development loans etc.) and it is not involved in the environmental aspects of small holder cash cropping.

3. Capital intensive cash cropping which is organized on land alienated from traditional ownership, partly on the basis of the perceived utility of that land for a particular form of cash cropping. Consequently, the land chosen for capital intensive cash cropping is generally suitable for the crop to be grown. As previously mentioned this is not necessarily the case in the small holder cash cropping sector. Capital intensive crop production is either for export (e.g. coffee, cacao crops) or for imported food replacement (e.g. processed sugar, beef) and it is organized mostly on a plantation or nuclear estate basis. Development in this sector involves either direct government initiatives or close co-operation with developers in the provision of infrastructure and capital. Environmental planning and management to maximize returns is regarded as an area of direct government concern.

The differences between these sectors are sufficiently great to make an assessment of the productivity of a particular crop/environment combination unique to the economic sector under which its potential would be realized. For instance, arabica coffee can be grown profitably on steep slopes under low input small holder cash cropping management, but it would not be profitable in a similar environment with large capital input.

Environmental Assessment

The most widely used techniques to establish the potential of the natural resources of an area for agricultural production are those derived within the context of 'western' agricultural experience. In principle these techniques operate on the basis of an assessment of the constraints imposed by the natural resources on agricultural production. Since the determination of the nature of such constraints to agricultural production can only be made in the context of the relevant agricultural (farming) system, the application of these techniques to other regions can lead to incorrect or inappropriate assessments of land use potential.

An absolute constraint under one agricultural system may be of positive benefit under another. For example, resource assessment for large scale capital intensive agricultural development would apply constraint criteria that take into account the possible use of machinery, fertilizers and associated managerial inputs. In this form of assessment low slope and absence of large surface stones are important evaluation factors, in order to minimize labour effort and allow access by machinery. However, in PNG the largest proportion of the rural population lives in highland and steepland areas with relatively high rainfall (2000 to 4000 mm per annum), and utilizes farming systems in which both food and cash crops are grown within the same subsistence resource use framework. Subsistence evaluation would place little importance on surface stones, while moderate slopes would be advantageous in so far as they provide adequate surface drainage. In addition, low soil fertility may be easily overcome by the application of fertilizer and be assessed as only a slight limitation in a capital intensive cash cropping system, whereas it may present a much more serious limitation to use in a subsistence system. Clearly the production constraint criteria valid for large scale western agricultural development are not relevant to the largest economic sector of PNG agriculture, the subsistence sector.

Any assessment of resource potential for agricultural development, particularly in regard to environmental planning in PNG, then needs to take into account not only the relevant crop/environment relationships but also the sector under which development is to take place and, consequently, the particular agricultural system to be employed.

Thus, to the usual land evaluation questions of 'Which is the best place to grow this crop?' and 'Which crop is most suited to this place?' one may add the question 'Under which agricultural system and sector is it best to organize this cropping?' and also the implied question 'Can traditional agricultural systems be modified to diversify and increase production over the long-term?'

Consequently, in PNG the nature of environmental planning, whether traditional, modified traditional (as in village-based cash cropping), or directly by the State, is itself an important factor in resource assessment.

The problem of environmental assessment is further confounded by a wide local diversity of resource type and distribution in PNG. Typically landforms vary from very steep rugged mountains to plains subject to intermittent or permanent inundation, a consequence of annual rainfall regimes which vary spatially from 1000 mm to 10000 mm. In response to this environmental diversity a great range of traditional agricultural systems have been developed for the reliable production of subsistence food supplies. These vary from near permanent highland root cropping, employing specialized composting and drainage techniques, to long fallow shifting cultivation. Horticulture is practised successfully both in terms of productivity and conservation on slopes in excess of 30 degrees under high rainfall and on land which is regularly inundated. All traditional PNG farming systems have the characteristic that they are very closely attuned to the detail of their local environment, thus, making it difficult to evaluate their applicability to other environments of only slightly dissimilar character.

Given a wide diversity of environments, agricultural systems and economic organization the approach adopted in attempting this resource assessment has been to:

- analyze the nature and distribution of natural resources relevant to agriculture.
- to determine to what degree and extent these resources are currently used.
- assess the adequacy of current 'agricultural systems' for food and cash crop production.

This approach aims to develop a basis for understanding the extent and operation of existing and potential crop/environment relationships in relation to population distribution and resource use in order to determine:

- how land that is not currently used might be most appropriately employed for food and cash cropping.
- how production can be intensified and maintained on land that is already being used while avoiding adverse environmental consequences and declines in long-term production.

Methodology

It is clear that this approach required investigations of a large number of Interrelated components. A diagram showing the major components and their role in the organization of the project is presented in Fig. 23.1. All data have been integrated spatially resulting in some 4500 mapping units being delineated and each has been described in terms related to agricultural productivity. An indication of the type of data in the information system is presented in Fig. 23.2, which shows for one mapped area its resources, population andland use characteristics. Briefly, the major components of the project are:

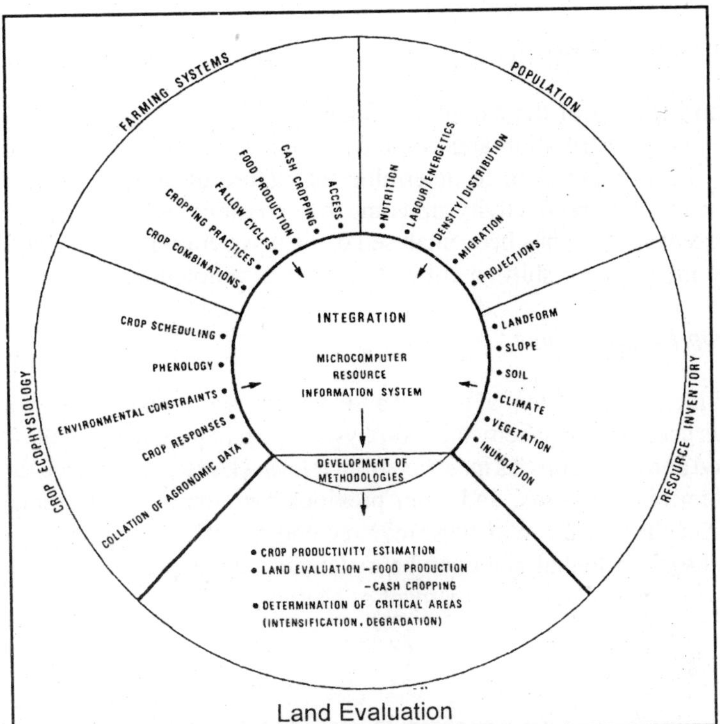

Fig. 23.1: Organisation of Major Components of Papua New Guinea Agricultural Resource Assessment Project

Resource Inventory

Basic environmental information used in land evaluation required the mapping and description of land areas in Papua New Guinea in terms of parameters related to agricultural productivity (e.g., landform, soils and climate), and a tabulated resource inventory has been prepared for the whole of PNG (Fig. 23.2).

Population

Using the 1980 National Census figures for all villages, the distribution of population within the mapped areas and compilation of demographic and other social information relevant to agricultural resource use, including data on nutritional status, was compiled to determine the level of current use of resources and the adequacy of food production systems.

Farming Systems

Identification of the extent and intensity of present agricultural land use, crop distribution and cropping practices in relation to resources has been undertaken to determine the nature of current production systems, their productivity limits and their possibilities for improvement. Present landuse has been analysed using a system for identifying land use intensity for shifting cultivation from air photographs.

Crop Ecophysiology

To identify the potential of used and unused areas for particular crops it was necessary to specify the eco-physiological requirements of the main food and cash crops, as indicated from relevant literature, from the survey of farming systems, and from previous agronomic experimentation within the country. With these requirements specified, the potential crops and their potential yield can be matched to the appropriate, available environments (see Development of Methodologies).

Integration

Development of a microcomputer-based resource information system was required to facilitate storage, interrogation and retrieval of information from all the previous components. Although a large volume of data was involved, a relatively simple and cost-effective means of manipulation is needed to permit the system to be established and used in Papua New Guinea.

PROVINCE 16 East New Britain
DISTRICT 3 Rabaul
3 Rabaul
RMU No. 2
LAT. 4 deg 10 min S
LONG. 152 deg 28 min E
AREA 51 sq. km

RESOURCE DESCRIPTORS
++++++++++++++
LANDFORM Raised coral reefs and associated back reef plains

Rocktype	Limestone		
SLOPE	2 degree	ALTITUDE	0-600 M
	2-5 degrees	MAX TEMP	32-39 deg C
Relief	Very low 10-30 m	MIN TEMP	27-23 degC

RAINFALL

Annual	2000-2500 mm
Seas Var	100-200 mm to 200 mm
Deficit	Irregular, moderate deficit
INUNDATION	Water logged area
Extent	<20%
Soil	Tropudalfs Moderately weathered soils with their finer textured subsoils Eutrandepts Slightly to moderately weathered ash soils with high (>=50%) subsoil BS values Fluvaquents Poorly drained, undifferentiated soils with high (>=0.2%) or fluctuating org C contents to >=125 cm
VEGETATION	See land Use Medium-crowned lowland hill forest

SOIL ATTRIBUTES
++++++++++++++

SOIL 1 Tropudalfs

STONINESS	Not stony/rocky (<1%)		
DEPTH	Deep (>1m)		
DRAINAGE	imperfectly drained		
REACTION	Weakly acid to neutral	AVAIL WATER CAPACITY	
SALINITY	None	0-25 cm	Very low
CATION EXCH	Moderate (10-25 meg %)	0-50 cm	moderate
BASE SAT'N	Moderate (20-60%)	0-100 cm	High
% NITROGEN	Moderate (0.2-0.5%)	MIN RESERVE	Moderate
AVAIL P	Moderate (10-20 ppm)	TEXTURE 1	Very fine
EXCH K	Moderate (0.2-0.6 meg%)	TEXTURE 2	Very fine
ERODIBILITY	Moderate	ANION FIX'N	No problem

SOIL 2 Eutrandepts

STONEINESS	not stony/rocky (<1%)		
DEPTH	deep (>1m)		
DRAINAGE	Well drained		
REACTION	weakly acid to neutral	AVAIL WATER CAPACITY	
SALTINITY	None	0-25 cm	Low
CATION EXCH	Moderate (10-25meg%)	0-50 cm	Moderate
BASE SAT'N	High (>60%)	0-100 cm	High
% NITROGEN	High (>0.5%)	MIN RESERVE	High
AVAIL P	Low (10ppm)	TEXTURE 1	Medium
EXCH K	Moderate (0.2-0.6 meg%)	TEXTURE 2	Medium
ERODIBILITY	Very low	ANION FIX'N	High

SOIL 3 fluvaquents

STONEINESS	Not stoney/rocky (<1%)		
DEPTH	Deep (>1m)		
DRAINAGE	Poorly to very poorly drained		
REACTION	Wealkly acid to neutral	AVAIL WATER CAPACITY	
SALTINITY	None	0-28 cm	Very low
CATION EXCH	High (>25 meg%)	0-50 cm	Moderate
BASE SAT'N	High (>60%)	0-100 cm	High
% NITROGEN	Moderate (0.2-0.5%)	MIN RESERVE	High
AVAIL P	High (>20 ppm)	TEXTURE 1	Very fine
EXCH K	High (>0.6 meg%)	TEXTURE 2	Very fine
ERODIBILITY	Moderate	ANION FIX'N	No problem

POTENTIAL CONSTRAINTS

LAND USE
+++++++++
'USED' AREA 51 Sq km = 100% of the total area

POPULATION DENSITY

Total pop.	4241
Density on total area	83 persons/sq km
Density on 'used' area	83 persons/sq km

LAND USE INTENSITY

Plantation and other non-garden uses	19 sq km
<1% current usage/10-20% anthrop, veg	32 sq km
TOTAL 'USED'	51 sq km

REGROWTH

Mixture of tall and short woody	32 sq km
No fallow (but totally used)	19 sq km

NON-SUBSISTENCE USE
Coconuts (+ or – cacao/coffee)

SMALLHOLDER ECONOMIC ACTIVITY (as % of total households)

Total households 881
Total villages 18

Activity	No.	%	Activity	No.	%
Coffee	0	0	spices	0	0
Tea	0	0	foodcrops	233	26
Cocoa	288	33	fish	288	33
Rubber	0	0	cattle	0	0
C' nut/copra	818	93	pigs	12	1

FARMING SYSTEM INFORMATION Available

POPULATIONS AND RURAL VILLAGES
+++++++++++++++++++++++++++++++

Total Population		Males	Females	Total
		2191	2050	4241
District 3 Rabaul		Division 5 DUKE OF YORK ISLANDS		
4	URUKUK	113	99	212
5	MOLOT	144	121	265
6	MAREN	153	48	106
7	BUTLIVUAN	140	119	259
8	PIRTOP	113	122	235
9	WAIRA	104	112	216
10	WATARA	78	71	149
11	NABUAL	151	131	282
12	INOLO	104	93	197
13	KABATIRAI	82	82	168
14	KUMAINA	71	61	132
15	NAKUKUR 1	127	119	246
16	NAKUKUR 2	146	172	318
17	KABILOMO	295	265	560
18	URAKUKAR	115	104	219
19	KABAKIAI	74	65	139
20	KUMLOKOR	93	87	180
21	INLIMUT	88	73	161

Fig. 23.2: Example of Papua New Guinea agricultural resource information for one mapping unit East-New Britain

All information is held in an integrated form in a micro-computer-based resource information system.

An analysis of data for all mapping units was undertaken to identify the dominant agricultural resource types in the country. This classification of resource types provides the framework for analysis of agricultural productivity.

Development of Methodologies

In the absence of techniques of land evaluation appropriate to Papua New Guinea conditions, it was necessary to develop methods for estimation of crop productivity, resource constraint criteria, and identification of areas where food/cash crop production systems were inadequate to support the current population. This required use of the resource information system for development and testing of agricultural resource assessment methods that were appropriate to Papua New Guinea conditions.

Land Evaluation

The methods referred to above allow evaluation of the potential expansion of food production and the intensification and modification of village-based food and cash crop production systems. Those areas where resources appear inadequate to support present population numbers under current food production systems and those areas where land degradation could occur were identified. Conversely, unused land was evaluated for its agricultural potential.

Conclusion

The information compiled in the course of the project and methods developed using that information provides Papua New Guinea for the first time with country-wide coverage and knowledge of the nature and current use of its natural resources for agriculture, and the potential of those resources for future agricultural change and expansion. In particular, Papua New Guinea will benefit from the major outputs of the project in the following ways:

1. A detailed inventory of natural resources related to agriculture is available for the whole country in co-ordinated,

accessible form, both as published maps and documents and also as a computer-based resource information system which facilitates updating, extension, interrogation and analysis for specific purposes.

2. The inventory also provides information on the degree to which the natural resources are currently being used for food and cash crop production and the manner in which they are being used. The populations and individual villages associated with each type of agricultural landuse also have been accurately determined.
3. An assessment will be provided for the whole country of the potential of its natural resources for agricultural development of food and cash crops under existing and modified forms of cropping practices. The assessment will relate to individual crops and crop combinations, and will aim to identify 'critical' limits of intensification at which declining productivity, soil erosion and/or malnutrition, etc., might occur.

The ultimate outcome of the project will be the provision of a basic framework for informed decision-making relating to the following areas:

1. Planning of agricultural development at both national and provincial levels.
2. Extrapolation and transfer of results from agricultural experiment stations to field situations and, equally, extrapolation of results of field studies of particular farming systems to other areas identified as having similar sets of resources.
3. Development of infrastructure related to agriculture, including such factors as: access, in relation to development potential and current use (i.e., transport planning); the ability of resources to provide food for an increasing population (i.e., health planning); the nature and variability of the Papua New Guinea natural environment (i.e., conservation, environmental impact studies).

24

Economics of Conserving Degraded Land for Agriculture

A Case Study

HRIDAI R. YADAV

Introduction

Reclamation of degraded land and its economic viability depends on the agro-climatic conditions and proportionate required inputs and subsequent output accrued from the reclaimed degraded land. The economic viability of the degraded land reclamation cannot provide proper profit within the limited time frame because the land which is lying degraded from several years requires few years to restore the fertility status of the soil. During the beginning years it is very difficult to obtain the optimum output, but, in the subsequent years output increases and the input ratio is required. The reclamation cost also varies according to suitability and capability of the land. In this study an effort had been made to select the usar land problematic soil in Palia village in Gauriganj block of Sultanpur district. The reclamation of degraded land can be taken as an essential and worthwhile exercise from the point of view of economic and environmental development by bringing additional degraded land under use. The pressure of human and cattle population is increasing rapidly extension of cultivated land has been stagnant from several years. The major factor for it is that exploitation of such uncultivated lands has not been within the reach of the ordinary degraded land patta allottee beneficiary. Most of the degraded lands are not suitable for agricultural operation. Reclamation of degraded land is time taking and costly affair. Adoption of such measures for degraded land accentuates soil erosion is not desirable from the long-term planning point of view. In view of the above constraints, it is essential that the pros and cons of degraded land reclamation are ample specifically demonstrated to the all concerned, so that they adopt the most appropriate remedial measures. Though high expenditure is involved in practicing most of the remedial measures in the initial stages, subsequently, the farmers begin to derive considerable benefit from the reclaimed degraded land. The farmers can be included to adopt conservation of degraded land only by disseminating to them information regarding the economic benefits in the form of additional foodgrain, fodder, fuelwood, fibre, fruits, fisheries, timber, vegetables etc. production which ultimately paves the way for socio-economic development and improve ecological imbalances of the area. The economics of degraded land reclamation is closely linked with management aspect. The cost of reclamation depends upon the nature and extent of selected patch of degraded land. Attempts have been made to reclaim the *usar* degraded land for paddy and wheat crop cultivation, agro-forestry and social forestry programmes. The details of the input involved in the reclamation of *usar* degraded land for agriculture, agro-forestry and social-forestry in the owned patta allotted land of the SC beneficiaries and details of the output and the benefit achieved from the reclaimed patch of *usar* degraded land are analysed.

Economics of Conserving Degraded Land for Crop Cultivation

Economics of reclamation of usar degraded land for crop cultivation in the selected patch of *usar* land with the involvement of beneficiaries belongs to Palia village located in front of the Institute. The beneficiary did not instal tubewells, but, the Institute installed one tubewell and one bore pipe and assisted the farmers in providing the irrigation facility in which they were sharing the cost of the diesel for lifting the water through the diesel engine. During the first year of reclamation all the inputs were provided to the farmers by the Institute. This was done by making available the various subsidies and the financial support for land levelling etc., under the Jawahar Rojgar Yojna Scheme. During the first year the reclamation of *usar* degraded land was done to deep ploughing, leaching and flushing organic and inorganic amendments and *dhaincha* growing as green manuring. In addition to such reclamation process, the mixing of *Jalkumbhi* with water in the soil had been done and the water was filled for atleast three months in the field, then, the paddy transplantation was done in the month of July. It is noteworthy exercise that the reclamation of such *usar* degraded land for the crop cultivation was done through adopting C_2 scientific technology which is economically viable, technically feasible, socially acceptable and involves very low input and better output. The cost incurred on different inputs and form operations have been presented in Table 24.1. The application of gypsum and pyrite application was not done because of its higher price but the application of organic and inorganic amendments was adopted. An initial investment of Rs. 11,400 per hectare was incurred for the reclamation of *usar* degraded land for bunding and levelling.

Table 24.1: Cost of *Usar* Degraded Land Reclamation and Crop Cultivation During the First Year

Particular	*Cost per Hectare (Rs.)*
Soil reclamation	
Bunding	250.00
Levelling	2000.00
Land preparation	2000.00
Impounding of Water	3500.00
Organic and inorganic amendments	1000.00
Jalkumbhi labour charge	1050.00
Transportation, application, mixing	1600.00
Total	**11400.00**
Rice cultivation	
Nursery raising	500.00
Seedling uprooting, transplanting	350.00
Irrigations (Instt. Tubewell) diesel cost	800.00
Fertilizers	1000.00
Insecticides/Fungicides	250.00
Labour cost	500.00
Harvesting and threshing	500.00
Total	**3900.00**
Wheat cultivation	
Field cultivation	400.00
Seed and sowing	500.00
Fertilizers	1000.00
Irrigation (diesel cost)	400.00
Harvesting and threshing	200.00
Labour Cost	400.00
Total	**2900.00**

The cost of rice and wheat cultivation was Rs. 3900 and Rs. 2900 per hectare respectively. However, the cost of Rs. 5100 for rice and Rs.3450 per hectare for wheat was incurred when the water was hired, while during the cist year the water irrigation facility was made available by the institute.

Thus, the total return from rice and wheat were Rs. 4500 and Rs. 1280 per hectare respectively during the first year. The return from wheat crop was less which may be due to the fact that some of the fields could not be levelled properly. In addition to the initial *p*H, usarisation levels were also high. Even after one year Ec during wheat crop was 4.8 mmhos/cm and *p*H was 9.6 which were not favourable for wheat crop. Thus, it is a fruitful exercise to reclaim the degraded usar land for crop cultivation if planned and implemented properly on scientific basis. Such reclamation procedures are technically feasible, economically viable and socially acceptable to the rural poor which will not only regenerate the degraded ecological imbalances of the area, but, also improve the socio-economic conditions of the deprived rural poor.

Conclusion

The reclamation of degraded land and its economic feasibility depends on the agro-climatic conditions and proportionate required inputs and subsequent outputs accrued from the reclamation of degraded land. The economic vaibility of the degraded land reclamation cannot provide proper profit within limited time frame, because the land which is lying degraded for several years requires few years to restore the fertility status of the soil. During the beginning years, it is very difficult to obtain the optimum output but in the subsequent years the output increases and the input ratio reduces. The reclamation cost also varies according to the suitability and capability of the land. In this study, an attempt has been made to select the *usar* land problematic soil in Palia village. Attempt have been made to reclaim the *usar* degraded land for paddy and wheat crop cultivation, agroforestry and social-forestry programmes on the patta allotted *usar* degraded land to the scheduled caste beneficiary.

The economics of reclamation of *usar* degraded land for crop cultivation indicates that an initial investment of Rs. 11400 per hectare was needed, provided various resources as well as different operations were available on subsidised rates. However, in case no subsidy was provided to the farmers, this initial investment may increase by 1/2 times. The cost of rice and wheat cultivation was Rs. 3900 and Rs. 2900 per hectare respectively. However, the cost of Rs. 5100 for rice and Rs. 3450 per hectare for wheat was incurred when the water was hired, while during the first year the water irrigation facility was made available by the Institute. The total return from rice and wheat was Rs. 4500 and Rs. 1280 per hectare respectively during the first year. The return from wheat crop was less which may be due to the fact that some of the fields could not be levelled properly. In addition to the initial *p*H, usarization levels were also high. Thus, it is a fruitful exercise in reclaiming the degraded *usar* land for crop cultivation if planned and implemented properly on scientific lines.

Thus, it may be concluded that reclamation of degraded land is an economically viable scheme if planned and implemented on technically feasible and scientific lines with the people's involvement and their participation for economic development to generate employment and increases the income of the deprived rural poor. It has been observed that the reclamation of degraded land is economically viable, technically feasible, socially acceptable and agro-climatically possible if a systematic approach is adopted because it is a time taking process and requires heavy investment at the initial stage. It will not only generate the employment and increase their income, but also improve the socio-economic conditions and ecological imbalances of the areas. Also, it will fulfil the increasing requirements of the growing human and cattle population.

25

Strategies for Conserving Degraded Land

HRIDAI R. YADAV

Introduction

Since 1960 great strides have been made in agricultural production through the application of science and technology which helped in transforming Indian agriculture from subsistent type into a commercial farming system. The input of research and development efforts is reflected in the achievement of self-sufficiency in foodgrain production from 51 million tonnes in 1950-51 to a record production of over 200 million tonnes in recent years. Despite these achievements, the agricultural economy of our country continues to face serious challenges due to our increasing population, depleting land fertility, dry land and flood problems, and shrinking non-renewable energy sources. The five decades planning and development experience in India has amply demonstrated that implementation of sectoral programmes for fulfilling the requirements of priorities does not necessarily lead to specification of local needs, while the micro-level sectoral planning has admittedly led to noticeable gains at the local level. The impact has been uneven and has created problems and regional imbalances. With the accelerated growth of agriculture farming, agro-forestry, social-forestry new problems are emerging. The existing research system is under great strain as the future research will necessarily be more complex, more difficult and more costly. There would be a need to step up mission oriented basic research particularly for the wasteland which has a great potential for the development. Moreover the technology generating institutions also have focused their attention towards cropping system for irrigated as well as for assured rainfall areas whereas the problems of dryland, flood, wasteland areas have yet to catch attention. There is a dearth of appropriate technology suitable for wasteland and yet whatever technologies are available they are not reaching to ultimate users, the farmers. For the speedy diffusion of available innovations on wasteland a well organised system to transfer of technology needs to be developed.

Due to an ever increasing pressure on limited land surface there is need to accelerate the land productivity through the technology of farming, agro-forestry, social forestry to combat with the shortage of foodgrain, fuel-wood, fodder, fibre, fruits, fisheries, timber etc. Moreover about 60 per cent big farmers in irrigated areas are interested to grow the crops, agro-forestry and social-forestry trees either in the form of pure farming, orchards or forestry or in association of arable crops. However, few farmers hesitate to plant fuel-*cum*-fodder trees due to some of the reasons:

(i) Trees create the problems in agricultural operation and ultimately reduce the crop yields.
(ii) The need of fuelwood will be met out by branches of fruit trees drawing at their own accords.
(iii) Protection of the saplings in field conditions is more difficult specially during the summer season.
(iv) Lack of seed materials and technology know-how of raising and maintenance of the seedlings.
(v) Shortage of water during dry period in the establishment period of saplings.
(vi) Lack of marketing infrastructure for wood and its products to assure remunerative grains.

Various constraints in agriculture farming, fruit plantation social-forestry and agro-forestry for farmers participation on degraded land and its reclamation are as follows:

- The wastelands are degraded, difficult in access and have scarcity of irrigation. There is need to community infrastructure.
- Grazing by stray animals is a serious threat to the fruit plants upto 5-6 years in its plantation. Therefore, cooperative efforts, on wasteland utilization is essential.

- Farmers who are owning or allotted wastelands generally do not have resources which makes them skeptical in availing loan for such purposes.
- Whatever we are planning for fruit plantations the cooperative marketing or processing facilities need to form .an integral part of it.
- Farmers are not aware of wastelands techniques for fruits, afforestation, crops etc.
- The lands on lease are often not converted into profitable units with much investment due to apprehension that the land could be taken back by the Government.
- There is no access to training, guidance, input supply, credit etc. for the farmers owning wastelands.
- A rural poor bothers first for his bread and livelihood, thus for any wasteland development programme, wage earning provision be associated in his long run process of planting trees and maintaining them over a period as a part of anti-poverty programme.
- A farmer even after earning livelihood would like to depend on local forest or community plantation for fuel and fodder.
- Most of community lands after allotment are not taken up together by all allottees and sporadic efforts do not help to solve their problems.
- Not many successful examples on wasteland development exist to motivate farmers for fruit plantation.
- Small farmers cannot survive only on few fruit plants and the income is also seasonal hence more employment and income opportunities are required.

The use of appropriate channel in transmiting the information of wasteland technology is of great importance. Though we are not as advanced as Western countries, but India how now move very fast in the recent years for the transfer of technology. The extension workers are not able to make full use of sophisticated system due to lack of skill and proper training and the transferring the technology has limited scope due to high level of illiteracy in the rural areas. The farmer is the ultimate user of technology. He accepts and adopts when it satisfies his requirements. His attitude, knowledge about technology skill to adopt it and host of other factors make him to think several times before making the final decision. In general there is a fashion to blame the farmers and the extension workers are not adopting the farm technology quickly after it is made available to them but our farmers are great economist and they take the time to analyse the cost and benefit ratio of the technology. After it is found economically viable, technologically adoptable, socially justifiable and politically acceptable, culturally profitable, it is adopted otherwise rejected. In case of cultivation, agro-forestry and social-forestry in the wasteland the scattered small holdings with low investment capacity of the farmers intiate a serious thing for adoption and diffusion of the technology. In view of the such complex condition a great challenge is before the scientists in generating the suitable technology suited to the needs of such farmers.

Development of wastelands has been one of the priority concerns by putting them to sustainable use. Wastelands development has strong social and economic dimensions which relate to increasing the liability of Biomass specially fuelwood, fodder, fibre, fruits, food and wood and the need of adequate employment and income generation. Thus such programme should create general awareness and help faster comprehensive people's participation to make the programme extensive and one for the people and of the people. Therefore, the involvement of Panchayat is crucial to promote sustainable participatory management of Agro-Afforestation on wastelands particularly those of community degraded land.

"Panchayat should be encouraged to take an active part in the farming and implementation of agro-afforestation on wastelands in their Panchayat degraded lands. Indeed we consider it essential that they should do so, for the successful execution of such schemes of rural reconstruction and development largely depends on the cooperation and participation of the people, that cooperation and participation should be sought and obtained through the people's local representatives, that is through the Panchayats."

The technology development and extension for wasteland reclamation, nursery raising, plantation maintenance and followup action have one of the major components for the people's participation for massive afforestation programme. The importance of technology development for reclamation of wastelands have been given much importance for implementation through the people's participation. For developing various technology centres for its wider propagation.

Strategies for the wasteland development to fulfil the increasing demand of growing cattle and human population had not been given due importance in the planning while the Department of Wasteland Development has given much importance to combat the increasing requirements of fuelwood and fodder under the social-forestry programmes which has not been found so successful because on the one hand such scattered programme with a particular objective of restoring the ecological imbalances so far could not provide momentum for the people's participation and hence mostly it had been unsuccessful programme. Therefore, there should be an integrated approach of developing the degraded lands not only to the fuelwood and fodder programmes but it should incorporate the foodgrain, fibre, fruit, timberwood, fisheries and other commercial production system as per the suitability and capability of the land and according to the requirement and interests of the local poor. In view of the above, a survey had been conducted selecting village-Palia, Block-Gauriganj, District-Sultanpur, U.P. where mostly the *usar* land is available. The village micro plan based on the watershed and village boundary had been developed, questionnaire had been framed and the survey had been conducted to know the requirements of the local poor and accordingly the whole village action plan had been developed and the soil treatment plan as per the capability of soil had been also formulated. The attempt have been made to involve the village people in the formulation of the village level action plan in their own land as well as the panchayat land and as per their requirements, the degraded wasteland reclamation plan for the agriculture, agro-forestry and social-forestry had been developed. The enclosed map provides clear indication with location of the availability of the wasteland and planning for its reclamation for various uses as per the requirement of the people and to ensure the sustainable development and their continued participation.

To ensure the continued participation for sustainable development, to restore the ecological imbalances of the village to generate employment, improve the socio-economic conditions of the deprived rural poor, a Panchayat Level Committee on "Agro-Afforestation on Wasteland Management" (AAWM) to train, motivate, demonstrate, educate the rural poor for new methods of farming technologies of reclaiming the wastelands, agro-forestry and social-forestry have been constituted. Suggested office bearers of the Committee are as follows:

Chairman	– Sarpanch/Pradhan
Secretary	– Panchayat Secretary
Member	– 5 members of Panchayat
	– 1 Forest Department Representative
	– 1 Horticulture Department Representative
	– 5 Land Less Labours (beneficiary)
	– 2 Panchayat women members
	– 1 Revenue Official (Patwari)
	– 2 Trainers or demonstrators

Village level micro action plan for reclamation of the degraded land a questionaire had been developed in which details of the population—male, female, cast-wise population information, activity-wise engaged people in various trades, landuse pattern source-wise irrigation system, its area, cropping pattern, area under crops, average production and annual production, total number of animals and its types and annual product per unit, afforestation programme on various lands, the types of planted species, the use of fuelwood by the various groups, its requirement, need of the fodder and requirement of the plants by the various groups of the villages and the details of the available land, its ownership pattern for planting, fodder, use of water-logged land, its use and various suggestions for the qualitative and quantitative improvement of the agriculture farming, agro-forestry and social-forestry programmes on degraded land have been surveyed in detail and accordingly the plan was formulated.

From the selected village beneficiaries had been selected and each unit of different wasteland types have been selected for the reclamation purposes for agriculture agro-forestry and social-forestry to meet the increasing demand of the growing human and cattle population.

The various operations for the agriculture, agro-forestry and social-forestry to meet, fulfil the agro requirements of the local rural poor and various strategies adopted, technologies demonstrated, concerned beneficiaries in coordination with agro-afforestation on wasteland management committee of the Village Panchayat Palia are as follows:

Strategies for Conservation of Degraded Land for Agro-forestry

The Government through its own resources have spent huge amount in the five year plans. Yet achievements in terms of plant survival has been very poor. It is due to the fact that the afforestation including social-forestry and agro-forestry has remained a Government programme with very little involvement of the farmers of the village. Another loss in terms of loosing confidence about success of plantation of wasteland has also been obvious. Thus the social-forestry and agro-forestry has to succeed only if there is active involvement of people right from plantation to grow stage of 4-5 years and even afterwards. In its maintenance for securing farmers participation the following points may be given due importance :

- There should be a nodal organisation/department responsible for wasteland development at district level. One of the potential institutions could be the H.G.Ks. with multi-disciplinary approach to coordinate and implement the envisaged activities through different departments/ specialists.
- Plantation on wastelands whether on community or on individual land should be taken up as anti-poverty programme for the rural poor by paying him wages for the rural poor for the labour on account of plantation.
- Involve schools for nursery raising and mass awareness campaigns in villages.
- Encourage decentralized nurseries for employment of youth and women in the villages with substantial subsidy to meet initial cost.
- Form tree growing cooperatives of people on community land on long-term basis with their ownership rights on trees.
- Organise frequent meetings at every level to listen to the participating farmers.
- Fodder and fuel requirement of cooperative growers should be met on regular basis as part of the project.
- For each village we must have integrated landuse plan of the wastelands and farmers interested in a particular activity/ enterprise should be identified.
- Farmers selection for wasteland development should be done after 2-3 orientation and training meetings of their representatives and executing agencies.
- Each village should have a demonstration unit of wasteland development of about one hectare showing all possible uses and units over there.

- At each cluster of 8-10 hectare wasteland drainage, irrigation service roads etc., should be sponsored by Government and managed by the farmers on cost to cost payment basis.
- Arrange credit and supply of input to facilitate in a manner that continuity is maintained on long-term basis.
- Farmers' cooperatives should be encouraged to have their own service units for supply of inputs, marketing and processing of fruits to make these projects sustainable under the technical guidance of the nodal agencies.
- The allotment of wastelands to individual and cooperative growers should be done in open meetings by high level officers of the district in presence of representatives and lower level executing agency.
- There is need to rehabilitate youth on wastelands by setting up demonstration units and running nurseries and their participation for input supply, marketing and processing.
- The wastelands if not utilized within 3 years after giving possession should be transferred to other *bonafide* persons of the same village.
- Mass media literatures, night meetings and village exhibitions should be organised regularly as supporting activity for other farmers of the same or the neighbouring village.
- Voluntary agencies, schools and farmers' groups must be encouraged for maximum participation in wasteland development programme.
- Settlement procedure should encourage allottees to stay in the villages with the assets developed by them.
- There should be built in mechanism to give financial support for care and maintenance of plan.
- Plantation for fruits by small, marginal and landless farmers must be fully subsidized.
- Fruit/timber based industries should be promoted at appropriate level.
- Each district may hold inter-institutional, inter-departmental and inter-village level competitions in relation to wasteland development programme.

Development of Agro-afforestation in acre of *usar* land for Aonla and Guvava orchards with spacing of 8m × 8m and Aonla 60 plants and Guvava 44 plants include land preparation work, layout, digging and filling of pits, planting material (including 10 extra for gap filling), planting work, manures and fertilizer application, irrigation, interculture operation, plant protection, fencing (ridge making and planting of bushes and various miscellaneous activities for the proper growth of plants should be scientifically and technically managed with Technical Parameters for mixed plantation of Aonla and Guvava in *usar* land.

	Aonla	*Guvava*
Varieties	Chakiya, Francis, Kanchan, Krishna	L-49
Spacing	8 m × 8 m	8 m × 8 m
Plant population	60 plants	44 plants
Plantation time	July-September	July-September
Pit Size	1 × 1 × 1 m	1 × 1 × 1 m
Planting Mode	More than one variety should be planted to avoid in compatibility.	Same
Preparation for Planting	While digging the pit care should be taken that upper soil and lower soil should not be mixed. The sand 20 kg., FYM 50 kg/pit and gypsum 10 kg./pit should be applied in the pit.	Same
Manures & Fertilizers	*Manure*—Compost 20 kg./pit during second year and afterwards on incremental dose of 10 kg./pit/year upto 10th year may be applied. Thereafter 8 constant dose of 10th year.	Compost 20 kg./pit during 2nd year and from 3rd year onwards. A constant dose of 30 kg./pit should be applied.

Grassroots level training institutions in the different fields like crop production, vegetable, farming, fruits, fibres, forestry, fisheries and allied subjects. These research and development training institution could serve as district level institution for wasteland development and could coordinate with the concerned departments like agriculture, horticulture, soil conservation, forestry and other related agencies with the main role of transfer of technology through training and follow up action programme. The development of the wasteland require multi-disciplinary approach and research and development demonstration institutions have already a matching structure which would perform following role in wasteland development for agro-afforestation:

(i) Identification of wasteland in the district and classification of the same into the categories specified by the Government of India.

(ii) Study soil problems and reasons of the wasteland its increasing or decreasing trend and its possibility of reclamation and utilization through economically viable technologies.

(iii) Preparing economically, physically and technically feasible plan which is also socially acceptable.

(iv) Building up manpower pool to work at grassroots level through 3-6 months practical training for wasteland development.

(v) Establishing and maintaining nurseries for supply of trustworthy fruit plants, forestry plants and vegetable seedlings.

(vi) Helping young farmers to establish and maintain private nurseries and linking these nurseries with local plantation sites.

(vii) Undertaking pioneering work on the problem lands to serve as first line extension work.

(viii) Arranging short courses for the school teachers and staff of the Development Blocks and other related departments on reclamation of typical wastelands.

(ix) Training of the beneficiaries holding possession of the wastelands and identified for reclamation.

(x) Organising awareness camps in the villages and ensuring people participation in implementation of the programme by giving appropriate incentives.

(xi) Screening colour slides, video films and other methods.

(xii) Organizing exhibitions and field days on the work sites.

(xiii) HGKs could implement on farm research related to wasteland to serve as a very effective link between farmers and the scientists.

It is very difficult to formulate a uniform programme for all research and development demonstration extension institutions for development of wastelands because all the districts will not have the similar problems. However, some technical programmes can still be generalised for different areas :

- Survey identification and classification of wasteland.
- Preparing perspective landuse plan of the wasteland development.
- Testing of water quality of waterlogged areas, cleaning of water, layout and development of fish tank/fisheries development of pisciculture and paddy-*cum*-fish culture in other areas.
- Testing of soil and water in the usar lands, reclamation of usar land for crop production, social forestry, orchards. Application of plantation techniques, care and maintenance of plants.
- Raising nurseries in polythene bags and nursery beds; care and maintenance of nurseries and other nursery raising techniques specially budding and grafting for plant improvement.
- Scientific cultivation of crop on usar lands.
- Soil conservation practices on usar land, revine lands and undulated lands.
- Suitable agronomic practices and cropping systems to convert monocropping area into double cropping area or to convert into agro-forestry, social-forestry and orchards.
- Identification of suitable species for fuelwood, fodder, fibre, fruit plants and their plantation percentage per unit and other horticultural practices for different types of wastelands may be identified as per the details on next page.
- Social-forestry techniques on different types of land including identification and selection of appropriate species to suit the different soil conditions and farmers requirements.
- Agro-forestry techniques on degraded land.
- Crop production technologies and cropping system.
- Silvi-pastoral management and fodder management for livestock production based on reclamation of degraded land.
- Recycling of waste in reclamation and development of degraded land.
- On farm research in all the relevant areas of developing degraded land.

Group of species	Plantation percentage	Species scientific name	Speicies Hindi name
A. Fuel wood	25	1. *Acacia Tortillies*	Israeli Babool
		2. *Acacia Nilotica*	Babool
		3. *Zizyphus Mauritianu*	Ber
		4. *Azadirachta Indica*	Neem
		5. *Albizia Lebbeck*	Siris
		6. *Casia fistula*	Amaltash
		7. *Casuarina equiset Folia*	Kaijurina
		8. *Delonix Regia*	Gulmohar
B. Fodder	25	1. *Prosopis Juliflora*	Muscat
		2. *Prosopis Cineraria*	Jhand
		3. *Leuconena Leucocephal*	Subabool
C. Wood	15	1. *Dalbergia Sissoo*	Sisham
		2. *Acacia Catechu*	Khair
D. Fibre	10	1. *Morus Alba*	Shahtoot
E. Fruits	25	1. *Mauritiana*	Ber
		2. *Emblica Officinalis*	Anwala
		3. *Psidium Guvava*	Amrud
		4. *Lemon*	Nimbu
		5. *Caricapapaya*	Papita
		6. *Peech*	Adu
		7. *Tomarindus Indica*	Imli
		8. *Kinnu*	Kinnu
		9. *Karonda*	Karonda

Conclusion

Thus, the various strategies for the conservation of degraded wastelands for agro-forestry may be adopted for the reclamation of degraded wastelands to meet and fulfil the increasing demand of the human and cattle population. The importance of the local people for their continued participation, in the planning implementation maintenance, management and sharing of the usufructs may also be given proper attention. The needs of the local poor for the fuelwood, fodder, fibre, fruits, foodgrains, fisheries, timberwood may also be looked not before forming the micro action plan. The formation of agro-afforestation on wasteland management committee and the selection of beneficiaries, site and species choice should have common concurrence of the village as whole. The selection of the agro-technologies for the conservation of degraded land, the choice of technology for the agro-forestry also be planned as per the desire of the local people for their continued participation for sustainable development to generage employment increasing their income, conditions of the deprived rural poor. The agro-technologies and the strategies, problems faced by the farmers and hurdles in the farming and plantation programmes are several which can be solved within the village system through the Research and Development, demonstration extension institutions in close coordination with the District Administration and such agro-technologies which are adoptable, economically viable, socially justifiable, politically acceptable may be demonstrated to meet the increasing demand of the rural poor. An integrated approach for the landuse, population stabilization, sustainable agriculture for subsistance farming, greening of the land adopting methods of tree crop farming for protection of the forest and good quality lands and proper conservation of bio-mass may also be demonstrated to the rural poor. The planning and people's policy to meet their demands as per the capability and suitability of the land may be given due attention in the planning process in the direct participation of the panchayat as it has been practically demonstrated in village Palia by farming the agro-afforestation on wastelands management committee. It had been also found very successful. Thus, the village level micro action plan questionaire should be formulated and proper survey of the village should be completed to know the available land resources, natural and human resources, requirements of the local people so that accordingly as per their participation, interest, the micro action plan to conserve the degraded land for the agro-forestry, social-forestry and agricultural purposes may be visualized, planted, formulated the ever increasing human and cattle population may be solved by the growth of the degraded land may be checked and ecological imbalances of the area may be restored. Such programmes will have multiple impact and replication in the neighbourhood areas, it will improve the socio-economic condition of the deprived rural poor if planned and implemented on technically scientific lines.

26

Reclamation of Sagar Island, West Bengal
Environmental Problems and Human Responses

SUNANDO BANDYOPADHYAY

Located at the south-western corner of the Ganga delta, the Sagar island (Extension: 21°37′N to 21°57′N and 88°02′E to 88°11′E) is a 214.9 km^2 coastal low-lying area reclaimed from the mangrove forests called Sundarban during the early 19th century. Bounded in the east and in the west by two major tidal rivers of the region, the Hooghly and the Baratala, the Sagar's southern strand is open to the Bay of Bengal (Fig. 26.1). Along with the small outlying island of Ghoramara at its northern tip, it forms a development block in South 24-Parganas district of West Bengal.

Brief History of Reclamation and Peopling

Beginning from the times of the Mahabharata, about 1st century B.C. (Mohanty, 1986), the name of the Sagar island has found its way into a number of ancient scriptures (Dutta, 1935, 1990; Dey, 1983), historical accounts and travel anthologies (Sarkar, 1971; Chattopadhyay, 1980) because of its strategic location at the mouth of the Ganga delta and as a site of religious importance. The wide range of archaeological finds that have been dated to be from the early historical period (c. 3rd century B.C.-7th century A.D.) through the early medieval period (c. 9th-12th century A.D.) and later times also be taken a long, though probably not uninterrupted continuation of human inhabitance in the island (Dutta, 1950, 1989; Mitra, 1963; Haldar, 1985; Chakraborty, 1983). The island has also been named as a principal port of King Pratapaditya during the late 17th century (Mukherjee, 1912; Mitra, 1965).

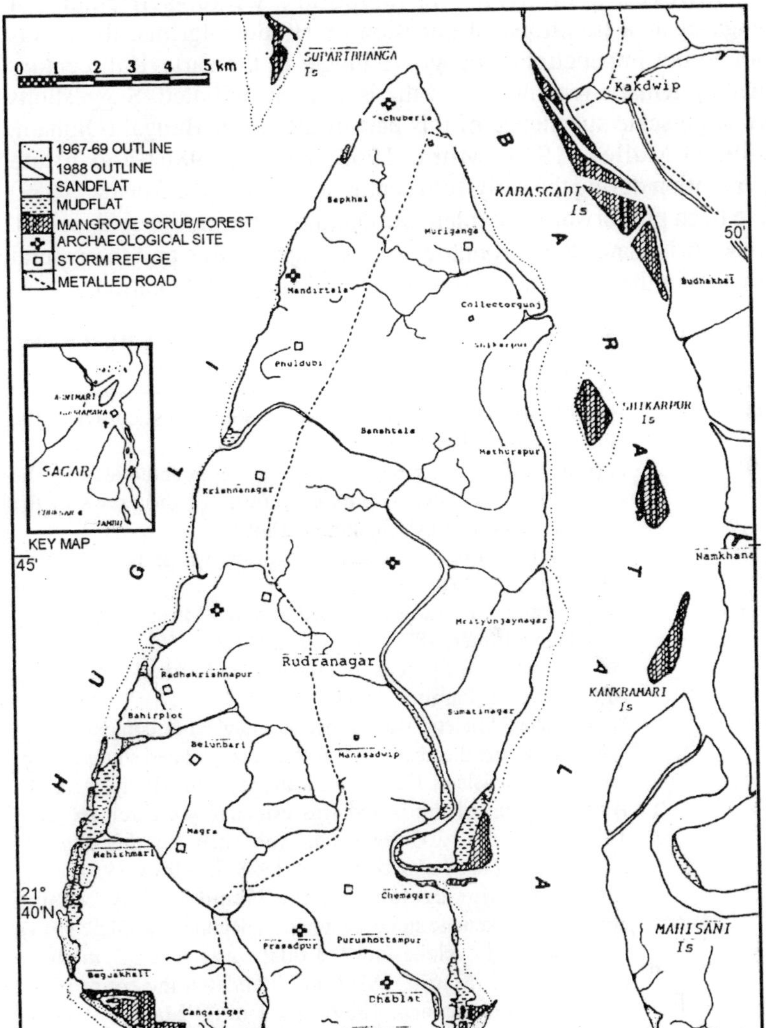

Fig. 26.1: Map of Sagar island and its surrounding areas (based on 1988 IRS-1A LISS-II imagery: F.C.C. and classified). The 1967-69 outline of some of the islands (based on Survey of India toposheet No. 79C/1 and 79C/2 has also been shown to indicate the extent of erosion for a period of approximately 20 years. Most of the mudflat and sandflat areas are liable to tidal inundation during highest high-tides.

However, apart from the temporary winter-settlement of Gangasagar, a traditional destination of Hindu pilgrims, there was nothing but impenetrable mangrove jungle in the early 19th century when systematic reclamation of the island was initiated. Suggestions like large-scale subsitence of this part of the lower Bengal (Oldham, 1939; O'Malley, 1914; Mitra, 1963; Rudra, 1986) and pirate intervention during the early 16th century (*The Calcutta Review*, 1859) have been put forward to explain the decline of the earlier settlements. Table 26.1 relates the chronology of the major events and the natural disasters in the early part of this modern phase of reclamation.

Table 26.1: Reclamation of the Sagar Island: Chronology of the major events (1808-1920)

1808	:	A light-house was constructed at the south-west corner of the island (Hunter, 1875).
1810	:	A project of cleaning Sagar island was conceptualized by the Government in order to provide refuge for the crews of the ships wrecked nearby (Chapman, 1869).
1811	:	The first lease of clearing and cultivation was granted (Hunter, 1875; Pargiter, 1889).
1813-14	:	Sagar island's area was reckoned at 580.9 km^2 by a survey by Lt. Blane (Hunter, 1875; Pargiter, 1934)*.
1817	:	An inquiry into the process of reclamation resulted in annulling of the scheme (Pargiter, 1934).
1819	:	"Sagar Island Society" was formed as a joint stock company and it stated to clear and embank the northern, central and south-eastern sections of the Island. Cultivators started to settle (Pargiter, 1934).
1820	:	About 10 km^2 of the island was effectively cleared (Hunter, 1879). A route to Gangasagar was built for the pilgrims (*Hamilton's East India Gazetteer*, 1828, in Mitra, 1954).
1823	:	The first major cyclone hit the island in July causing considerable damage since reclamation begun (O'Malley, 1914).
1833	:	On May 31, a cyclone-induced tidal surge rose 3.7 m above ordinary level (Martin, 1836) and inundated the entire island under 2.1 m (Chapman, 1809) to 3.1 m (O'Malley, 1914) of water and destroyed almost everything. More than 85% of the 7,000 inhabitants were killed (Chapman, 1869). The society threw up the scheme "in despair" (Pargiter, 1934, p. 116).
1834-35	:	The ownership of the northern blocks was transferred and the

* This figure, clearly an overestimation (see Table 26.2), is still found in the Census of India Handbooks (cf: Mitra, 1953; Ray, 1963; Ghosh, 1973, 1982) and other Government literature.

		Government started supporting infrastructural facilities in exchange of making salt for it (Pargiter, 1934).
1840-52	:	In June 1845, October 1848, and June, 1852, severe cyclonic storms caused serious damages. Reclamation was temporarily abandoned in the south-eastern section (Dhablat) for want of fresh water (O'Malley, 1914). Cyclones, though less severe, also occurred in May 1840, April 1850 and October 1851 (Harrison, 1909).
1852-53	:	"Salt-rules", a new Government regulation, benefited the salt-making trade and the island proposed (Pargiter, 1934).
1862-63	:	A survey revealed 41.7 km^2 of the total island area had been cleared and the remaining part was dense jungle (Pargiter, 1934). The area under cultivation was about 33 km^2 (Chapman, 1860).
1864	:	On October 5, a cyclone and the consequent tidal wave swept across the island "with great force and wrought great havoc" Pargiter, 1934, p. 117. Some of the estimates of its height above the ground had been 3.4 m (Hunter, 1875), under 4 m (Rundell, 1903) and 4.6 m (Beadle, 1903; O'Malley, 1914). Of the 5,625 inhabitants 73.6% were killed (Chapman, 1869).
1866	:	The island-inhabitants "suffered severely" in a famine (Lane, 1869, p. 11).
1867	:	A storm surge reduced the area under cultivation to just 3.7 km^2 and killed 5 out of the 787 inhabitants on November 1 and 2. All sections of the island were wholly or partly abandoned except the south-eastern part which was prospering under an Indian proprietor (Chapman, 1869).
1871	:	Construction of storm refugees, according to a specific site-plan, was made mandatory for the grant owners in the island (Pargiter, 1934).
1876	:	Another cylone passed over the island (Mitra, 1963; Reznov, 1984).
1880	:	Lease of the northern and central blocks were transferred for the first time to an Indian. Rapid clearing of the area for cultivation followed (Ascoli, 1921).
1897	:	An earthquake caused submergence of a part of the island's southern extremity and detached the northern section of Sagar (Mud Point or Ghoamara) from the main island (Datta, 1950).*

* There is some uncertainty about exactly when this breaching took place. O'Malley (1914) wrote that the 1867 cyclone "appeared to cut a channel straight across the island, dividing it into two halves" (p. 136). However, there is no evidence of this in the 1874 map of Thuillier ("District 24-Pergunnahs"; 1 : 253,440). Maiti (1989) has proposed this date to be 1903 but he has not supported it with any evidence. As chronological studies of old maps indicate, the event must have taken place sometime between 1887 and 1922-23.

1898-1901	:	Leasing of the whole island was completed (Ascoli, 1921).
1904	:	An inspection into the settled areas revealed deplorable conditions (Ascoli, 1921).
1911	:	Sunderban was declared as a reserved forest (Das, 1990). Sagar island was, however, outside its bounds.
1915	:	Only 5.1 km^2 of the island area was found to be under cultivation. A post of colonization officer was created (Ascoli, 1921).
1916-20	:	Systematic clearing and settling continued with periodic reviews and strategy revisions (Ascoli, 1921).

By the end of World War I, the institutional aspects of colonization were completed in Sagar, and it was left for the migrating settlers, mostly coastal people from the neighouring Medinipur district across the Hooghly, to push the frontier of Sundarban out of the island (Table 26.2). Officially, the last phase of reclamation was completed here between 1951 and 1971, when the Banstala and Shikarpur jungles of the central Sagar were cleared for the refugees from East Pakistan (Mukherjee, 1983). Today, the island is a far cry from the time when, as Wilson (1862) has described, "tigers lurked in the jungle and not unfrequently carried off the pilgrims" (Hunter, 1875, p. 103). The only prominent (protected) mangrove patch (Mainly *Phoenix paludosa* with scattered *Ceriops decandra*) is restricted in its south-western extremity and covers just 1.9 km^2 of area (Fig. 26.1). At present, not only there is no land available in the island for further reclamation, but also the marginal areas are getting eroded continuously (Table 26.2). This, viewed in the perspective of a growing population (Table 26.3), highlights the need for protection of the agricultural areas from further diminution.

The Problems

Nature and Location

Exposure to tide-water and remobilized coastal sand are the two major hazards faced by the inhabitants of the Sagar island.

Here, tide-water is involved in two problems: coastal erosion in the fringe areas and inundation of agricultural land. While inundations are by and large episodic events, caused by cyclonic storm-surges, coastal erosion can be both episodic or continuous—operating on every highest high-tides, specially during the monsoons. The episodic

Table 26.2: Changing Area and Forest Cover of Sagar Island (1978-1988)

Source	*Year*	*Scale*	*Total Area (in km^2)*	*Forested Area (in km^2)*	*Rate of Loss (–)/ Gain (+) of Area (in $km\ yr^{-2}$)*	*Rate of Maximum Transgression with Locality (in $m\ yr^{-2}$)*
1. J. Rennell's Bengal Atlas: Sheet No. 1	1778	1:760320	443.8	443.8		
2. H.L. Thuillier's Map of District 24-Pergunnahs (Sheet No. 121 of Atlas of India)	1874	1:253440	293.4	293.4	–1.6 (1778-1874)	73.8 (1778-1884): in the south-central
3. R.A. Thuillier's Map of District 24-Pergunnahs (Sheet No. 121 of Atlas of India.	1887	1:253440	256.1	201.8	–2.9 (1874-87)	148.5 (1874-87): in the south-central (Gangasagar)
4. Survey of India's Sheet No. 79C	1922-23	1:253440	247.8	not shown	–0.2 (1887-1992)	54.4 (1887-1922): in the south-west (Dhablat)
5. Survey of India's Sheet No. 79 C/1 and 79 C/2	1942	1:63360	229.6	19.2	–0.9 (1922-42)	69.3 (1922-42): in the south-west (Dhablat)
6. Survey of India's Sheet No. 79 C/1 and 79 C/2	1967-69	1:50000	224.5	5.2	–0.2 (1942-68)	34.7 (1942-68): in the north-west (Collectorgunj)
7. Aerial photographs (mosaic of 47 photos spread in five runs)	1977	1:53500	224.7	4.9	+0.03 (1968-77)	29.4 (1968-77): in the south-west (Basantapur)
8. IRS-1A LISS-II imagery (standard F.C.C. and classified: mosaic of six scenes)	1988	1:100000	214.9	2.7	–0.9 (1977-88)	23.9 (1977-88): in the west-central (Sumatinagar)

Table 26.3: Growth of Population in the Sagar Island (1872-1991)

Year	*Population (including the outer islands*)*	*Index*	*Population (excluding the outer islands)*	*Index*
1872	8381	100		
1881	10072	120		
1891	11881	142		
1901	15065	180		
1911	16975	203		
1921	19445	232		
1931	31505	376		
1941	44941	536		
1951	51463	614	48606	100
1961	73629	879	69587	143
1971	91229	1089	86569	178
1981	111228	1327	106672	219
1991 (estimated)	131150	1565	126027	259

* These islands got detached from the Sagar in 1903. (See Table 26.1 and Fig. 26.1 for details). However, their population figures could not be separated from those of the main island prior to 1951 because of non-availability of data.

Source: Compiled from : Mitra, 1954; Ray, 1963; Ghosh, 1973, 1982.

storm surges, however, are far more dangerous. Twelve hours of pounding by the extra-powerful waves during a cyclone can be equivalent to a century's worth of normal wave action (Tifft, 1985). Affecting all the three sides of the triangle-shaped island, the localities of coastal erosion, in response to changing processes and dynamics, have shown considerable shifting in the past 200 years. In isolated patches, land accretion has also taken place (Bandyopadhyay, 1990). This accounts for the slight increase in the total area of the island between 1967-69 and 1977 (Table 26.2). The zones currently undergoing erosion have been shown in Fig. 26.1.

In Sagar, sand flats and sand dunes are confined in the sea-facing southern coast and the southern part of the eastern and western peripheries overlooking the Hooghy and the Baratala respectively. The dunes, attaining a maximum height of 8.1 m, form a near-continuous belt between Gangasagar and Dhablat in the western part of the southern coast, while the remaining part is mainly occupied by sand flats and occasional muddy patches. Consequently, dune encroachment and sand blasting over agricultural areas concern mainly the bay-facing stretches of southern Sagar. This includes the accreting Raspur-Basantapur section (sand blasting and dune migration) with an abundant sand supply in the west and the eroding Beguakhali section (sand blasting only) in the south-eastern corner. Aided by strong on-shore winds, sand progradation is mostly operative during the dry pre-monsoonal season of March, April and May.

Evidences

Recurrence interval of the severe cyclonic storms that repeatedly affected the island during its early history of colonization (Table 26.1) has shown a tendency to increase in the later times. Since 1921 about seven major stroms have hit the island apart from a few minor ones (Maiti, 1989). None of these has been destructive to any large extent except a 1942 event.

Sagar's southern coast-line is retreating at an alarming rate (Table 26.2). The well-known Kapil temple of Gangasagar where one of the largest Indian festivals is held every January (average attendance in the three-day fair: approximately 750,000 people), had to be relocated thrice since the old one, described in detail by Wilson (1862), was submerged during the 1897 earthquake (Dutta, 1950). An entire *mouza* called Bishalakshipur was transgressed by the sea between 1942 and 1969. At present, many other coastal villages are also undergoing active erosion. These include Sumatinagar, Mrityunjaynagar, Phuldubi, Beguakhali (Plate 26.1), Bahirplot, Shibpur, Shikarpur and the archaeological site of Mandirtala among others. This problem has recently been reported by Banerjee (1992). [It may be mentioned here that Jothimani and Garg (1991) have shown that tidal ingress has caused desertation of villages in the Rann of Kachchh, Gujarat, in recent times. Coastal settlements in Medinipur district (West Bengal) and other parts of the reclaimed Sundarban also face similar threats.]

An uninterrupted survey of the island's sea-beach was conducted by the Geological Survey of India between 1984 and 1989. It indicated that "*en mass* block-erosion" was taking place in the eastern (Dhablat) section of the beach, while the Gangasagar-Raspur part was accreting. The maximum values of beach-face lowering and rising had been 1.68 m and 2.22 m respectively (Chakraborty, 1989; Bandopadhyay and Chakraborty, 1990). Profile sampling and seasonal beach mapping by the author since February 1990, also connote similar results for the eastern section and on-going erosion for the western

(Beguakhali-Gangasagar) section. In the beach itself, eroding bottom clay sequences that form prominent breaks of slope in the beach profiles, remnants of obliterated mangroves (mainly *Heritiera fomes*) and other village-associated trees (*Ficus benghalensis*, *Borassus Clavalifer*, *Phoenix sylvestris*, etc.) as well as wave-cut frontal dunes also indicate active erosion (Bandyopadhyay, 1990).

Plate 26.1: The eroding village of Beguakhali, Sagar island, in June, 1991.

Between 1984 and 1989, the coastal dune belt of the Sagar has retreated 14.5 m at the rate of 2.9 m yr^{-1} (Bandopadhyay and Chakraborty, 1990, which, in this case, is almost synonymous with advancement of the sea. In later years, between synonymous with advancement of the sea. In later years, between February 1990, and February 1992, the rates of sand encroachment over agricultural areas have shown variance between 0.2 m yr^{-1} and 22.6 m yr^{-1} in various sampling sites along the coast (Plate 26.2).

The Responses

Embankments

Embanking the coast-line and the major tidal channels, apart from completely blocking the smaller ones, had been the usual reclamation

Plate 26.2: Progradation of dunes over agricultural areas in the eastern end of Raspur-Gokulnagar, Sagar island.

procedure of the Sagar island like elsewhere in the Sundarban. These are done in order to prevent inundation of the marginal low-lying areas by the highest high-tide or storm-surges. The forests are cleared subsequently. A widely practised process in many areas of the world, the problem associated with reclamation of the low-lying coastal areas is that, by keeping out silt-laden tidal water, the region remains for ever lower than the highest high-tide and/or storm-surge levels. In the Sundarban, it was too late when this was realized (e.g. by Ascoli, 1921) and a large part of the region was already reclaimed or leased out. For example, Adams-Williams in his book *History of Rivers in the Gangetic Delta: 1750-1918* had opined that, in the Sundarban, "river requirements must ever remain the essential condition of any extension of reclamation" and that, "it must be the policy of the future to arrest reclamation in that area till the tidal spill has done its work (and) to avoid heavy embankments until the height of the land is a sufficient protection against the highest tides" (Ascoli, 1921, 159).

The existing embankments of the Sagar Island are mostly earthen and require constant maintenance. They are clearly inadequate for the sustained storm-waves of the summer monsoons (June to September) let alone the cyclonic surges, and breaches are not uncommon (Plate 26.3). Maintained mostly by the village panchayats, these walls are generally repaired just before the onset of the monsoons every year. (The Sagar has nine independently elected Panchayats comprising 41 villages in all. Funds for most of the State or Central Government's development projects are routed through them). This is hardly the proper time for it because, the constructional material does not get the proper time to settle into a cohesive body before the rainy season sets in and washes them out. Political considerations in giving priority to repairs in certain areas are also not unheard of. In the island, the outer embankments are partly double with an intervening gap that ranges from 50 m to 200 m. Between them, regularly spaced cross-embankments, about 150 m apart, are also built to prevent water from inundating a large area in case a breach occurs. There are, however, quite a few localities where only a single embankment exists along the coast—among these, the one at the Botkhali region of Dhablat is extremely vulnerable.

Two sea-facing brick-lined embankments were built in the Basantpur-Raspur section and the Dhablat-Shibpur area in 1963 by the State Government's Department of Irrigation and Waterways. While the former has now got burried under accumulating sands, parts of the latter have recently been completely wahsed away, rendering 32 families homeless. [These families have now formed squatting settlements along the current (formerly inner) embankment over-looking the sea. A similar case of squatting settlers has also been cited by Elahi (1989) from the eroding western bank of the

Plate 26.3: Eroding marginal embankments, Sagar island. (These can be co-mpared with Fig. 26.2)

(a) A breached sea-facing brick-lined embankment at Botkhali, Shibpur, in February 1991.

(b) A part of an embankment overlooking the Baratala at Kach-uberia in June, 1991. The bamboo fences were erected after a part of the embankment collapsed.

Jamuna in northern Bangladesh.] Though they work well in protecting river bank erosion, these embankments, built by pitching brick-blocks and cementing them together over an earthen base, are easily penetrated by the breaking waves. The waves wash away the mud, causing the entire structure to collapse. The constructional details of the typical embankments used in the Sagar island have been given in Fig. 26.2.

In the south-east corner of the island (Beguakhali), a fairly elaborate scheme using concrete break-waters was implemented in 1975 to save a semaphore station. This time, though the structures did not disintegrate, beach materials from their bases were eroded away (which could have been caused by wave-reflection) and the defences gave in.

Storm Refuges

As described in Table 26.1, in 1871, the Government made it mandatory for the grant-owners to construct storm refuges for the settling cultivators according to pre-laid specifications (Fig. 26.2). Planned by J.O. Mynes, a Superintending Engineer of that time, these were meant to supply fresh drinking water as well as shelter in the case of total innundation by saline water during a cyclonic storm (Chapman, 1869; Pargiter, 1934). According to Thuillier's 1886 map of *District Midnapore* (1:253, 440), in which the Sagar island forms a part, the first of these refuges was constructed in Kachuberia at the northern tip of the island (Fig. 26.1). At present, though in a degraded condition, 11 storm refuges are, still, found in the island. A few of these were last used during a 1942 cyclone. As a survey of the refuges has revealed, their construction, however, did not follow the specifications exactly.

Afforestation

To prevent sand encroachment, green belts using *Casuarina equisetifolia* and, in a few places, *Accacia accacia* have been created by the villagers of the southern Sagar (through the Panchayats or at a private level) since 1976. A notable exception of this is Beguakhali, where no agricultural area is directly threatened. The protective wind-breaks have worked most satisfactorily in Basantapur (Satyabatipur) and Dhablat (Shibpur) where several rows of *Casuarina equisetifolia*

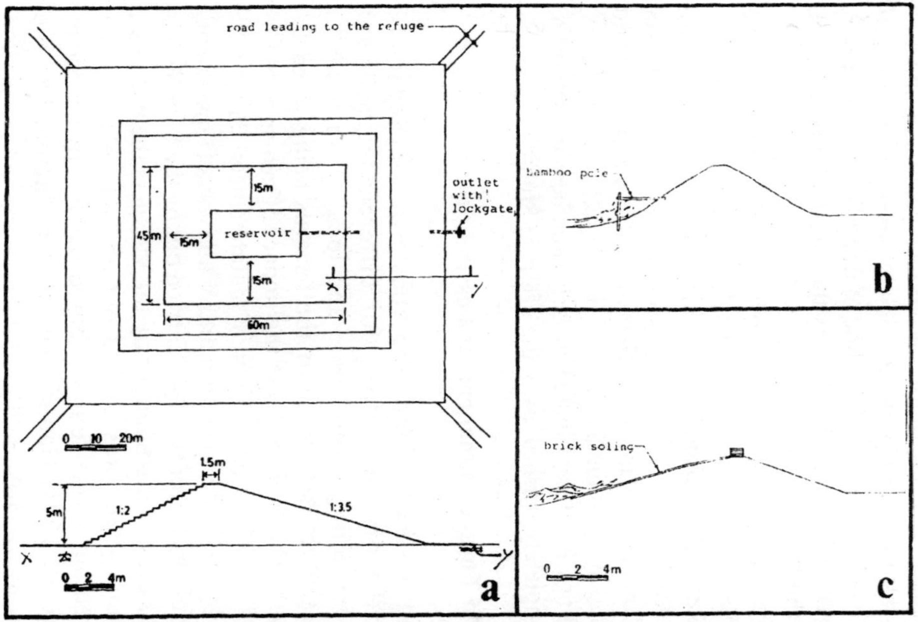

Fig. 26.2: (a) Plan (above) and section (below) of storm refuges as specified in the 1871 plan (based on data in Pargiter, 1934, and field surveys).
(b) Section of the typical earthen embankments used in Sagar. The wooden barrier acts as a buffer between the breakers and the embankment.
(c) Section of the typical brick embankments used in the isalnd (both 2b and 2c are based on field measurements).

have been planted to raise a man-made forest. In other areas, trees have been grown over an embankment (constructed in 1976) in a linear fashion. This has created a new series of back-dunes which have now started to overcome the barrier (Plate 26.1), making the respite a short-lived one. In Shibpur, though the afforestation programme initiated by the collective effort of the villagers has completely checked dune migration for the time being, this situation is not going to last for long. Coastal erosion in this region has already removed what used to be a 5.8 m high line of frontal dunes in February 1990, and, currently, has started to destroy the forest originally created at the back of the frontal dunes.

On a different role, vegetation has also been used to prevent coastal erosion in the Sagar. For example, artificially planted *Avecinnia alba* trees have worked well in ensuring bank stabilization at the Chemagari confluence. In August 1991, seeds of *Avecinnia* were air-dropped over the Bahirplot (Radhakrishnapur) sandflats of south-western Sagar and were row-planted in the Shibpur mudflats of the south-east. At present, while the seedings have germinated in large numbers in Bahirplot, the sea has completely washed away the effort in Shibpur.

Evaluation and Future Management Possibilities

Despite being a small island, the coasts of the Sagar are characteristically diverse, calling for different management programmes depending on the time and locality. In order to ascertain the relative importance of the hazards being faced by the coastal inhabitants and to assess the impact of management of the existing infrastructure (embankment maintenance: done by the Panchayats or by the State Irrigation and Waterways Department) or the newer projects (afforestation: carried out by the Panchayats or by the State Forest Department or by the villagers themselves), a sample opinion survey was carried out on randomly selected families in three out of the four sea-board hamlets of the Sagar island in February 1991. Gangasagar was not included in the survey because, with a large section of the non-resident population related with tourism-related jobs, it is characteristically quite different from the other settlements of the island. Among the rest, Raspur-Gokulnagar is a small linear settlement that is constituted by just 18 families—all of whom were interviewed. A summary of the results of this survey, which shows a general dissatisfaction concerning the progress of the management works, have been given in Table 26.4.

As seen earlier, permanency of the earthen embankments of the Sagar can never be guaranteed under a sustained storm-wave condition. Laterite boulders, which have been used with some short-term success in Digha and Haldia for the prevention of erosion, can be experimentally brought over the water, to the island from Medinipur. However, this needs a great deal of funding apart from foresight—because it is not definite whether they will be suitable for the conditions prevailing in the Sagar. Often the long-term effect of human modification of coastal environment is unpredictable and it should be attempted only after adequate research on the possible feedbacks (Bruun, 1971; Goudie, 1986). Perhaps, a more practical thing would be to mobilize the existing resources in a rational framework. Strict and time-bound periodic maintenance of the embankments would probably make a longer way into the core of the problem than building costly but wrongly designed brick embankments.

The role of the mangroves, as coastal stabilizers, cannot be over-emphasised (Hellier, 1988) and the sooner the erosion-prone sections of the island opt for forming a mangrove-buffer between the sea and the embankments the better. Paul (1991) has recommended *Avicennia alba* and *Avicennia oficinalis* for re-establishment of the mangrove-barrier in the deforested mud flats of the Sundarban. The reason of the recent failure of the *Avicennia* plantation scheme in Shibpur must have been the choice of location and time—the first was well inside the high-tide line in an extremely erosive coastal stretch and the second, in the monsoon season.

From a different view-point, a scheme has been suggested by Mukherjee (1976) for permanently raising the reclaimed coastal low-lying areas above the tidal or storm-surge levels. According to his plan, the silt-carrying high-tide water, using sluices, should be let in daily from February to June to inundate the land adjacent to the embanked tidal channels and be drained out, saving a 15 to 20 cm deep standing water, during the low-tides. This, however, has to be drained out completely at the beginning of the monsoon and, for the rest of the year, paddy (salt-tolerant species if needed) can be cultivated in the fresh water available from the rains. In this scheme, aquaculture is also possible if the sluices are protected by nets of suitable mesh.

Table 26.4: Sample Opinion Survey of Three Sea-Board Villages of the Sagar Island (February 1991): A Summary of the Findings

		Villages		
		Shibpur (Dhablat)	*Raspur-Gokulnagar*	*Beguakhali*
A1	Most critical problem(s) being faced by the village:			
	(a) Coastal erosion	96.2%	0%	64.7%
	(b) Dunal encroachment	0%	83.4%	0%
	(c) Salt-water incursion	3.8%	0%	14.7%
	(a) and (b)	0%	16.6%	0%
	(a), (b) and (c)	0%	0%	20.6%
A2	Families intending to leave their parental home because of the problems they are facing:	76.9%	0%	29.4%
B1	Families feeling endangered because of coastal erosion:	96.2%	22.2%	85.3%
B2	Families satisfied with protection offered by the embankments:	3.8%	77.8%	14.7%
B3	Agency best maintaining the embankments:			
	(a) Panchayat	79.9%	66.7%	55.9%
	(b) State Irrigation Department	23.1%	38.9%	44.1%
B4	Families losing all or part of their landholdings due to delluviation:	42.1%	77.8%	35.3%
B5	Families changing their profession (e.g. from farming to fishing) because of delluviation:	34.6%	0%	14.7%
C1	Families bring part of their land because of dune progradation:	3.8%	77.8%	50 %
C2	Families satisfied with the protection offered by the vegetative barriers (afforestation):	100%	55.6%	17.6%

(Contd.)

(Contd.)

C3	Agency best carrying out the afforestation programme:	11.5%	77.8%	14.7%
	(a) Panchayat			
	(b) State Forest Department	–	5.5%	–
	(c) Collective effort	76.9%	16.7%	–
D1	Total number of families residing in the hamlet	161	18	103
D2	Number of families surveyed:	52	18	34
D3	Average size of the families (adults + children)	4.2 + 4.6	4.9 + 4.6	4.1 + 4.4
D4	Number of families all of whose members are illiterate:	8	8	5

Note: (1) In A1, B3 and C3, the figures represent per cent of families favouring a certain possibility (e.g. in A1, 96.2% of families feel coastal erosion is the most critical problem being faced by their village).

(2) In C3, not all of the families answered.

(3) in D1, the sources of the figures are respective Panchayats.

For stabilization of the dunes, it is suggested that the use of *Casuarina equisetifolia* should be discontinued. Not only this species has failed to check dune migration unless planted to create a man-made forest, but also it has inhibited growth of the natural dune binders by contributing a highly acidic leaf-litter. (Though not apparent in the Sagar, consumption of this species as fuel has degenerated the afforested areas of the nearby Bakkhali region, about 15 km in the east, across the Baratala). Further, as Chakrabarti (1991) has observed, these tall trees, unlike creepers, are unable to withstand strong winds and sometimes get uprooted. While rows of *Casuarina equisetifolia* can be used as the final defence against migrating dunes, growth of natural dune colonizers like *Ipomoea pes-carpae, Launaea Sarmentosa, Cyperus exaltatus* and, to some extent, Opuntea dillenii should be promoted on the dune itself. *Pandanus faccicularis* can be grown in the dune slacks. Experience from the Sagar island has shown that, in regions sheltered from a high degree of anthropogenic pressure and grazing activity (e.g. east of the Gangasagar sand flat), these plants have stabilized coastal dunes quite satisfactorily and have checked dune migration altogether. In other parts, human intervention has notably reduced their effectiveness—one bald patch often acting as a nucleus of a blow-out.

The fact that no highly destructive cyclone has lashed the Sagar island since 1942 simply indicates the high probability of such an event in near future. While the old storm refuges are mostly unusable, evacuation drills or newer infrastructural facilities like concrete storm shelters that had saved thousands of lives in the devastating 1991 cyclone of Bangladesh (Moreau *et al.*, 1991) are unknown in the island. It seems that future negligence in this aspect may prove extremely costly for the island's inhabitants.

Conclusion

From the standpoint of the settlers, some of the reasons for human occupance of the hazard-prone regions are: superior economic opportunity, lack of alternative opportunities and high ratios of reserve to potential loss (Natural Hazards Research Working Paper No. 16, 1970). All of these are partly or fully true for the reclaimed regions of the Sundarban.

Chronological study of maps, serial photos and satellite imageries indicate that the coast of the Indian Sundarban—specially its reclaimed part—is steadily getting eroded since Rennell prepared the first map of the region using modern survey techniques in 1778-80. It seems that the phase of delta building has been over in this zone for the past several years and, in all probability, this trend is going to continue in the future.

In 1867, Chapman wrote: "Sagar island is more valuable as a break-water to save the mainland from full destructive force of storm waves than as a precarious field for agriculture." (Chapman, 1869, 7). The opinion of Adams-Williams (Ascoli, 1921) has already been quoted. Some of the later authors dealing with the Sundarban region also did not approve of the reclamation process and suggested various schemes to facilitate deltatic accretion (e.g. Mukherjee, 1969, 1973; Pramanic and Sinha, 1972, etc.)

While it is generally true that premature reclamation of the coastal low lands stops the natural process of delta building, whether it can be applied to a region where deltaic accretion has practically stopped seems debatable. Reclamation of the Sagar island can, thus, be evaluated from two opposing viewpoints. It either has been a fruitful long-term attempt (periodic loss of life and property notwithstanding) that has made most out of a fertile strip of land bound for oblivion, or it has unnecessarily exposed a section of the population to a hazardous environment.

Acknowlegements

Sincere thanks are expressed to Mr. Kanailal Das, Calcutta University, for his support in conducting the field surveys. Thanks are also due to Prof. M.K. Bandopadhyay, Mr. Subir Bera, Ms. Bina Das and Mr. Subrata Ghosh for their help.

REFERENCES

Ascoli, F.D., (1921). *A Revenue History of the Sundarbans from 1870 to 1920*, The Bengal Secretariat Book Depot: 76:79, 142-55, 158-59.

Bandopadhyay, P.C. and Chakraborty, S.C., (1990). "Repeat beach mapping and survey profiling at Bakkhali, Sagar islands, 27-Parganas (South), West Bengal", *Records, Geol. Surv. Ind.*, 123(3): 27.

Bandopadhyay, S., (1990). "Evolution of the Sagar island coast-line, West Bengal, between 1923 and 1990", in B.K. Roy (ed.), *Cartography for Development of Outlying States and Islands of India*, 2, Monography No. 10, Nat. Atlas and Thematic Mapping Org.: 68-69.

Beadle, J.P., (1903). "Note on the progress of the late hurricane (dated October

25, 1864)", *Prepare from 1864 to 1873 Regarding the Cyclone Wave of 1864 and its Effect on the Hooghly Embankments etc.*, Bengal Secretariat Press, Calcutta: 2.

Bruun, P., (1971). "Coastal research and its economic justification", in J.A. Steers (ed.), *Introduction to Coastline Development*, Macmillan, London: 204-25.

Chakrabarti, P., (1991). "Process response system analysis in the macrotidal estuarine and mesotidal coastal plain of eastern India", in R. Vaidyanadhan (ed.), *Quaternary Deltas of India*, Mem. Geol. Soc. Ind., 22: 165-81.

Chakrabarti, S.K. (1983). "Archaeological treasures of 24-Parganas in the Indian Museum" (in Bengali), *24-Parganas Archaeological Conference*, Baruipur: 79-82.

Chakraborty, S.C., (1989). "Repeat beach mapping and survey profiling at Bakkhali, Sagar Islands, 24-Parganas district, West Bengal", *Records, Geol. Surv. Ind.*, 122(3): 13.

Chapman, R.B., (1869). "Official Paper No. 103CE" (dated December 28, 1867), *Correspondence Relating to the Settlement of Saugor Island for 1869:* Bengal Secretariat Book Depot. Calcutta: 1-9.

Chattopadhyay, S., (1880). *Periplus of the Erythrean Sea and Ptolemy on Ancient Geography of India*, Prajna, Calcutta: 120-21, 134-42.

Das. S., (1990). "Human interference in the ecology of Sundarban, West Bengal", *Indian Journal of Landscape Systems and Ecological Studies*, 13(2): 83-86.

Dey, G.S., (1983). Copper inscriptions and coins found in 24-Parganas (in Bengali), *24-Parganas Archaeological Conference*, Baruipur: 71-76.

Dutta, K., (1935). A brief historical account of Sundarbans (in Bengali), in Sen, D.C., *Greater Bengal* (in Bengali), 2, Calcutta University Pub., Calcutta: 1126-32.

Dutta, K., (1950). "Western Sundarbans in ancient times" (in Bengali), *Probasi* [Reprinted in *24-Parganas Archaeological Conference* (1983), Baruipur]: 12-18.

Datta, K., (1989). *The Past of South 24-Parganas* (in Bengali), 1, (Edited by S. Bhattacharyya and H. Majumdar), Sundarban Regional Museum; Baruipur: 32-33.

Elahi, K.M., (1989). "Population displacement due to riverbank erosion of the Jamuna in Bangladesh", in J.I. Clarke, P. Curson, S.L. Kayastha, and P. Nag, (eds.): *Population and Disaster*, Blackwell, Oxford: 81-97.

Ghose, B., (1978). *District Census Handbook of Twentyfour Parganas, West Bengal, 1971*, 22(10-B): 352-53.

Ghose, S.N., (1982). *District Census Handbook of 24-Parganas, 1981*, 23(13-B): 468-69.

Goudie, A., (1986). *The Human Impact on the Natural Environment*, (2nd edn.), Basil-Blackwell Ltd., Oxford: 232-42.

Haldar, N., (1983). "Archaeological Treasures of Diamond Harbour" sub-division (in Bengali), *24-Parganas Archaeological Conference*, Baruipur: 55-57.

Harrison, H.L., (1909). *Bengal Embankment Manual,* Bengal Secretariat Press, Calcutta: xxxi-xxxvi.

Hellier, C., (1988). "The mangrove wastelands", *The Ecologist,* 18(2): 77-79.

Hunter, W.W., (1879). *A Statistical Account of Bengal,* 2, Trubner and Co., London: 102-6, 259-60.

Jothimani. P. and Garg, J.K., (1991). "Mapping and monitoring of tidal ingress in Banni plains, Kachchh, Gujarat, using multi-temporal satellite data" (Abstr.), *Souvenir and Abstracts of Int. Sem. on Monitoring Geosystems Perspectives for the 21st Century,* December 6-9, 1991, Delhi University: 35.

Lane, T.B. (1869). Official Paper No. 1971B (dated April, 16th 1868). *Correspondence Relating to the Settlement of Saugor Island for 1869*, Bengal Secretariat Book Depot, Calcutta : 11.

Maiti, J., (1989). *Holy Pilgrimage Gangasagar* (in Bengali), published by A.K. Maiti, Sagar Isl. : 50-58.

Martin, R., (1836). *Notes on Medical Topography of Calcutta:* 84, 151. (cited in Chapman, 1869: 3).

Mitchell, B., (1979). *Geography and Resource Analysis*, Longman, London : 217-20.

Mitra, A., (1954). *District Census Handbook of 24-Parganas, West Bengal, 1951*: 3, 440-44, cvi-cviii.

Mitra, S.C., (1963). *History of Jessore and Khulna* (in Bengali), 1, 3rd edition (edited by S.S. Mitra), Dasgupta and Co. Pvt. Ltd., Calcutta : 61-67, 73, 155-56.

——, (1965). *History of Jessore and Khulna* (in Bengali), 2, 2nd edition (edited by S.S. Mitra), Dasgupta and Co. Pvt. Ltd., Calcutta : 153-54, 205-6, 223.

Mohanty, J.N., (1988). Indian Philosophy, *Encyclopaedia Britannica*, Macropaedia-21, 15th edition, Encycl. Britannica Inc., Chicago : 180-201.

Moreau, R., Shahriar, H. and Whitmore, J., (1991). "Death in the winds", *Newsweek*, 117(19) : 10-14.

Mukherjee, K.N., (1969). Nature and problems of neo-reclamation in Sundarbans, *Geographical Review of India,* 31(4) : 1-9.

——, (1976). Harmonious solution of the basic problem of Sundarbans reclamation, *Geographical Review of India*, 38(3) : 311-15.

——, (1983). History of settlement in the Sundarbans of West Bengal, *Ind. Jour. Landscape Systems,* 6 (1 and 2) : 1-19.

Mukherjee, R.K. (1912). *Indian Shipping : A History of the Sea-borne Trades, and the Maritime Activity of the Indians form the Earliest Times,* Longman Green and Co., Calcutta : 21-26.

Natural Hazards Research Working Paper No. 16 (1970). Suggestions for Comparative Field Observations on Natural Hazards, Dept. of Geography, Toronto University, Toronto. (Cited in Mitchell, 1979 : 217-20).

O'Malley, L.S.S., (1914). *Bengal District Gazetteers—24-Parganas,* Bengal Secretariat Book Depot, Calcutta : 13-14, 135-37, 254-58.

Oldham, R.D., (1939). *A Manual of the Geology of India and Burma,* 3 (Revised and re-written by E.H. Pascoe), 3rd edition (1964 reprint). Geological, Survey of India : 1986-90.

Pargiter, F.E., (1889). The Sundarbans, *Calcutta Review*, 178 : 280-301.

Pargiter, (1934). *A Revenue History of the Sundarbans from 1765 to 1870,* Bengal Government Press, Alipur : 115-18.

Paul, A.K., (1991). Effective management strategies for the coast of West Bengal, *Geographical Review of India,* 53(1) : 60-74.

Pramanik, H.R. and Sinha, G., (1972). Development of coastal areas in western Sundarbans, *Proceedings of the Seminar on Geomorphology, Geohydrology and Geotechnics of the Lower Ganga Basin,* Indian Institute of Technology, Kharagpur : C7-C15.

Ray, B., (1963). *District Census Handbook of 24-Parganas, West Bengal, 1961,* 2: 290-95.

Reznov, I.A., (1984). *Catastrophes in Earth History*, Mir Publishers, Moscow: 113, 139.

Rudra, K., (1986). *The History of Development of the Bhagirathi-Hooghly River System and some Connected Considerations,* unpublished Ph.D. thesis, Dept. of Geography, Calcutta University, Calcutta : 31-39.

Randell, F.E., (1903). Note of the protective works constructed on either banks of the river at the mouth of the Hooghly (dated February 26th 1868), *Papers from 1863 to 1873 Regarding the Cyclone Wave of 1864 and its Effect on the Hooghly Embankments etc.*, Bengal Secretariat Press, Calcutta : 7.

Sarkar, D.C., (1971). *Studies in the Geography of Ancient and Medieval India,* Motilal-Banarasi Dass, Delhi : 213-14.

The Calcutta Review (1859). The Gangetic Delta (a summary of a number of articles compiled from various sources) : 1-25.

Tifft, S., (1985). Erratic killers, *Time*, 125(23) : 11.

Wilson, H.H. (1862). *Essays on the religion of the Hindus,* 2: 164-69. (Cited in Hunter, 1875: 103-4).

27

Wetland Management—Traditional Rights and Recreational Uses

The Tonda Wildlife Management Area of Papua New Guinea

P. EATON

Land Tenure and Conservation

The relationship of land tenure to conservation has long been recognized as a significant one. Over 300 years ago, Grotius (1625) wrote: "The right of occupation rests upon the fact that most things become exhausted after promiscuous use". More recently, Hardin (1968) has made us aware of "the tragedy of the commons" where each individual following his own short-term interests in exploiting limited natural resources may bring ruin to all. One of the most valuable functions of a land tenure system is that it provides a motive for managing renewable resources so that they may be enjoyed in the future; it also provides a means to do this by controlling access to these resources.

The existence of proprietary rights should encourage careful stewardship of land and resources. Unfortunately, concern for long-term interests and consequent responsible management have not always been a feature of western systems of individual tenure or of wetland management. Today, it is often a case of public pressure and government regulations being necessary to prevent private landowners destroying or degrading the natural environment. In contrast, many tribal societies with traditional forms of tenure still maintain communal controls that prevent overexploitation of resources, but are now struggling to protect their customary rights and territories against encroachments by outsiders. In this type of situation, conservation policies will be more effective if they attempt to protect and formalize indigenous rights and customary practices. This case study describes efforts that have been made to do this in Papua New Guinea.

Customary Tenure in Papua New Guinea

In Papua New Guinea, 97 per cent of the land is held under customary tenure. Land is owned by the kinship group or clan; individual usage rights are inherited by birth through membership of a particular lineage. There are a multiplicity of different rights which include those to clear and cultivate land, to build houses, to hunt, to fish, to gather firewood and other forest products. The rights vary in strength and permanence; some are held by individuals and others by the whole group. Land ownership is rarely documented, registered or subject to survey. Instead, knowledge of rights and the natural features which form land boundaries is passed down by word of mouth from one generation to the next. There are generally strict communal controls on the transfer of land outside the group.

The customary tenure systems have helped to conserve resources in a number of different ways. Access to land and resources is limited to those holding customary rights; outsiders are excluded from farming, hunting and fishing in a group's territory. Certain localized scarce resources are jealously guarded; these include bird of paradise display trees, bush fowl nesting grounds and beaches where turtles lay eggs. Bird of paradise feathers are valuable for decoration and ceremonial purposes; bush fowl and turtle eggs are used for food and are also sold. Within the group itself, overexploitation of marine and wildlife species is discouraged. In the traditional subsistence economy, enough food should be produced to meet the needs of the group, but to kill a surplus of game or fish is regarded as wasteful and anti-social behaviour. There may also be controls on certain hunting and fishing methods which are considered too effective or indiscriminate; these include nets with fine mesh, poisons, explosives and firearms. Stocks of wildlife and fish are also conserved by moratoria in times of scarcity and during breeding seasons. In addition, some animals and particular areas may be protected by taboos which often have magical or religious origins but also help to protect wildlife species and their habitats.

Traditional conservation and tenure helped to maintain a balance between rural societies and the natural resources that sustained them. Unfortunately, this balance is now being disturbed by outside influences, new technologies and the cash economy. Customary landowners have become concerned that their traditional rights and controls are being ignored and that wildlife is becoming scarce. The development of wildlife management areas has been an attempt to solve these problems.

Wildlife Management Areas

The legislation responsible for creating these areas is the Fauna (Protection and Control) Act. This legislation contains provision for the protection of certain endangered species; these may be only hunted by indigenous Papua New Guineans using traditional hunting methods and for customary non-commercial purposes. The Act also provides for the establishment of certain types of protected area on customary land. The most significant of these are the wildlife management areas.

These areas may only be designated after consultation with the owners of the land and with local authorities. A wildlife management committee is formed from representatives of the customary landowners and this committee draws up rules for the protection and management of wildlife resources in their areas. The rules and boundaries are approved by the Minister for Environment and Conservation and then officially published in the National Gazette which gives them legal status.

The rules of the different areas vary depending on the particular situation and problems. Some provide complete protection for certain species, others prescribe hunting and fishing methods, there are often quotas on numbers killed; all seek to prohibit or control hunting by outsiders (those who do not hold traditional rights in the area).

Wildlife management areas have proved to be popular with customary landowners because, in the absence of any system for registering land titles, they help to formalize their rights and legalize the boundaries of their territories. There are at present 16 areas and many more have been proposed (Fig. 27.1). The remainder of this paper is concerned with the largest of these areas and the first to be developed—the Tonda Wildlife Management Area.

Tonda Wildlife Management Area

Tonda was established in 1975 and has an area of approximately 5900 km^2 (Fig. 27.2). It is located in the extreme southwest of Papua New Guinea. It stretches inland for about 50 km from the Torres Straits; the Indonesian frontier forms its western boundary and the Mai Kussa River its eastern boundary.

The whole region is low and flat, rarely rising more than 20 m above sea level. The main rivers are the Rivers Bensbach and Morehead which meander across the western plains, and in the east, the tidal estuaries of the Wasi and Mai Kussa which join to form Strachan Island. There are large areas of swamp and during the wet season, usually from November to March, much of the region is inundated by flood-waters. These gradually recede in the middle of the year, leaving marshy depressions, small lakes and lagoons.

The total annual rainfall is generally between 1500 and 2000 mm; there is considerable annual as well as seasonal variation. The characteristic vegetation is savanna grassland with a coastal fringe of mangroves and further inland melaleuca forest, mixed woodlands and isolated pandanus palms.

The whole region is rich in wildlife. There are large herds of rusa deer *(Cervus timorensis rusa)* which have moved into the area from Irian Jaya, the western part of New Guinea, where they were introduced by the Dutch about 60 years ago. The agile wallaby *(Macropus agilis)* is very common and there are many of the smaller marsupials. Freshwater and salt-water crocodiles (*Crocodilus porosus* and *Crocodilus novaeguinae),* turtles and large monitor lizards *(Varanus* spp.) are found in the swamps and rivers. There are many varieties of fish, large barramundi *(Lates calcifer)* are especially plentiful. There is a profusion of bird species. These include large numbers of different types of herons, egrets, cormorants, ibises, ducks and magpie geese *(Anseranus semipal-mata*), also spectacular larger birds such as the Australian pelican *(Pelecanus conspicillatus),* double-wattled cassowary (*Casuarius casuarius),* black-necked stork (*Xenorhynchus asiaticus),* brolga crane (*Grus rubicunda*) and the Australian bustard (*Ardeotis australis*). Birds of prey include the white-breasted sea eagle (*Haliaetus leucogaster*), whistling kite (*Haliaster sphenurus*) and osprey (*Pandon haliaetus*).

The area is very sparsely populated; the last census in 1980 gave a total population of 1239, an average density of only 0.21 people

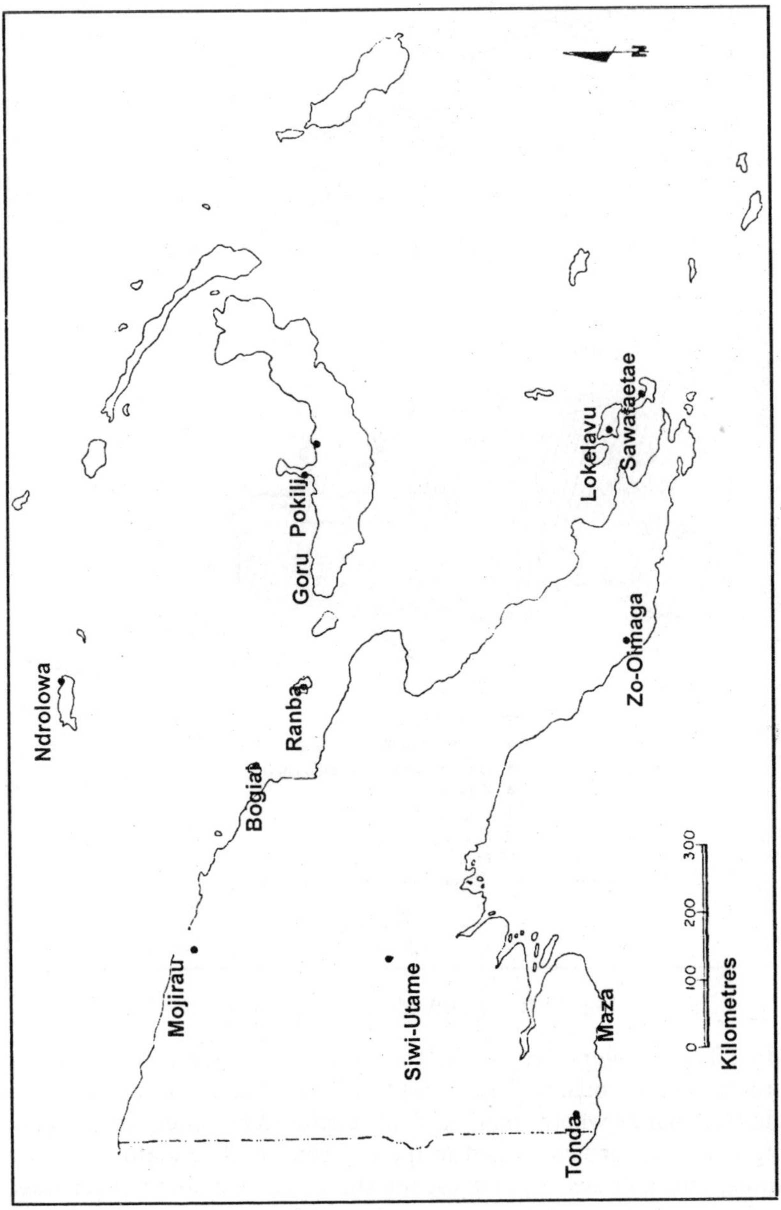

Fig. 27.1: Location of Wildlife Management Areas

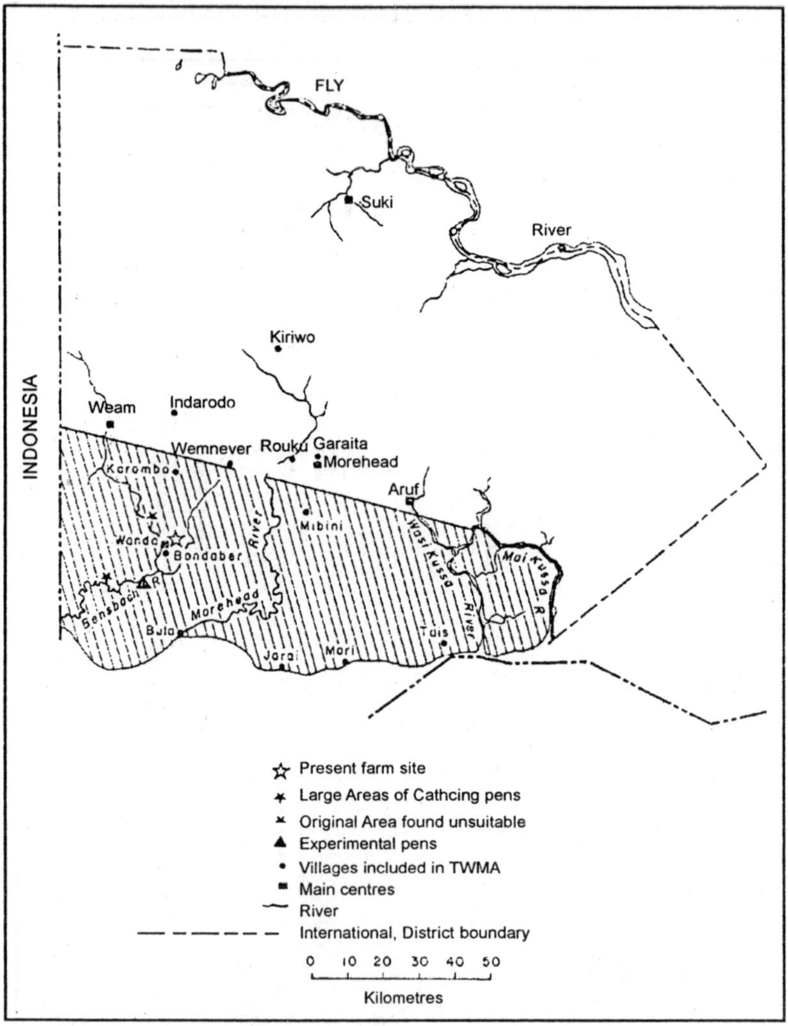

Fig. 27.2: Tonda Wildlife Management Area

km^{-2}. The villagers live mainly by shifting cultivation on the poorly drained acidic soils, with the most fertile areas being the alluvium on the river banks where small gardens, enclosed by fences to keep out pig and deer, are cultivated in the dry season. The main crops are yams, taro and sweet potatoes, but there are also some vegetables, fruit and tobacco, while sago is collected from the swamps.

Hunting plays an important part in both the cash and subsistence economies. Wallabies, wild pig and other animals are hunted by traditional methods using bows and arrows, snares, spears and dogs. Initially, the people were unwilling to eat deer as it was not part of their traditional diet, but venison is now becoming increasingly popular. Fish is an important part of the diet, which may also be supplemented by turtle and megapode (*Megapodus freycinet*) eggs. Wildlife also has other uses, for example bird plumes are used for personal decoration and monitor lizard skins are used for drums.

Crocodile skins provide a source of income. The hunting of crocodiles and the trade in their skins is controlled by the government through the Crocodile Trade Protection Act which sets maximum and minimum limits on the size of crocodiles killed in order to protect breeding and immature animals. In the villages there are several small crocodile farms where young ones are kept until they reach maturity. In somewhat similar fashion, young cassowaries are also reared in captivity. There have been cases of cassowaries being air-lifted to the New Guinea Highlands where they are in great demand for food at wedding feasts.

At one stage the government started a deer-farming project and various proposals have been made by private companies to set up meat-processing and exporting joint ventures. None of these has yet been implemented.

The most important commercial enterprise is based on the Bensbach Wildlife Lodge. This provides accommodation and also organizes hunting and fishing for tourists. The lodge is under expatriate management but employs a number of local workers.

Concern over hunting by outsiders was a major reason for setting up a wildlife management area. A committee was formed with representatives from the different villages of the area. Management rules were drawn up which included the following: the restriction on the hunting of deer and duck by outsiders, the requirement of a licence for hunting and fishing, the setting of quotas of a maximum number of five deer and five duck, the charging of royalties, prohibition of nets for fishing, and shooting from vehicles or boats and designation of areas in which hunting was banned.

Charging royalties is one means by which traditional landowners can obtain income from recreational hunting by tourists. Half of the royalties collected are paid to those with particular rights to the land where the hunting or fishing takes place; the other half is deposited in a bank trust account to be used for the development and welfare of the whole area.

At present, hunting by tourists does not seem to pose any major threat to wildlife resources in the area. It is confined to deer, duck and barramundi, and there is no evidence that their numbers are being depleted. In addition, there are a growing number of visitors who are more interested in birdwatching and photography than shooting. The impact of the villagers' own hunting has been limited by the low population density, traditional hunting methods and by the fact that animals are generally only killed for subsistence purposes.

Certain problems have occurred in the management of the area. One is the predatory activities of dogs, both feral and village dogs which are left free to roam the plains and swamps. They hunt in packs and their victims are usually young or female deer. Another problem is the activities of poachers from Indonesia. They have been found setting nets across the mouth of the Bensbach river. At times when the barramundi migrate and breed this could have serious effects on the fish population. In addition, poachers catch crocodiles and outsize skins are smuggled across the border.

The management committee themselves have not always been very effective in enforcing the area's rules. This is partly because the population is very scattered and tends to migrate seasonally. Communication is difficult and meetings are hard to arrange. There are complaints that the royalties are not always properly collected, distributed and used. Another grievance of the local people is lack of support from the government. Wildlife officers were once active in the area, initiating and assisting projects, but cuts in public expenditure have meant a reduction in their numbers and in extension work.

The future of the Tonda area is still uncertain. It is in one of the poorest and most remote parts of the country. The people feel they need more government services and economic development. Land use surveys (Bleeker and Paijmans, 1971) indicate that much of the region is unsuitable for agriculture or forestry. The most appropriate types of development would seem to be those directed towards wildlife management and a limited operation of tourism. The wildlife management area has proved to be an important means of involving customary landowners in these activities, but if this unique wetland is to retain its unspoilt character both national and international assistance may be needed to reinforce and complement local initiatives.

REFERENCES

Bleeker, P. and Paijmans, K., 1971. Soils of the Morehead-Kiunga area. *CSIRO Land Research Series 29*.

Grotius, H., 1625. *De Jure Belli ac Pacis*. Translated by F.W. Kelsey, Clarendon Press, Oxford, 1925.

Hardin, G., 1968. The tragedy of the commons. *Science*, 162: 1243-48.

28

Wasteland and Their Reclamation in Damodar River Basin

R. THAKUR

Introduction

Land is our basic resource. It has different roles. It is a productive economic factor in agriculture, forestry, grazing, fishing and mining. It is considered as a foundation for social prestige and is the basis of wealth and political power. Its utilization determines the pace of India's economic growth. Land resources of our country are facing various problems from the past few decades. Increasing population pressure on land demands more from existing fixed land resources. Ill effects of development like mining operations, destruction of forest cover, mismanaged irrigation, waterlogging, salinity and unscientific agricultural practices are responsible for degradation of land resources. Adverse effects of environmental forces are also adding to the increasing menace of degradation.

In order to meet the demands of ever increasing population and to achieve the cherished goal of sustainable development, reclamation and utilization of wasteland is inevitable. According to National Wasteland Development Board, 37.5 per cent of Indian geographical area is wasteland. Land, which is degraded and presently lying unutilized is wasteland. The vast stretches and varieties of wasteland that exist throughout the length and breadth of the country are the areas, which attract attention as the potential lands that could be identified, developed and put to gainful uses. In recent times, utilization of wasteland is gaining momentum for better use of land resources and for expansion of area under cultivation. Various attempts have been made by the government and academic institutions to promote and utilize wasteland effectively. Utilization of wasteland is a complicated issue which involves various dimensions and themes. Combining these dimensions into a form of structure is urgent priority and need of the time.

In the present study, efforts have been made as how to utilize wasteland in the Damodar river basin. The study provides detail information on utilization of wasteland which includes mapping, classification and reclamation of wastelands. Such studies may help in reducing pressure of population on land and also to meet agricultural demand for the growing population. Utilization of land has almost reached at saturation point. It is, therefore, desirable to utilize wasteland and evaluate it on the basis of its potential so that intelligent decision can be taken to utilize it for different purposes and needs.

The Concept and Meaning of Wasteland

The concept, definition and classification of wasteland is highly controversial and debatable. Standardisation of the definition of wasteland is imperative in the light of various organizations take categorized wasteland differently. But wasteland is a piece of land lying uninhabited, uncultivated and left over after use or no longer serving any purpose. The term 'wasteland' denoting this meaning has now almost disappeared, because in many cases these common lands are of much value as open space. In other words, the view is held that hardly there is land, which is not being used at the moment and as such, can rarely be termed as a waste.

A definition based on economic potential and actual return from land seemed to receive some acceptance. Any land providing less than 20 per cent of its economic potential is wasteland. This definition does not seem helpful for many reasons, as it depends on productivity, which, in turn, depends on the state of technology and its usage. The productive potential of land increases with improvement in technology, so much so that actual increase in production is a function of adaptation and utilization of improved technology over a period of time. Thus, the definition makes wastelands a function of state of technology factor of its acceptance and time. Besides, because of its heavy bias on economics, it neglects ecological consideration. Thus, any land, which is giving proper economic returns, but is an ecological hazard, shall not be counted as a wasteland. The National Wasteland Development Board under the Ministry of Environment and Forests defined wasteland as that "land which is presently lying unused or which is not being used to its optimum potential due to some constraints". In national perspective no land is wasteland and there should be optimum utilization of all the available land to derive maximum benefit.

Existing Studies

The available literature relevant for the present study is as follows: Yadav and Aggarwal (1959), Academy of Science of USSR (1958), Patil (1966), Yadav (1967;1984), Prasad and Yadav (1969), Singh (1978), Jha (1984), Singh (1985), Bhumla and Khare (1987), Sharma, Tripathi and Sharma (1988), Shukla (1988), Kumar and Pandey (1989), Kumar (1989), Singh (1992), and Mohammad (1988). Studies on reclamation of wasteland are vast and diverse. Most of the works are done by government organizations. Their works are based on the physical, morphometric and other factors. Anthropogenic factors are neglected. But the combined aspects may provide an ideal model for the utilization of wasteland which is the core of study.

The Study Area

The Damodar river basin lies in the states of Jharkhand and West Bengal. It occupies 13425 sq km area of Gondwana trough in the middle of the Chotanagpur Plateau. It consists of Dhanbad, Bokaro, Hazaribag, Giridih and some parts of Ranchi and Palamau districts of Jharkhand and mainly Bankura and Burdwan districts of West Bengal. The region is well marked for having a chain of India's most important coal bearing areas. It is a part of the heavily industrialized region of India across Jharkhand-Bengal border, well known for concentration of industrial, mineral and power resources (Fig. 28.1).

In the hilly areas of Jharkhand, the well marked Damodar river basin runs east-west through the middle of Chotanagpur plateau. The Damodar river emerges from a highly dissected plateau surface in the Palamau district of Jharkhand at a height of approximately 610 metres above sea level. The river flows first eastward and then southward for 540 km until it joins the Hooghly river about 50 km downstream of

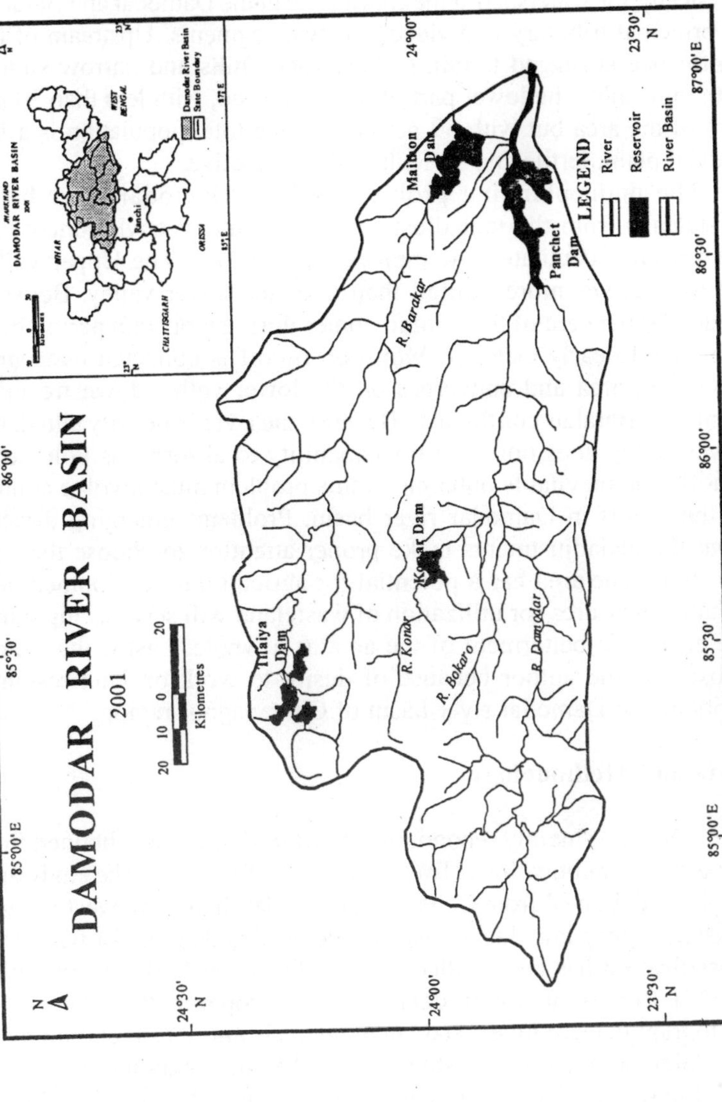

Fig. 28.1: Location of Damodar River Basin

Kolkata. Out of which 290 km lie in the state of Jharkhand and is considered the Upper Damodar basin and the remaining length of 248 km in West Bengal and is considered the lower Damodar basin. Physically, the watershed at the confluence of the Damodar and Barakar, its principal tributary is divided into two segments. Upstream of the confluence is rugged terrain of bare rocky hills and narrow valleys with thin soils. The lower part of the watershed, with less than 30 per cent of the area but with 59 per cent of the total population is a flat alluvial plain, fertile and agriculturally productive.

The main planning problems of the Damodar river basin wastelands from the maladjustment in its natural environment that have been accentuated by improper human use. The Upper valley region receives more rainfall than does the lower valley. Between 80 and 90 per cent of the rainfall comes during monsoon period from late June to early October. Monsoon runoff is collected over large catchment area and converges on the lower valley downstream of Damodar-Barakar confluence. Because the river is heavily silted, the lower valley does not have the capability to absorb this volume of runoff. The inevitable outcome to this problem must involve control of the runoff in Damodar river basin. Problems emerging directly from the maladjustments make proper attention to choose the area for study. The area has a potential for agricultural development and suitable measures for utilization of wasteland will serve as input into the economic betterment of the area as a whole. Lastly, the area is chosen by the author because of desire to work on land resource problems of Damodar river basin of Chotanagpur region.

Data and Methodology

The study uses mainly secondary data which have been obtained from government publications. Transformation of region of the study area has been collected from Census Atlas of Jharkhand and West Bengal. Wasteland map and data on various determinants used for wasteland classification has been collected from Damodar Valley Corporation (DVC). Representation of data through a proper methodology using cartographic techniques, statistical analysis and interpretation helps in achieving objective of study and makes the study more effective and impressive. The district is used as a unit of study because the work is application-oriented. Secondly, it is structured in such a way for which a district is more suitable for study area. Further, as district is a recognized unit of socio-economic development in various government plans and all the government policies and projects on wasteland are applicable on administrative units which make easier to collect data and informations. Cartographic methods have been used to show distribution of wastelands in river basin.

Distribution and Types of Wasteland

The distribution of wasteland depends upon its distribution and classification and criteria used for definition. In the present study wasteland classification is based on National Wasteland Development Board. According to this classification, wasteland in Damodar river basin consists of the following types which are ravines, gullied land, derelict land, waterlogged land, degraded forest land and weed infected areas. Detailed distribution of these lands is given below:

Ravinous Wasteland

A ravine is a deep narrow gorge, worn out by a stream of torrent of water. It is a long narrow depression in the earth surface, rather smaller than a valley but larger than a gully. Several gullies often lead to a ravine and several ravines to a valley (Moore, 1976 p. 182).

- *Gullied land:* Gullies are the result of the localised surface run off. It affects the friable unconsolidated material resulting in the formation of perceptible channels in undulating terrain of a maximum depth of 3 m. These are the primary stages of excessive land dissection followed by their networking leading to the development of ravinous land.
- *Ravinous land:* This category of land contains system of gullies running more or less parallel to each other in deep alluvial soil and entering into a nearby river flowing much lower than the surrounding tablelands. The ravines are the extensive systems of gullies developed along river courses. It can be classified into three sub-categories, proceeding from the watershed divided to the riverside and thereafter passing through table land first and the peripheral lands latter. They are called: (i) Shallow (3 to 6m), (ii) Medium (6 to 9m) and (iii) Deep (more than 9m). The land along every river in the district focus this menace, the

most prone are river Damodar and Barakar. The problem of eroded land has not only posed an ecological threat but also created social problem. on the basis of the magnitude of the problem of soil erosion the ravine wasteland can also be determined into two categories, they are: (i) areas where the problem is more acute and which are dominated by a net work of deep gullies and wild ravines and (ii) area where gullies and ravines are not very deep and dense and which occupy a comparatively narrow zone along the river banks.

According to Sharma (1980) it is a zone of moderately severe ravine erosion. In Jharkhand, 6 lakh hectares of land are suffering from severe ravine erosion out of which 3.9 lakh hectares fall in Damodar river basin. Here, the problem is most acute in Hazaribag, Bokaro, Giridih, Palamau, Ranchi, Dhanbad and Santhal Parganas districts, out of which the first six districts fall in Damodar river basin. Table 28.1 (Fig. 28.2), indicates the area under ravines in Damodar river basin. The district of Hazaribag, Bokaro and Giridih covers nearly 50 per cent of the ravined area out of the total river basin, whereas Dhanbad and Palamau districts have only 7 and 3 per cent respectively.

The ravines are more developed on the relatively level or undulating surfaces of the Ranchi and Hazaribag peneplains and adjoining belts than on the steep scarps slope. The bold, high and steep scarps are generally free from ravines because of their general inaccessibility to man and forest cover is relatively dense. This is also partly due to the absence of soil and sediment on steep rocky stones. It is the gentler and lower slopes of the scarps where forest cover has been thinned or removed so that the ravines are seen.

Table 28.1: Area Under Ravines in Damodar River Basin

District	*Area Under Ravines (Lac Hectares)*	*Percentage of Total Area*
Hazaribag, Bokaro & Giridih	1.7	17
Ranchi	1.2	12
Palamau	0.7	7
Dhanbad	0.3	3
Total	3.9	39

Source: Calculated by the author.

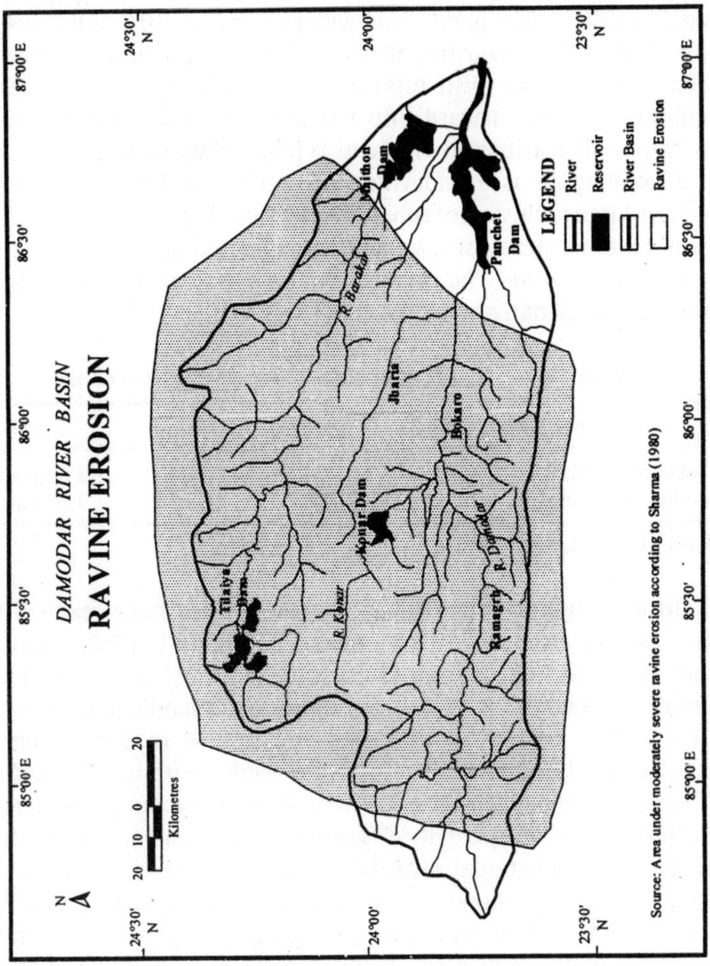

Fig. 28.2: Ravine Erosion in Damodar River Basin

The worst type of ravine erosion is seen in Jamui and Giridih subdivision in the north of Chotanagpur. Ravine erosion almost of equal magnitude occurs further west in the Hazaribag peneplain (Barakar valley). The gentler and wider scarps (25-30 km) that connect the central Upper Hazaribag plateau (650 mts) with the lower Northern Hazaribag Plateau (330 mts) are also ravined. This ravine belt continues southwest-ward into Palamau and Ranchi districts. The environs of Hazaribag town are also plagued by ravines.

Chotanagpur is a wide tract of granites and gneisses. Granite contains large inclusion of schist. These rocks have prominent jointing due to tectonic processes, which have affected headward erosion of ravines in this zone. The ravines find their way along the joints and, hence, are very narrow with vertical side walls.

Table 28.2: Classification of Damodar Ravines and Gullies

Particulars of the ravines	*Shallow*	*Medium*	*Deeper*
Depth in metres	0-1	1-3	3 and more
Width in metres	0-15	1.5-3.5	3 and more

Source: H.S. Sharma, (1980).

In the Chotanagpur plateau region, ravines have reached their base level of erosion down to gneissi and granitic rock. Therefore, their extension or retrogression longitudinally and side-wise is minimized considerably. In India, demand for land is increasing at a fast rate, any attempt made in the direction of reclaiming unused, denuded and less productive areas for useful purposes is worthy of the time and money spent on it. There are many reclamation measures that have been adopted in different parts of the world. In India, particularly in Damodar river basin, reclamation of wastelands has been practiced traditionally, and not on modern scientific lines. Some of the methods were successful but later on proved to be temporary and short-lived. While some other measures failed to show any response at all. Now, newer technology is available for reclamation and they are developed on sound and scientific principles. Any wasteland reclamation and development programme aims at achieving the following objective: (a) to improve the physical conditions and fertility of soil, (b) to improve the availability and quality of water, (c) to prevent the shifting of soil, landslides and flooding and (d) to conserve the biological resources of the land for sustainable use.

The remedies for the reclamation of different wasteland types in totality cannot be uniform because for different wasteland types, different reclamation methods are required. The different departments of agriculture, forest and wasteland reclamation and the Damodar Valley Corporation in this region do not have any co-ordination which creates a certain amount of confusion. This is true, particularly, of the Hazaribag area where the Damodar Valley Corporation of the State Government was working side by side. The following measures were adopted in the affected areas:

(1) Construction of embankments parallel to the contours. These barriers against drainage control seasonal runoff and arrest the sediments washed down by sheet erosion above the embankments which run across the gullies, hence, the latter are automatically plugged by the embankment.
(2) Small masonary and earthen dams across individual gullies have been constructed.

Remedies for Reclamation of Ravine Land

Several factors are responsible for the formation of ravines in the region. Clearance of forests in this belt seems to be mostly responsible for ravine formation which reduces the infiltration and increases the runoff. Further, uncontrolled grazing, moderate annual rainfall, downpour frequency of greater intensity, pronounced vertical difference between the general ground level and the river bed level and extreme dryness of the soil due to easy drainage and high porosity are responsible in one way or the other in the formation of ravine land. Some authentic steps are taken to reclaim and to utilize these lands.

The first step in this direction is to know the extent of the land under ravine and then a survey should be conducted to assess whether the ravine land is suitable for agricultural purpose after reclamation or it is to be devoted for forest or grasslands. Along with that, topographical sheets should be prepared to know the nature of the gullies and ravines. The second step to assess whether the depth of ravine land is shallow, mechanical (tractor) reclamation measures can be used for levelling the ravine land and bullock power can also be used for terracing and levelling the land. According to slope and terraces, the field should be divided into different plots and strong bunds should be constructed around the field to check the erosion and water flow. Suitable drains should be made for removing excess water. Land preparation and ploughing should be done according to the nature of soil. Diversion channels can be constructed to reduce the erosion by gullies. Testing of the soil shall be done to know the deficiencies of the soil. Area where gullies/ravines land has acquired severe form can be utilized fór plantation. Erosion resistant trees can be grown here which in the long run not only check erosion but also help to meet the fuel demand and wood supply in the locality.

In the agricultural field which is prepared, farming should be done on scientific basis. Crop rotation should be given emphasis as it helps to check soil loss and runoff. A mixed cropping and inter-cropping practices have also been found very effective agronomic measures for soil erosion control. In order to retain and safe disposal of rain water, contour bonding with varying cross-sections depending upon length and degree of slope, soil texture and vegetable cover at different vertical intervals have been found very effective. The experience of previous years shows that wholesale levelling of ravines to join agricultural land is not economical. Also afforestation will not check ravines from retrogression as the runoff will still cause damage and water erosion at ravine heads will continue. Again the land holders who have lost their agricultural lands in the ravines will need part of it to be restored for production of crops. Hence, a balance land use plan has to be suggested, i.e. reclamation for agricultural land of shallow and medium ravines, and horticulture, afforestation and grassland development for deeper ravines should be done.

Before reclamation work begins a few things should be kept in mind: firstly, those lands are only to be reclaimed for agriculture where irrigation can be made available. Secondly, grassland areas should be developed only when they can be tied up with projects of dairy and animal husbandry. Thirdly, afforestation should be soil conservation-oriented. Wildlife reserves may also be planned where possible. Afforestation belt should be continuous along the river and not in isolated patches. Ravine lands are under the ownership of the government, Gaon Samaj and private ownership. Patches of Gaon Samaj land should be eliminated from reclamation blocks by exchange of land. Land consolidation work should also be done, and ownership boundaries should be scientifically planned. Crop management practices in reclaimed ravine land should include crop rotation and crop combination. To control soil erosion, contour farming, strip cropping and terracing should be done. If the above mentioned measures are taken into consideration, then, it is possible to reclaim ravine land which will at the same time enhance the land resource potential and economic conditions of the region.

Remedies for Reclamation of Waterlogged Land

To present the reclamation remedies for waterlogged land, the Damodar river basin has been surveyed. The watershed of the basin is divided into two segments: the upper valley and the lower valley regions. The upper valley receives more annual rainfall at Konar 1,346 mm and Maithon 1,261 mm, respectively. While the average annual rainfall in lower valley is 1,100 mm. Monsoon runoff is collected over a large catchment area and converges on the lower valley. Because the river is heavily silted, the lower valley does not have the capacity to absorb this volume of runoff. The inevitable outcome of this situation is recurrent and devastating floods in the lower valleys affect the agricultural activity in the region.

Remedial measures usually employed to solve the problem of waterlogging by construction of seven multipurpose dams on the Damodar River and its main tributaries. Two of the dams at Panchet Hill and Aiyar were to be on the Damodar while three at Maithon, Deolbari, and Tilaiya were to be on the Barakar, and one each on two of the minor tributaries, the Bokaro and the Konar. This occurs when there is excessive water seepage from the dams and when the soil in the surrounding areas reaches its saturation point. The Damodar Valley Corporation has envisaged a number of drainage channels, 564 km long for flushing the waterlogged areas, especially, the standing pools of water in the lower Damodar basin.

Waterlogged areas lying in the region can be reclaimed with afforestation of suitable species and trees. The preparatory step is to remove the excess water by constructing proper drainage and the planted trees will clog the pores, stop the upward movement of water and help in reclaiming the waterlogged conditions. The soil along both the sides of the river shows variability in physical and chemical condition. Trees adopted to the soil conditions, if planted in sufficient numbers, are capable of minimizing seepage in the long run. Seeding of good size should be used for planting. Irrigation may also be provided during summer months to accelerate the growth of plants so that by ensuring rains the plants are sufficiently established to withstand waterlogging. This technique has successfully been tried by Research Institute. Apart from this, regular meetings should be held between the personnel of the canal/dam irrigation department and the farmers for the use of canal water, for irrigation in a proper quantum according to the requirements of the field.

Remedies for Reclamation of Derelict Land from Mineral Extraction

To present the reclamation remedies of derelict land from mineral extraction especially from coal extraction has been surveyed. The situation on the bank of river Damodar is well known for its concentration of industrial mineral resources, particularly, most important coal bearing areas. Industrial minerals like fireclay, graphite in Dhanbad, sands near river Damodar, crystaline limestone in western part of the basin, iron ore in Dhanbad, quartz, bauxite, copper, lead, mica and manganese are abundant (Fig. 28.3).

The Gondwana sedimentary rocks have coal deposits in the upper and middle sections of the Damodar basin. The progress of coal mining, its heaps, and disturbance of local drainage because of the mining operations have all damaged the basin's cultivation, and left derelict land wherever mining operations have taken place. Wastelands due to mining and due to heaps of waste materials are most prominent around Jharia and Raniganj coal fields. But, recently, new fields have been developed in the western part of the valley which again means plenty of wasteland in the western portion of the Damodar basin.

Table 28.3: Spatial Patterns of Coal Mining Areas

State	*District*	*Coal Fields*	*Area (in km^2)*	*Reserve (Million Tons)*	*Percentage of India's (Production/Year)*
West Begal	Burdwan	Raniganj			
	Birbhum	Raniganj			
	Dhanbad	1. Raniganj and Mugma	1500	1329	2.80
		2. Jharia	440	15180	31.71
	Bokaro	1. Bokaro and Chandrapura	N.A.	3040	N.A.
Jharkhand	Hazaribag	1. Ramgarh	100	200	6.20
		2. N. Karanpura	1560	10750	5.80
		3. S. Karanpura	—	—	—
	Giridih	1. Giridih	N.A.	4	0.80

Source: Joshi (1978); Basu (1984).

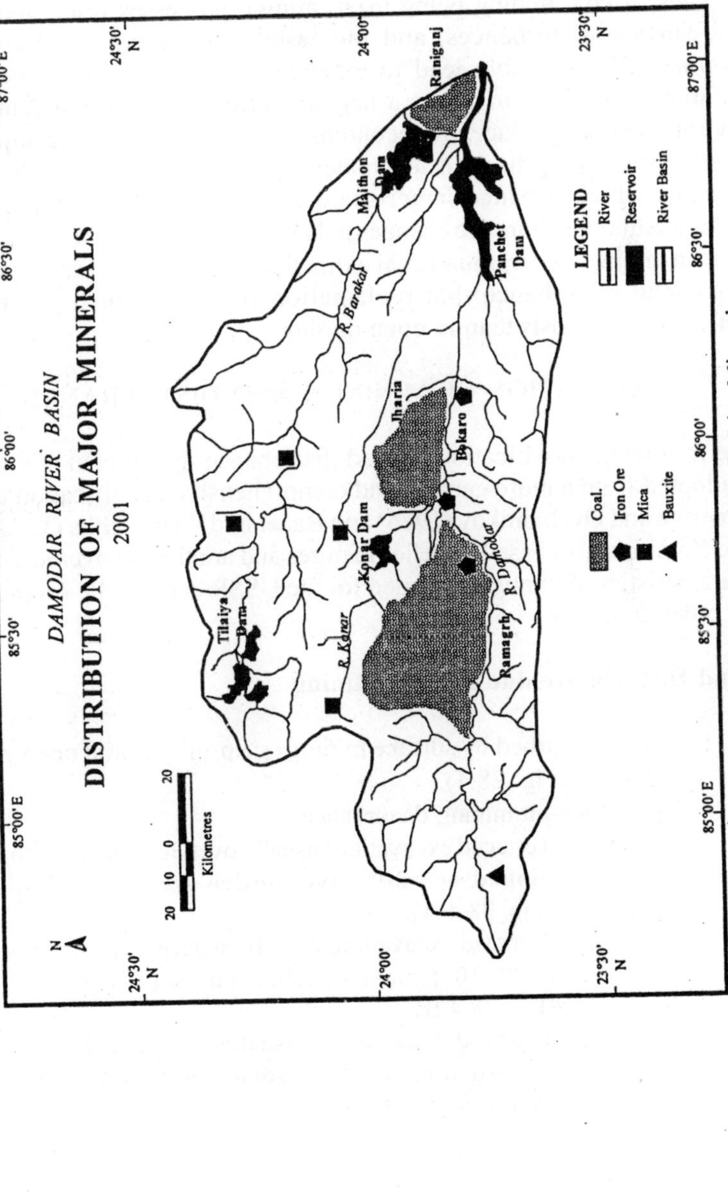

Fig. 28.3: Distribution of Major Minerals

Table 28.3 shows the coalfields arranged according to administrative divisions within which they fall in Damodar river basin and bring about land-surface disturbances. Irrespective of the actual methods of coal mining being used, mining processes bring about land-surface disturbances, and increased mining expanded coal supplies will inevitably lead to extended land disturbance. Such disturbed land tends to create a negative effect on the surrounding environment and reduces its economic value. Generally speaking, progress in mining has led to greater use of open coal extraction methods which produce larger-scale disturbances on the earth's surface. Although dramatic changes in landscape may occur as a result of open mining, underground coal extraction on occasion causes such gross land disturbance that reclamation runs into much greater difficulties and costs than in open mining.

CLASSIFICATION OF MINING LAND DISTURBANCE

The following classification of land disturbance due to coal mining is adopted from a more general and comprehensive classification by Motorina and Ovchinnikov (1975) and Bauer and Weinitschke (1973). The classifications based on relief features and another on overburden characteristics. Although designed for the USSR can also be adopted for other countries.

Land Disturbance due to Coal Mining

1. Land disturbed by surface mining (strip-mining and open-pit mining) (Fig. 28.4).
   1.1 Open-pit mining disturbance
      1.1.1 Terraced excavations usually over 30 m deep; deposit dipped at >30°, overburden stored externally (Fig. 28.4 A).
      1.1.2 Terraced excavations over 10 m deep; deposit dipped at 8°-30°; most overburden stored externally (Fig. 28.4 B).
      1.1.3 Terraced excavations usually 10-30 m deep with deposit dipped at 8°, some internal storage of overburden (Fig. 28.4 C).

1.2 Strip-mining disturbance

1.2.1 Area strip-mining of horizontal deposits relatively near the surface (Fig. 28.4 D).

1.2.2 Contour strip-mining of horizontal or steeply dipped deposits in mountainous regions (Fig. 28.4 E).

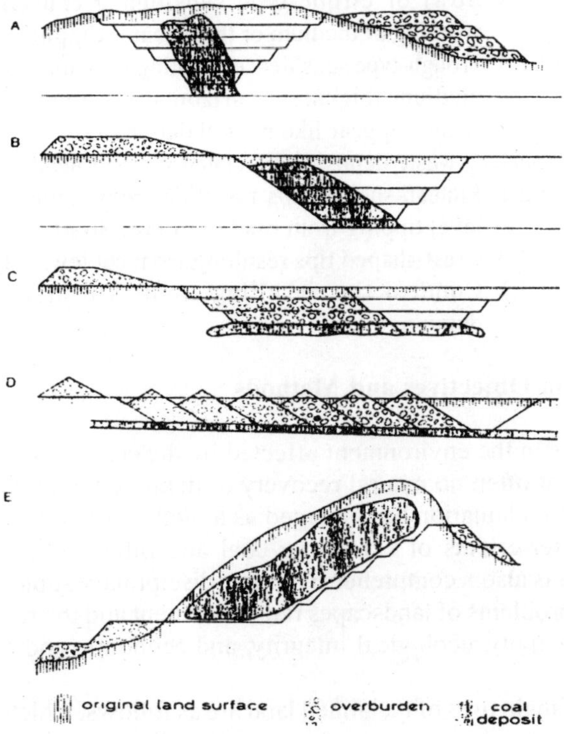

A. Open pit deposit deeply dipping;

B. Open pit with medium dip to deposit;

C. Open pit with horizontal deposit;

D. Conventional area strip-mining;

E. Contour stip-mining of deeply dipped deposit;

Source: Chadwick and Lindman (1982), p. 32.

Fig. 28.4: Land Disturbance by Mining

2. Land disturbed underground (deep) mining:
   - 2.1 Land subsidence
     - 2.1.1 Canyon subsidence caused by working medium or thick seams that dip steeply (> 45°).
     - 2.1.2 Terraced subsidence resulting from the working of seams that show 27° – 45° dipping and where the land surface slopes.
     - 2.1.3 Bowl or cirque-type subsidence caused by the working of medium or thick seams dipping upto 27°.
     - 2.1.3 Trough-type subsidence resulting from mining low and medium thickness, horizontal or slightly inclined seams; appear like natural depressions.
   - 2.2 Surface waste deposits associated with pit heads.
     - 2.2.1 Plateau-shaped tips resulting from single or multi-level tipping from road or rail transport.
     - 2.2.2 Crest-shaped tips resulting from cableway dumping.
     - 2.2.3 Comical tips resulting from skip or tip-wagon dumping

Reclamation Objectives and Methods

The changes in the environment affected by the coal industry are so profound that often no natural recovery of disturbed landscapes can occur. Land reclamation has emerged as a method of countering the negative after-effects of extracting coal and other mineral. Land reclamation is also a comprehensive inter-disciplinary subject which covers the problems of landscapes redevelopment and the restoration of its productivity, ecological integrity, and economic and aesthetic value.

The six main uses of reclaimed land are as follows, which depend on natural and socio-economic factors of locality:

(i) Agriculture — arable land, orchards, or grazing land;
(ii) Forestry — commercial or non-commercial forests;
(iii) Recreation — recreation zone, parks or public open spaces;
(iv) Water use — fishing, swimming, boating, yachting;
(v) Construction — sites for light industry, houses or service, purposes;
(vi) Wildlife habitats — wilderness areas.

These uses are closely interrelated and often form a comprehensive development in an area of extracted deposits.

Strip-mining Techniques in Land Reclamation

Experts in Czechoslovakia believe that the opening pioneer cuts in surface mining operations can be located in such a way that, at the final stage of mining, overburden and soil material are strategically placed for the final stages of reclamation work. This approach makes it possible to provide the best soil at the surface of reclaimed land when levelling the area. When large horizontal coal deposits are mined in USSR, GDR or FRG, by surface mining, open pits are arranged in such a way that when each new pit is opened spoil is disposed of in the old mined-out pit. This technique provides for maximal filling of old pits and a reduction in the areas needed for external waste tips. A large number of operational improvements have occurred in recent years in the USA in the surface mining of coal.

Weed-infected Areas

This problem occurs wherever there is the presence of water in the soil. Since weeds come under the hardier varieties of plants, they have the peculiar characteristic of coming up even in the worst of climatic conditions and also grow and breed rapidly. In fact, they invade areas of crop cultivation also if proper care is not taken. The only remedy for their control is to continuously plough the land (turn the topsoil) or to use weedicides, otherwise they pose a threat to occupy all the empty space where cultivation can be done. In the Damodar river basin, weed-infected areas are found all along the dams and water reservoirs.

Reclamation Remedies of Upland

The bank of Damodar river in upper part has been taken into consideration to present reclamation remedies of uplands. Problems of water retention and soil erosion due to sheet wash are two such problems, which make, it uneconomic to utilise these lands for agriculture. Therefore, the first step to reclaim upland area should involve, checking the soil erosion due to sheet wash, help accumulation of silt from the slopes and growing fuel, fodder and economic species of trees. Uneven sloppy surface is the main hindrance to utilise uplands. Kankar nodules dominate the upland, which further pose difficulties for the utilisation of upland area for agriculture purpose. Providing irrigation to these lands is another difficult task because of high slope and low groundwater retention

Though afforestation is the better way to utilise these lands, agricultural activity is also possible; but, it needs huge economic incentive. The upland areas located in the eastern part of Hazaribag district are areas with lesser slope. They contain good soil depth, which can be taken up for growing agricultural crops after bunding and constructing suitable water harvesting. These areas should be ploughed and divided into sufficient compartments according to the slope, *kankars* should be thrown out of field and soil testing should be done to know the physio-chemical status of soil. Suitable agriculture crops can be grown here. Strip cropping should be given preference to check sheet wash and erosion. Contour cultivation can also be emphasized if required. In contour cultivation, each furrow, which lies approximately on the level, intercepts flowing water, hold it and allow it to soak into the soil.

Patches of upland which are located on the bank of Barakar river are high, uneven and predominant with *kankar* can be utilised for afforestation. These patches are difficult to reclaim for cultivation as heavy expenditure will be needed and nature of soil cannot ensure for good economic returns. Afforestation is only suitable way to reclaim these upland patches. Tree species should be planted here which in long-term bind the soil and reduce the rate of erosion and provide fuel and fodder to dwellers.

Further Suggestions

It is abundantly clear that wasteland reclamation is applied in approach which depends upon local conditions and nature of wasteland. The reclamation of wastelands is not an easy task and requires heavy investment and further research so that methods could be developed with less capital investment. But any programme of wasteland reclamation, no matter how much priority has been given, will not be successful until some important measures to support it from periphery are not taken. The following suggestions are given to support and create a overall structure of wasteland development:

- The whole programme of land reclamation and afforestation must be made people's programme by involving local people, particularly the weaker sections of the society.
- The data provided by various agencies for wastelands lack uniform application. It should be verified and its feasible figures can be decided.
- Future locations of settlements, industries and roads etc. should be promoted on wastelands.
- New technology of plant breeding and tissue culture for afforestation and crop production should be applied on larger scale.
- The commercial and co-operative agencies should be fully involved for requisite financial inputs and consumption loans for afforestation and reclamation programme.
- There should be much more involvement of women's group in wastelands improvement programme.
- The wastelands can also be given to the Forest Development Corporation for development of production forestry.
- The experts of various fields, such as agronomists, forestry economists, hydrologists, geographers, botanists and so on to come out from their respective pigeon holes to devise plans for wasteland reclamation.
- For wasteland reclamation, improvement in surface, drainage, soil erosion and waterlogging must be done. The sheet and gully erosion can be checked by ground cover bunding.
- Whenever the owners of the wastelands are not willing to make their land productive, the government should take over such lands and bring them under suitable utilisation.
- Every land owner whether in rural or urban areas must bring at least 10 per cent of his land under green cover.
- National Wasteland Development Board should work as a catalystic agent. It should formulate basic policies and guidelines for making the wastelands productive through various methods and cropping patterns.

Thus, it should be understood that like other development programmes the wasteland development programme is the programme of the people, by the people and for the people, and they expected to make a greater contribution to the development process and objectives. Need of hour is not to take isolated efforts but to create a system involving every one, common people and the government. All have some role to play. We can succeed to mitigate this problem and judiciously utilize our land resources.

REFERENCES

Bali, J.S. (1984) "Watershed management to fight drought", *Souvenir International Symposium on Hydrological Aspects of Droughts*, New Delhi, 61-66.

Basu, M. (1984) "The Damodar valley coalfields: A geographical study", in A. Ramesh (ed) *Contributions to Indian Geography*, New Delhi: Heritage Publishers, 150-164.

Bradshaw. A.D. and Chadwick, M.J. (1980) *The Restoration of Land*, Oxford: Blackwell, 73-188.

Chadwick, M.J. and Lindman, N. (eds) (1982) *Environment Implications of Expanded Coal Utilization*, New York: Pergamon Press, 31-51.

Goodman, G.T. and Chadwick, M.J. (eds) (1978) *Environmental Management of Mineral Wastes*, Netherlands: Sijthoff and Noordhoff International Publishers: 1-84.

Grim, C.E. and Hill, R.D. (1974) *Environmental Protection in Surface Mining of Coal, EPA*—670/2-74-013, Ohio, USA.

Hutnik, R.J. and Davis, G. (1973) "Ecology and reclamation of devastated land", Vol. I, II, New York: Gordon and Breach.

Hutnik, R.J. and Davis, G. (1973) "Reclamation of coal mine land in the United States as compared with Ruhr", in G.T. Goodman and M.J. Chadwick (ed) (1978) *Environmental Management of Mineral Wastes*, Netherlands: Sijthoff and Noordhoff International Publishers,71-83.

Joshi, K.L. (1978) *Geography of India: Resources and Regional Development*, New Delhi: NCERT.

Jha, V.C. (1987) "Wasteland types and their effective utilization in Birbhum District", *The Deccan Geographer*, 25(2 & 3): 231-242.

Kausch, P. (1979) "Brown coal opencast mining and landscaping in Rhineland", *Energy Research*, 3: 275-288.

Motorina, L.V. and Zabelina, N.M. (1968) The Recultivation of Land Damaged by the Mining Industry—A Review of Literature, All Union Scientific and Technical Institute for Agriculture: Moscow (Russian).

Motorina, L.V. (1975) *Experience of Reclamation of Land Disturbed by Mining in the USSR and Abroad*, Moscow.

Motorina, L.V. and Ovchinnikov, V.A. (1975) *Industry and the Recultivation of Land*, Moscow: Mis'l.

Prasad, M. (2008) "Impact of new mining technology on land degradation in coal fields of Chotanagpur", in B. Thakur (ed) *Perspectives in Resource Management in Developing Countries,* Vol. 3: *Ecological Degradation of Land*, New Delhi: Concept, 212-231.

Saha, S.K. (1979) "River basin planning in the Damodar valley of India", *The Geographical Review, 69(3):*273-306.

Schaller, F.W. and Sutton, P. (1978) *Reclamation of Drastically Disturbed Lands*, American Society of Agronomy: Madison Wisconsin.

Sharma, H.S. (1980) *Ravine Erosion in India*, New Delhi: Concept.

Yadav, H.R. (1985) *Reclaiming Wastelands*, New Delhi: Concept, pp. 100-105, 117-119.

Yadav, H.R. (1985) "Determinants and utilization of banjar land: A case study of district Sultanpur", *Geographical Review of India*, 47(3): 6-9.

Yadav, H.R. (1989) *The Concept of Wasteland: Dimension of Wasteland Development*, New Delhi: Concept, 3-7.

Index